Talk to the Hand!

Recent Doonesbury Books by G. B. Trudeau

Read My Lips, Make My Day, Eat Quiche and Die!
Give Those Nymphs Some Hooters!
You're Smokin' Now, Mr. Butts!
I'd Go With the Helmet, Ray
Welcome to Club Scud!
What Is It, Tink, Is Pan in Trouble?
Quality Time on Highway 1
Washed Out Bridges and Other Disasters
In Search of Cigarette Holder Man
Doonesbury Nation
Virtual Doonesbury
Planet Doonesbury
Buck Wild Doonesbury
Duke 2000: Whatever It Takes
The Revolt of the English Majors
Peace Out, Dawg!
Got War?

Special Collections

The Doonesbury Chronicles
Doonesbury's Greatest Hits
The People's Doonesbury
Doonesbury Dossier: The Reagan Years
Doonesbury Deluxe: Selected Glances Askance
Recycled Doonesbury: Second Thoughts on a Gilded Age
Action Figure!
The Portable Doonesbury
Flashbacks: Twenty-Five Years of Doonesbury
The Bundled Doonesbury

A DOONESBURY BOOK

Talk to the Hand!

BY G. B. TRUDEAU

Andrews McMeel
Publishing

Kansas City

DOONESBURY is distributed internationally by Universal Press Syndicate.

04 05 06 07 08 BAM 10 9 8 7 6 5 4 3 2 1

ISBN: 0-7407-4671-5

Library of Congress Catalog Card Number: 2004106218

DOONESBURY may be viewed on the Internet at
www.doonesbury.com and www.ucomics.com.

──── **ATTENTION: SCHOOLS AND BUSINESSES** ────

Andrews McMeel books are available at quantity discounts with bulk purchase for educational, business, or sales promotional use. For information, please write to: Special Sales Department, Andrews McMeel Publishing, 4520 Main Street, Kansas City, Missouri 64111.

"People need somebody to watch over them. Ninety-five percent of the people in the world need to be told what to do and how to behave."

—Arnold Schwarzenegger

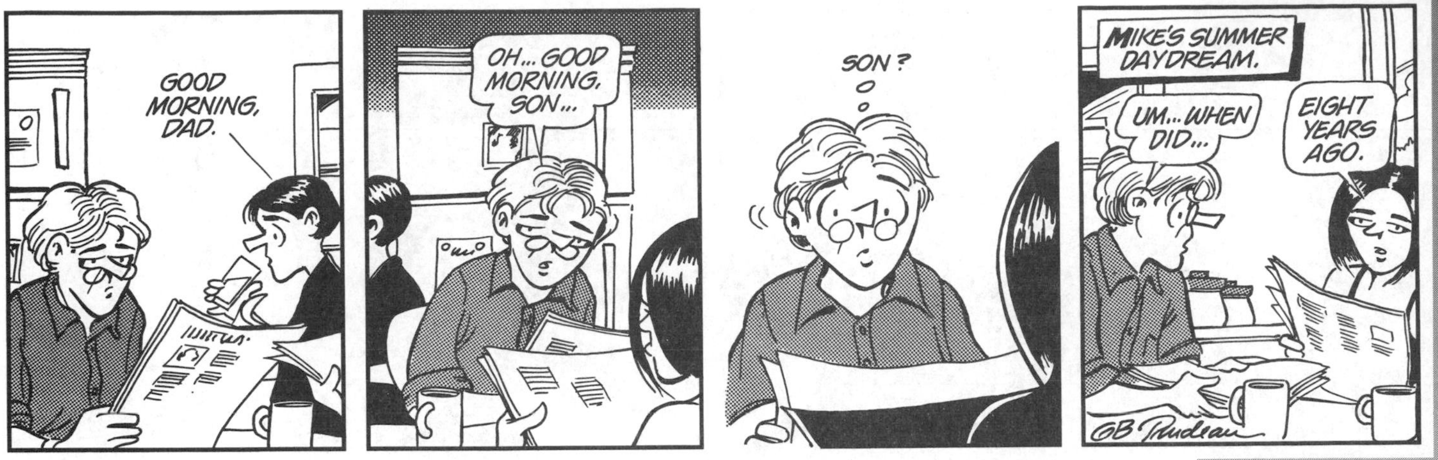
GOOD MORNING, DAD.
OH... GOOD MORNING, SON...
SON?
MIKE'S SUMMER DAYDREAM.
UM... WHEN DID...
EIGHT YEARS AGO.
GB Trudeau

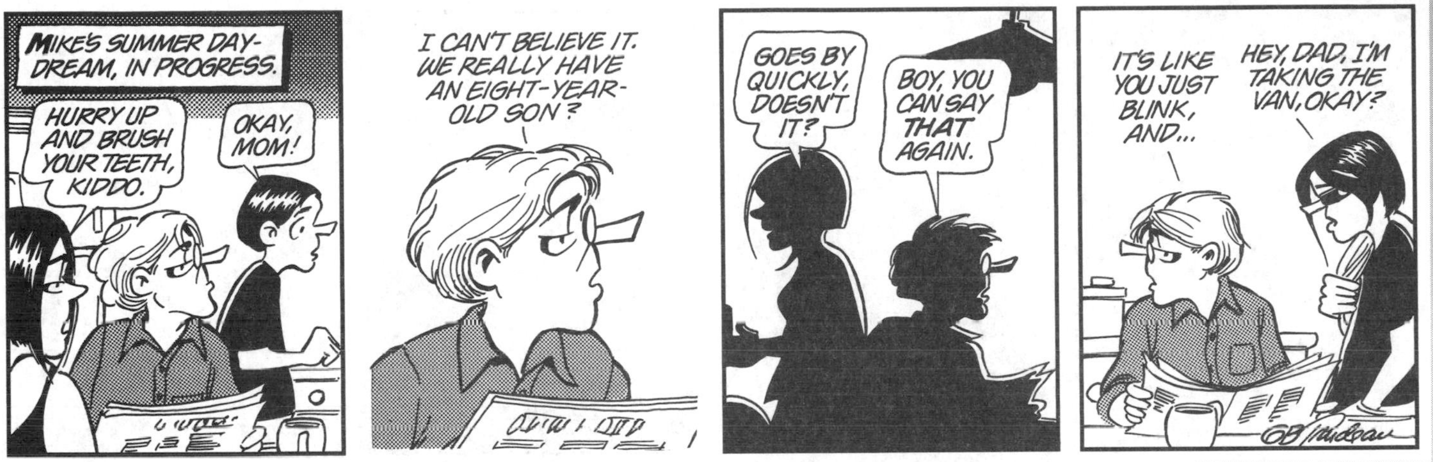
MIKE'S SUMMER DAY-DREAM, IN PROGRESS.
HURRY UP AND BRUSH YOUR TEETH, KIDDO.
OKAY, MOM!
I CAN'T BELIEVE IT. WE REALLY HAVE AN EIGHT-YEAR-OLD SON?
GOES BY QUICKLY, DOESN'T IT?
BOY, YOU CAN SAY THAT AGAIN.
IT'S LIKE YOU JUST BLINK, AND...
HEY, DAD, I'M TAKING THE VAN, OKAY?
GB Trudeau

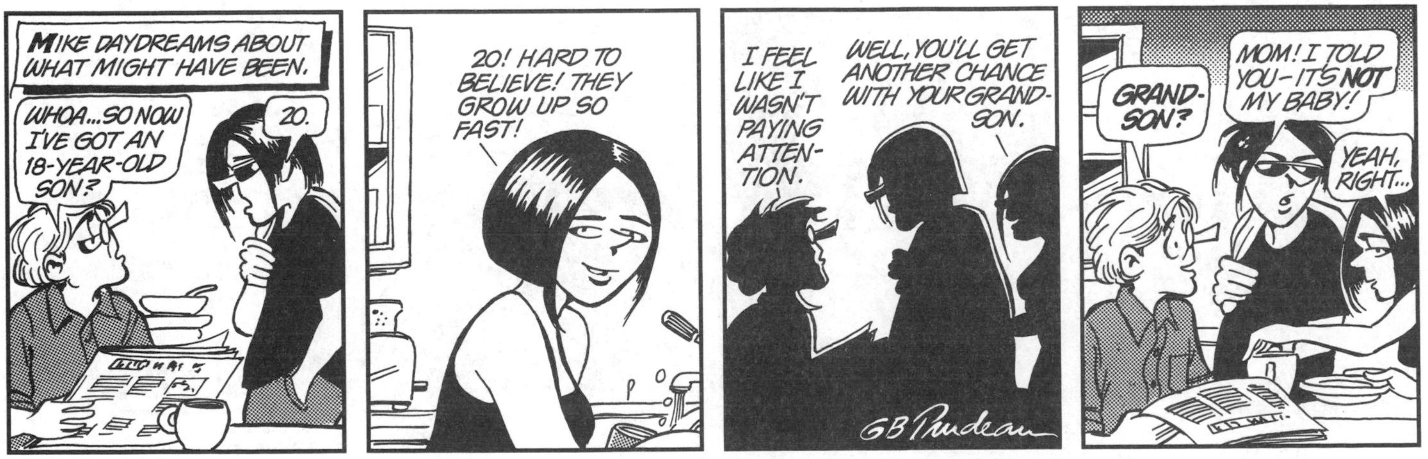
MIKE DAYDREAMS ABOUT WHAT MIGHT HAVE BEEN.
WHOA... SO NOW I'VE GOT AN 18-YEAR-OLD SON?
20.
20! HARD TO BELIEVE! THEY GROW UP SO FAST!
I FEEL LIKE I WASN'T PAYING ATTEN-TION.
WELL, YOU'LL GET ANOTHER CHANCE WITH YOUR GRAND-SON.
GB Trudeau
GRAND-SON?
MOM! I TOLD YOU– IT'S NOT MY BABY!
YEAH, RIGHT...

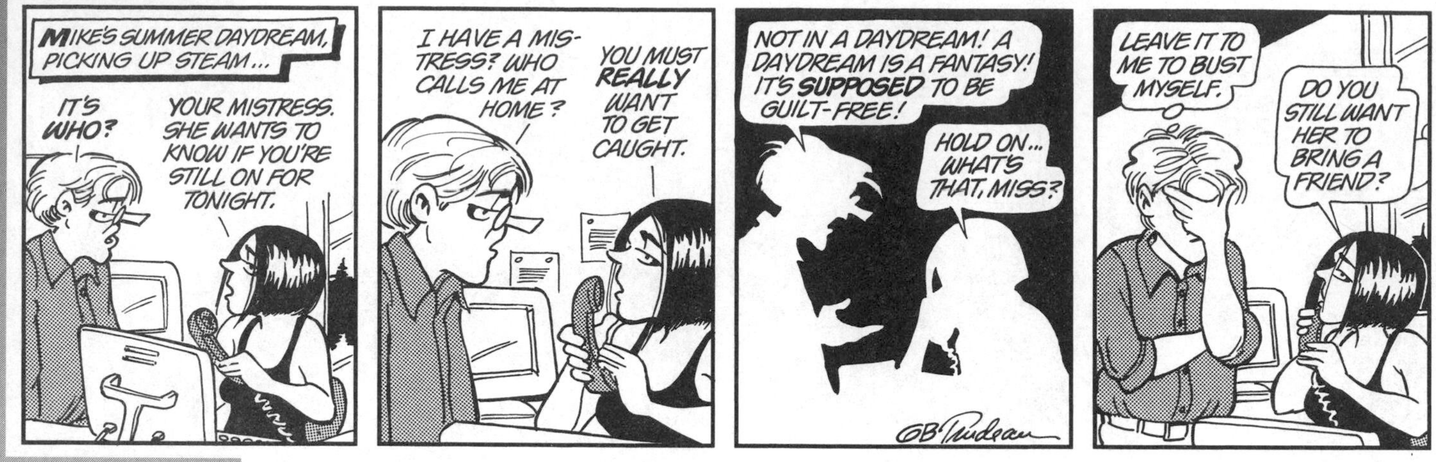
MIKE'S SUMMER DAYDREAM, PICKING UP STEAM...
IT'S WHO?
YOUR MISTRESS. SHE WANTS TO KNOW IF YOU'RE STILL ON FOR TONIGHT.
I HAVE A MISTRESS? WHO CALLS ME AT HOME?
YOU MUST REALLY WANT TO GET CAUGHT.
NOT IN A DAYDREAM! A DAYDREAM IS A FANTASY! IT'S SUPPOSED TO BE GUILT-FREE!
HOLD ON... WHAT'S THAT, MISS?
LEAVE IT TO ME TO BUST MYSELF.
DO YOU STILL WANT HER TO BRING A FRIEND?

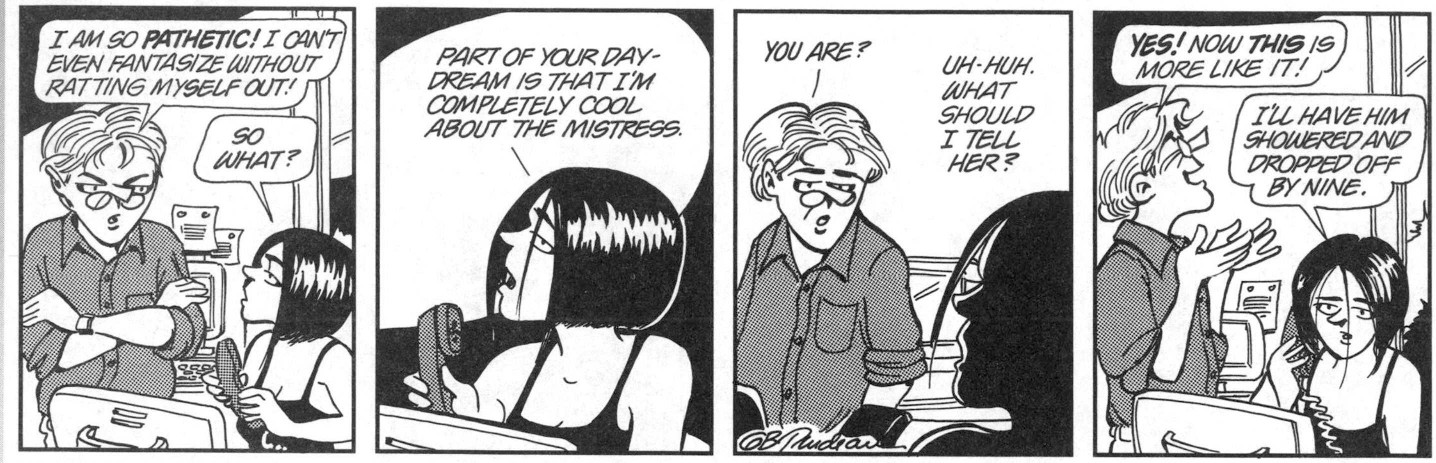
I AM SO PATHETIC! I CAN'T EVEN FANTASIZE WITHOUT RATTING MYSELF OUT!
SO WHAT?
PART OF YOUR DAYDREAM IS THAT I'M COMPLETELY COOL ABOUT THE MISTRESS.
YOU ARE?
UH-HUH. WHAT SHOULD I TELL HER?
YES! NOW THIS IS MORE LIKE IT!
I'LL HAVE HIM SHOWERED AND DROPPED OFF BY NINE.

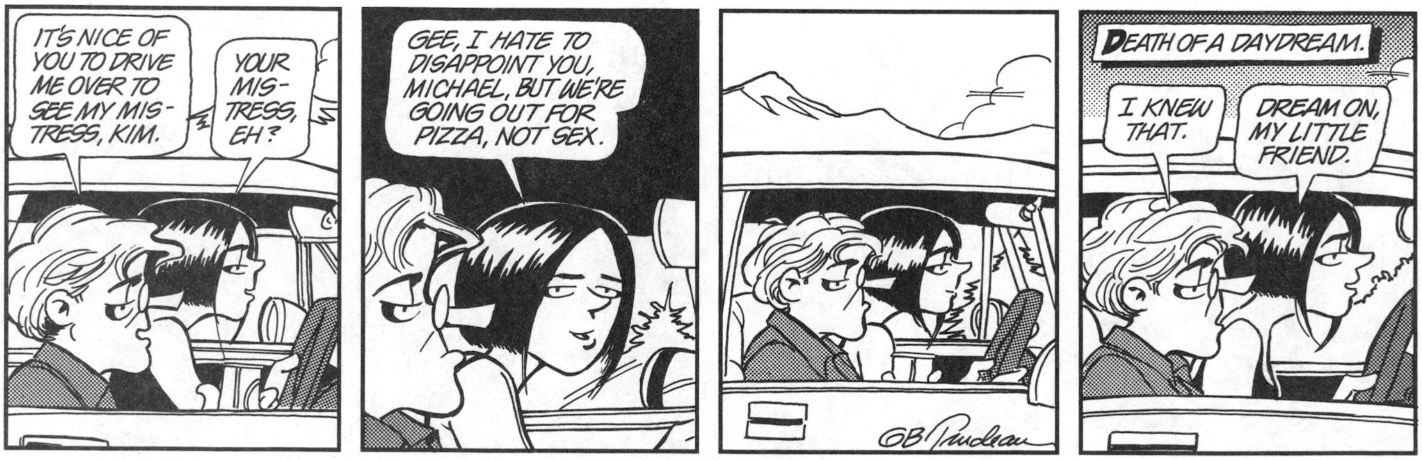
IT'S NICE OF YOU TO DRIVE ME OVER TO SEE MY MISTRESS, KIM.
YOUR MISTRESS, EH?
GEE, I HATE TO DISAPPOINT YOU, MICHAEL, BUT WE'RE GOING OUT FOR PIZZA, NOT SEX.
DEATH OF A DAYDREAM.
I KNEW THAT.
DREAM ON, MY LITTLE FRIEND.

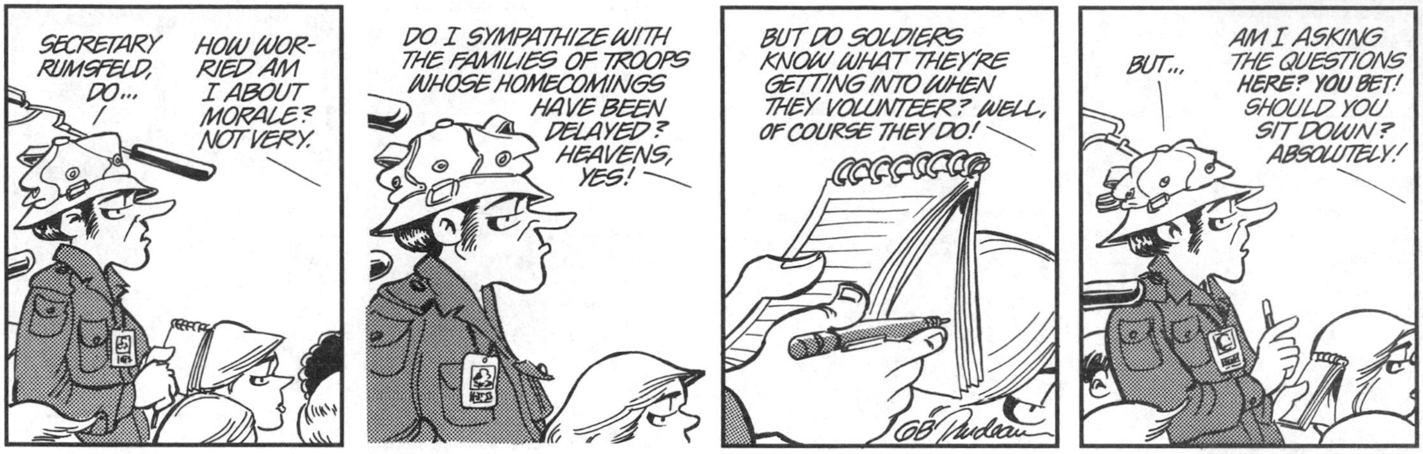
SECRETARY RUMSFELD, DO...
HOW WORRIED AM I ABOUT MORALE? NOT VERY.
DO I SYMPATHIZE WITH THE FAMILIES OF TROOPS WHOSE HOMECOMINGS HAVE BEEN DELAYED? HEAVENS, YES!
BUT DO SOLDIERS KNOW WHAT THEY'RE GETTING INTO WHEN THEY VOLUNTEER? WELL, OF COURSE THEY DO!
BUT...
AM I ASKING THE QUESTIONS HERE? YOU BET! SHOULD YOU SIT DOWN? ABSOLUTELY!

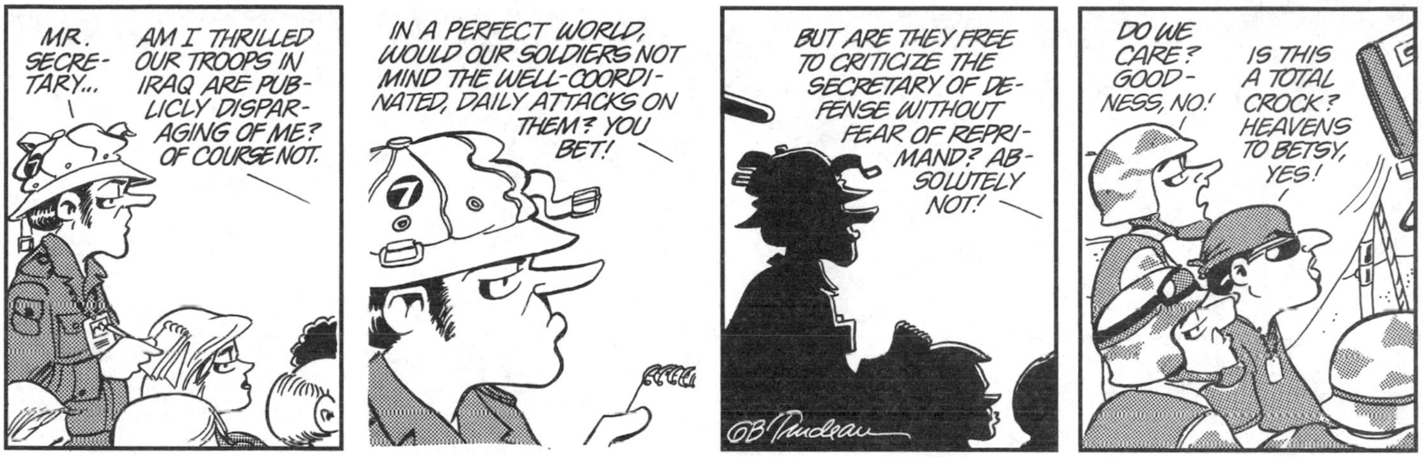
MR. SECRETARY...
AM I THRILLED OUR TROOPS IN IRAQ ARE PUBLICLY DISPARAGING OF ME? OF COURSE NOT.
IN A PERFECT WORLD, WOULD OUR SOLDIERS NOT MIND THE WELL-COORDINATED, DAILY ATTACKS ON THEM? YOU BET!
BUT ARE THEY FREE TO CRITICIZE THE SECRETARY OF DEFENSE WITHOUT FEAR OF REPRIMAND? ABSOLUTELY NOT!
DO WE CARE? GOODNESS, NO!
IS THIS A TOTAL CROCK? HEAVENS TO BETSY, YES!

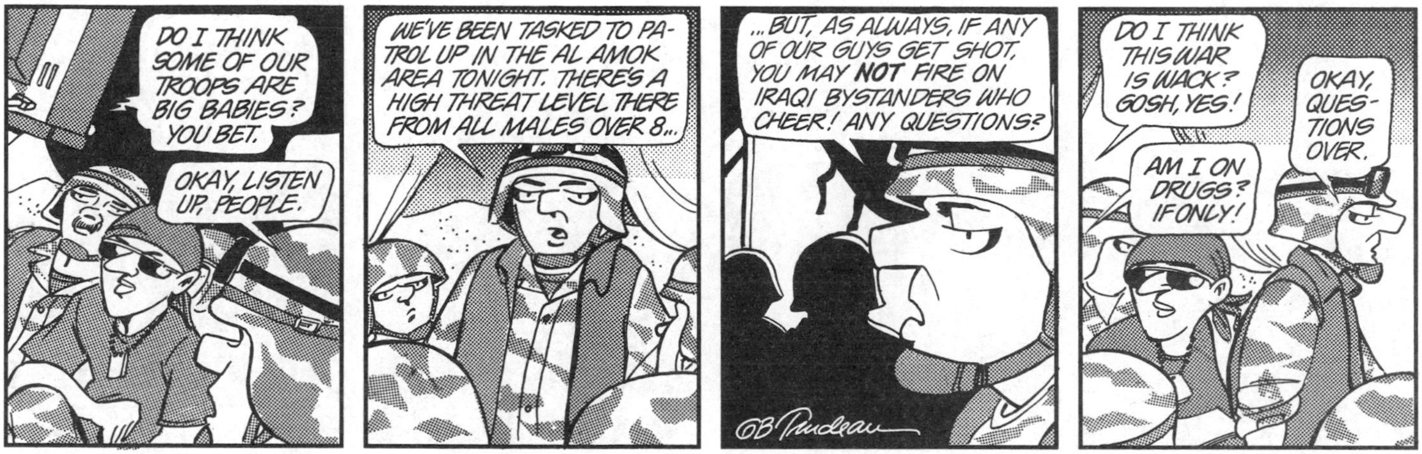
DO I THINK SOME OF OUR TROOPS ARE BIG BABIES? YOU BET.
OKAY, LISTEN UP, PEOPLE.
WE'VE BEEN TASKED TO PATROL UP IN THE AL AMOK AREA TONIGHT. THERE'S A HIGH THREAT LEVEL THERE FROM ALL MALES OVER 8...
...BUT, AS ALWAYS, IF ANY OF OUR GUYS GET SHOT, YOU MAY NOT FIRE ON IRAQI BYSTANDERS WHO CHEER! ANY QUESTIONS?
DO I THINK THIS WAR IS WACK? GOSH, YES!
AM I ON DRUGS? IF ONLY!
OKAY, QUESTIONS OVER.

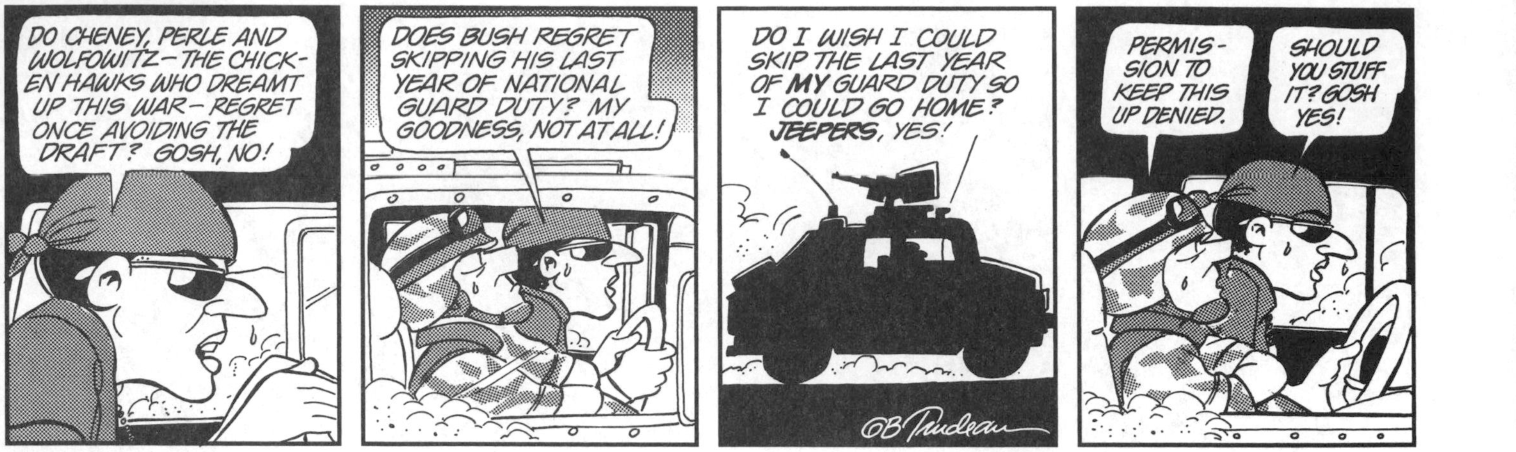
DO CHENEY, PERLE AND WOLFOWITZ—THE CHICKEN HAWKS WHO DREAMT UP THIS WAR—REGRET ONCE AVOIDING THE DRAFT? GOSH, NO!
DOES BUSH REGRET SKIPPING HIS LAST YEAR OF NATIONAL GUARD DUTY? MY GOODNESS, NOT AT ALL!
DO I WISH I COULD SKIP THE LAST YEAR OF **MY** GUARD DUTY SO I COULD GO HOME? **JEEPERS**, YES!
PERMISSION TO KEEP THIS UP DENIED.
SHOULD YOU STUFF IT? GOSH YES!
©B Trudeau

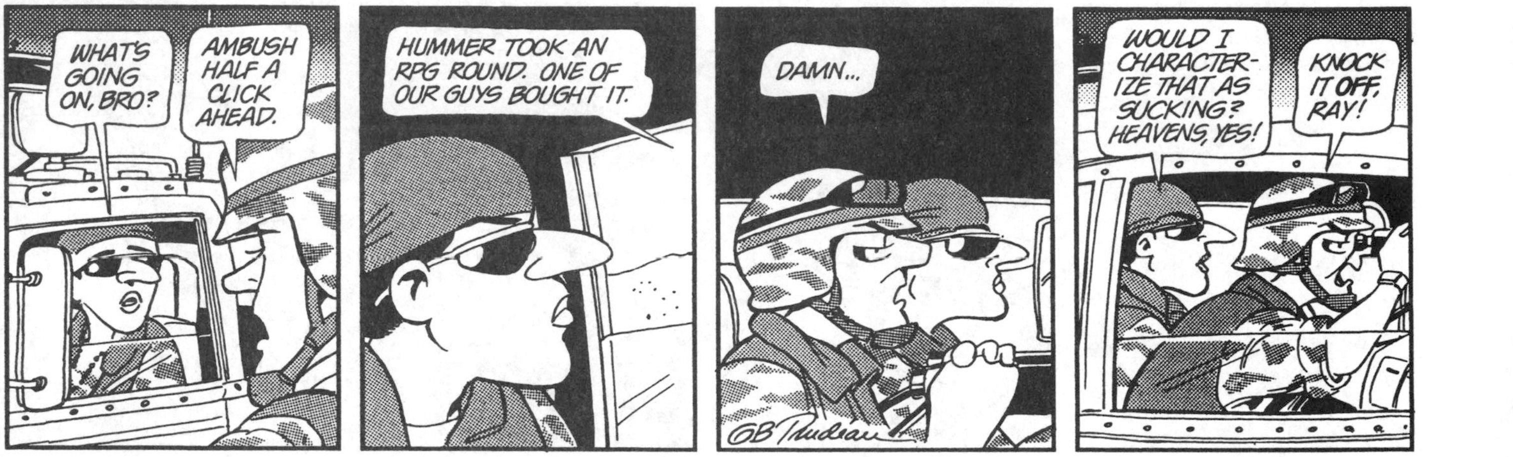
WHAT'S GOING ON, BRO?
AMBUSH HALF A CLICK AHEAD.
HUMMER TOOK AN RPG ROUND. ONE OF OUR GUYS BOUGHT IT.
DAMN...
WOULD I CHARACTERIZE THAT AS SUCKING? HEAVENS, YES!
KNOCK IT **OFF**, RAY!
©B Trudeau

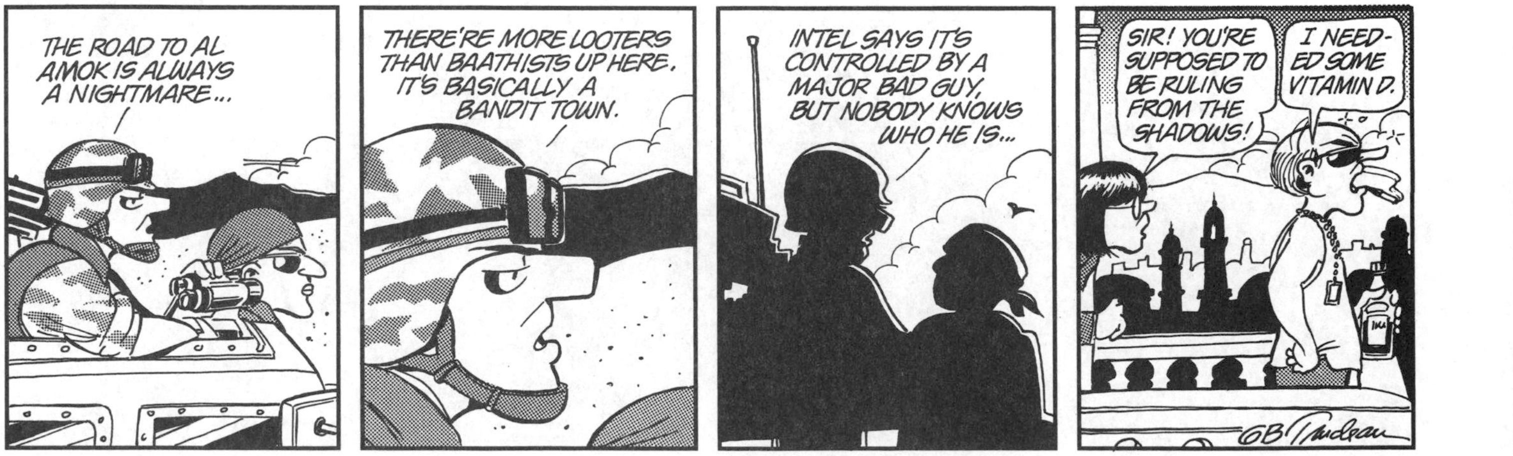
THE ROAD TO AL AMOK IS ALWAYS A NIGHTMARE...
THERE'RE MORE LOOTERS THAN BAATHISTS UP HERE. IT'S BASICALLY A BANDIT TOWN.
INTEL SAYS IT'S CONTROLLED BY A MAJOR BAD GUY, BUT NOBODY KNOWS WHO HE IS...
SIR! YOU'RE SUPPOSED TO BE RULING FROM THE SHADOWS!
I NEEDED SOME VITAMIN D.
©B Trudeau

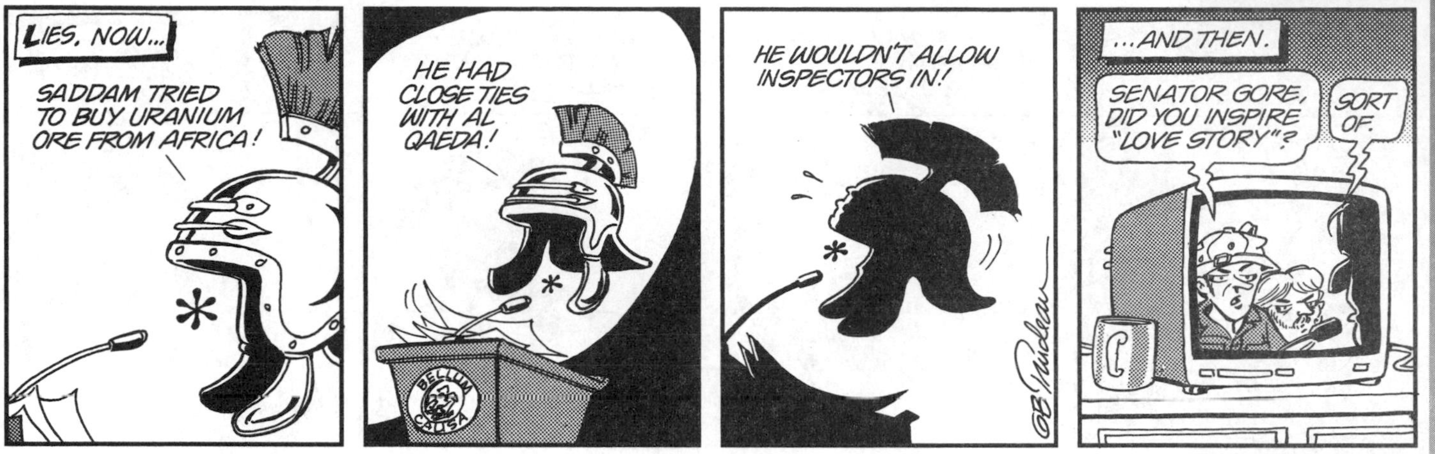
LIES, NOW...
SADDAM TRIED TO BUY URANIUM ORE FROM AFRICA!
HE HAD CLOSE TIES WITH AL QAEDA!
BELLUM CAUSA
HE WOULDN'T ALLOW INSPECTORS IN!
...AND THEN.
SENATOR GORE, DID YOU INSPIRE "LOVE STORY"?
SORT OF.

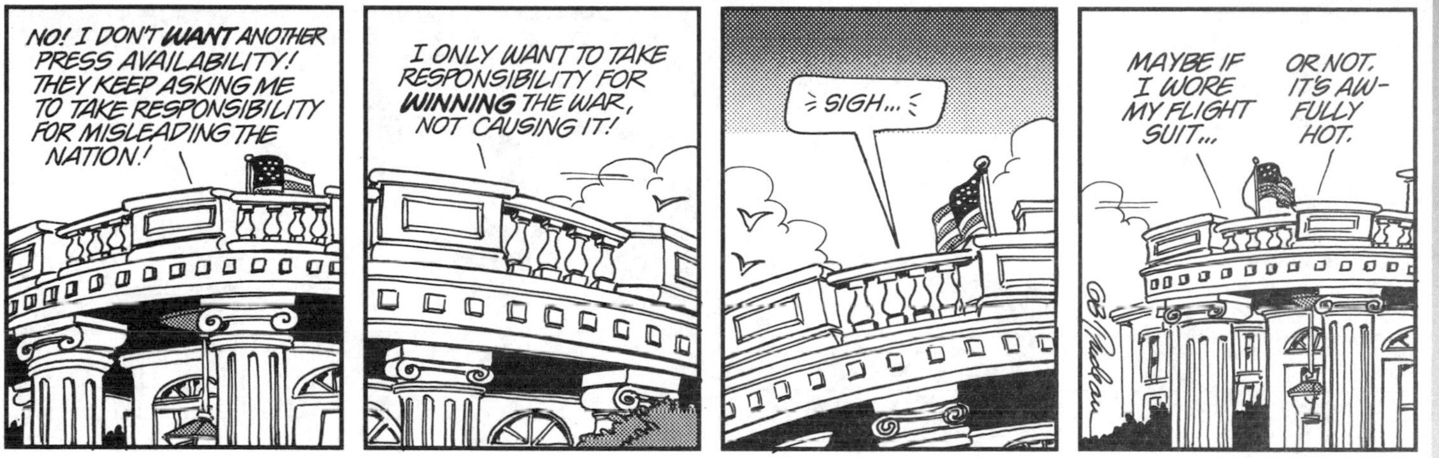
NO! I DON'T WANT ANOTHER PRESS AVAILABILITY! THEY KEEP ASKING ME TO TAKE RESPONSIBILITY FOR MISLEADING THE NATION!
I ONLY WANT TO TAKE RESPONSIBILITY FOR WINNING THE WAR, NOT CAUSING IT!
SIGH...
MAYBE IF I WORE MY FLIGHT SUIT...
OR NOT. IT'S AWFULLY HOT.

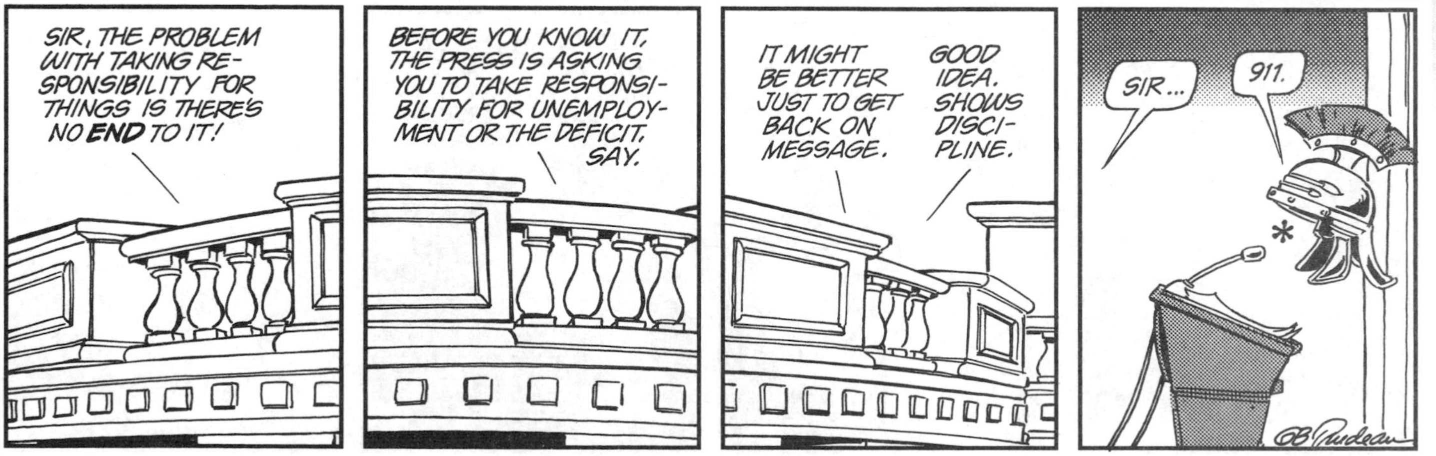
SIR, THE PROBLEM WITH TAKING RESPONSIBILITY FOR THINGS IS THERE'S NO END TO IT!
BEFORE YOU KNOW IT, THE PRESS IS ASKING YOU TO TAKE RESPONSIBILITY FOR UNEMPLOYMENT OR THE DEFICIT, SAY.
IT MIGHT BE BETTER JUST TO GET BACK ON MESSAGE.
GOOD IDEA. SHOWS DISCIPLINE.
SIR...
911.

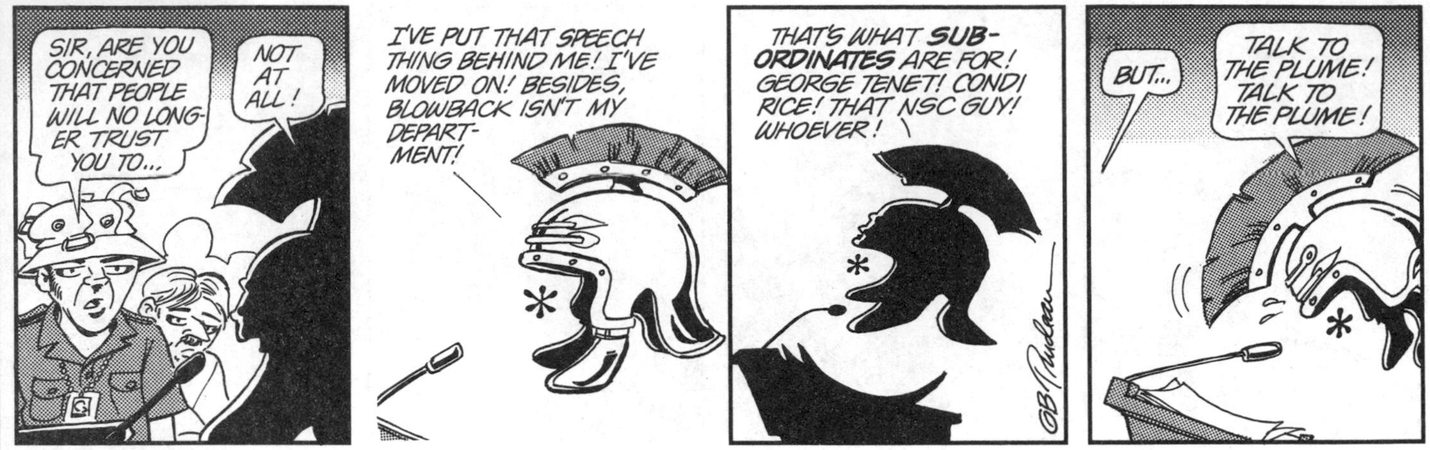
SIR, ARE YOU CONCERNED THAT PEOPLE WILL NO LONGER TRUST YOU TO...
NOT AT ALL!
I'VE PUT THAT SPEECH THING BEHIND ME! I'VE MOVED ON! BESIDES, BLOWBACK ISN'T MY DEPARTMENT!
THAT'S WHAT **SUBORDINATES** ARE FOR! GEORGE TENET! CONDI RICE! THAT NSC GUY! WHOEVER!
BUT...
TALK TO THE PLUME! TALK TO THE PLUME!

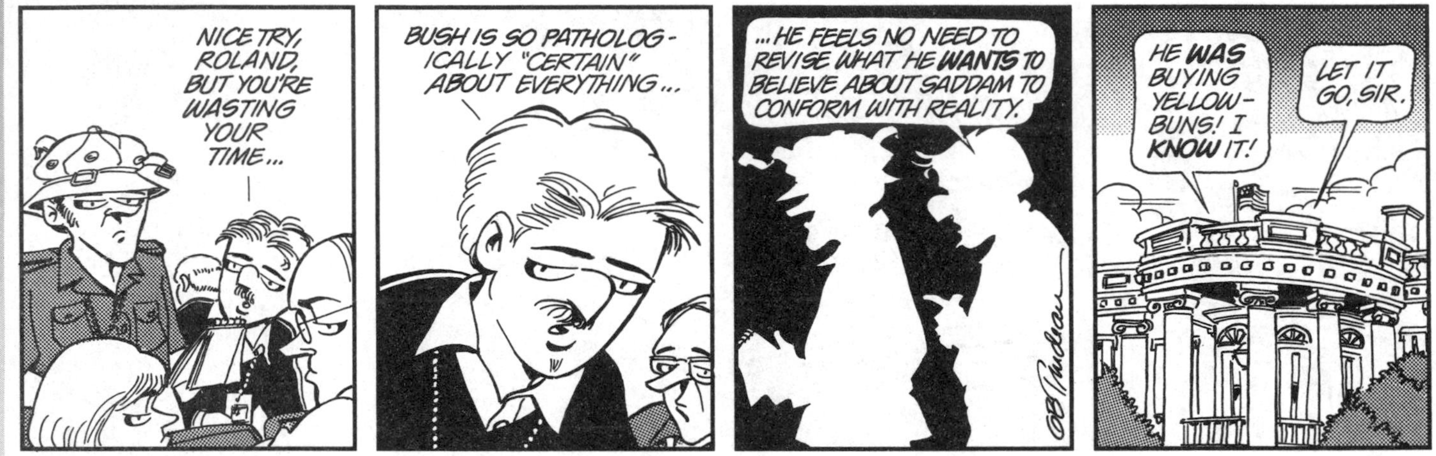
NICE TRY, ROLAND, BUT YOU'RE WASTING YOUR TIME...
BUSH IS SO PATHOLOGICALLY "CERTAIN" ABOUT EVERYTHING...
...HE FEELS NO NEED TO REVISE WHAT HE **WANTS** TO BELIEVE ABOUT SADDAM TO CONFORM WITH REALITY.
HE **WAS** BUYING YELLOW-BUNS! I **KNOW** IT!
LET IT GO, SIR.

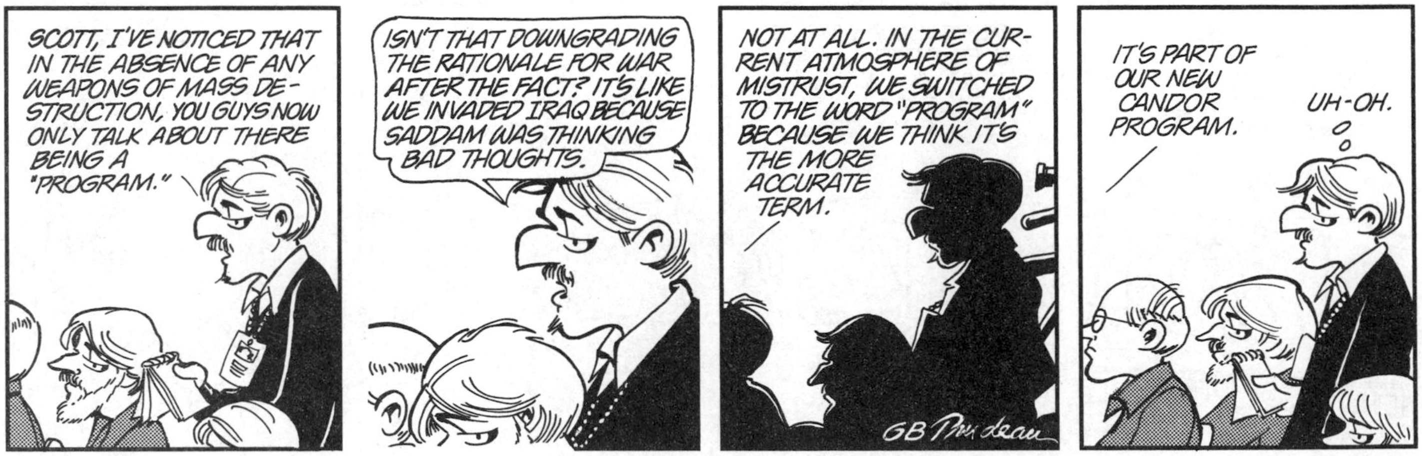
SCOTT, I'VE NOTICED THAT IN THE ABSENCE OF ANY WEAPONS OF MASS DESTRUCTION, YOU GUYS NOW ONLY TALK ABOUT THERE BEING A "PROGRAM."
ISN'T THAT DOWNGRADING THE RATIONALE FOR WAR AFTER THE FACT? IT'S LIKE WE INVADED IRAQ BECAUSE SADDAM WAS THINKING BAD THOUGHTS.
NOT AT ALL. IN THE CURRENT ATMOSPHERE OF MISTRUST, WE SWITCHED TO THE WORD "PROGRAM" BECAUSE WE THINK IT'S THE MORE ACCURATE TERM.
IT'S PART OF OUR NEW CANDOR PROGRAM.
UH-OH.

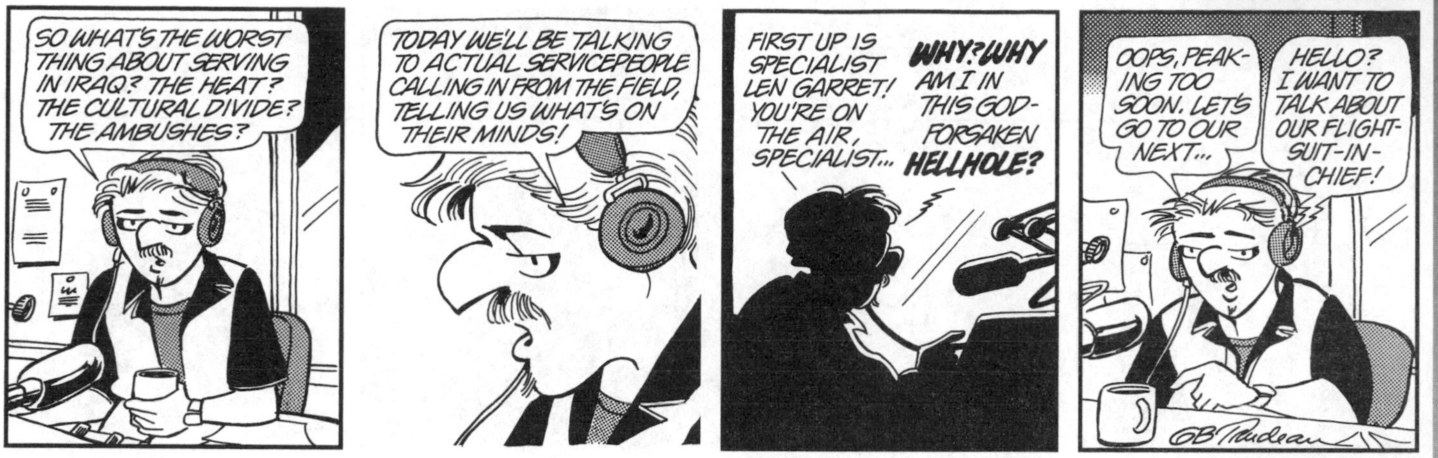
SO WHAT'S THE WORST THING ABOUT SERVING IN IRAQ? THE HEAT? THE CULTURAL DIVIDE? THE AMBUSHES?
TODAY WE'LL BE TALKING TO ACTUAL SERVICEPEOPLE CALLING IN FROM THE FIELD, TELLING US WHAT'S ON THEIR MINDS!
FIRST UP IS SPECIALIST LEN GARRET! YOU'RE ON THE AIR, SPECIALIST...
WHY? WHY AM I IN THIS GOD-FORSAKEN HELLHOLE?
OOPS, PEAKING TOO SOON. LET'S GO TO OUR NEXT...
HELLO? I WANT TO TALK ABOUT OUR FLIGHT-SUIT-IN-CHIEF!
GB Trudeau

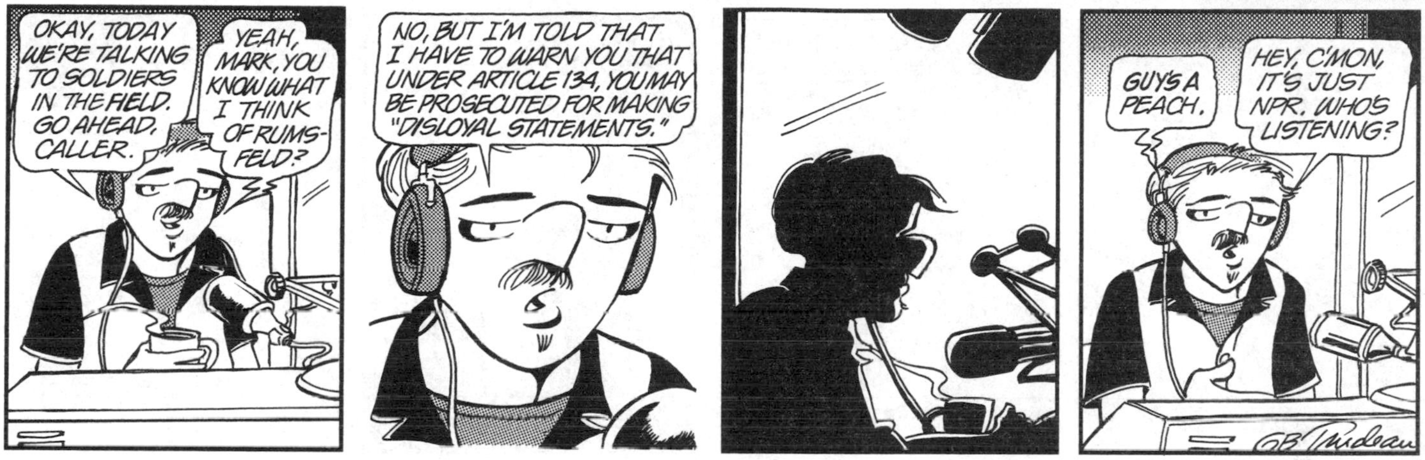
OKAY, TODAY WE'RE TALKING TO SOLDIERS IN THE FIELD. GO AHEAD, CALLER.
YEAH, MARK, YOU KNOW WHAT I THINK OF RUMSFELD?
NO, BUT I'M TOLD THAT I HAVE TO WARN YOU THAT UNDER ARTICLE 134, YOU MAY BE PROSECUTED FOR MAKING "DISLOYAL STATEMENTS."
GUY'S A PEACH.
HEY, C'MON, IT'S JUST NPR. WHO'S LISTENING?
GB Trudeau

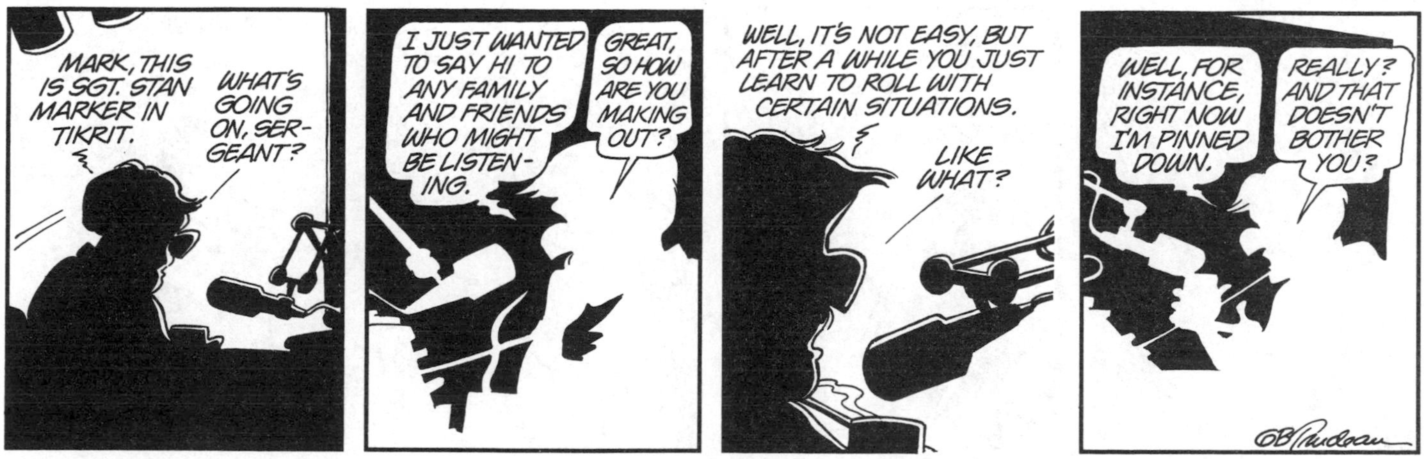
MARK, THIS IS SGT. STAN MARKER IN TIKRIT.
WHAT'S GOING ON, SERGEANT?
I JUST WANTED TO SAY HI TO ANY FAMILY AND FRIENDS WHO MIGHT BE LISTENING.
GREAT, SO HOW ARE YOU MAKING OUT?
WELL, IT'S NOT EASY, BUT AFTER A WHILE YOU JUST LEARN TO ROLL WITH CERTAIN SITUATIONS.
LIKE WHAT?
WELL, FOR INSTANCE, RIGHT NOW I'M PINNED DOWN.
REALLY? AND THAT DOESN'T BOTHER YOU?
GB Trudeau

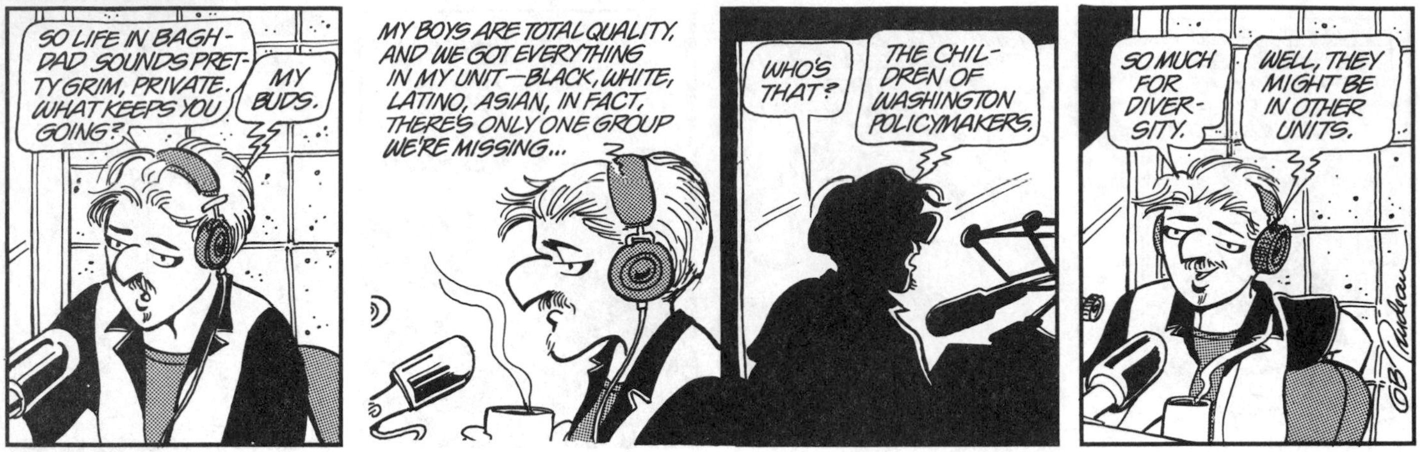
SO LIFE IN BAGHDAD SOUNDS PRETTY GRIM, PRIVATE. WHAT KEEPS YOU GOING?
MY BUDS.
MY BOYS ARE TOTAL QUALITY, AND WE GOT EVERYTHING IN MY UNIT—BLACK, WHITE, LATINO, ASIAN, IN FACT, THERE'S ONLY ONE GROUP WE'RE MISSING...
WHO'S THAT?
THE CHILDREN OF WASHINGTON POLICYMAKERS.
SO MUCH FOR DIVERSITY.
WELL, THEY MIGHT BE IN OTHER UNITS.

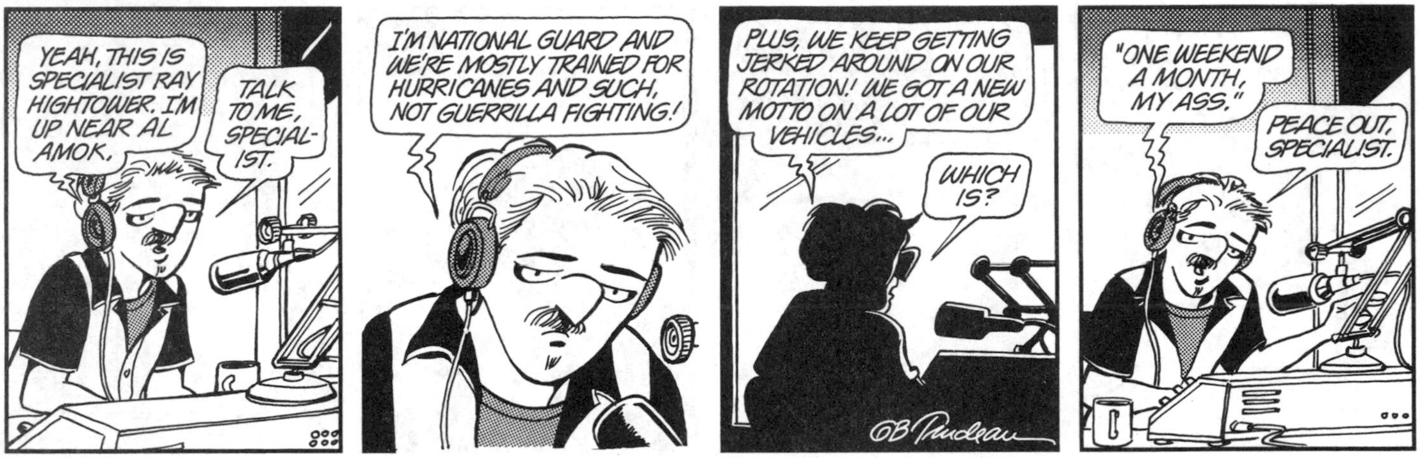
YEAH, THIS IS SPECIALIST RAY HIGHTOWER. I'M UP NEAR AL AMOK.
TALK TO ME, SPECIALIST.
I'M NATIONAL GUARD AND WE'RE MOSTLY TRAINED FOR HURRICANES AND SUCH, NOT GUERRILLA FIGHTING!
PLUS, WE KEEP GETTING JERKED AROUND ON OUR ROTATION! WE GOT A NEW MOTTO ON A LOT OF OUR VEHICLES...
WHICH IS?
"ONE WEEKEND A MONTH, MY ASS."
PEACE OUT, SPECIALIST.

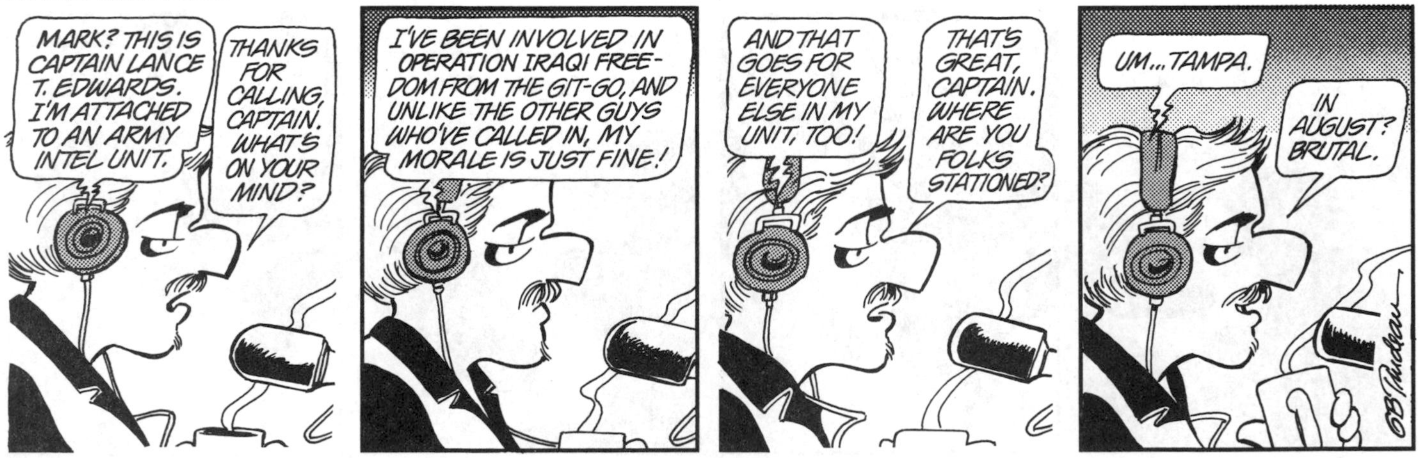
MARK? THIS IS CAPTAIN LANCE T. EDWARDS. I'M ATTACHED TO AN ARMY INTEL UNIT.
THANKS FOR CALLING, CAPTAIN. WHAT'S ON YOUR MIND?
I'VE BEEN INVOLVED IN OPERATION IRAQI FREEDOM FROM THE GIT-GO, AND UNLIKE THE OTHER GUYS WHO'VE CALLED IN, MY MORALE IS JUST FINE!
AND THAT GOES FOR EVERYONE ELSE IN MY UNIT, TOO!
THAT'S GREAT, CAPTAIN. WHERE ARE YOU FOLKS STATIONED?
UM... TAMPA.
IN AUGUST? BRUTAL.

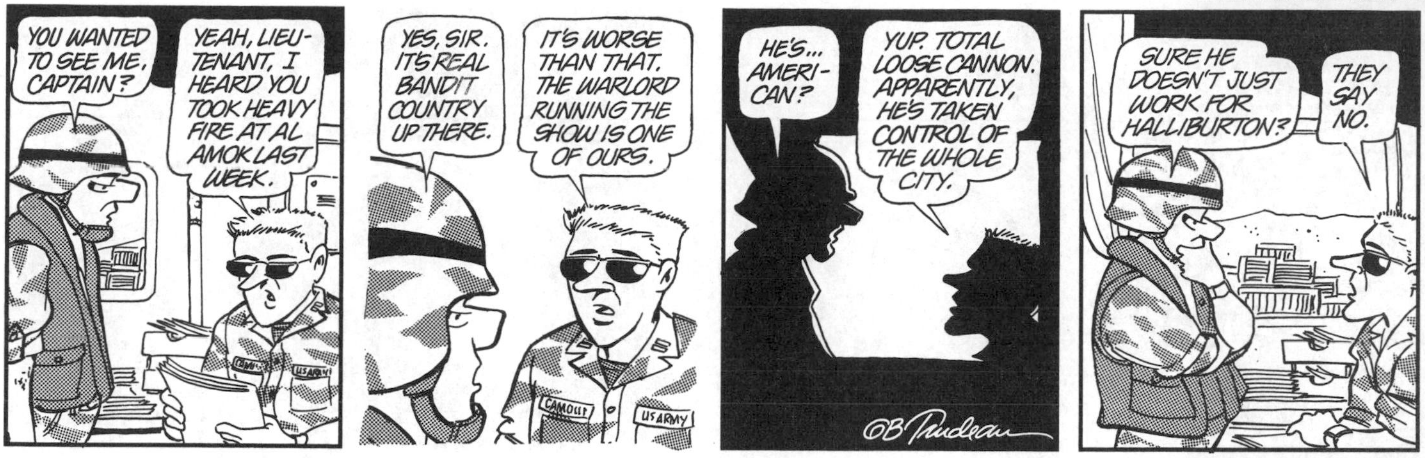
YOU WANTED TO SEE ME, CAPTAIN?
YEAH, LIEU-TENANT, I HEARD YOU TOOK HEAVY FIRE AT AL AMOK LAST WEEK.
YES, SIR. IT'S REAL BANDIT COUNTRY UP THERE.
IT'S WORSE THAN THAT. THE WARLORD RUNNING THE SHOW IS ONE OF OURS.
HE'S... AMERI-CAN?
YUP. TOTAL LOOSE CANNON. APPARENTLY, HE'S TAKEN CONTROL OF THE WHOLE CITY.
SURE HE DOESN'T JUST WORK FOR HALLIBURTON?
THEY SAY NO.

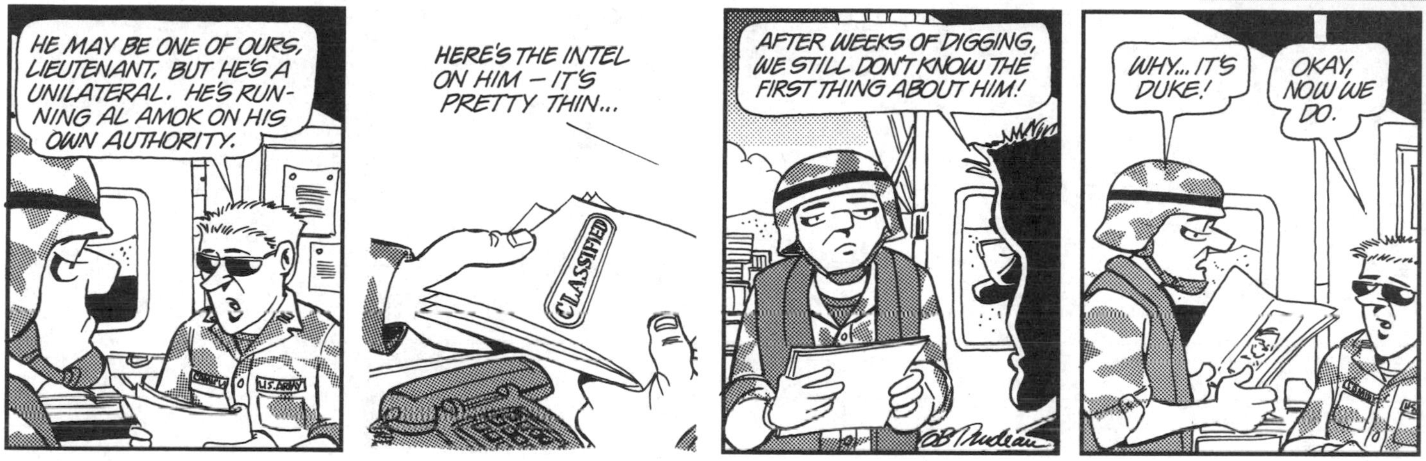
HE MAY BE ONE OF OURS, LIEUTENANT, BUT HE'S A UNILATERAL. HE'S RUN-NING AL AMOK ON HIS OWN AUTHORITY.
HERE'S THE INTEL ON HIM — IT'S PRETTY THIN...
CLASSIFIED
AFTER WEEKS OF DIGGING, WE STILL DON'T KNOW THE FIRST THING ABOUT HIM!
WHY... IT'S DUKE!
OKAY, NOW WE DO.

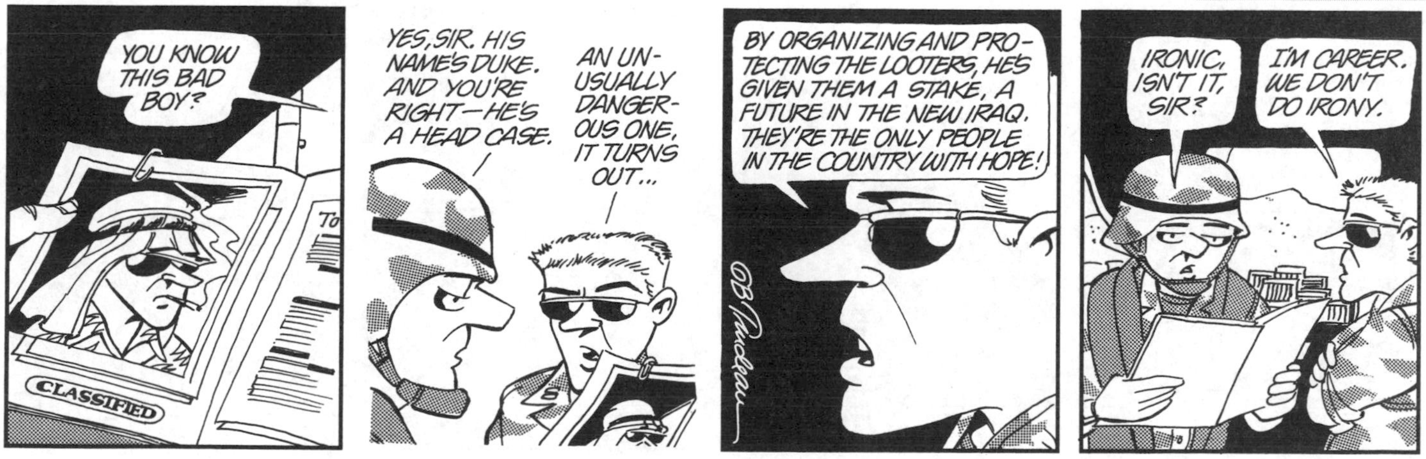
YOU KNOW THIS BAD BOY?
CLASSIFIED
YES, SIR. HIS NAME'S DUKE. AND YOU'RE RIGHT—HE'S A HEAD CASE.
AN UN-USUALLY DANGER-OUS ONE, IT TURNS OUT...
BY ORGANIZING AND PRO-TECTING THE LOOTERS, HE'S GIVEN THEM A STAKE, A FUTURE IN THE NEW IRAQ. THEY'RE THE ONLY PEOPLE IN THE COUNTRY WITH HOPE!
IRONIC, ISN'T IT, SIR?
I'M CAREER. WE DON'T DO IRONY.

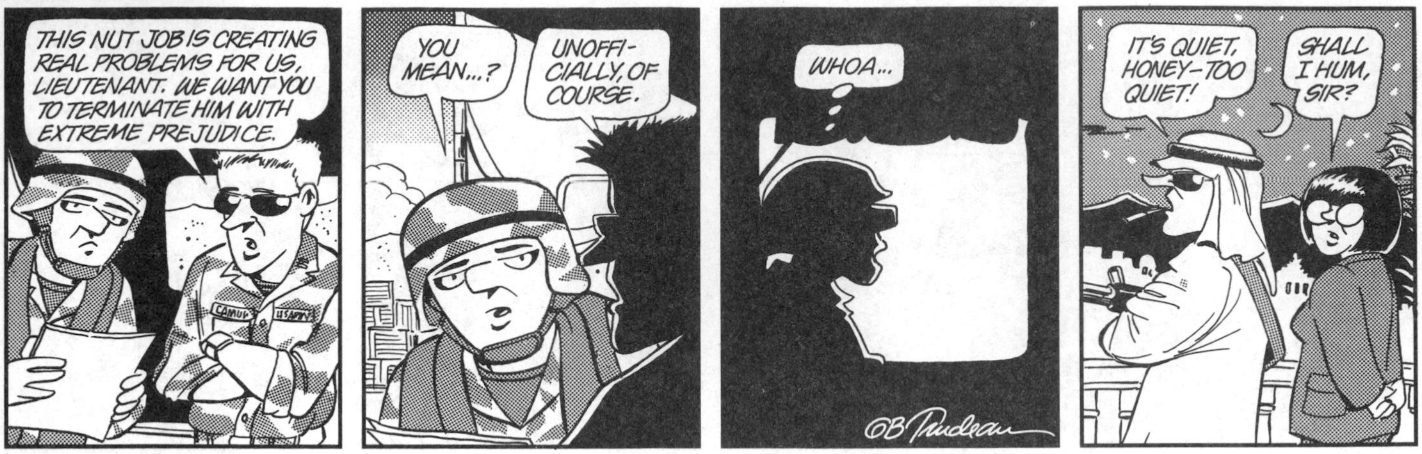
THIS NUT JOB IS CREATING REAL PROBLEMS FOR US, LIEUTENANT. WE WANT YOU TO TERMINATE HIM WITH EXTREME PREJUDICE.
YOU MEAN...?
UNOFFICIALLY, OF COURSE.
WHOA...
IT'S QUIET, HONEY–TOO QUIET!
SHALL I HUM, SIR?

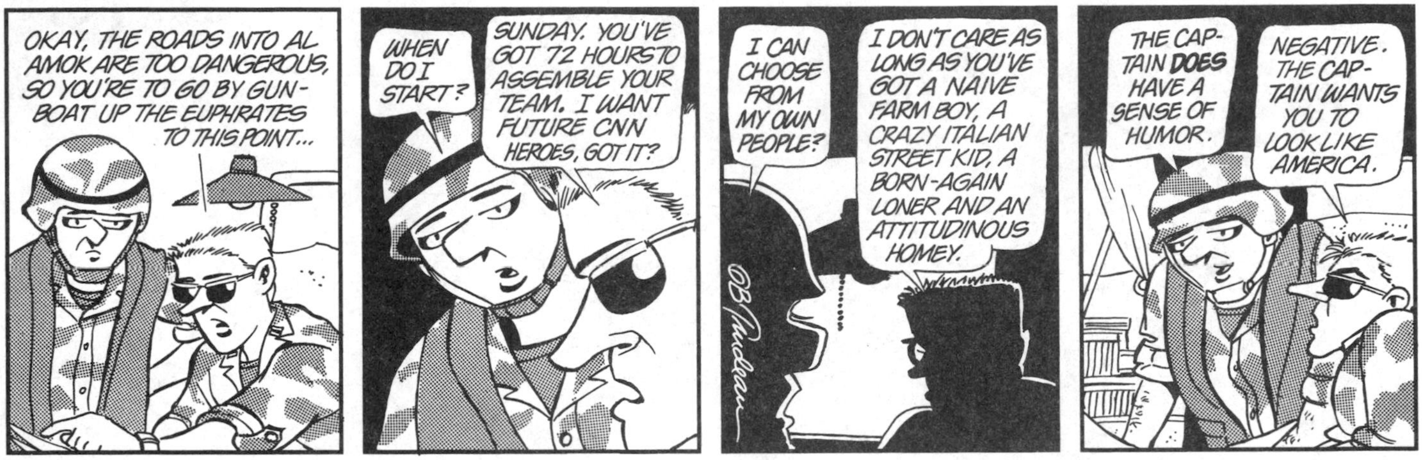
OKAY, THE ROADS INTO AL AMOK ARE TOO DANGEROUS, SO YOU'RE TO GO BY GUNBOAT UP THE EUPHRATES TO THIS POINT...
WHEN DO I START?
SUNDAY. YOU'VE GOT 72 HOURS TO ASSEMBLE YOUR TEAM. I WANT FUTURE CNN HEROES, GOT IT?
I CAN CHOOSE FROM MY OWN PEOPLE?
I DON'T CARE AS LONG AS YOU'VE GOT A NAIVE FARM BOY, A CRAZY ITALIAN STREET KID, A BORN-AGAIN LONER AND AN ATTITUDINOUS HOMEY.
THE CAPTAIN DOES HAVE A SENSE OF HUMOR.
NEGATIVE. THE CAPTAIN WANTS YOU TO LOOK LIKE AMERICA.

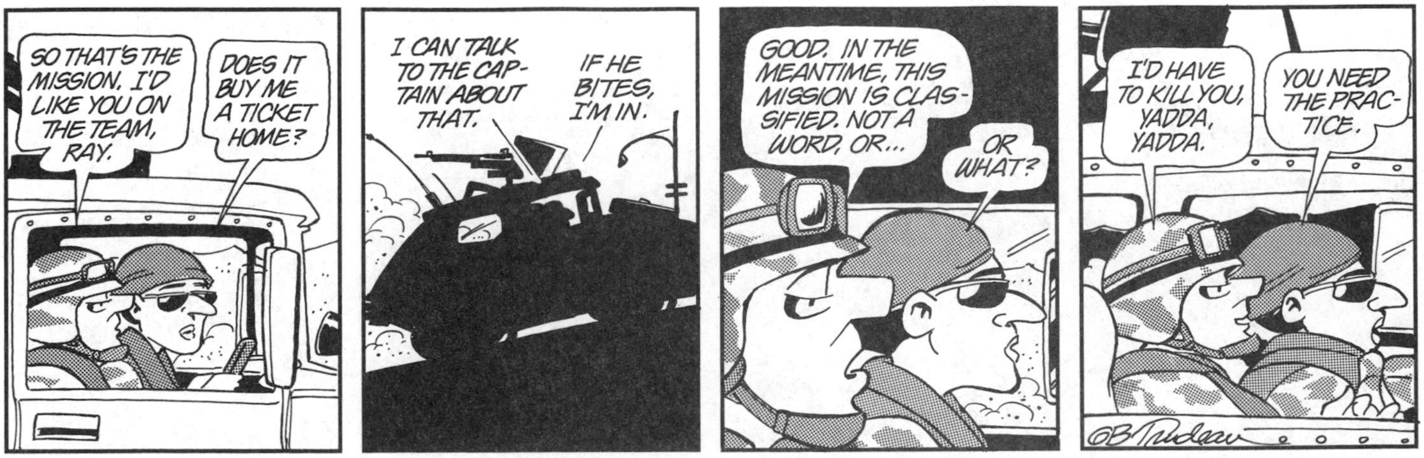
SO THAT'S THE MISSION. I'D LIKE YOU ON THE TEAM, RAY.
DOES IT BUY ME A TICKET HOME?
I CAN TALK TO THE CAPTAIN ABOUT THAT.
IF HE BITES, I'M IN.
GOOD. IN THE MEANTIME, THIS MISSION IS CLASSIFIED. NOT A WORD, OR...
OR WHAT?
I'D HAVE TO KILL YOU, YADDA, YADDA.
YOU NEED THE PRACTICE.

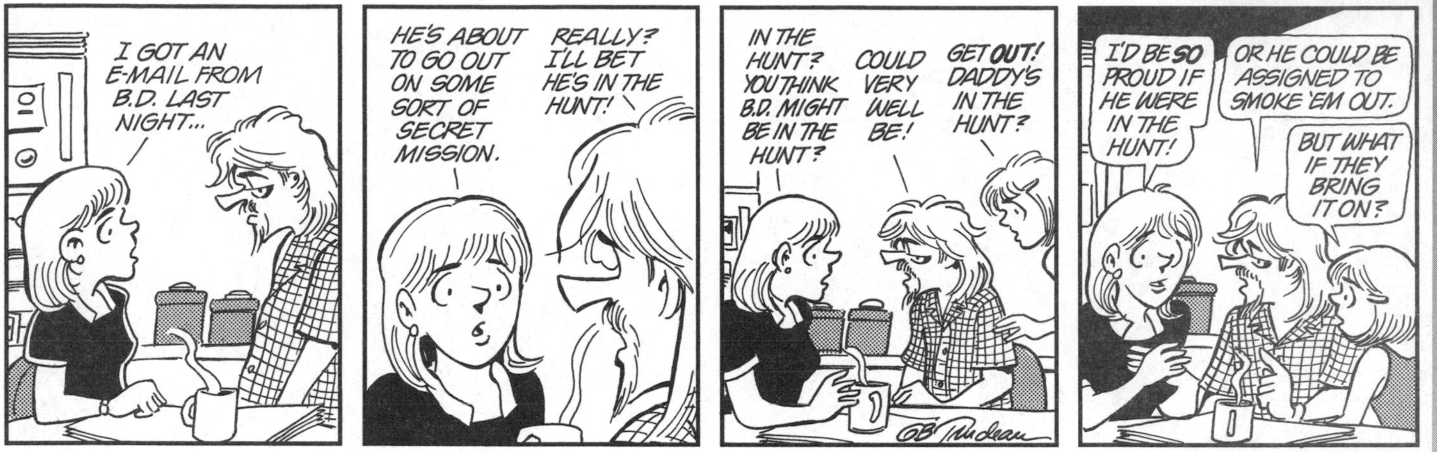
I GOT AN E-MAIL FROM B.D. LAST NIGHT...
HE'S ABOUT TO GO OUT ON SOME SORT OF SECRET MISSION.
REALLY? I'LL BET HE'S IN THE HUNT!
IN THE HUNT? YOU THINK B.D. MIGHT BE IN THE HUNT?
COULD VERY WELL BE!
GET **OUT**! DADDY'S IN THE HUNT?
I'D BE **SO** PROUD IF HE WERE IN THE HUNT!
OR HE COULD BE ASSIGNED TO SMOKE 'EM OUT.
BUT WHAT IF THEY BRING IT ON?

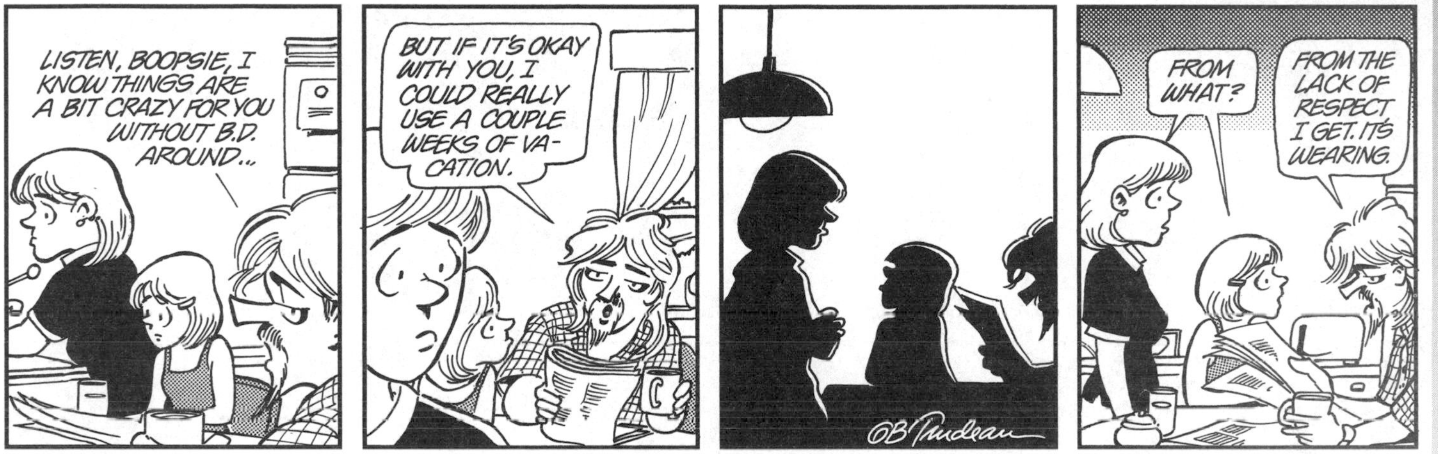
LISTEN, BOOPSIE, I KNOW THINGS ARE A BIT CRAZY FOR YOU WITHOUT B.D. AROUND...
BUT IF IT'S OKAY WITH YOU, I COULD REALLY USE A COUPLE WEEKS OF VA- CATION.
FROM WHAT?
FROM THE LACK OF RESPECT I GET. IT'S WEARING.

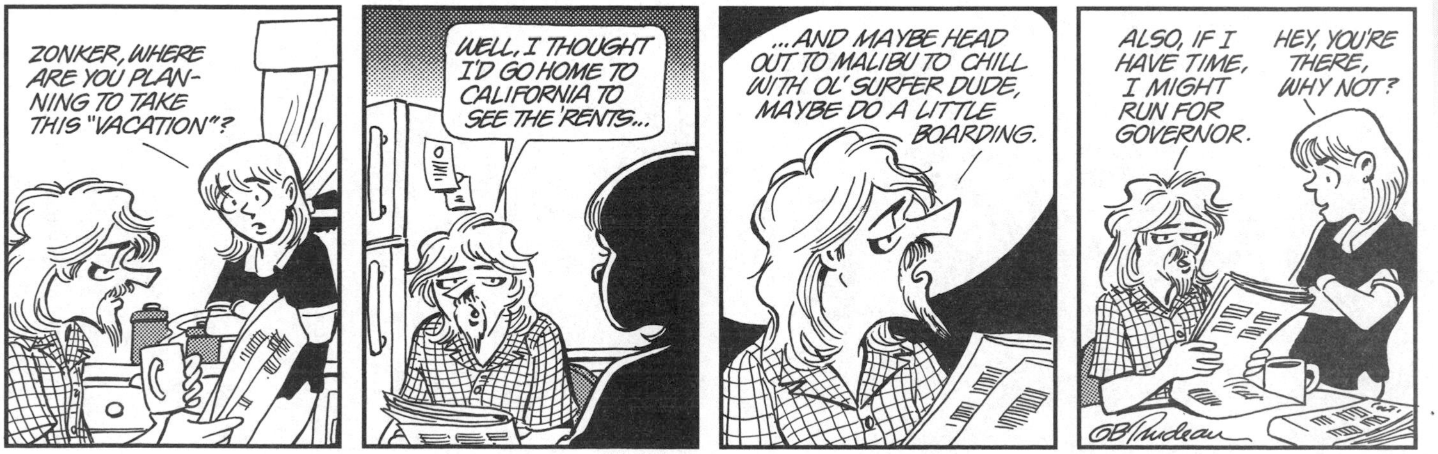
ZONKER, WHERE ARE YOU PLAN- NING TO TAKE THIS "VACATION"?
WELL, I THOUGHT I'D GO HOME TO CALIFORNIA TO SEE THE 'RENTS...
...AND MAYBE HEAD OUT TO MALIBU TO CHILL WITH OL' SURFER DUDE, MAYBE DO A LITTLE BOARDING.
ALSO, IF I HAVE TIME, I MIGHT RUN FOR GOVERNOR.
HEY, YOU'RE THERE, WHY NOT?

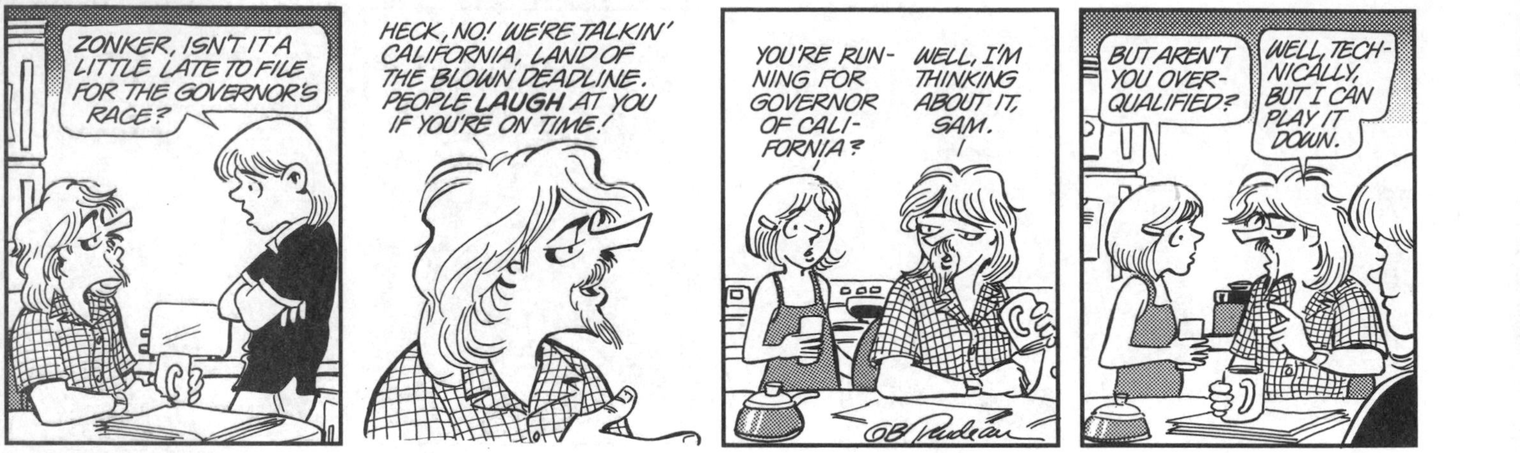
ZONKER, ISN'T IT A LITTLE LATE TO FILE FOR THE GOVERNOR'S RACE?
HECK, NO! WE'RE TALKIN' CALIFORNIA, LAND OF THE BLOWN DEADLINE. PEOPLE LAUGH AT YOU IF YOU'RE ON TIME!
YOU'RE RUNNING FOR GOVERNOR OF CALIFORNIA?
WELL, I'M THINKING ABOUT IT, SAM.
BUT AREN'T YOU OVERQUALIFIED?
WELL, TECHNICALLY, BUT I CAN PLAY IT DOWN.

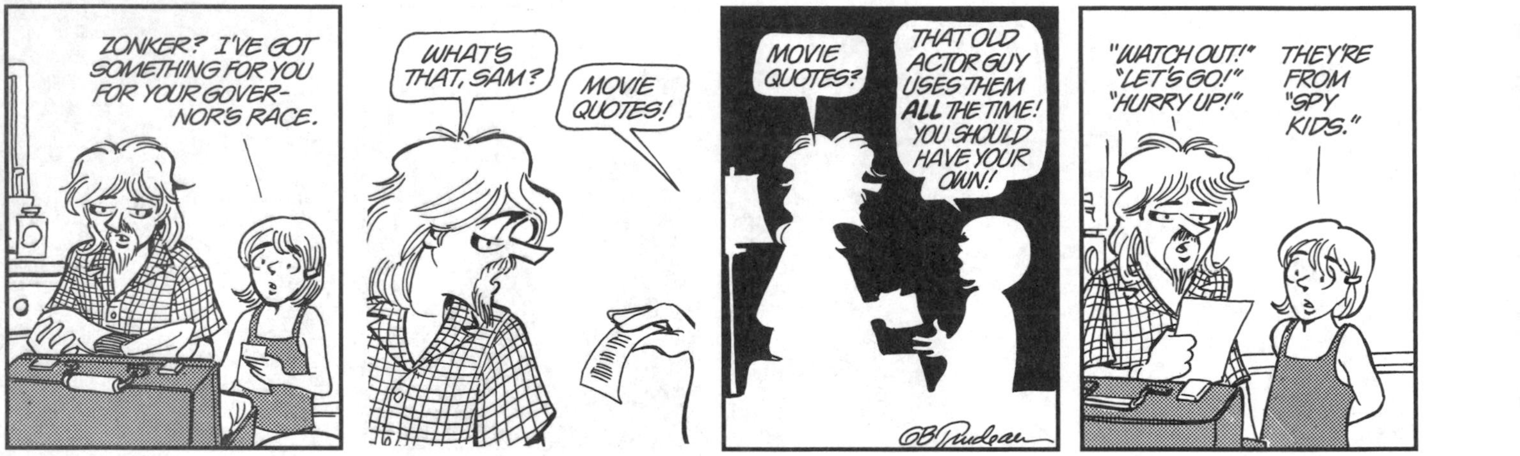
ZONKER? I'VE GOT SOMETHING FOR YOU FOR YOUR GOVERNOR'S RACE.
WHAT'S THAT, SAM?
MOVIE QUOTES!
MOVIE QUOTES?
THAT OLD ACTOR GUY USES THEM ALL THE TIME! YOU SHOULD HAVE YOUR OWN!
"WATCH OUT!" "LET'S GO!" "HURRY UP!"
THEY'RE FROM "SPY KIDS."

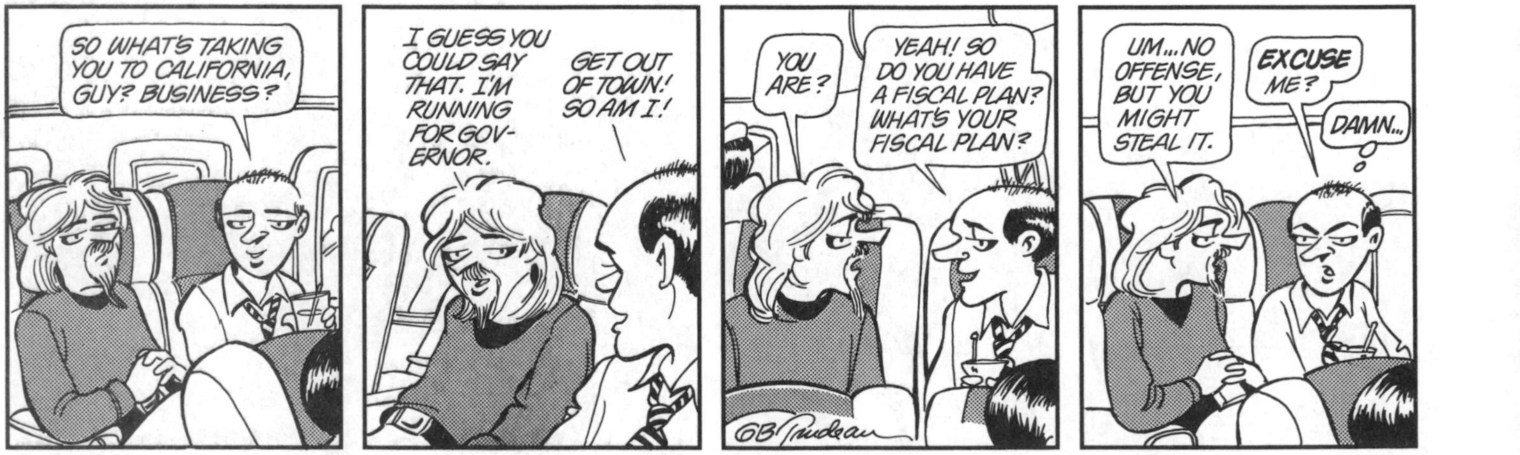
SO WHAT'S TAKING YOU TO CALIFORNIA, GUY? BUSINESS?
I GUESS YOU COULD SAY THAT. I'M RUNNING FOR GOVERNOR.
GET OUT OF TOWN! SO AM I!
YOU ARE?
YEAH! SO DO YOU HAVE A FISCAL PLAN? WHAT'S YOUR FISCAL PLAN?
UM...NO OFFENSE, BUT YOU MIGHT STEAL IT.
EXCUSE ME?
DAMN...

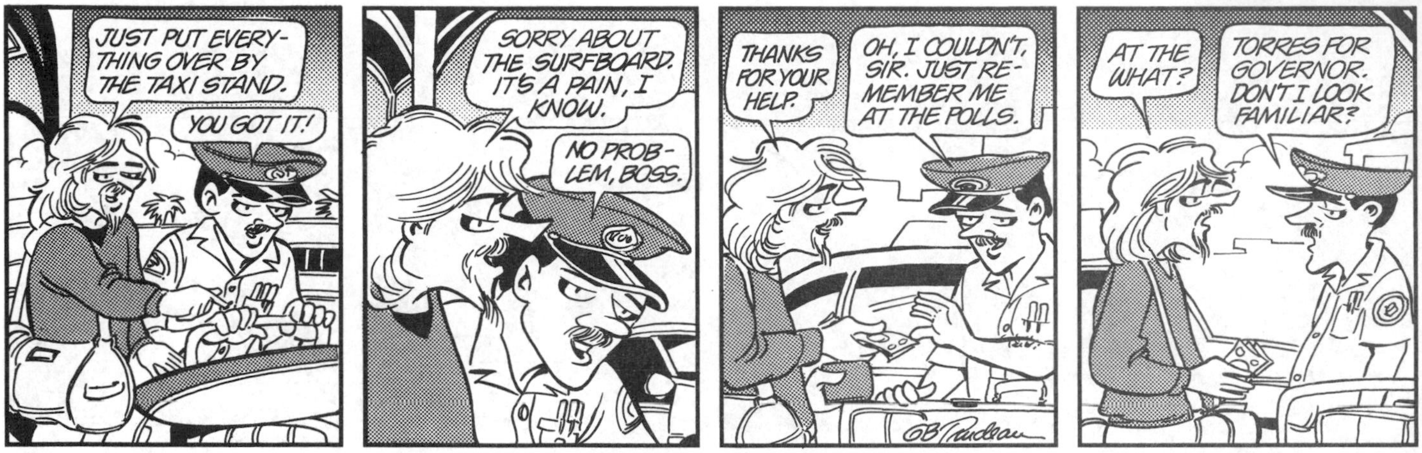
JUST PUT EVERY-THING OVER BY THE TAXI STAND.
YOU GOT IT!
SORRY ABOUT THE SURFBOARD. IT'S A PAIN, I KNOW.
NO PROB-LEM, BOSS.
THANKS FOR YOUR HELP.
OH, I COULDN'T, SIR. JUST RE-MEMBER ME AT THE POLLS.
AT THE WHAT?
TORRES FOR GOVERNOR. DON'T I LOOK FAMILIAR?

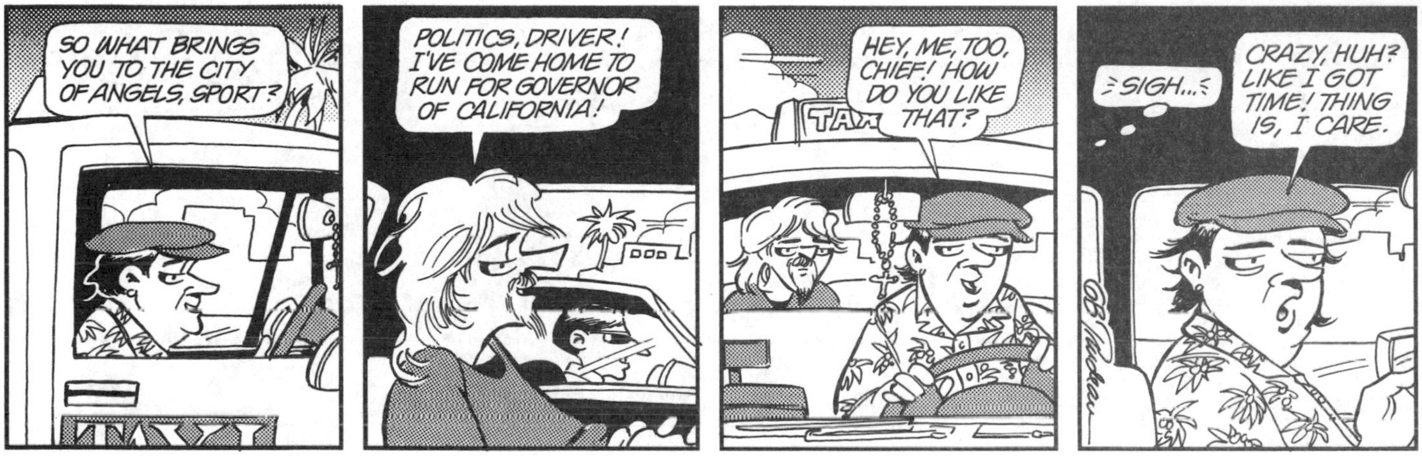
SO WHAT BRINGS YOU TO THE CITY OF ANGELS, SPORT?
POLITICS, DRIVER! I'VE COME HOME TO RUN FOR GOVERNOR OF CALIFORNIA!
HEY, ME, TOO, CHIEF! HOW DO YOU LIKE THAT?
SIGH...
CRAZY, HUH? LIKE I GOT TIME! THING IS, I CARE.

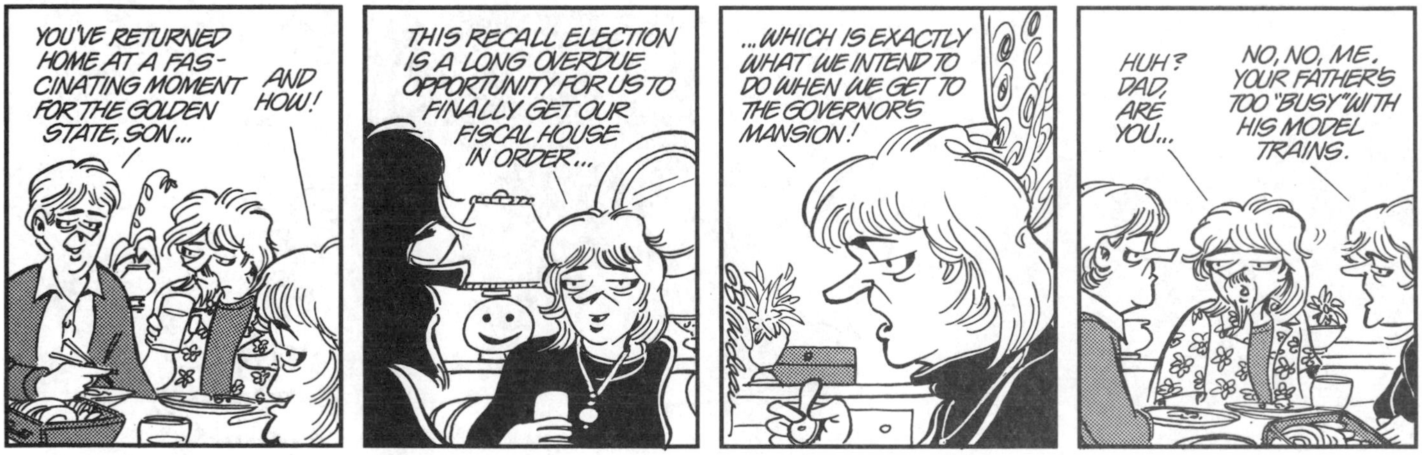
YOU'VE RETURNED HOME AT A FAS-CINATING MOMENT FOR THE GOLDEN STATE, SON...
AND HOW!
THIS RECALL ELECTION IS A LONG OVERDUE OPPORTUNITY FOR US TO FINALLY GET OUR FISCAL HOUSE IN ORDER...
...WHICH IS EXACTLY WHAT WE INTEND TO DO WHEN WE GET TO THE GOVERNOR'S MANSION!
HUH? DAD, ARE YOU...
NO, NO, ME. YOUR FATHER'S TOO "BUSY" WITH HIS MODEL TRAINS.

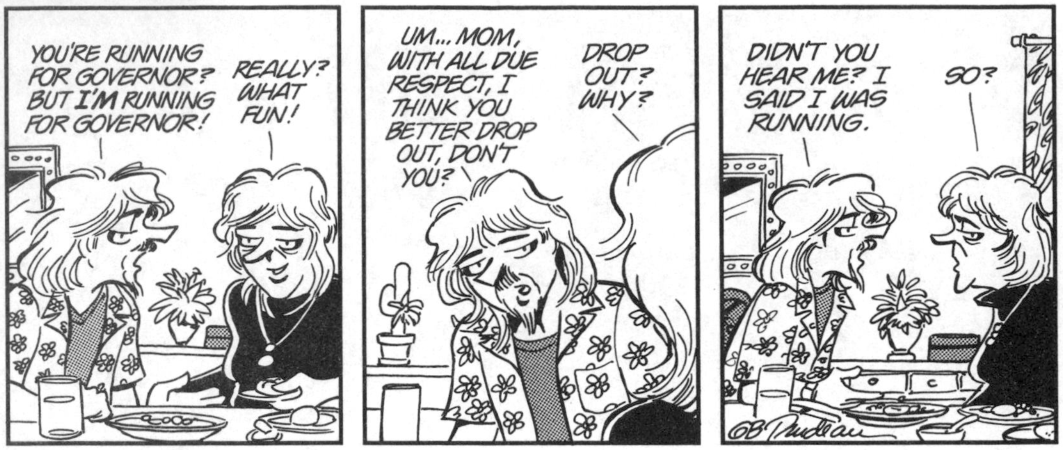
YOU'RE RUNNING FOR GOVERNOR? BUT I'M RUNNING FOR GOVERNOR!
REALLY? WHAT FUN!
UM... MOM, WITH ALL DUE RESPECT, I THINK YOU BETTER DROP OUT, DON'T YOU?
DROP OUT? WHY?
DIDN'T YOU HEAR ME? I SAID I WAS RUNNING.
SO?
MOM! GET REAL! I'D CLEAN YOUR CLOCK!
OH, YEAH? BRING IT ON, BUD-DY BOY!

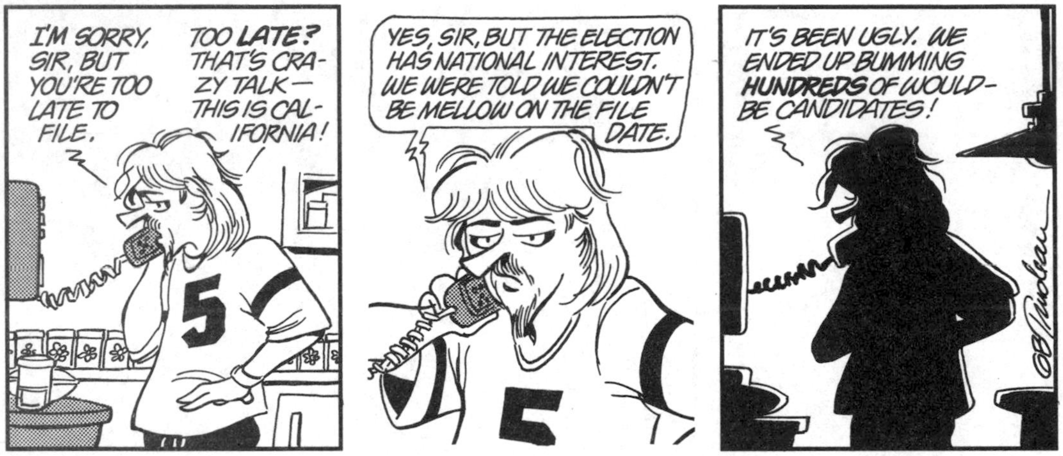
I'M SORRY, SIR, BUT YOU'RE TOO LATE TO FILE.
TOO LATE? THAT'S CRA-ZY TALK— THIS IS CAL-IFORNIA!
YES, SIR, BUT THE ELECTION HAS NATIONAL INTEREST. WE WERE TOLD WE COULDN'T BE MELLOW ON THE FILE DATE.
IT'S BEEN UGLY. WE ENDED UP BUMMING HUNDREDS OF WOULD-BE CANDIDATES!
I MYSELF...
DON'T SAY IT!

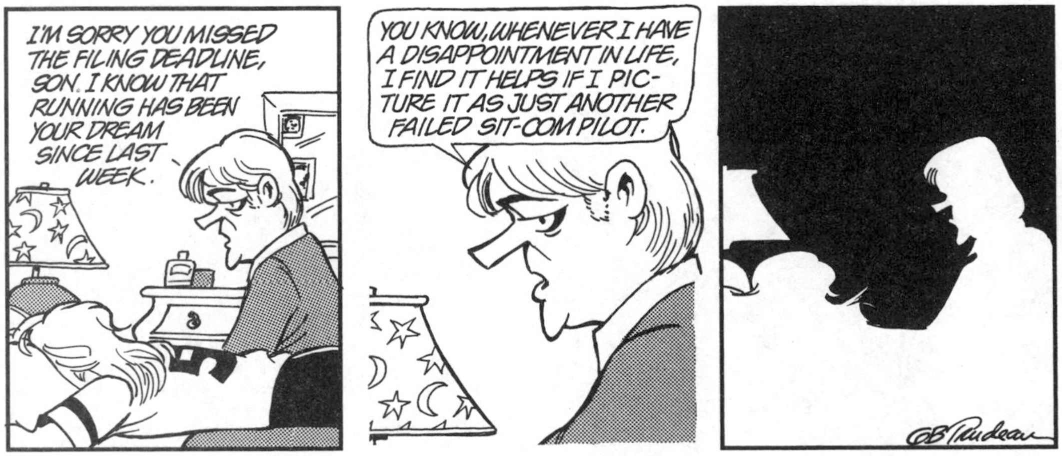
I'M SORRY YOU MISSED THE FILING DEADLINE, SON. I KNOW THAT RUNNING HAS BEEN YOUR DREAM SINCE LAST WEEK.
YOU KNOW, WHENEVER I HAVE A DISAPPOINTMENT IN LIFE, I FIND IT HELPS IF I PIC-TURE IT AS JUST ANOTHER FAILED SIT-COM PILOT.
YOU'RE RIGHT... I FEEL BETTER.
SEE, IF YOU CHEAPEN IT, IT DOESN'T HURT AS MUCH.

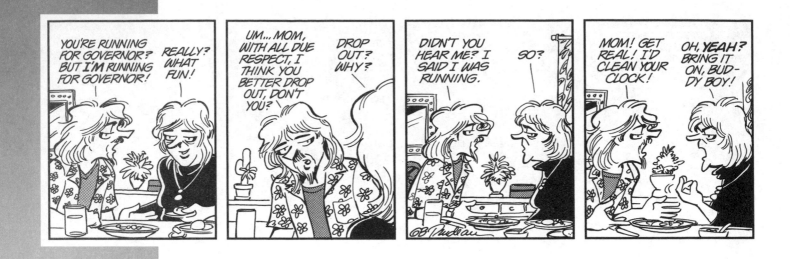

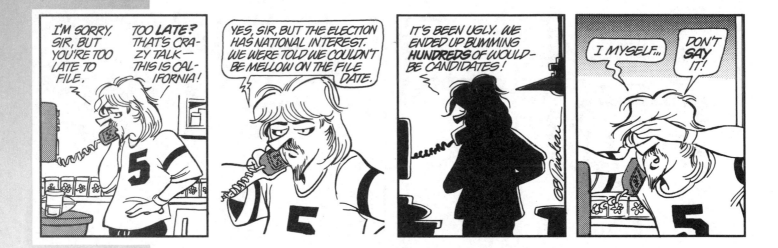

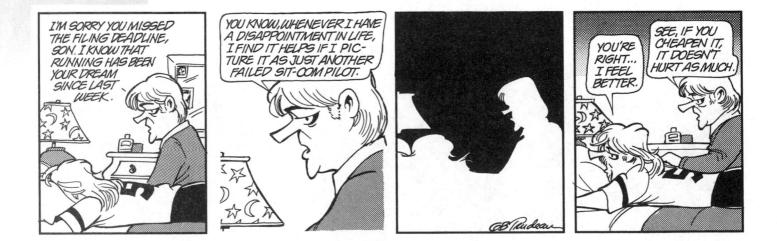

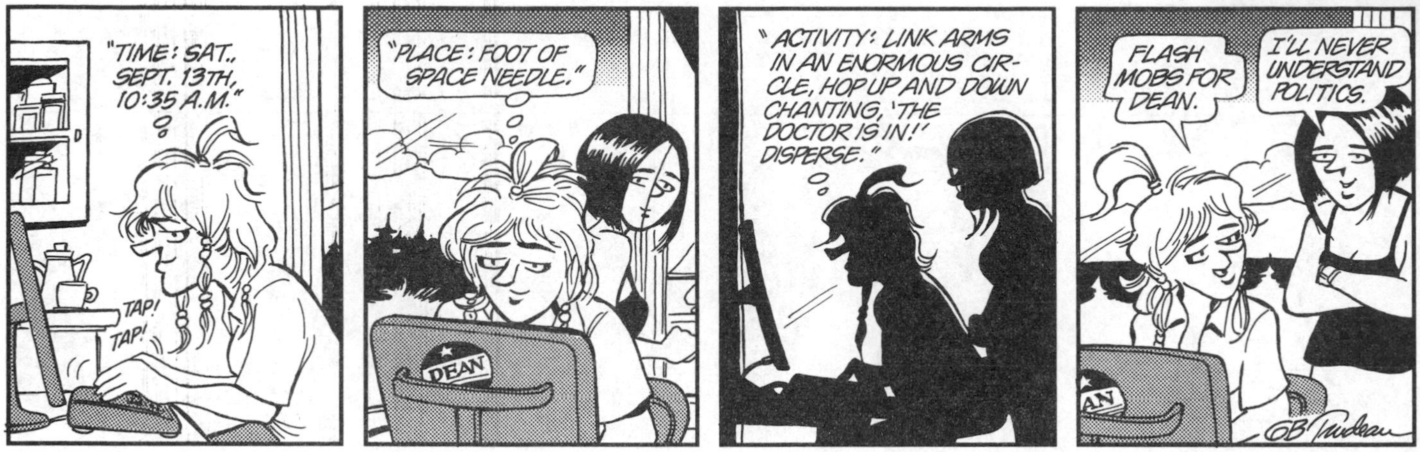
"TIME: SAT., SEPT. 13TH, 10:35 A.M."
TAP! TAP!
"PLACE: FOOT OF SPACE NEEDLE."
DEAN
"ACTIVITY: LINK ARMS IN AN ENORMOUS CIRCLE, HOP UP AND DOWN CHANTING, 'THE DOCTOR IS IN!' DISPERSE."
FLASH MOBS FOR DEAN.
I'LL NEVER UNDERSTAND POLITICS.

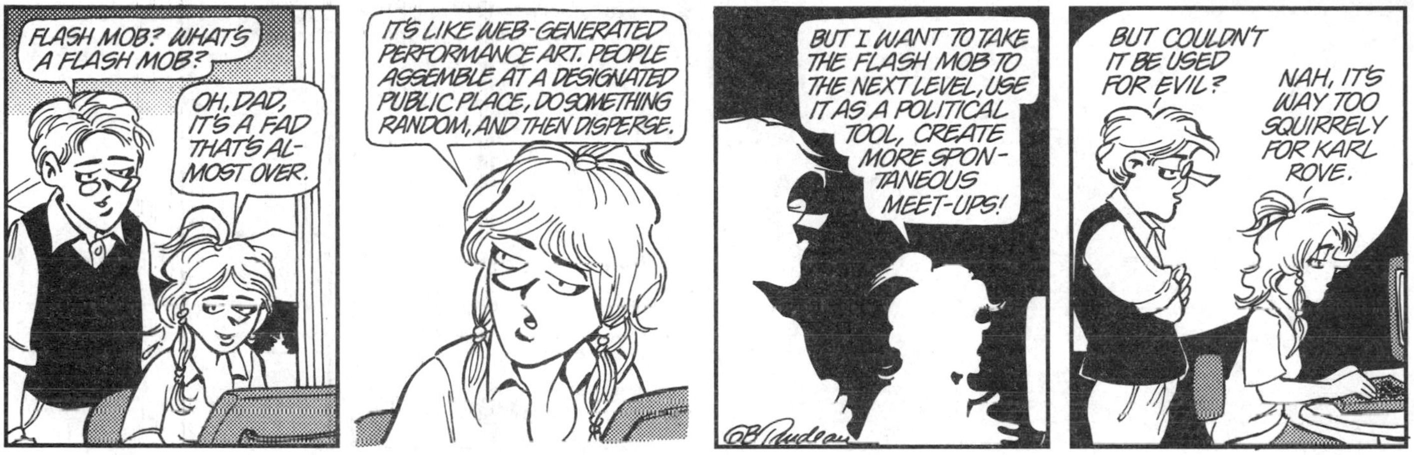
FLASH MOB? WHAT'S A FLASH MOB?
OH, DAD, IT'S A FAD THAT'S ALMOST OVER.
IT'S LIKE WEB-GENERATED PERFORMANCE ART. PEOPLE ASSEMBLE AT A DESIGNATED PUBLIC PLACE, DO SOMETHING RANDOM, AND THEN DISPERSE.
BUT I WANT TO TAKE THE FLASH MOB TO THE NEXT LEVEL, USE IT AS A POLITICAL TOOL, CREATE MORE SPONTANEOUS MEET-UPS!
BUT COULDN'T IT BE USED FOR EVIL?
NAH, IT'S WAY TOO SQUIRRELY FOR KARL ROVE.

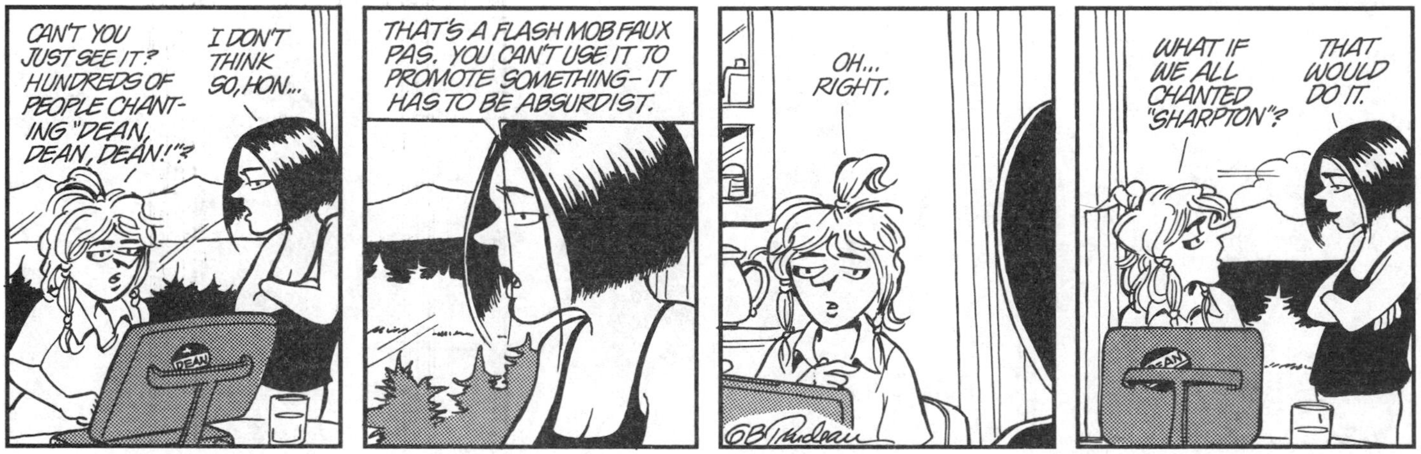
CAN'T YOU JUST SEE IT? HUNDREDS OF PEOPLE CHANTING "DEAN, DEAN, DEAN!"?
I DON'T THINK SO, HON...
DEAN
THAT'S A FLASH MOB FAUX PAS. YOU CAN'T USE IT TO PROMOTE SOMETHING– IT HAS TO BE ABSURDIST.
OH... RIGHT.
WHAT IF WE ALL CHANTED "SHARPTON"?
THAT WOULD DO IT.

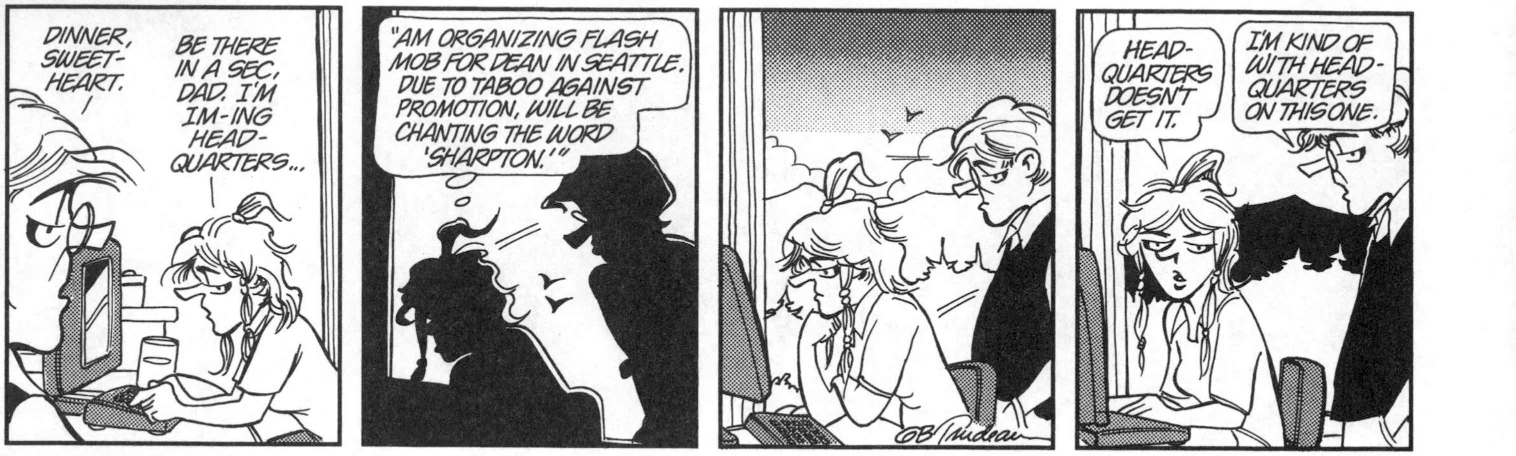
DINNER, SWEET-HEART.
BE THERE IN A SEC, DAD. I'M IM-ING HEAD-QUARTERS...
"AM ORGANIZING FLASH MOB FOR DEAN IN SEATTLE. DUE TO TABOO AGAINST PROMOTION, WILL BE CHANTING THE WORD 'SHARPTON.'"
HEAD-QUARTERS DOESN'T GET IT.
I'M KIND OF WITH HEAD-QUARTERS ON THIS ONE.

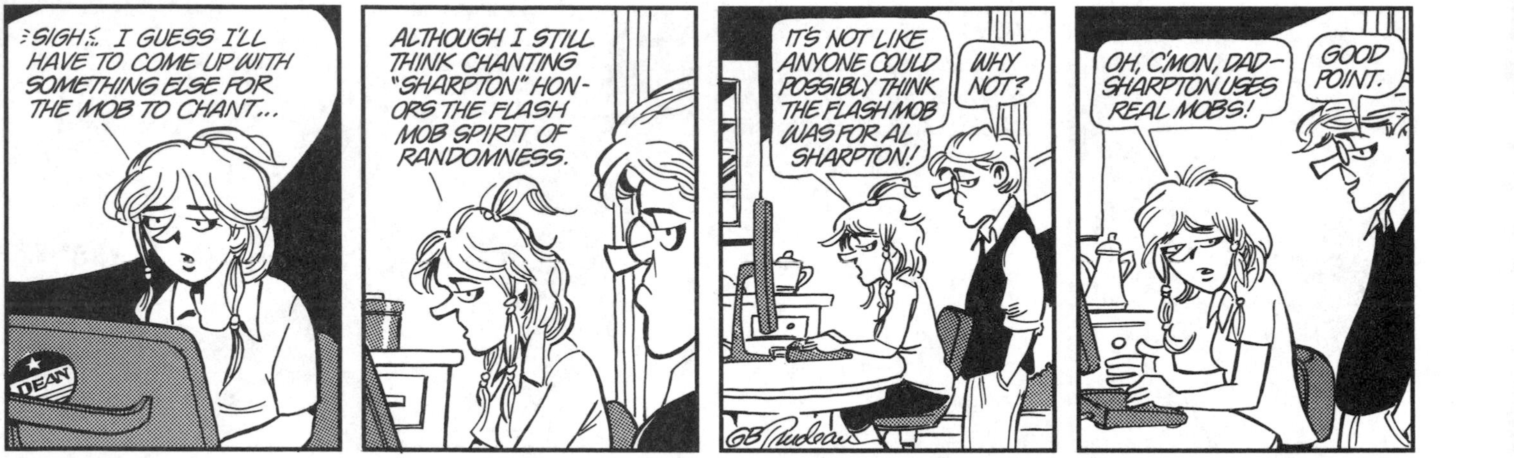
SIGH... I GUESS I'LL HAVE TO COME UP WITH SOMETHING ELSE FOR THE MOB TO CHANT...
DEAN
ALTHOUGH I STILL THINK CHANTING "SHARPTON" HON-ORS THE FLASH MOB SPIRIT OF RANDOMNESS.
IT'S NOT LIKE ANYONE COULD POSSIBLY THINK THE FLASH MOB WAS FOR AL SHARPTON!
WHY NOT?
OH, C'MON, DAD–SHARPTON USES REAL MOBS!
GOOD POINT.

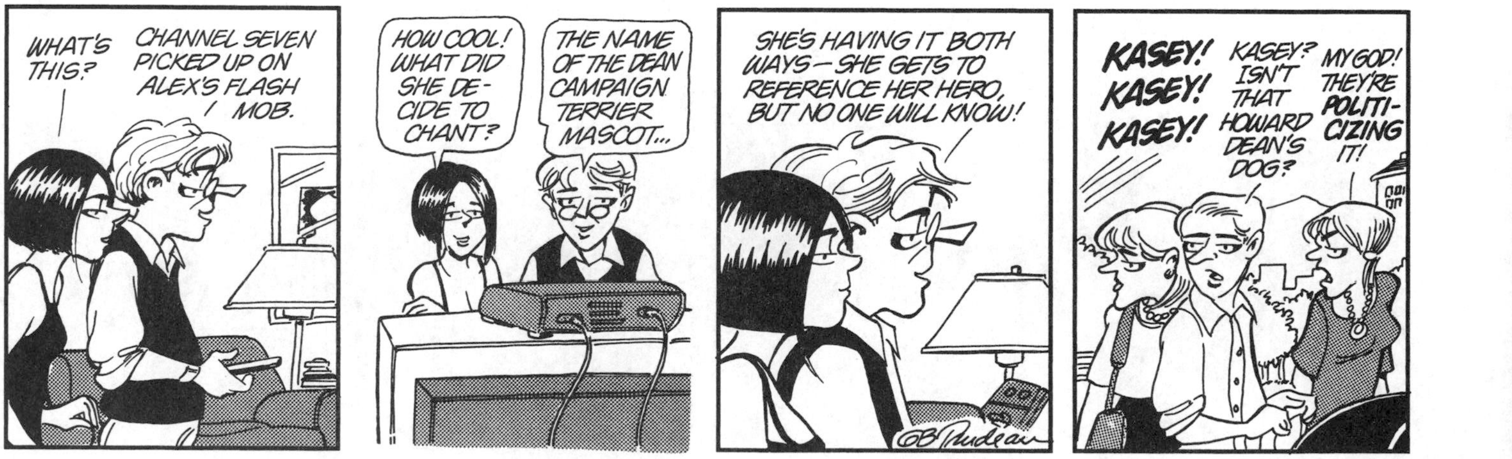
WHAT'S THIS?
CHANNEL SEVEN PICKED UP ON ALEX'S FLASH MOB.
HOW COOL! WHAT DID SHE DE-CIDE TO CHANT?
THE NAME OF THE DEAN CAMPAIGN TERRIER MASCOT...
SHE'S HAVING IT BOTH WAYS–SHE GETS TO REFERENCE HER HERO, BUT NO ONE WILL KNOW!
KASEY! KASEY! KASEY!
KASEY? ISN'T THAT HOWARD DEAN'S DOG?
MY GOD! THEY'RE POLITI-CIZING IT!

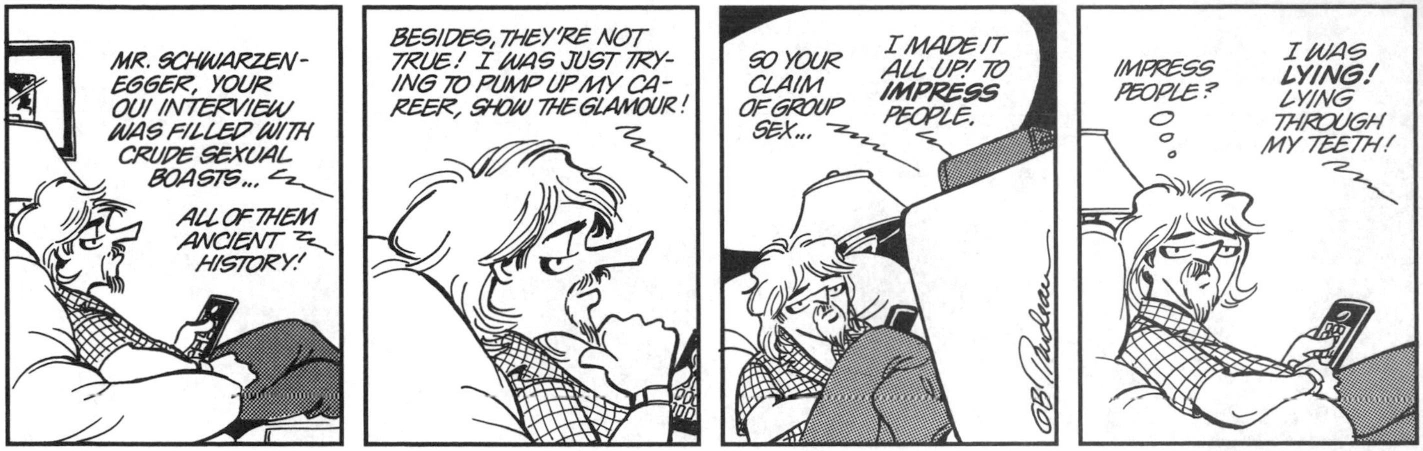

MR. SCHWARZEN-EGGER, YOUR OUI INTERVIEW WAS FILLED WITH CRUDE SEXUAL BOASTS...
ALL OF THEM ANCIENT HISTORY!
BESIDES, THEY'RE NOT TRUE! I WAS JUST TRYING TO PUMP UP MY CAREER, SHOW THE GLAMOUR!
SO YOUR CLAIM OF GROUP SEX...
I MADE IT ALL UP! TO IMPRESS PEOPLE.
IMPRESS PEOPLE?
I WAS LYING! LYING THROUGH MY TEETH!

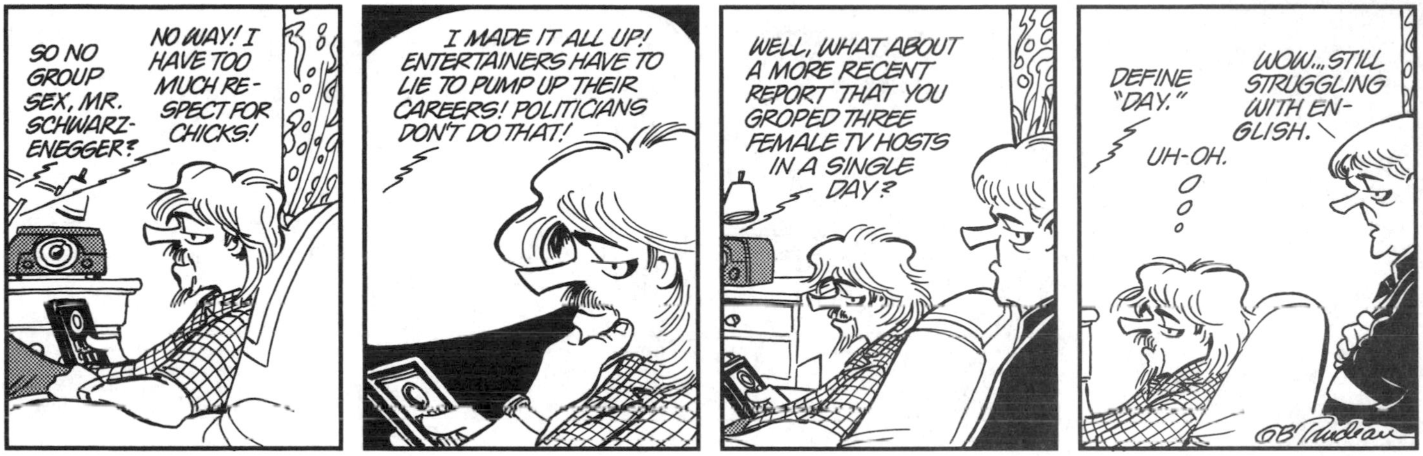

SO NO GROUP SEX, MR. SCHWARZENEGGER?
NO WAY! I HAVE TOO MUCH RESPECT FOR CHICKS!
I MADE IT ALL UP! ENTERTAINERS HAVE TO LIE TO PUMP UP THEIR CAREERS! POLITICIANS DON'T DO THAT!
WELL, WHAT ABOUT A MORE RECENT REPORT THAT YOU GROPED THREE FEMALE TV HOSTS IN A SINGLE DAY?
DEFINE "DAY."
UH-OH.
WOW... STILL STRUGGLING WITH ENGLISH.

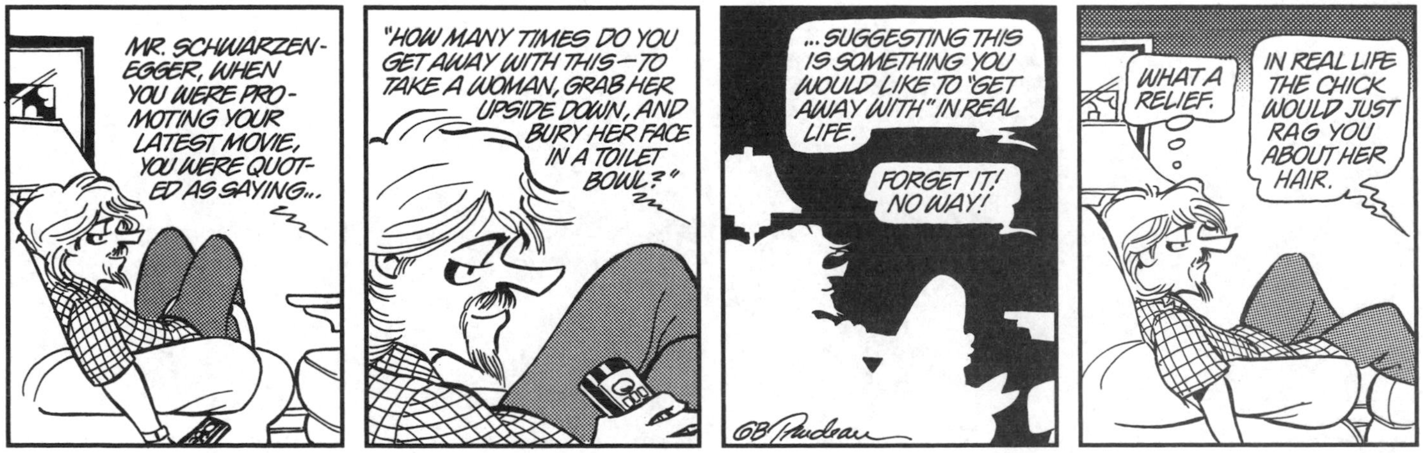

MR. SCHWARZENEGGER, WHEN YOU WERE PROMOTING YOUR LATEST MOVIE, YOU WERE QUOTED AS SAYING...
"HOW MANY TIMES DO YOU GET AWAY WITH THIS—TO TAKE A WOMAN, GRAB HER UPSIDE DOWN, AND BURY HER FACE IN A TOILET BOWL?"
...SUGGESTING THIS IS SOMETHING YOU WOULD LIKE TO "GET AWAY WITH" IN REAL LIFE.
FORGET IT! NO WAY!
WHAT A RELIEF.
IN REAL LIFE THE CHICK WOULD JUST RAG YOU ABOUT HER HAIR.

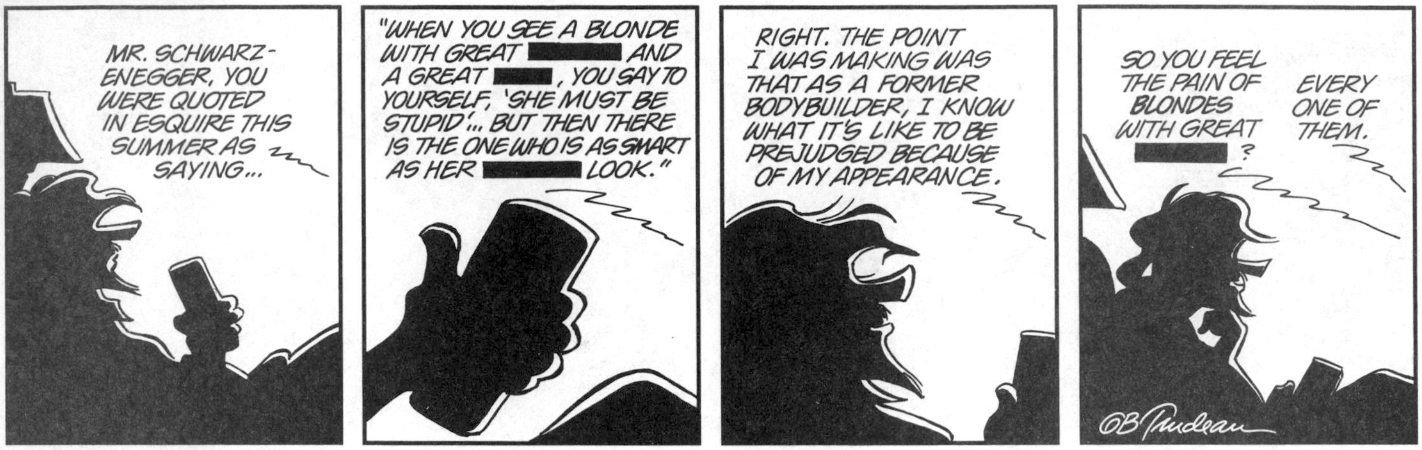
MR. SCHWARZ-ENEGGER, YOU WERE QUOTED IN ESQUIRE THIS SUMMER AS SAYING...
"WHEN YOU SEE A BLONDE WITH GREAT [redacted] AND A GREAT [redacted], YOU SAY TO YOURSELF, 'SHE MUST BE STUPID'... BUT THEN THERE IS THE ONE WHO IS AS SMART AS HER [redacted] LOOK."
RIGHT. THE POINT I WAS MAKING WAS THAT AS A FORMER BODYBUILDER, I KNOW WHAT IT'S LIKE TO BE PREJUDGED BECAUSE OF MY APPEARANCE.
SO YOU FEEL THE PAIN OF BLONDES WITH GREAT [redacted]?
EVERY ONE OF THEM.
©B Trudeau

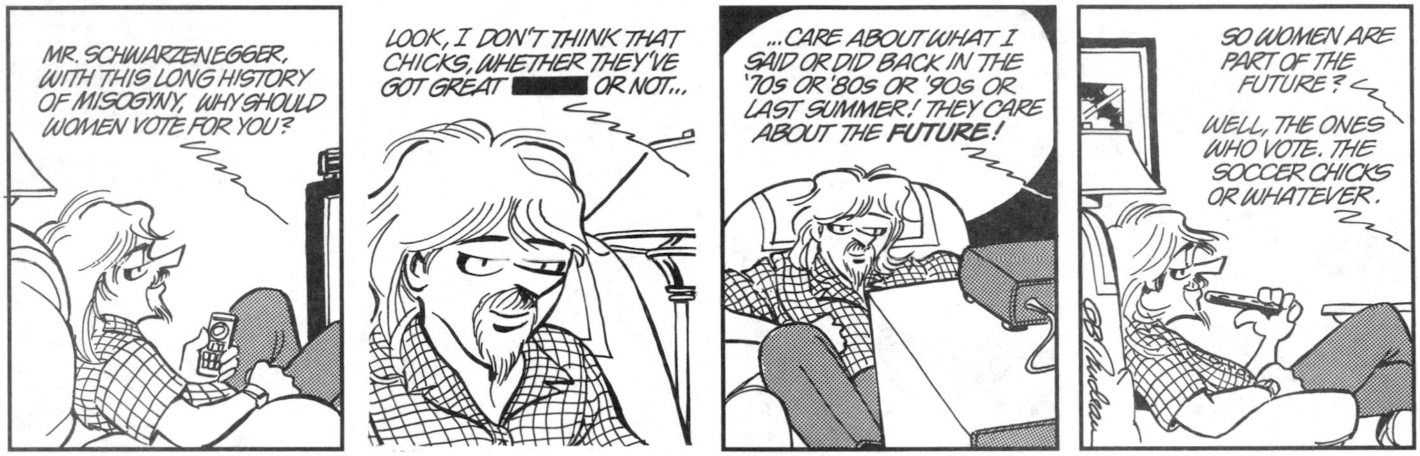
MR. SCHWARZENEGGER, WITH THIS LONG HISTORY OF MISOGYNY, WHY SHOULD WOMEN VOTE FOR YOU?
LOOK, I DON'T THINK THAT CHICKS, WHETHER THEY'VE GOT GREAT [redacted] OR NOT...
...CARE ABOUT WHAT I SAID OR DID BACK IN THE '70s OR '80s OR '90s OR LAST SUMMER! THEY CARE ABOUT THE FUTURE!
SO WOMEN ARE PART OF THE FUTURE?
WELL, THE ONES WHO VOTE. THE SOCCER CHICKS OR WHATEVER.
GB Trudeau

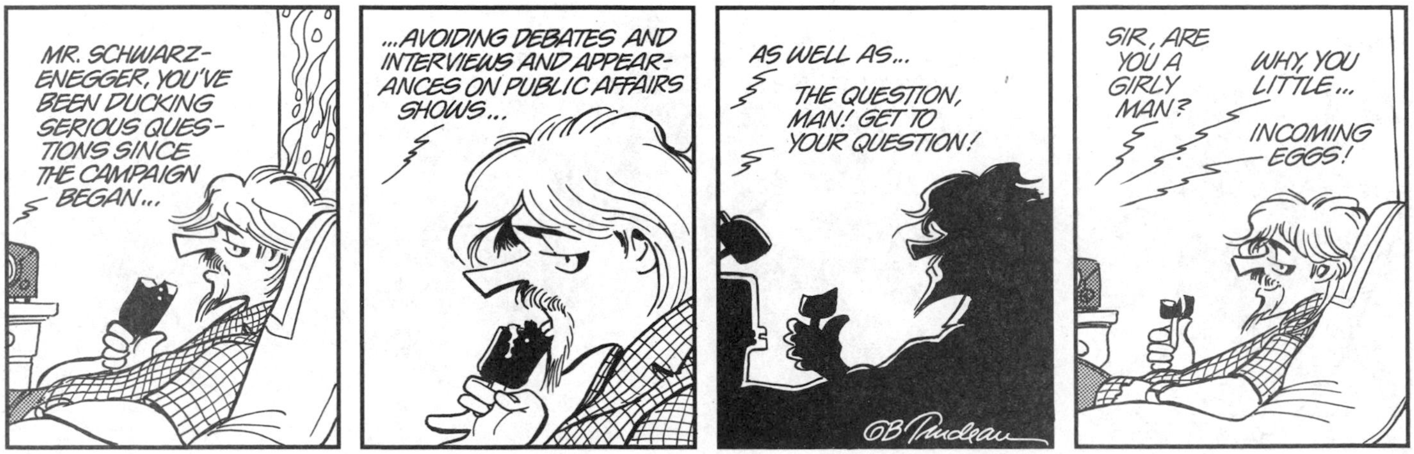
MR. SCHWARZ-ENEGGER, YOU'VE BEEN DUCKING SERIOUS QUES-TIONS SINCE THE CAMPAIGN BEGAN...
...AVOIDING DEBATES AND INTERVIEWS AND APPEAR-ANCES ON PUBLIC AFFAIRS SHOWS...
AS WELL AS...
THE QUESTION, MAN! GET TO YOUR QUESTION!
©B Trudeau
SIR, ARE YOU A GIRLY MAN?
WHY, YOU LITTLE...
INCOMING EGGS!

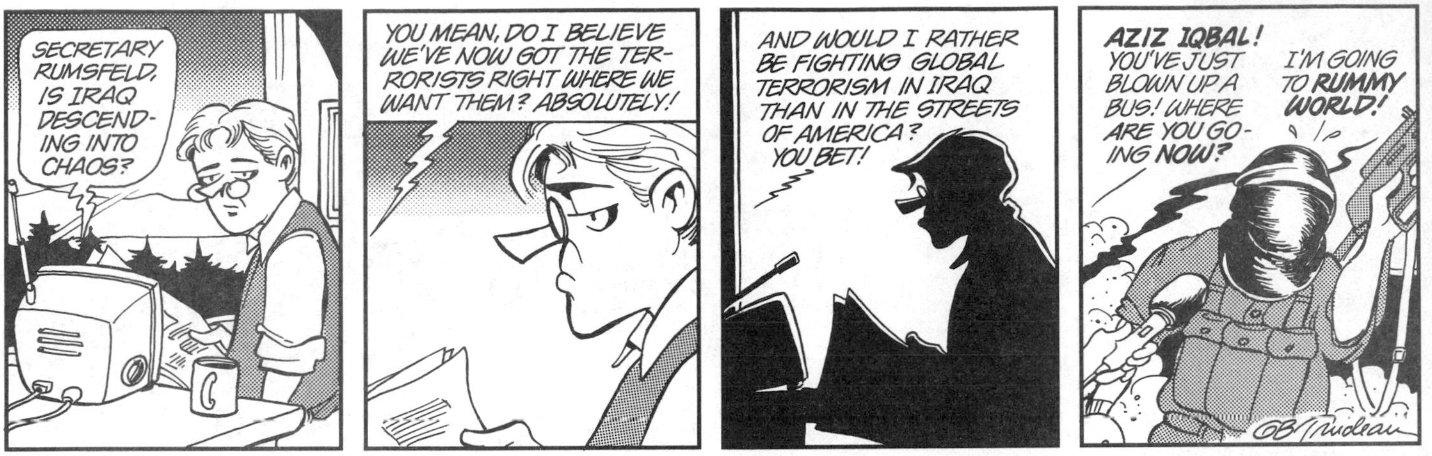
SECRETARY RUMSFELD, IS IRAQ DESCENDING INTO CHAOS?
YOU MEAN, DO I BELIEVE WE'VE NOW GOT THE TERRORISTS RIGHT WHERE WE WANT THEM? ABSOLUTELY!
AND WOULD I RATHER BE FIGHTING GLOBAL TERRORISM IN IRAQ THAN IN THE STREETS OF AMERICA? YOU BET!
AZIZ IQBAL! YOU'VE JUST BLOWN UP A BUS! WHERE ARE YOU GOING NOW?
I'M GOING TO RUMMY WORLD!

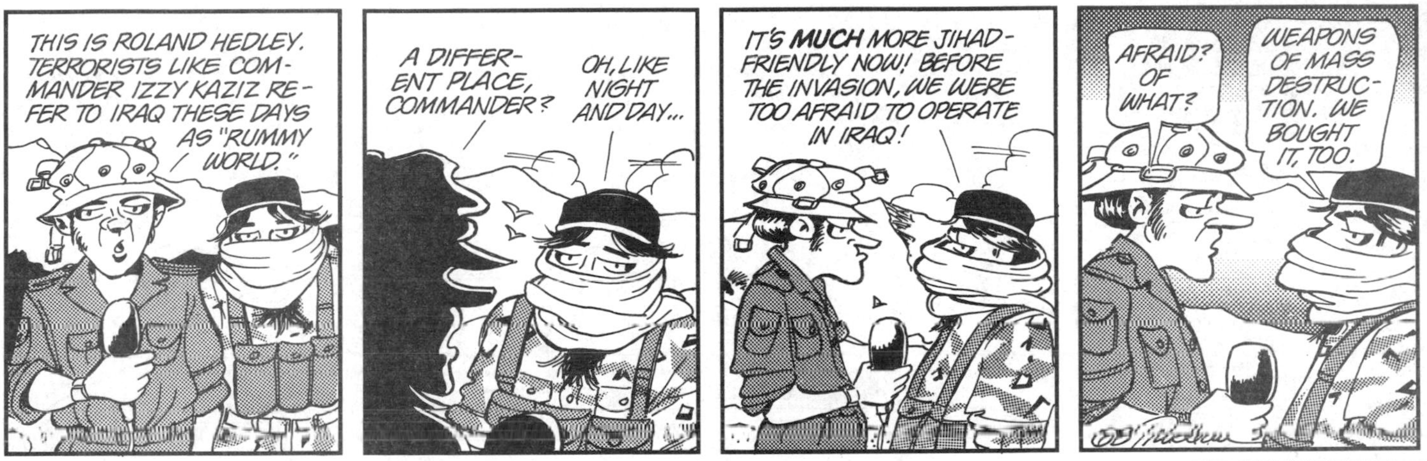
THIS IS ROLAND HEDLEY. TERRORISTS LIKE COMMANDER IZZY KAZIZ REFER TO IRAQ THESE DAYS AS "RUMMY WORLD."
A DIFFERENT PLACE, COMMANDER?
OH, LIKE NIGHT AND DAY...
IT'S MUCH MORE JIHAD-FRIENDLY NOW! BEFORE THE INVASION, WE WERE TOO AFRAID TO OPERATE IN IRAQ!
AFRAID? OF WHAT?
WEAPONS OF MASS DESTRUCTION. WE BOUGHT IT, TOO.

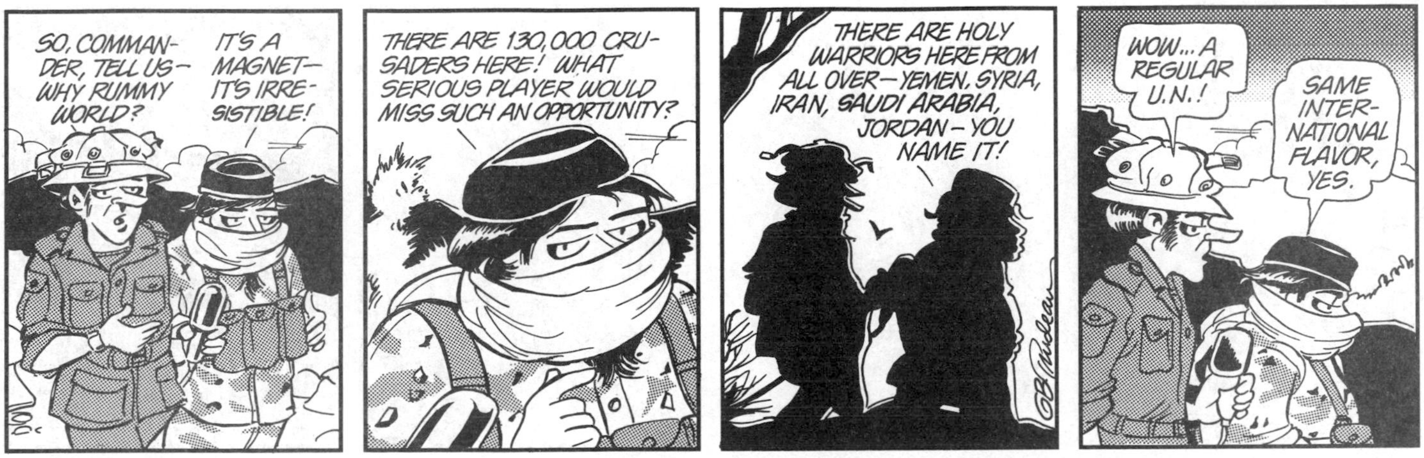
SO, COMMANDER, TELL US— WHY RUMMY WORLD?
IT'S A MAGNET— IT'S IRRESISTIBLE!
THERE ARE 130,000 CRUSADERS HERE! WHAT SERIOUS PLAYER WOULD MISS SUCH AN OPPORTUNITY?
THERE ARE HOLY WARRIORS HERE FROM ALL OVER—YEMEN, SYRIA, IRAN, SAUDI ARABIA, JORDAN—YOU NAME IT!
WOW... A REGULAR U.N.!
SAME INTERNATIONAL FLAVOR, YES.

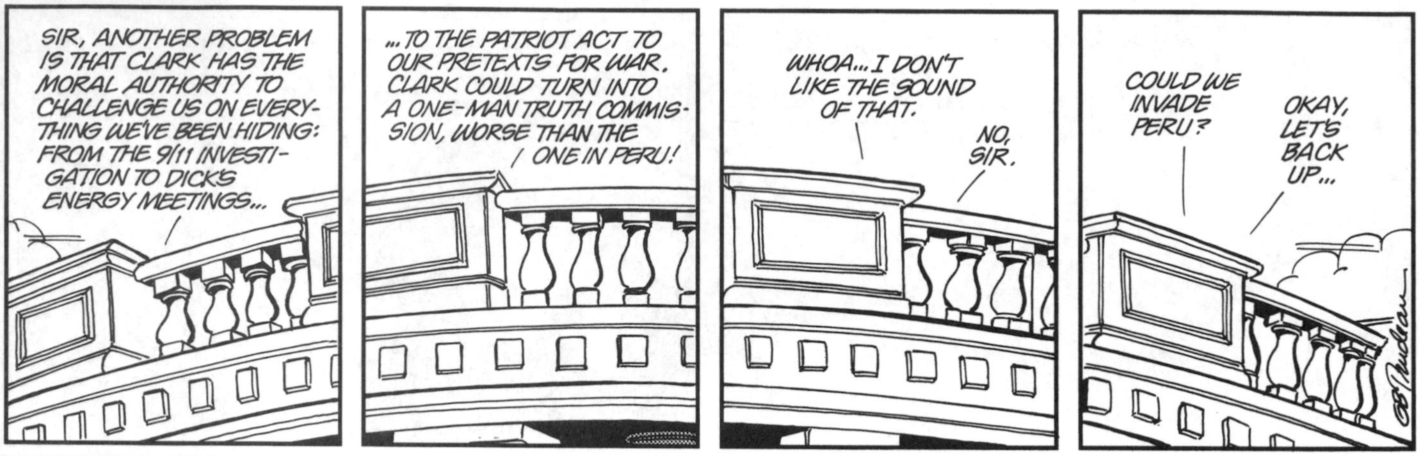
SIR, ANOTHER PROBLEM IS THAT CLARK HAS THE MORAL AUTHORITY TO CHALLENGE US ON EVERYTHING WE'VE BEEN HIDING: FROM THE 9/11 INVESTIGATION TO DICK'S ENERGY MEETINGS...
...TO THE PATRIOT ACT TO OUR PRETEXTS FOR WAR. CLARK COULD TURN INTO A ONE-MAN TRUTH COMMISSION, WORSE THAN THE ONE IN PERU!
WHOA... I DON'T LIKE THE SOUND OF THAT.
NO, SIR.
COULD WE INVADE PERU?
OKAY, LET'S BACK UP...

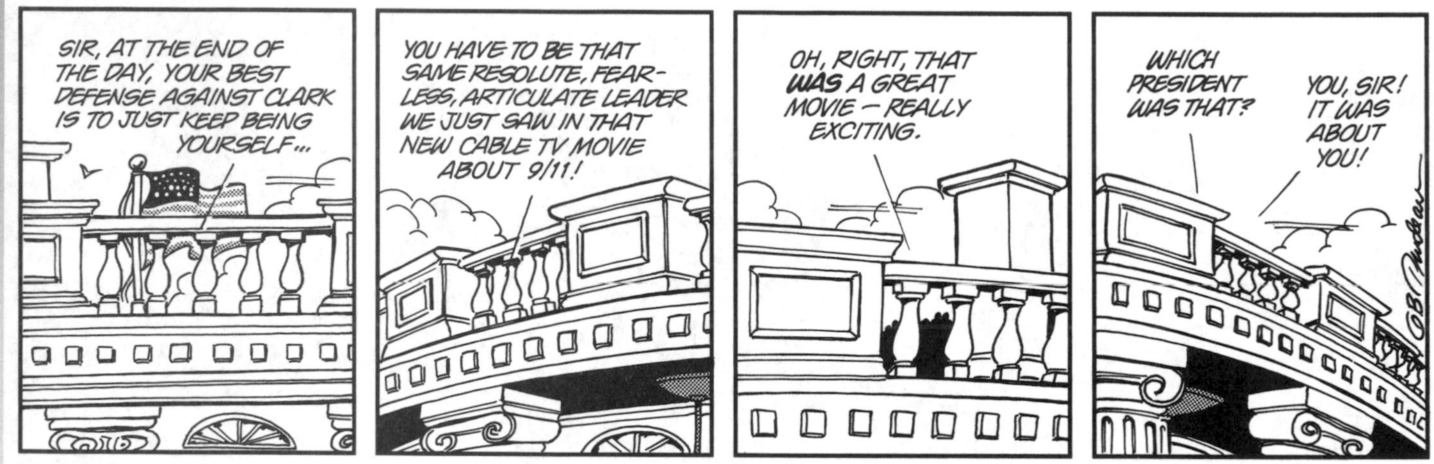
SIR, AT THE END OF THE DAY, YOUR BEST DEFENSE AGAINST CLARK IS TO JUST KEEP BEING YOURSELF...
YOU HAVE TO BE THAT SAME RESOLUTE, FEARLESS, ARTICULATE LEADER WE JUST SAW IN THAT NEW CABLE TV MOVIE ABOUT 9/11!
OH, RIGHT, THAT **WAS** A GREAT MOVIE — REALLY EXCITING.
WHICH PRESIDENT WAS THAT?
YOU, SIR! IT WAS ABOUT YOU!

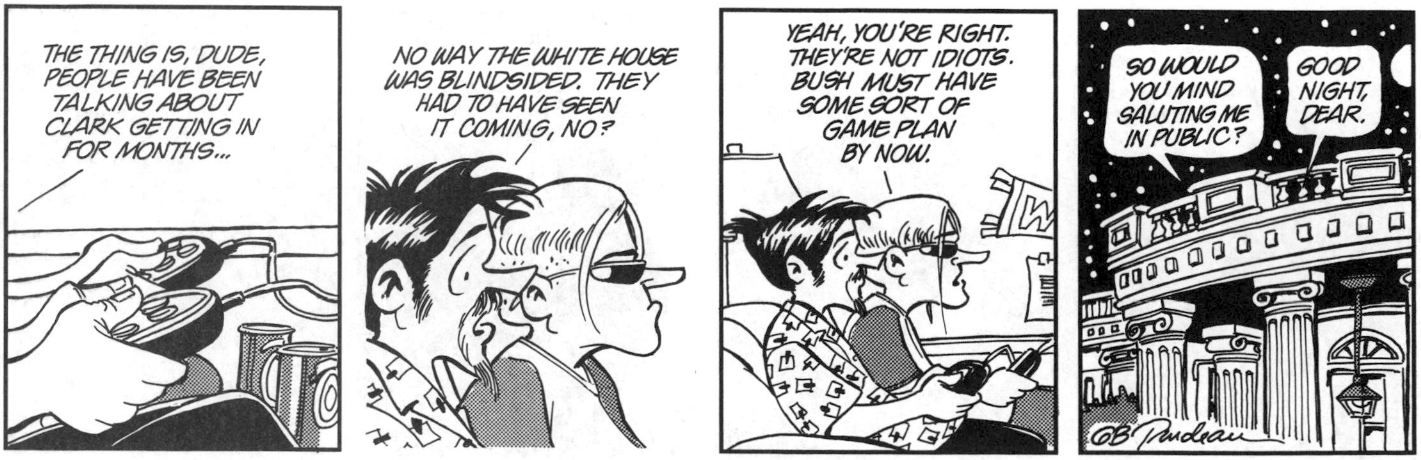
THE THING IS, DUDE, PEOPLE HAVE BEEN TALKING ABOUT CLARK GETTING IN FOR MONTHS...
NO WAY THE WHITE HOUSE WAS BLINDSIDED. THEY HAD TO HAVE SEEN IT COMING, NO?
YEAH, YOU'RE RIGHT. THEY'RE NOT IDIOTS. BUSH MUST HAVE SOME SORT OF GAME PLAN BY NOW.
SO WOULD YOU MIND SALUTING ME IN PUBLIC?
GOOD NIGHT, DEAR.

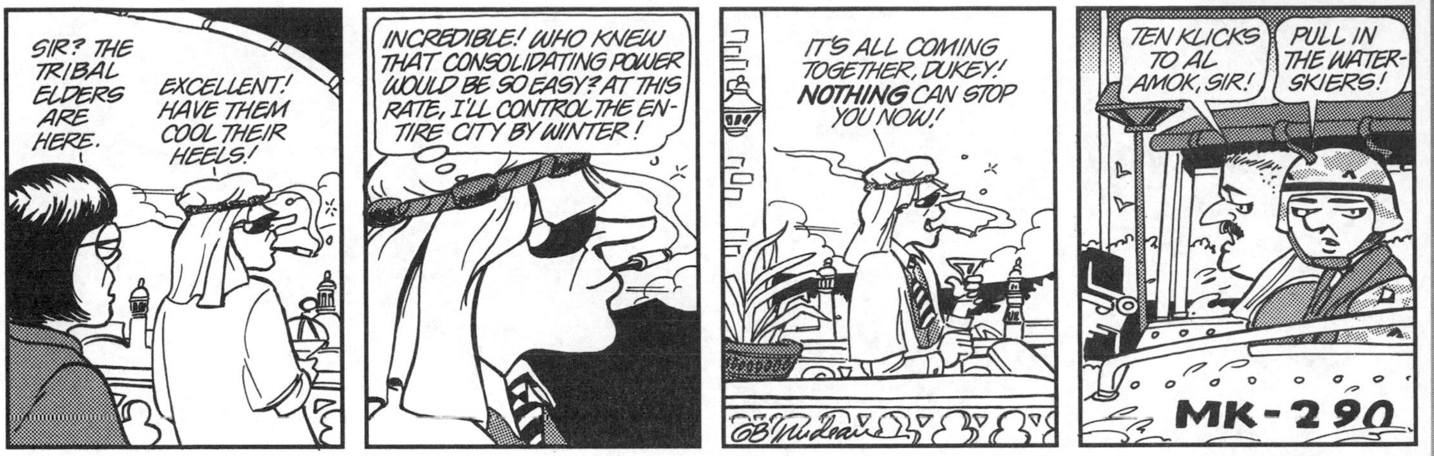
SIR? THE TRIBAL ELDERS ARE HERE.
EXCELLENT! HAVE THEM COOL THEIR HEELS!
INCREDIBLE! WHO KNEW THAT CONSOLIDATING POWER WOULD BE SO EASY? AT THIS RATE, I'LL CONTROL THE ENTIRE CITY BY WINTER!
IT'S ALL COMING TOGETHER, DUKEY! NOTHING CAN STOP YOU NOW!
TEN KLICKS TO AL AMOK, SIR!
PULL IN THE WATER-SKIERS!
MK-290

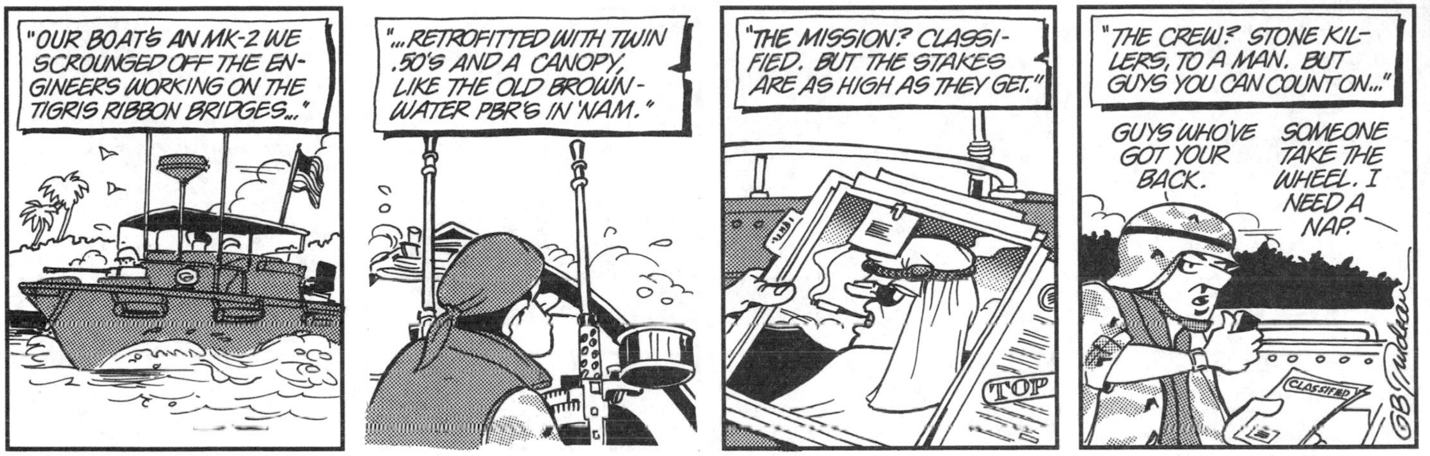
"OUR BOAT'S AN MK-2 WE SCROUNGED OFF THE ENGINEERS WORKING ON THE TIGRIS RIBBON BRIDGES..."
"...RETROFITTED WITH TWIN .50'S AND A CANOPY, LIKE THE OLD BROWN-WATER PBR'S IN 'NAM."
"THE MISSION? CLASSIFIED. BUT THE STAKES ARE AS HIGH AS THEY GET."
TOP
"THE CREW? STONE KILLERS, TO A MAN. BUT GUYS YOU CAN COUNT ON..."
GUYS WHO'VE GOT YOUR BACK.
SOMEONE TAKE THE WHEEL. I NEED A NAP.
CLASSIFIED

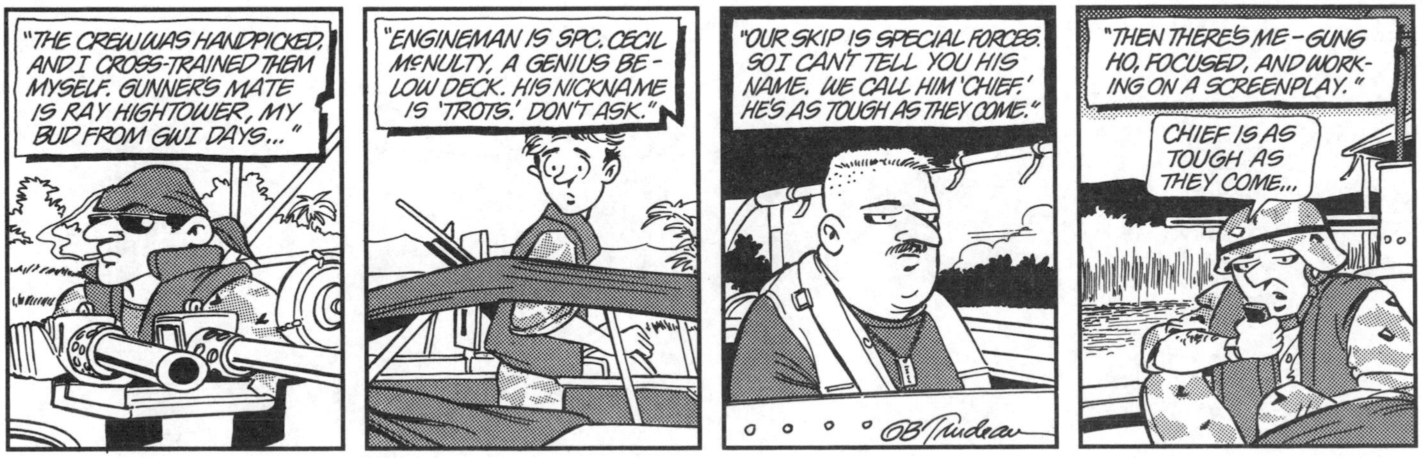
"THE CREW WAS HANDPICKED, AND I CROSS-TRAINED THEM MYSELF. GUNNER'S MATE IS RAY HIGHTOWER, MY BUD FROM GW1 DAYS..."
"ENGINEMAN IS SPC. CECIL McNULTY, A GENIUS BELOW DECK. HIS NICKNAME IS 'TROTS.' DON'T ASK."
"OUR SKIP IS SPECIAL FORCES, SO I CAN'T TELL YOU HIS NAME. WE CALL HIM 'CHIEF.' HE'S AS TOUGH AS THEY COME."
"THEN THERE'S ME – GUNG HO, FOCUSED, AND WORKING ON A SCREENPLAY."
CHIEF IS AS TOUGH AS THEY COME...

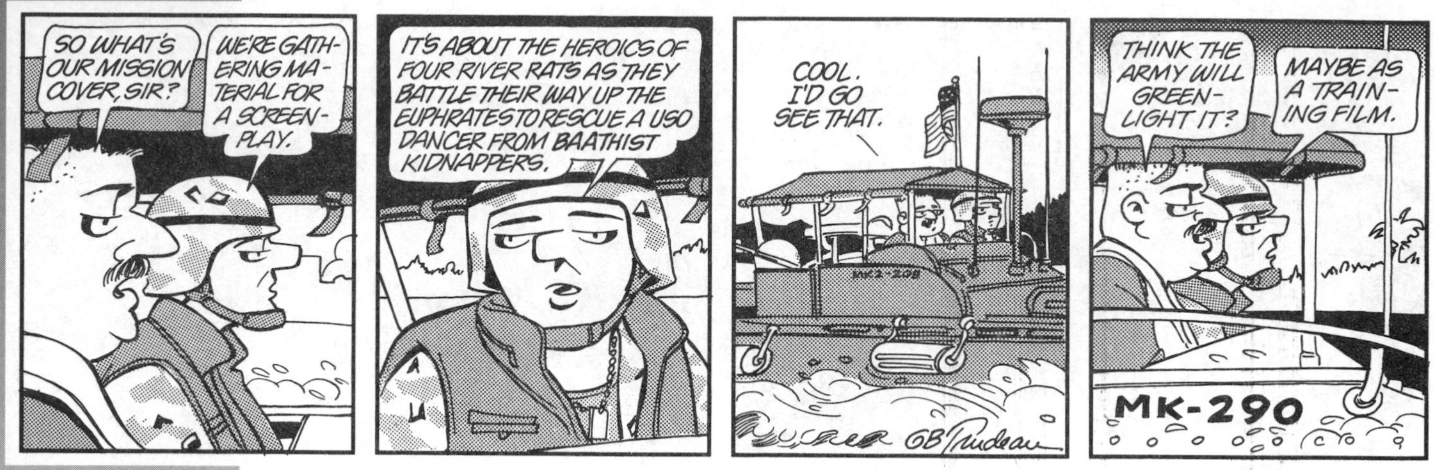
SO WHAT'S OUR MISSION COVER, SIR?
WE'RE GATHERING MATERIAL FOR A SCREENPLAY.
IT'S ABOUT THE HEROICS OF FOUR RIVER RATS AS THEY BATTLE THEIR WAY UP THE EUPHRATES TO RESCUE A USO DANCER FROM BAATHIST KIDNAPPERS.
COOL. I'D GO SEE THAT.
THINK THE ARMY WILL GREEN-LIGHT IT?
MAYBE AS A TRAINING FILM.
MK-290

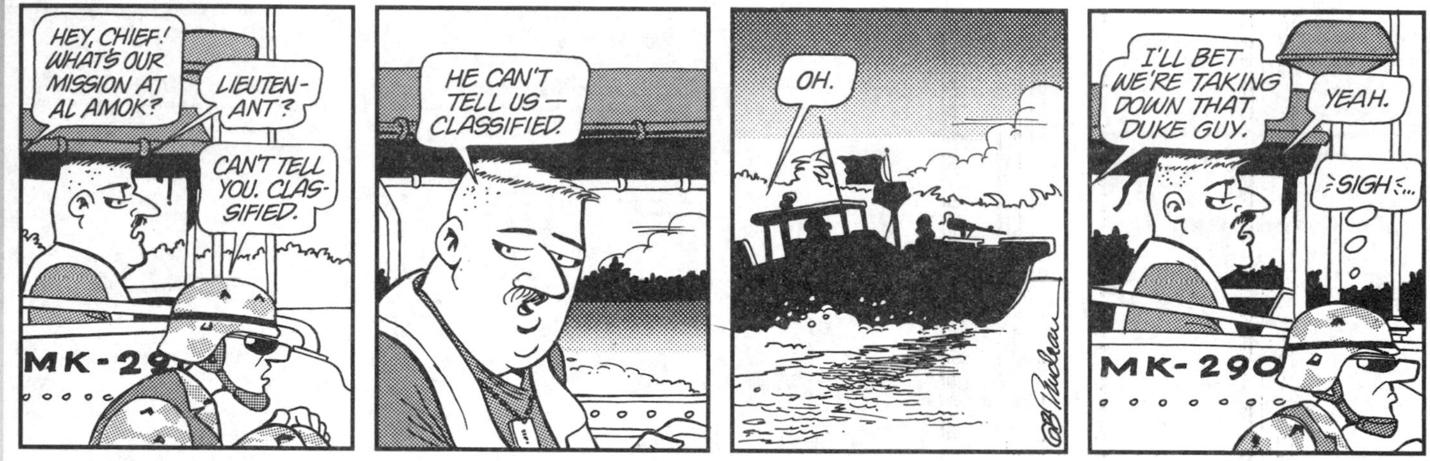
HEY, CHIEF! WHAT'S OUR MISSION AT AL AMOK?
LIEUTENANT?
CAN'T TELL YOU. CLASSIFIED.
HE CAN'T TELL US — CLASSIFIED.
OH.
I'LL BET WE'RE TAKING DOWN THAT DUKE GUY.
YEAH.
SIGH...
MK-290

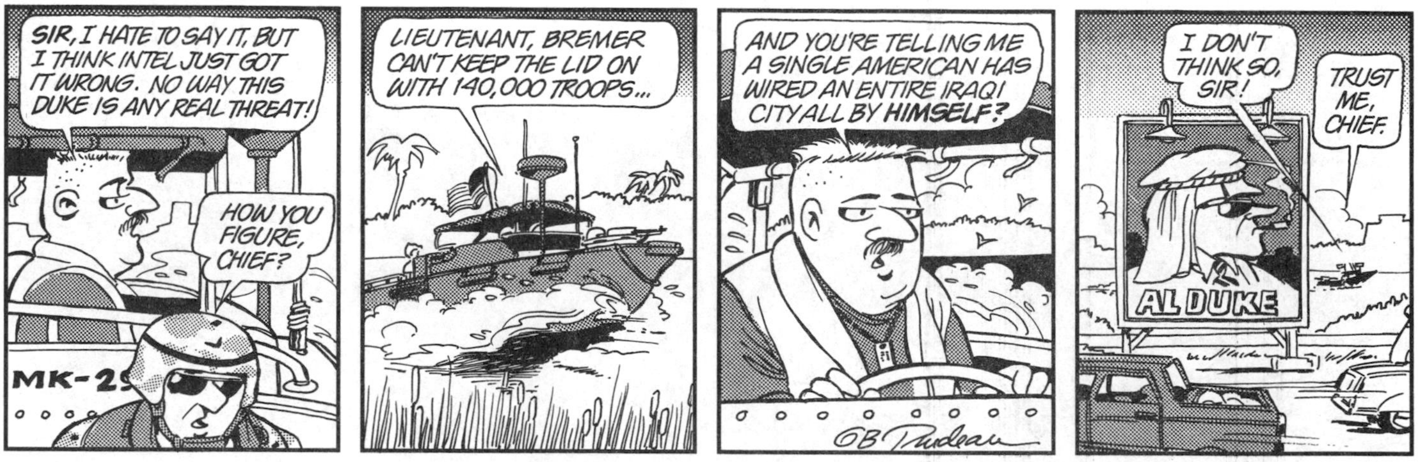
SIR, I HATE TO SAY IT, BUT I THINK INTEL JUST GOT IT WRONG. NO WAY THIS DUKE IS ANY REAL THREAT!
HOW YOU FIGURE, CHIEF?
LIEUTENANT, BREMER CAN'T KEEP THE LID ON WITH 140,000 TROOPS...
AND YOU'RE TELLING ME A SINGLE AMERICAN HAS WIRED AN ENTIRE IRAQI CITY ALL BY HIMSELF?
I DON'T THINK SO, SIR!
TRUST ME, CHIEF.
AL DUKE

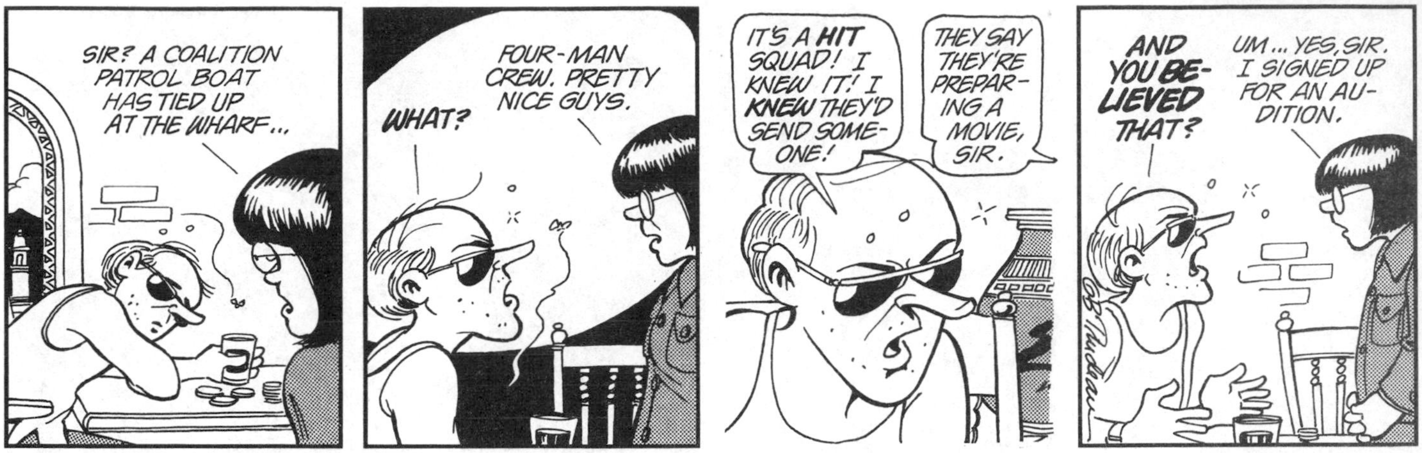
SIR? A COALITION PATROL BOAT HAS TIED UP AT THE WHARF...
WHAT?
FOUR-MAN CREW. PRETTY NICE GUYS.
IT'S A HIT SQUAD! I KNEW IT! I KNEW THEY'D SEND SOMEONE!
THEY SAY THEY'RE PREPARING A MOVIE, SIR.
AND YOU BELIEVED THAT?
UM... YES, SIR. I SIGNED UP FOR AN AUDITION.

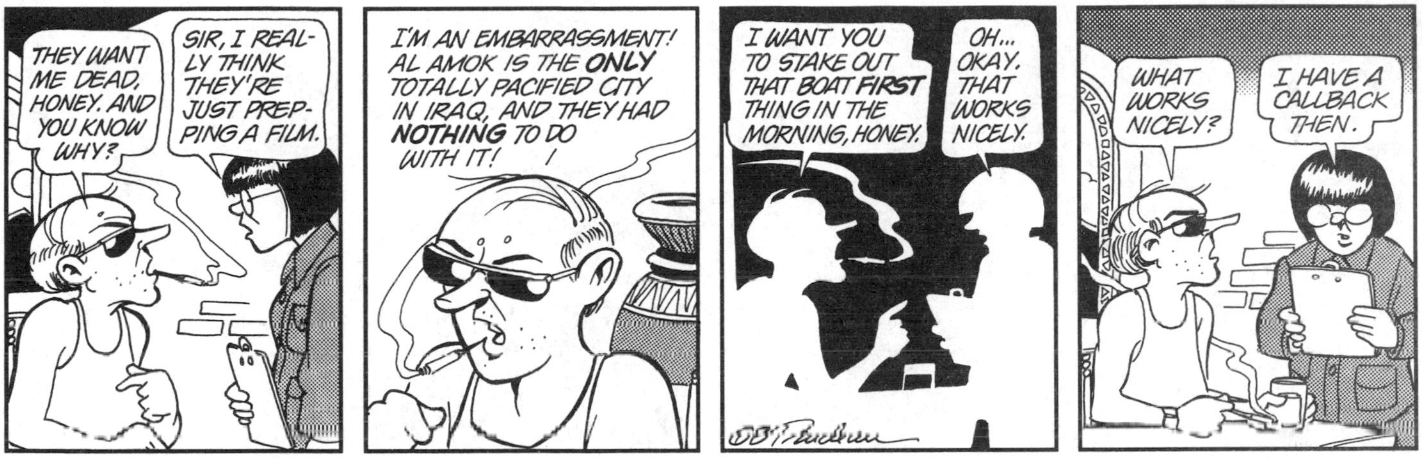
THEY WANT ME DEAD, HONEY. AND YOU KNOW WHY?
SIR, I REALLY THINK THEY'RE JUST PREPPING A FILM.
I'M AN EMBARRASSMENT! AL AMOK IS THE ONLY TOTALLY PACIFIED CITY IN IRAQ, AND THEY HAD NOTHING TO DO WITH IT!
I WANT YOU TO STAKE OUT THAT BOAT FIRST THING IN THE MORNING, HONEY.
OH... OKAY. THAT WORKS NICELY.
WHAT WORKS NICELY?
I HAVE A CALLBACK THEN.

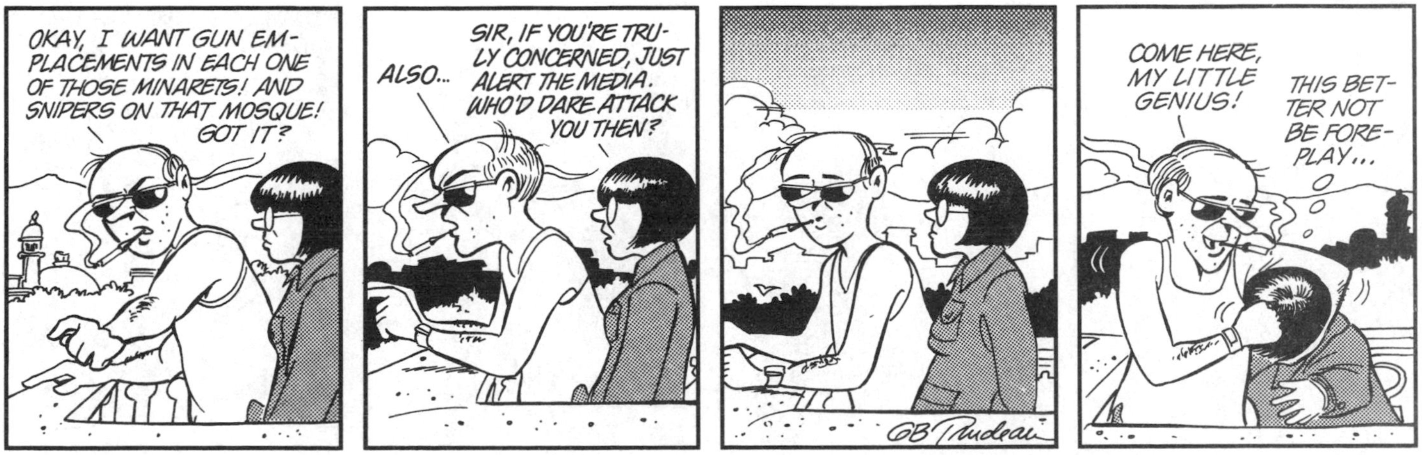
OKAY, I WANT GUN EMPLACEMENTS IN EACH ONE OF THOSE MINARETS! AND SNIPERS ON THAT MOSQUE! GOT IT?
ALSO...
SIR, IF YOU'RE TRULY CONCERNED, JUST ALERT THE MEDIA. WHO'D DARE ATTACK YOU THEN?
COME HERE, MY LITTLE GENIUS!
THIS BETTER NOT BE FOREPLAY...

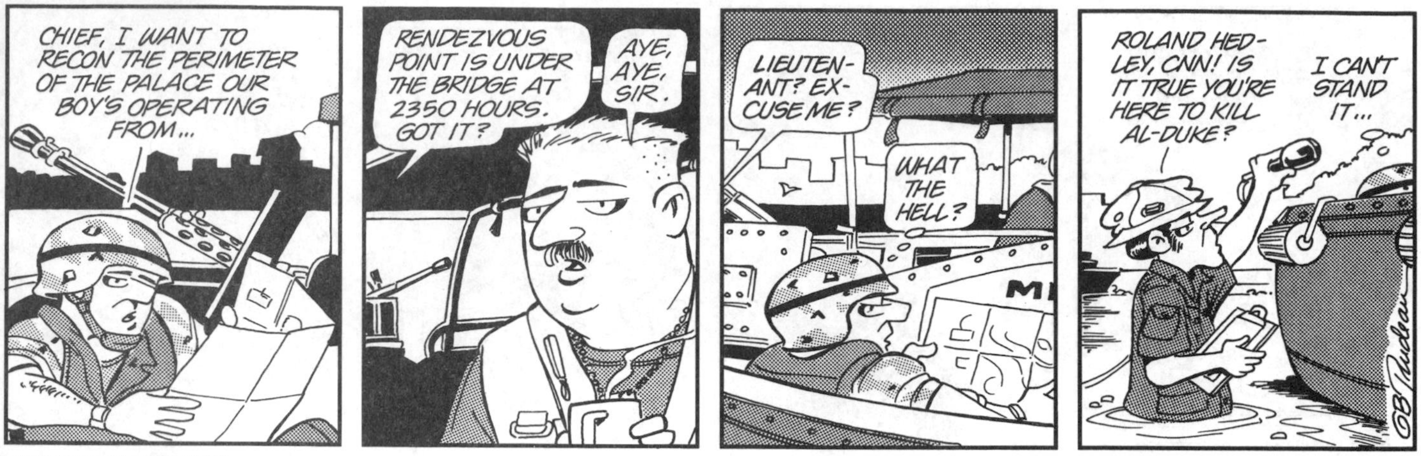
CHIEF, I WANT TO RECON THE PERIMETER OF THE PALACE OUR BOY'S OPERATING FROM...
RENDEZVOUS POINT IS UNDER THE BRIDGE AT 2350 HOURS. GOT IT?
AYE, AYE, SIR.
LIEUTEN-ANT? EX-CUSE ME?
WHAT THE HELL?
ROLAND HED-LEY, CNN! IS IT TRUE YOU'RE HERE TO KILL AL-DUKE?
I CAN'T STAND IT...

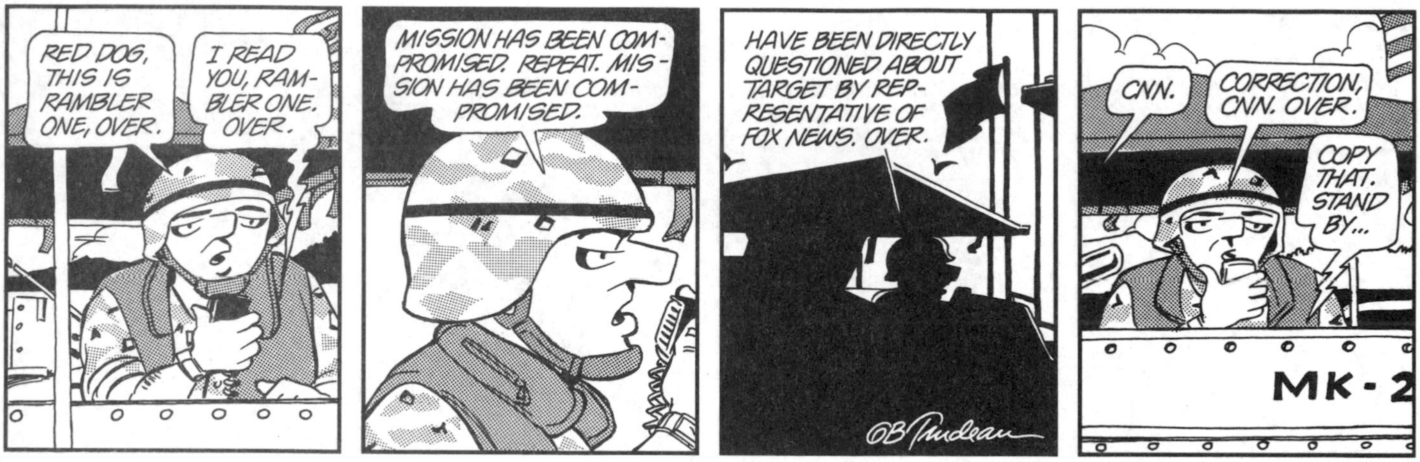
RED DOG, THIS IS RAMBLER ONE, OVER.
I READ YOU, RAM-BLER ONE. OVER.
MISSION HAS BEEN COM-PROMISED. REPEAT. MIS-SION HAS BEEN COM-PROMISED.
HAVE BEEN DIRECTLY QUESTIONED ABOUT TARGET BY REP-RESENTATIVE OF FOX NEWS. OVER.
CNN.
CORRECTION, CNN. OVER.
COPY THAT. STAND BY...
MK-2

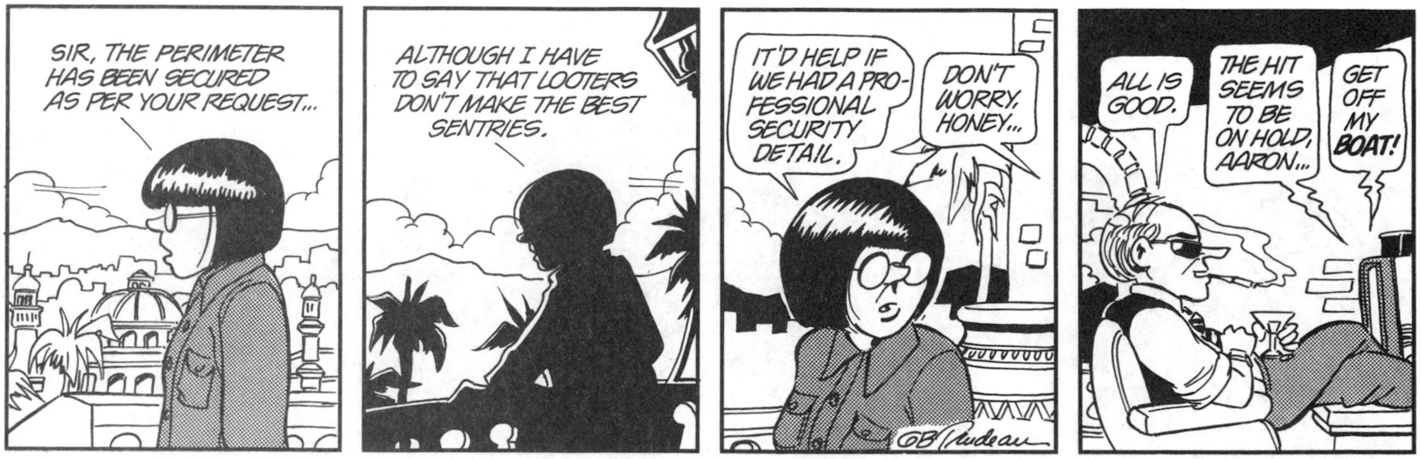
SIR, THE PERIMETER HAS BEEN SECURED AS PER YOUR REQUEST...
ALTHOUGH I HAVE TO SAY THAT LOOTERS DON'T MAKE THE BEST SENTRIES.
IT'D HELP IF WE HAD A PRO-FESSIONAL SECURITY DETAIL.
DON'T WORRY, HONEY...
ALL IS GOOD.
THE HIT SEEMS TO BE ON HOLD, AARON...
GET OFF MY BOAT!

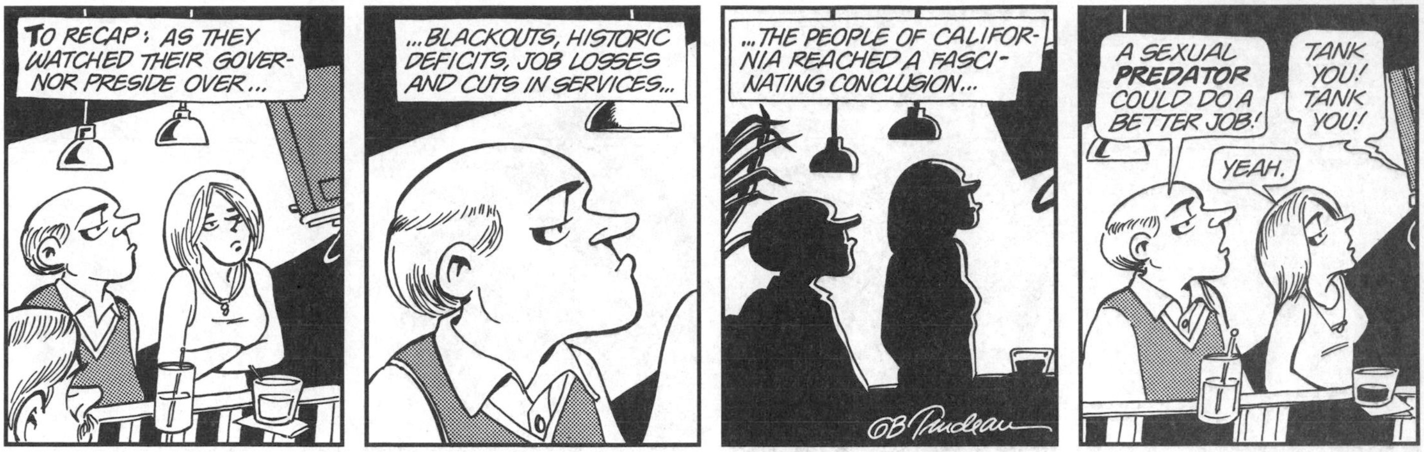
TO RECAP: AS THEY WATCHED THEIR GOVERNOR PRESIDE OVER...
...BLACKOUTS, HISTORIC DEFICITS, JOB LOSSES AND CUTS IN SERVICES...
...THE PEOPLE OF CALIFORNIA REACHED A FASCINATING CONCLUSION...
A SEXUAL PREDATOR COULD DO A BETTER JOB!
TANK YOU! TANK YOU!
YEAH.

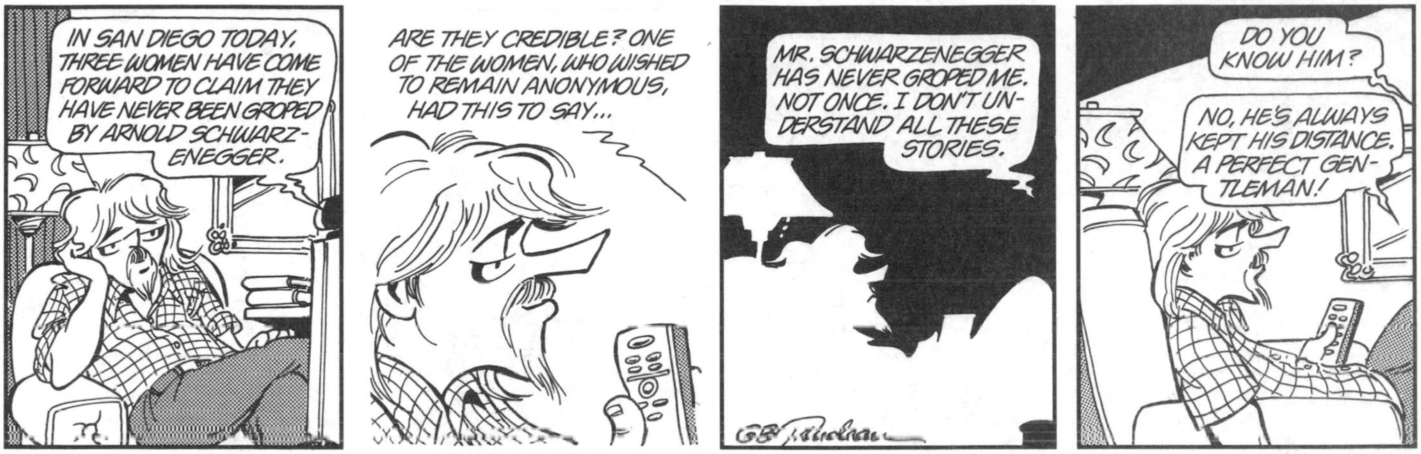
IN SAN DIEGO TODAY, THREE WOMEN HAVE COME FORWARD TO CLAIM THEY HAVE NEVER BEEN GROPED BY ARNOLD SCHWARZENEGGER.
ARE THEY CREDIBLE? ONE OF THE WOMEN, WHO WISHED TO REMAIN ANONYMOUS, HAD THIS TO SAY...
MR. SCHWARZENEGGER HAS NEVER GROPED ME. NOT ONCE. I DON'T UNDERSTAND ALL THESE STORIES.
DO YOU KNOW HIM?
NO, HE'S ALWAYS KEPT HIS DISTANCE. A PERFECT GENTLEMAN!

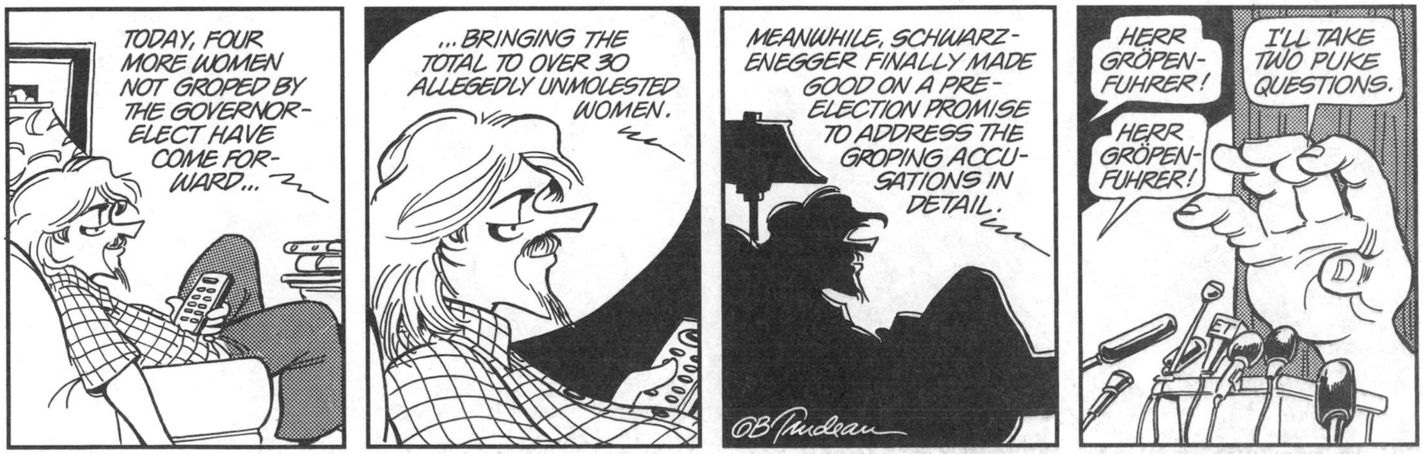
TODAY, FOUR MORE WOMEN NOT GROPED BY THE GOVERNOR-ELECT HAVE COME FORWARD...
...BRINGING THE TOTAL TO OVER 30 ALLEGEDLY UNMOLESTED WOMEN.
MEANWHILE, SCHWARZENEGGER FINALLY MADE GOOD ON A PRE-ELECTION PROMISE TO ADDRESS THE GROPING ACCUSATIONS IN DETAIL.
HERR GRÖPENFUHRER!
HERR GRÖPENFUHRER!
I'LL TAKE TWO PUKE QUESTIONS.

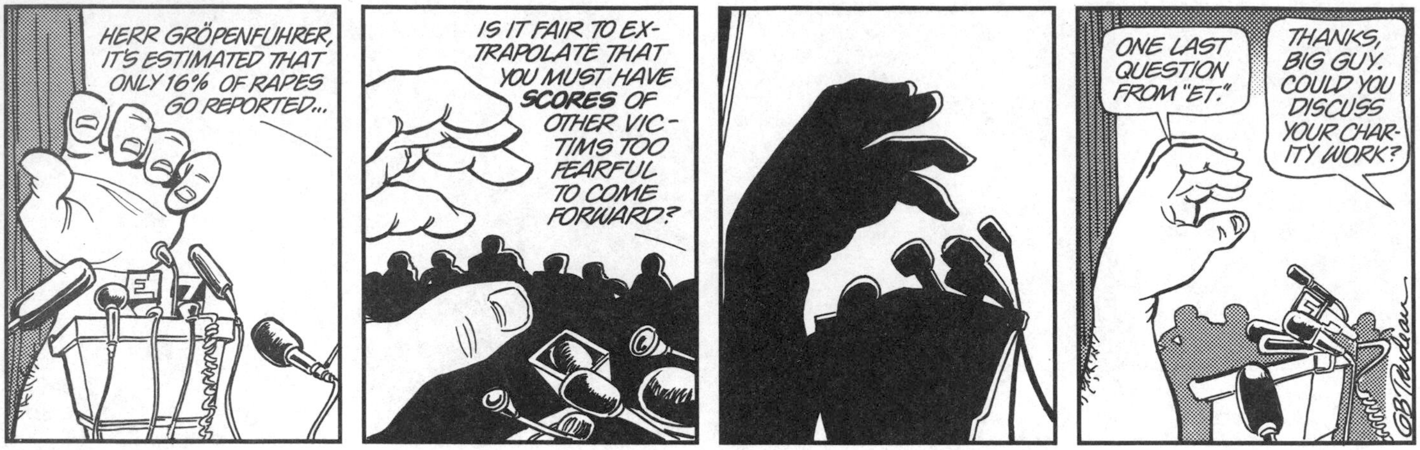
HERR GRÖPENFUHRER, IT'S ESTIMATED THAT ONLY 16% OF RAPES GO REPORTED...
IS IT FAIR TO EXTRAPOLATE THAT YOU MUST HAVE SCORES OF OTHER VICTIMS TOO FEARFUL TO COME FORWARD?
ONE LAST QUESTION FROM "ET."
THANKS, BIG GUY. COULD YOU DISCUSS YOUR CHARITY WORK?

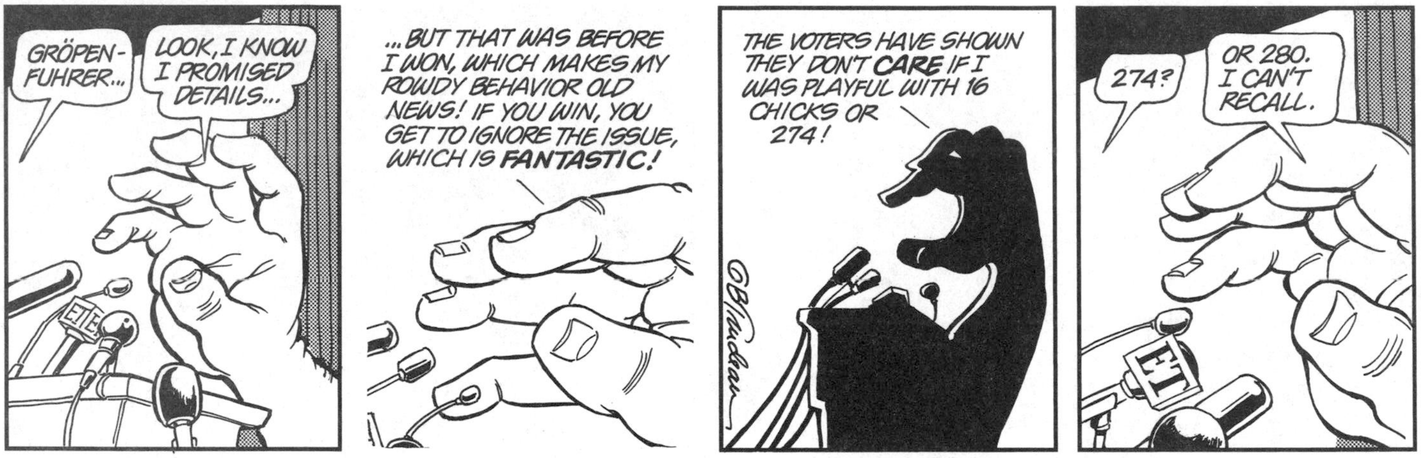
GRÖPENFUHRER...
LOOK, I KNOW I PROMISED DETAILS...
...BUT THAT WAS BEFORE I WON, WHICH MAKES MY ROWDY BEHAVIOR OLD NEWS! IF YOU WIN, YOU GET TO IGNORE THE ISSUE, WHICH IS FANTASTIC!
THE VOTERS HAVE SHOWN THEY DON'T CARE IF I WAS PLAYFUL WITH 16 CHICKS OR 274!
274?
OR 280. I CAN'T RECALL.

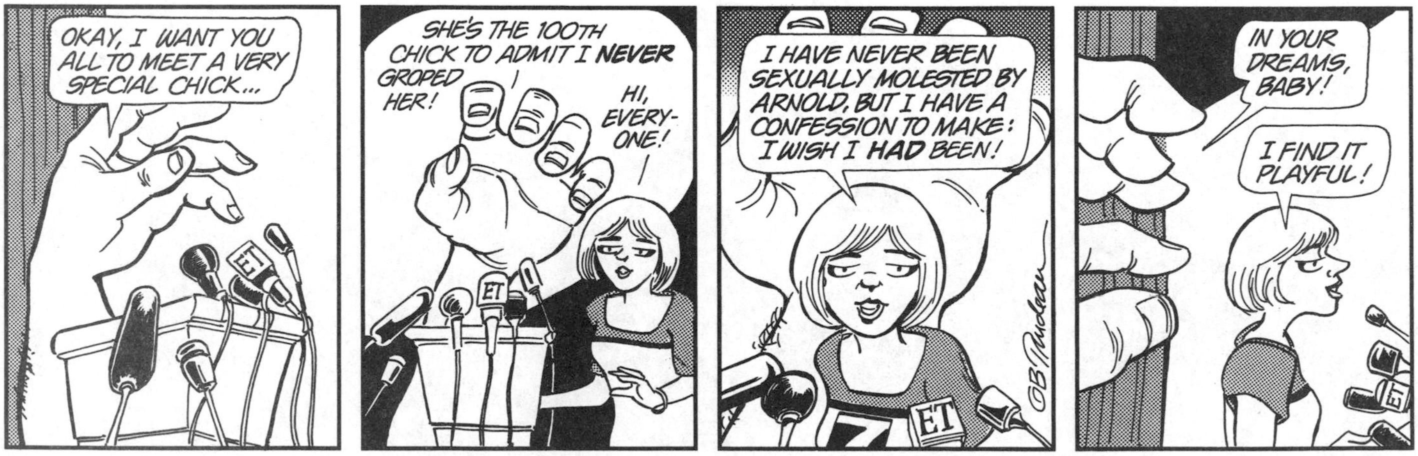
OKAY, I WANT YOU ALL TO MEET A VERY SPECIAL CHICK...
SHE'S THE 100TH CHICK TO ADMIT I NEVER GROPED HER!
HI, EVERYONE!
I HAVE NEVER BEEN SEXUALLY MOLESTED BY ARNOLD, BUT I HAVE A CONFESSION TO MAKE: I WISH I HAD BEEN!
IN YOUR DREAMS, BABY!
I FIND IT PLAYFUL!

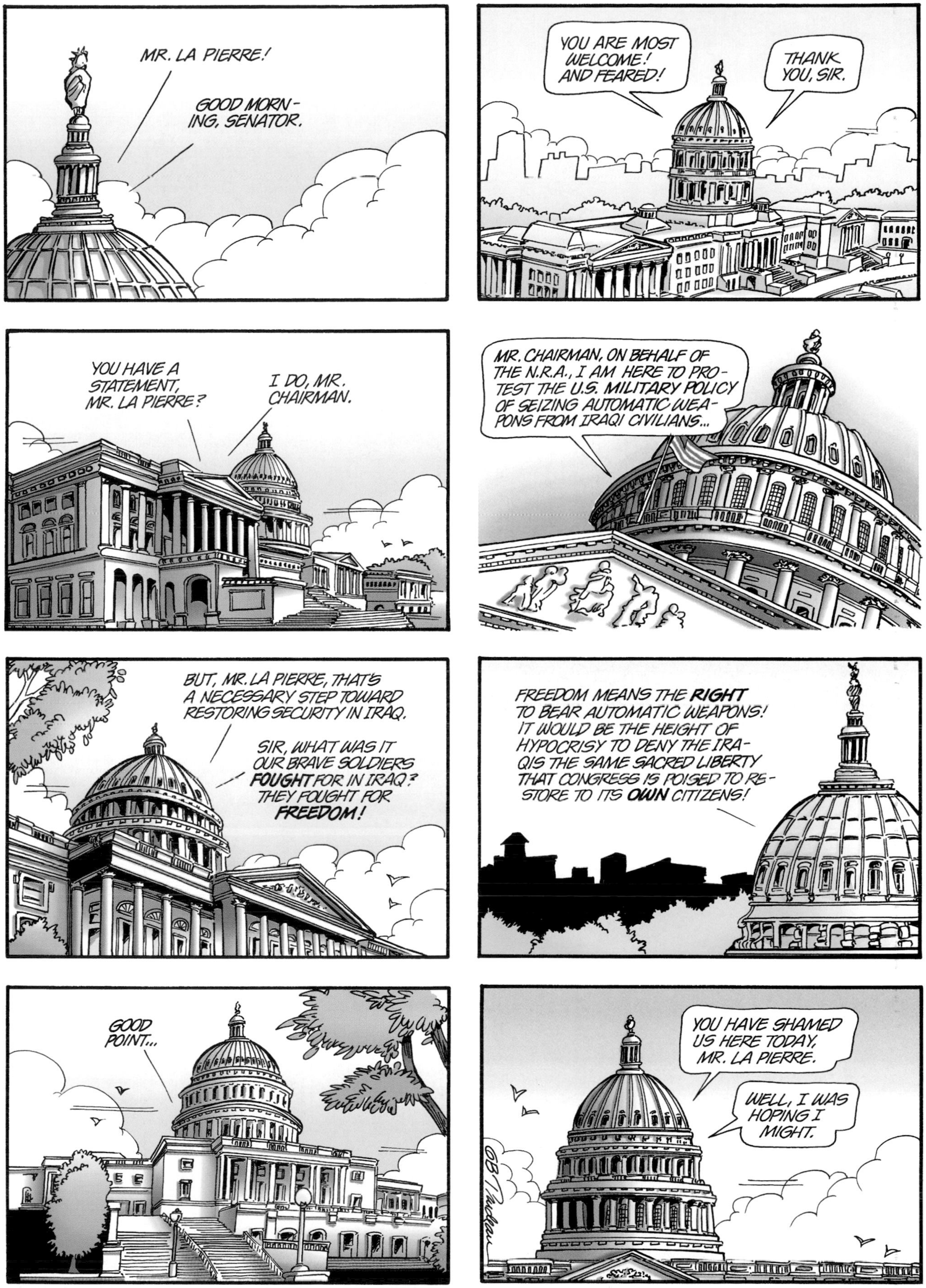
MR. LA PIERRE!
GOOD MORNING, SENATOR.
YOU ARE MOST WELCOME! AND FEARED!
THANK YOU, SIR.
YOU HAVE A STATEMENT, MR. LA PIERRE?
I DO, MR. CHAIRMAN.
MR. CHAIRMAN, ON BEHALF OF THE N.R.A., I AM HERE TO PROTEST THE U.S. MILITARY POLICY OF SEIZING AUTOMATIC WEAPONS FROM IRAQI CIVILIANS...
BUT, MR. LA PIERRE, THAT'S A NECESSARY STEP TOWARD RESTORING SECURITY IN IRAQ.
SIR, WHAT WAS IT OUR BRAVE SOLDIERS FOUGHT FOR IN IRAQ? THEY FOUGHT FOR FREEDOM!
FREEDOM MEANS THE RIGHT TO BEAR AUTOMATIC WEAPONS! IT WOULD BE THE HEIGHT OF HYPOCRISY TO DENY THE IRAQIS THE SAME SACRED LIBERTY THAT CONGRESS IS POISED TO RESTORE TO ITS OWN CITIZENS!
GOOD POINT...
YOU HAVE SHAMED US HERE TODAY, MR. LA PIERRE.
WELL, I WAS HOPING I MIGHT.

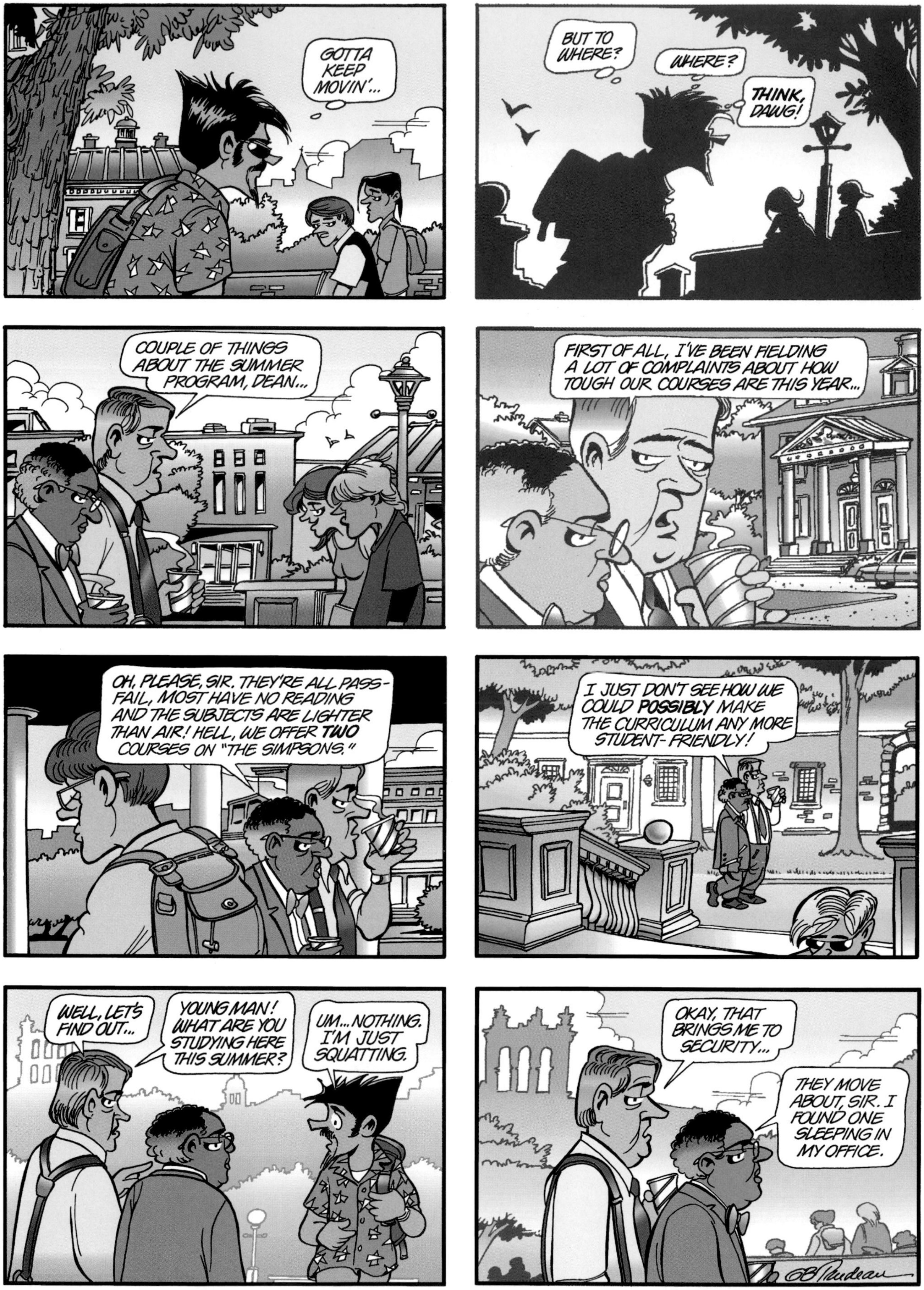
GOTTA KEEP MOVIN'...
BUT TO WHERE?
WHERE?
THINK, DAWG!
COUPLE OF THINGS ABOUT THE SUMMER PROGRAM, DEAN...
FIRST OF ALL, I'VE BEEN FIELDING A LOT OF COMPLAINTS ABOUT HOW TOUGH OUR COURSES ARE THIS YEAR...
OH, PLEASE, SIR. THEY'RE ALL PASS-FAIL, MOST HAVE NO READING AND THE SUBJECTS ARE LIGHTER THAN AIR! HELL, WE OFFER TWO COURSES ON "THE SIMPSONS."
I JUST DON'T SEE HOW WE COULD POSSIBLY MAKE THE CURRICULUM ANY MORE STUDENT-FRIENDLY!
WELL, LET'S FIND OUT...
YOUNG MAN! WHAT ARE YOU STUDYING HERE THIS SUMMER?
UM...NOTHING. I'M JUST SQUATTING.
OKAY, THAT BRINGS ME TO SECURITY...
THEY MOVE ABOUT, SIR. I FOUND ONE SLEEPING IN MY OFFICE.

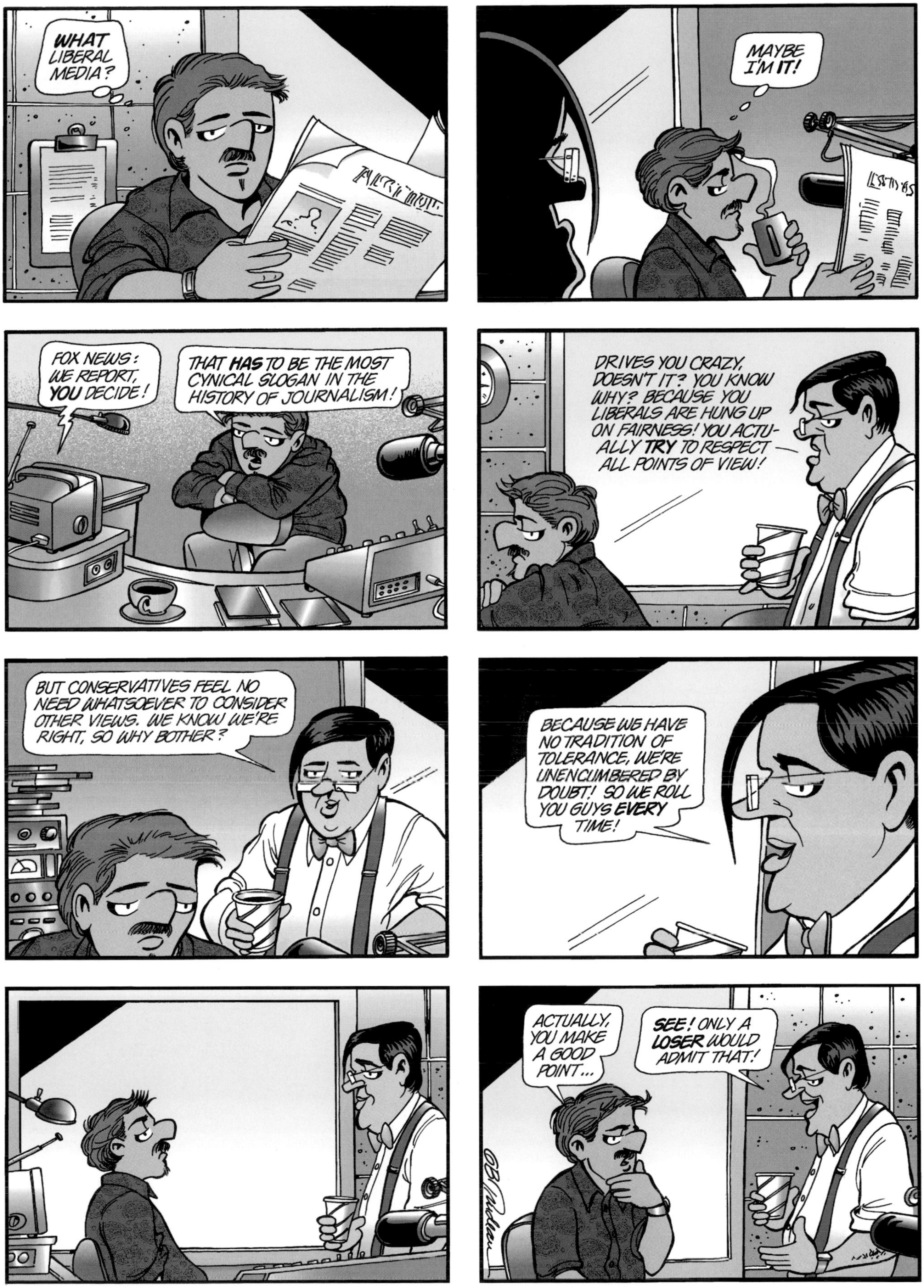
WHAT LIBERAL MEDIA?
MAYBE I'M IT!
FOX NEWS: WE REPORT, YOU DECIDE!
THAT HAS TO BE THE MOST CYNICAL SLOGAN IN THE HISTORY OF JOURNALISM!
DRIVES YOU CRAZY, DOESN'T IT? YOU KNOW WHY? BECAUSE YOU LIBERALS ARE HUNG UP ON FAIRNESS! YOU ACTUALLY TRY TO RESPECT ALL POINTS OF VIEW!
BUT CONSERVATIVES FEEL NO NEED WHATSOEVER TO CONSIDER OTHER VIEWS. WE KNOW WE'RE RIGHT, SO WHY BOTHER?
BECAUSE WE HAVE NO TRADITION OF TOLERANCE, WE'RE UNENCUMBERED BY DOUBT! SO WE ROLL YOU GUYS EVERY TIME!
ACTUALLY, YOU MAKE A GOOD POINT...
SEE! ONLY A LOSER WOULD ADMIT THAT!

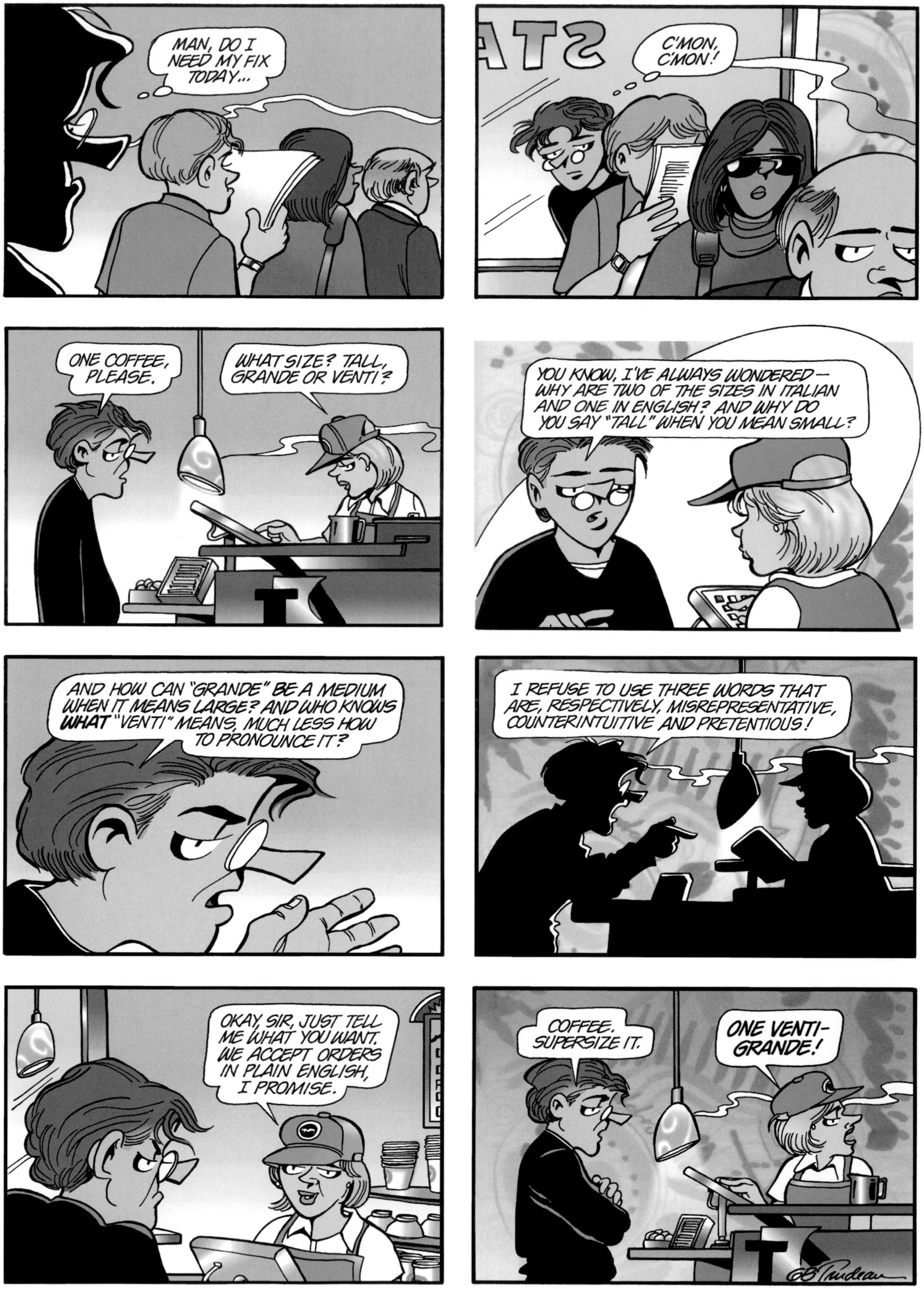
MAN, DO I NEED MY FIX TODAY...
C'MON, C'MON!
ONE COFFEE, PLEASE.
WHAT SIZE? TALL, GRANDE OR VENTI?
YOU KNOW, I'VE ALWAYS WONDERED— WHY ARE TWO OF THE SIZES IN ITALIAN AND ONE IN ENGLISH? AND WHY DO YOU SAY "TALL" WHEN YOU MEAN SMALL?
AND HOW CAN "GRANDE" BE A MEDIUM WHEN IT MEANS LARGE? AND WHO KNOWS **WHAT** "VENTI" MEANS, MUCH LESS HOW TO PRONOUNCE IT?
I REFUSE TO USE THREE WORDS THAT ARE, RESPECTIVELY, MISREPRESENTATIVE, COUNTERINTUITIVE AND PRETENTIOUS!
OKAY, SIR, JUST TELL ME WHAT YOU WANT. WE ACCEPT ORDERS IN PLAIN ENGLISH, I PROMISE.
COFFEE. SUPERSIZE IT.
ONE VENTI-GRANDE!
GB Trudeau

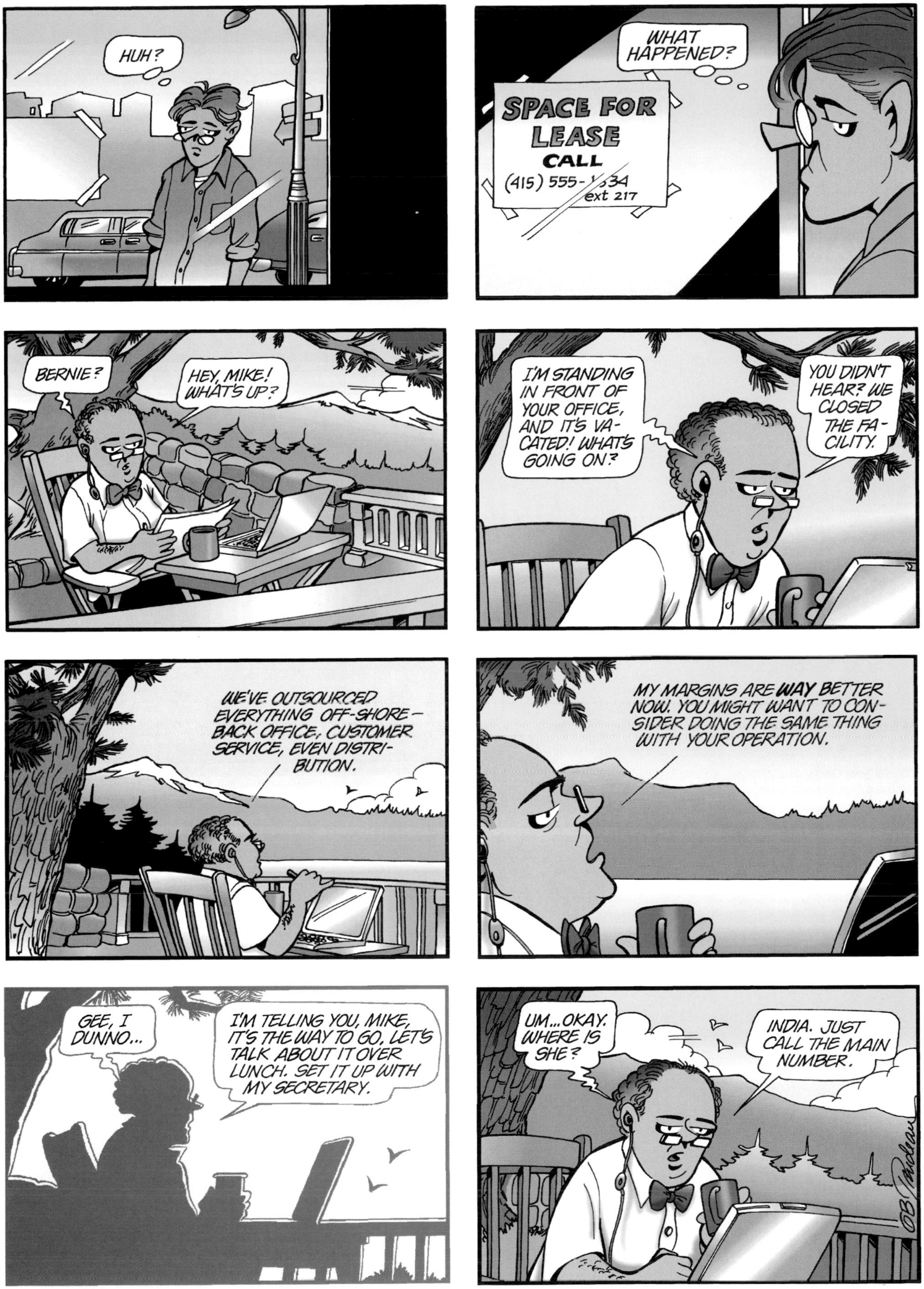

HUH?
WHAT HAPPENED?
SPACE FOR LEASE
CALL
(415) 555-1334
ext 217
BERNIE?
HEY, MIKE! WHAT'S UP?
I'M STANDING IN FRONT OF YOUR OFFICE, AND IT'S VACATED! WHAT'S GOING ON?
YOU DIDN'T HEAR? WE CLOSED THE FACILITY.
WE'VE OUTSOURCED EVERYTHING OFF-SHORE – BACK OFFICE, CUSTOMER SERVICE, EVEN DISTRIBUTION.
MY MARGINS ARE **WAY** BETTER NOW. YOU MIGHT WANT TO CONSIDER DOING THE SAME THING WITH YOUR OPERATION.
GEE, I DUNNO...
I'M TELLING YOU, MIKE, IT'S THE WAY TO GO. LET'S TALK ABOUT IT OVER LUNCH. SET IT UP WITH MY SECRETARY.
UM...OKAY. WHERE IS SHE?
INDIA. JUST CALL THE MAIN NUMBER.

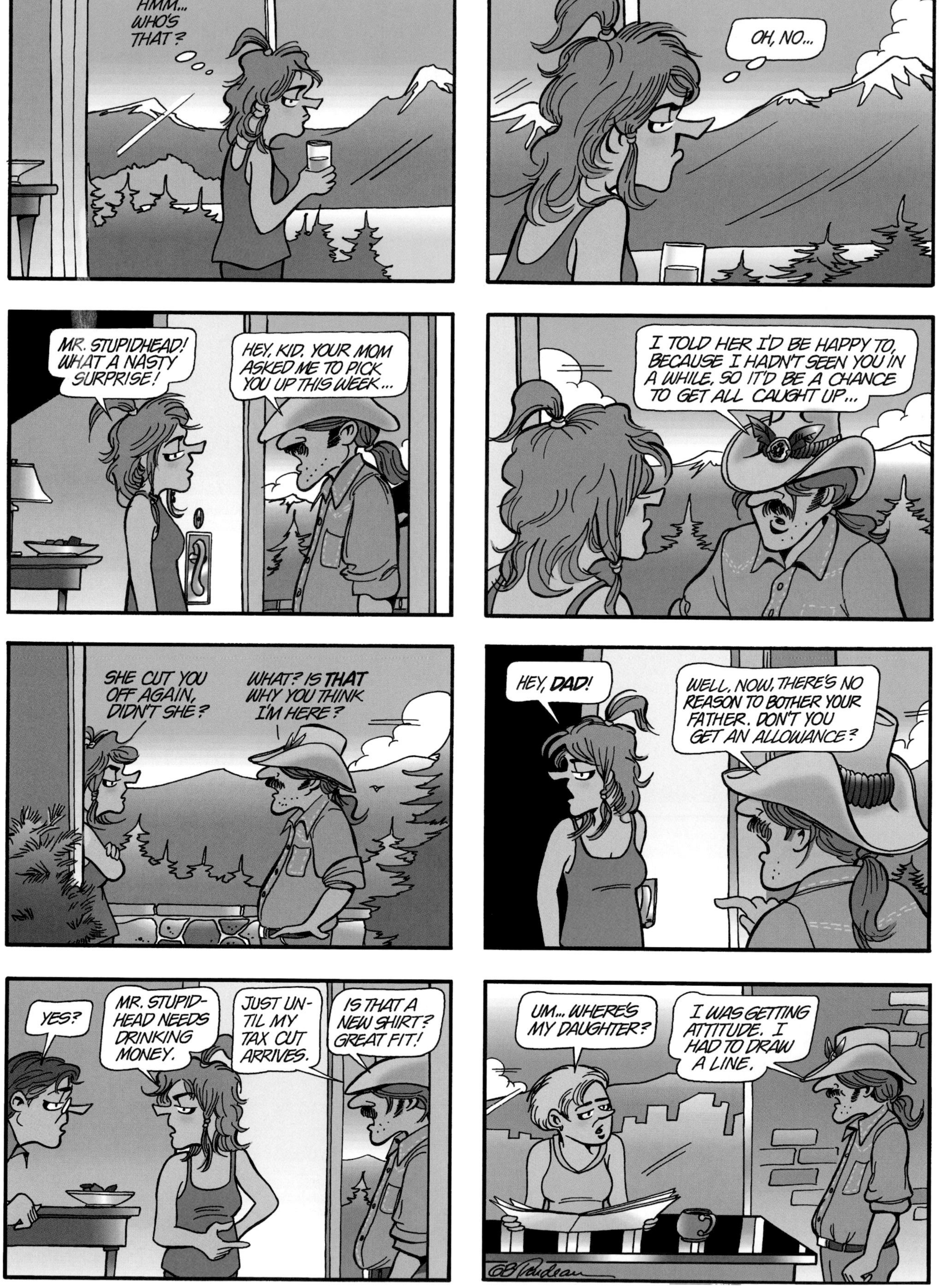

HMM... WHO'S THAT?
OH, NO...
MR. STUPIDHEAD! WHAT A NASTY SURPRISE!
HEY, KID. YOUR MOM ASKED ME TO PICK YOU UP THIS WEEK...
I TOLD HER I'D BE HAPPY TO, BECAUSE I HADN'T SEEN YOU IN A WHILE, SO IT'D BE A CHANCE TO GET ALL CAUGHT UP...
SHE CUT YOU OFF AGAIN, DIDN'T SHE?
WHAT? IS **THAT** WHY YOU THINK I'M HERE?
HEY, **DAD**!
WELL, NOW, THERE'S NO REASON TO BOTHER YOUR FATHER. DON'T YOU GET AN ALLOWANCE?
YES?
MR. STUPID-HEAD NEEDS DRINKING MONEY.
JUST UN-TIL MY TAX CUT ARRIVES.
IS THAT A NEW SHIRT? GREAT FIT!
UM... WHERE'S MY DAUGHTER?
I WAS GETTING ATTITUDE. I HAD TO DRAW A LINE.

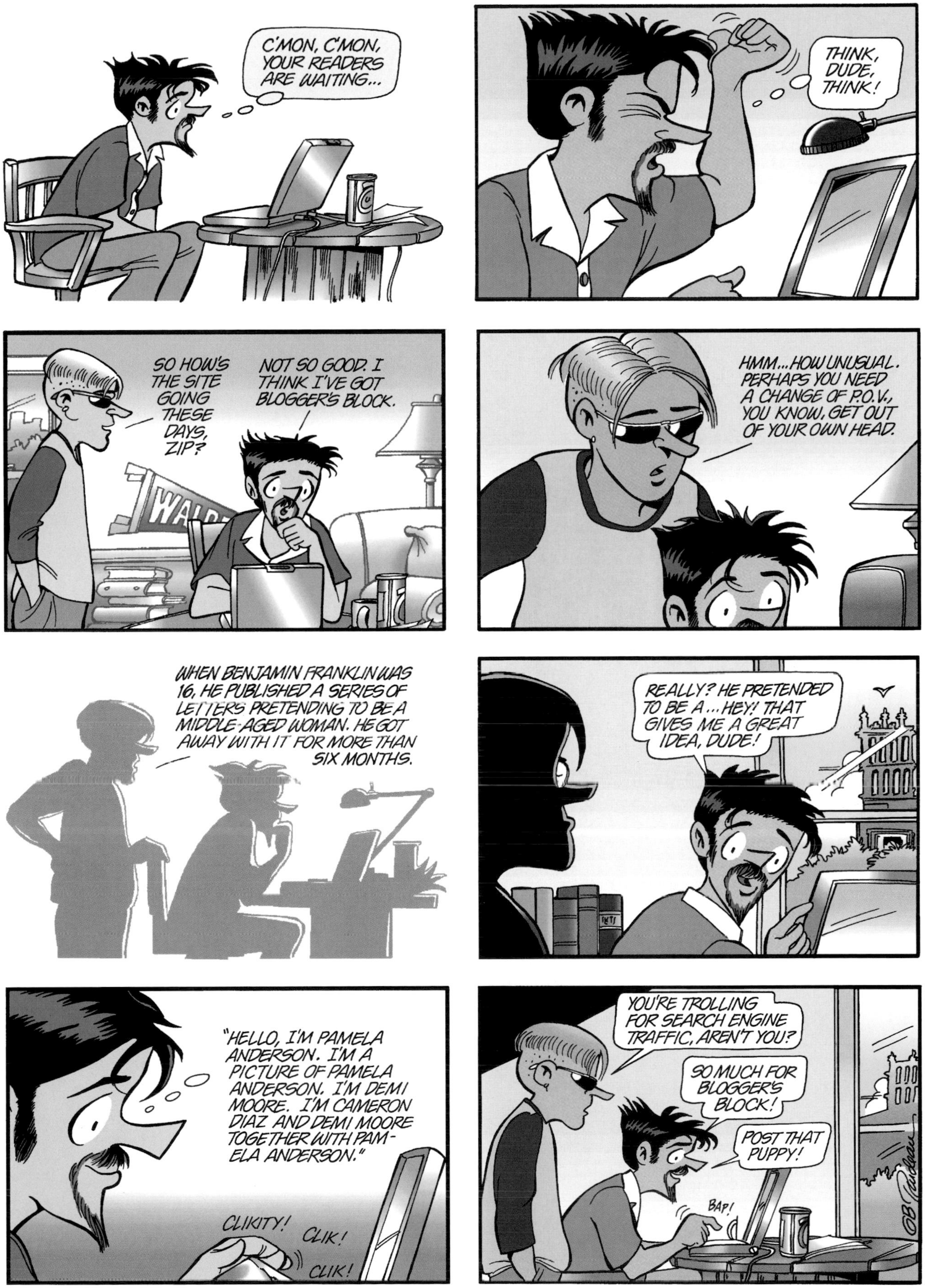
C'MON, C'MON, YOUR READERS ARE WAITING...
THINK, DUDE, THINK!
SO HOW'S THE SITE GOING THESE DAYS, ZIP?
NOT SO GOOD. I THINK I'VE GOT BLOGGER'S BLOCK.
HMM...HOW UNUSUAL. PERHAPS YOU NEED A CHANGE OF P.O.V., YOU KNOW, GET OUT OF YOUR OWN HEAD.
WHEN BENJAMIN FRANKLIN WAS 16, HE PUBLISHED A SERIES OF LETTERS PRETENDING TO BE A MIDDLE-AGED WOMAN. HE GOT AWAY WITH IT FOR MORE THAN SIX MONTHS.
REALLY? HE PRETENDED TO BE A ... HEY! THAT GIVES ME A GREAT IDEA, DUDE!
"HELLO, I'M PAMELA ANDERSON. I'M A PICTURE OF PAMELA ANDERSON. I'M DEMI MOORE. I'M CAMERON DIAZ AND DEMI MOORE TOGETHER WITH PAMELA ANDERSON."
CLIKITY! CLIK! CLIK!
YOU'RE TROLLING FOR SEARCH ENGINE TRAFFIC, AREN'T YOU?
SO MUCH FOR BLOGGER'S BLOCK!
POST THAT PUPPY!
BAP!

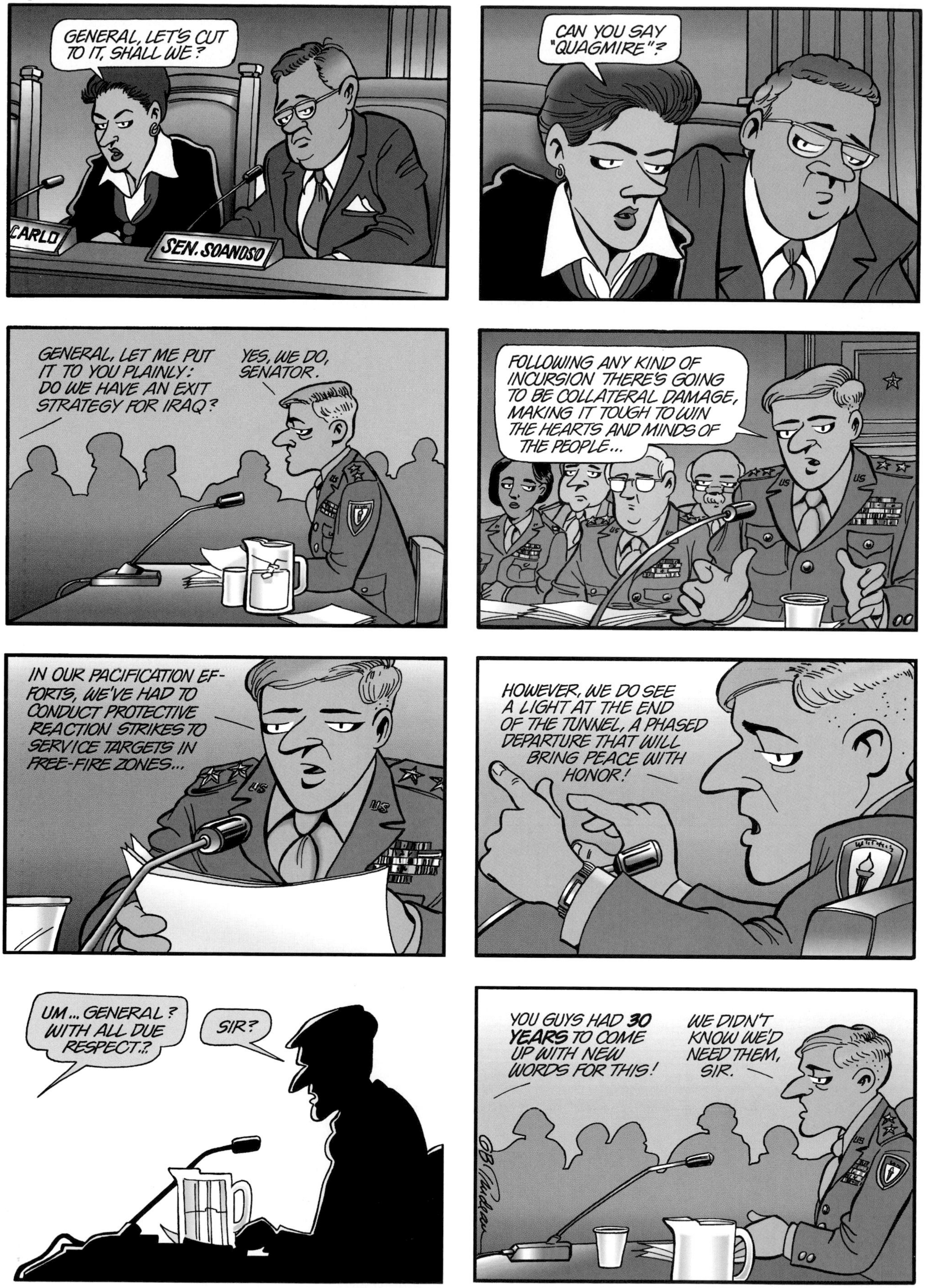
GENERAL, LET'S CUT TO IT, SHALL WE?
CARLO
SEN. SOANDSO
CAN YOU SAY "QUAGMIRE"?
GENERAL, LET ME PUT IT TO YOU PLAINLY: DO WE HAVE AN EXIT STRATEGY FOR IRAQ?
YES, WE DO, SENATOR.
FOLLOWING ANY KIND OF INCURSION THERE'S GOING TO BE COLLATERAL DAMAGE, MAKING IT TOUGH TO WIN THE HEARTS AND MINDS OF THE PEOPLE...
IN OUR PACIFICATION EF-FORTS, WE'VE HAD TO CONDUCT PROTECTIVE REACTION STRIKES TO SERVICE TARGETS IN FREE-FIRE ZONES...
HOWEVER, WE DO SEE A LIGHT AT THE END OF THE TUNNEL, A PHASED DEPARTURE THAT WILL BRING PEACE WITH HONOR!
UM... GENERAL? WITH ALL DUE RESPECT..?
SIR?
YOU GUYS HAD **30 YEARS** TO COME UP WITH NEW WORDS FOR THIS!
WE DIDN'T KNOW WE'D NEED THEM, SIR.

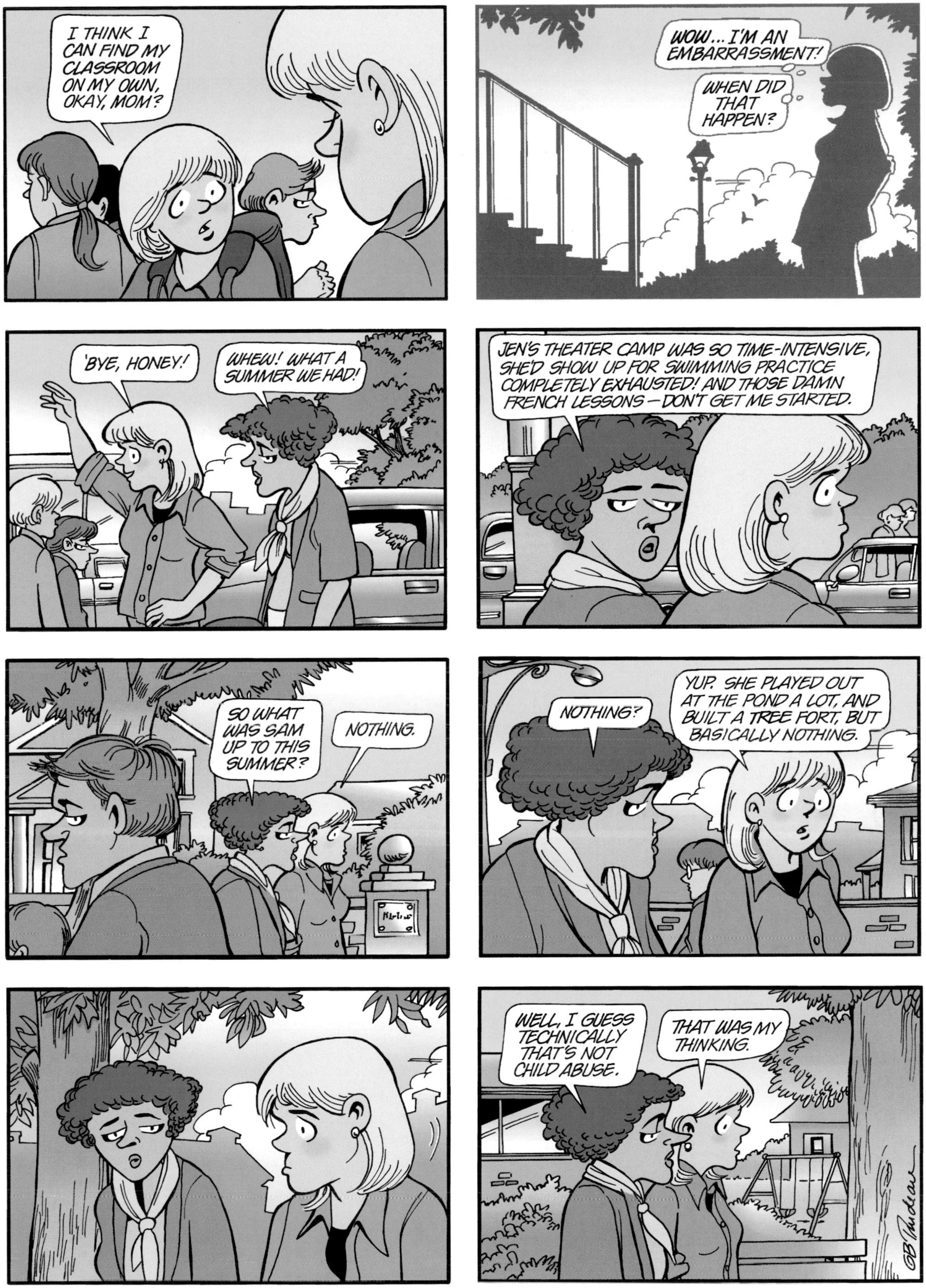
I THINK I CAN FIND MY CLASSROOM ON MY OWN, OKAY, MOM?
WOW... I'M AN EMBARRASSMENT!
WHEN DID THAT HAPPEN?
'BYE, HONEY!
WHEW! WHAT A SUMMER WE HAD!
JEN'S THEATER CAMP WAS SO TIME-INTENSIVE, SHE'D SHOW UP FOR SWIMMING PRACTICE COMPLETELY EXHAUSTED! AND THOSE DAMN FRENCH LESSONS — DON'T GET ME STARTED.
SO WHAT WAS SAM UP TO THIS SUMMER?
NOTHING.
NOTHING?
YUP. SHE PLAYED OUT AT THE POND A LOT, AND BUILT A TREE FORT, BUT BASICALLY NOTHING.
WELL, I GUESS TECHNICALLY THAT'S NOT CHILD ABUSE.
THAT WAS MY THINKING.

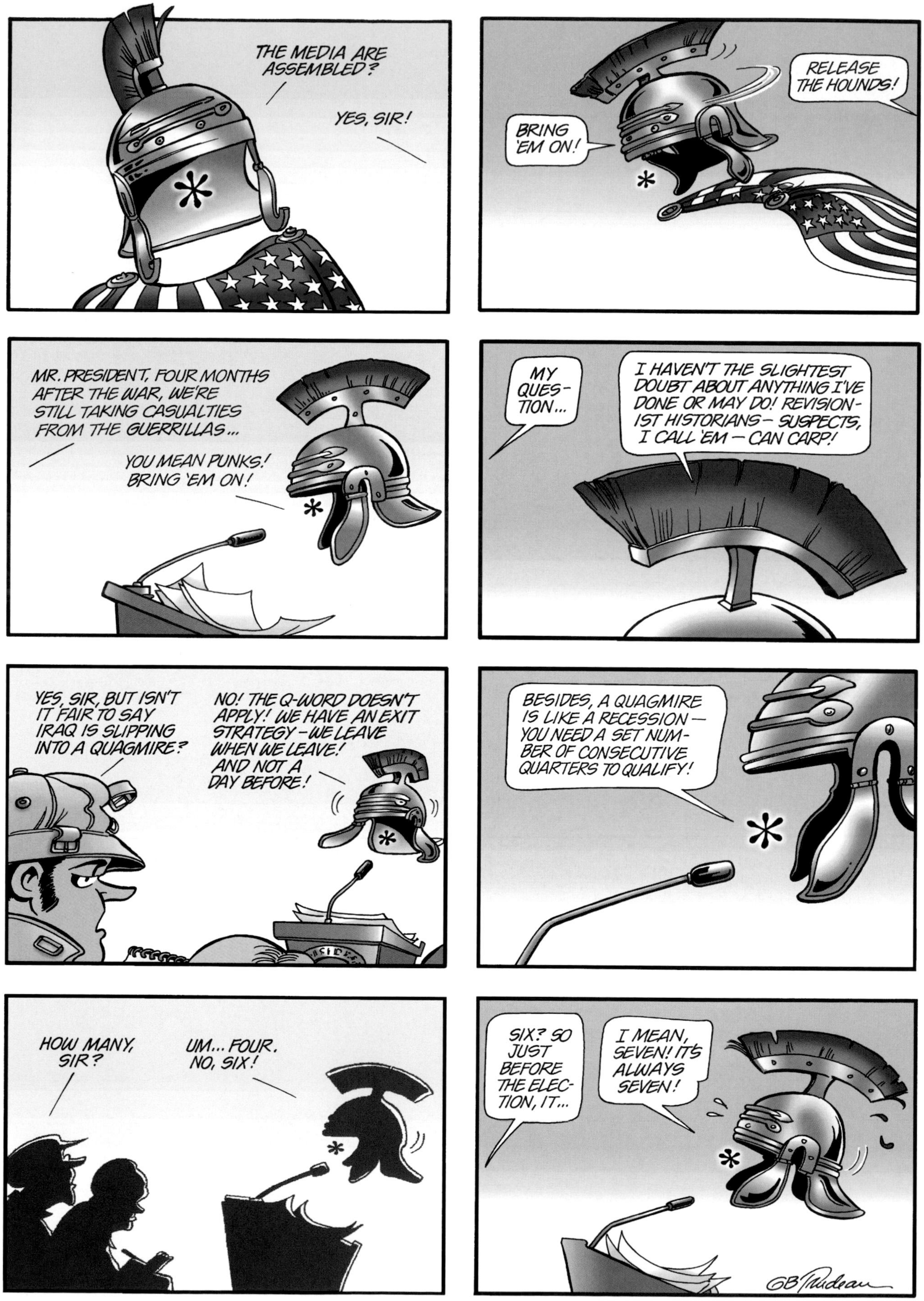
THE MEDIA ARE ASSEMBLED?
YES, SIR!
RELEASE THE HOUNDS!
BRING 'EM ON!
MR. PRESIDENT, FOUR MONTHS AFTER THE WAR, WE'RE STILL TAKING CASUALTIES FROM THE GUERRILLAS...
YOU MEAN PUNKS! BRING 'EM ON!
MY QUES-TION...
I HAVEN'T THE SLIGHTEST DOUBT ABOUT ANYTHING I'VE DONE OR MAY DO! REVISION-IST HISTORIANS— SUSPECTS, I CALL 'EM — CAN CARP!
YES, SIR, BUT ISN'T IT FAIR TO SAY IRAQ IS SLIPPING INTO A QUAGMIRE?
NO! THE Q-WORD DOESN'T APPLY! WE HAVE AN EXIT STRATEGY—WE LEAVE WHEN WE LEAVE! AND NOT A DAY BEFORE!
BESIDES, A QUAGMIRE IS LIKE A RECESSION — YOU NEED A SET NUM-BER OF CONSECUTIVE QUARTERS TO QUALIFY!
HOW MANY, SIR?
UM... FOUR. NO, SIX!
SIX? SO JUST BEFORE THE ELEC-TION, IT...
I MEAN, SEVEN! IT'S ALWAYS SEVEN!
GB Trudeau

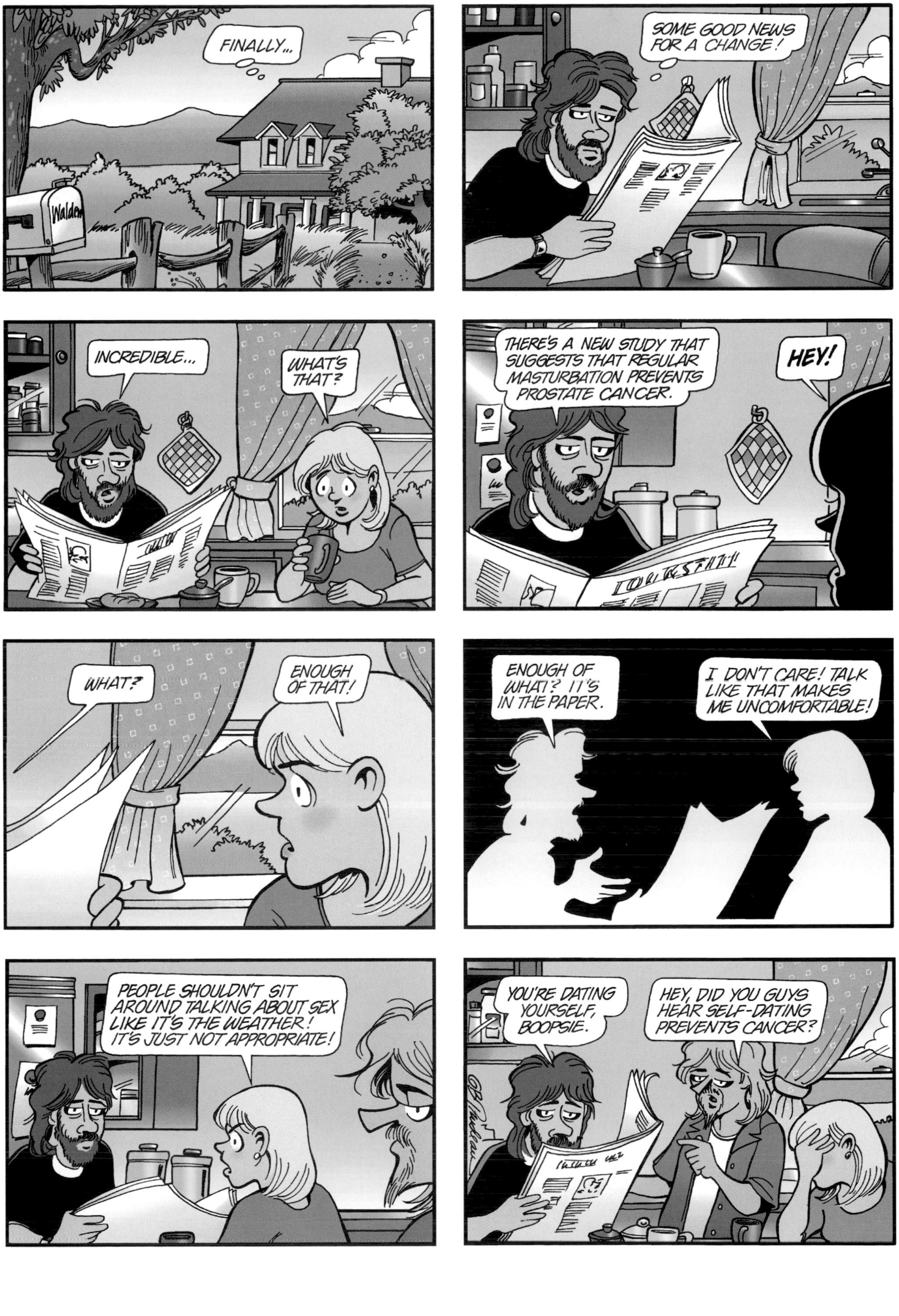
FINALLY...
Walden
SOME GOOD NEWS FOR A CHANGE!
INCREDIBLE...
WHAT'S THAT?
THERE'S A NEW STUDY THAT SUGGESTS THAT REGULAR MASTURBATION PREVENTS PROSTATE CANCER.
HEY!
WHAT?
ENOUGH OF THAT!
ENOUGH OF WHAT? IT'S IN THE PAPER.
I DON'T CARE! TALK LIKE THAT MAKES ME UNCOMFORTABLE!
PEOPLE SHOULDN'T SIT AROUND TALKING ABOUT SEX LIKE IT'S THE WEATHER! IT'S JUST NOT APPROPRIATE!
YOU'RE DATING YOURSELF, BOOPSIE.
HEY, DID YOU GUYS HEAR SELF-DATING PREVENTS CANCER?

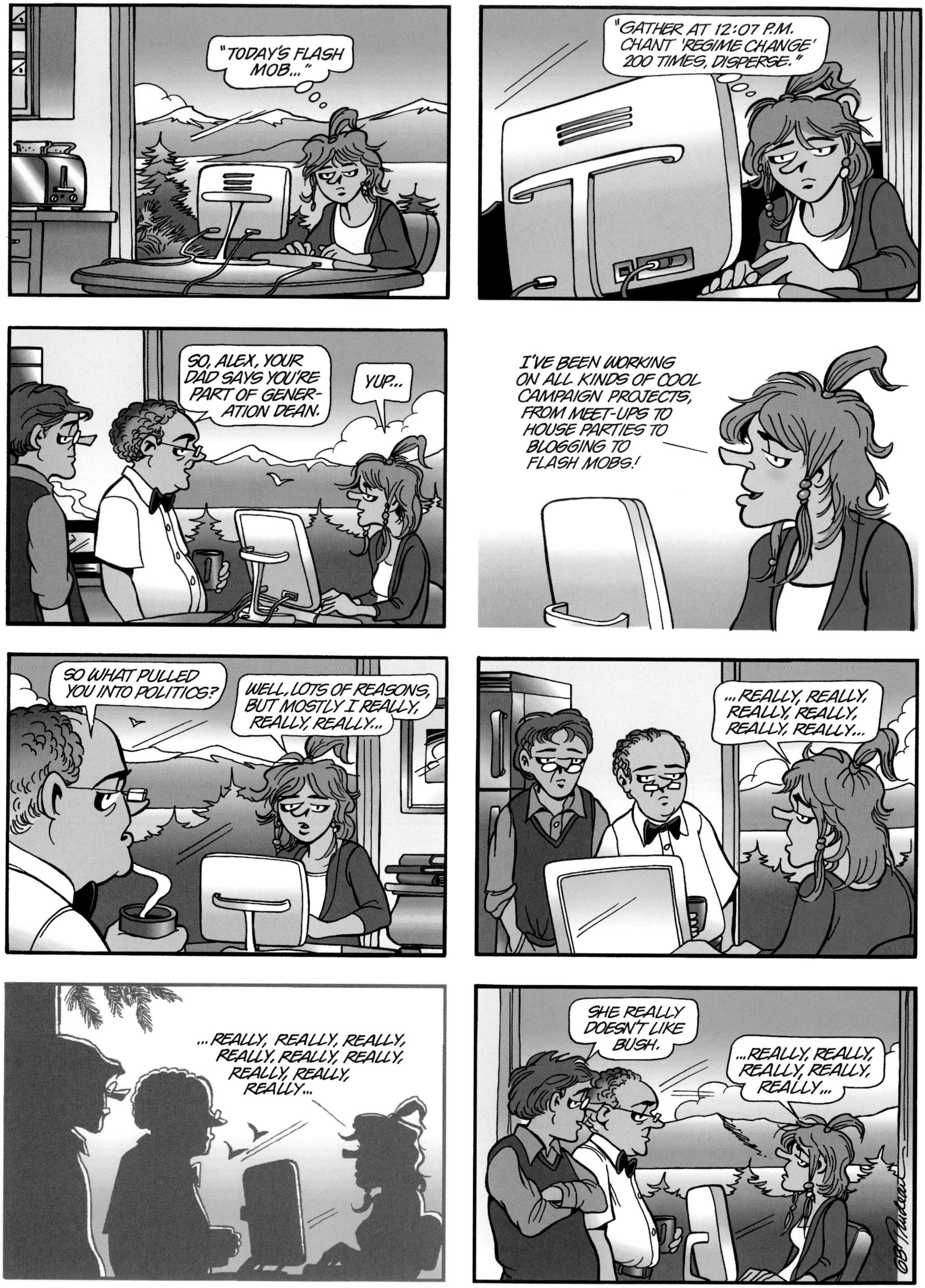
"TODAY'S FLASH MOB..."
"GATHER AT 12:07 P.M. CHANT 'REGIME CHANGE' 200 TIMES, DISPERSE."
SO, ALEX, YOUR DAD SAYS YOU'RE PART OF GENERATION DEAN.
YUP...
I'VE BEEN WORKING ON ALL KINDS OF COOL CAMPAIGN PROJECTS, FROM MEET-UPS TO HOUSE PARTIES TO BLOGGING TO FLASH MOBS!
SO WHAT PULLED YOU INTO POLITICS?
WELL, LOTS OF REASONS, BUT MOSTLY I REALLY, REALLY, REALLY...
...REALLY, REALLY, REALLY, REALLY, REALLY, REALLY...
...REALLY, REALLY, REALLY, REALLY, REALLY, REALLY, REALLY, REALLY, REALLY...
SHE REALLY DOESN'T LIKE BUSH.
...REALLY, REALLY, REALLY, REALLY, REALLY...

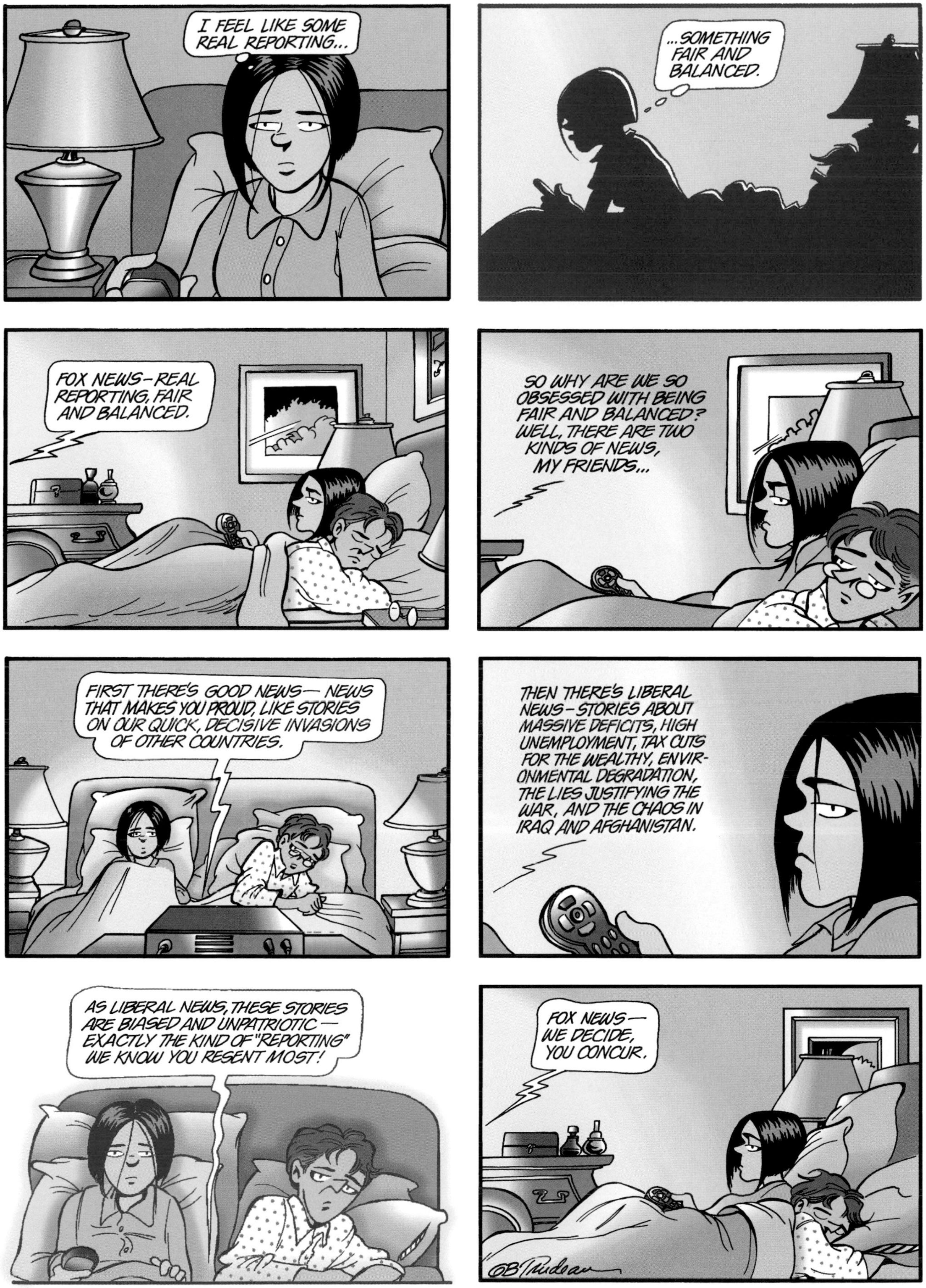
I FEEL LIKE SOME REAL REPORTING...
...SOMETHING FAIR AND BALANCED.
FOX NEWS—REAL REPORTING, FAIR AND BALANCED.
SO WHY ARE WE SO OBSESSED WITH BEING FAIR AND BALANCED? WELL, THERE ARE TWO KINDS OF NEWS, MY FRIENDS...
FIRST THERE'S GOOD NEWS— NEWS THAT MAKES YOU PROUD, LIKE STORIES ON OUR QUICK, DECISIVE INVASIONS OF OTHER COUNTRIES.
THEN THERE'S LIBERAL NEWS—STORIES ABOUT MASSIVE DEFICITS, HIGH UNEMPLOYMENT, TAX CUTS FOR THE WEALTHY, ENVIRONMENTAL DEGRADATION, THE LIES JUSTIFYING THE WAR, AND THE CHAOS IN IRAQ AND AFGHANISTAN.
AS LIBERAL NEWS, THESE STORIES ARE BIASED AND UNPATRIOTIC— EXACTLY THE KIND OF "REPORTING" WE KNOW YOU RESENT MOST!
FOX NEWS— WE DECIDE, YOU CONCUR.
©B. Trudeau

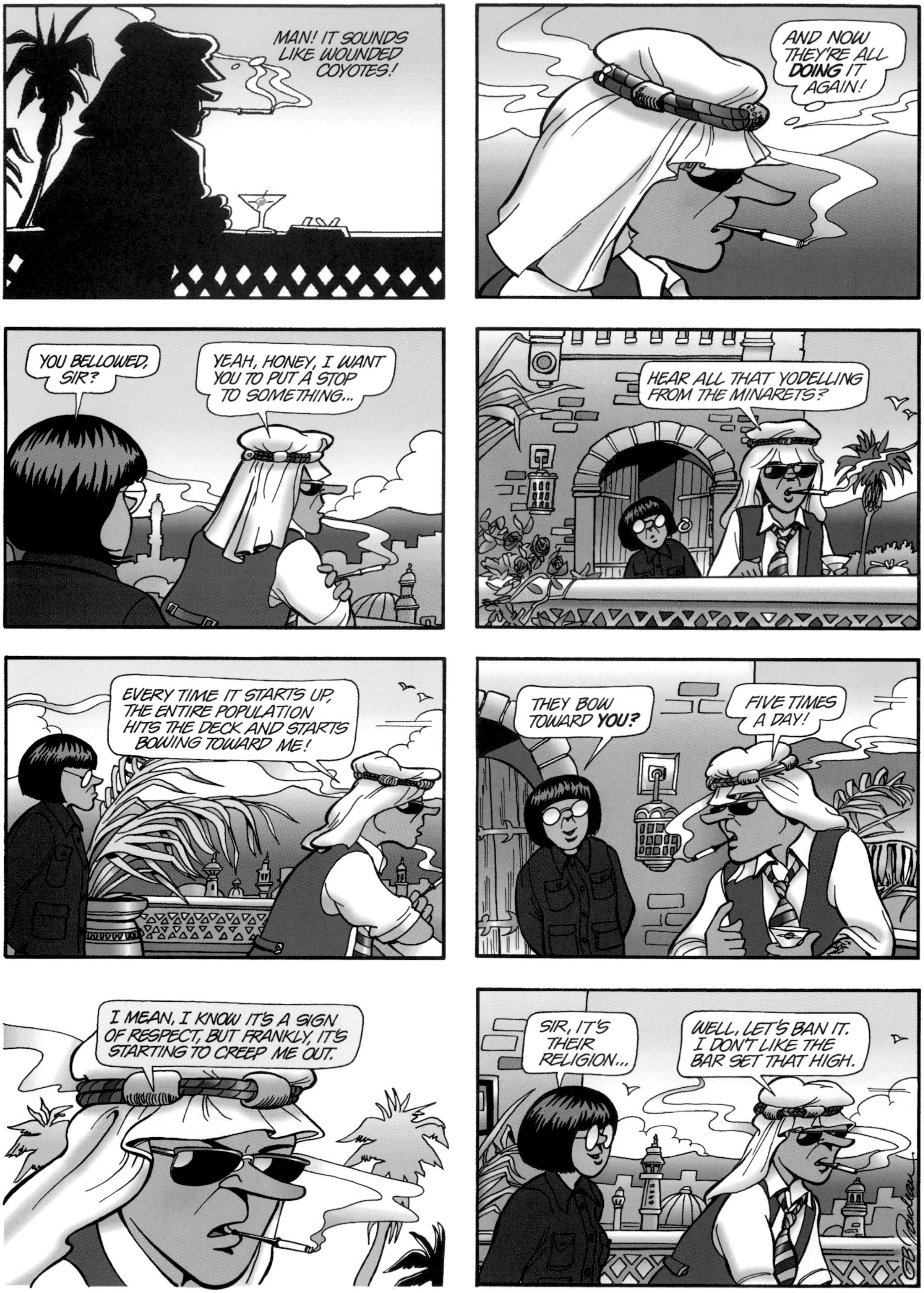
MAN! IT SOUNDS LIKE WOUNDED COYOTES!
AND NOW THEY'RE ALL **DOING** IT AGAIN!
YOU BELLOWED, SIR?
YEAH, HONEY, I WANT YOU TO PUT A STOP TO SOMETHING...
HEAR ALL THAT YODELLING FROM THE MINARETS?
EVERY TIME IT STARTS UP, THE ENTIRE POPULATION HITS THE DECK AND STARTS BOWING TOWARD ME!
THEY BOW TOWARD **YOU?**
FIVE TIMES A DAY!
I MEAN, I KNOW IT'S A SIGN OF RESPECT, BUT FRANKLY, IT'S STARTING TO CREEP ME OUT.
SIR, IT'S THEIR RELIGION...
WELL, LET'S BAN IT. I DON'T LIKE THE BAR SET THAT HIGH.

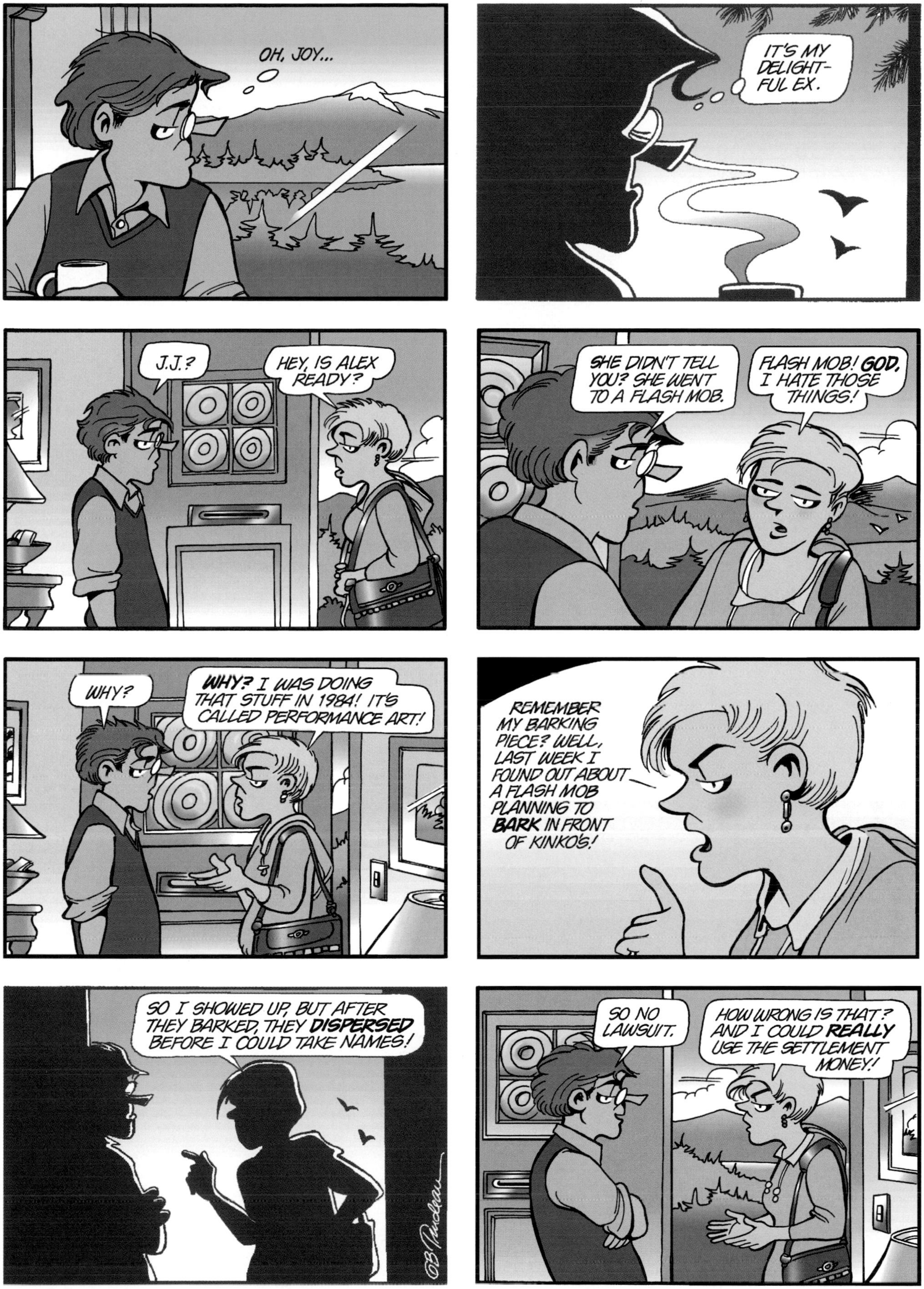

OH, JOY...
IT'S MY DELIGHTFUL EX.
J.J.?
HEY, IS ALEX READY?
SHE DIDN'T TELL YOU? SHE WENT TO A FLASH MOB.
FLASH MOB! GOD, I HATE THOSE THINGS!
WHY?
WHY? I WAS DOING THAT STUFF IN 1984! IT'S CALLED PERFORMANCE ART!
REMEMBER MY BARKING PIECE? WELL, LAST WEEK I FOUND OUT ABOUT A FLASH MOB PLANNING TO BARK IN FRONT OF KINKO'S!
SO I SHOWED UP, BUT AFTER THEY BARKED, THEY DISPERSED BEFORE I COULD TAKE NAMES!
SO NO LAWSUIT.
HOW WRONG IS THAT? AND I COULD REALLY USE THE SETTLEMENT MONEY!

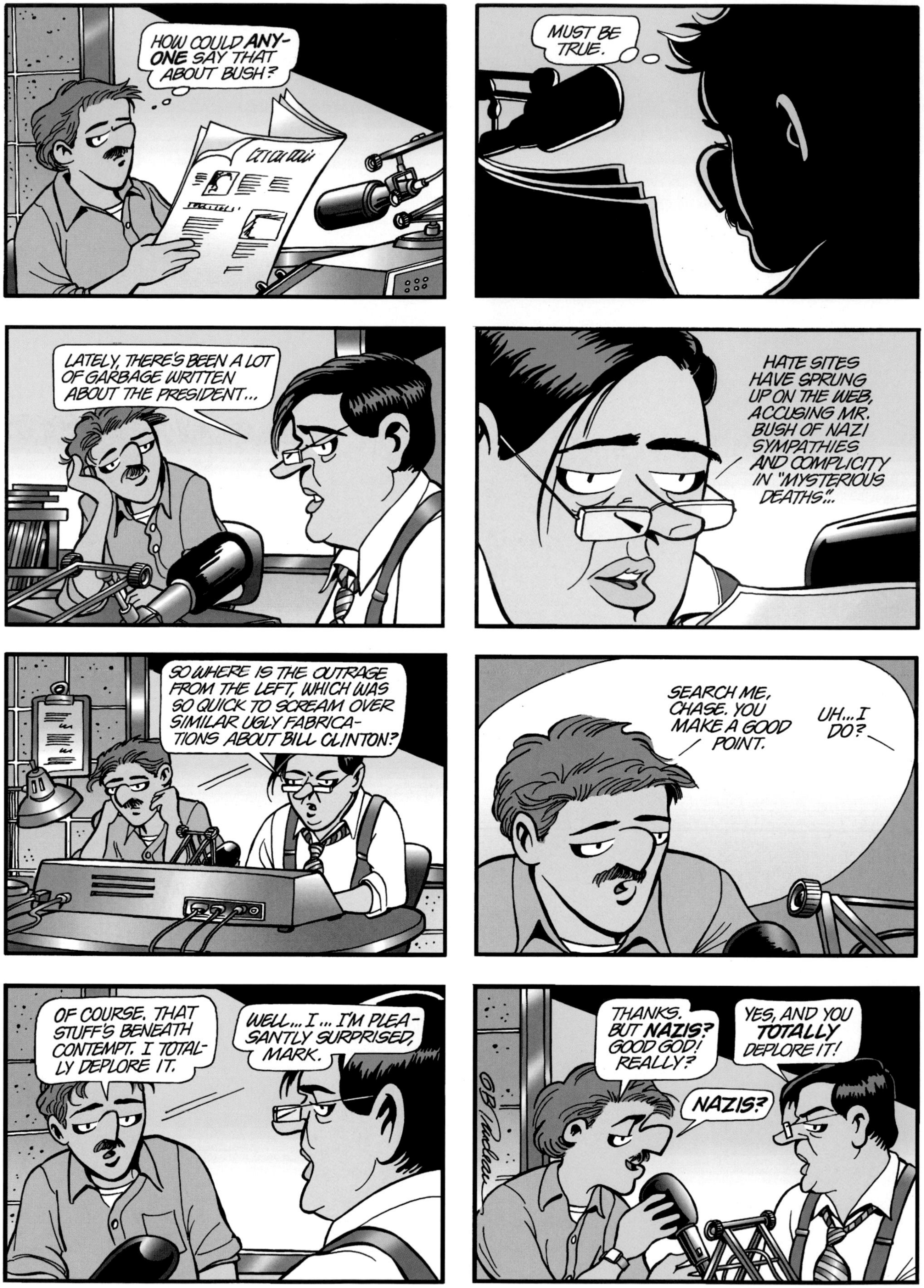
HOW COULD ANYONE SAY THAT ABOUT BUSH?
MUST BE TRUE.
LATELY, THERE'S BEEN A LOT OF GARBAGE WRITTEN ABOUT THE PRESIDENT...
HATE SITES HAVE SPRUNG UP ON THE WEB, ACCUSING MR. BUSH OF NAZI SYMPATHIES AND COMPLICITY IN "MYSTERIOUS DEATHS."...
SO WHERE IS THE OUTRAGE FROM THE LEFT, WHICH WAS SO QUICK TO SCREAM OVER SIMILAR UGLY FABRICATIONS ABOUT BILL CLINTON?
SEARCH ME, CHASE. YOU MAKE A GOOD POINT.
UH... I DO?
OF COURSE. THAT STUFF'S BENEATH CONTEMPT. I TOTALLY DEPLORE IT.
WELL... I... I'M PLEASANTLY SURPRISED, MARK.
THANKS. BUT NAZIS? GOOD GOD! REALLY?
YES, AND YOU TOTALLY DEPLORE IT!
NAZIS?

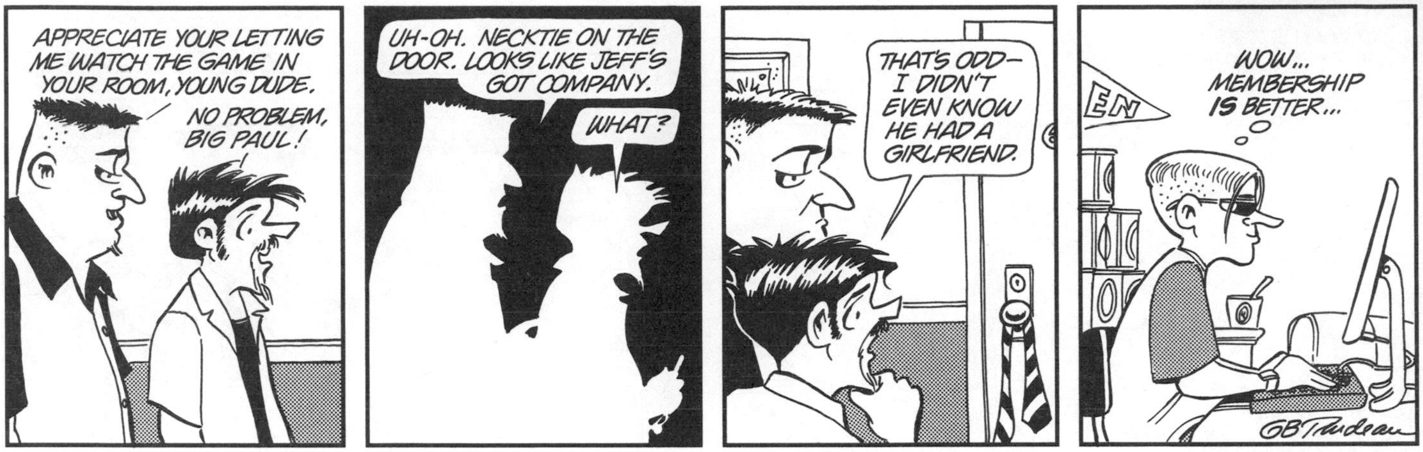
APPRECIATE YOUR LETTING ME WATCH THE GAME IN YOUR ROOM, YOUNG DUDE.
NO PROBLEM, BIG PAUL!
UH-OH. NECKTIE ON THE DOOR. LOOKS LIKE JEFF'S GOT COMPANY.
WHAT?
THAT'S ODD— I DIDN'T EVEN KNOW HE HAD A GIRLFRIEND.
WOW... MEMBERSHIP IS BETTER...

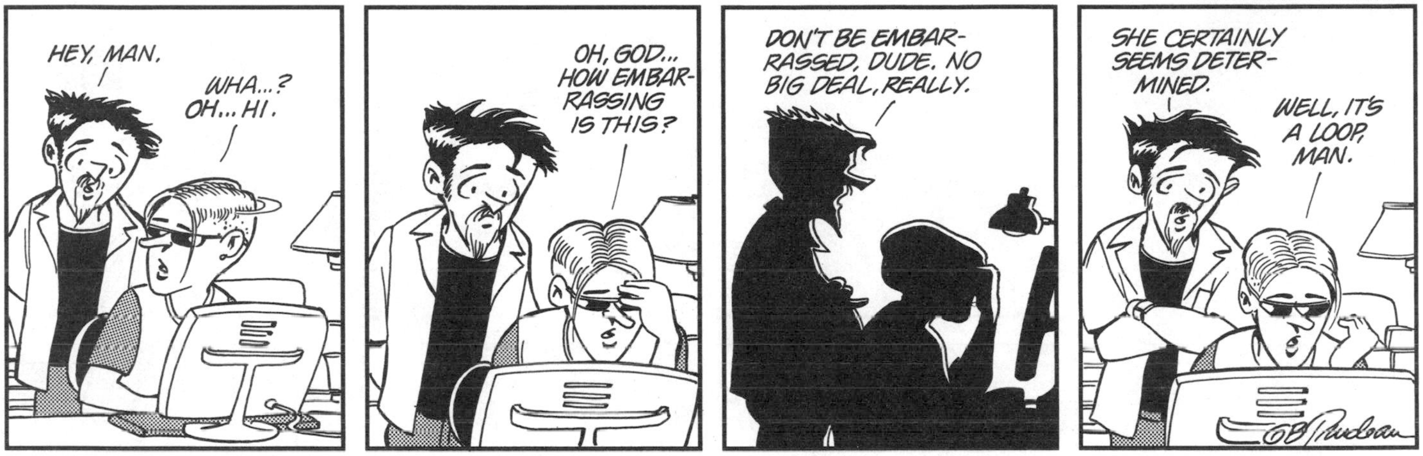
HEY, MAN.
WHA...? OH... HI.
OH, GOD... HOW EMBARRASSING IS THIS?
DON'T BE EMBARRASSED, DUDE. NO BIG DEAL, REALLY.
SHE CERTAINLY SEEMS DETERMINED.
WELL, IT'S A LOOP, MAN.

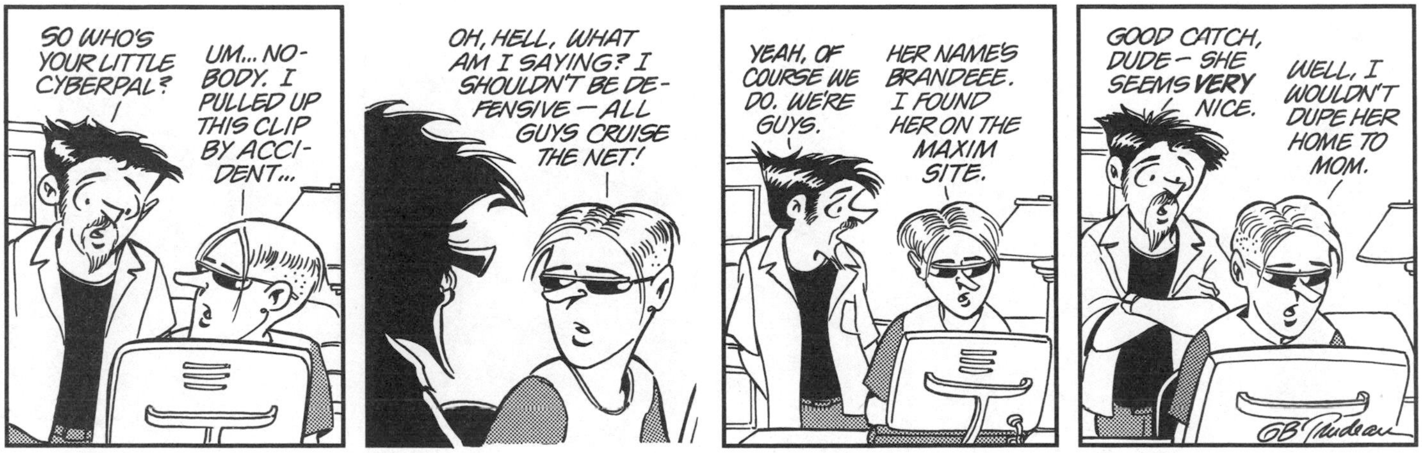
SO WHO'S YOUR LITTLE CYBERPAL?
UM... NOBODY. I PULLED UP THIS CLIP BY ACCIDENT...
OH, HELL, WHAT AM I SAYING? I SHOULDN'T BE DEFENSIVE — ALL GUYS CRUISE THE NET!
YEAH, OF COURSE WE DO. WE'RE GUYS.
HER NAME'S BRANDEEE. I FOUND HER ON THE MAXIM SITE.
GOOD CATCH, DUDE— SHE SEEMS VERY NICE.
WELL, I WOULDN'T DUPE HER HOME TO MOM.

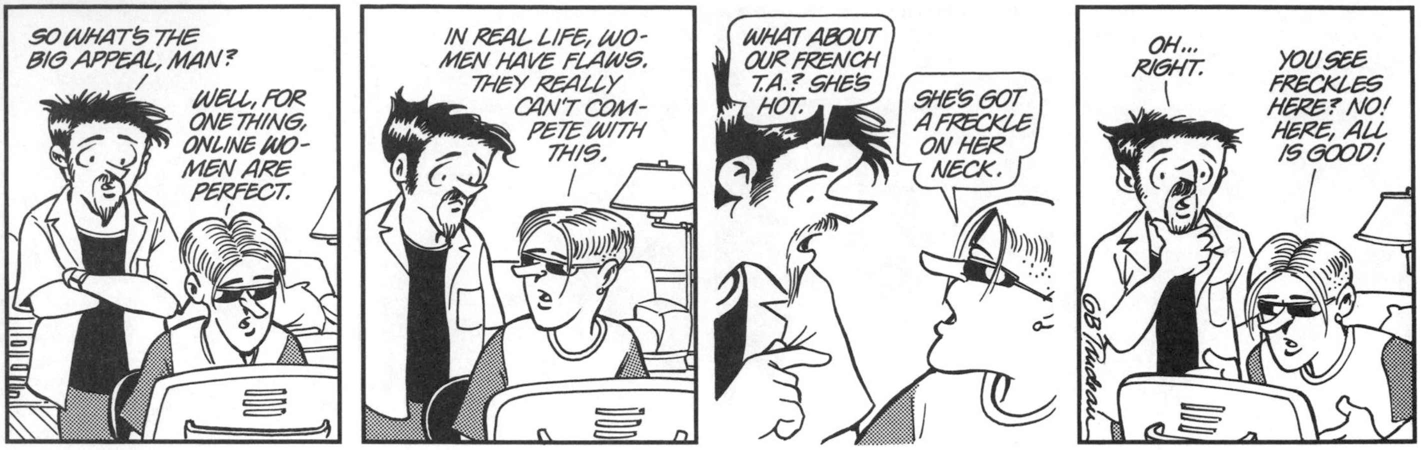
SO WHAT'S THE BIG APPEAL, MAN?
WELL, FOR ONE THING, ONLINE WOMEN ARE PERFECT.
IN REAL LIFE, WOMEN HAVE FLAWS. THEY REALLY CAN'T COMPETE WITH THIS.
WHAT ABOUT OUR FRENCH T.A.? SHE'S HOT.
SHE'S GOT A FRECKLE ON HER NECK.
OH... RIGHT.
YOU SEE FRECKLES HERE? NO! HERE, ALL IS GOOD!

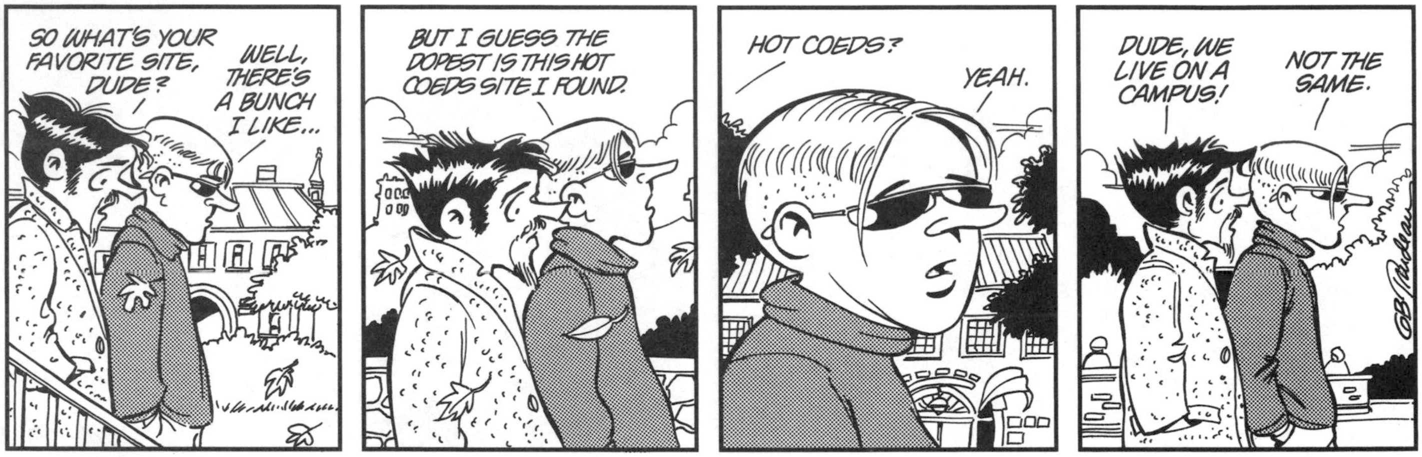
SO WHAT'S YOUR FAVORITE SITE, DUDE?
WELL, THERE'S A BUNCH I LIKE...
BUT I GUESS THE DOPEST IS THIS HOT COEDS SITE I FOUND.
HOT COEDS?
YEAH.
DUDE, WE LIVE ON A CAMPUS!
NOT THE SAME.

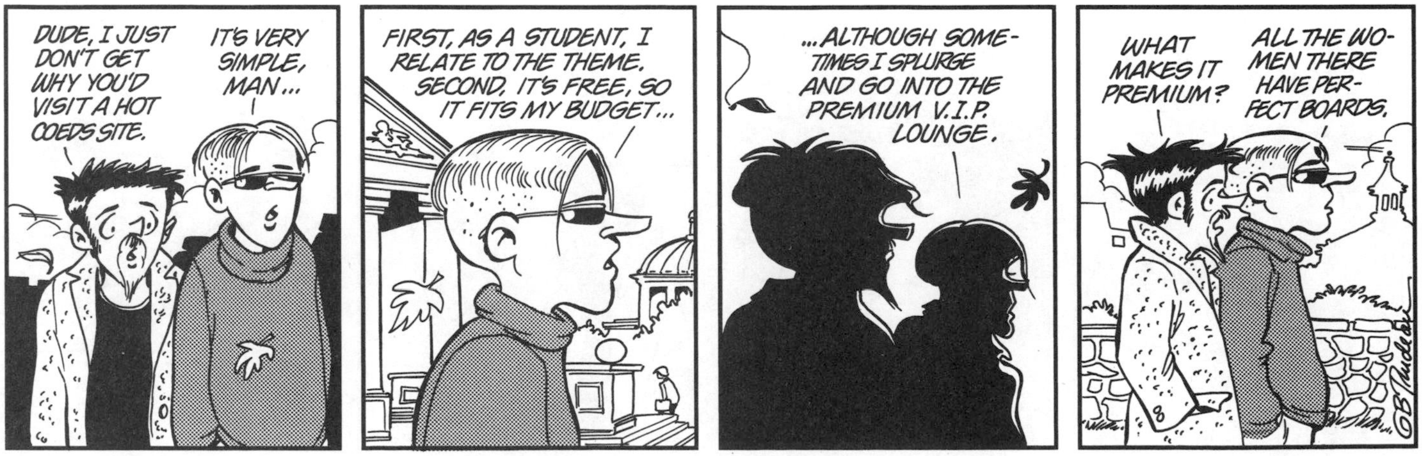
DUDE, I JUST DON'T GET WHY YOU'D VISIT A HOT COEDS SITE.
IT'S VERY SIMPLE, MAN...
FIRST, AS A STUDENT, I RELATE TO THE THEME. SECOND, IT'S FREE, SO IT FITS MY BUDGET...
...ALTHOUGH SOMETIMES I SPLURGE AND GO INTO THE PREMIUM V.I.P. LOUNGE.
WHAT MAKES IT PREMIUM?
ALL THE WOMEN THERE HAVE PERFECT BOARDS.

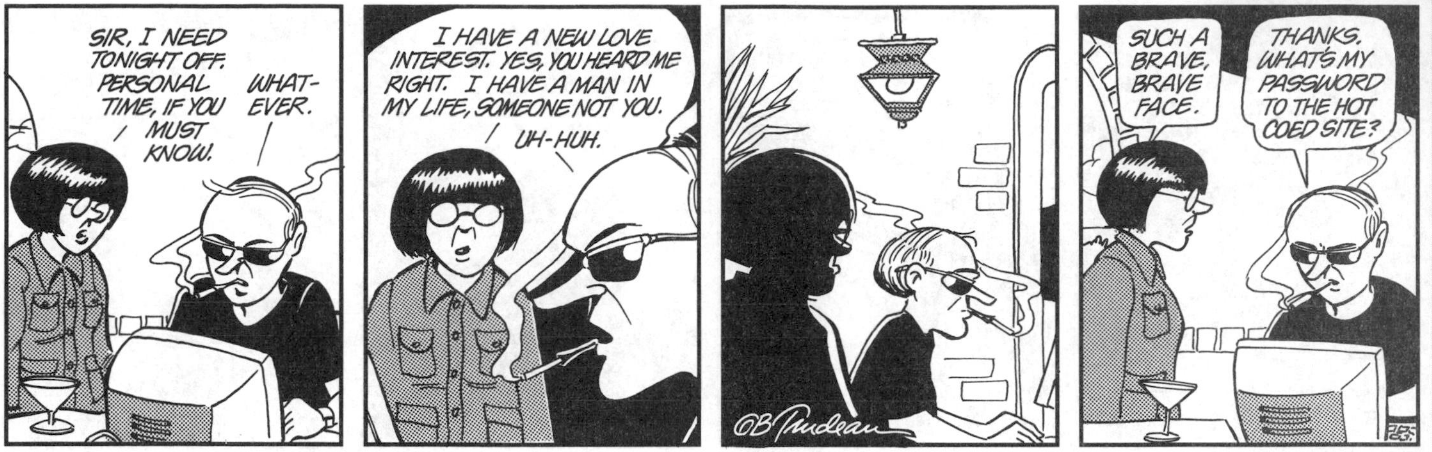
SIR, I NEED TONIGHT OFF. PERSONAL TIME, IF YOU MUST KNOW.
WHAT-EVER.
I HAVE A NEW LOVE INTEREST. YES, YOU HEARD ME RIGHT. I HAVE A MAN IN MY LIFE, SOMEONE NOT YOU.
UH-HUH.
SUCH A BRAVE, BRAVE FACE.
THANKS. WHAT'S MY PASSWORD TO THE HOT COED SITE?

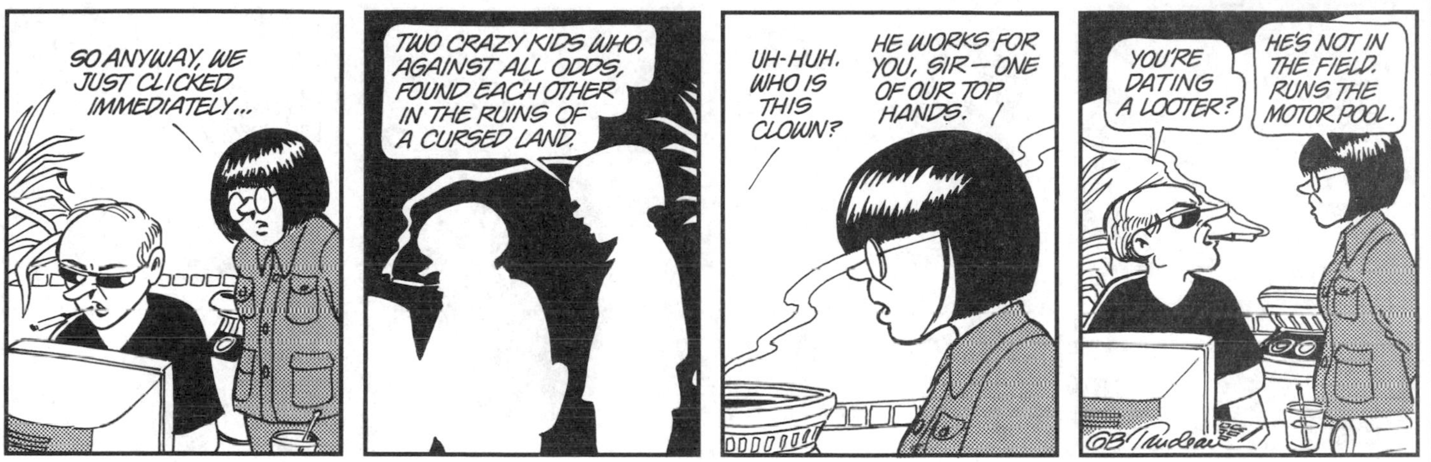
SO ANYWAY, WE JUST CLICKED IMMEDIATELY...
TWO CRAZY KIDS WHO, AGAINST ALL ODDS, FOUND EACH OTHER IN THE RUINS OF A CURSED LAND.
UH-HUH. WHO IS THIS CLOWN?
HE WORKS FOR YOU, SIR—ONE OF OUR TOP HANDS.
YOU'RE DATING A LOOTER?
HE'S NOT IN THE FIELD. RUNS THE MOTOR POOL.

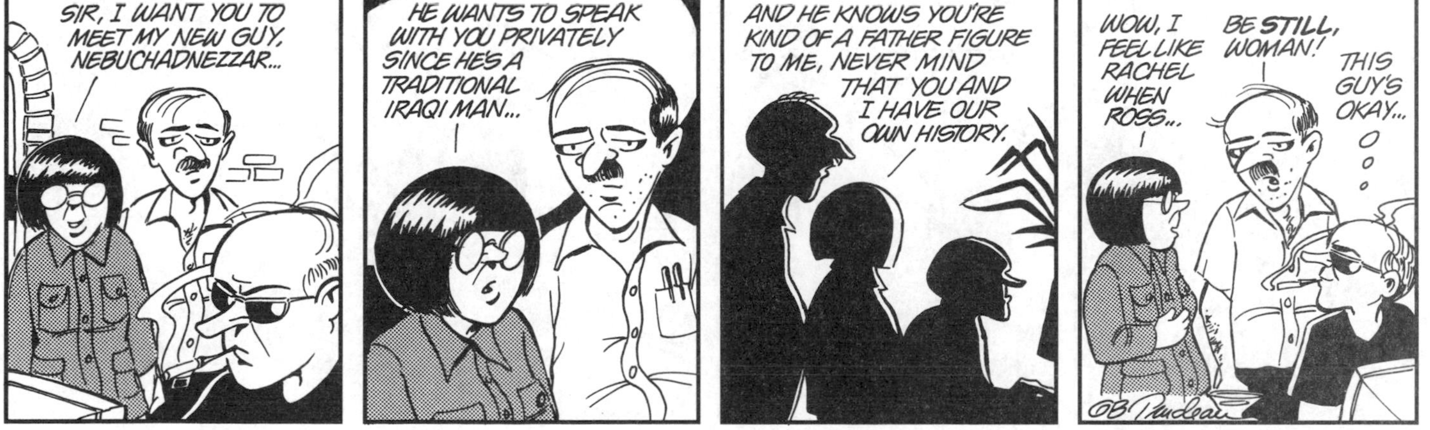
SIR, I WANT YOU TO MEET MY NEW GUY, NEBUCHADNEZZAR...
HE WANTS TO SPEAK WITH YOU PRIVATELY SINCE HE'S A TRADITIONAL IRAQI MAN...
AND HE KNOWS YOU'RE KIND OF A FATHER FIGURE TO ME, NEVER MIND THAT YOU AND I HAVE OUR OWN HISTORY.
WOW, I FEEL LIKE RACHEL WHEN ROSS...
BE STILL, WOMAN!
THIS GUY'S OKAY...

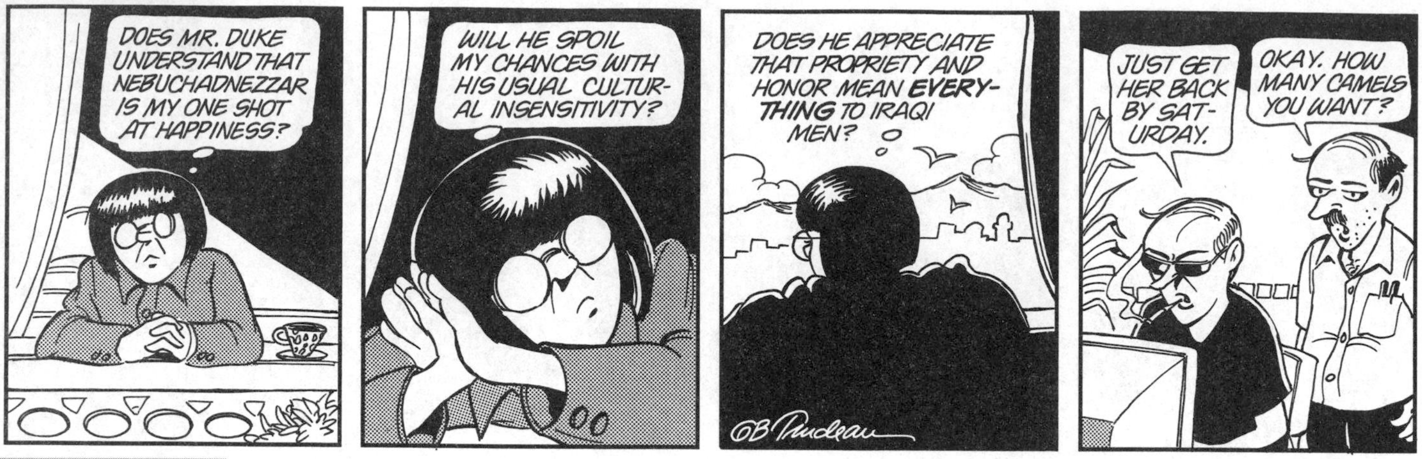
DOES MR. DUKE UNDERSTAND THAT NEBUCHADNEZZAR IS MY ONE SHOT AT HAPPINESS?
WILL HE SPOIL MY CHANCES WITH HIS USUAL CULTURAL INSENSITIVITY?
DOES HE APPRECIATE THAT PROPRIETY AND HONOR MEAN **EVERYTHING** TO IRAQI MEN?
JUST GET HER BACK BY SATURDAY.
OKAY. HOW MANY CAMELS YOU WANT?
©B Trudeau

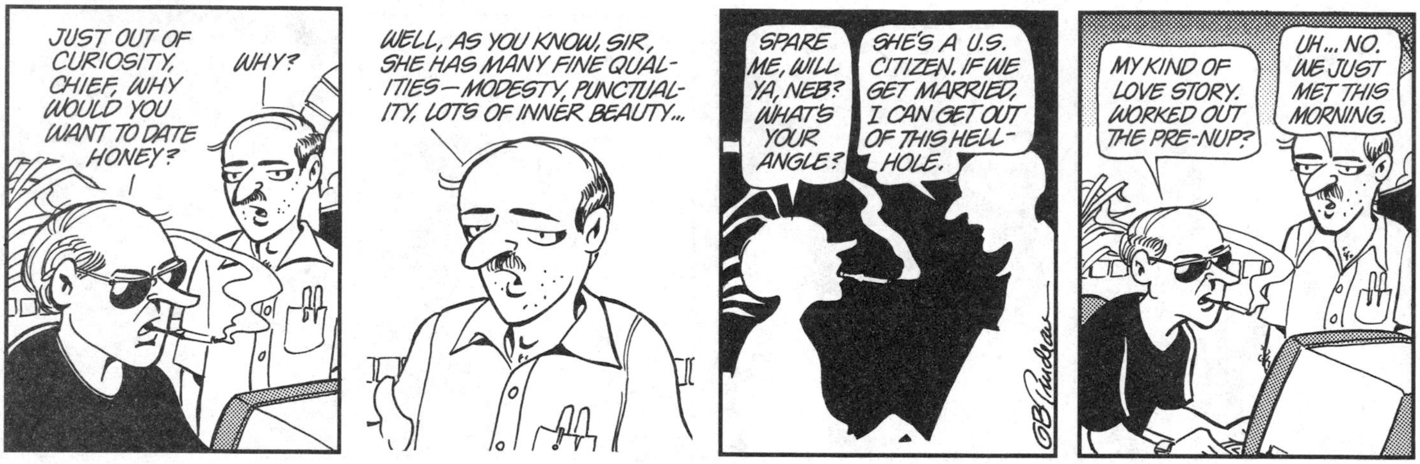
JUST OUT OF CURIOSITY, CHIEF, WHY WOULD YOU WANT TO DATE HONEY?
WHY?
WELL, AS YOU KNOW, SIR, SHE HAS MANY FINE QUALITIES—MODESTY, PUNCTUALITY, LOTS OF INNER BEAUTY...
SPARE ME, WILL YA, NEB? WHAT'S YOUR ANGLE?
SHE'S A U.S. CITIZEN. IF WE GET MARRIED, I CAN GET OUT OF THIS HELL-HOLE.
©B Trudeau
MY KIND OF LOVE STORY. WORKED OUT THE PRE-NUP?
UH... NO. WE JUST MET THIS MORNING.

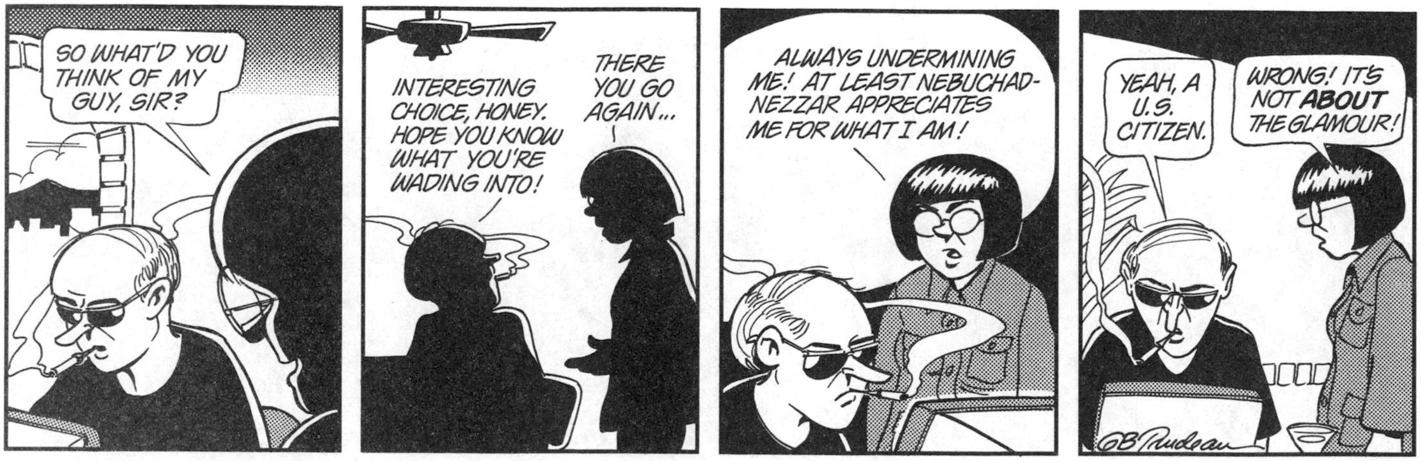
SO WHAT'D YOU THINK OF MY GUY, SIR?
INTERESTING CHOICE, HONEY. HOPE YOU KNOW WHAT YOU'RE WADING INTO!
THERE YOU GO AGAIN...
ALWAYS UNDERMINING ME! AT LEAST NEBUCHADNEZZAR APPRECIATES ME FOR WHAT I AM!
YEAH, A U.S. CITIZEN.
WRONG! IT'S NOT **ABOUT** THE GLAMOUR!
©B Trudeau

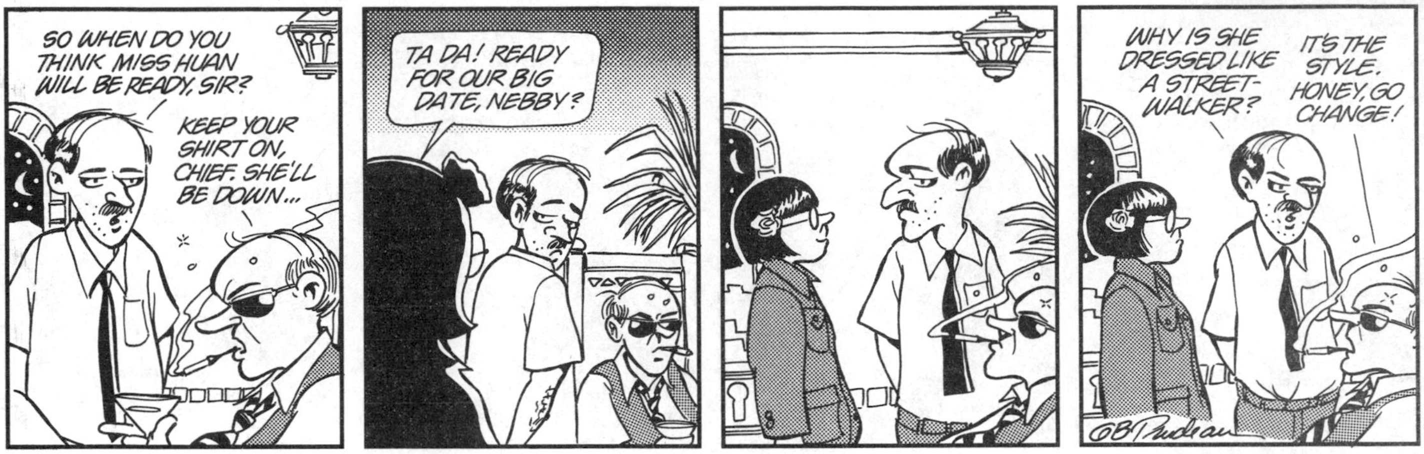
SO WHEN DO YOU THINK MISS HUAN WILL BE READY, SIR?
KEEP YOUR SHIRT ON, CHIEF. SHE'LL BE DOWN...
TA DA! READY FOR OUR BIG DATE, NEBBY?
WHY IS SHE DRESSED LIKE A STREET-WALKER?
IT'S THE STYLE. HONEY, GO CHANGE!

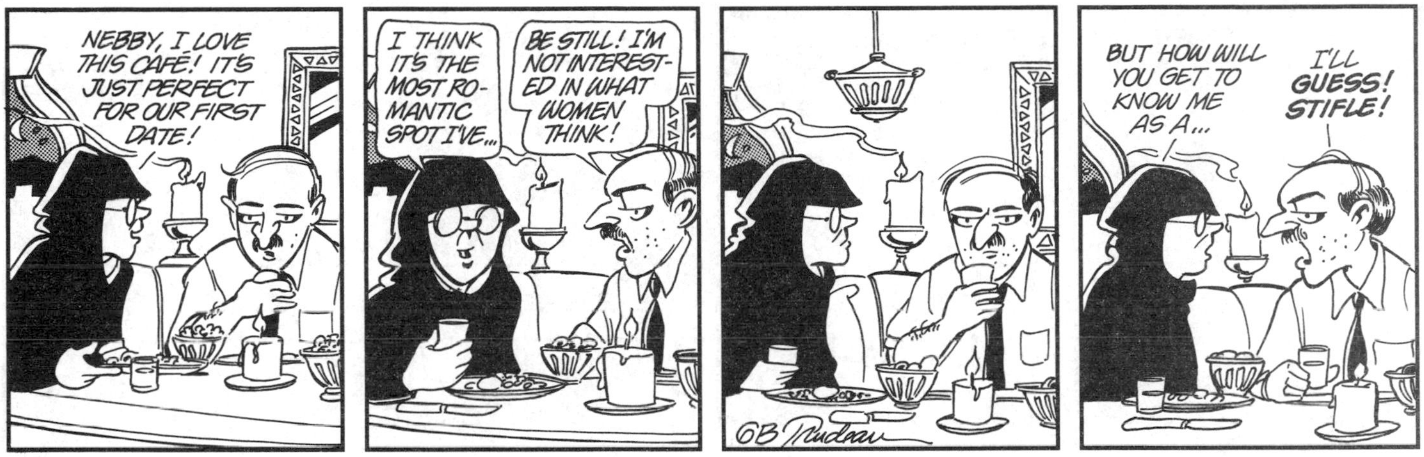
NEBBY, I LOVE THIS CAFÉ! IT'S JUST PERFECT FOR OUR FIRST DATE!
I THINK IT'S THE MOST RO-MANTIC SPOT I'VE...
BE STILL! I'M NOT INTEREST-ED IN WHAT WOMEN THINK!
BUT HOW WILL YOU GET TO KNOW ME AS A...
I'LL GUESS! STIFLE!

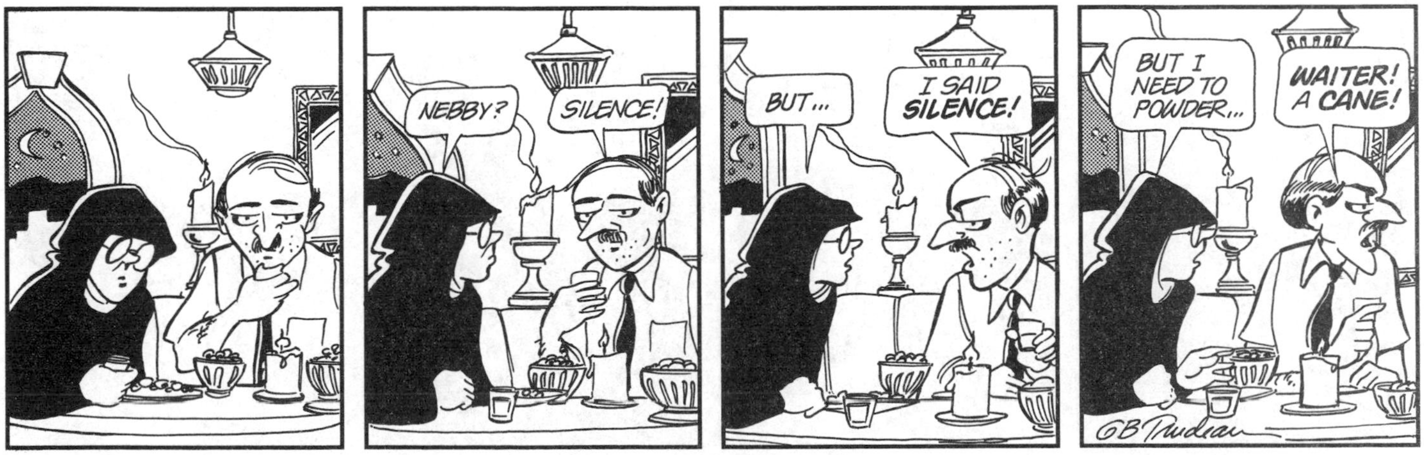
NEBBY?
SILENCE!
BUT...
I SAID SILENCE!
BUT I NEED TO POWDER...
WAITER! A CANE!

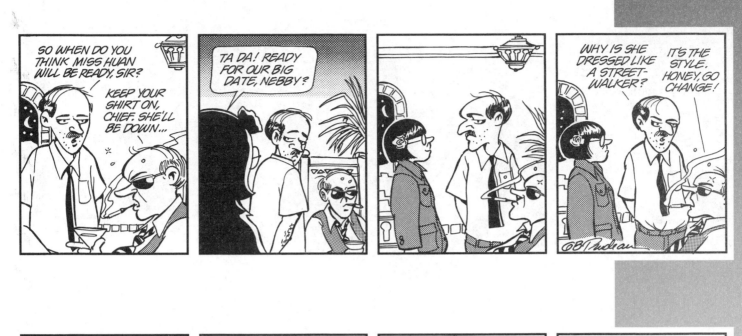

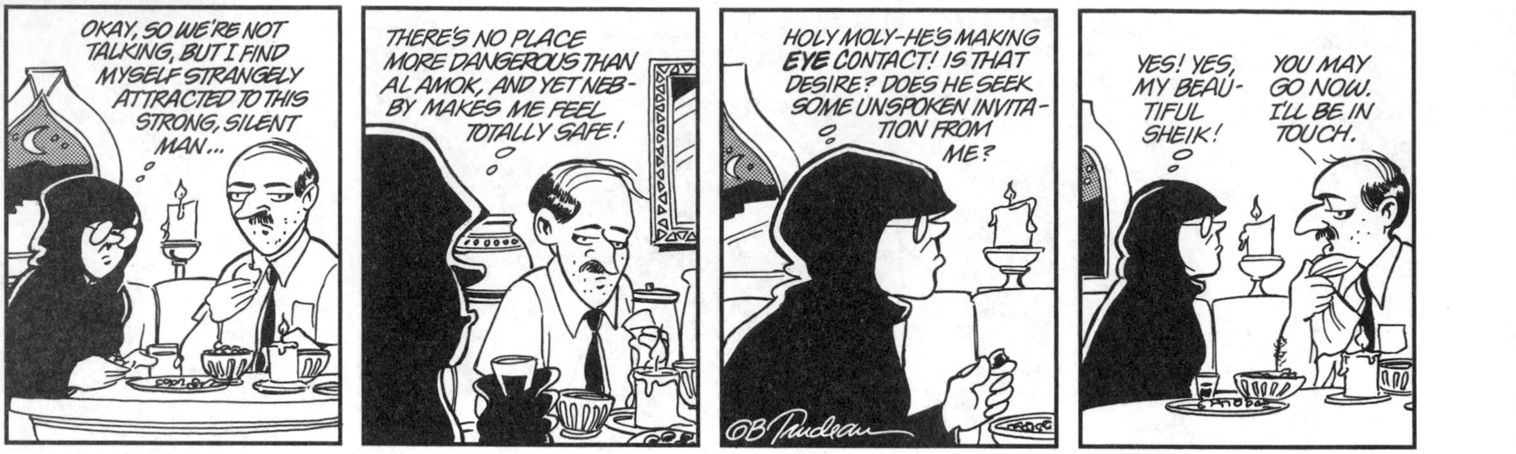
OKAY, SO WE'RE NOT TALKING, BUT I FIND MYSELF STRANGELY ATTRACTED TO THIS STRONG, SILENT MAN...
THERE'S NO PLACE MORE DANGEROUS THAN AL AMOK, AND YET NEBBY MAKES ME FEEL TOTALLY SAFE!
HOLY MOLY–HE'S MAKING EYE CONTACT! IS THAT DESIRE? DOES HE SEEK SOME UNSPOKEN INVITATION FROM ME?
YES! YES, MY BEAUTIFUL SHEIK!
YOU MAY GO NOW. I'LL BE IN TOUCH.

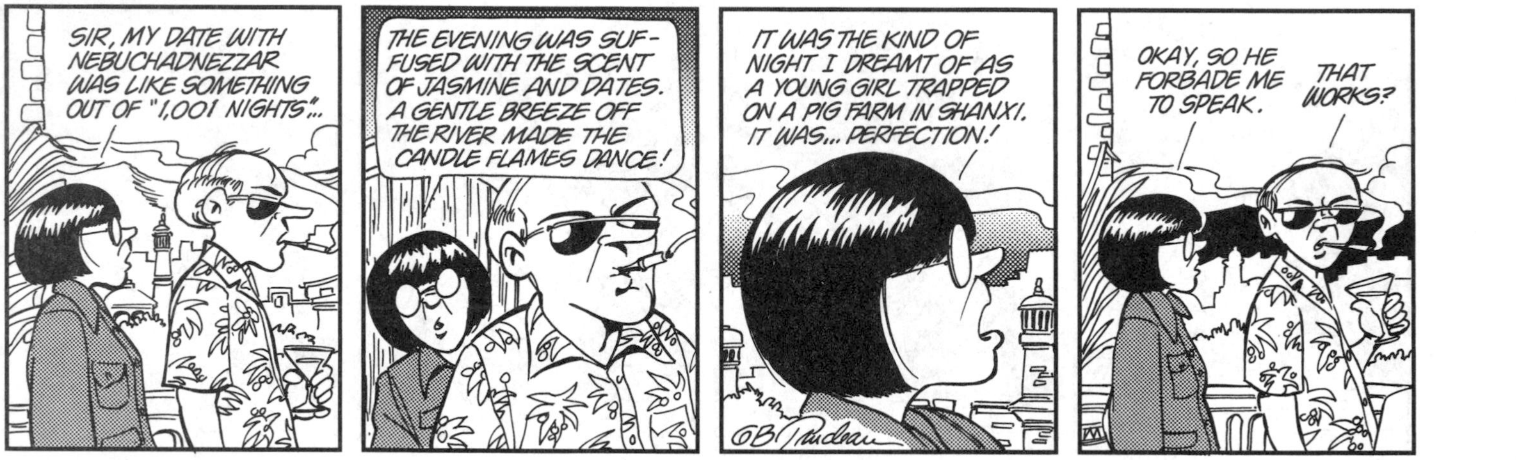
SIR, MY DATE WITH NEBUCHADNEZZAR WAS LIKE SOMETHING OUT OF "1,001 NIGHTS"...
THE EVENING WAS SUFFUSED WITH THE SCENT OF JASMINE AND DATES. A GENTLE BREEZE OFF THE RIVER MADE THE CANDLE FLAMES DANCE!
IT WAS THE KIND OF NIGHT I DREAMT OF AS A YOUNG GIRL TRAPPED ON A PIG FARM IN SHANXI. IT WAS... PERFECTION!
OKAY, SO HE FORBADE ME TO SPEAK.
THAT WORKS?

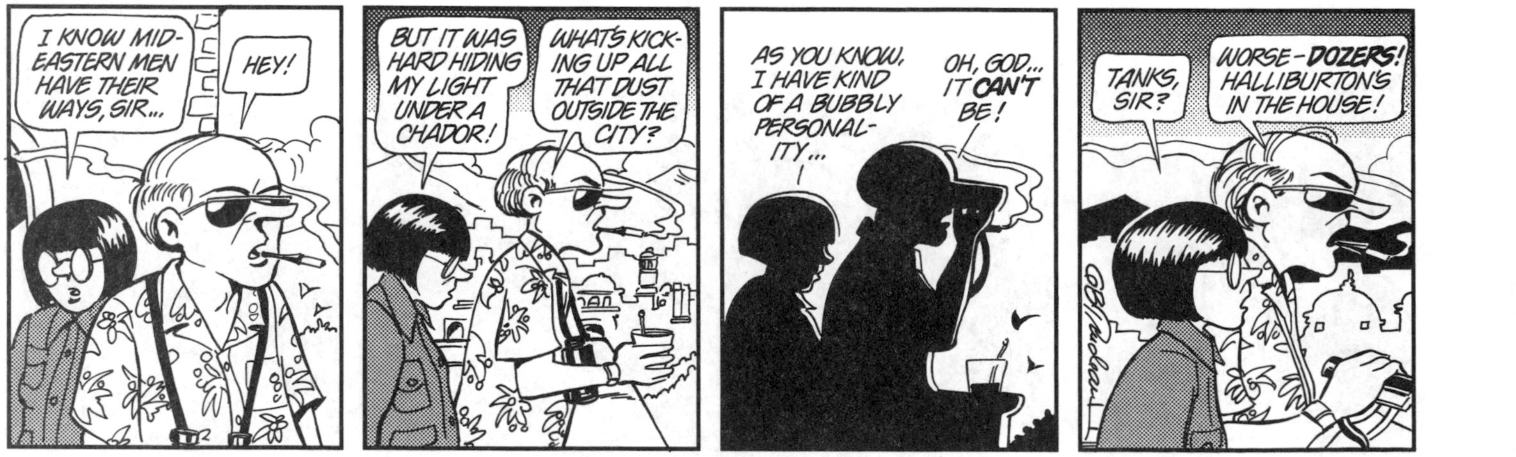
I KNOW MID-EASTERN MEN HAVE THEIR WAYS, SIR...
HEY!
BUT IT WAS HARD HIDING MY LIGHT UNDER A CHADOR!
WHAT'S KICKING UP ALL THAT DUST OUTSIDE THE CITY?
AS YOU KNOW, I HAVE KIND OF A BUBBLY PERSONALITY...
OH, GOD... IT CAN'T BE!
TANKS, SIR?
WORSE–DOZERS! HALLIBURTON'S IN THE HOUSE!

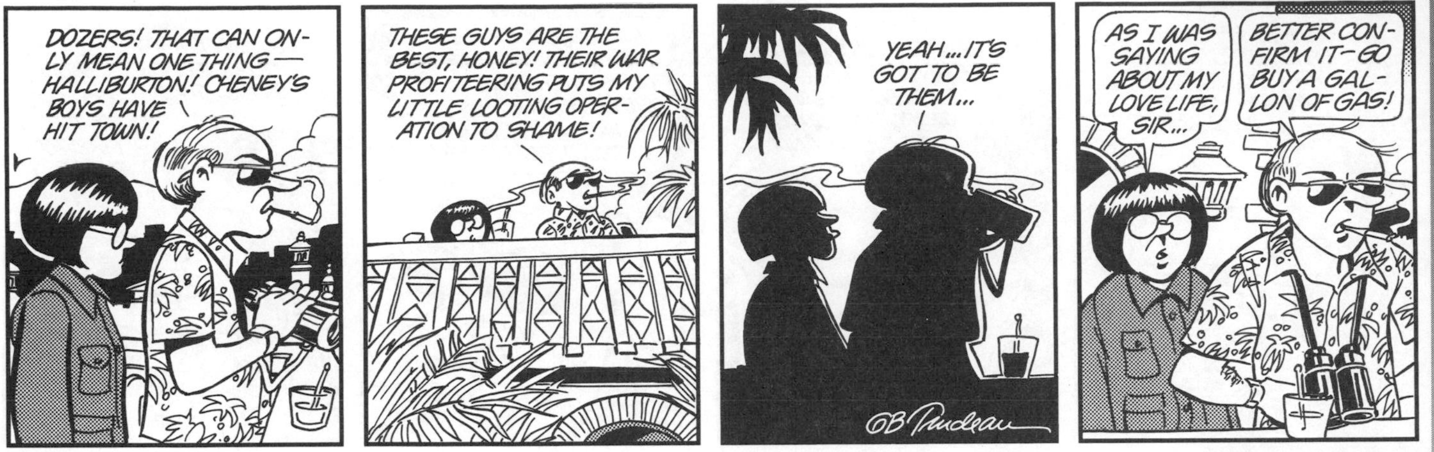
DOZERS! THAT CAN ONLY MEAN ONE THING — HALLIBURTON! CHENEY'S BOYS HAVE HIT TOWN!
THESE GUYS ARE THE BEST, HONEY! THEIR WAR PROFITEERING PUTS MY LITTLE LOOTING OPERATION TO SHAME!
YEAH... IT'S GOT TO BE THEM...
AS I WAS SAYING ABOUT MY LOVE LIFE, SIR...
BETTER CONFIRM IT– GO BUY A GALLON OF GAS!

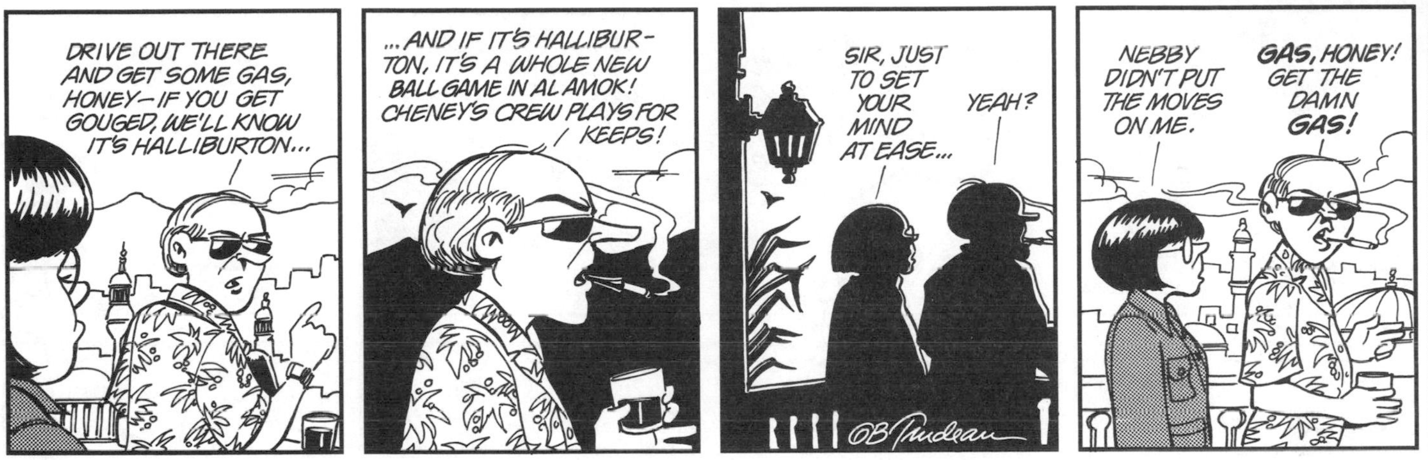
DRIVE OUT THERE AND GET SOME GAS, HONEY– IF YOU GET GOUGED, WE'LL KNOW IT'S HALLIBURTON...
... AND IF IT'S HALLIBURTON, IT'S A WHOLE NEW BALL GAME IN AL AMOK! CHENEY'S CREW PLAYS FOR KEEPS!
SIR, JUST TO SET YOUR MIND AT EASE...
YEAH?
NEBBY DIDN'T PUT THE MOVES ON ME.
GAS, HONEY! GET THE DAMN GAS!

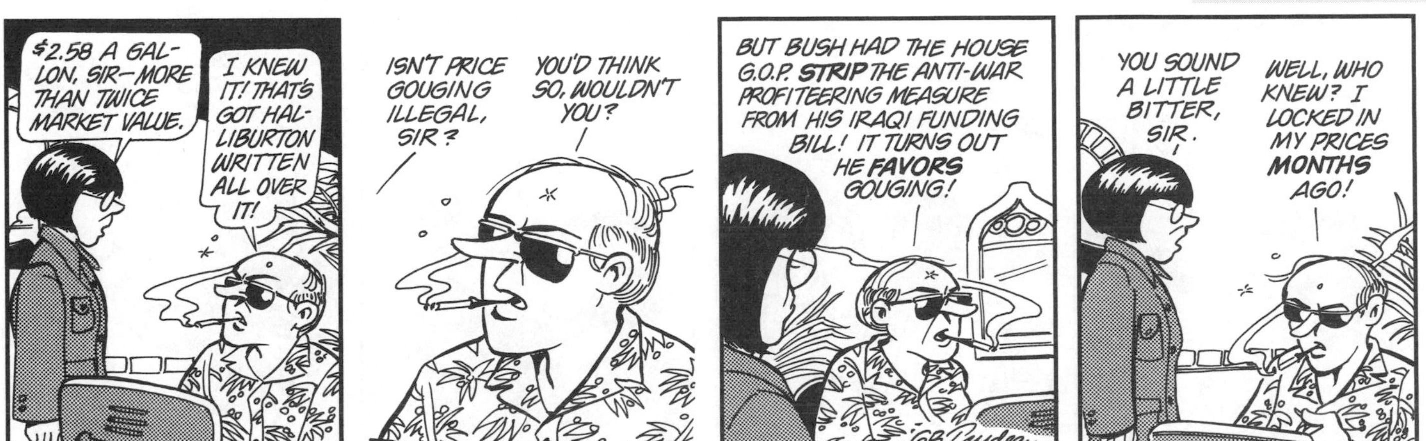
$2.58 A GALLON, SIR– MORE THAN TWICE MARKET VALUE.
I KNEW IT! THAT'S GOT HALLIBURTON WRITTEN ALL OVER IT!
ISN'T PRICE GOUGING ILLEGAL, SIR?
YOU'D THINK SO, WOULDN'T YOU?
BUT BUSH HAD THE HOUSE G.O.P. STRIP THE ANTI-WAR PROFITEERING MEASURE FROM HIS IRAQI FUNDING BILL! IT TURNS OUT HE FAVORS GOUGING!
YOU SOUND A LITTLE BITTER, SIR.
WELL, WHO KNEW? I LOCKED IN MY PRICES MONTHS AGO!

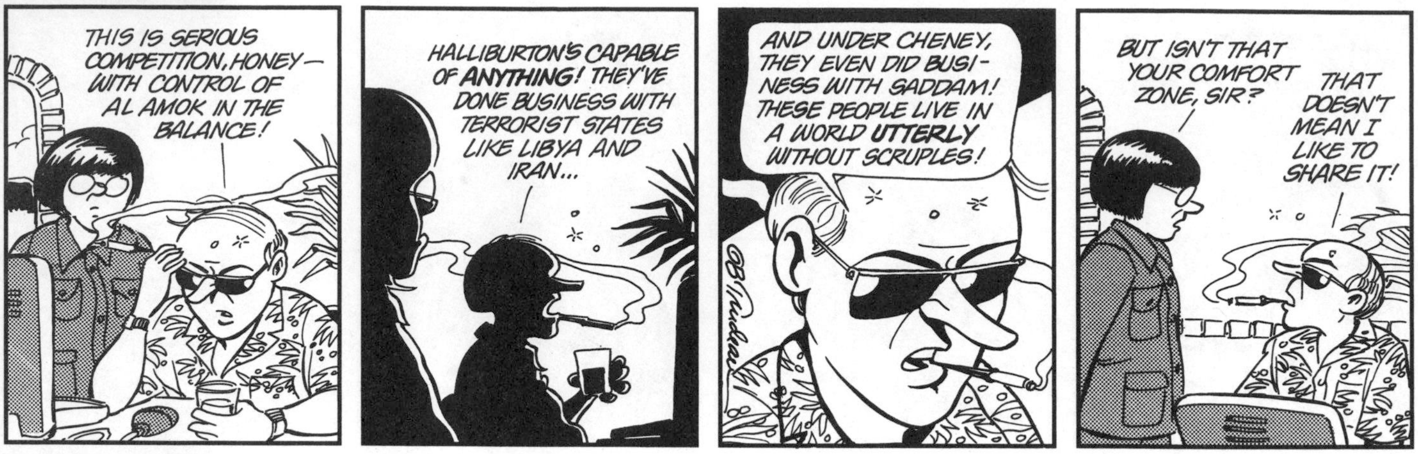
THIS IS SERIOUS COMPETITION, HONEY— WITH CONTROL OF AL AMOK IN THE BALANCE!
HALLIBURTON'S CAPABLE OF ANYTHING! THEY'VE DONE BUSINESS WITH TERRORIST STATES LIKE LIBYA AND IRAN...
AND UNDER CHENEY, THEY EVEN DID BUSINESS WITH SADDAM! THESE PEOPLE LIVE IN A WORLD UTTERLY WITHOUT SCRUPLES!
BUT ISN'T THAT YOUR COMFORT ZONE, SIR?
THAT DOESN'T MEAN I LIKE TO SHARE IT!

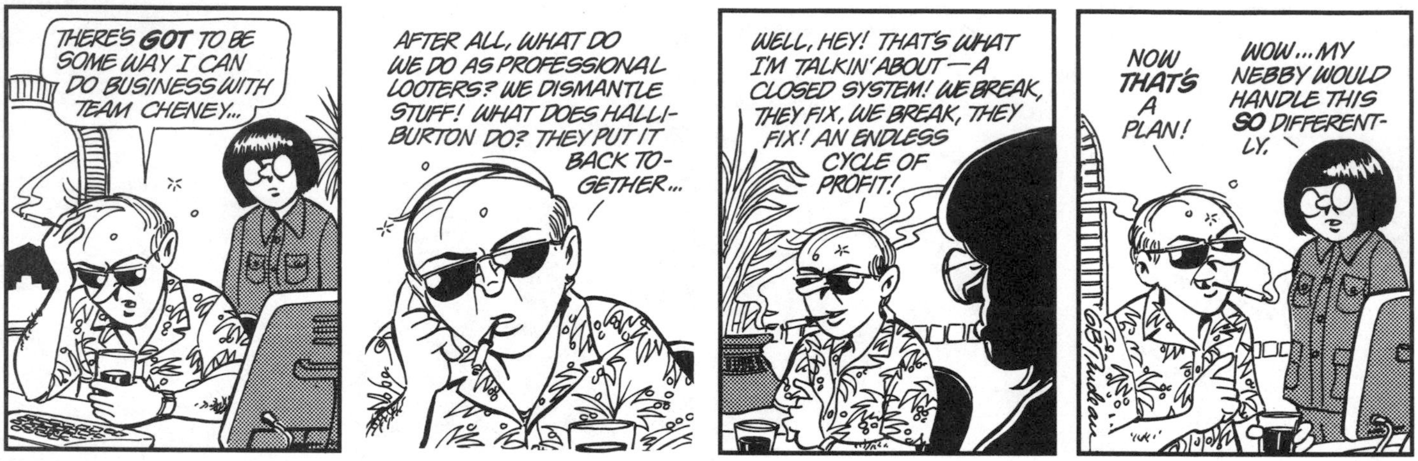
THERE'S GOT TO BE SOME WAY I CAN DO BUSINESS WITH TEAM CHENEY...
AFTER ALL, WHAT DO WE DO AS PROFESSIONAL LOOTERS? WE DISMANTLE STUFF! WHAT DOES HALLIBURTON DO? THEY PUT IT BACK TOGETHER...
WELL, HEY! THAT'S WHAT I'M TALKIN' ABOUT—A CLOSED SYSTEM! WE BREAK, THEY FIX, WE BREAK, THEY FIX! AN ENDLESS CYCLE OF PROFIT!
NOW THAT'S A PLAN!
WOW... MY NEBBY WOULD HANDLE THIS SO DIFFERENTLY.

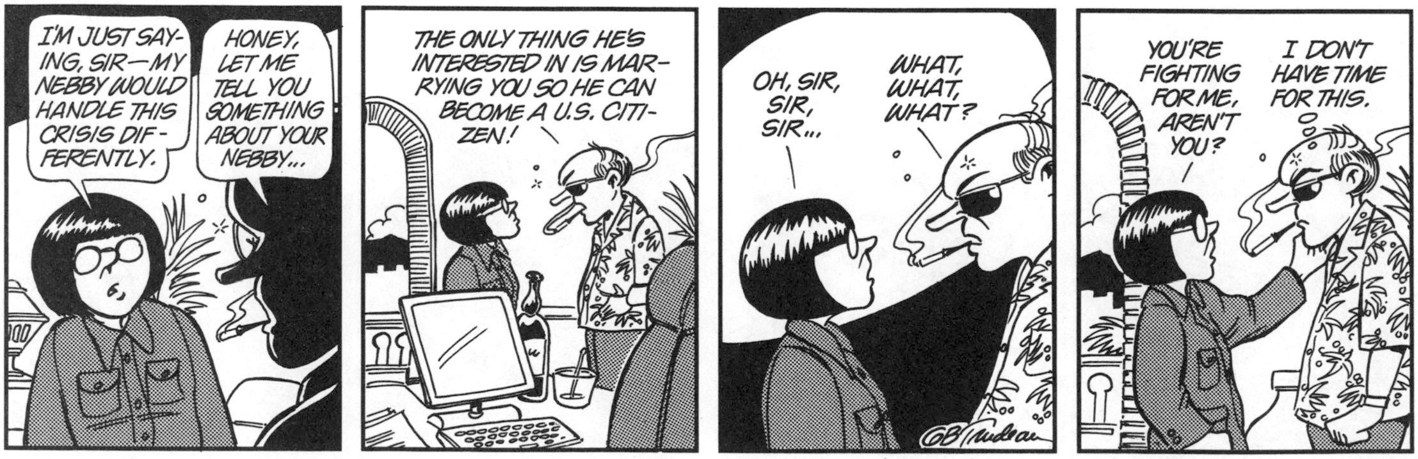
I'M JUST SAYING, SIR—MY NEBBY WOULD HANDLE THIS CRISIS DIFFERENTLY.
HONEY, LET ME TELL YOU SOMETHING ABOUT YOUR NEBBY...
THE ONLY THING HE'S INTERESTED IN IS MARRYING YOU SO HE CAN BECOME A U.S. CITIZEN!
OH, SIR, SIR, SIR...
WHAT, WHAT, WHAT?
YOU'RE FIGHTING FOR ME, AREN'T YOU?
I DON'T HAVE TIME FOR THIS.

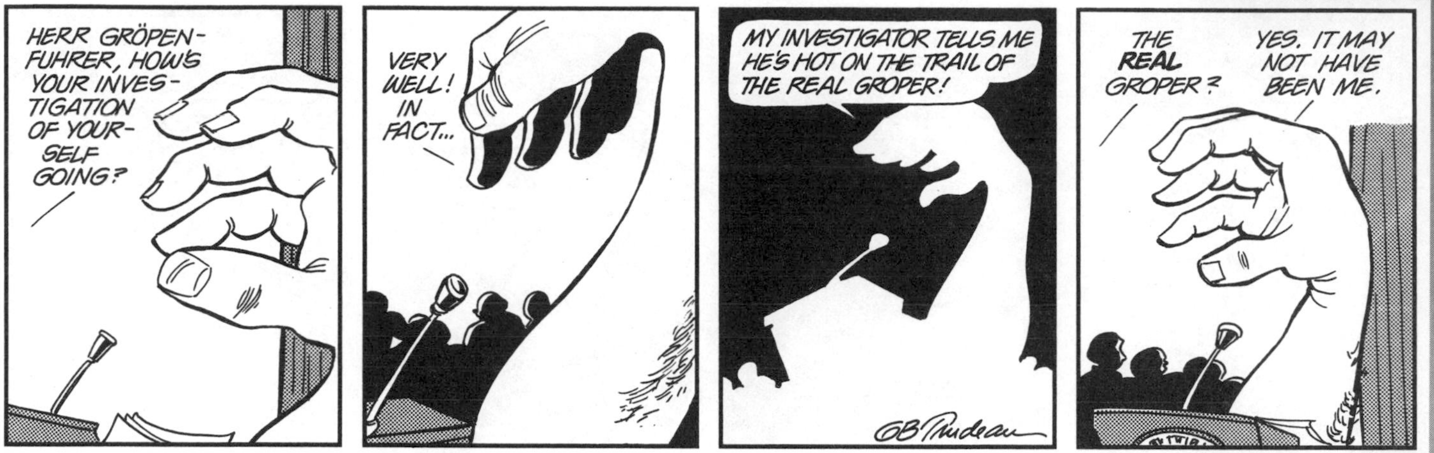
HERR GRÖPENFUHRER, HOW'S YOUR INVESTIGATION OF YOURSELF GOING?
VERY WELL! IN FACT...
MY INVESTIGATOR TELLS ME HE'S HOT ON THE TRAIL OF THE REAL GROPER!
THE **REAL** GROPER?
YES. IT MAY NOT HAVE BEEN ME.
GB Trudeau

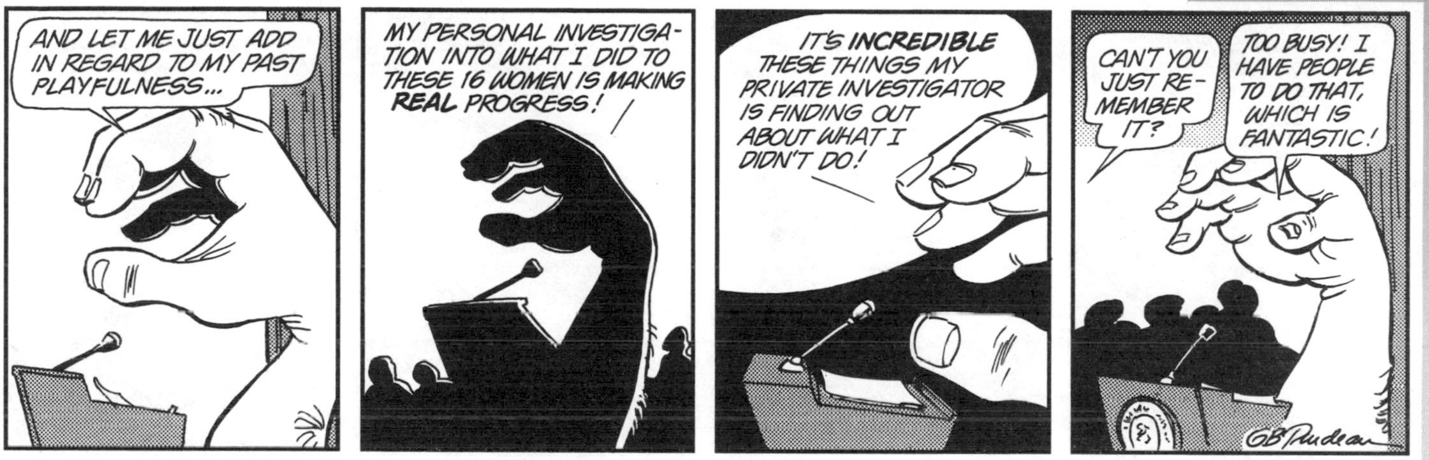
AND LET ME JUST ADD IN REGARD TO MY PAST PLAYFULNESS...
MY PERSONAL INVESTIGATION INTO WHAT I DID TO THESE 16 WOMEN IS MAKING **REAL** PROGRESS!
IT'S **INCREDIBLE** THESE THINGS MY PRIVATE INVESTIGATOR IS FINDING OUT ABOUT WHAT I DIDN'T DO!
CAN'T YOU JUST REMEMBER IT?
TOO BUSY! I HAVE PEOPLE TO DO THAT, WHICH IS FANTASTIC!
GB Trudeau

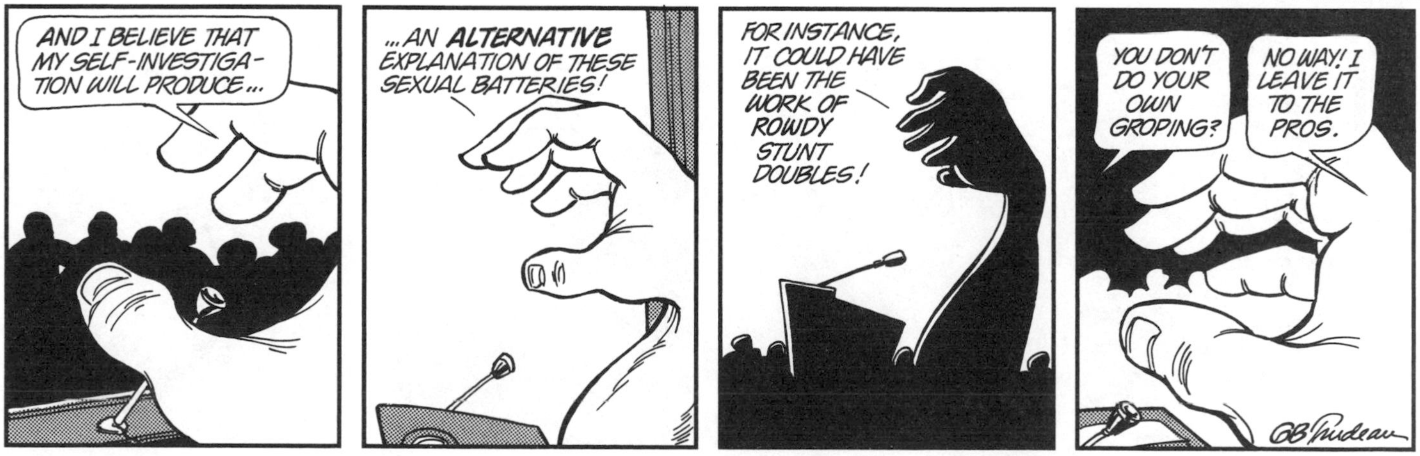
AND I BELIEVE THAT MY SELF-INVESTIGATION WILL PRODUCE...
...AN **ALTERNATIVE** EXPLANATION OF THESE SEXUAL BATTERIES!
FOR INSTANCE, IT COULD HAVE BEEN THE WORK OF **ROWDY** STUNT DOUBLES!
YOU DON'T DO YOUR OWN GROPING?
NO WAY! I LEAVE IT TO THE PROS.
GB Trudeau

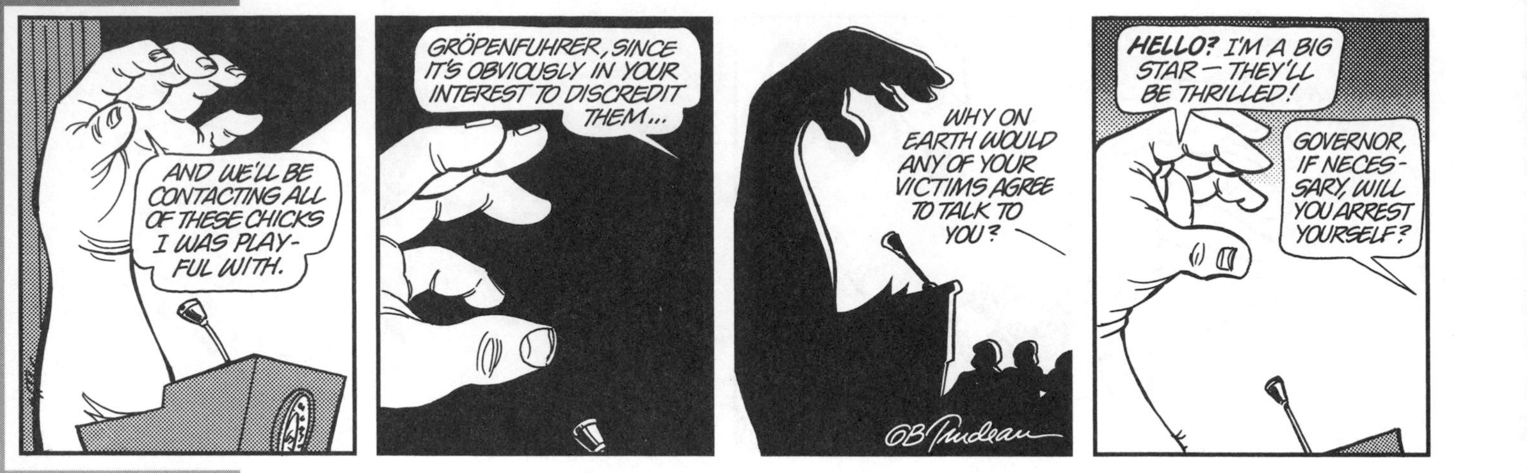
AND WE'LL BE CONTACTING ALL OF THESE CHICKS I WAS PLAYFUL WITH.
GRÖPENFUHRER, SINCE IT'S OBVIOUSLY IN YOUR INTEREST TO DISCREDIT THEM...
WHY ON EARTH WOULD ANY OF YOUR VICTIMS AGREE TO TALK TO YOU?
HELLO? I'M A BIG STAR — THEY'LL BE THRILLED!
GOVERNOR, IF NECESSARY, WILL YOU ARREST YOURSELF?

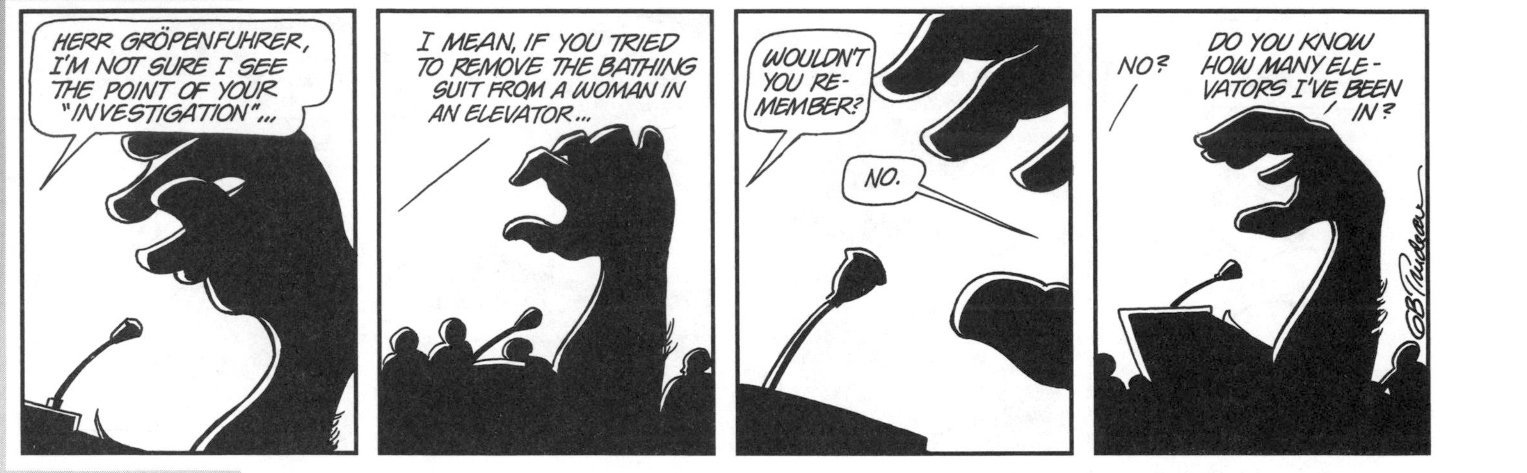
HERR GRÖPENFUHRER, I'M NOT SURE I SEE THE POINT OF YOUR "INVESTIGATION"...
I MEAN, IF YOU TRIED TO REMOVE THE BATHING SUIT FROM A WOMAN IN AN ELEVATOR...
WOULDN'T YOU REMEMBER?
NO.
NO?
DO YOU KNOW HOW MANY ELEVATORS I'VE BEEN IN?

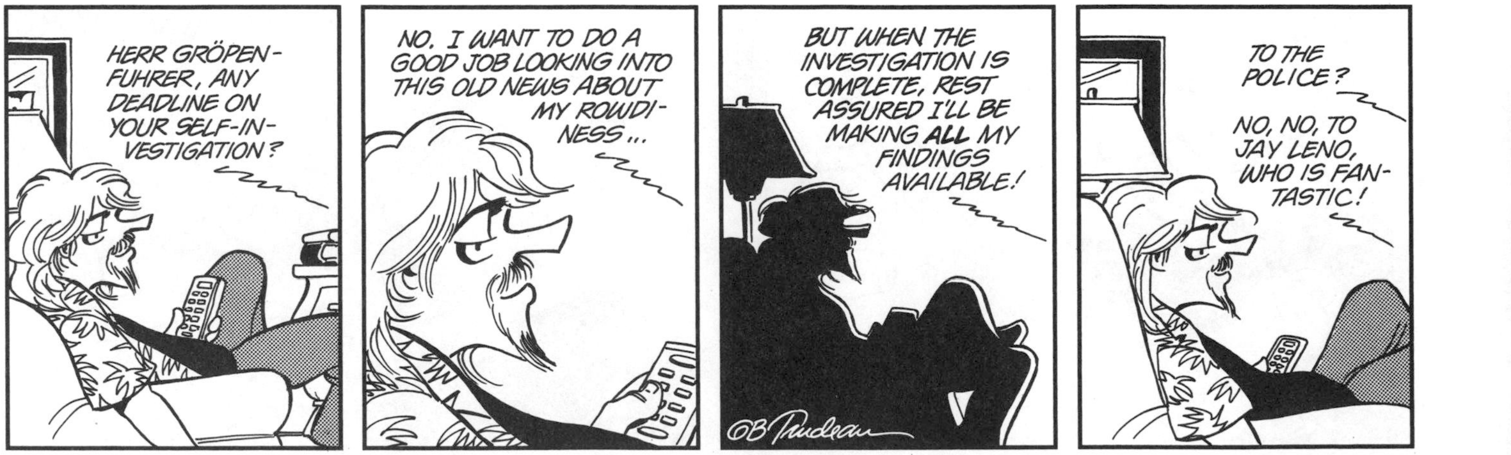
HERR GRÖPENFUHRER, ANY DEADLINE ON YOUR SELF-INVESTIGATION?
NO. I WANT TO DO A GOOD JOB LOOKING INTO THIS OLD NEWS ABOUT MY ROWDINESS...
BUT WHEN THE INVESTIGATION IS COMPLETE, REST ASSURED I'LL BE MAKING ALL MY FINDINGS AVAILABLE!
TO THE POLICE?
NO, NO, TO JAY LENO, WHO IS FANTASTIC!

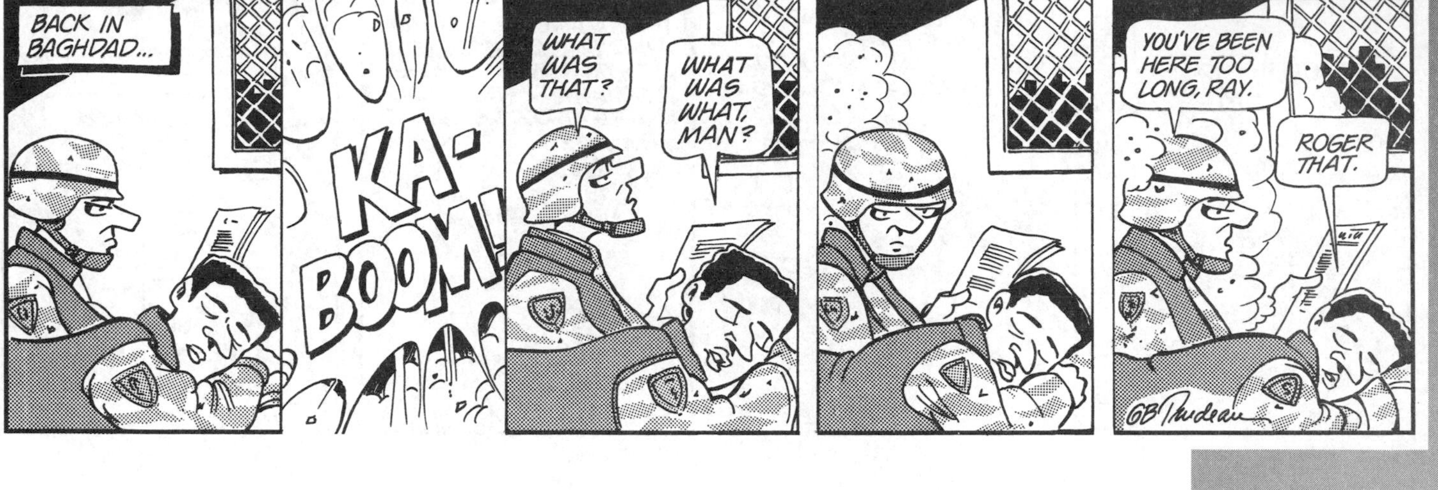
BACK IN BAGHDAD...
KA-BOOM!
WHAT WAS THAT?
WHAT WAS WHAT, MAN?
YOU'VE BEEN HERE TOO LONG, RAY.
ROGER THAT.

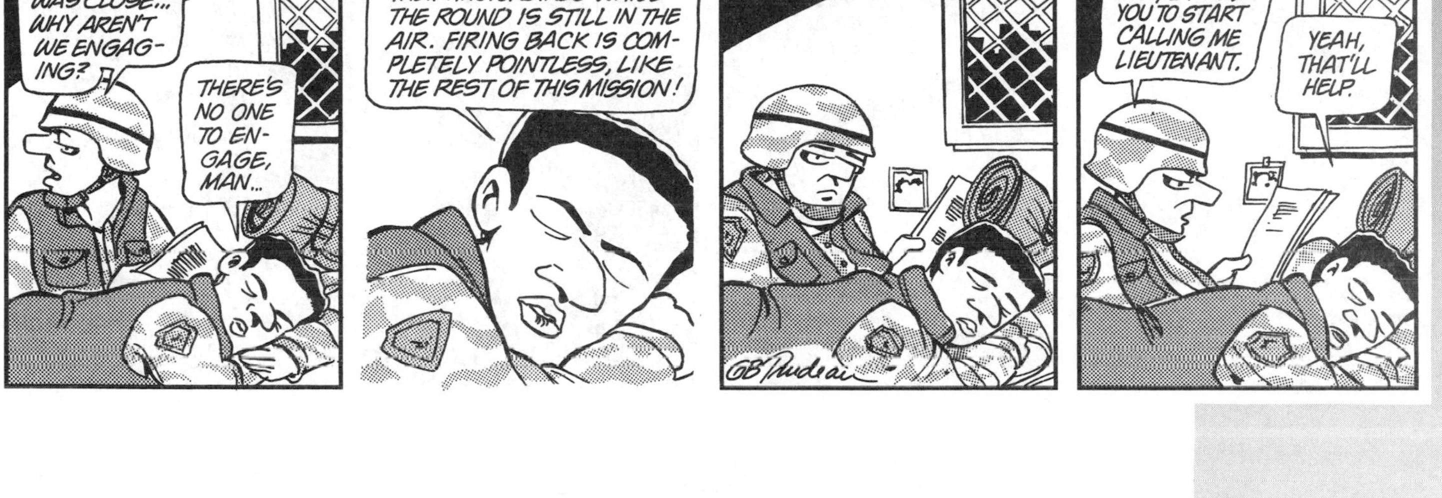
THAT LAST ONE WAS CLOSE... WHY AREN'T WE ENGAGING?
THERE'S NO ONE TO ENGAGE, MAN...
THE HAJIS PEEL OUT ON THEIR MOTORBIKES WHILE THE ROUND IS STILL IN THE AIR. FIRING BACK IS COMPLETELY POINTLESS, LIKE THE REST OF THIS MISSION!
RAY, I NEED YOU TO START CALLING ME LIEUTENANT.
YEAH, THAT'LL HELP.

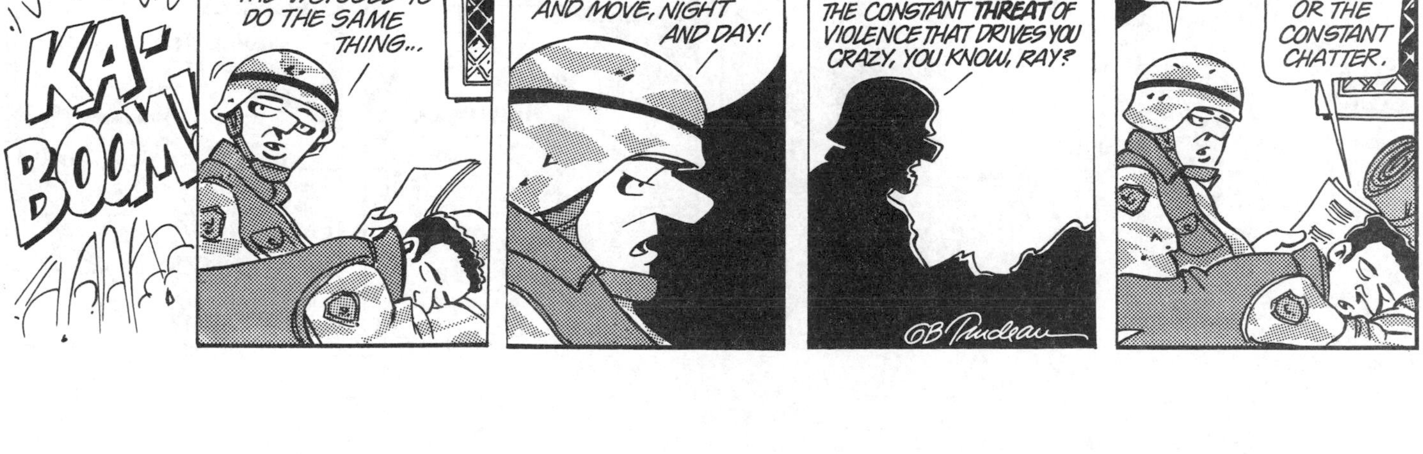
KA-BOOM!
YOU KNOW, WHEN I WAS IN NAM, THE V.C. USED TO DO THE SAME THING...
LAUNCH A MORTAR ROUND AT A FIREBASE AND MOVE — LAUNCH AND MOVE, NIGHT AND DAY!
A COUPLE OF FIGHTERS COULD KEEP AN ENTIRE BATTALION ON EDGE. IT'S THE CONSTANT THREAT OF VIOLENCE THAT DRIVES YOU CRAZY, YOU KNOW, RAY?
RAY?
YEAH, THAT OR THE CONSTANT CHATTER.

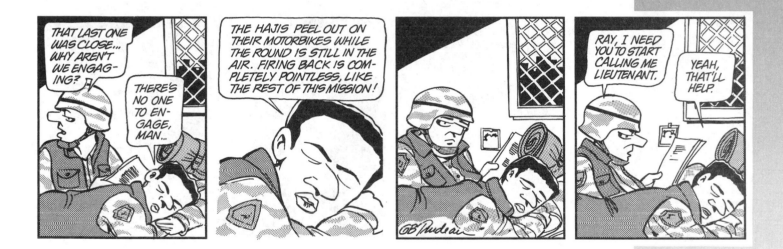

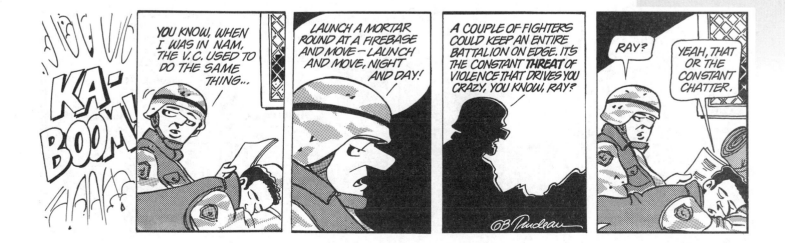

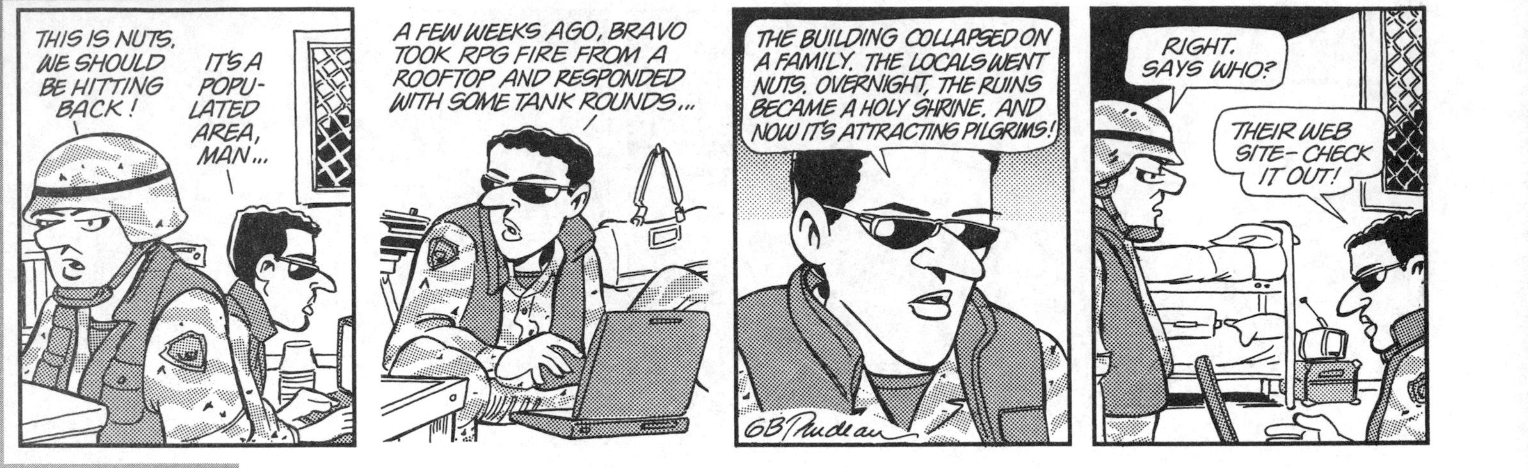
THIS IS NUTS. WE SHOULD BE HITTING BACK!
IT'S A POPU-LATED AREA, MAN...
A FEW WEEKS AGO, BRAVO TOOK RPG FIRE FROM A ROOFTOP AND RESPONDED WITH SOME TANK ROUNDS...
THE BUILDING COLLAPSED ON A FAMILY. THE LOCALS WENT NUTS. OVERNIGHT, THE RUINS BECAME A HOLY SHRINE. AND NOW IT'S ATTRACTING PILGRIMS!
RIGHT. SAYS WHO?
THEIR WEB SITE–CHECK IT OUT!

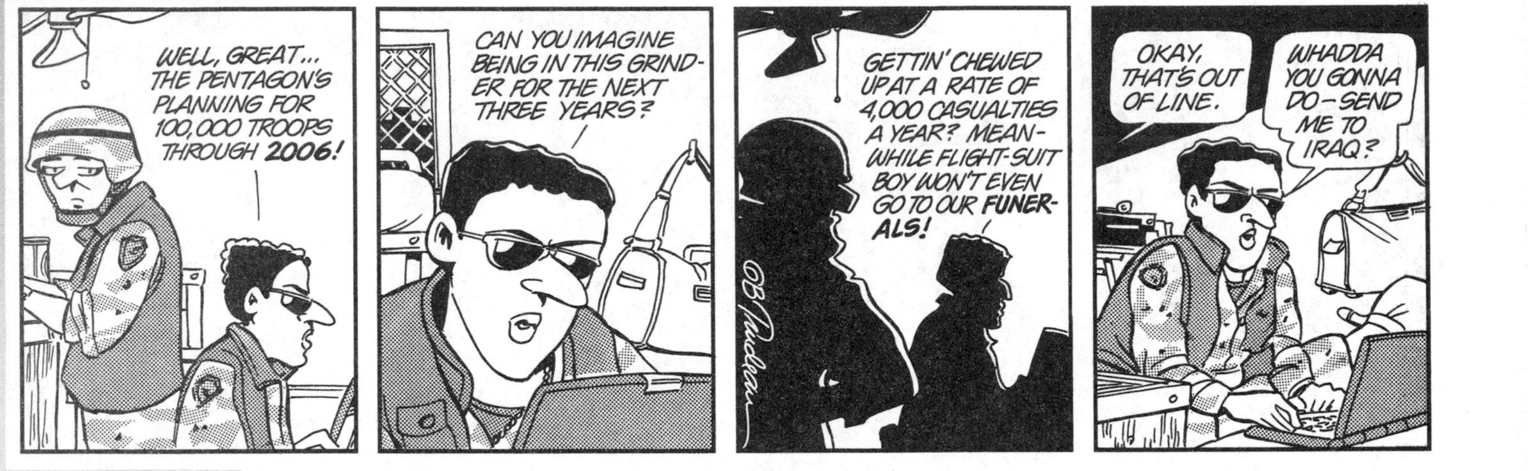
WELL, GREAT... THE PENTAGON'S PLANNING FOR 100,000 TROOPS THROUGH **2006**!
CAN YOU IMAGINE BEING IN THIS GRIND-ER FOR THE NEXT THREE YEARS?
GETTIN' CHEWED UP AT A RATE OF 4,000 CASUALTIES A YEAR? MEAN-WHILE FLIGHT-SUIT BOY WON'T EVEN GO TO OUR **FUNER-ALS**!
OKAY, THAT'S OUT OF LINE.
WHADDA YOU GONNA DO–SEND ME TO IRAQ?

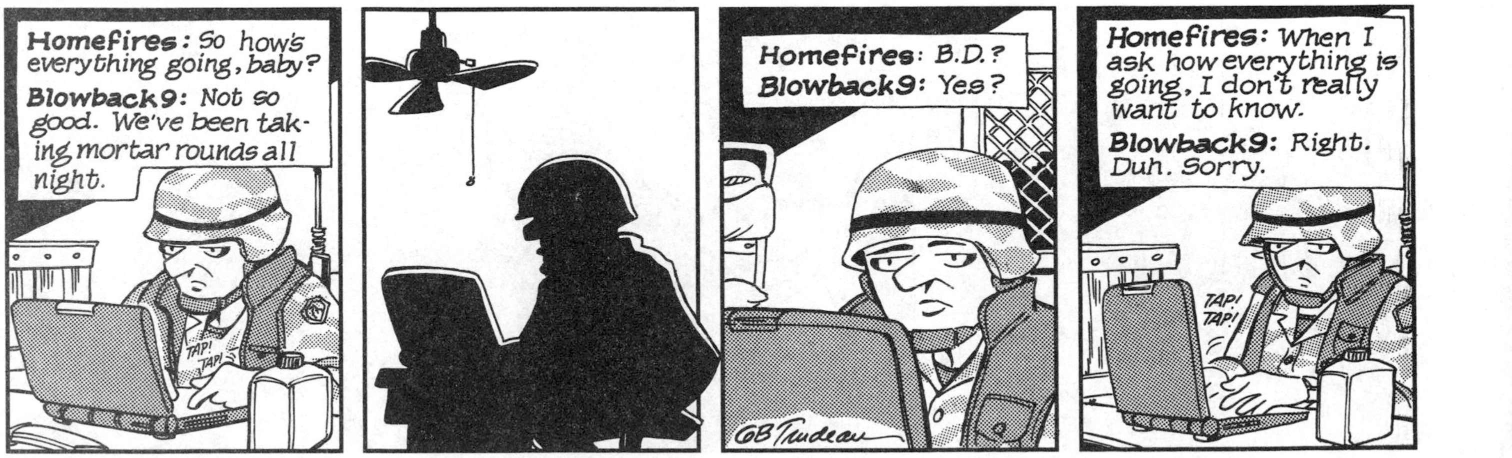
Homefires: So how's everything going, baby?
Blowback9: Not so good. We've been tak-ing mortar rounds all night.
TAP! TAP!
Homefires: B.D.?
Blowback9: Yes?
Homefires: When I ask how everything is going, I don't really want to know.
Blowback9: Right. Duh. Sorry.
TAP! TAP!

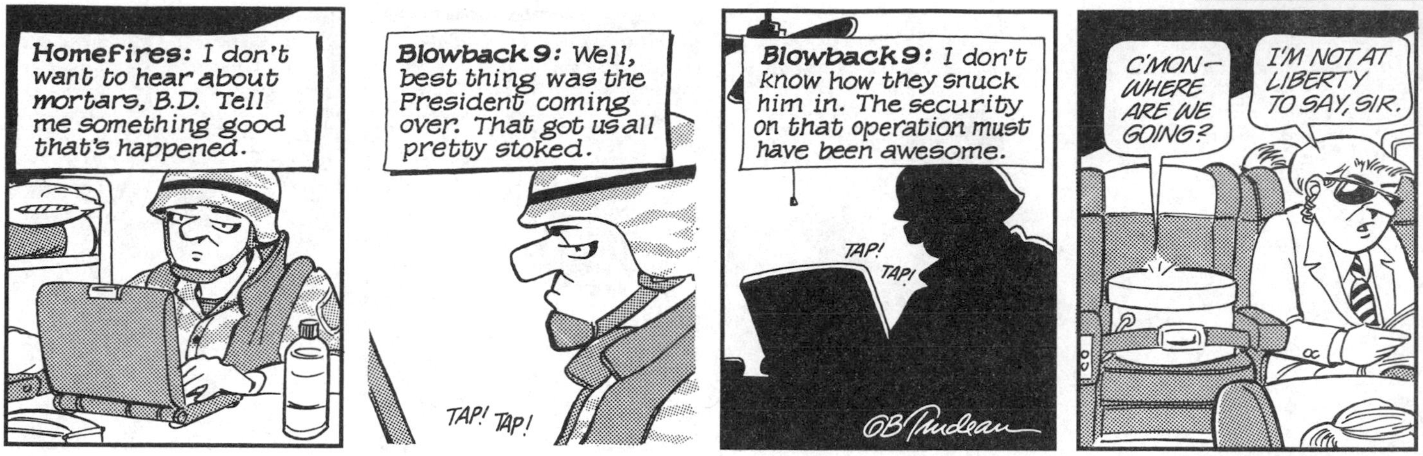
Homefires: I don't want to hear about mortars, B.D. Tell me something good that's happened.
Blowback 9: Well, best thing was the President coming over. That got us all pretty stoked.
TAP! TAP!
Blowback 9: I don't know how they snuck him in. The security on that operation must have been awesome.
TAP! TAP!
GB Trudeau
C'MON—WHERE ARE WE GOING?
I'M NOT AT LIBERTY TO SAY, SIR.

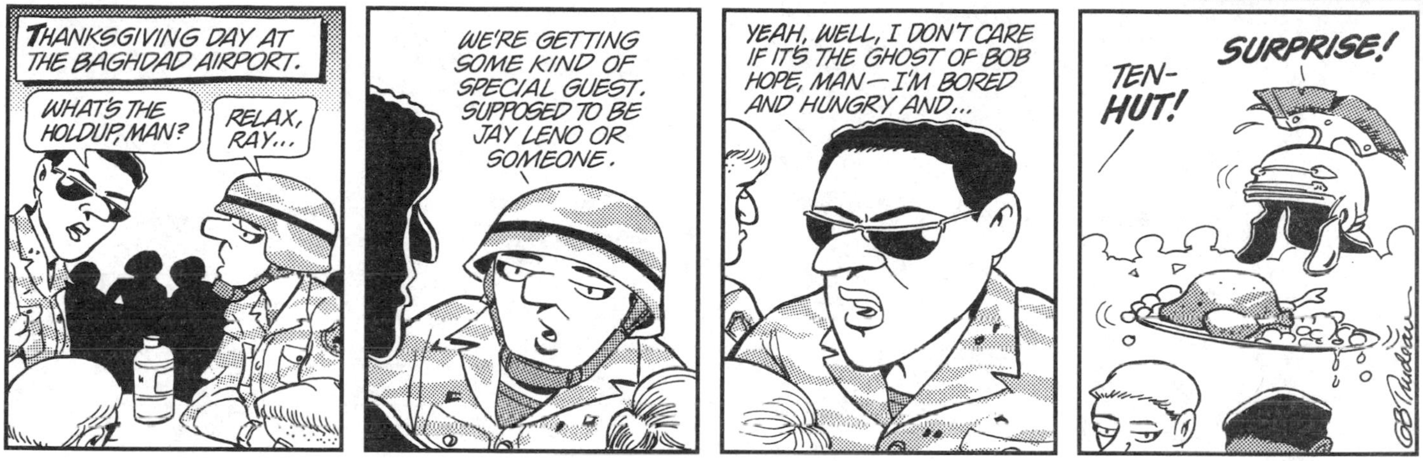
THANKSGIVING DAY AT THE BAGHDAD AIRPORT.
WHAT'S THE HOLDUP, MAN?
RELAX, RAY...
WE'RE GETTING SOME KIND OF SPECIAL GUEST. SUPPOSED TO BE JAY LENO OR SOMEONE.
YEAH, WELL, I DON'T CARE IF IT'S THE GHOST OF BOB HOPE, MAN—I'M BORED AND HUNGRY AND...
TEN-HUT!
SURPRISE!
GB Trudeau

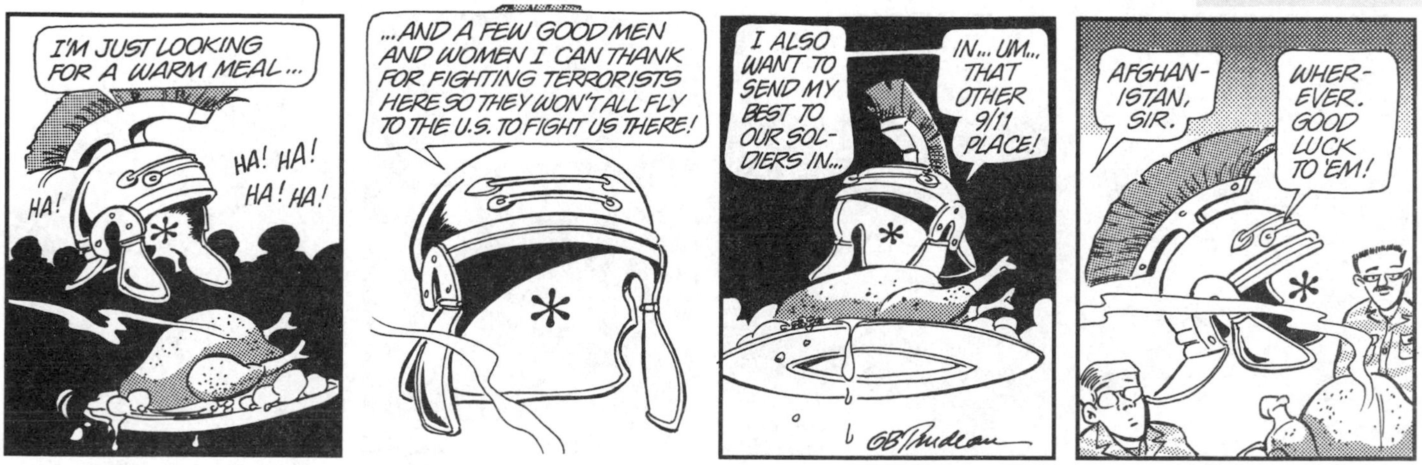
I'M JUST LOOKING FOR A WARM MEAL...
HA!
HA! HA! HA! HA!
...AND A FEW GOOD MEN AND WOMEN I CAN THANK FOR FIGHTING TERRORISTS HERE SO THEY WON'T ALL FLY TO THE U.S. TO FIGHT US THERE!
I ALSO WANT TO SEND MY BEST TO OUR SOLDIERS IN...
IN... UM... THAT OTHER 9/11 PLACE!
GB Trudeau
AFGHANISTAN, SIR.
WHEREVER. GOOD LUCK TO 'EM!

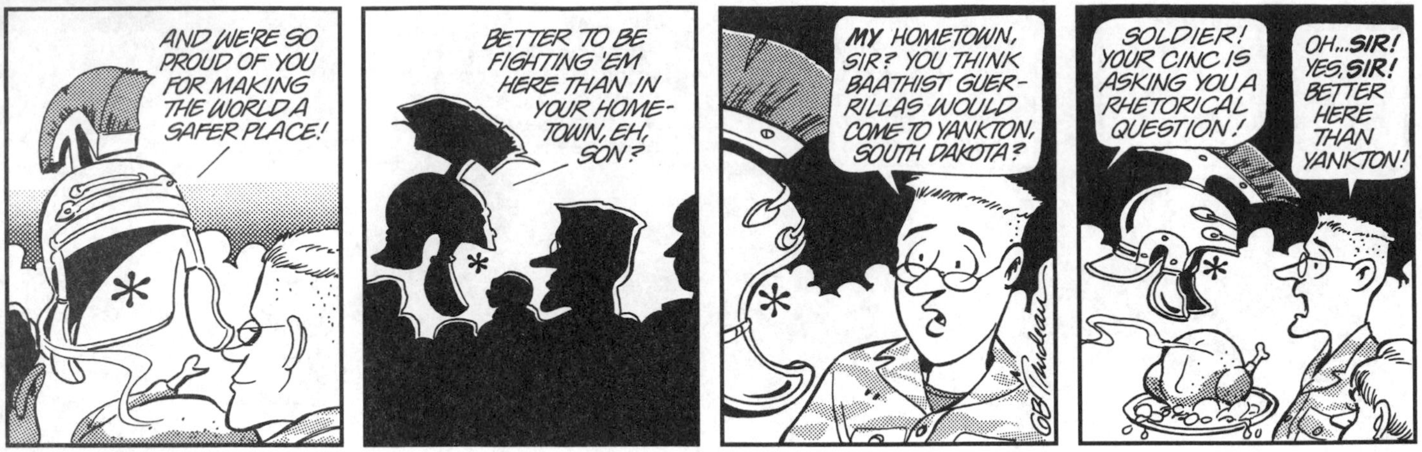
AND WE'RE SO PROUD OF YOU FOR MAKING THE WORLD A SAFER PLACE!
BETTER TO BE FIGHTING 'EM HERE THAN IN YOUR HOME-TOWN, EH, SON?
MY HOMETOWN, SIR? YOU THINK BAATHIST GUER-RILLAS WOULD COME TO YANKTON, SOUTH DAKOTA?
SOLDIER! YOUR CINC IS ASKING YOU A RHETORICAL QUESTION!
OH... SIR! YES, SIR! BETTER HERE THAN YANKTON!

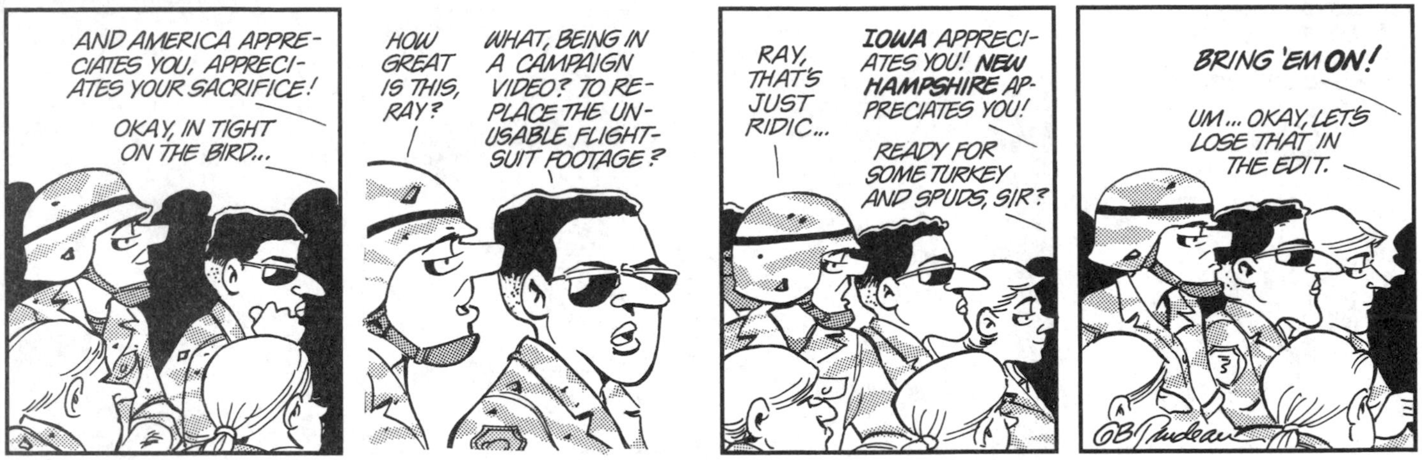
AND AMERICA APPRE-CIATES YOU, APPRECI-ATES YOUR SACRIFICE!
OKAY, IN TIGHT ON THE BIRD...
HOW GREAT IS THIS, RAY?
WHAT, BEING IN A CAMPAIGN VIDEO? TO RE-PLACE THE UN-USABLE FLIGHT-SUIT FOOTAGE?
RAY, THAT'S JUST RIDIC...
IOWA APPRECI-ATES YOU! NEW HAMPSHIRE AP-PRECIATES YOU!
READY FOR SOME TURKEY AND SPUDS, SIR?
BRING 'EM ON!
UM... OKAY, LET'S LOSE THAT IN THE EDIT.

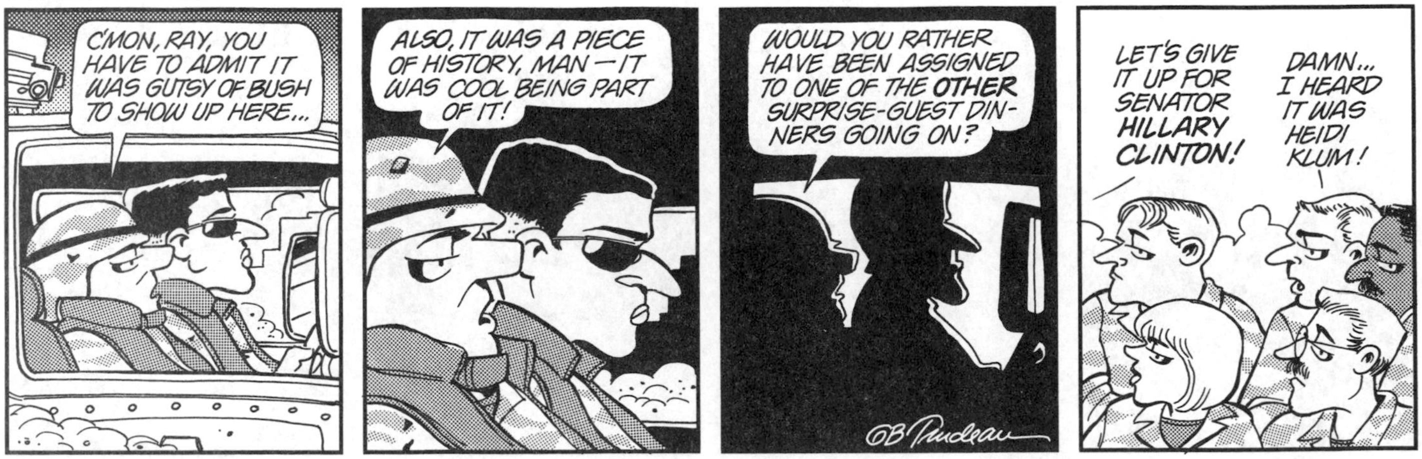
C'MON, RAY, YOU HAVE TO ADMIT IT WAS GUTSY OF BUSH TO SHOW UP HERE...
ALSO, IT WAS A PIECE OF HISTORY, MAN — IT WAS COOL BEING PART OF IT!
WOULD YOU RATHER HAVE BEEN ASSIGNED TO ONE OF THE OTHER SURPRISE-GUEST DIN-NERS GOING ON?
LET'S GIVE IT UP FOR SENATOR HILLARY CLINTON!
DAMN... I HEARD IT WAS HEIDI KLUM!

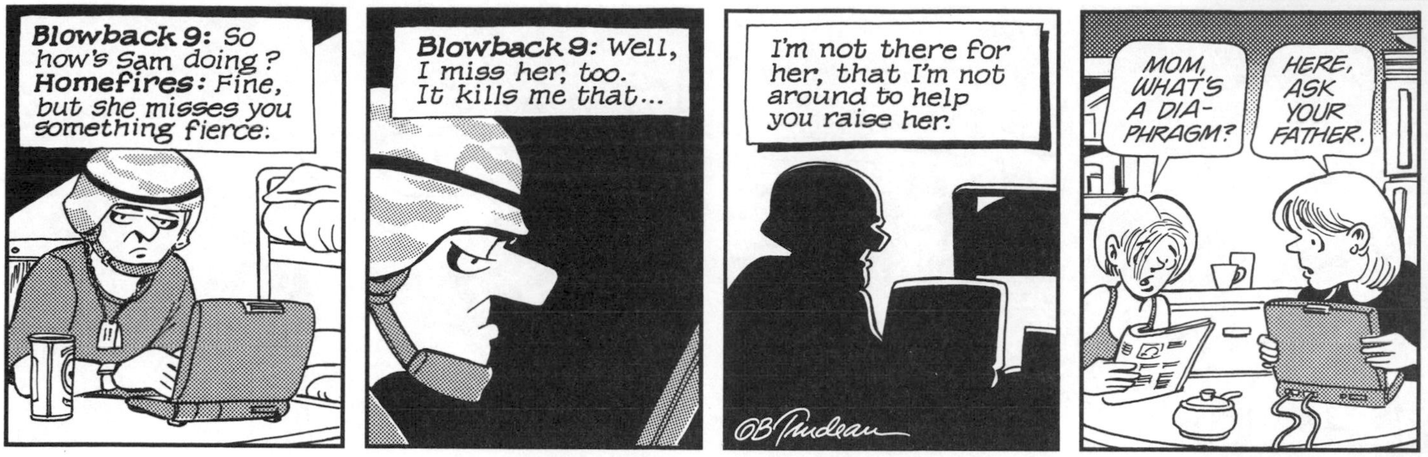
Blowback 9: So how's Sam doing? Homefires: Fine, but she misses you something fierce.
Blowback 9: Well, I miss her, too. It kills me that...
I'm not there for her, that I'm not around to help you raise her.
MOM, WHAT'S A DIA-PHRAGM?
HERE, ASK YOUR FATHER.

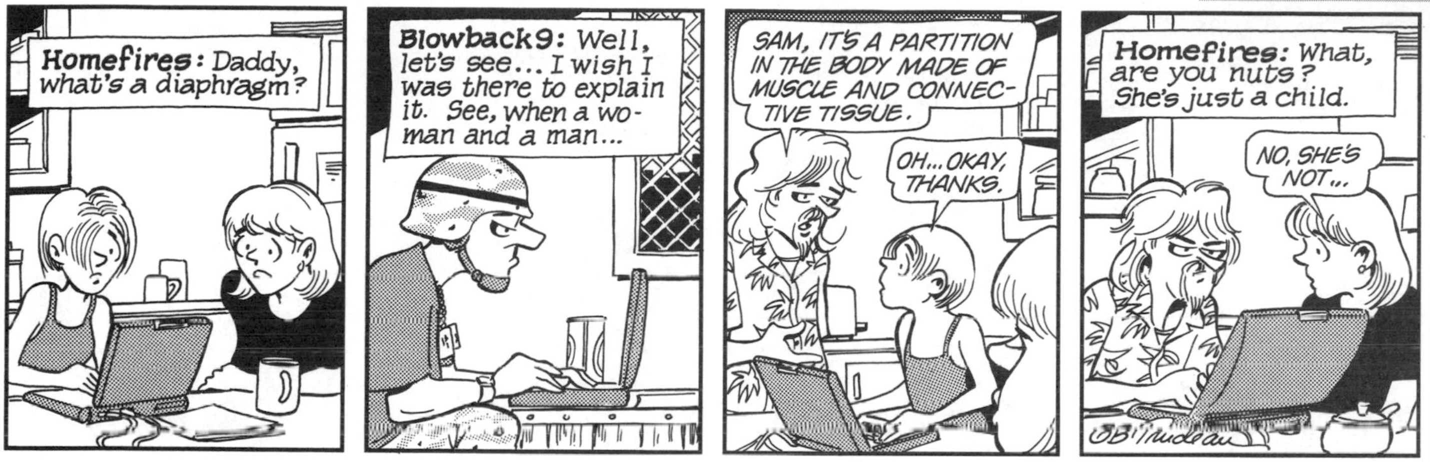
Homefires: Daddy, what's a diaphragm?
Blowback 9: Well, let's see... I wish I was there to explain it. See, when a wo-man and a man...
SAM, IT'S A PARTITION IN THE BODY MADE OF MUSCLE AND CONNEC-TIVE TISSUE.
OH... OKAY, THANKS.
Homefires: What, are you nuts? She's just a child.
NO, SHE'S NOT...

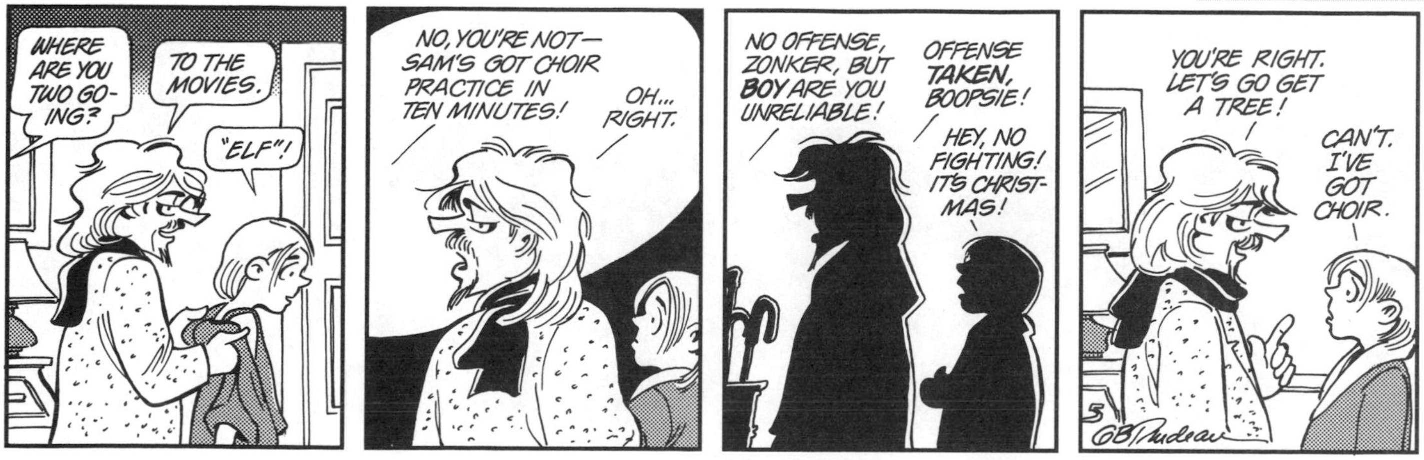
WHERE ARE YOU TWO GO-ING?
TO THE MOVIES.
"ELF"!
NO, YOU'RE NOT— SAM'S GOT CHOIR PRACTICE IN TEN MINUTES!
OH... RIGHT.
NO OFFENSE, ZONKER, BUT BOY ARE YOU UNRELIABLE!
OFFENSE TAKEN, BOOPSIE!
HEY, NO FIGHTING! IT'S CHRIST-MAS!
YOU'RE RIGHT. LET'S GO GET A TREE!
CAN'T. I'VE GOT CHOIR.

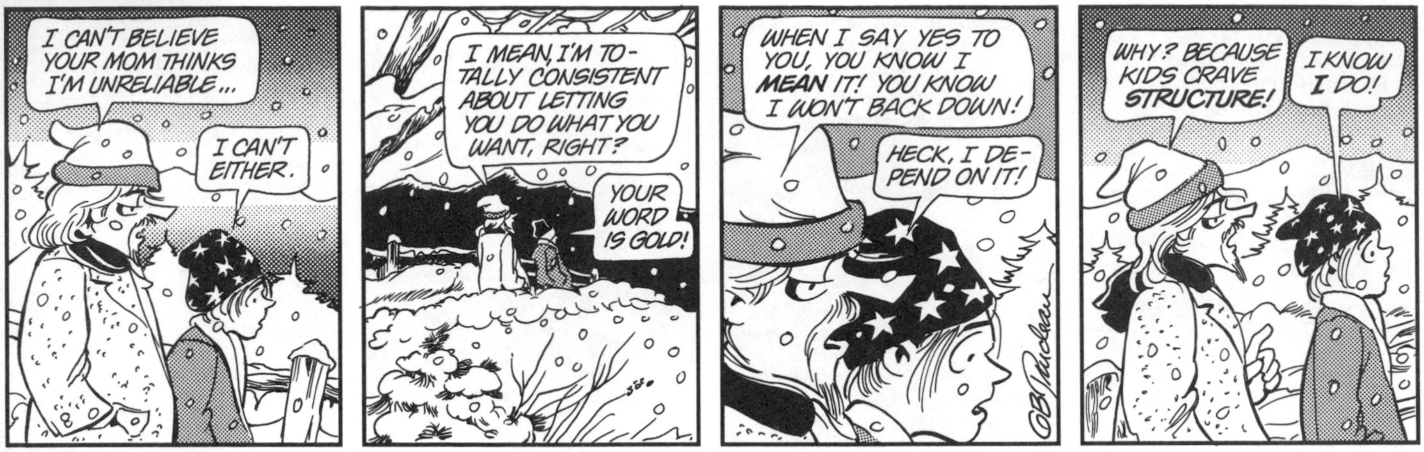
I CAN'T BELIEVE YOUR MOM THINKS I'M UNRELIABLE...
I CAN'T EITHER.
I MEAN, I'M TO-TALLY CONSISTENT ABOUT LETTING YOU DO WHAT YOU WANT, RIGHT?
YOUR WORD IS GOLD!
WHEN I SAY YES TO YOU, YOU KNOW I MEAN IT! YOU KNOW I WON'T BACK DOWN!
HECK, I DE-PEND ON IT!
WHY? BECAUSE KIDS CRAVE STRUCTURE!
I KNOW I DO!

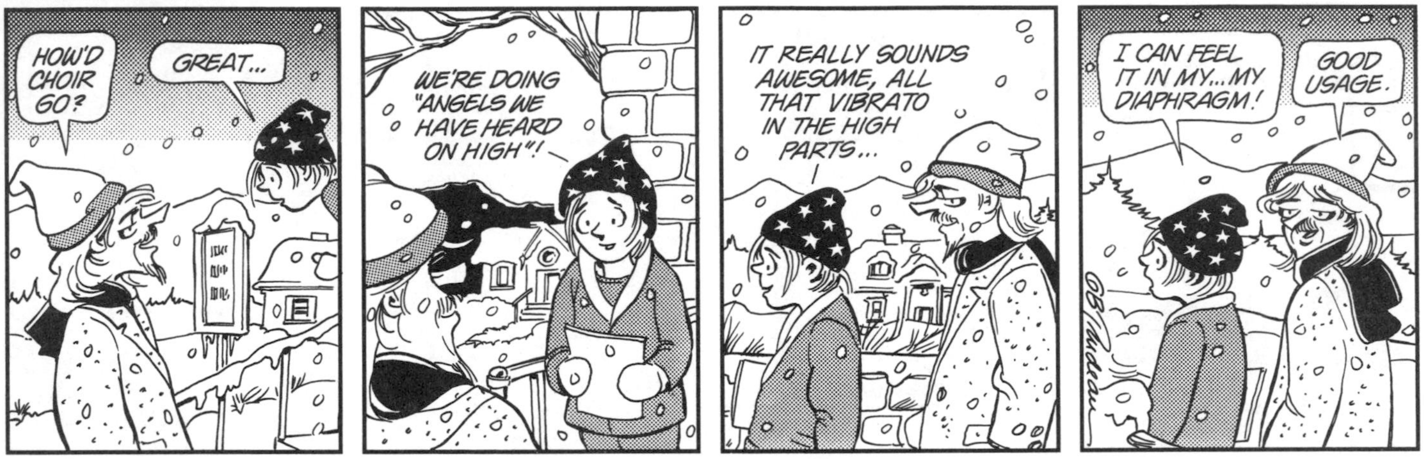
HOW'D CHOIR GO?
GREAT...
WE'RE DOING "ANGELS WE HAVE HEARD ON HIGH"!
IT REALLY SOUNDS AWESOME, ALL THAT VIBRATO IN THE HIGH PARTS...
I CAN FEEL IT IN MY...MY DIAPHRAGM!
GOOD USAGE.

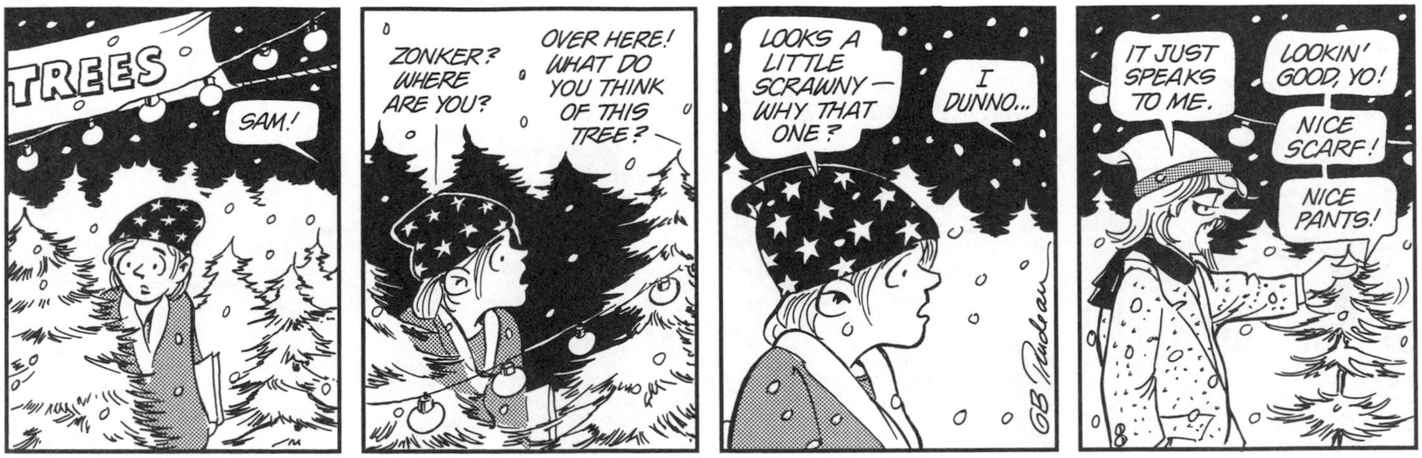
TREES
SAM!
ZONKER? WHERE ARE YOU?
OVER HERE! WHAT DO YOU THINK OF THIS TREE?
LOOKS A LITTLE SCRAWNY— WHY THAT ONE?
I DUNNO...
IT JUST SPEAKS TO ME.
LOOKIN' GOOD, YO!
NICE SCARF!
NICE PANTS!

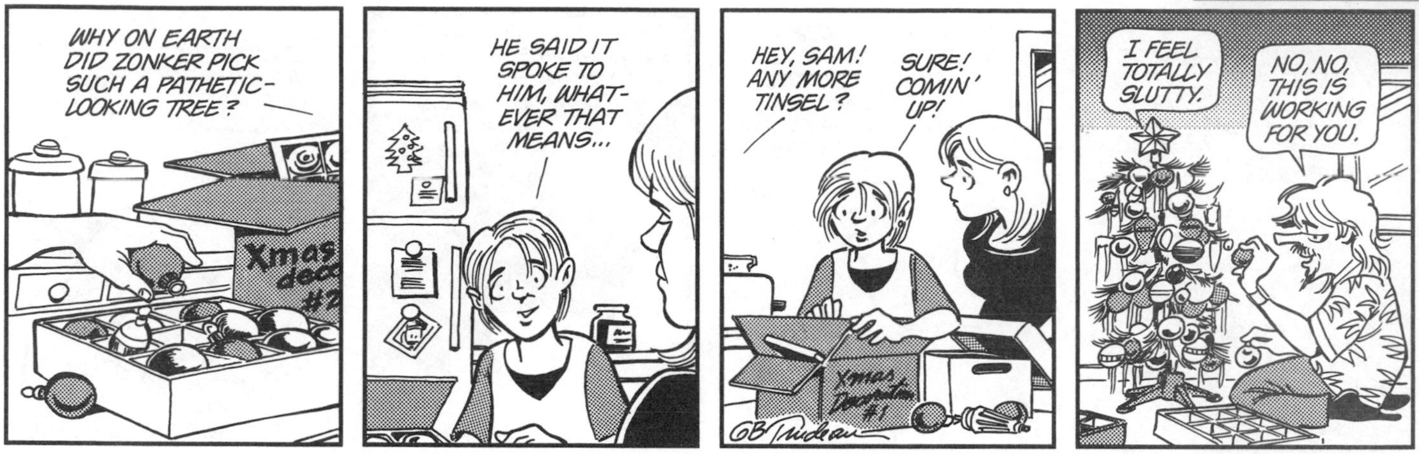
WHY ON EARTH DID ZONKER PICK SUCH A PATHETIC-LOOKING TREE?
HE SAID IT SPOKE TO HIM, WHATEVER THAT MEANS...
HEY, SAM! ANY MORE TINSEL?
SURE! COMIN' UP!
I FEEL TOTALLY SLUTTY.
NO, NO, THIS IS WORKING FOR YOU.

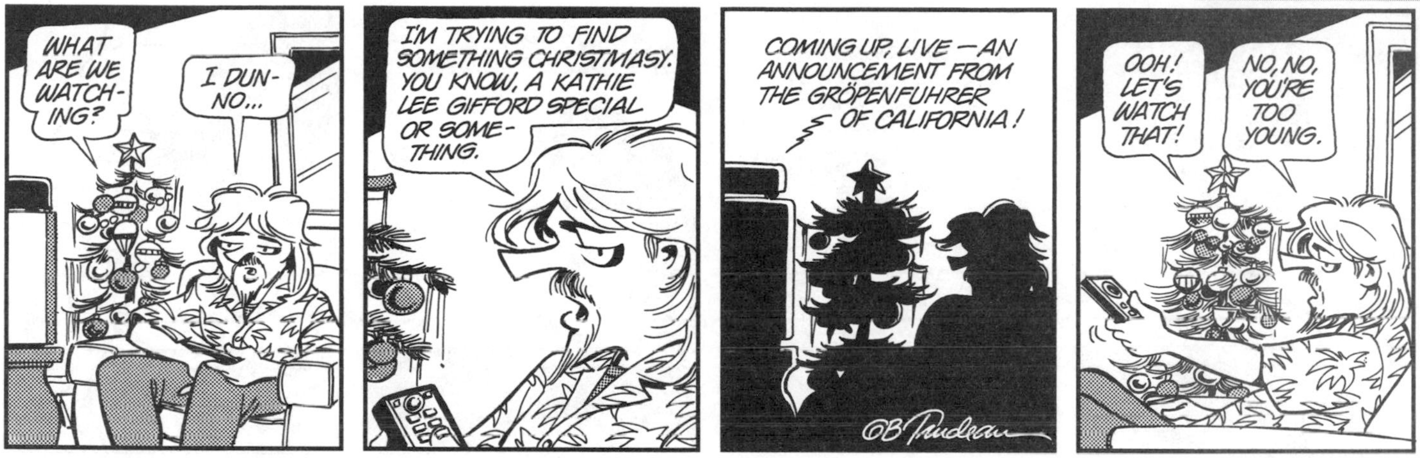
WHAT ARE WE WATCHING?
I DUNNO...
I'M TRYING TO FIND SOMETHING CHRISTMASY. YOU KNOW, A KATHIE LEE GIFFORD SPECIAL OR SOMETHING.
COMING UP, LIVE — AN ANNOUNCEMENT FROM THE GRÖPENFUHRER OF CALIFORNIA!
OOH! LET'S WATCH THAT!
NO, NO, YOU'RE TOO YOUNG.

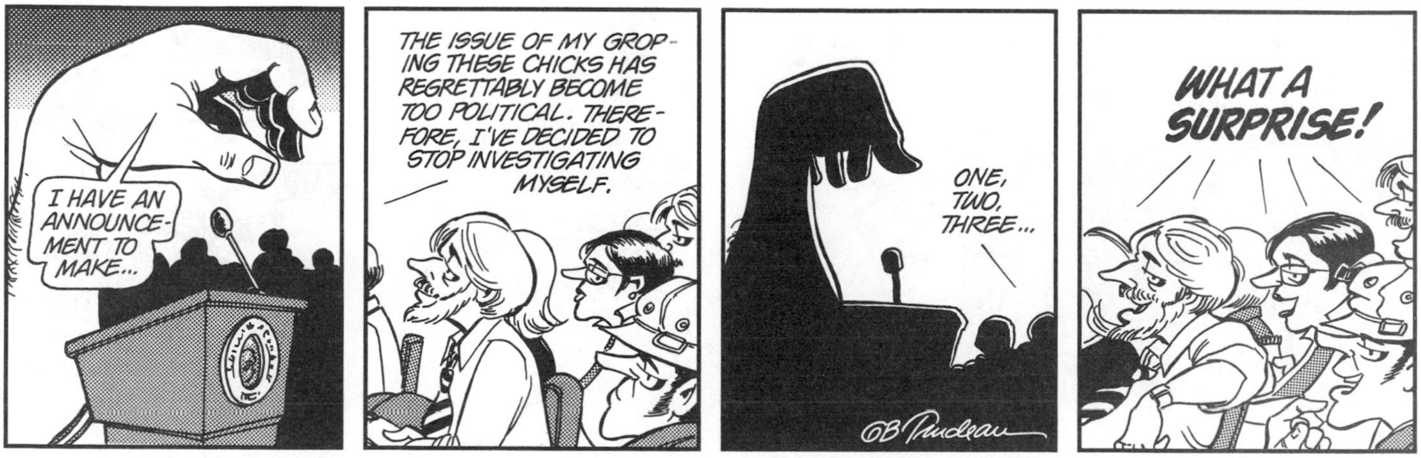
I HAVE AN ANNOUNCEMENT TO MAKE...
THE ISSUE OF MY GROPING THESE CHICKS HAS REGRETTABLY BECOME TOO POLITICAL. THEREFORE, I'VE DECIDED TO STOP INVESTIGATING MYSELF.
ONE, TWO, THREE...
WHAT A SURPRISE!

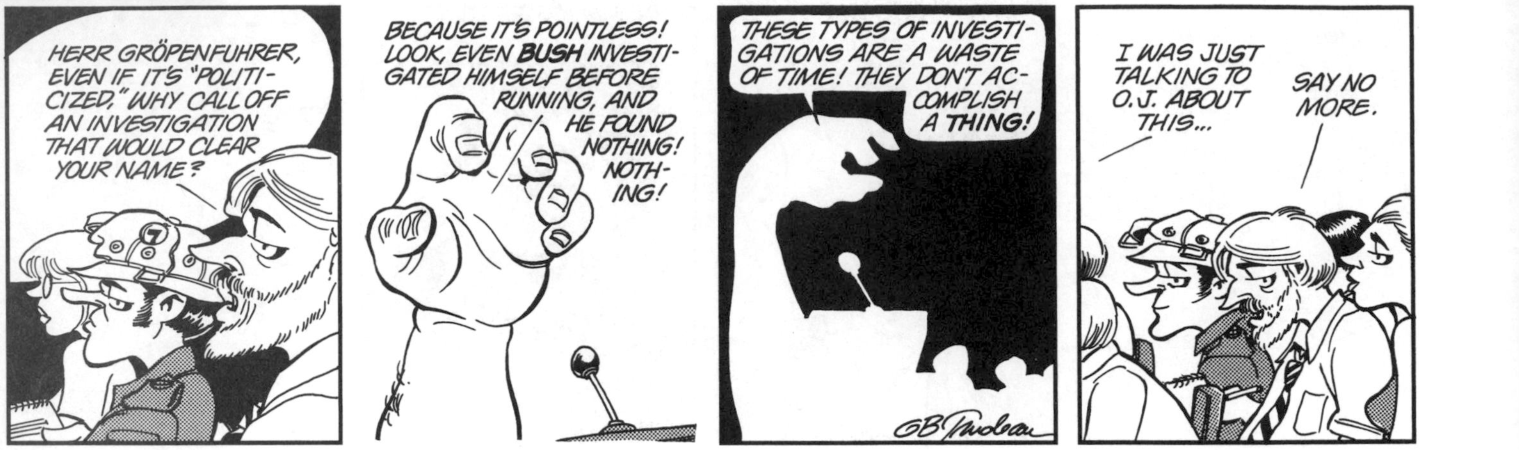
HERR GRÖPENFUHRER, EVEN IF IT'S "POLITICIZED," WHY CALL OFF AN INVESTIGATION THAT WOULD CLEAR YOUR NAME?
BECAUSE IT'S POINTLESS! LOOK, EVEN BUSH INVESTIGATED HIMSELF BEFORE RUNNING, AND HE FOUND NOTHING! NOTHING!
THESE TYPES OF INVESTIGATIONS ARE A WASTE OF TIME! THEY DON'T ACCOMPLISH A THING!
I WAS JUST TALKING TO O.J. ABOUT THIS...
SAY NO MORE.

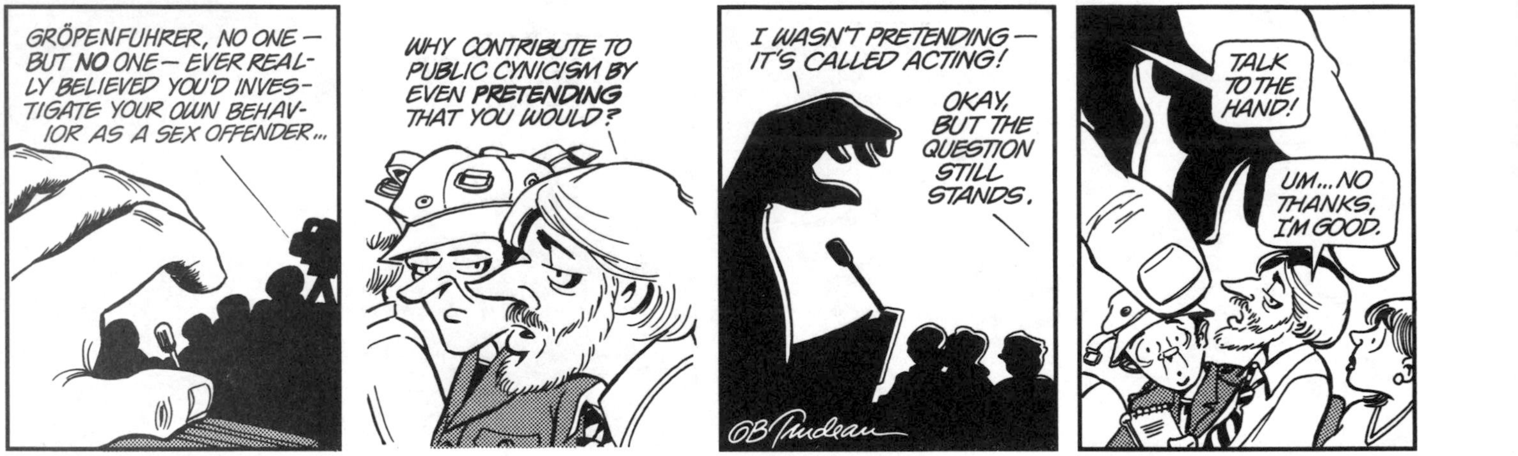
GRÖPENFUHRER, NO ONE — BUT NO ONE — EVER REALLY BELIEVED YOU'D INVESTIGATE YOUR OWN BEHAVIOR AS A SEX OFFENDER...
WHY CONTRIBUTE TO PUBLIC CYNICISM BY EVEN PRETENDING THAT YOU WOULD?
I WASN'T PRETENDING — IT'S CALLED ACTING!
OKAY, BUT THE QUESTION STILL STANDS.
TALK TO THE HAND!
UM... NO THANKS, I'M GOOD.

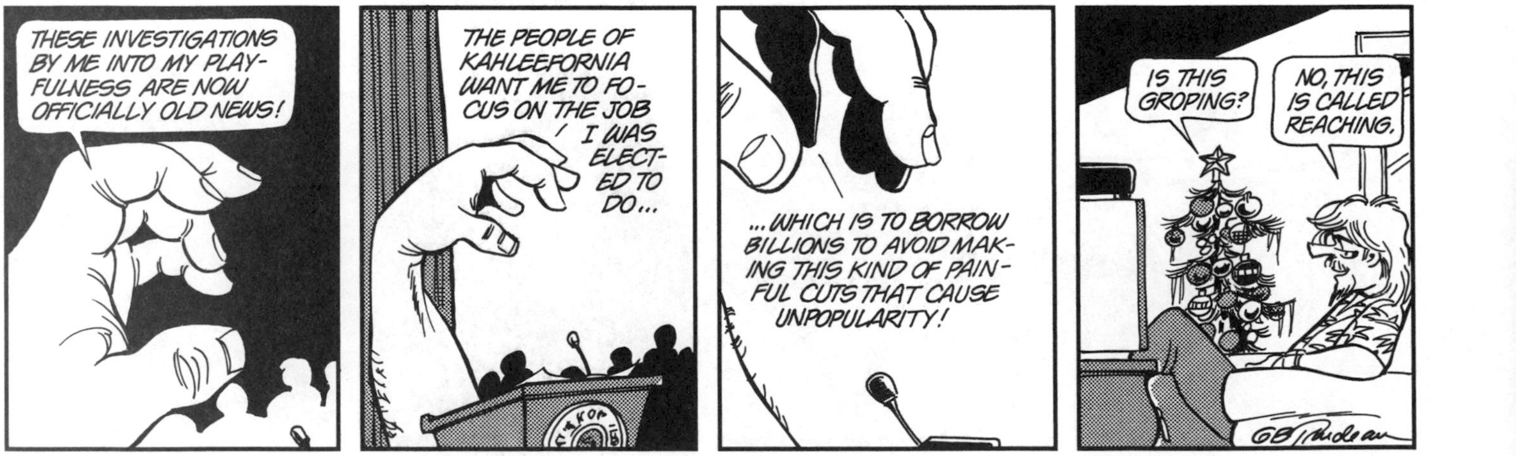
THESE INVESTIGATIONS BY ME INTO MY PLAYFULNESS ARE NOW OFFICIALLY OLD NEWS!
THE PEOPLE OF KAHLEEFORNIA WANT ME TO FOCUS ON THE JOB I WAS ELECTED TO DO...
...WHICH IS TO BORROW BILLIONS TO AVOID MAKING THIS KIND OF PAINFUL CUTS THAT CAUSE UNPOPULARITY!
IS THIS GROPING?
NO, THIS IS CALLED REACHING.

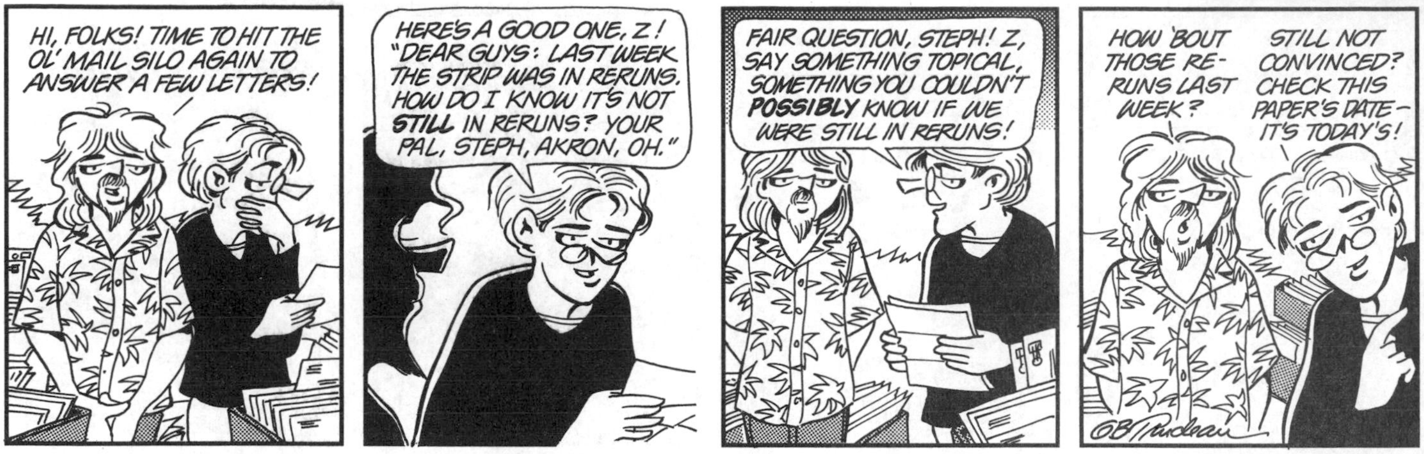
HI, FOLKS! TIME TO HIT THE OL' MAIL SILO AGAIN TO ANSWER A FEW LETTERS!
HERE'S A GOOD ONE, Z! "DEAR GUYS: LAST WEEK THE STRIP WAS IN RERUNS. HOW DO I KNOW IT'S NOT **STILL** IN RERUNS? YOUR PAL, STEPH, AKRON, OH."
FAIR QUESTION, STEPH! Z, SAY SOMETHING TOPICAL, SOMETHING YOU COULDN'T **POSSIBLY** KNOW IF WE WERE STILL IN RERUNS!
HOW 'BOUT THOSE RE-RUNS LAST WEEK?
STILL NOT CONVINCED? CHECK THIS PAPER'S DATE– IT'S TODAY'S!

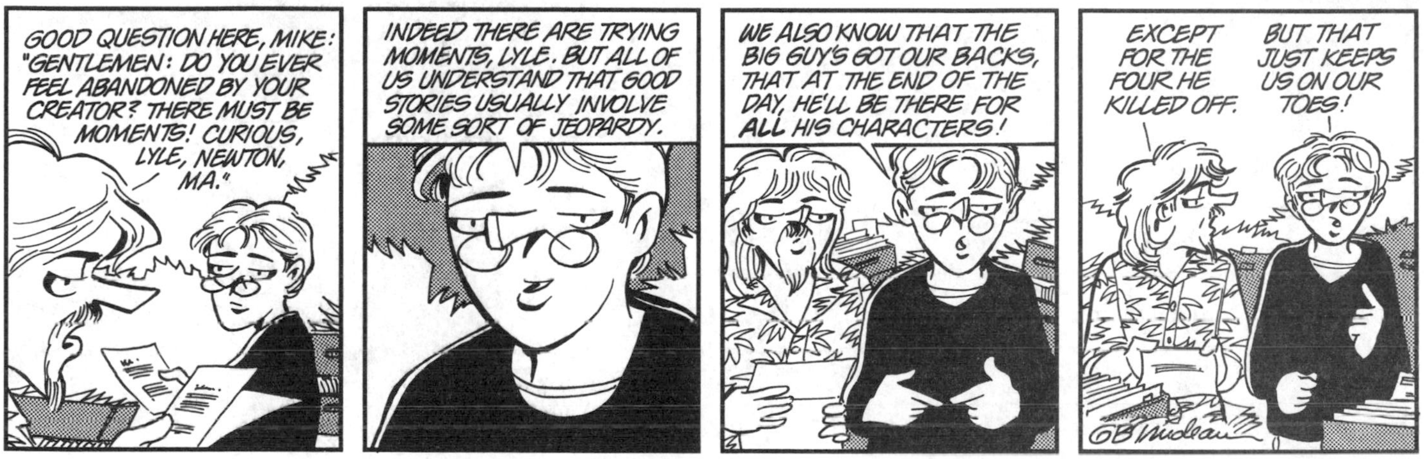
GOOD QUESTION HERE, MIKE: "GENTLEMEN: DO YOU EVER FEEL ABANDONED BY YOUR CREATOR? THERE MUST BE MOMENTS! CURIOUS, LYLE, NEWTON, MA."
INDEED THERE ARE TRYING MOMENTS, LYLE. BUT ALL OF US UNDERSTAND THAT GOOD STORIES USUALLY INVOLVE SOME SORT OF JEOPARDY.
WE ALSO KNOW THAT THE BIG GUY'S GOT OUR BACKS, THAT AT THE END OF THE DAY, HE'LL BE THERE FOR **ALL** HIS CHARACTERS!
EXCEPT FOR THE FOUR HE KILLED OFF.
BUT THAT JUST KEEPS US ON OUR TOES!

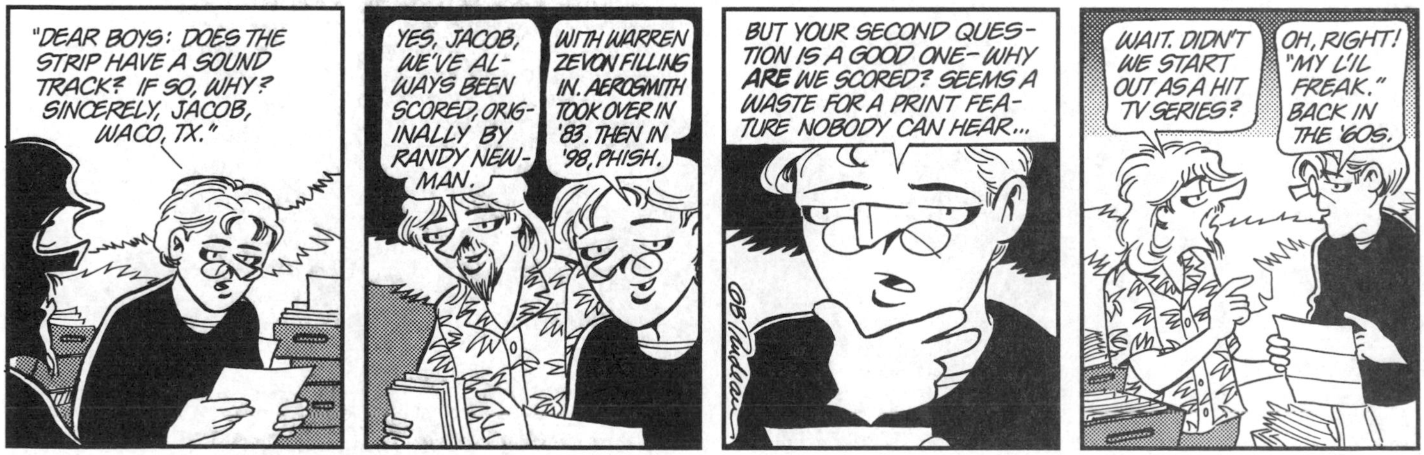
"DEAR BOYS: DOES THE STRIP HAVE A SOUND TRACK? IF SO, WHY? SINCERELY, JACOB, WACO, TX."
YES, JACOB, WE'VE AL-WAYS BEEN SCORED, ORIG-INALLY BY RANDY NEW-MAN.
WITH WARREN ZEVON FILLING IN. AEROSMITH TOOK OVER IN '83. THEN IN '98, PHISH.
BUT YOUR SECOND QUES-TION IS A GOOD ONE– WHY **ARE** WE SCORED? SEEMS A WASTE FOR A PRINT FEA-TURE NOBODY CAN HEAR...
WAIT. DIDN'T WE START OUT AS A HIT TV SERIES?
OH, RIGHT! "MY L'IL FREAK." BACK IN THE '60S.

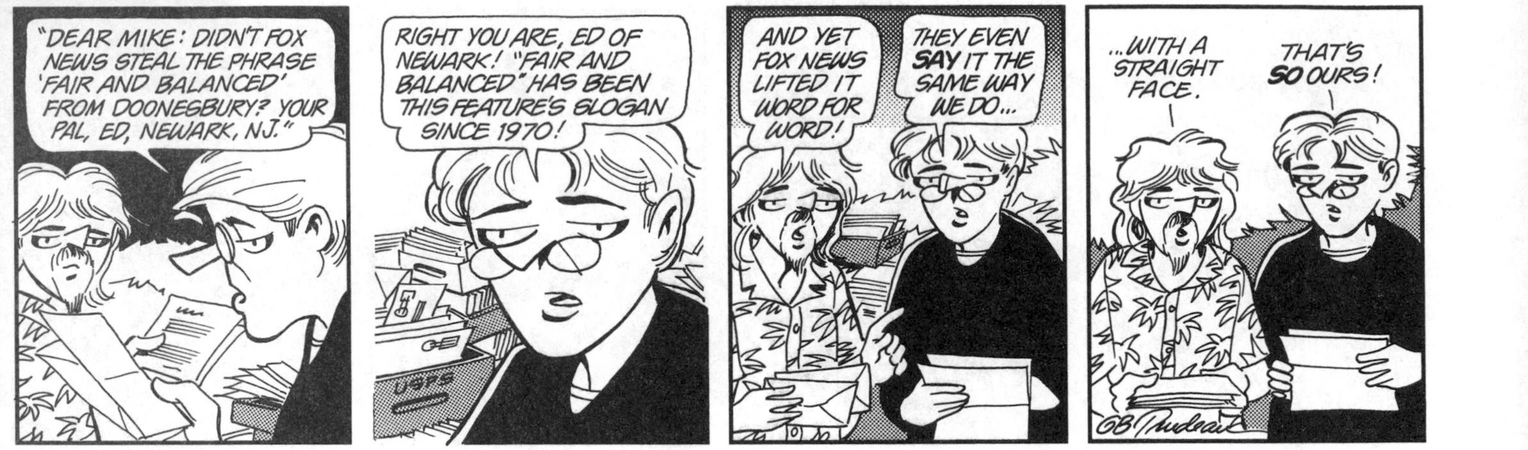
"DEAR MIKE: DIDN'T FOX NEWS STEAL THE PHRASE 'FAIR AND BALANCED' FROM DOONESBURY? YOUR PAL, ED, NEWARK, NJ."
RIGHT YOU ARE, ED OF NEWARK! "FAIR AND BALANCED" HAS BEEN THIS FEATURE'S SLOGAN SINCE 1970!
AND YET FOX NEWS LIFTED IT WORD FOR WORD!
THEY EVEN SAY IT THE SAME WAY WE DO...
...WITH A STRAIGHT FACE.
THAT'S SO OURS!

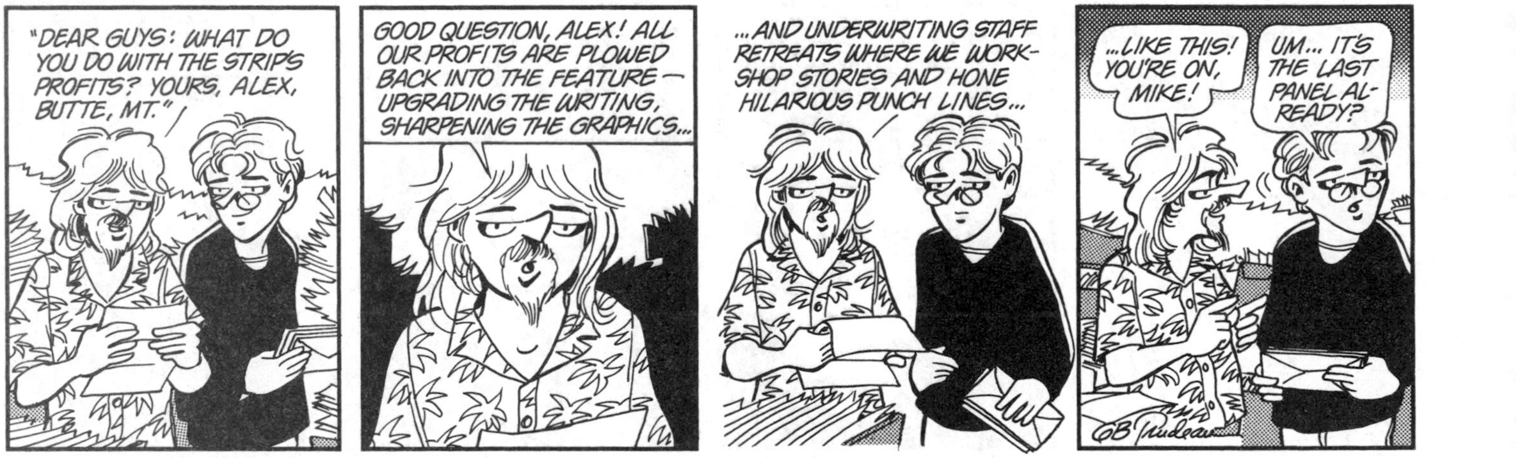
"DEAR GUYS: WHAT DO YOU DO WITH THE STRIP'S PROFITS? YOURS, ALEX, BUTTE, MT."
GOOD QUESTION, ALEX! ALL OUR PROFITS ARE PLOWED BACK INTO THE FEATURE — UPGRADING THE WRITING, SHARPENING THE GRAPHICS...
...AND UNDERWRITING STAFF RETREATS WHERE WE WORKSHOP STORIES AND HONE HILARIOUS PUNCH LINES...
...LIKE THIS! YOU'RE ON, MIKE!
UM... IT'S THE LAST PANEL ALREADY?

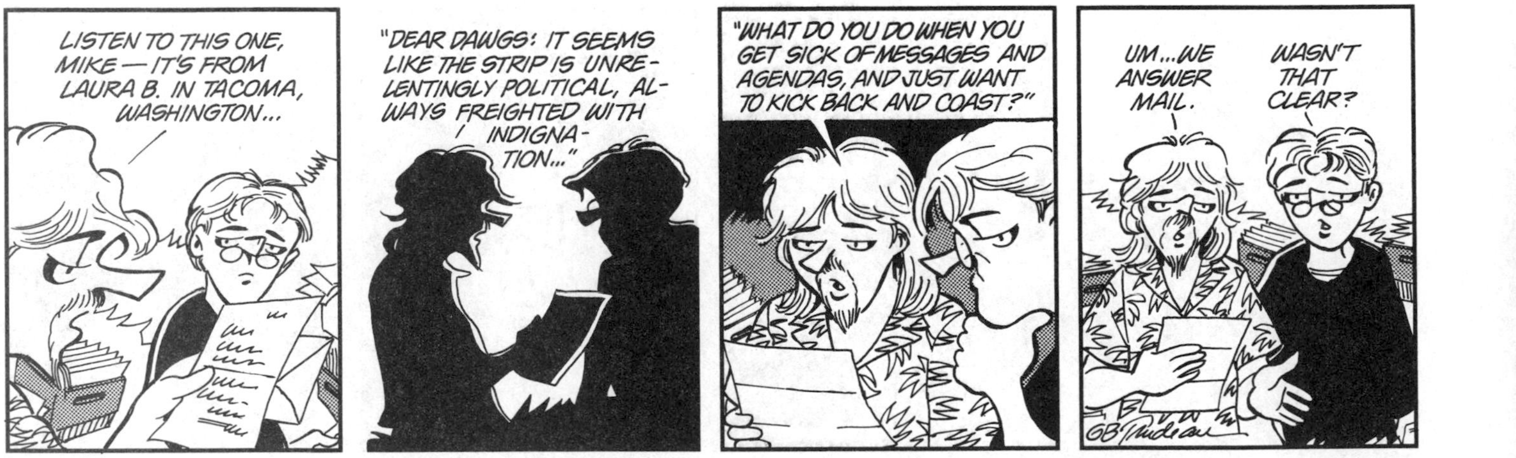
LISTEN TO THIS ONE, MIKE — IT'S FROM LAURA B. IN TACOMA, WASHINGTON...
"DEAR DAWGS: IT SEEMS LIKE THE STRIP IS UNRELENTINGLY POLITICAL, ALWAYS FREIGHTED WITH INDIGNATION..."
"WHAT DO YOU DO WHEN YOU GET SICK OF MESSAGES AND AGENDAS, AND JUST WANT TO KICK BACK AND COAST?"
UM...WE ANSWER MAIL.
WASN'T THAT CLEAR?

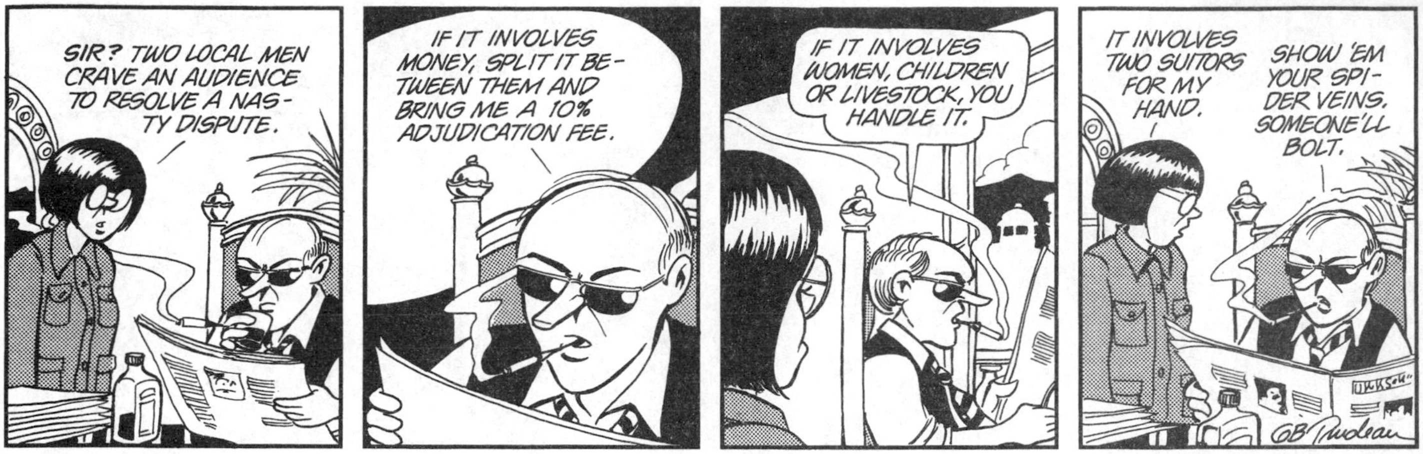
SIR? TWO LOCAL MEN CRAVE AN AUDIENCE TO RESOLVE A NASTY DISPUTE.
IF IT INVOLVES MONEY, SPLIT IT BETWEEN THEM AND BRING ME A 10% ADJUDICATION FEE.
IF IT INVOLVES WOMEN, CHILDREN OR LIVESTOCK, YOU HANDLE IT.
IT INVOLVES TWO SUITORS FOR MY HAND.
SHOW 'EM YOUR SPIDER VEINS. SOMEONE'LL BOLT.

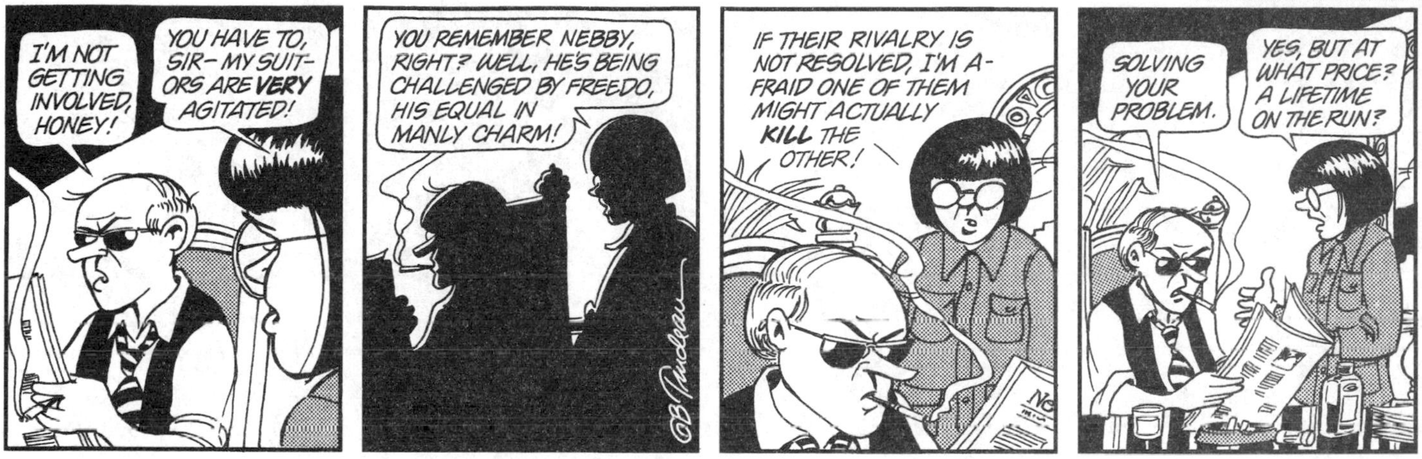
I'M NOT GETTING INVOLVED, HONEY!
YOU HAVE TO, SIR– MY SUITORS ARE VERY AGITATED!
YOU REMEMBER NEBBY, RIGHT? WELL, HE'S BEING CHALLENGED BY FREEDO, HIS EQUAL IN MANLY CHARM!
IF THEIR RIVALRY IS NOT RESOLVED, I'M AFRAID ONE OF THEM MIGHT ACTUALLY KILL THE OTHER!
SOLVING YOUR PROBLEM.
YES, BUT AT WHAT PRICE? A LIFETIME ON THE RUN?

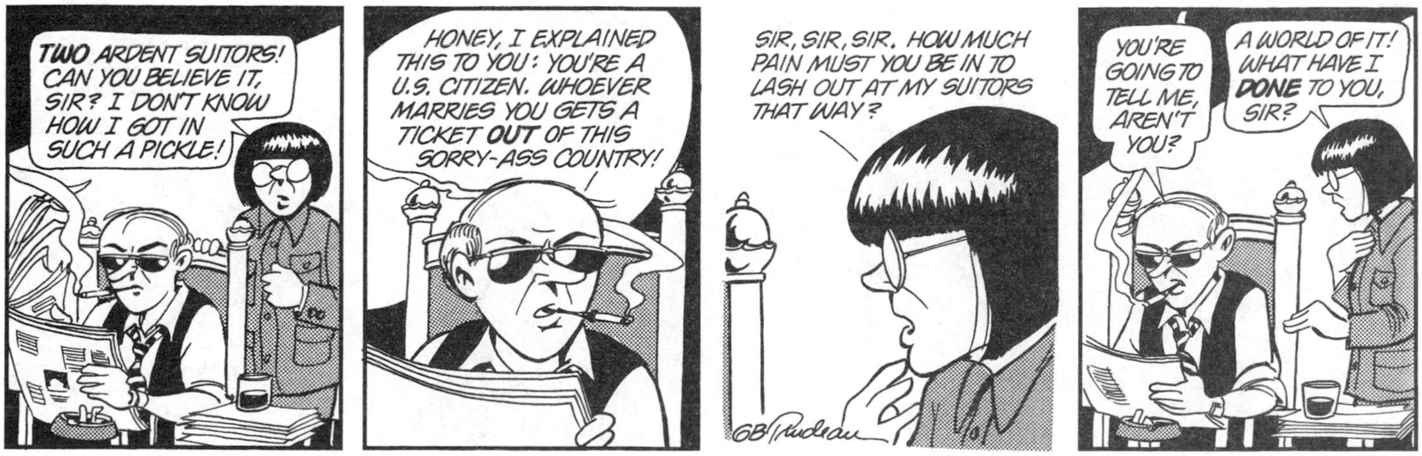
TWO ARDENT SUITORS! CAN YOU BELIEVE IT, SIR? I DON'T KNOW HOW I GOT IN SUCH A PICKLE!
HONEY, I EXPLAINED THIS TO YOU: YOU'RE A U.S. CITIZEN. WHOEVER MARRIES YOU GETS A TICKET OUT OF THIS SORRY-ASS COUNTRY!
SIR, SIR, SIR. HOW MUCH PAIN MUST YOU BE IN TO LASH OUT AT MY SUITORS THAT WAY?
YOU'RE GOING TO TELL ME, AREN'T YOU?
A WORLD OF IT! WHAT HAVE I DONE TO YOU, SIR?

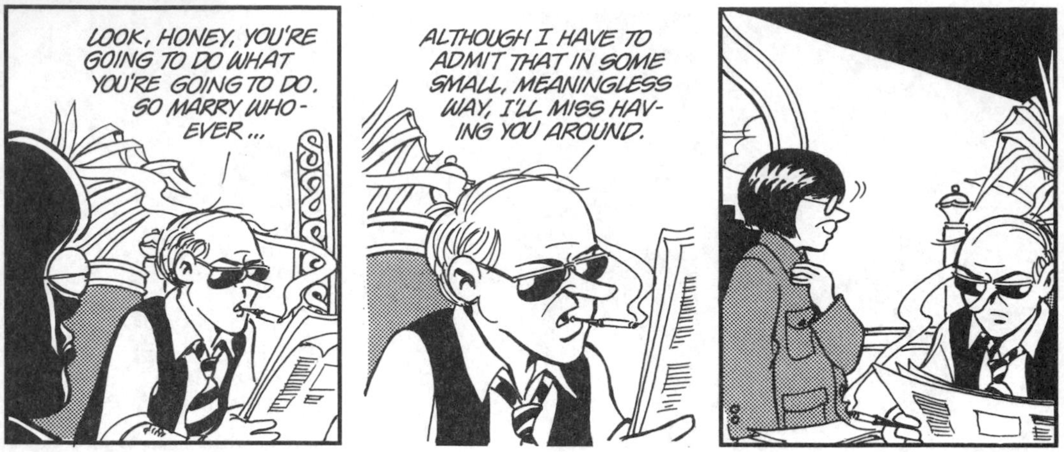
LOOK, HONEY, YOU'RE GOING TO DO WHAT YOU'RE GOING TO DO. SO MARRY WHO-EVER...
ALTHOUGH I HAVE TO ADMIT THAT IN SOME SMALL, MEANINGLESS WAY, I'LL MISS HAVING YOU AROUND.
SCRAM! SHOO! BOTH OF YOU!
I KNOW I'M GOING TO REGRET THIS.
GB Trudeau

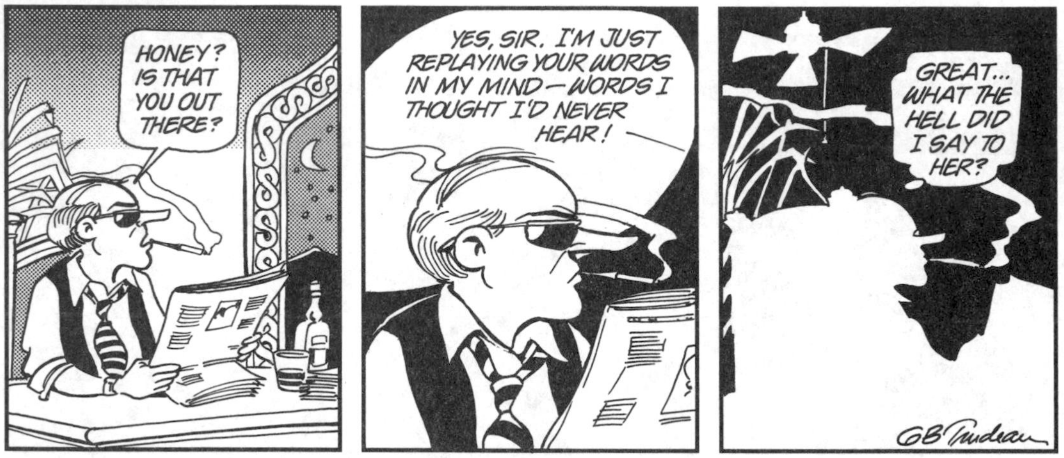
HONEY? IS THAT YOU OUT THERE?
YES, SIR. I'M JUST REPLAYING YOUR WORDS IN MY MIND—WORDS I THOUGHT I'D NEVER HEAR!
GREAT... WHAT THE HELL DID I SAY TO HER?
GB Trudeau
"IN SOME SMALL, MEANINGLESS WAY, I'D MISS YOU, HONEY!"
SIGH...

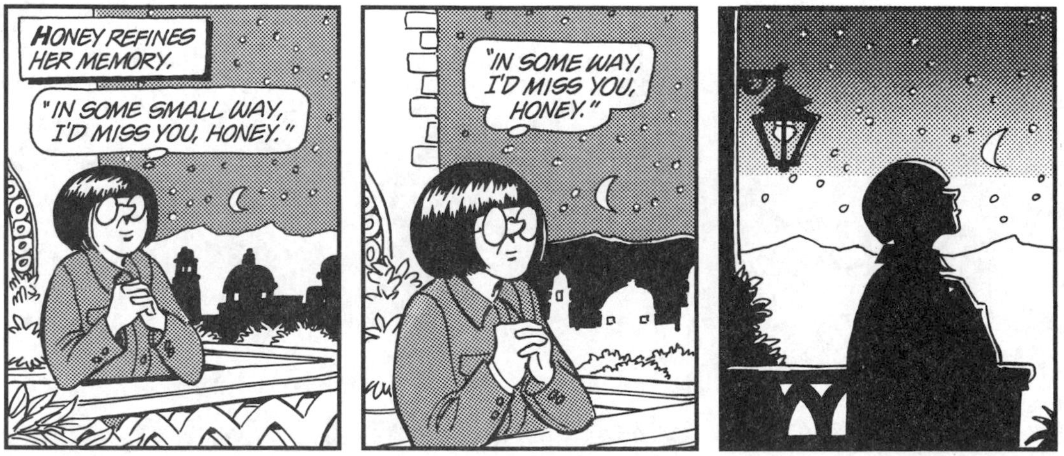
HONEY REFINES HER MEMORY.
"IN SOME SMALL WAY, I'D MISS YOU, HONEY."
"IN SOME WAY, I'D MISS YOU, HONEY."
"YOU COMPLETE ME, HONEY."
THERE WE GO.
GB Trudeau

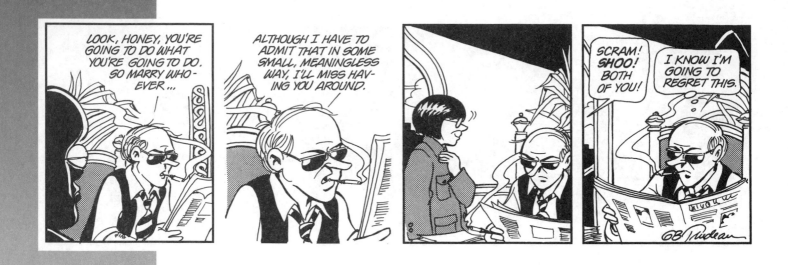

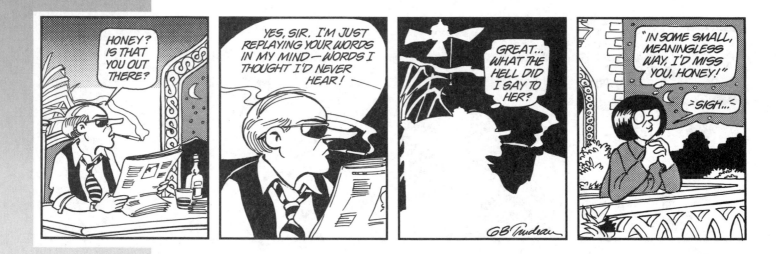

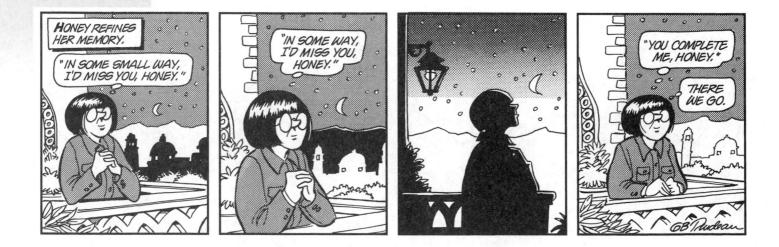

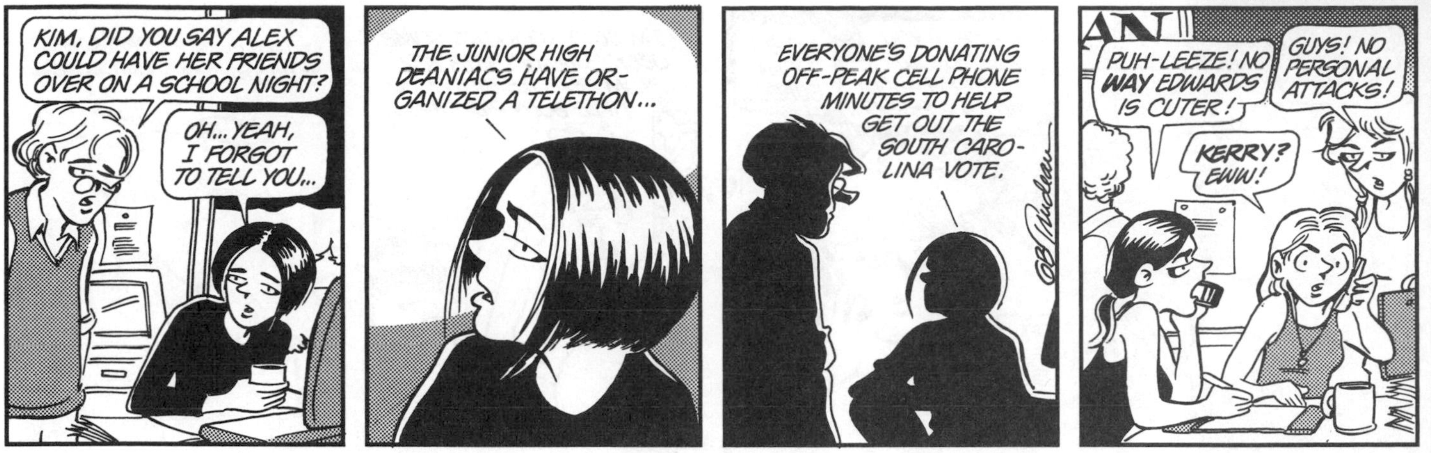
KIM, DID YOU SAY ALEX COULD HAVE HER FRIENDS OVER ON A SCHOOL NIGHT?
OH... YEAH, I FORGOT TO TELL YOU...
THE JUNIOR HIGH DEANIACS HAVE ORGANIZED A TELETHON...
EVERYONE'S DONATING OFF-PEAK CELL PHONE MINUTES TO HELP GET OUT THE SOUTH CAROLINA VOTE.
PUH-LEEZE! NO WAY EDWARDS IS CUTER!
GUYS! NO PERSONAL ATTACKS!
KERRY? EWW!

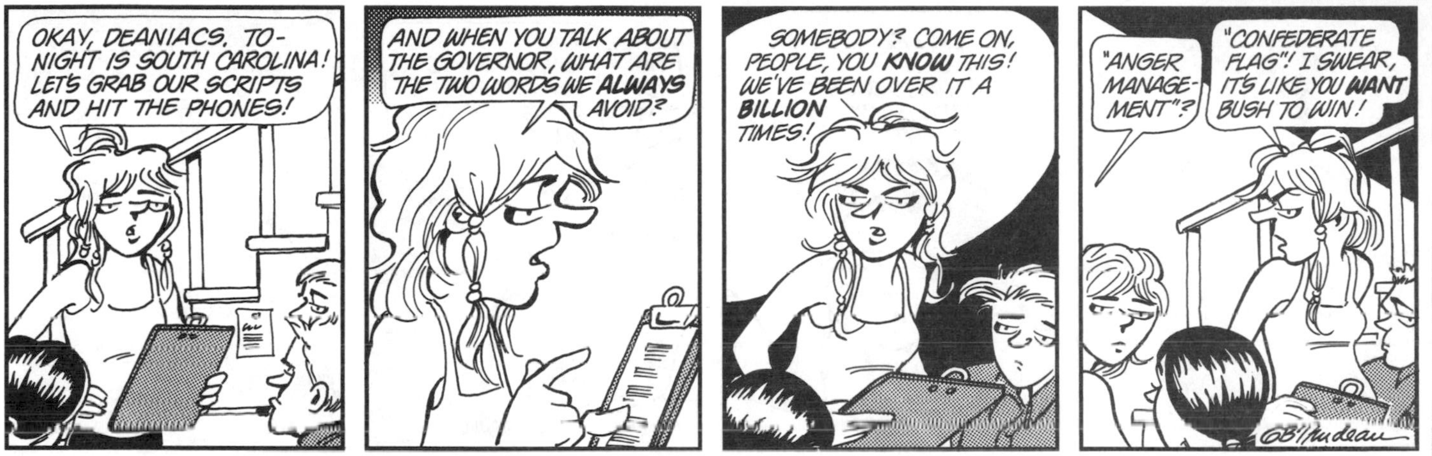
OKAY, DEANIACS, TONIGHT IS SOUTH CAROLINA! LET'S GRAB OUR SCRIPTS AND HIT THE PHONES!
AND WHEN YOU TALK ABOUT THE GOVERNOR, WHAT ARE THE TWO WORDS WE ALWAYS AVOID?
SOMEBODY? COME ON, PEOPLE, YOU KNOW THIS! WE'VE BEEN OVER IT A BILLION TIMES!
"ANGER MANAGEMENT"?
"CONFEDERATE FLAG"! I SWEAR, IT'S LIKE YOU WANT BUSH TO WIN!

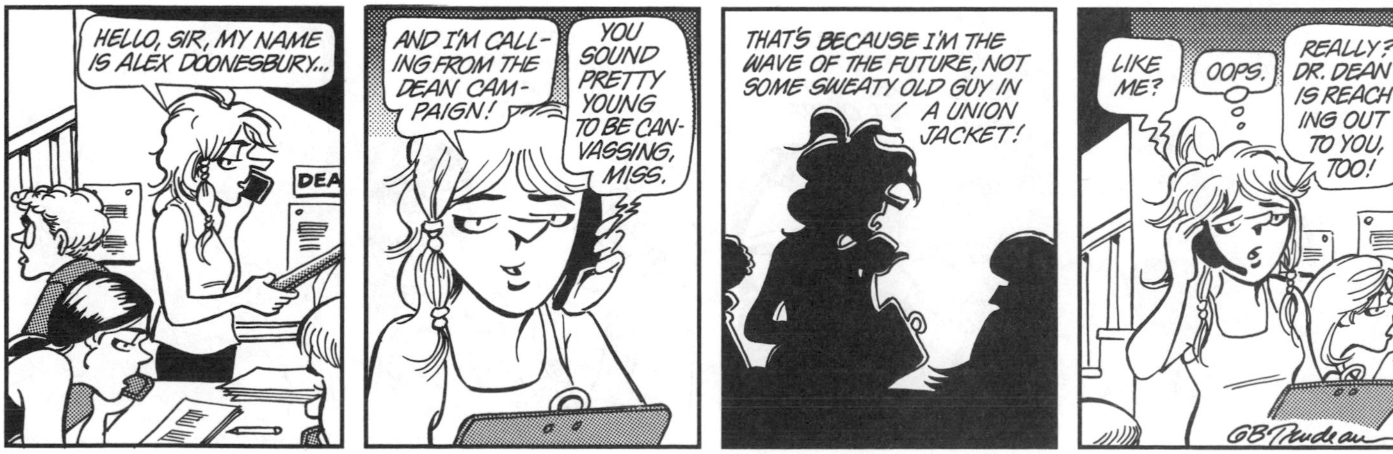
HELLO, SIR, MY NAME IS ALEX DOONESBURY...
DEA
AND I'M CALLING FROM THE DEAN CAMPAIGN!
YOU SOUND PRETTY YOUNG TO BE CANVASSING, MISS.
THAT'S BECAUSE I'M THE WAVE OF THE FUTURE, NOT SOME SWEATY OLD GUY IN A UNION JACKET!
LIKE ME?
OOPS.
REALLY? DR. DEAN IS REACHING OUT TO YOU, TOO!

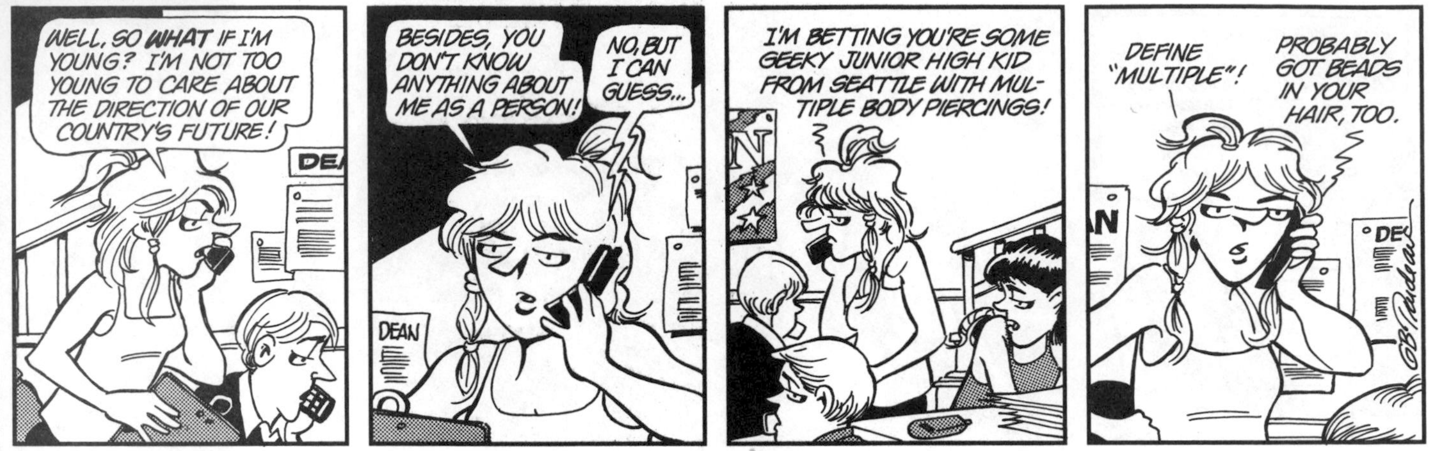
WELL, SO WHAT IF I'M YOUNG? I'M NOT TOO YOUNG TO CARE ABOUT THE DIRECTION OF OUR COUNTRY'S FUTURE!
DEAN
BESIDES, YOU DON'T KNOW ANYTHING ABOUT ME AS A PERSON!
NO, BUT I CAN GUESS...
DEAN
I'M BETTING YOU'RE SOME GEEKY JUNIOR HIGH KID FROM SEATTLE WITH MULTIPLE BODY PIERCINGS!
DEFINE "MULTIPLE"!
PROBABLY GOT BEADS IN YOUR HAIR, TOO.
DEAN

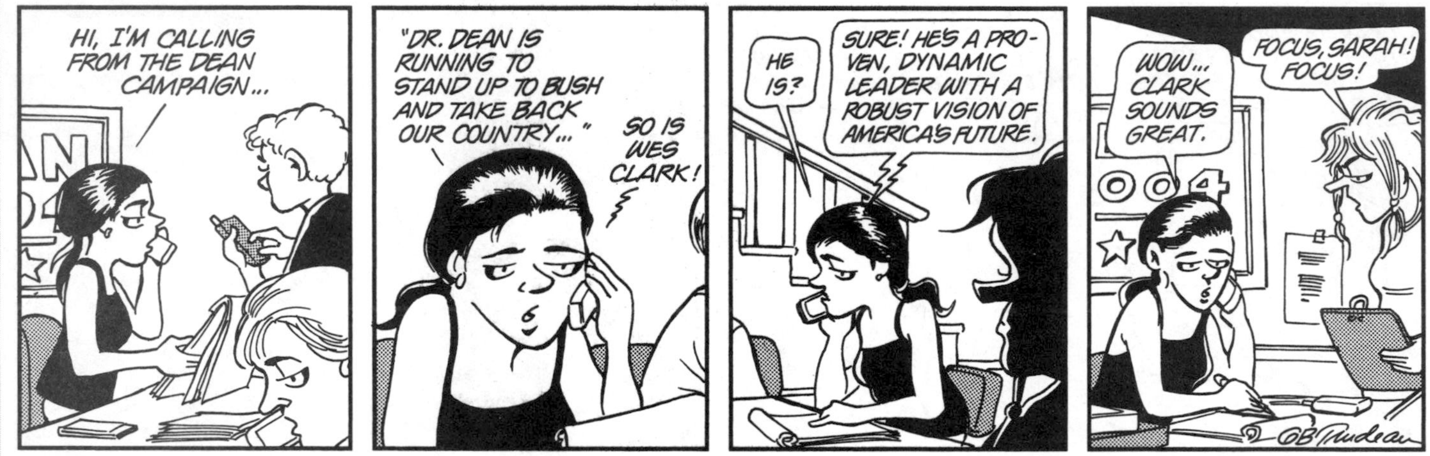
HI, I'M CALLING FROM THE DEAN CAMPAIGN...
"DR. DEAN IS RUNNING TO STAND UP TO BUSH AND TAKE BACK OUR COUNTRY..."
SO IS WES CLARK!
HE IS?
SURE! HE'S A PROVEN, DYNAMIC LEADER WITH A ROBUST VISION OF AMERICA'S FUTURE.
WOW... CLARK SOUNDS GREAT.
FOCUS, SARAH! FOCUS!

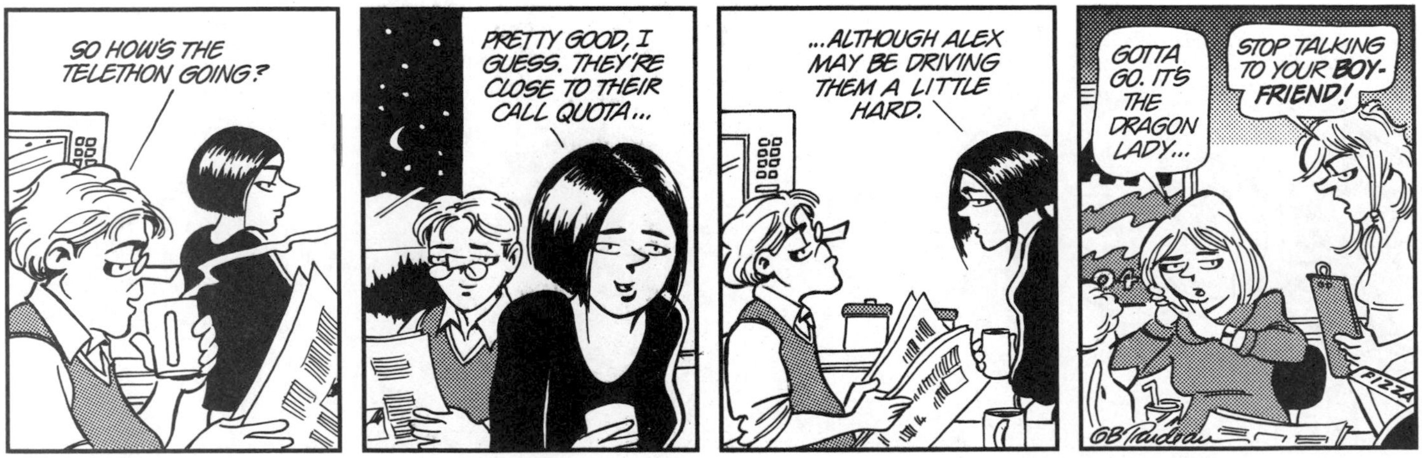
SO HOW'S THE TELETHON GOING?
PRETTY GOOD, I GUESS. THEY'RE CLOSE TO THEIR CALL QUOTA...
...ALTHOUGH ALEX MAY BE DRIVING THEM A LITTLE HARD.
GOTTA GO. IT'S THE DRAGON LADY...
STOP TALKING TO YOUR BOY-FRIEND!
PIZZA

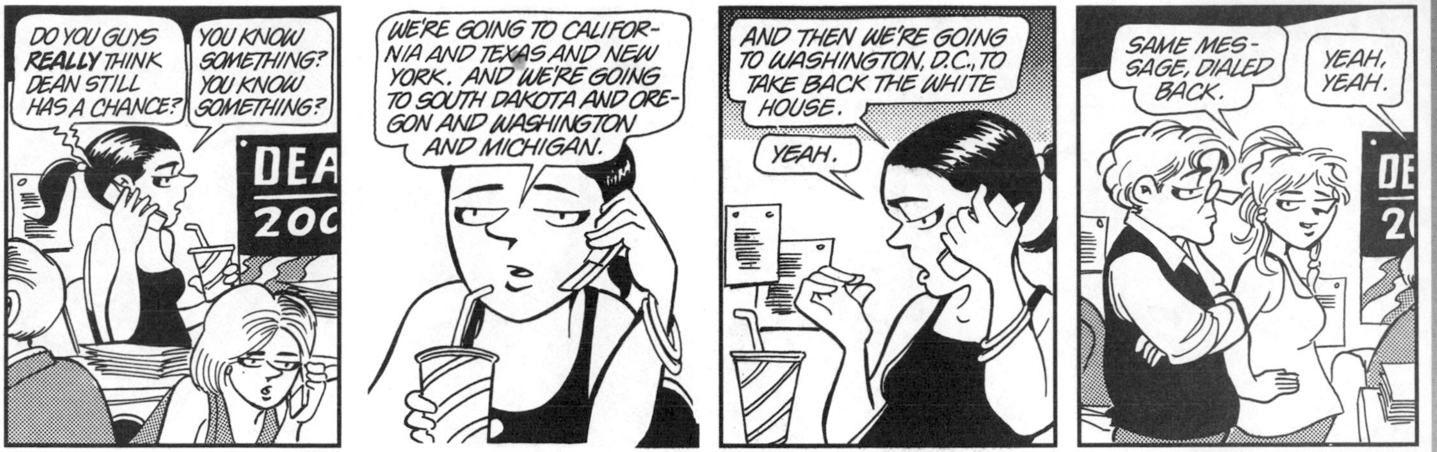
DO YOU GUYS REALLY THINK DEAN STILL HAS A CHANCE?
YOU KNOW SOMETHING? YOU KNOW SOMETHING?
DEA 200
WE'RE GOING TO CALIFORNIA AND TEXAS AND NEW YORK. AND WE'RE GOING TO SOUTH DAKOTA AND OREGON AND WASHINGTON AND MICHIGAN.
AND THEN WE'RE GOING TO WASHINGTON, D.C., TO TAKE BACK THE WHITE HOUSE.
YEAH.
SAME MESSAGE, DIALED BACK.
YEAH, YEAH.

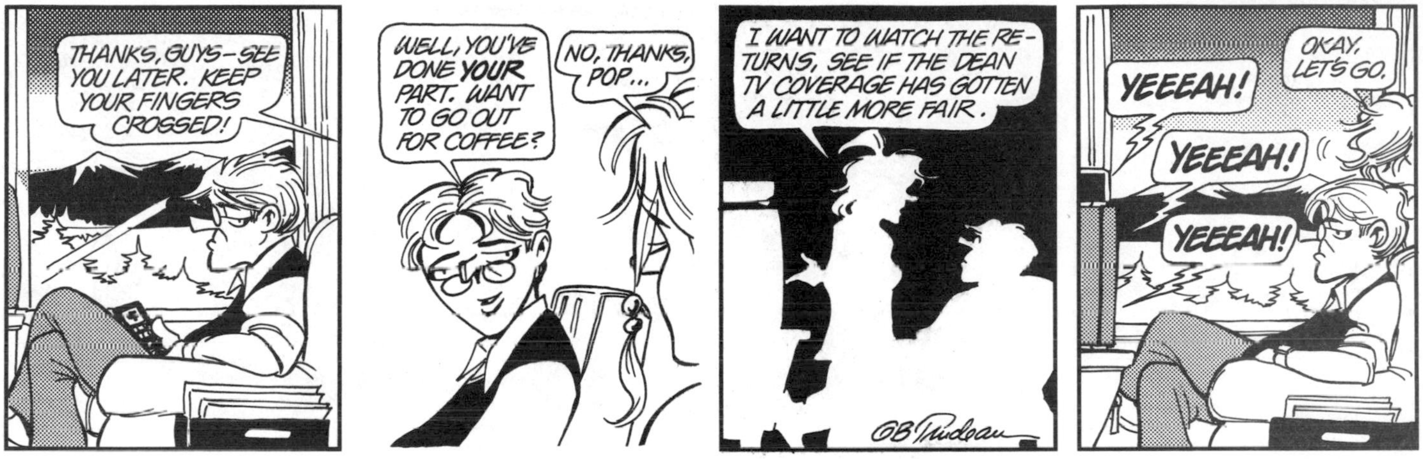
THANKS, GUYS—SEE YOU LATER. KEEP YOUR FINGERS CROSSED!
WELL, YOU'VE DONE YOUR PART. WANT TO GO OUT FOR COFFEE?
NO, THANKS, POP...
I WANT TO WATCH THE RETURNS, SEE IF THE DEAN TV COVERAGE HAS GOTTEN A LITTLE MORE FAIR.
YEEEAH!
YEEEAH!
YEEEAH!
OKAY, LET'S GO.

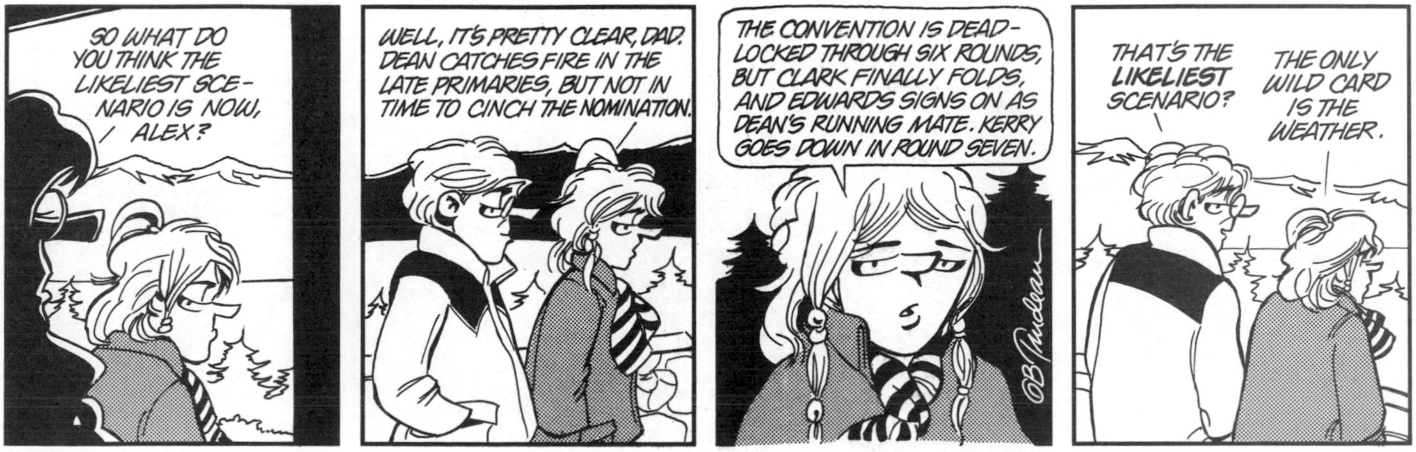
SO WHAT DO YOU THINK THE LIKELIEST SCENARIO IS NOW, ALEX?
WELL, IT'S PRETTY CLEAR, DAD. DEAN CATCHES FIRE IN THE LATE PRIMARIES, BUT NOT IN TIME TO CINCH THE NOMINATION.
THE CONVENTION IS DEADLOCKED THROUGH SIX ROUNDS, BUT CLARK FINALLY FOLDS, AND EDWARDS SIGNS ON AS DEAN'S RUNNING MATE. KERRY GOES DOWN IN ROUND SEVEN.
THAT'S THE LIKELIEST SCENARIO?
THE ONLY WILD CARD IS THE WEATHER.

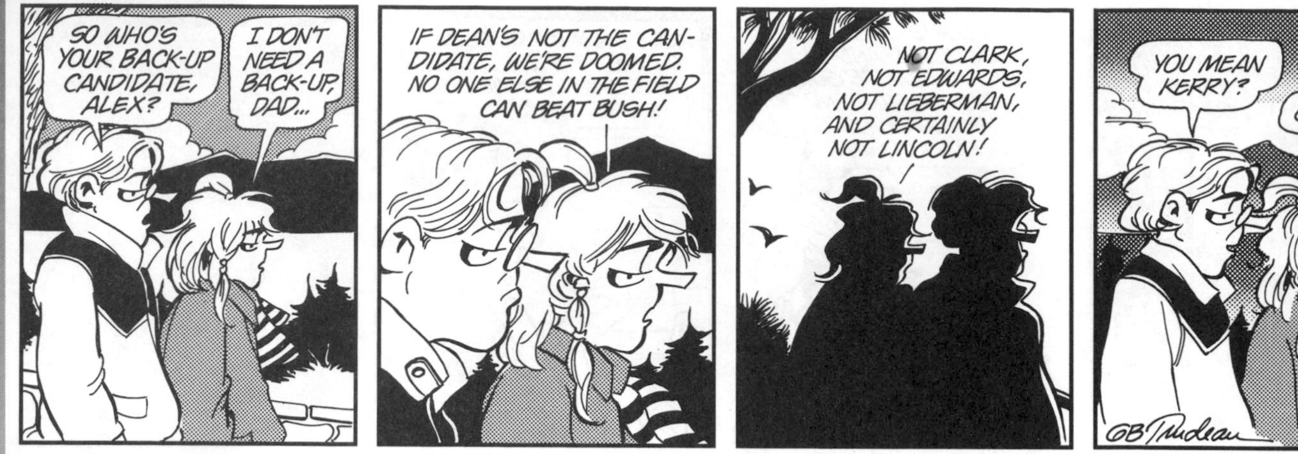
SO WHO'S YOUR BACK-UP CANDIDATE, ALEX?
I DON'T NEED A BACK-UP, DAD...
IF DEAN'S NOT THE CANDIDATE, WE'RE DOOMED. NO ONE ELSE IN THE FIELD CAN BEAT BUSH!
NOT CLARK, NOT EDWARDS, NOT LIEBERMAN, AND CERTAINLY NOT LINCOLN!
YOU MEAN KERRY?
GREAT.

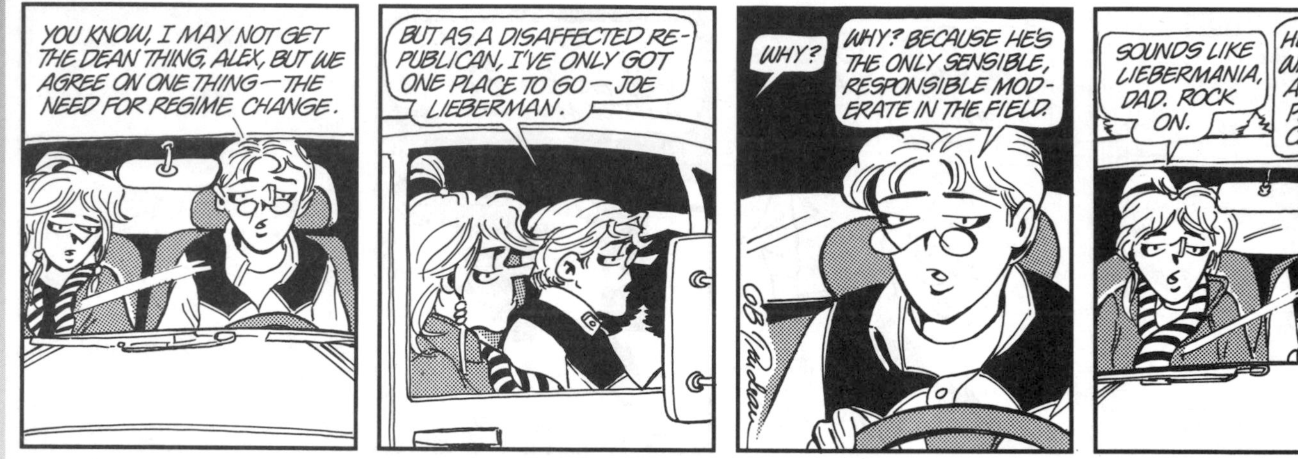
YOU KNOW, I MAY NOT GET THE DEAN THING, ALEX, BUT WE AGREE ON ONE THING—THE NEED FOR REGIME CHANGE.
BUT AS A DISAFFECTED REPUBLICAN, I'VE ONLY GOT ONE PLACE TO GO—JOE LIEBERMAN.
WHY?
WHY? BECAUSE HE'S THE ONLY SENSIBLE, RESPONSIBLE MODERATE IN THE FIELD.
SOUNDS LIKE LIEBERMANIA, DAD. ROCK ON.
HEY, WHAT'S WRONG WITH AN AGE-APPROPRIATE CANDIDATE?

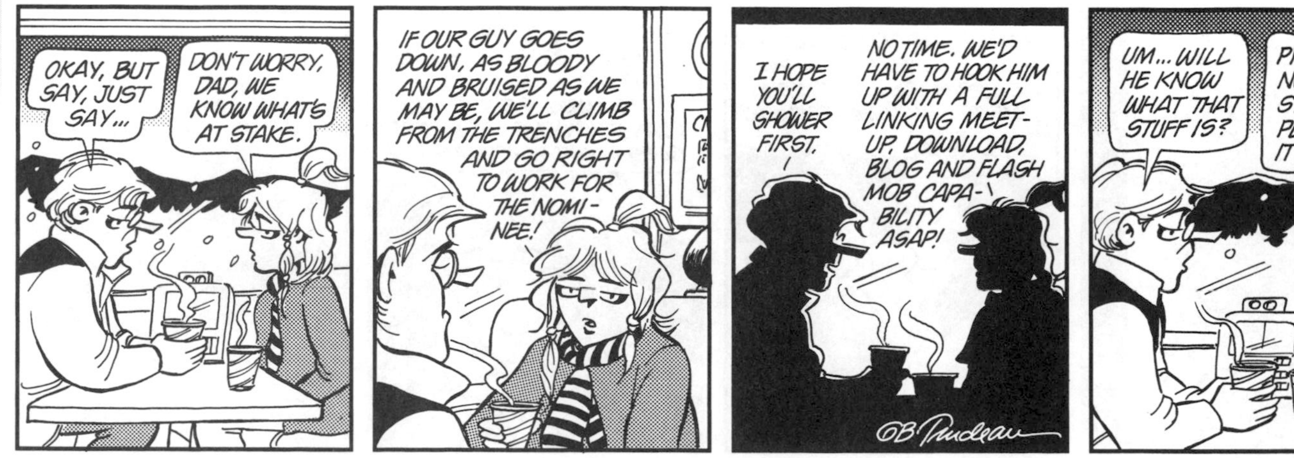
OKAY, BUT SAY, JUST SAY...
DON'T WORRY, DAD, WE KNOW WHAT'S AT STAKE.
IF OUR GUY GOES DOWN, AS BLOODY AND BRUISED AS WE MAY BE, WE'LL CLIMB FROM THE TRENCHES AND GO RIGHT TO WORK FOR THE NOMINEE!
I HOPE YOU'LL SHOWER FIRST.
NO TIME. WE'D HAVE TO HOOK HIM UP WITH A FULL LINKING MEET-UP, DOWNLOAD, BLOG AND FLASH MOB CAPABILITY ASAP!
UM... WILL HE KNOW WHAT THAT STUFF IS?
PROBABLY NOT. WE'RE STILL EXPLAINING IT TO DEAN.

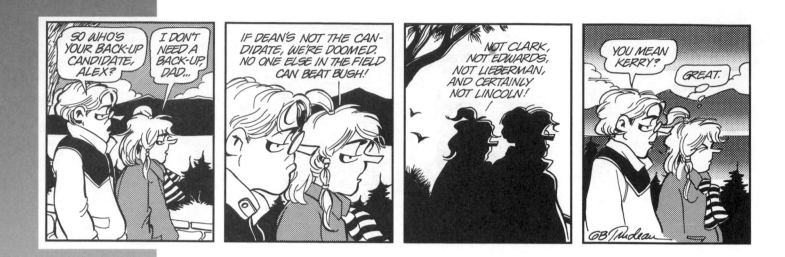

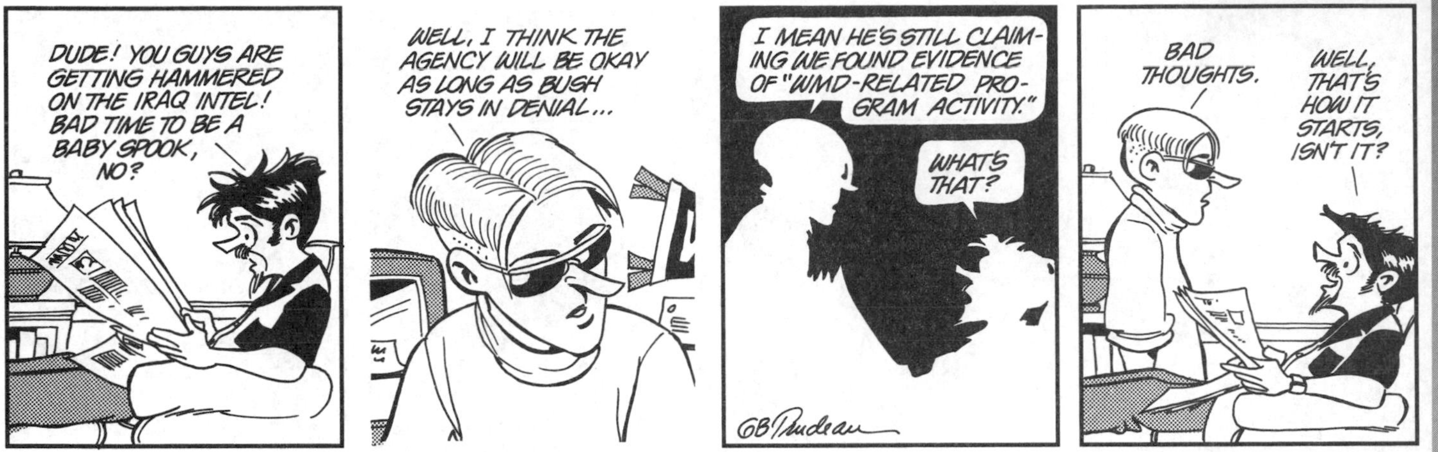
DUDE! YOU GUYS ARE GETTING HAMMERED ON THE IRAQ INTEL! BAD TIME TO BE A BABY SPOOK, NO?
WELL, I THINK THE AGENCY WILL BE OKAY AS LONG AS BUSH STAYS IN DENIAL...
I MEAN HE'S STILL CLAIMING WE FOUND EVIDENCE OF "WMD-RELATED PROGRAM ACTIVITY."
WHAT'S THAT?
BAD THOUGHTS.
WELL, THAT'S HOW IT STARTS, ISN'T IT?
GB Trudeau

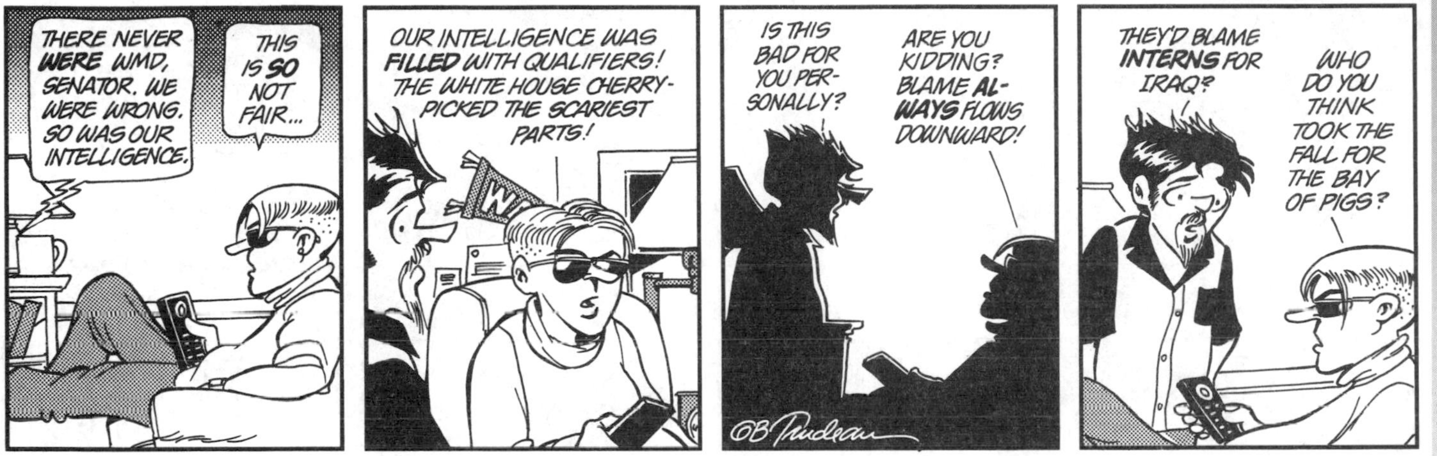
THERE NEVER **WERE** WMD, SENATOR. WE WERE WRONG. SO WAS OUR INTELLIGENCE.
THIS IS **SO** NOT FAIR...
OUR INTELLIGENCE WAS **FILLED** WITH QUALIFIERS! THE WHITE HOUSE CHERRY-PICKED THE **SCARIEST** PARTS!
IS THIS BAD FOR YOU PERSONALLY?
ARE YOU KIDDING? BLAME **ALWAYS** FLOWS DOWNWARD!
THEY'D BLAME **INTERNS** FOR IRAQ?
WHO DO YOU THINK TOOK THE FALL FOR THE BAY OF PIGS?
GB Trudeau

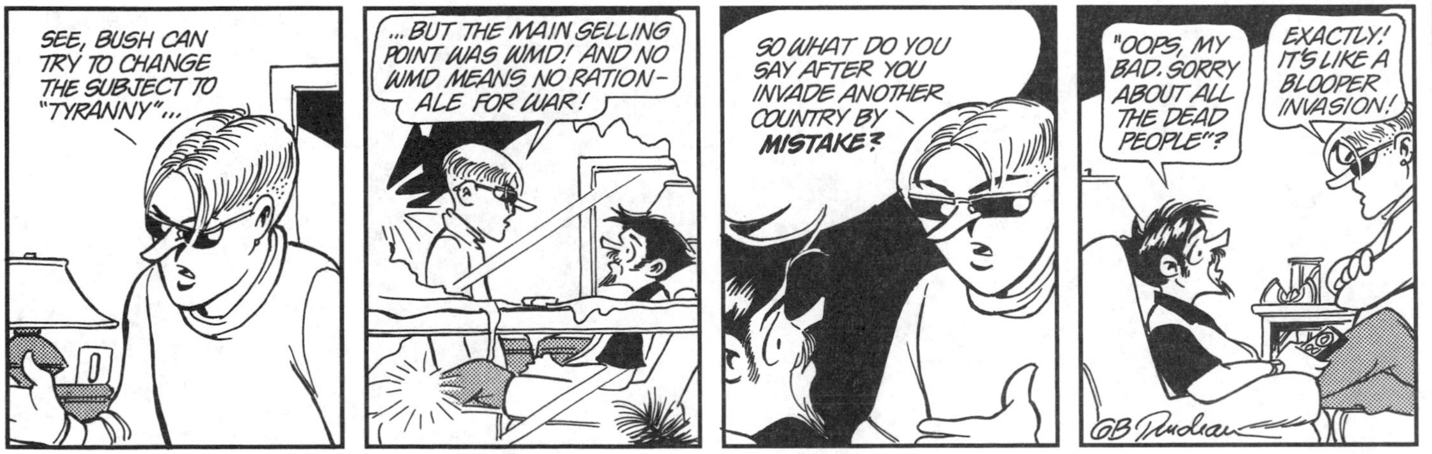
SEE, BUSH CAN TRY TO CHANGE THE SUBJECT TO "TYRANNY"...
...BUT THE MAIN SELLING POINT WAS WMD! AND NO WMD MEANS NO RATIONALE FOR WAR!
SO WHAT DO YOU SAY AFTER YOU INVADE ANOTHER COUNTRY BY **MISTAKE**?
"OOPS, MY BAD. SORRY ABOUT ALL THE DEAD PEOPLE"?
EXACTLY! IT'S LIKE A BLOOPER INVASION!
GB Trudeau

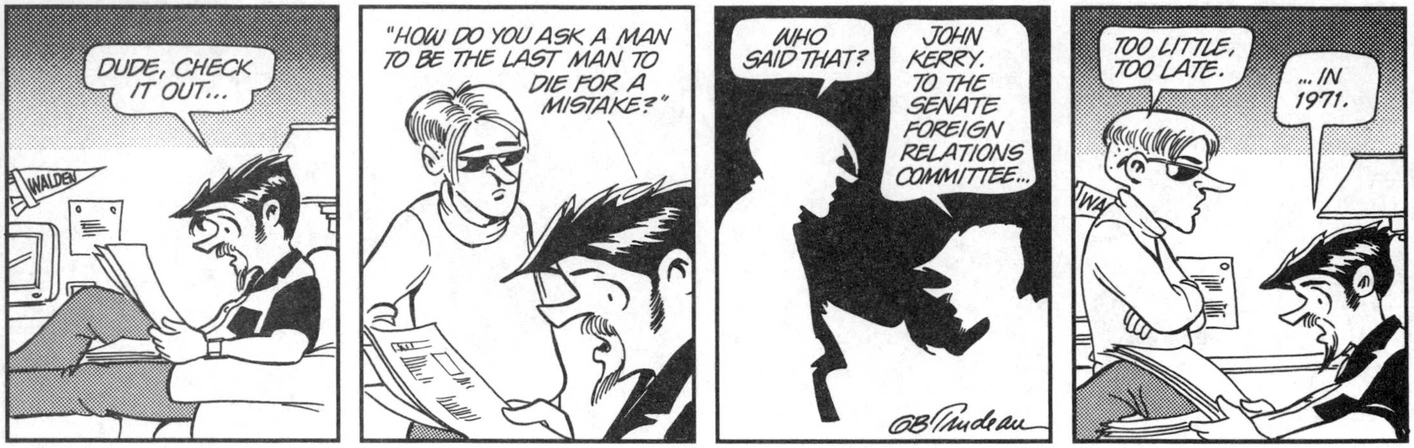
DUDE, CHECK IT OUT...
WALDEN
"HOW DO YOU ASK A MAN TO BE THE LAST MAN TO DIE FOR A MISTAKE?"
WHO SAID THAT?
JOHN KERRY. TO THE SENATE FOREIGN RELATIONS COMMITTEE...
©B Trudeau
TOO LITTLE, TOO LATE.
...IN 1971.

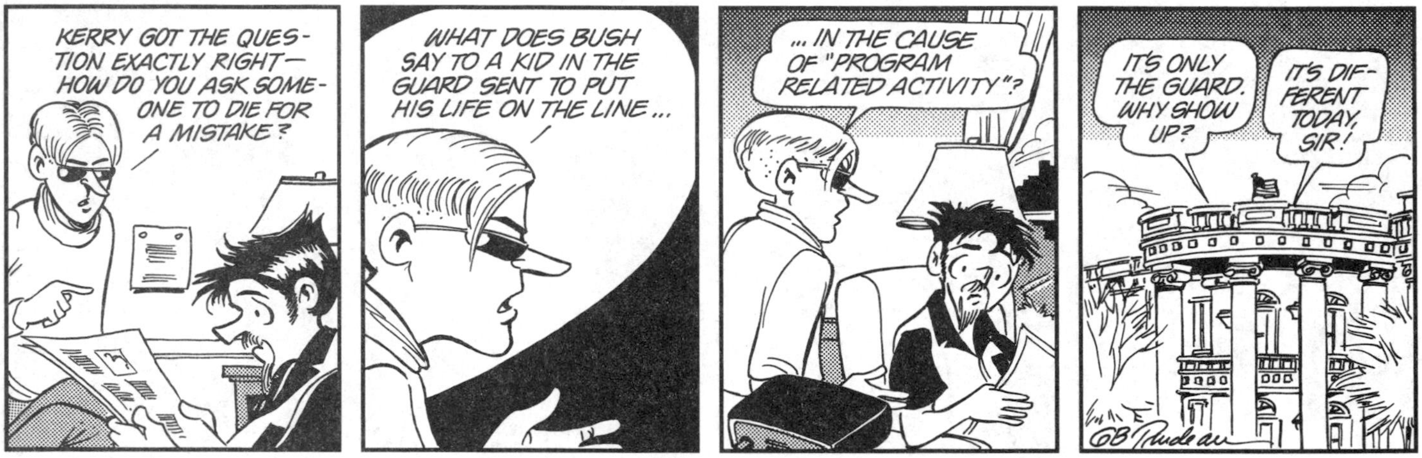
KERRY GOT THE QUESTION EXACTLY RIGHT—HOW DO YOU ASK SOMEONE TO DIE FOR A MISTAKE?
WHAT DOES BUSH SAY TO A KID IN THE GUARD SENT TO PUT HIS LIFE ON THE LINE...
...IN THE CAUSE OF "PROGRAM RELATED ACTIVITY"?
IT'S ONLY THE GUARD. WHY SHOW UP?
IT'S DIFFERENT TODAY, SIR!
©B Trudeau

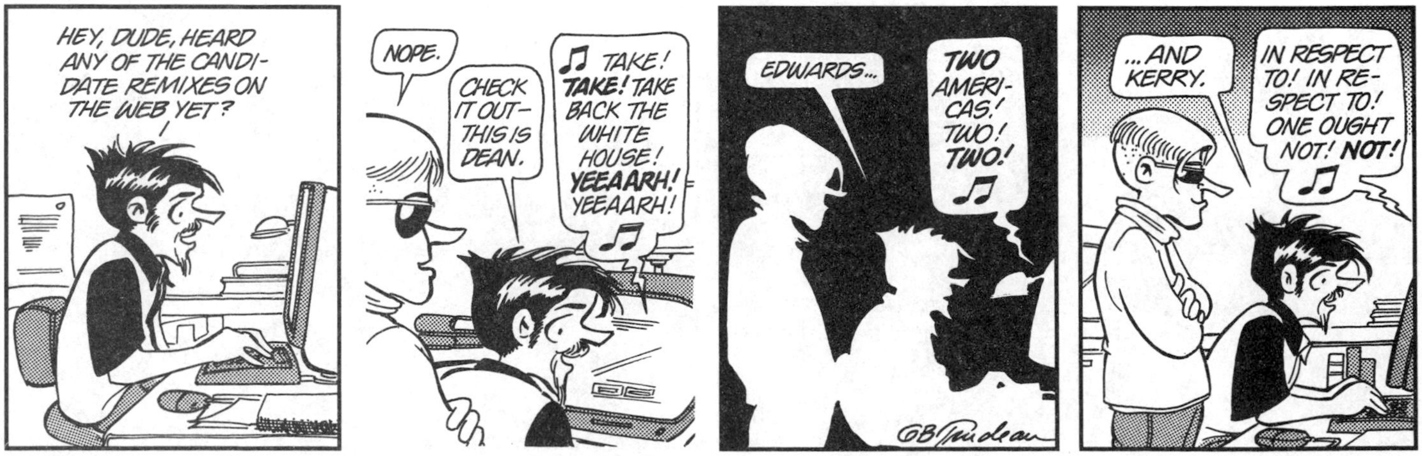
HEY, DUDE, HEARD ANY OF THE CANDIDATE REMIXES ON THE WEB YET?
NOPE.
CHECK IT OUT—THIS IS DEAN.
♫ TAKE! TAKE! TAKE BACK THE WHITE HOUSE! YEEAARH! YEEAARH!
♫
EDWARDS...
TWO AMERICAS! TWO! TWO!
♫
©B Trudeau
...AND KERRY.
IN RESPECT TO! IN RESPECT TO! ONE OUGHT NOT! NOT!
♫

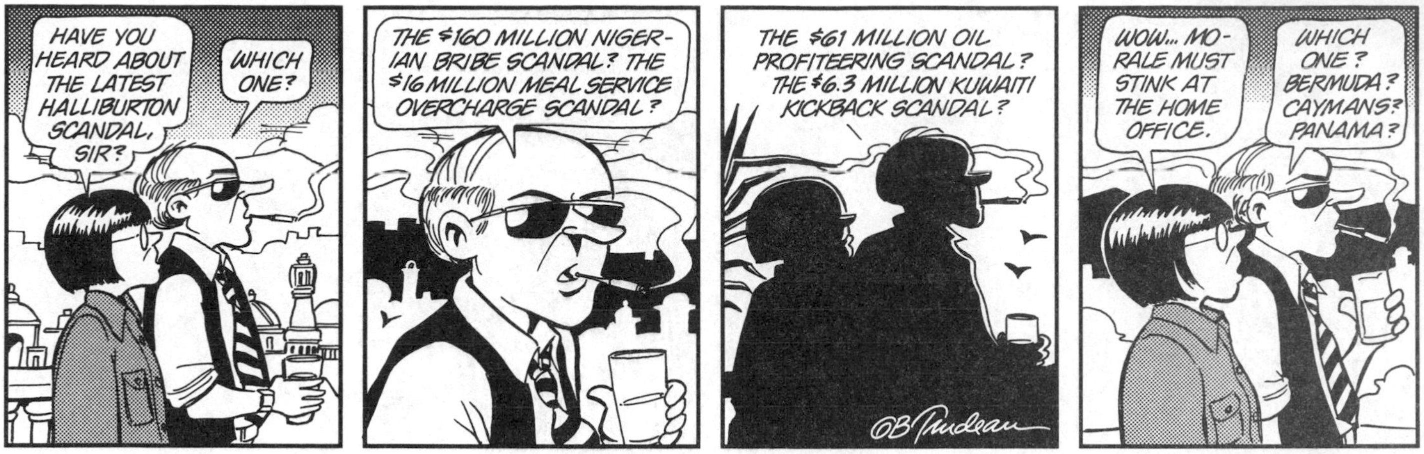
HAVE YOU HEARD ABOUT THE LATEST HALLIBURTON SCANDAL, SIR?
WHICH ONE?
THE $160 MILLION NIGERIAN BRIBE SCANDAL? THE $16 MILLION MEAL SERVICE OVERCHARGE SCANDAL?
THE $61 MILLION OIL PROFITEERING SCANDAL? THE $6.3 MILLION KUWAITI KICKBACK SCANDAL?
©B Trudeau
WOW... MORALE MUST STINK AT THE HOME OFFICE.
WHICH ONE? BERMUDA? CAYMANS? PANAMA?

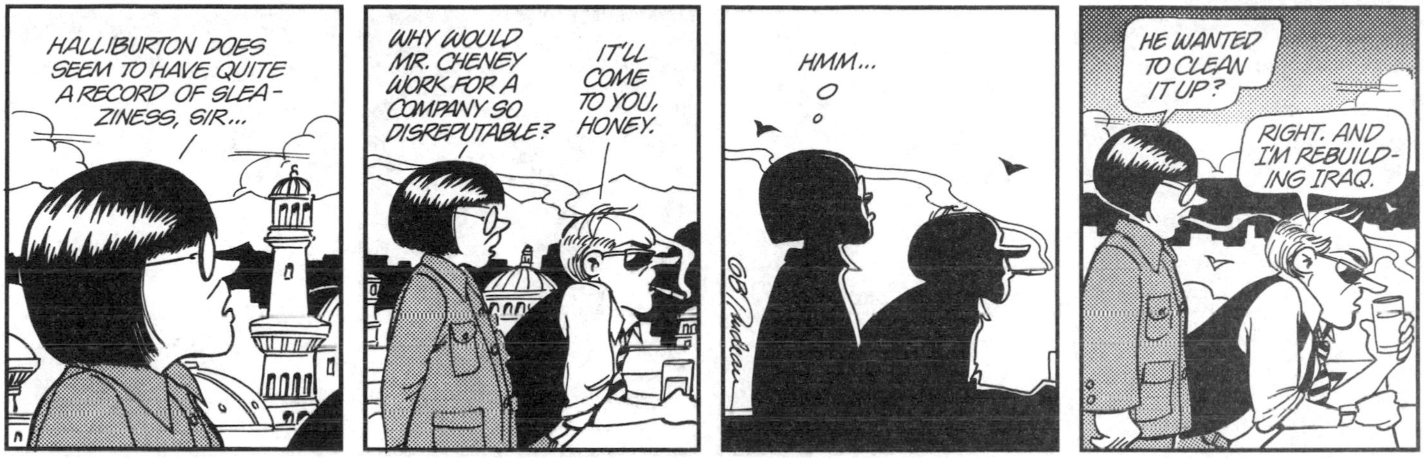
HALLIBURTON DOES SEEM TO HAVE QUITE A RECORD OF SLEAZINESS, SIR...
WHY WOULD MR. CHENEY WORK FOR A COMPANY SO DISREPUTABLE?
IT'LL COME TO YOU, HONEY.
©B Trudeau
HMM...
HE WANTED TO CLEAN IT UP?
RIGHT. AND I'M REBUILDING IRAQ.

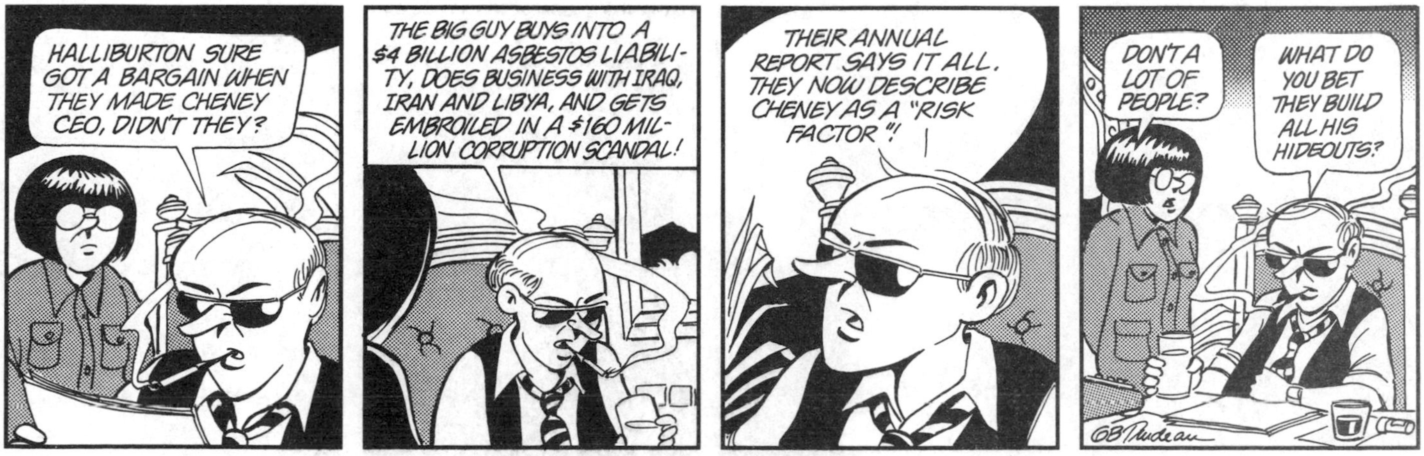
HALLIBURTON SURE GOT A BARGAIN WHEN THEY MADE CHENEY CEO, DIDN'T THEY?
THE BIG GUY BUYS INTO A $4 BILLION ASBESTOS LIABILITY, DOES BUSINESS WITH IRAQ, IRAN AND LIBYA, AND GETS EMBROILED IN A $160 MILLION CORRUPTION SCANDAL!
THEIR ANNUAL REPORT SAYS IT ALL. THEY NOW DESCRIBE CHENEY AS A "RISK FACTOR"!
DON'T A LOT OF PEOPLE?
WHAT DO YOU BET THEY BUILD ALL HIS HIDEOUTS?
©B Trudeau

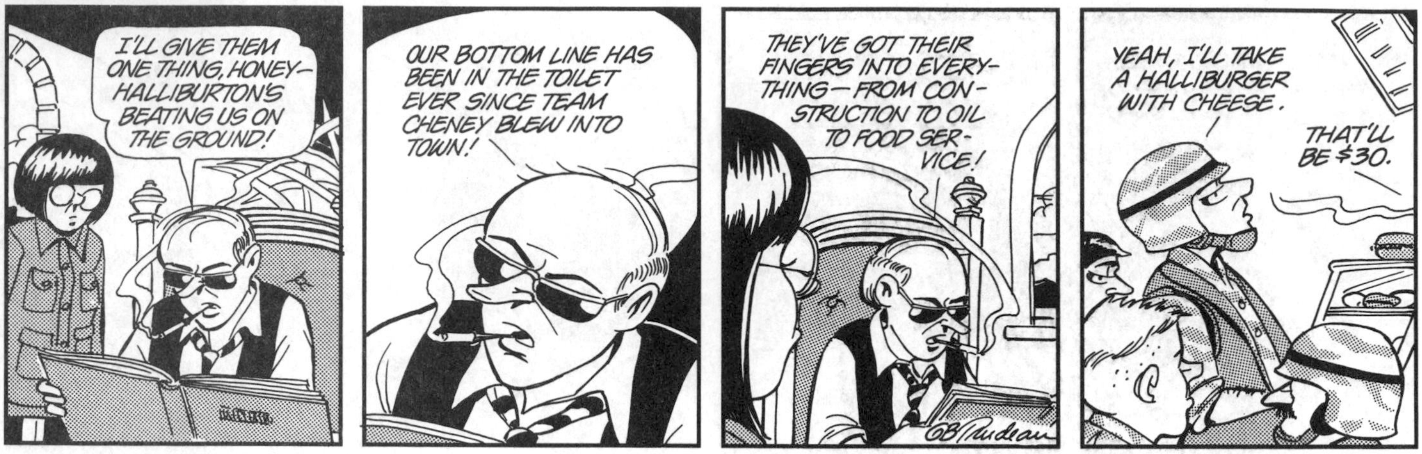
I'LL GIVE THEM ONE THING, HONEY—HALLIBURTON'S BEATING US ON THE GROUND!
OUR BOTTOM LINE HAS BEEN IN THE TOILET EVER SINCE TEAM CHENEY BLEW INTO TOWN!
THEY'VE GOT THEIR FINGERS INTO EVERYTHING—FROM CONSTRUCTION TO OIL TO FOOD SERVICE!
YEAH, I'LL TAKE A HALLIBURGER WITH CHEESE.
THAT'LL BE $30.

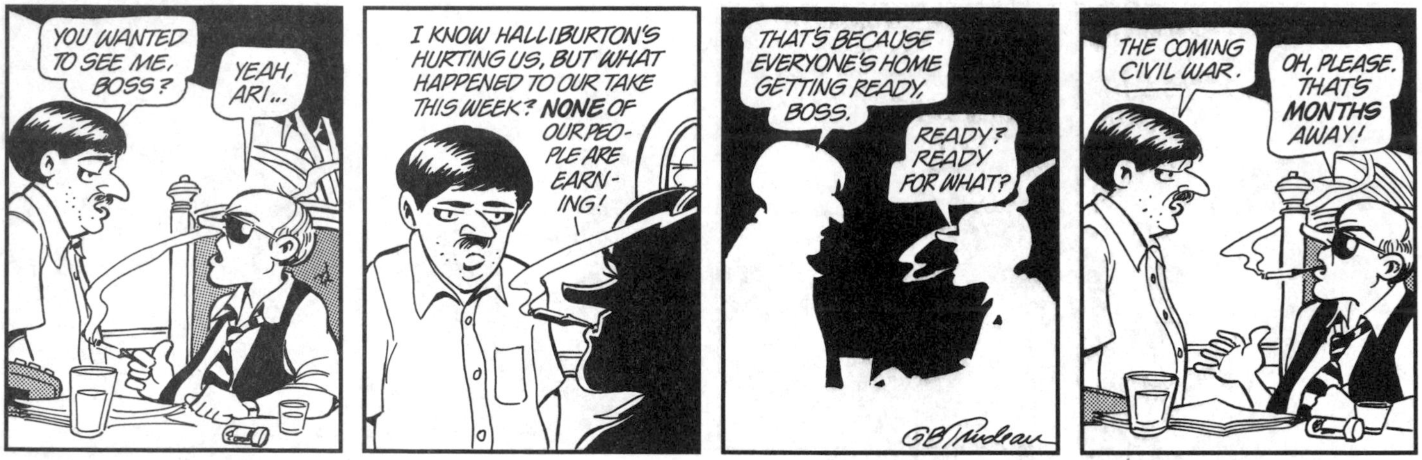
YOU WANTED TO SEE ME, BOSS?
YEAH, ARI...
I KNOW HALLIBURTON'S HURTING US, BUT WHAT HAPPENED TO OUR TAKE THIS WEEK? NONE OF OUR PEOPLE ARE EARNING!
THAT'S BECAUSE EVERYONE'S HOME GETTING READY, BOSS.
READY? READY FOR WHAT?
THE COMING CIVIL WAR.
OH, PLEASE. THAT'S MONTHS AWAY!

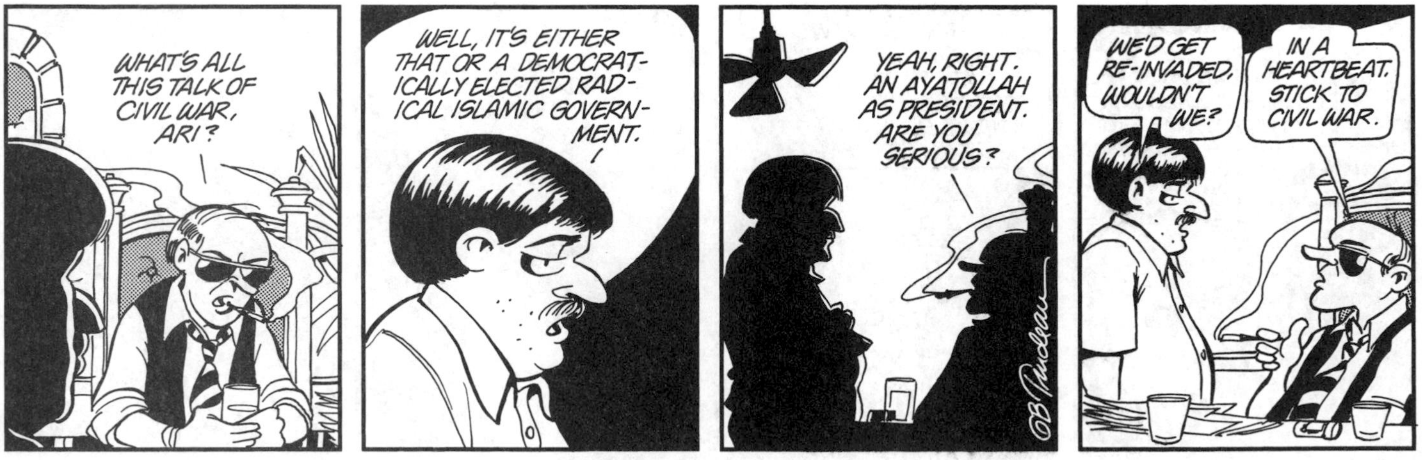
WHAT'S ALL THIS TALK OF CIVIL WAR, ARI?
WELL, IT'S EITHER THAT OR A DEMOCRATICALLY ELECTED RADICAL ISLAMIC GOVERNMENT.
YEAH, RIGHT. AN AYATOLLAH AS PRESIDENT. ARE YOU SERIOUS?
WE'D GET RE-INVADED, WOULDN'T WE?
IN A HEARTBEAT. STICK TO CIVIL WAR.

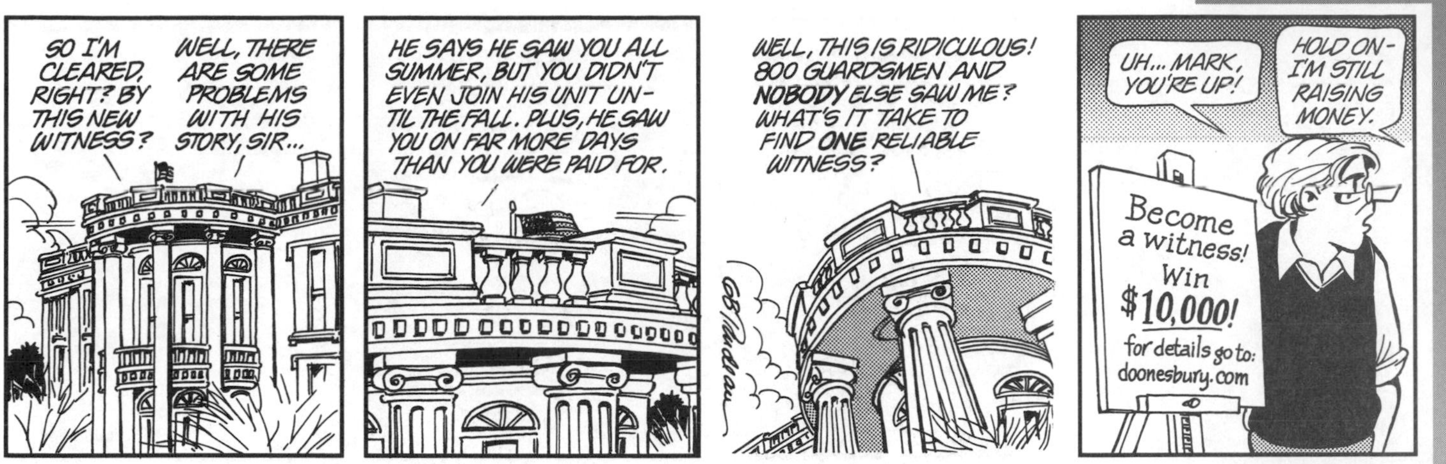
SO I'M CLEARED, RIGHT? BY THIS NEW WITNESS?
WELL, THERE ARE SOME PROBLEMS WITH HIS STORY, SIR...
HE SAYS HE SAW YOU ALL SUMMER, BUT YOU DIDN'T EVEN JOIN HIS UNIT UNTIL THE FALL. PLUS, HE SAW YOU ON FAR MORE DAYS THAN YOU WERE PAID FOR.
WELL, THIS IS RIDICULOUS! 800 GUARDSMEN AND NOBODY ELSE SAW ME? WHAT'S IT TAKE TO FIND ONE RELIABLE WITNESS?
UH... MARK, YOU'RE UP!
HOLD ON—I'M STILL RAISING MONEY.
Become a witness! Win $10,000! for details go to: doonesbury.com

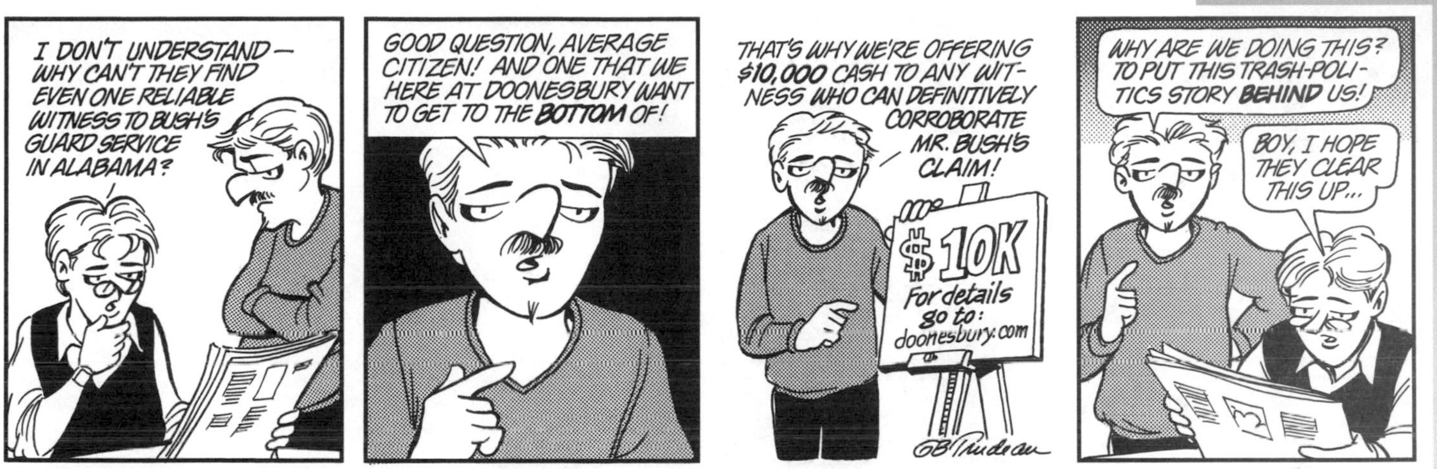
I DON'T UNDERSTAND—WHY CAN'T THEY FIND EVEN ONE RELIABLE WITNESS TO BUSH'S GUARD SERVICE IN ALABAMA?
GOOD QUESTION, AVERAGE CITIZEN! AND ONE THAT WE HERE AT DOONESBURY WANT TO GET TO THE BOTTOM OF!
THAT'S WHY WE'RE OFFERING $10,000 CASH TO ANY WITNESS WHO CAN DEFINITIVELY CORROBORATE MR. BUSH'S CLAIM!
$10K For details go to: doonesbury.com
WHY ARE WE DOING THIS? TO PUT THIS TRASH-POLITICS STORY BEHIND US!
BOY, I HOPE THEY CLEAR THIS UP...

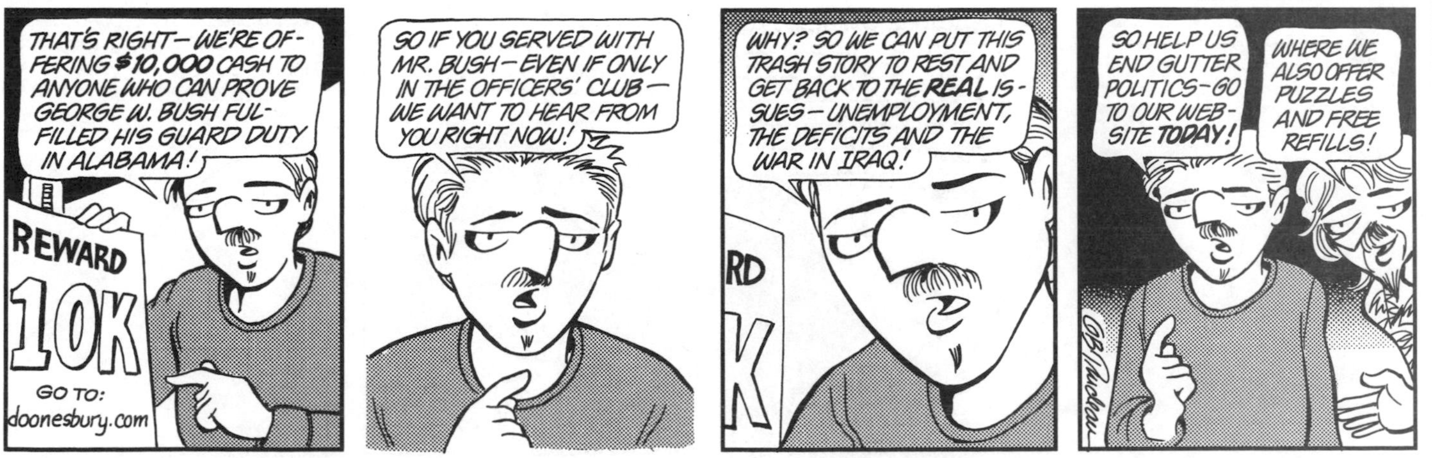
THAT'S RIGHT—WE'RE OFFERING $10,000 CASH TO ANYONE WHO CAN PROVE GEORGE W. BUSH FULFILLED HIS GUARD DUTY IN ALABAMA!
REWARD 10K GO TO: doonesbury.com
SO IF YOU SERVED WITH MR. BUSH—EVEN IF ONLY IN THE OFFICERS' CLUB—WE WANT TO HEAR FROM YOU RIGHT NOW!
WHY? SO WE CAN PUT THIS TRASH STORY TO REST AND GET BACK TO THE REAL ISSUES—UNEMPLOYMENT, THE DEFICITS AND THE WAR IN IRAQ!
SO HELP US END GUTTER POLITICS—GO TO OUR WEBSITE TODAY!
WHERE WE ALSO OFFER PUZZLES AND FREE REFILLS!

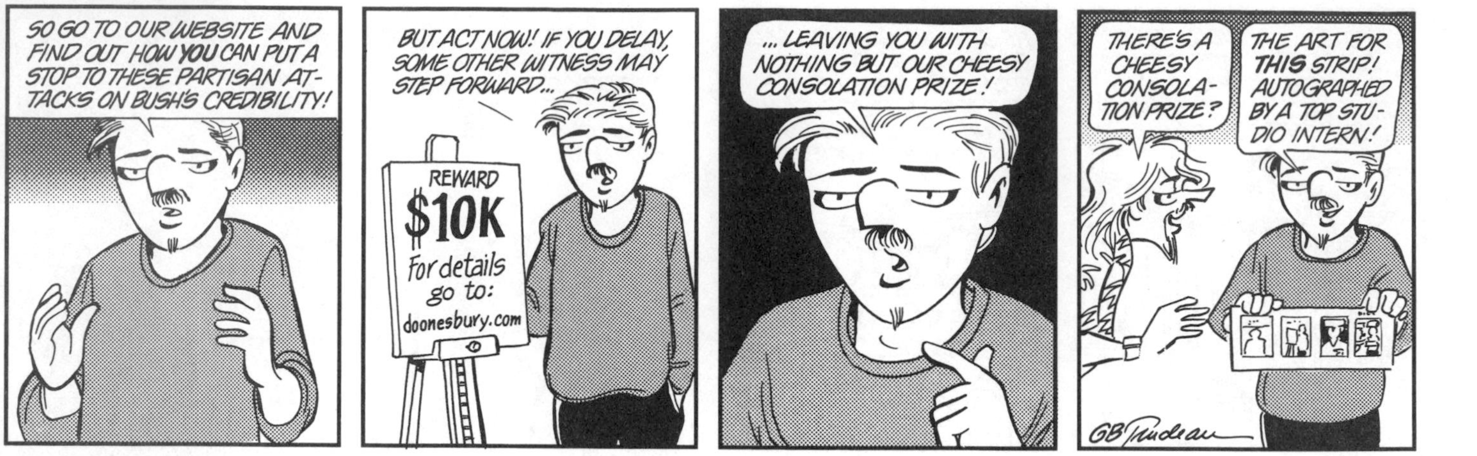
SO GO TO OUR WEBSITE AND FIND OUT HOW YOU CAN PUT A STOP TO THESE PARTISAN ATTACKS ON BUSH'S CREDIBILITY!
BUT ACT NOW! IF YOU DELAY, SOME OTHER WITNESS MAY STEP FORWARD...
REWARD
$10K
For details go to:
doonesbury.com
...LEAVING YOU WITH NOTHING BUT OUR CHEESY CONSOLATION PRIZE!
THERE'S A CHEESY CONSOLATION PRIZE?
THE ART FOR THIS STRIP! AUTOGRAPHED BY A TOP STUDIO INTERN!
GB Trudeau

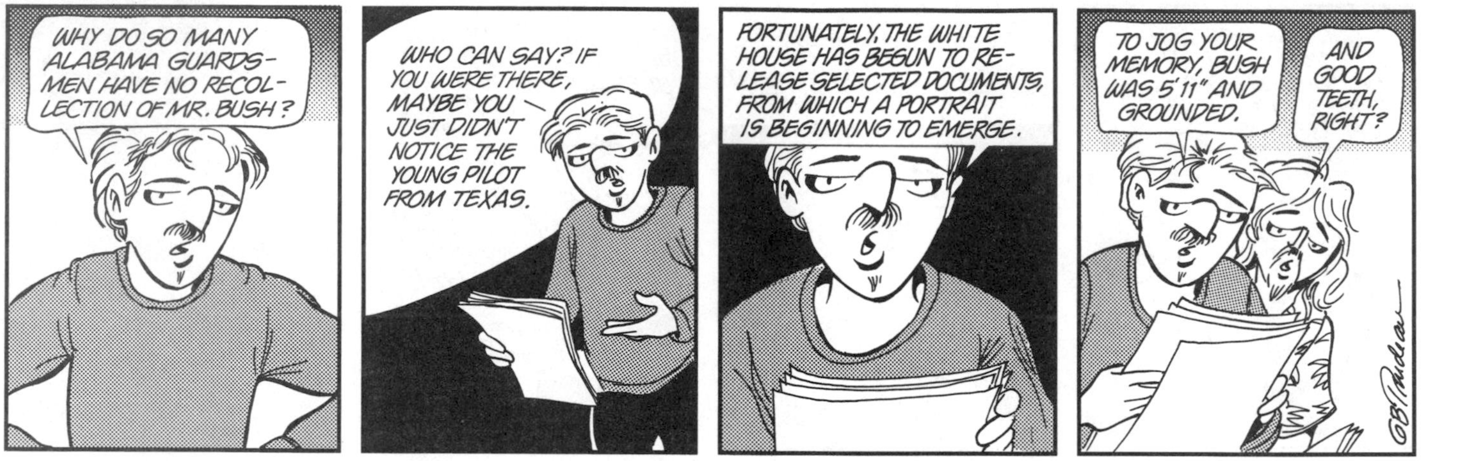
WHY DO SO MANY ALABAMA GUARDSMEN HAVE NO RECOLLECTION OF MR. BUSH?
WHO CAN SAY? IF YOU WERE THERE, MAYBE YOU JUST DIDN'T NOTICE THE YOUNG PILOT FROM TEXAS.
FORTUNATELY, THE WHITE HOUSE HAS BEGUN TO RELEASE SELECTED DOCUMENTS, FROM WHICH A PORTRAIT IS BEGINNING TO EMERGE.
TO JOG YOUR MEMORY, BUSH WAS 5'11" AND GROUNDED.
AND GOOD TEETH, RIGHT?
GB Trudeau

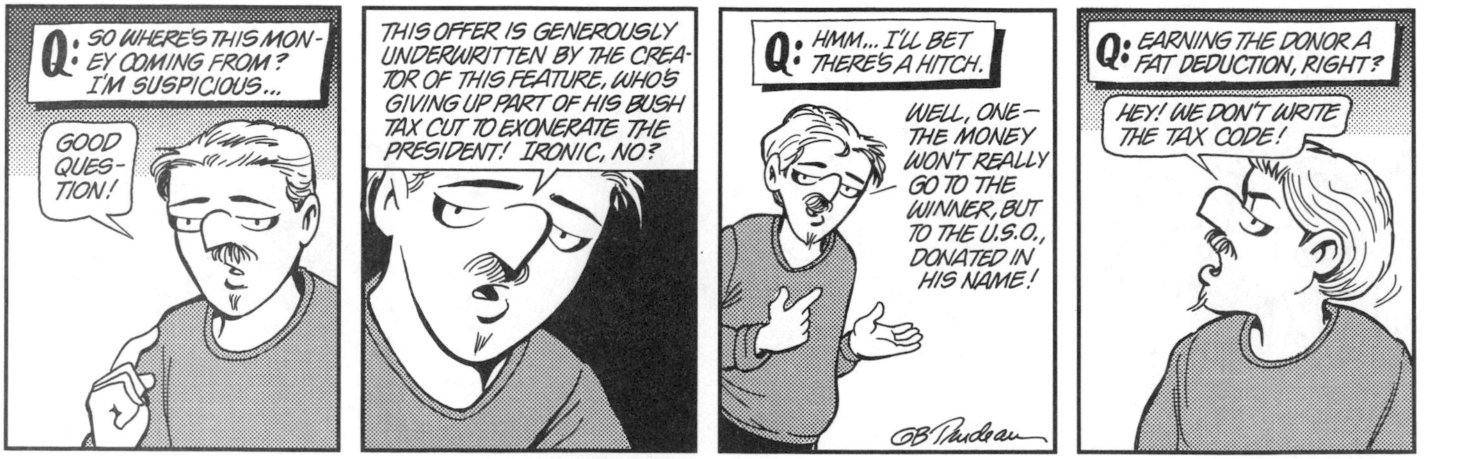
Q: SO WHERE'S THIS MONEY COMING FROM? I'M SUSPICIOUS...
GOOD QUESTION!
THIS OFFER IS GENEROUSLY UNDERWRITTEN BY THE CREATOR OF THIS FEATURE, WHO'S GIVING UP PART OF HIS BUSH TAX CUT TO EXONERATE THE PRESIDENT! IRONIC, NO?
Q: HMM... I'LL BET THERE'S A HITCH.
WELL, ONE — THE MONEY WON'T REALLY GO TO THE WINNER, BUT TO THE U.S.O., DONATED IN HIS NAME!
GB Trudeau
Q: EARNING THE DONOR A FAT DEDUCTION, RIGHT?
HEY! WE DON'T WRITE THE TAX CODE!

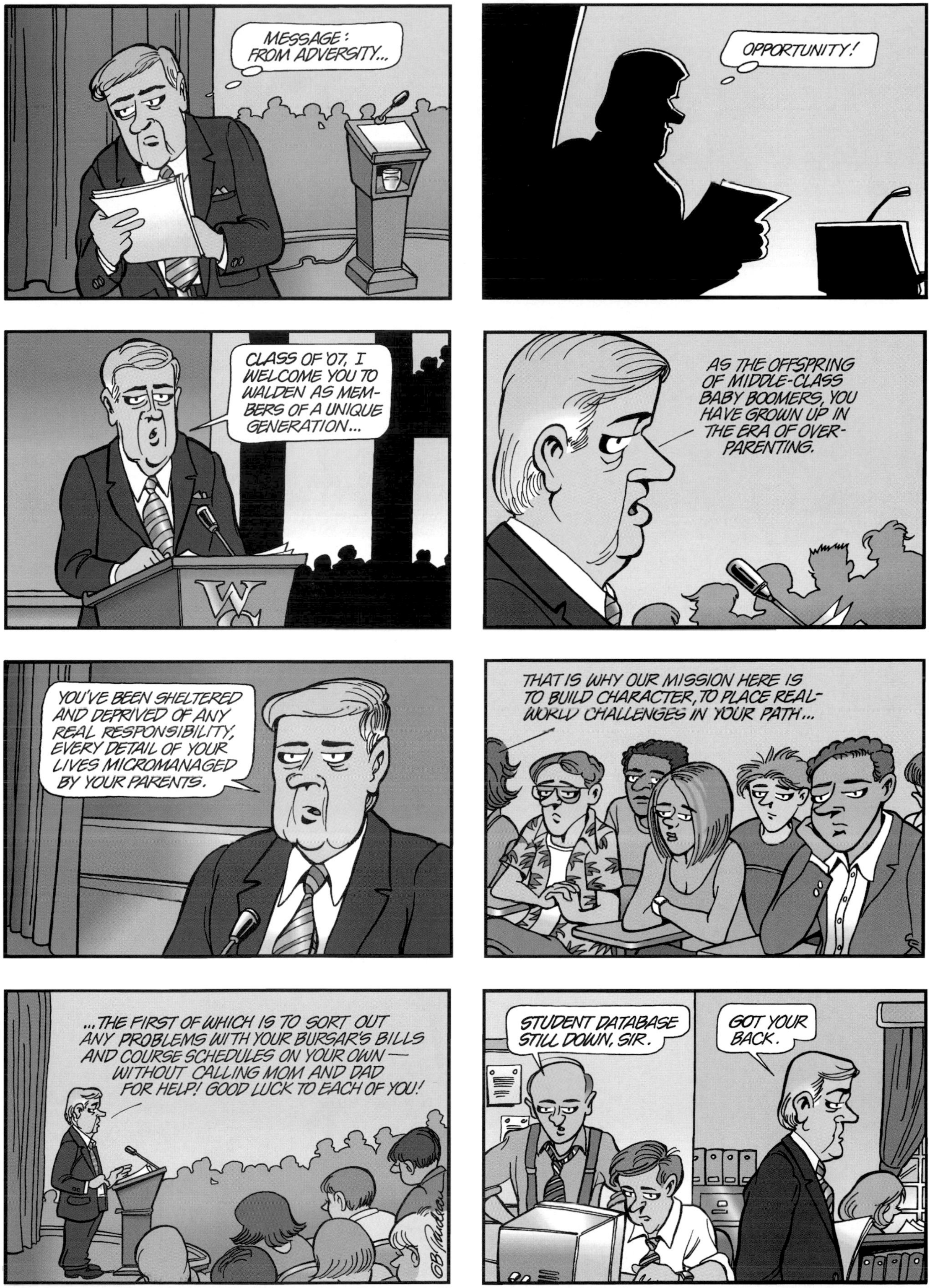
MESSAGE: FROM ADVERSITY...
OPPORTUNITY!
CLASS OF '07, I WELCOME YOU TO WALDEN AS MEMBERS OF A UNIQUE GENERATION...
AS THE OFFSPRING OF MIDDLE-CLASS BABY BOOMERS, YOU HAVE GROWN UP IN THE ERA OF OVER-PARENTING.
YOU'VE BEEN SHELTERED AND DEPRIVED OF ANY REAL RESPONSIBILITY, EVERY DETAIL OF YOUR LIVES MICROMANAGED BY YOUR PARENTS.
THAT IS WHY OUR MISSION HERE IS TO BUILD CHARACTER, TO PLACE REAL-WORLD CHALLENGES IN YOUR PATH...
...THE FIRST OF WHICH IS TO SORT OUT ANY PROBLEMS WITH YOUR BURSAR'S BILLS AND COURSE SCHEDULES ON YOUR OWN— WITHOUT CALLING MOM AND DAD FOR HELP! GOOD LUCK TO EACH OF YOU!
©B. Trudeau
STUDENT DATABASE STILL DOWN, SIR.
GOT YOUR BACK.

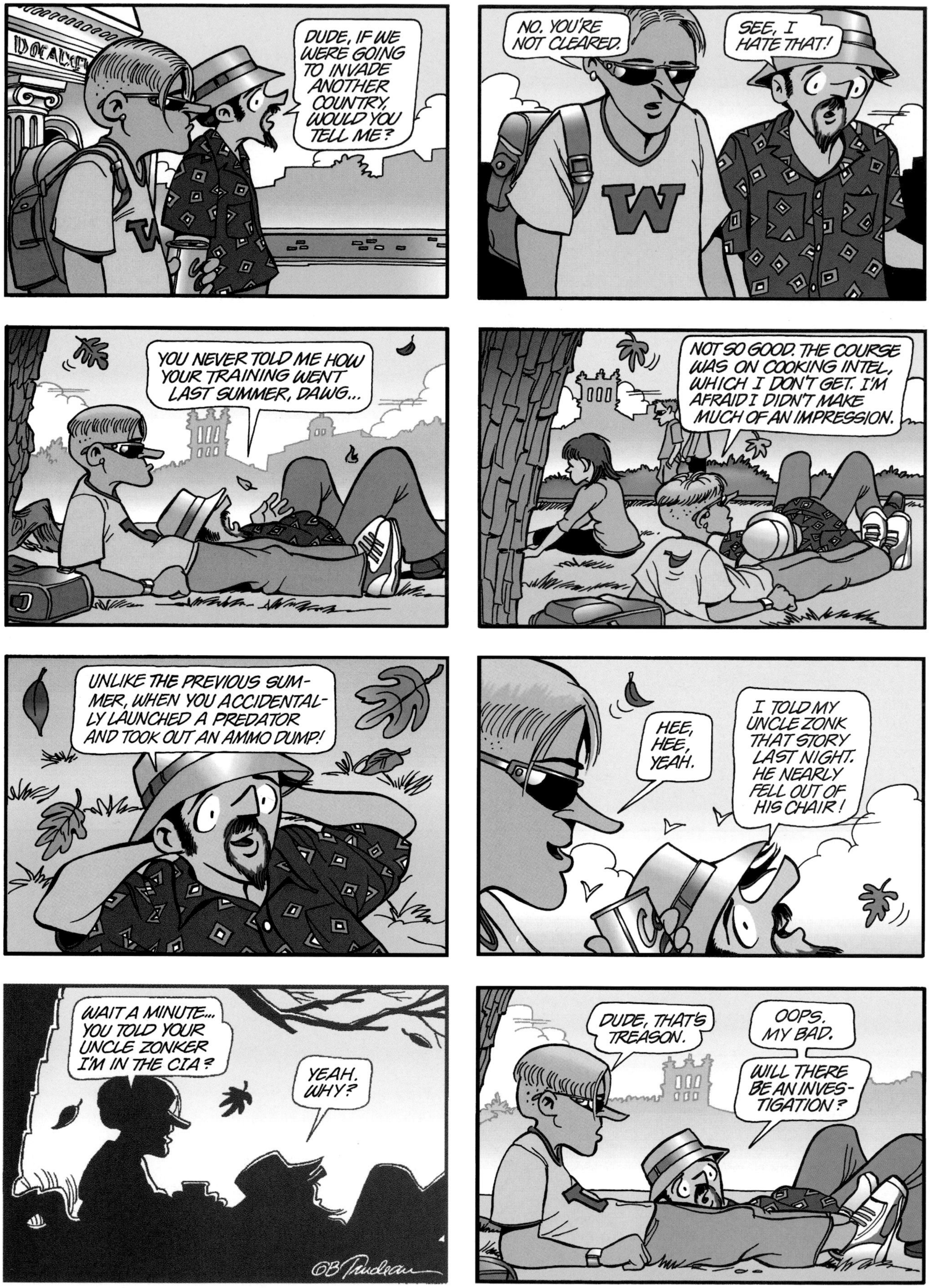
DUDE, IF WE WERE GOING TO INVADE ANOTHER COUNTRY, WOULD YOU TELL ME?
NO. YOU'RE NOT CLEARED.
SEE, I HATE THAT!
YOU NEVER TOLD ME HOW YOUR TRAINING WENT LAST SUMMER, DAWG...
NOT SO GOOD. THE COURSE WAS ON COOKING INTEL, WHICH I DON'T GET. I'M AFRAID I DIDN'T MAKE MUCH OF AN IMPRESSION.
UNLIKE THE PREVIOUS SUMMER, WHEN YOU ACCIDENTALLY LAUNCHED A PREDATOR AND TOOK OUT AN AMMO DUMP!
HEE, HEE, YEAH.
I TOLD MY UNCLE ZONK THAT STORY LAST NIGHT. HE NEARLY FELL OUT OF HIS CHAIR!
WAIT A MINUTE... YOU TOLD YOUR UNCLE ZONKER I'M IN THE CIA?
YEAH. WHY?
DUDE, THAT'S TREASON.
OOPS. MY BAD.
WILL THERE BE AN INVESTIGATION?
©B Trudeau

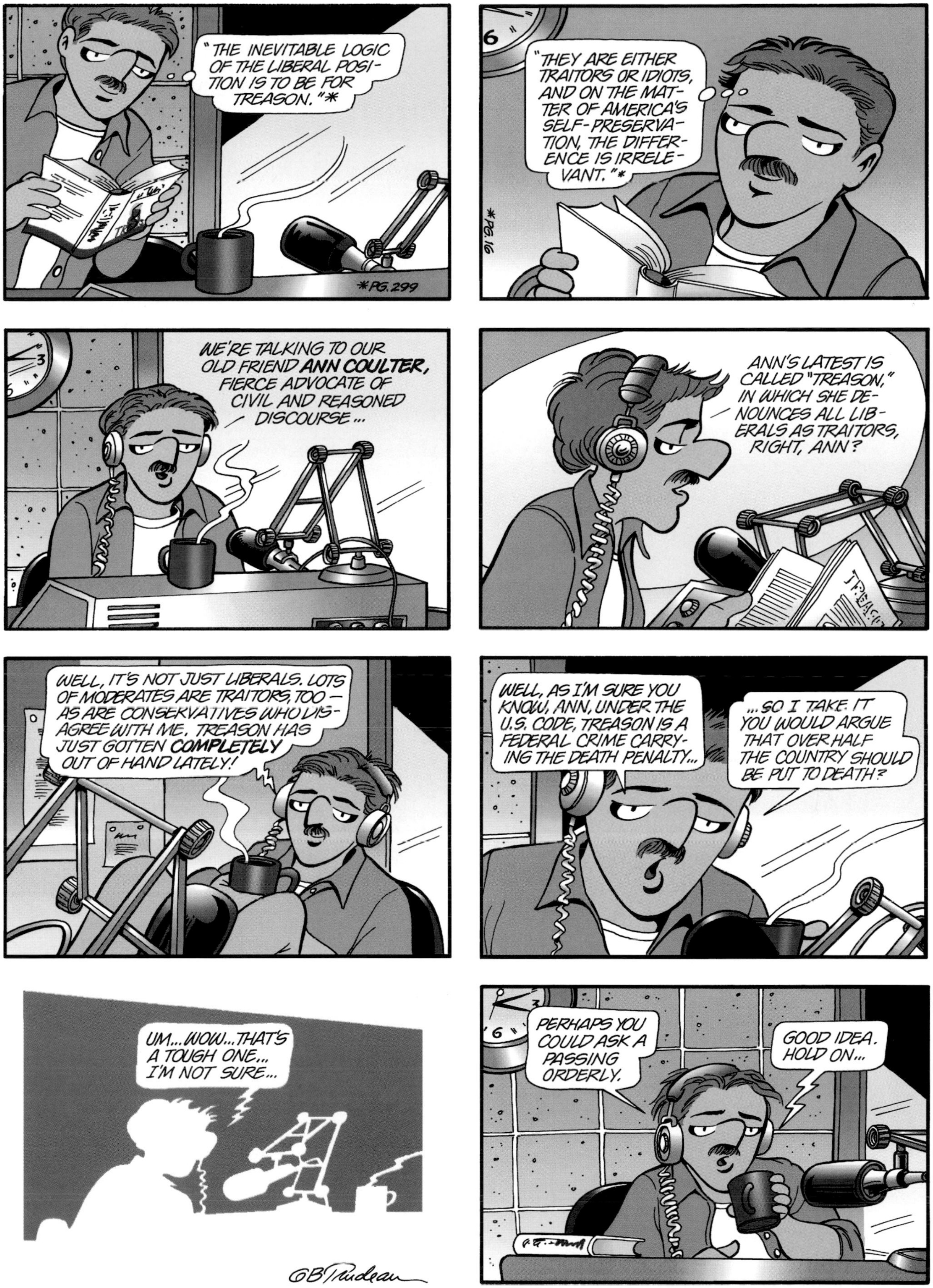

"THE INEVITABLE LOGIC OF THE LIBERAL POSITION IS TO BE FOR TREASON."*
*PG. 299
"THEY ARE EITHER TRAITORS OR IDIOTS, AND ON THE MATTER OF AMERICA'S SELF-PRESERVATION, THE DIFFERENCE IS IRRELEVANT."*
*PG. 16
WE'RE TALKING TO OUR OLD FRIEND **ANN COULTER,** FIERCE ADVOCATE OF CIVIL AND REASONED DISCOURSE...
ANN'S LATEST IS CALLED "TREASON," IN WHICH SHE DENOUNCES ALL LIBERALS AS TRAITORS, RIGHT, ANN?
WELL, IT'S NOT JUST LIBERALS. LOTS OF MODERATES ARE TRAITORS, TOO — AS ARE CONSERVATIVES WHO DISAGREE WITH ME. TREASON HAS JUST GOTTEN **COMPLETELY** OUT OF HAND LATELY!
WELL, AS I'M SURE YOU KNOW, ANN, UNDER THE U.S. CODE, TREASON IS A FEDERAL CRIME CARRYING THE DEATH PENALTY...
...SO I TAKE IT YOU WOULD ARGUE THAT OVER HALF THE COUNTRY SHOULD BE PUT TO DEATH?
UM...WOW...THAT'S A TOUGH ONE... I'M NOT SURE...
PERHAPS YOU COULD ASK A PASSING ORDERLY.
GOOD IDEA. HOLD ON...

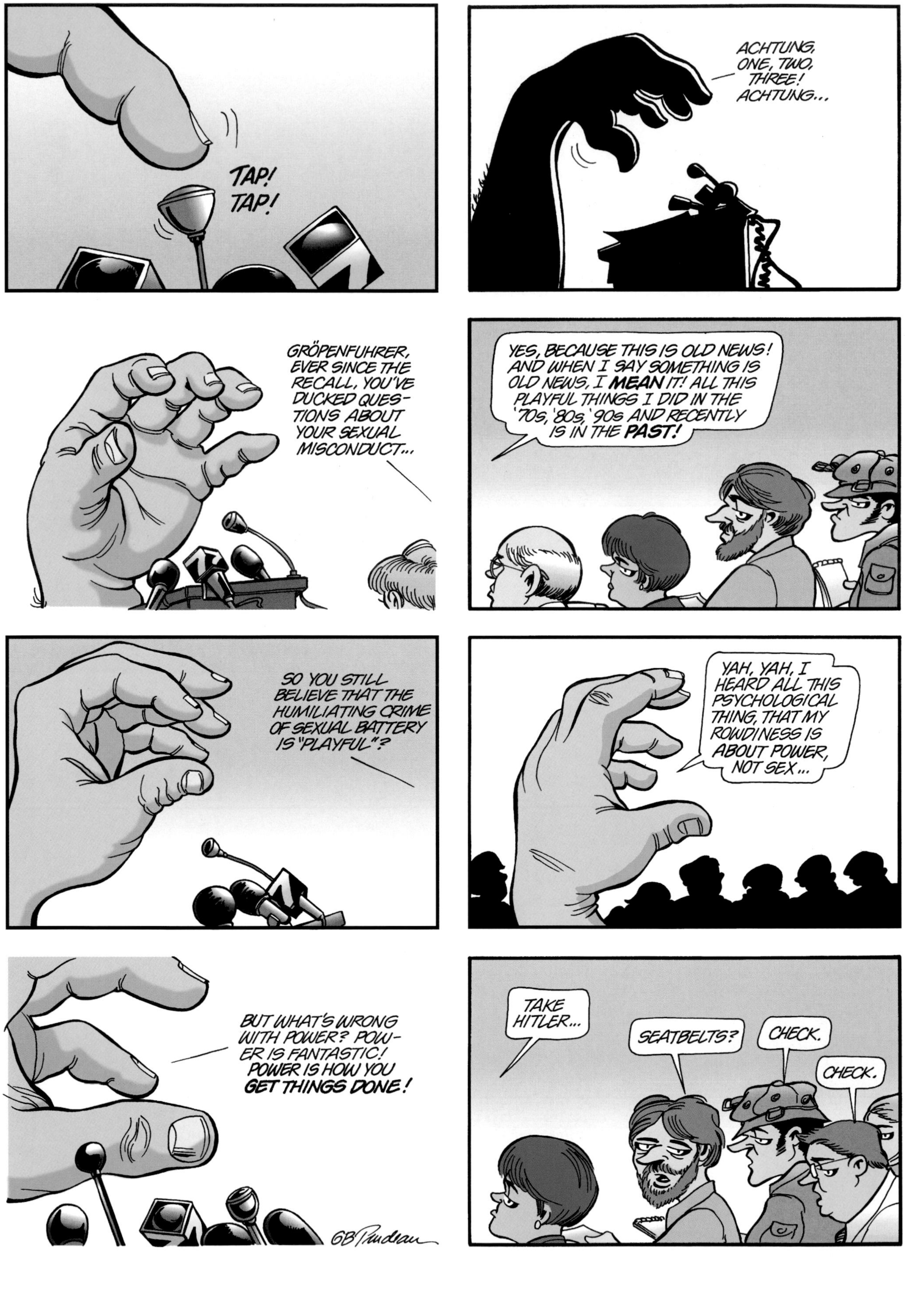

TAP! TAP!
ACHTUNG, ONE, TWO, THREE! ACHTUNG...
GRÖPENFUHRER, EVER SINCE THE RECALL, YOU'VE DUCKED QUESTIONS ABOUT YOUR SEXUAL MISCONDUCT...
YES, BECAUSE THIS IS OLD NEWS! AND WHEN I SAY SOMETHING IS OLD NEWS, I **MEAN** IT! ALL THIS PLAYFUL THINGS I DID IN THE '70s, '80s, '90s AND RECENTLY IS IN THE **PAST!**
SO YOU STILL BELIEVE THAT THE HUMILIATING CRIME OF SEXUAL BATTERY IS "PLAYFUL"?
YAH, YAH, I HEARD ALL THIS PSYCHOLOGICAL THING, THAT MY ROWDINESS IS ABOUT POWER, NOT SEX...
BUT WHAT'S WRONG WITH POWER? POWER IS FANTASTIC! POWER IS HOW YOU **GET THINGS DONE!**
TAKE HITLER...
SEATBELTS?
CHECK.
CHECK.
GB Trudeau

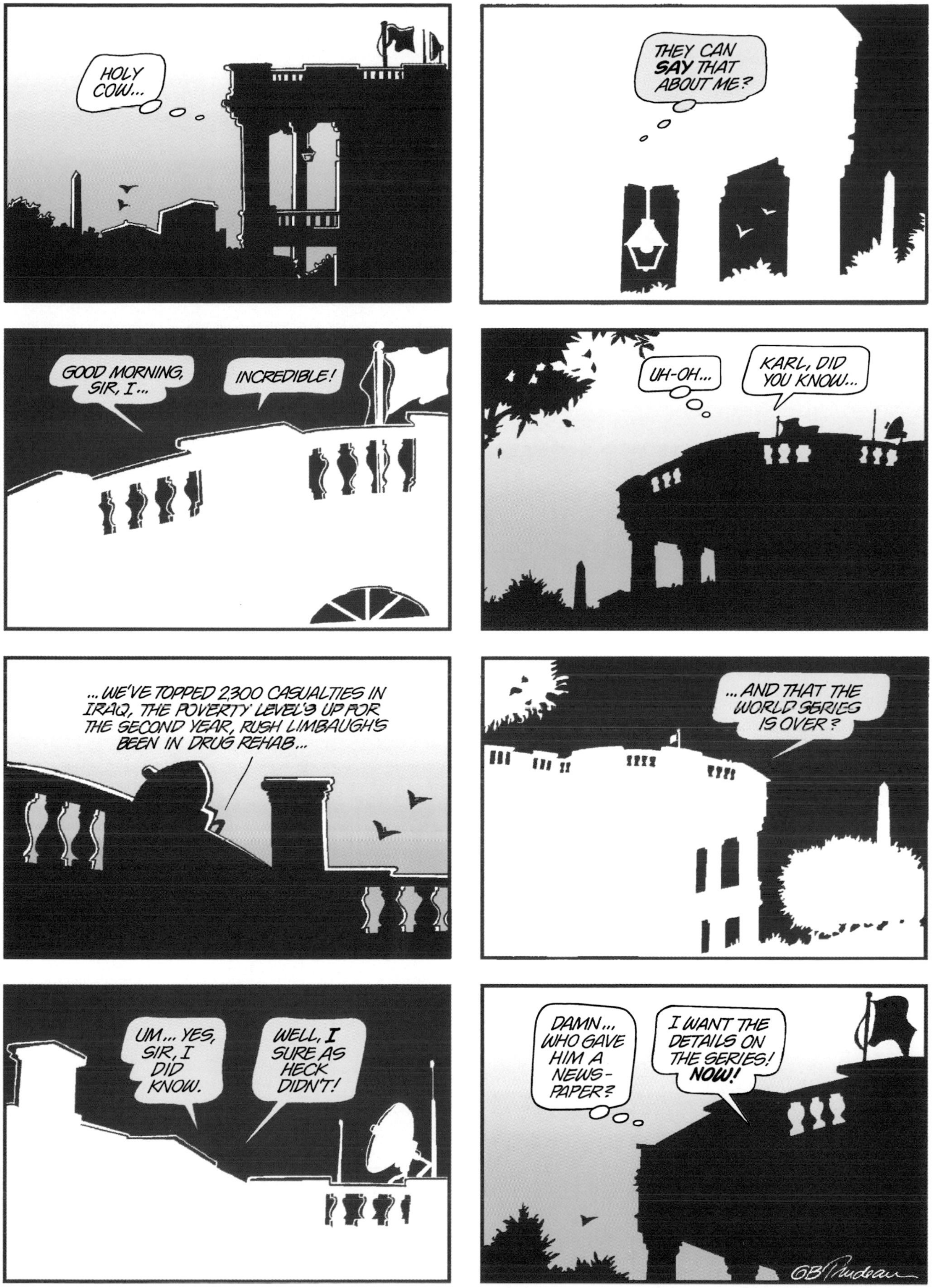

HOLY COW...
THEY CAN SAY THAT ABOUT ME?
GOOD MORNING, SIR, I...
INCREDIBLE!
UH-OH...
KARL, DID YOU KNOW...
...WE'VE TOPPED 2,300 CASUALTIES IN IRAQ, THE POVERTY LEVEL'S UP FOR THE SECOND YEAR, RUSH LIMBAUGH'S BEEN IN DRUG REHAB...
...AND THAT THE WORLD SERIES IS OVER?
UM... YES, SIR, I DID KNOW.
WELL, I SURE AS HECK DIDN'T!
DAMN... WHO GAVE HIM A NEWS-PAPER?
I WANT THE DETAILS ON THE SERIES! NOW!
©B Trudeau

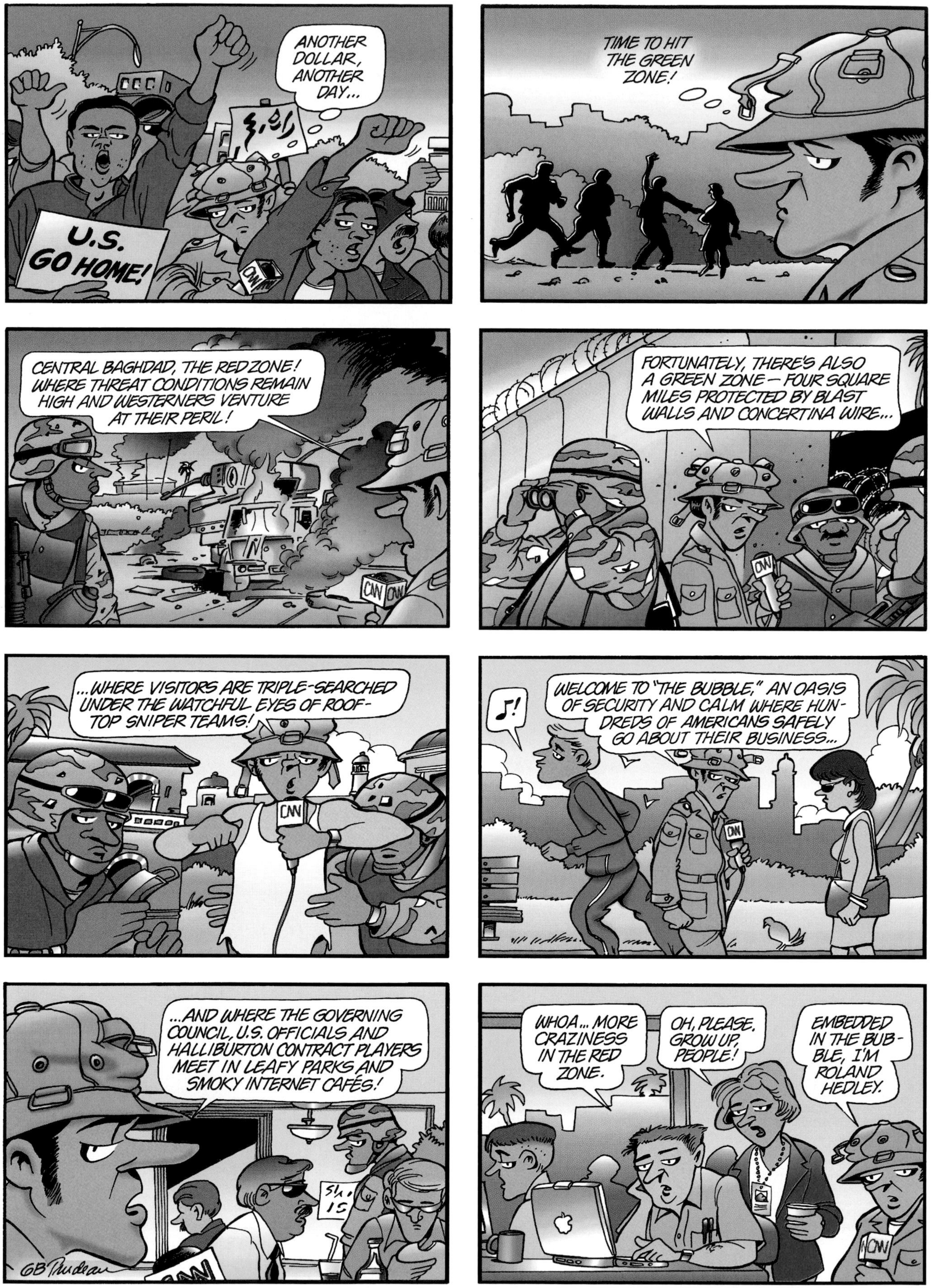
U.S. GO HOME!
ANOTHER DOLLAR, ANOTHER DAY...
TIME TO HIT THE GREEN ZONE!
CENTRAL BAGHDAD, THE RED ZONE! WHERE THREAT CONDITIONS REMAIN HIGH AND WESTERNERS VENTURE AT THEIR PERIL!
FORTUNATELY, THERE'S ALSO A GREEN ZONE — FOUR SQUARE MILES PROTECTED BY BLAST WALLS AND CONCERTINA WIRE...
...WHERE VISITORS ARE TRIPLE-SEARCHED UNDER THE WATCHFUL EYES OF ROOF-TOP SNIPER TEAMS!
♪!
WELCOME TO "THE BUBBLE," AN OASIS OF SECURITY AND CALM WHERE HUN-DREDS OF AMERICANS SAFELY GO ABOUT THEIR BUSINESS...
...AND WHERE THE GOVERNING COUNCIL, U.S. OFFICIALS AND HALLIBURTON CONTRACT PLAYERS MEET IN LEAFY PARKS AND SMOKY INTERNET CAFÉS!
GB Trudeau
WHOA... MORE CRAZINESS IN THE RED ZONE.
OH, PLEASE, GROW UP, PEOPLE!
EMBEDDED IN THE BUB-BLE, I'M ROLAND HEDLEY.

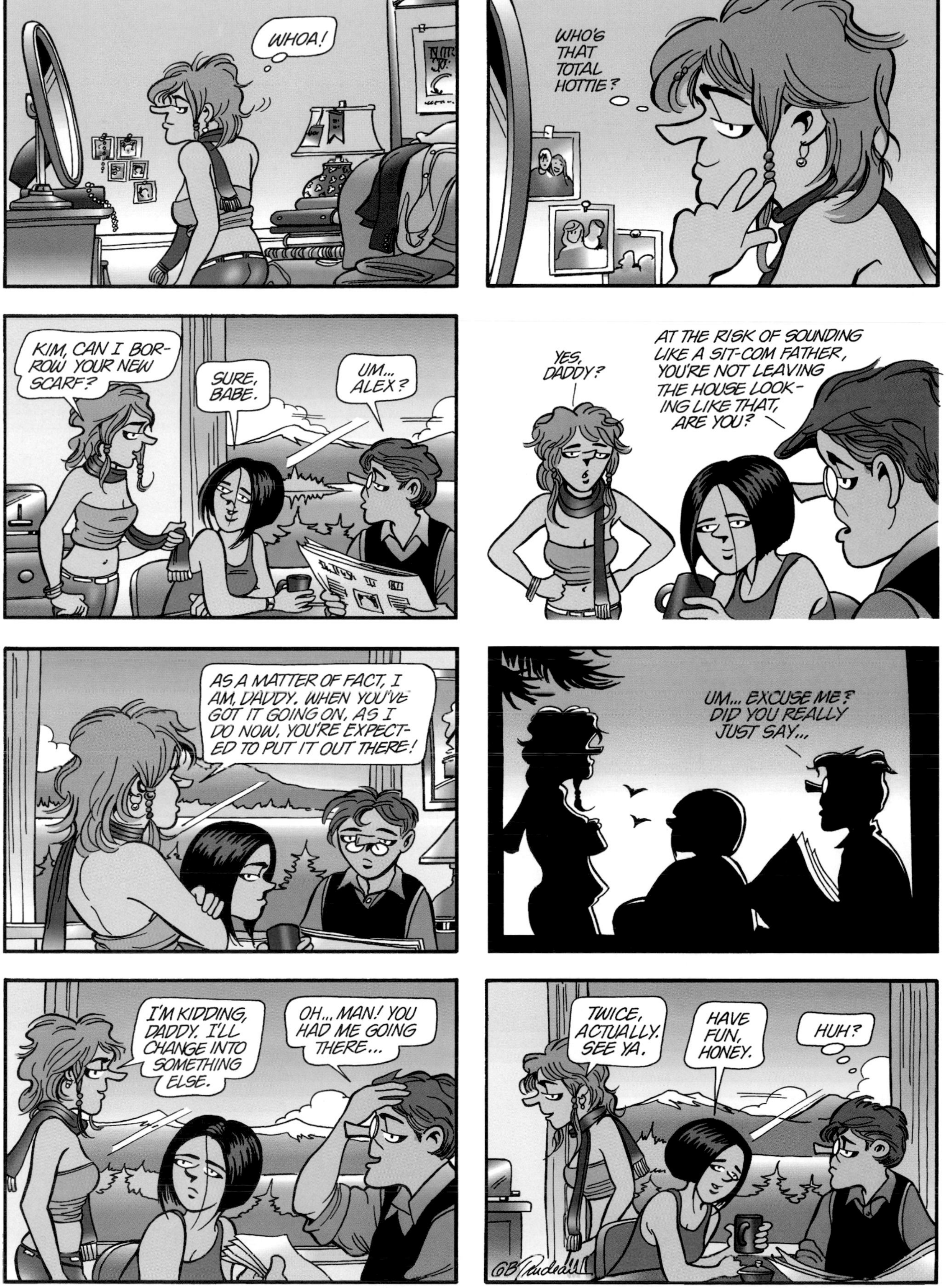
WHOA!
WHO'S THAT TOTAL HOTTIE?
KIM, CAN I BORROW YOUR NEW SCARF?
SURE, BABE.
UM... ALEX?
YES, DADDY?
AT THE RISK OF SOUNDING LIKE A SIT-COM FATHER, YOU'RE NOT LEAVING THE HOUSE LOOKING LIKE THAT, ARE YOU?
AS A MATTER OF FACT, I AM, DADDY. WHEN YOU'VE GOT IT GOING ON, AS I DO NOW, YOU'RE EXPECTED TO PUT IT OUT THERE!
UM... EXCUSE ME? DID YOU REALLY JUST SAY...
I'M KIDDING, DADDY. I'LL CHANGE INTO SOMETHING ELSE.
OH... MAN! YOU HAD ME GOING THERE...
TWICE, ACTUALLY. SEE YA.
HAVE FUN, HONEY.
HUH?

THINK I'LL SET A WHOLE NEW TONE FOR THE SHOW TODAY...

YEAH, RIGHT...

WHO AM I KIDDING?

ON THE LINE TODAY— A VERY BUSY MAN— RECENTLY REHABBED RADIO TALK ICON *RUSH LIMBAUGH!* WELCOME, MR. L!

THANK YOU, MY FRIEND.

SIR, I'VE GOT TO ASK YOU— DURING YOUR TIME OFF...

DID YOU FIND THAT YOU HAD ANY RE-GRETS AS YOU LOOKED BACK ON YOUR CAREER?

REGRETS? OVER WHAT?

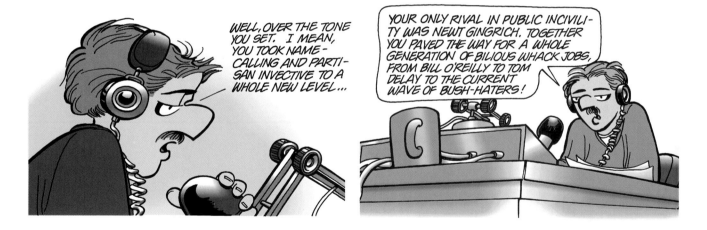

WELL, OVER THE TONE YOU SET. I MEAN, YOU TOOK NAME-CALLING AND PARTI-SAN INVECTIVE TO A WHOLE NEW LEVEL...

YOUR ONLY RIVAL IN PUBLIC INCIVIL-TY WAS NEWT GINGRICH. TOGETHER YOU PAVED THE WAY FOR A WHOLE GENERATION OF BILIOUS WHACK JOBS, FROM BILL O'REILLY TO TOM DELAY TO THE CURRENT WAVE OF BUSH-HATERS!

YOU GIVE ME TOO MUCH CREDIT, MY FRIEND...

NO, NO, I DON'T, I DON'T! YOU REALLY ARE THE *GODFATHER* OF THE POLITICS OF PERSONAL DESTRUCTION!

WELL, THAT'S RICH, COMING FROM...

SHUT UP, YOU HYPOCRITICAL, PILL-POPPING LARD MOUNTAIN!

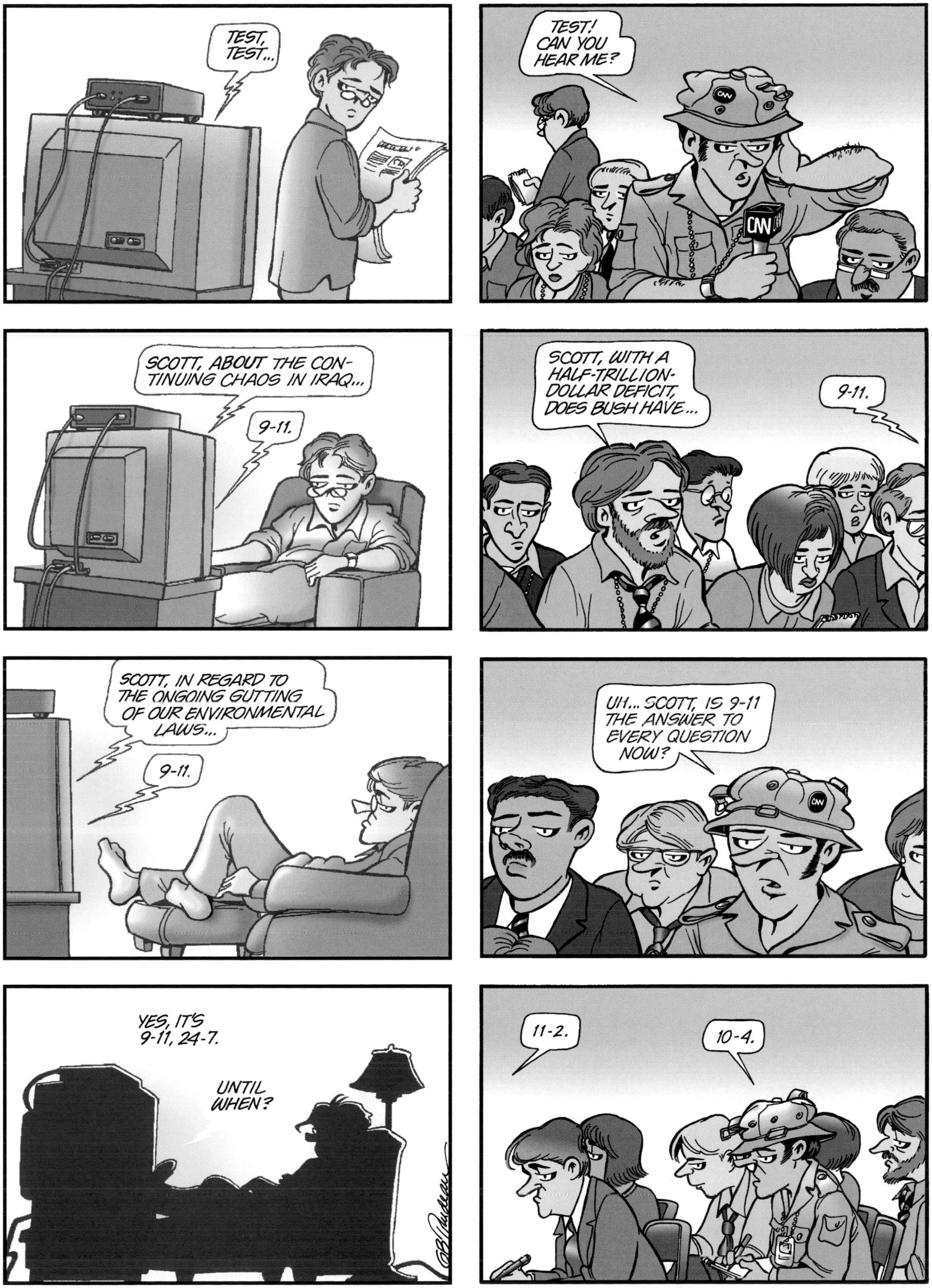
TEST, TEST...
TEST! CAN YOU HEAR ME?
SCOTT, ABOUT THE CONTINUING CHAOS IN IRAQ...
9-11.
SCOTT, WITH A HALF-TRILLION-DOLLAR DEFICIT, DOES BUSH HAVE...
9-11.
SCOTT, IN REGARD TO THE ONGOING GUTTING OF OUR ENVIRONMENTAL LAWS...
9-11.
UH... SCOTT, IS 9-11 THE ANSWER TO EVERY QUESTION NOW?
YES, IT'S 9-11, 24-7.
UNTIL WHEN?
11-2.
10-4.

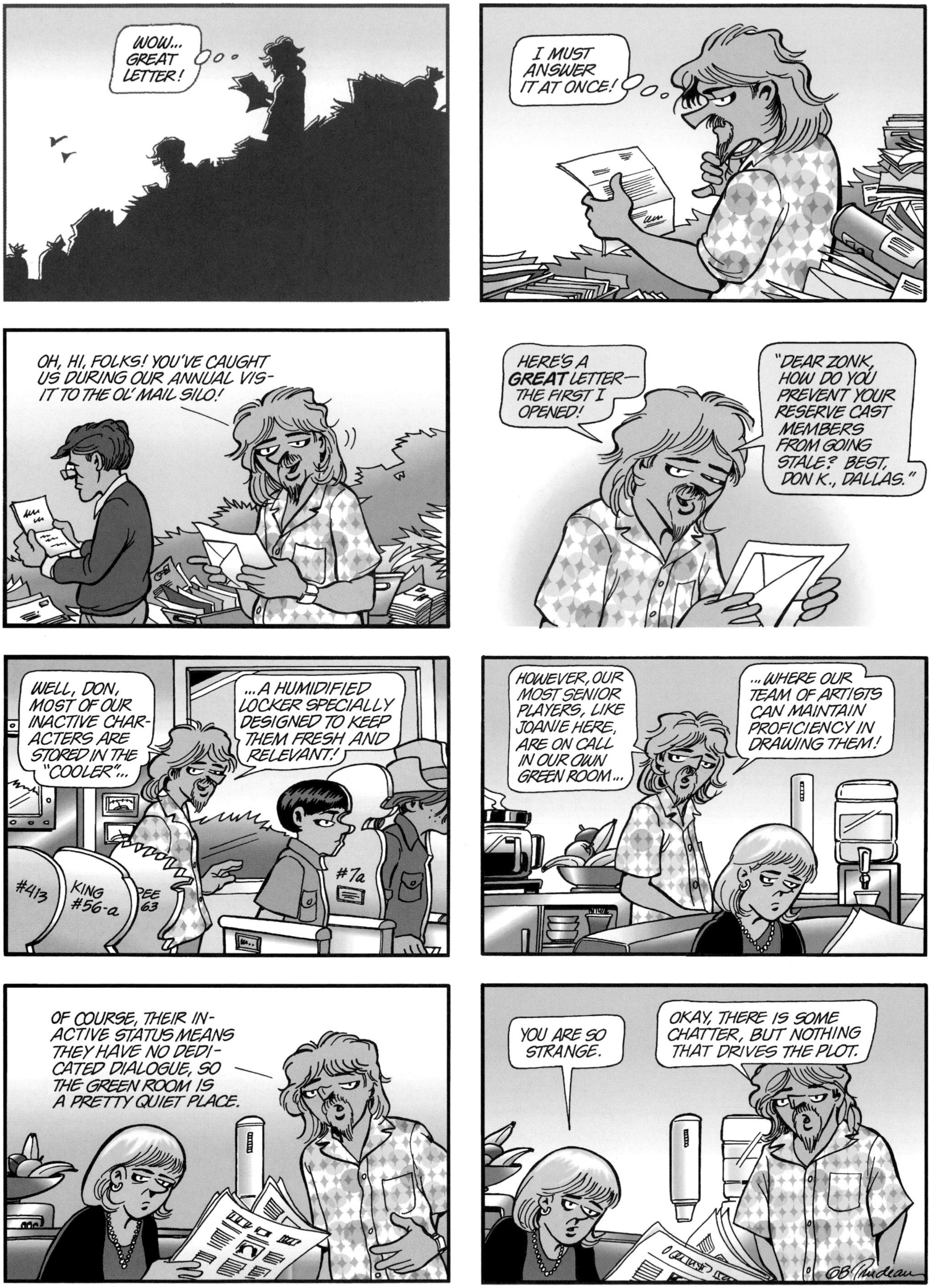
WOW... GREAT LETTER!
I MUST ANSWER IT AT ONCE!
OH, HI, FOLKS! YOU'VE CAUGHT US DURING OUR ANNUAL VISIT TO THE OL' MAIL SILO!
HERE'S A **GREAT** LETTER— THE FIRST I OPENED!
"DEAR ZONK, HOW DO YOU PREVENT YOUR RESERVE CAST MEMBERS FROM GOING STALE? BEST, DON K., DALLAS."
WELL, DON, MOST OF OUR INACTIVE CHARACTERS ARE STORED IN THE "COOLER"...
...A HUMIDIFIED LOCKER SPECIALLY DESIGNED TO KEEP THEM FRESH AND RELEVANT!
#413
KING #56-a
#7a
HOWEVER, OUR MOST SENIOR PLAYERS, LIKE JOANIE HERE, ARE ON CALL IN OUR OWN GREEN ROOM...
...WHERE OUR TEAM OF ARTISTS CAN MAINTAIN PROFICIENCY IN DRAWING THEM!
OF COURSE, THEIR INACTIVE STATUS MEANS THEY HAVE NO DEDICATED DIALOGUE, SO THE GREEN ROOM IS A PRETTY QUIET PLACE.
YOU ARE SO STRANGE.
OKAY, THERE IS SOME CHATTER, BUT NOTHING THAT DRIVES THE PLOT.
GB Trudeau

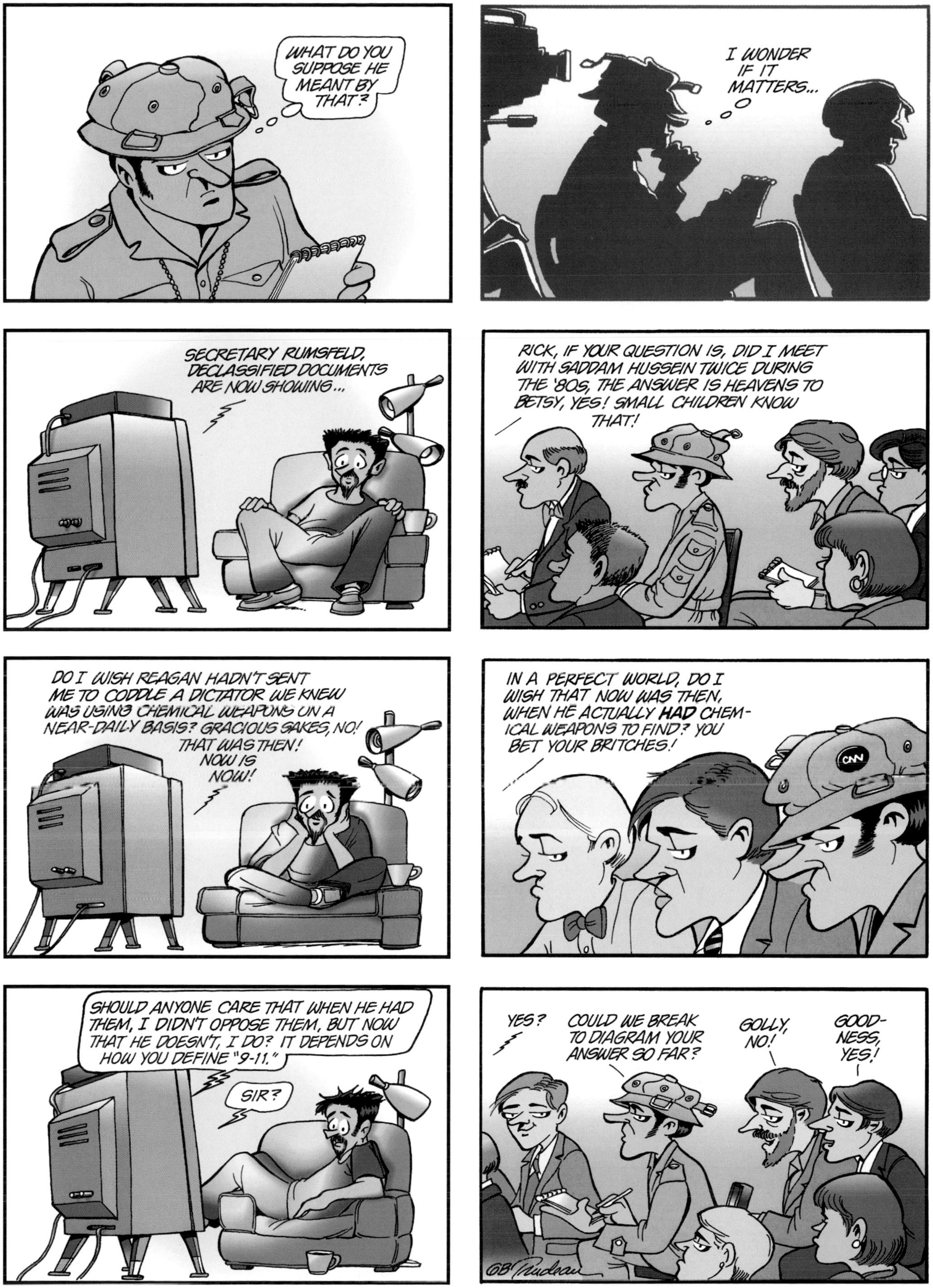
WHAT DO YOU SUPPOSE HE MEANT BY THAT?
I WONDER IF IT MATTERS...
SECRETARY RUMSFELD, DECLASSIFIED DOCUMENTS ARE NOW SHOWING...
RICK, IF YOUR QUESTION IS, DID I MEET WITH SADDAM HUSSEIN TWICE DURING THE '80S, THE ANSWER IS HEAVENS TO BETSY, YES! SMALL CHILDREN KNOW THAT!
DO I WISH REAGAN HADN'T SENT ME TO CODDLE A DICTATOR WE KNEW WAS USING CHEMICAL WEAPONS ON A NEAR-DAILY BASIS? GRACIOUS SAKES, NO! THAT WAS THEN! NOW IS NOW!
IN A PERFECT WORLD, DO I WISH THAT NOW WAS THEN, WHEN HE ACTUALLY HAD CHEMICAL WEAPONS TO FIND? YOU BET YOUR BRITCHES!
SHOULD ANYONE CARE THAT WHEN HE HAD THEM, I DIDN'T OPPOSE THEM, BUT NOW THAT HE DOESN'T, I DO? IT DEPENDS ON HOW YOU DEFINE "9-11."
SIR?
YES?
COULD WE BREAK TO DIAGRAM YOUR ANSWER SO FAR?
GOLLY, NO!
GOODNESS, YES!
GBTrudeau

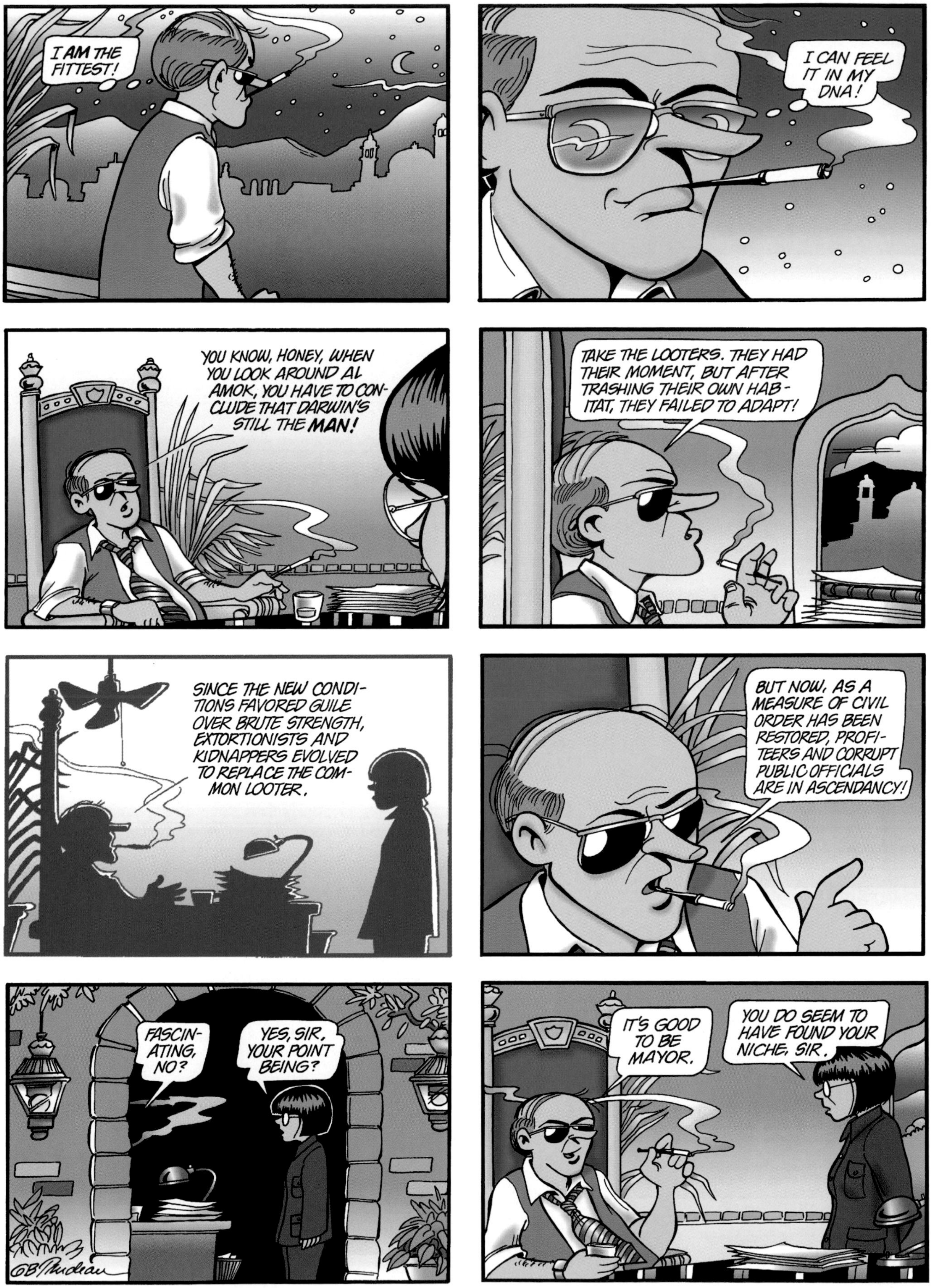
I AM THE FITTEST!
I CAN FEEL IT IN MY DNA!
YOU KNOW, HONEY, WHEN YOU LOOK AROUND AL AMOK, YOU HAVE TO CONCLUDE THAT DARWIN'S STILL THE MAN!
TAKE THE LOOTERS. THEY HAD THEIR MOMENT, BUT AFTER TRASHING THEIR OWN HABITAT, THEY FAILED TO ADAPT!
SINCE THE NEW CONDITIONS FAVORED GUILE OVER BRUTE STRENGTH, EXTORTIONISTS AND KIDNAPPERS EVOLVED TO REPLACE THE COMMON LOOTER.
BUT NOW, AS A MEASURE OF CIVIL ORDER HAS BEEN RESTORED, PROFITEERS AND CORRUPT PUBLIC OFFICIALS ARE IN ASCENDANCY!
FASCINATING, NO?
YES, SIR, YOUR POINT BEING?
IT'S GOOD TO BE MAYOR.
YOU DO SEEM TO HAVE FOUND YOUR NICHE, SIR.

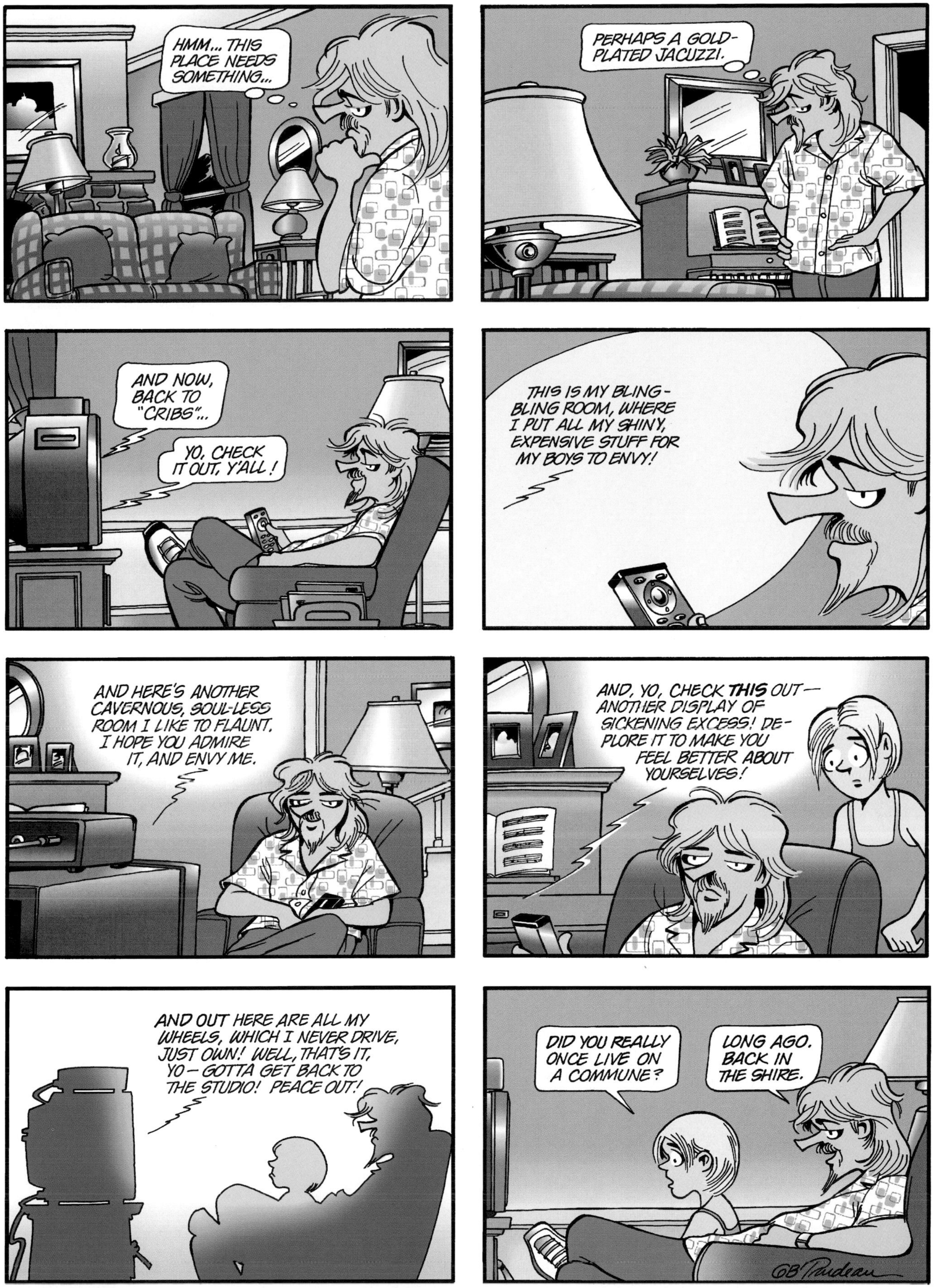
HMM... THIS PLACE NEEDS SOMETHING...
PERHAPS A GOLD-PLATED JACUZZI.
AND NOW, BACK TO "CRIBS"...
YO, CHECK IT OUT, Y'ALL!
THIS IS MY BLING-BLING ROOM, WHERE I PUT ALL MY SHINY, EXPENSIVE STUFF FOR MY BOYS TO ENVY!
AND HERE'S ANOTHER CAVERNOUS, SOUL-LESS ROOM I LIKE TO FLAUNT. I HOPE YOU ADMIRE IT, AND ENVY ME.
AND, YO, CHECK THIS OUT— ANOTHER DISPLAY OF SICKENING EXCESS! DE-PLORE IT TO MAKE YOU FEEL BETTER ABOUT YOURSELVES!
AND OUT HERE ARE ALL MY WHEELS, WHICH I NEVER DRIVE, JUST OWN! WELL, THAT'S IT, YO— GOTTA GET BACK TO THE STUDIO! PEACE OUT!
DID YOU REALLY ONCE LIVE ON A COMMUNE?
LONG AGO. BACK IN THE SHIRE.
GB Trudeau

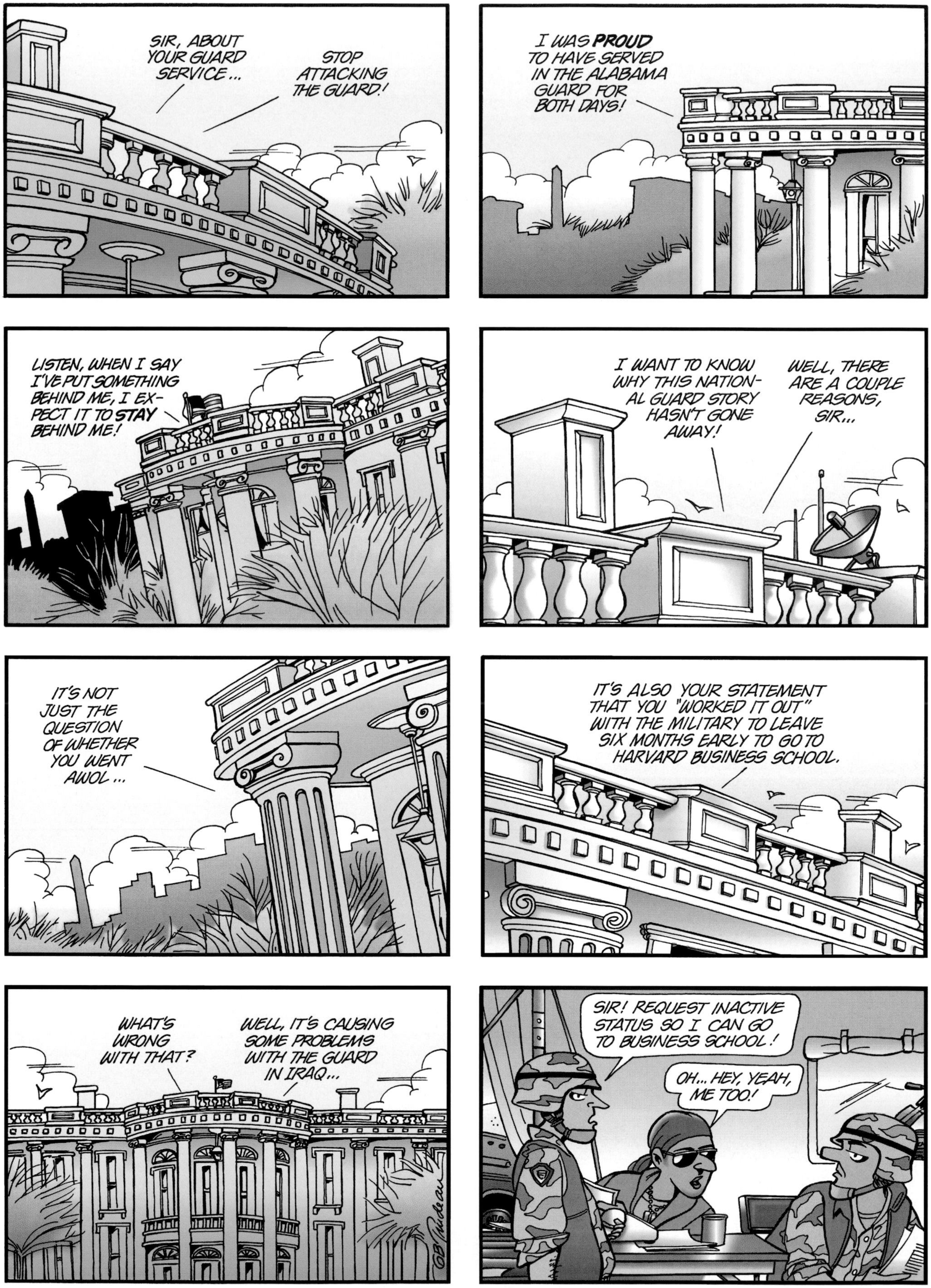
SIR, ABOUT YOUR GUARD SERVICE...
STOP ATTACKING THE GUARD!
I WAS **PROUD** TO HAVE SERVED IN THE ALABAMA GUARD FOR BOTH DAYS!
LISTEN, WHEN I SAY I'VE PUT SOMETHING BEHIND ME, I EXPECT IT TO **STAY** BEHIND ME!
I WANT TO KNOW WHY THIS NATIONAL GUARD STORY HASN'T GONE AWAY!
WELL, THERE ARE A COUPLE REASONS, SIR...
IT'S NOT JUST THE QUESTION OF WHETHER YOU WENT AWOL...
IT'S ALSO YOUR STATEMENT THAT YOU "WORKED IT OUT" WITH THE MILITARY TO LEAVE SIX MONTHS EARLY TO GO TO HARVARD BUSINESS SCHOOL.
WHAT'S WRONG WITH THAT?
WELL, IT'S CAUSING SOME PROBLEMS WITH THE GUARD IN IRAQ...
SIR! REQUEST INACTIVE STATUS SO I CAN GO TO BUSINESS SCHOOL!
OH... HEY, YEAH, ME TOO!

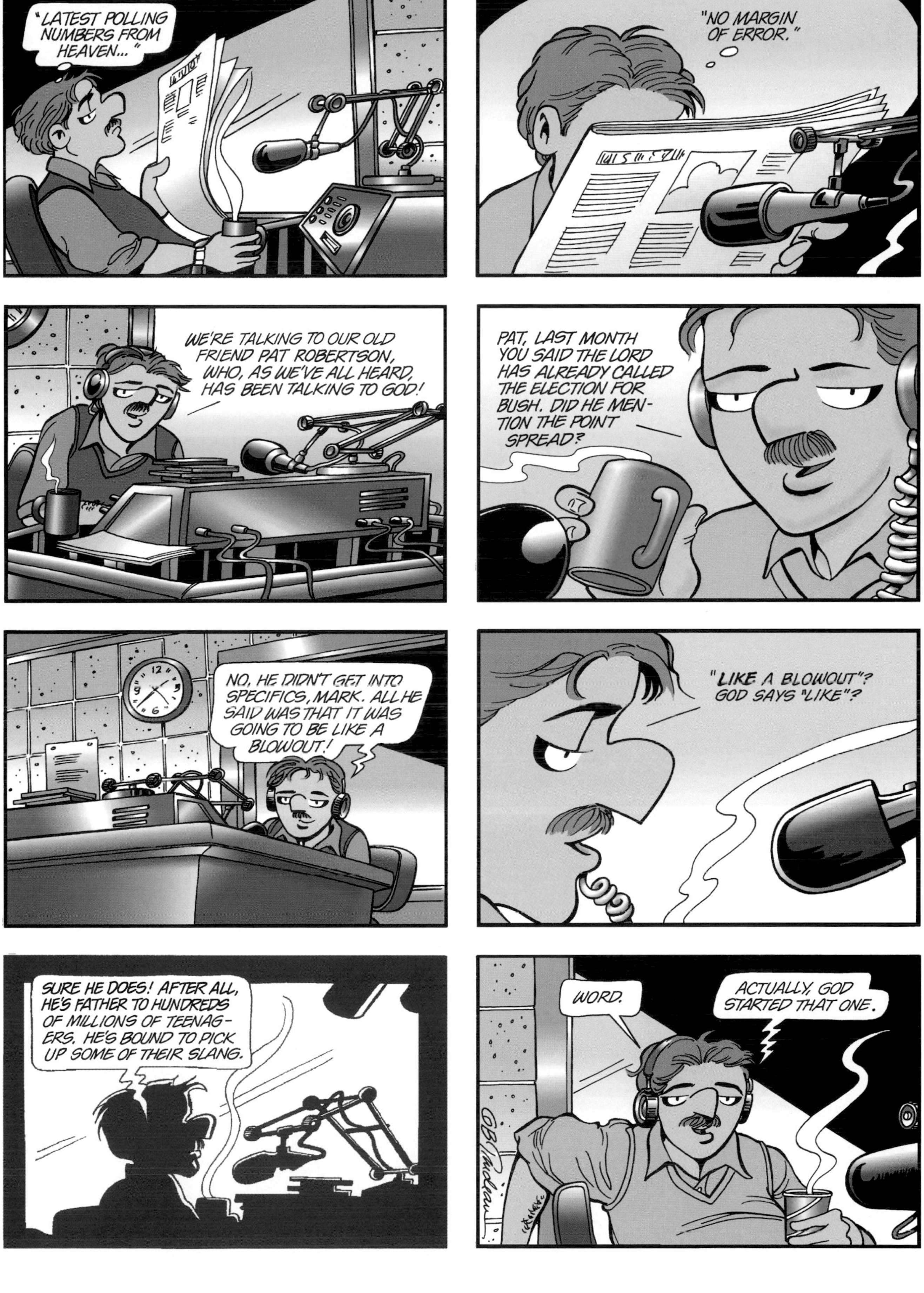
"LATEST POLLING NUMBERS FROM HEAVEN..."
"NO MARGIN OF ERROR."
WE'RE TALKING TO OUR OLD FRIEND PAT ROBERTSON, WHO, AS WE'VE ALL HEARD, HAS BEEN TALKING TO GOD!
PAT, LAST MONTH YOU SAID THE LORD HAS ALREADY CALLED THE ELECTION FOR BUSH. DID HE MENTION THE POINT SPREAD?
NO, HE DIDN'T GET INTO SPECIFICS, MARK. ALL HE SAID WAS THAT IT WAS GOING TO BE LIKE A BLOWOUT!
"LIKE A BLOWOUT"? GOD SAYS "LIKE"?
SURE HE DOES! AFTER ALL, HE'S FATHER TO HUNDREDS OF MILLIONS OF TEENAGERS. HE'S BOUND TO PICK UP SOME OF THEIR SLANG.
WORD.
ACTUALLY, GOD STARTED THAT ONE.

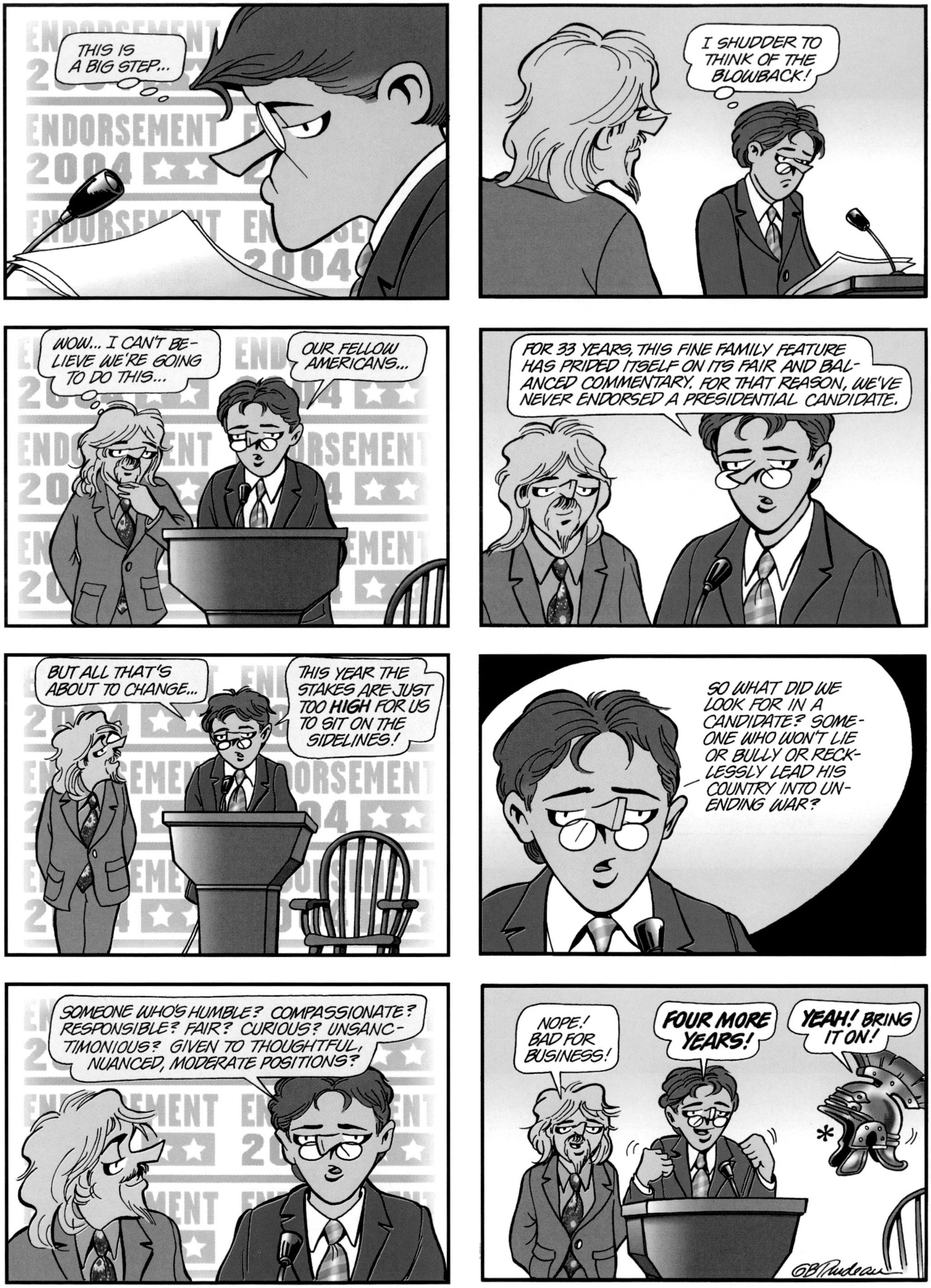

ENDORSEMENT 2004
THIS IS A BIG STEP...
I SHUDDER TO THINK OF THE BLOWBACK!
WOW... I CAN'T BE-LIEVE WE'RE GOING TO DO THIS...
OUR FELLOW AMERICANS...
FOR 33 YEARS, THIS FINE FAMILY FEATURE HAS PRIDED ITSELF ON ITS FAIR AND BAL-ANCED COMMENTARY. FOR THAT REASON, WE'VE NEVER ENDORSED A PRESIDENTIAL CANDIDATE.
BUT ALL THAT'S ABOUT TO CHANGE...
THIS YEAR THE STAKES ARE JUST TOO **HIGH** FOR US TO SIT ON THE SIDELINES!
SO WHAT DID WE LOOK FOR IN A CANDIDATE? SOME-ONE WHO WON'T LIE OR BULLY OR RECK-LESSLY LEAD HIS COUNTRY INTO UN-ENDING WAR?
SOMEONE WHO'S HUMBLE? COMPASSIONATE? RESPONSIBLE? FAIR? CURIOUS? UNSANC-TIMONIOUS? GIVEN TO THOUGHTFUL, NUANCED, MODERATE POSITIONS?
NOPE! BAD FOR BUSINESS!
FOUR MORE YEARS!
YEAH! BRING IT ON!
GBTrudeau

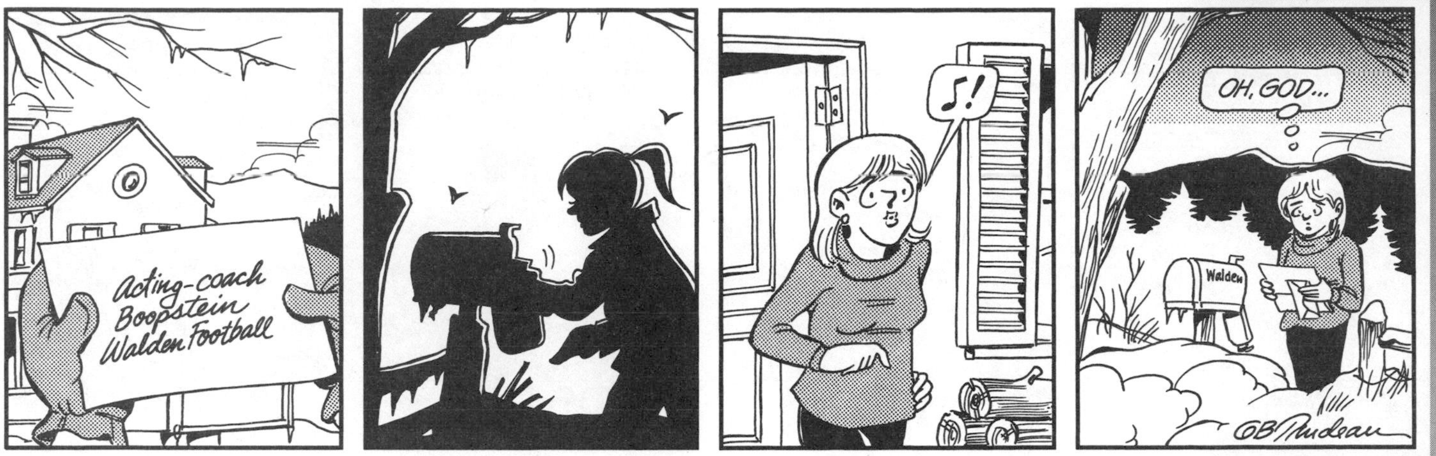
Acting-coach Boopstein Walden Football
♪!
Walden
OH, GOD...
©B Trudeau

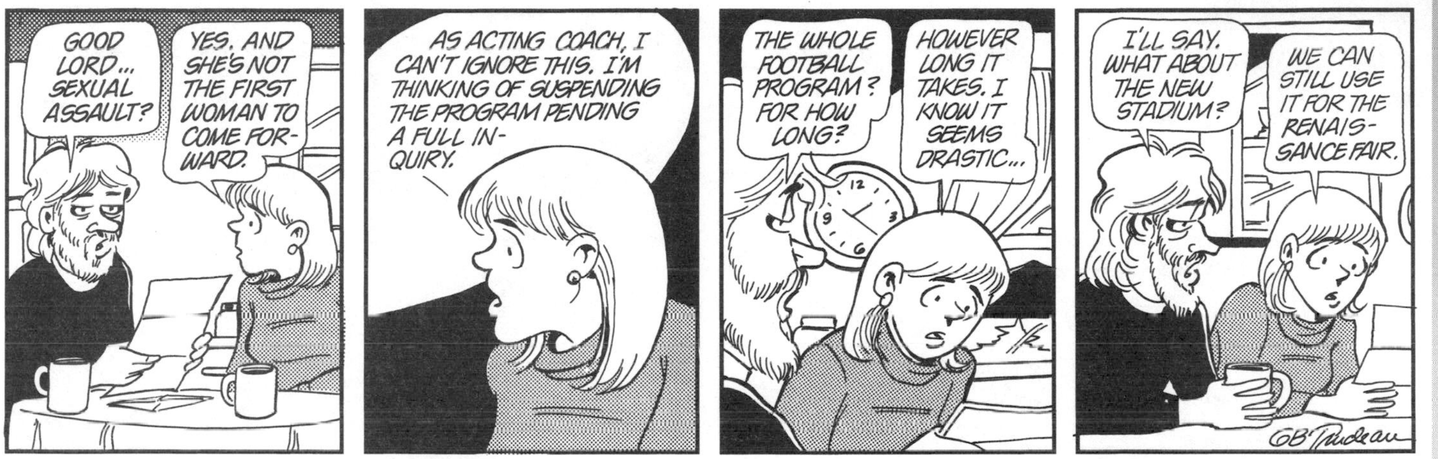
GOOD LORD... SEXUAL ASSAULT?
YES. AND SHE'S NOT THE FIRST WOMAN TO COME FORWARD.
AS ACTING COACH, I CAN'T IGNORE THIS. I'M THINKING OF SUSPENDING THE PROGRAM PENDING A FULL INQUIRY.
THE WHOLE FOOTBALL PROGRAM? FOR HOW LONG?
HOWEVER LONG IT TAKES. I KNOW IT SEEMS DRASTIC...
I'LL SAY. WHAT ABOUT THE NEW STADIUM?
WE CAN STILL USE IT FOR THE RENAISSANCE FAIR.
©B Trudeau

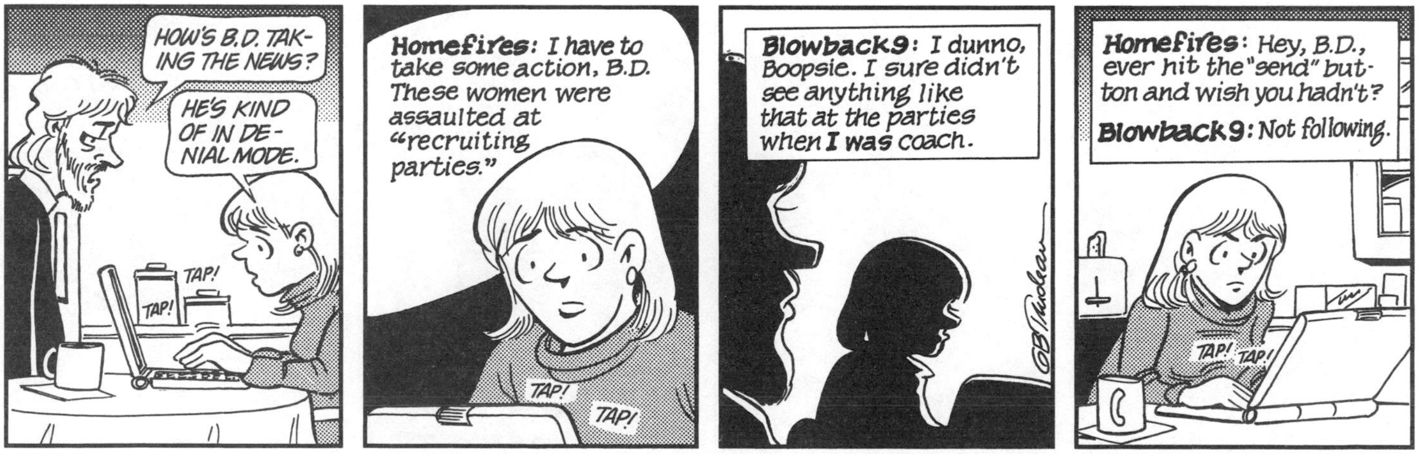
HOW'S B.D. TAKING THE NEWS?
HE'S KIND OF IN DENIAL MODE.
TAP!
TAP!
Homefires: I have to take some action, B.D. These women were assaulted at "recruiting parties."
TAP!
TAP!
Blowback9: I dunno, Boopsie. I sure didn't see anything like that at the parties when I was coach.
©B Trudeau
Homefires: Hey, B.D., ever hit the "send" button and wish you hadn't?
Blowback9: Not following.
TAP!
TAP!

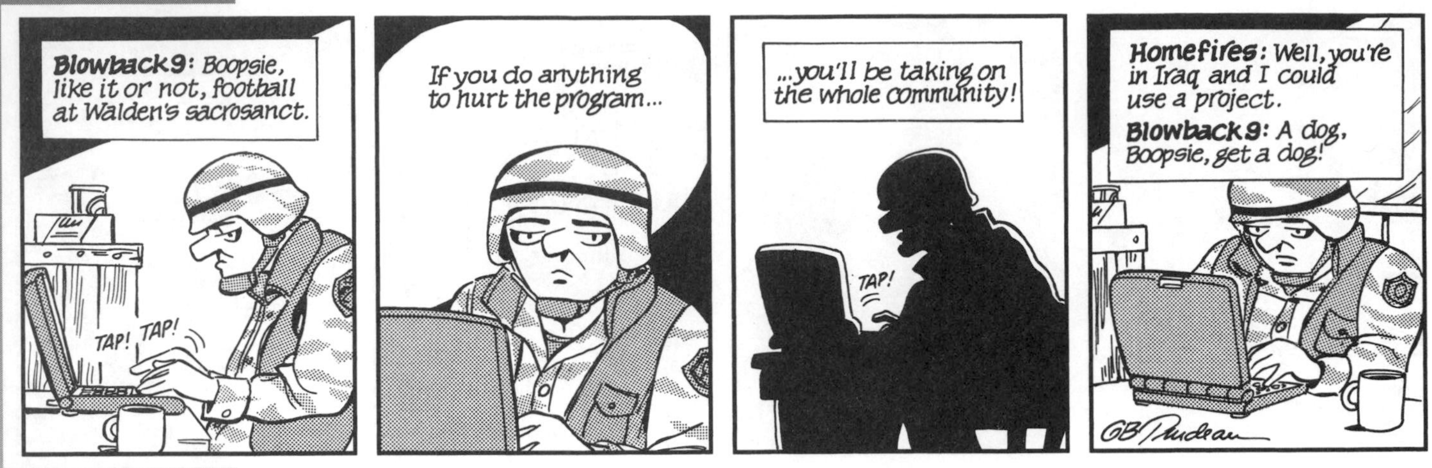
Blowback9: Boopsie, like it or not, football at Walden's sacrosanct.
TAP! TAP!
If you do anything to hurt the program...
...you'll be taking on the whole community!
TAP!
Homefires: Well, you're in Iraq and I could use a project.
Blowback9: A dog, Boopsie, get a dog!
GB Trudeau

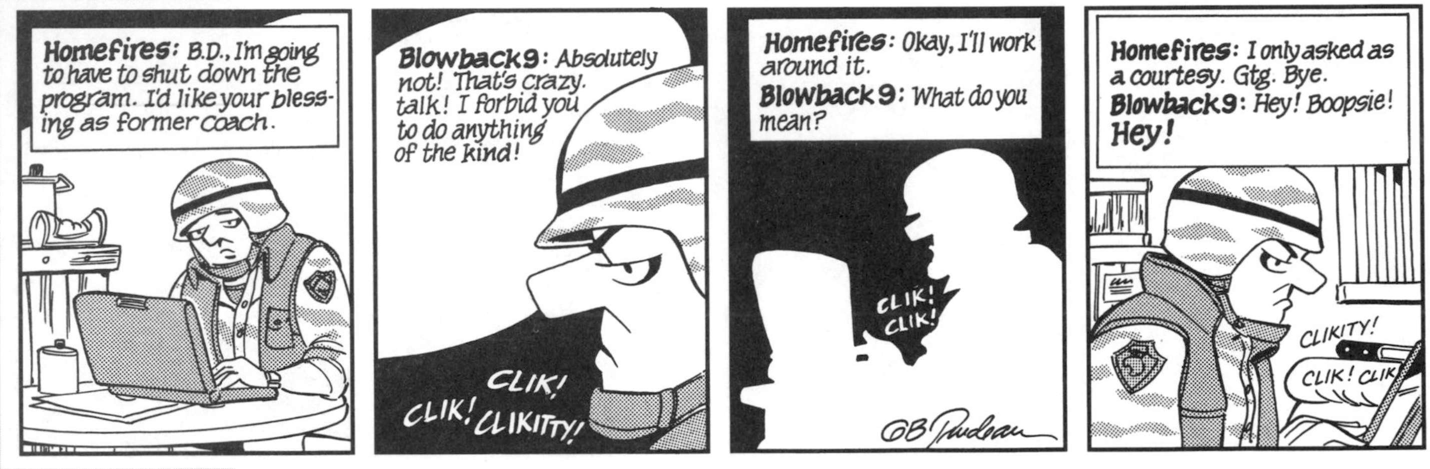
Homefires: B.D., I'm going to have to shut down the program. I'd like your blessing as former coach.
Blowback9: Absolutely not! That's crazy talk! I forbid you to do anything of the kind!
CLIK! CLIK! CLIKITTY!
Homefires: Okay, I'll work around it.
Blowback9: What do you mean?
CLIK! CLIK!
GB Trudeau
Homefires: I only asked as a courtesy. Gtg. Bye.
Blowback9: Hey! Boopsie! Hey!
CLIKITY!
CLIK! CLIK

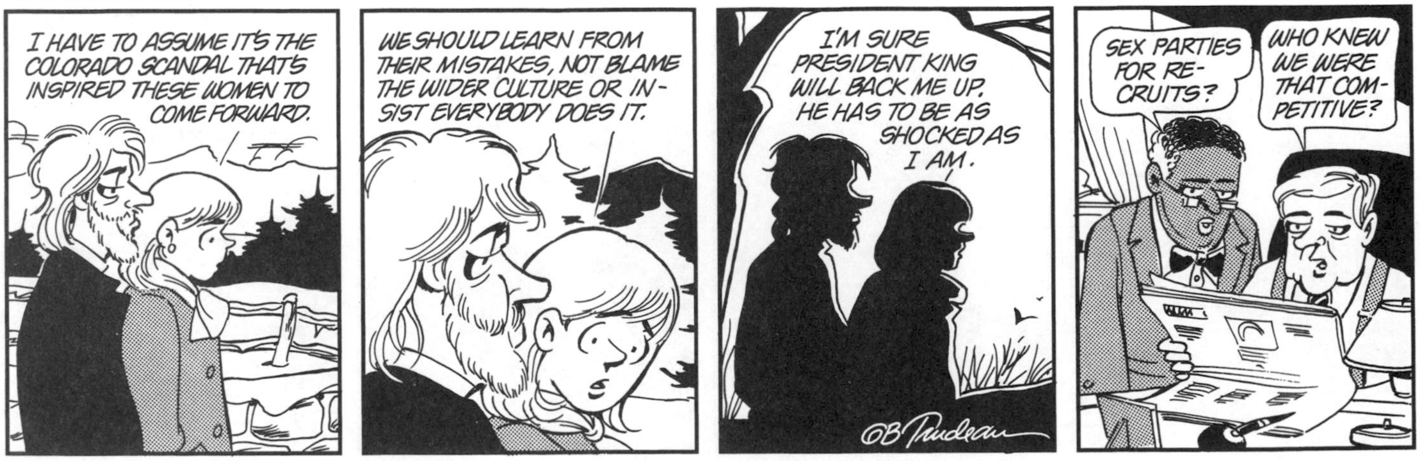
I HAVE TO ASSUME IT'S THE COLORADO SCANDAL THAT'S INSPIRED THESE WOMEN TO COME FORWARD.
WE SHOULD LEARN FROM THEIR MISTAKES, NOT BLAME THE WIDER CULTURE OR INSIST EVERYBODY DOES IT.
I'M SURE PRESIDENT KING WILL BACK ME UP. HE HAS TO BE AS SHOCKED AS I AM.
GB Trudeau
SEX PARTIES FOR RECRUITS?
WHO KNEW WE WERE THAT COMPETITIVE?

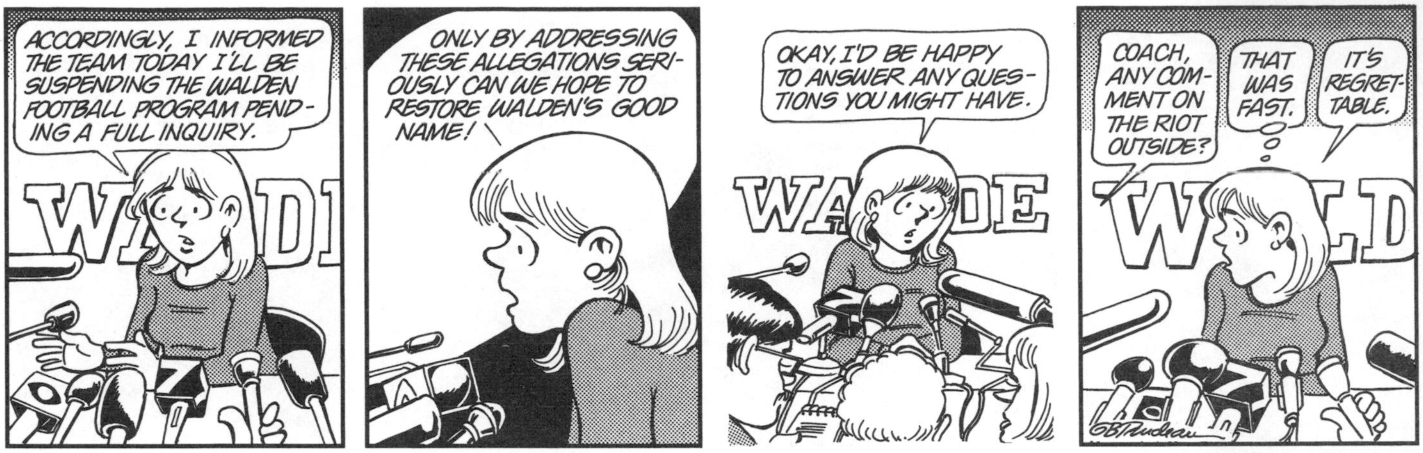
ACCORDINGLY, I INFORMED THE TEAM TODAY I'LL BE SUSPENDING THE WALDEN FOOTBALL PROGRAM PENDING A FULL INQUIRY.
ONLY BY ADDRESSING THESE ALLEGATIONS SERIOUSLY CAN WE HOPE TO RESTORE WALDEN'S GOOD NAME!
OKAY, I'D BE HAPPY TO ANSWER ANY QUESTIONS YOU MIGHT HAVE.
COACH, ANY COMMENT ON THE RIOT OUTSIDE?
THAT WAS FAST.
IT'S REGRETTABLE.

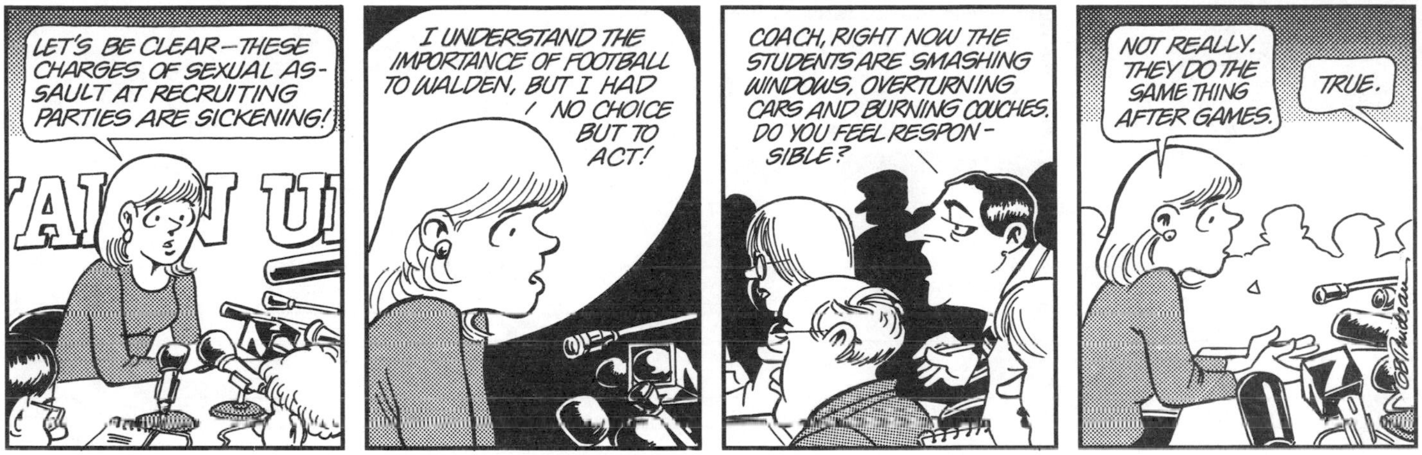
LET'S BE CLEAR—THESE CHARGES OF SEXUAL ASSAULT AT RECRUITING PARTIES ARE SICKENING!
I UNDERSTAND THE IMPORTANCE OF FOOTBALL TO WALDEN, BUT I HAD NO CHOICE BUT TO ACT!
COACH, RIGHT NOW THE STUDENTS ARE SMASHING WINDOWS, OVERTURNING CARS AND BURNING COUCHES. DO YOU FEEL RESPONSIBLE?
NOT REALLY. THEY DO THE SAME THING AFTER GAMES.
TRUE.

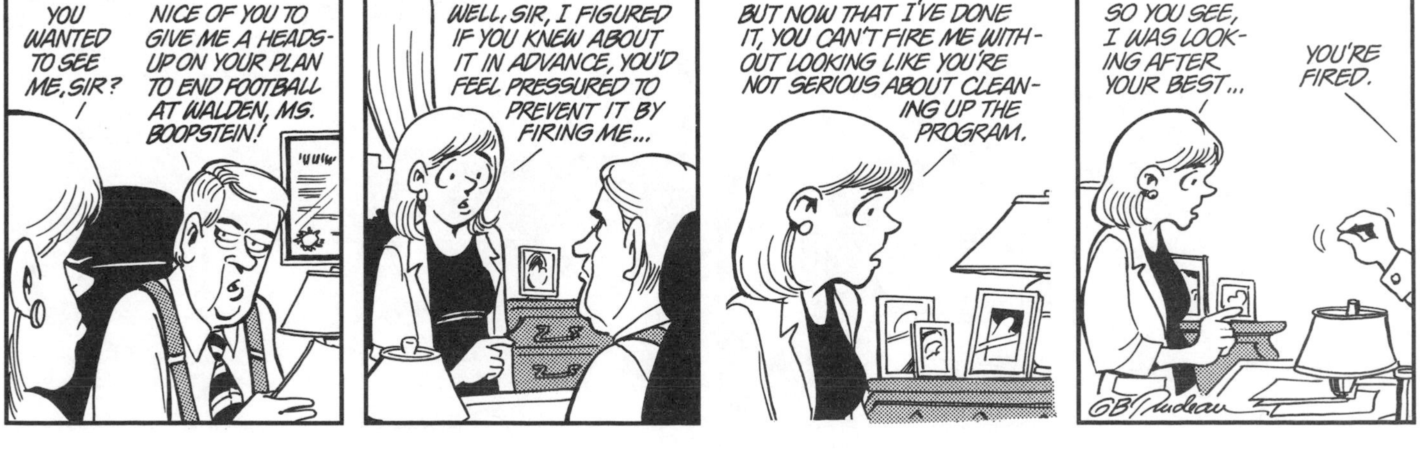
YOU WANTED TO SEE ME, SIR?
NICE OF YOU TO GIVE ME A HEADS-UP ON YOUR PLAN TO END FOOTBALL AT WALDEN, MS. BOOPSTEIN!
WELL, SIR, I FIGURED IF YOU KNEW ABOUT IT IN ADVANCE, YOU'D FEEL PRESSURED TO PREVENT IT BY FIRING ME...
BUT NOW THAT I'VE DONE IT, YOU CAN'T FIRE ME WITHOUT LOOKING LIKE YOU'RE NOT SERIOUS ABOUT CLEANING UP THE PROGRAM.
SO YOU SEE, I WAS LOOKING AFTER YOUR BEST...
YOU'RE FIRED.

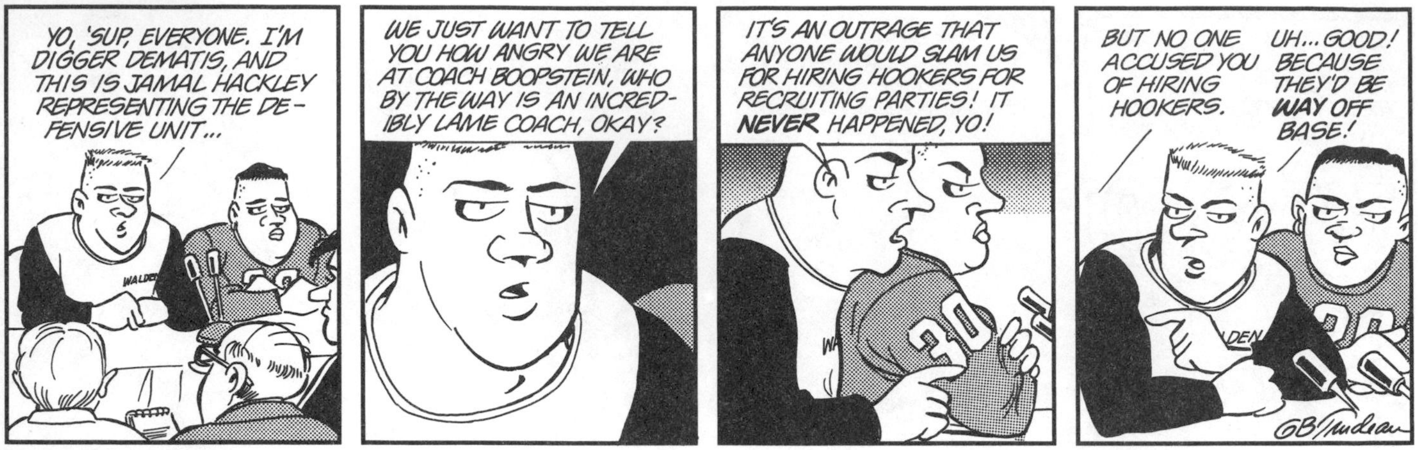
YO, 'SUP, EVERYONE. I'M DIGGER DEMATIS, AND THIS IS JAMAL HACKLEY REPRESENTING THE DE-FENSIVE UNIT...
WE JUST WANT TO TELL YOU HOW ANGRY WE ARE AT COACH BOOPSTEIN, WHO BY THE WAY IS AN INCRED-IBLY LAME COACH, OKAY?
IT'S AN OUTRAGE THAT ANYONE WOULD SLAM US FOR HIRING HOOKERS FOR RECRUITING PARTIES! IT NEVER HAPPENED, YO!
BUT NO ONE ACCUSED YOU OF HIRING HOOKERS.
UH...GOOD! BECAUSE THEY'D BE WAY OFF BASE!
GB Trudeau

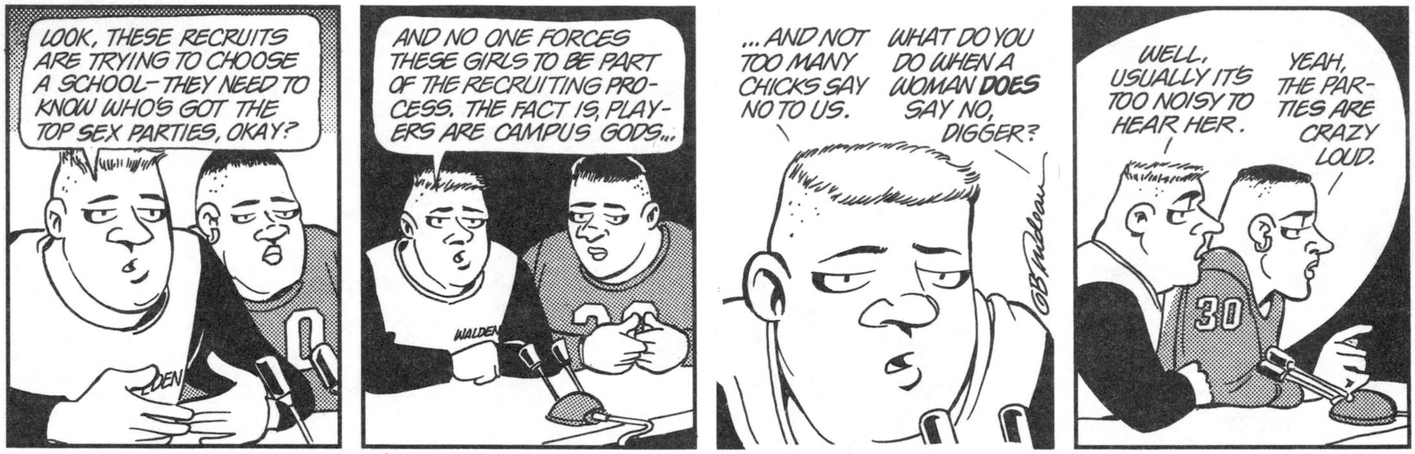
LOOK, THESE RECRUITS ARE TRYING TO CHOOSE A SCHOOL–THEY NEED TO KNOW WHO'S GOT THE TOP SEX PARTIES, OKAY?
AND NO ONE FORCES THESE GIRLS TO BE PART OF THE RECRUITING PRO-CESS. THE FACT IS, PLAY-ERS ARE CAMPUS GODS...
...AND NOT TOO MANY CHICKS SAY NO TO US.
WHAT DO YOU DO WHEN A WOMAN DOES SAY NO, DIGGER?
WELL, USUALLY IT'S TOO NOISY TO HEAR HER.
YEAH, THE PAR-TIES ARE CRAZY LOUD.

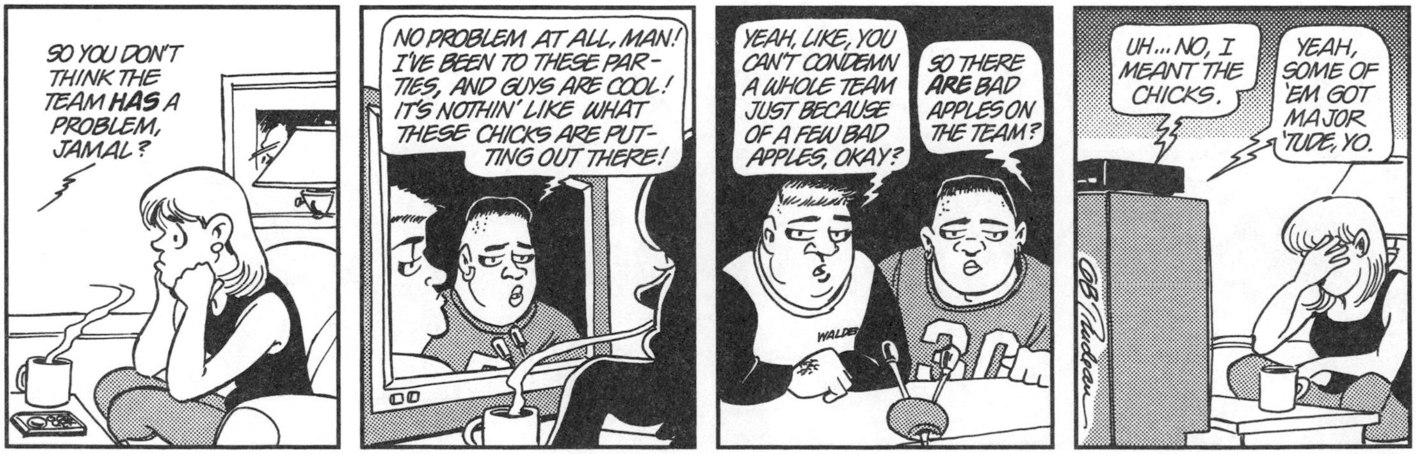
SO YOU DON'T THINK THE TEAM HAS A PROBLEM, JAMAL?
NO PROBLEM AT ALL, MAN! I'VE BEEN TO THESE PAR-TIES, AND GUYS ARE COOL! IT'S NOTHIN' LIKE WHAT THESE CHICKS ARE PUT-TING OUT THERE!
YEAH, LIKE, YOU CAN'T CONDEMN A WHOLE TEAM JUST BECAUSE OF A FEW BAD APPLES, OKAY?
SO THERE ARE BAD APPLES ON THE TEAM?
UH... NO, I MEANT THE CHICKS.
YEAH, SOME OF 'EM GOT MAJOR 'TUDE, YO.

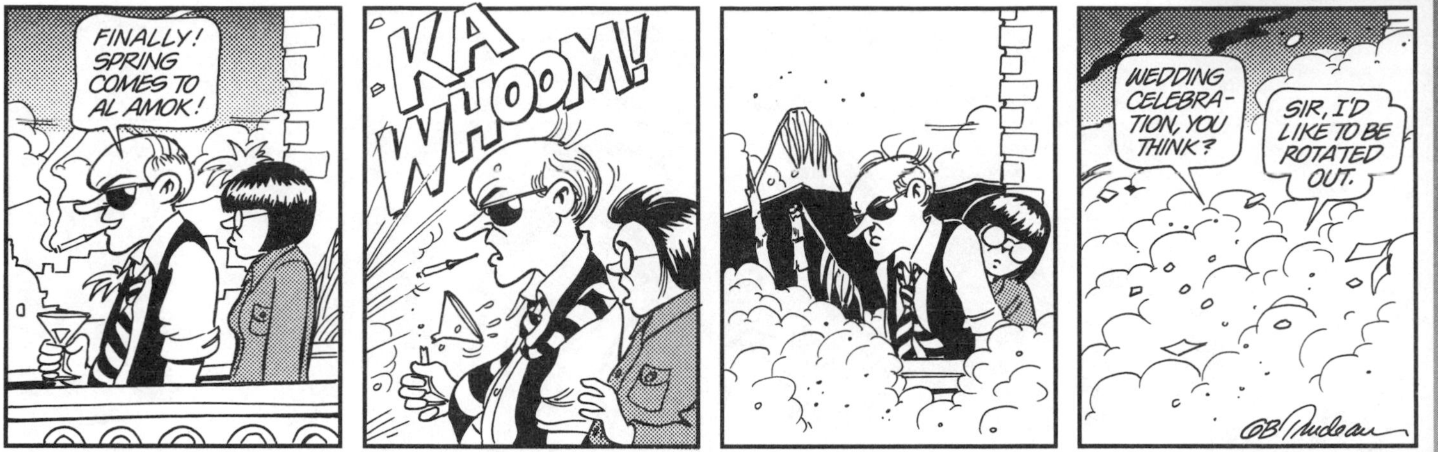
FINALLY! SPRING COMES TO AL AMOK!
KA WHOOM!
WEDDING CELEBRATION, YOU THINK?
SIR, I'D LIKE TO BE ROTATED OUT.

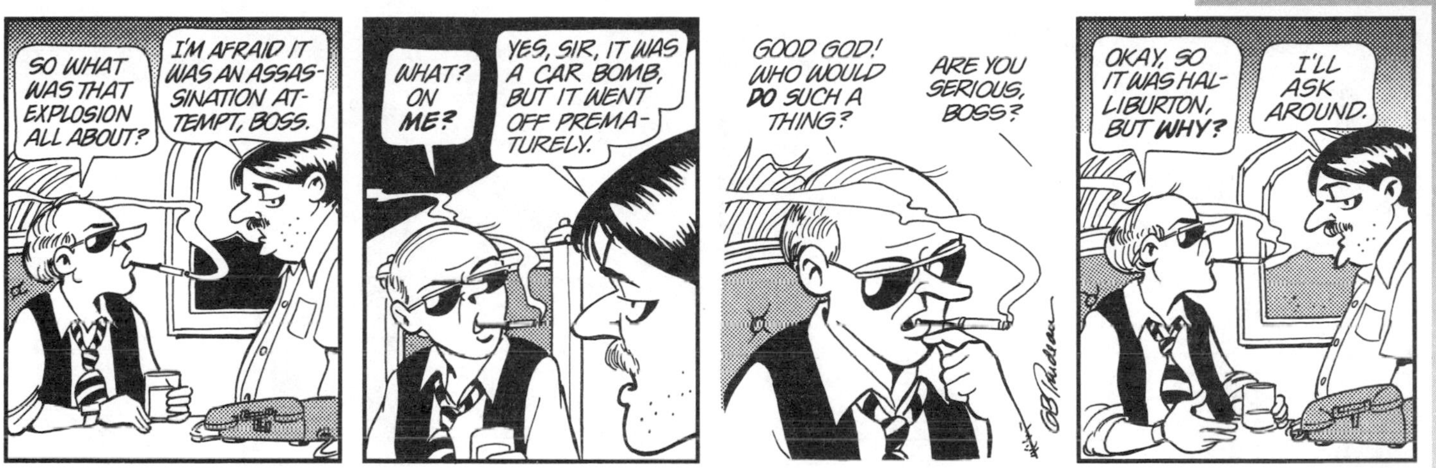
SO WHAT WAS THAT EXPLOSION ALL ABOUT?
I'M AFRAID IT WAS AN ASSASSINATION ATTEMPT, BOSS.
WHAT? ON **ME?**
YES, SIR, IT WAS A CAR BOMB, BUT IT WENT OFF PREMATURELY.
GOOD GOD! WHO WOULD **DO** SUCH A THING?
ARE YOU SERIOUS, BOSS?
OKAY, SO IT WAS HALLIBURTON, BUT **WHY?**
I'LL ASK AROUND.

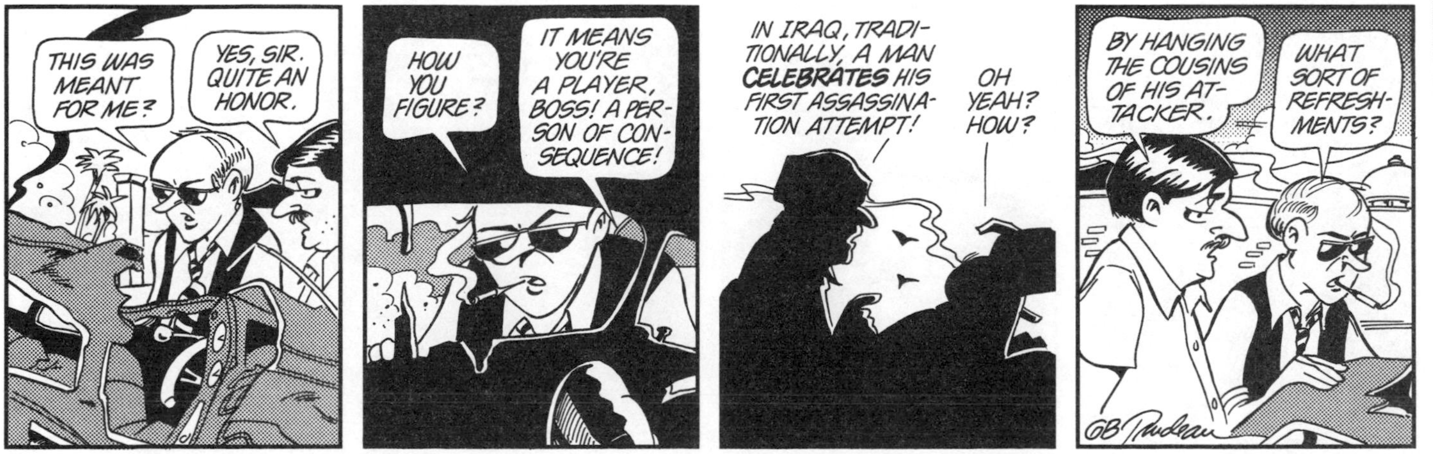
THIS WAS MEANT FOR ME?
YES, SIR. QUITE AN HONOR.
HOW YOU FIGURE?
IT MEANS YOU'RE A PLAYER, BOSS! A PERSON OF CONSEQUENCE!
IN IRAQ, TRADITIONALLY, A MAN **CELEBRATES** HIS FIRST ASSASSINATION ATTEMPT!
OH YEAH? HOW?
BY HANGING THE COUSINS OF HIS ATTACKER.
WHAT SORT OF REFRESHMENTS?

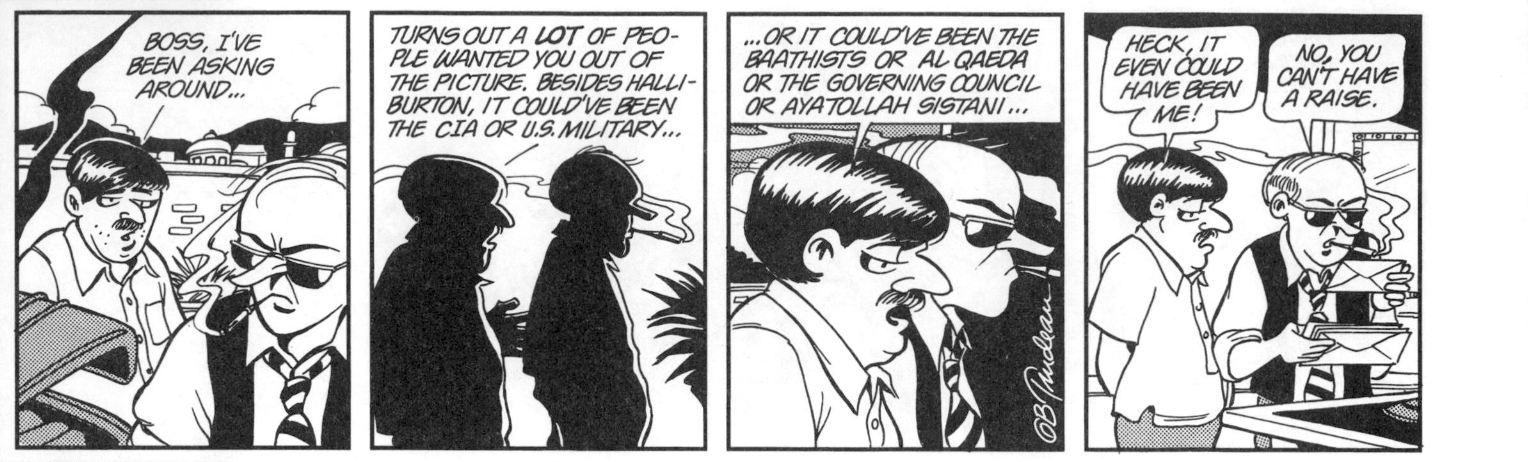
BOSS, I'VE BEEN ASKING AROUND...
TURNS OUT A LOT OF PEOPLE WANTED YOU OUT OF THE PICTURE. BESIDES HALLIBURTON, IT COULD'VE BEEN THE CIA OR U.S. MILITARY...
...OR IT COULD'VE BEEN THE BAATHISTS OR AL QAEDA OR THE GOVERNING COUNCIL OR AYATOLLAH SISTANI...
HECK, IT EVEN COULD HAVE BEEN ME!
NO, YOU CAN'T HAVE A RAISE.
GB Trudeau

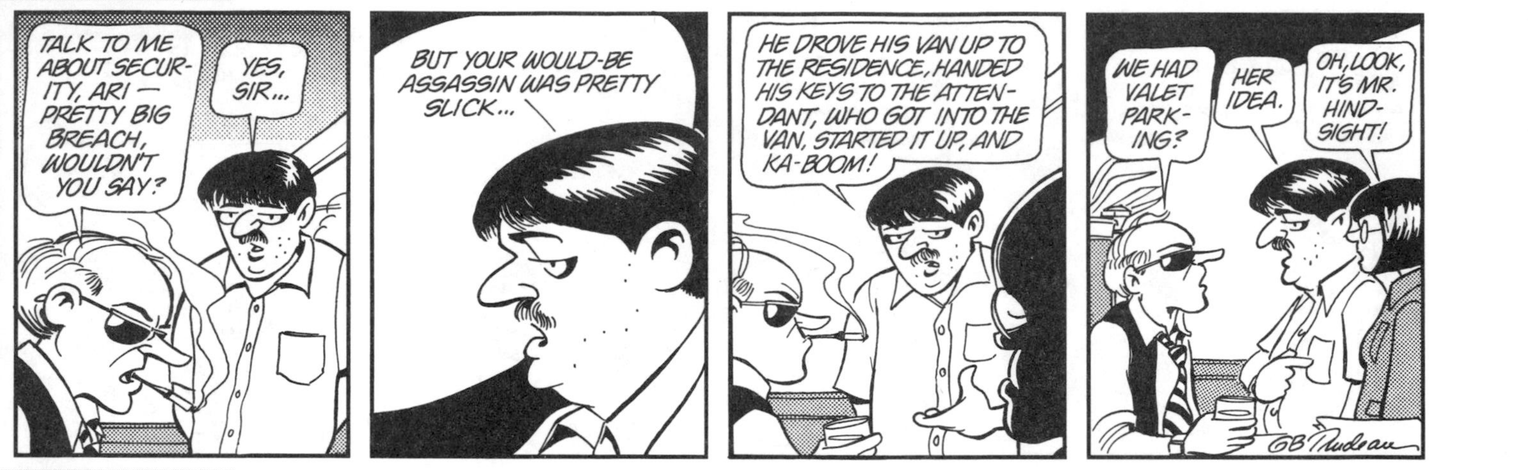
TALK TO ME ABOUT SECURITY, ARI — PRETTY BIG BREACH, WOULDN'T YOU SAY?
YES, SIR...
BUT YOUR WOULD-BE ASSASSIN WAS PRETTY SLICK...
HE DROVE HIS VAN UP TO THE RESIDENCE, HANDED HIS KEYS TO THE ATTENDANT, WHO GOT INTO THE VAN, STARTED IT UP, AND KA-BOOM!
WE HAD VALET PARKING?
HER IDEA.
OH, LOOK, IT'S MR. HINDSIGHT!
GB Trudeau

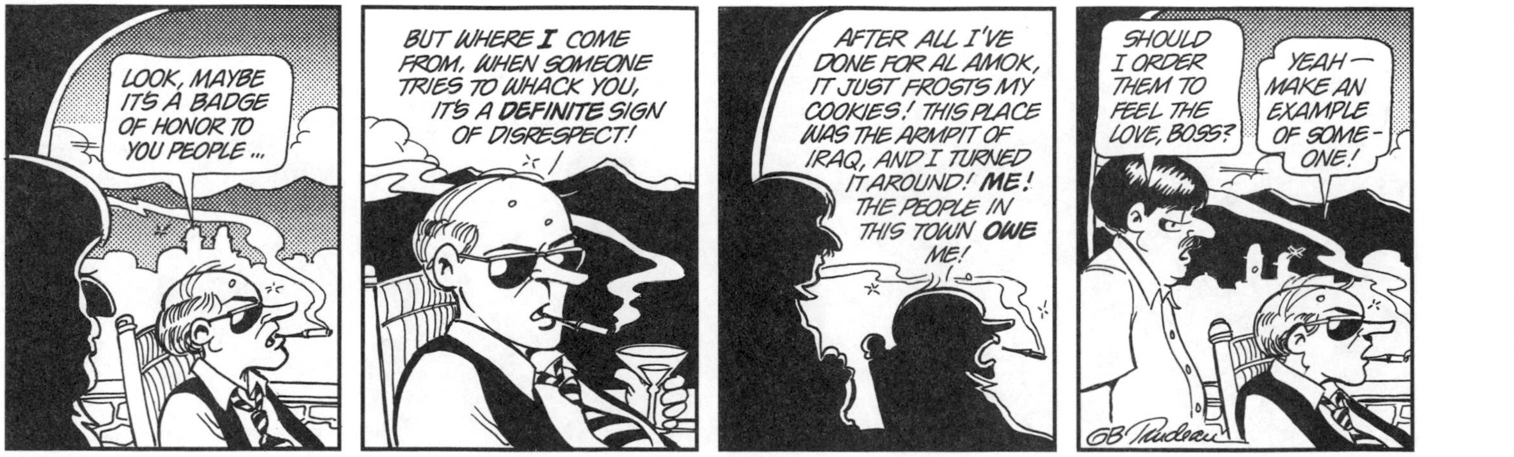
LOOK, MAYBE IT'S A BADGE OF HONOR TO YOU PEOPLE...
BUT WHERE I COME FROM, WHEN SOMEONE TRIES TO WHACK YOU, IT'S A DEFINITE SIGN OF DISRESPECT!
AFTER ALL I'VE DONE FOR AL AMOK, IT JUST FROSTS MY COOKIES! THIS PLACE WAS THE ARMPIT OF IRAQ, AND I TURNED IT AROUND! ME! THE PEOPLE IN THIS TOWN OWE ME!
SHOULD I ORDER THEM TO FEEL THE LOVE, BOSS?
YEAH — MAKE AN EXAMPLE OF SOMEONE!
GB Trudeau

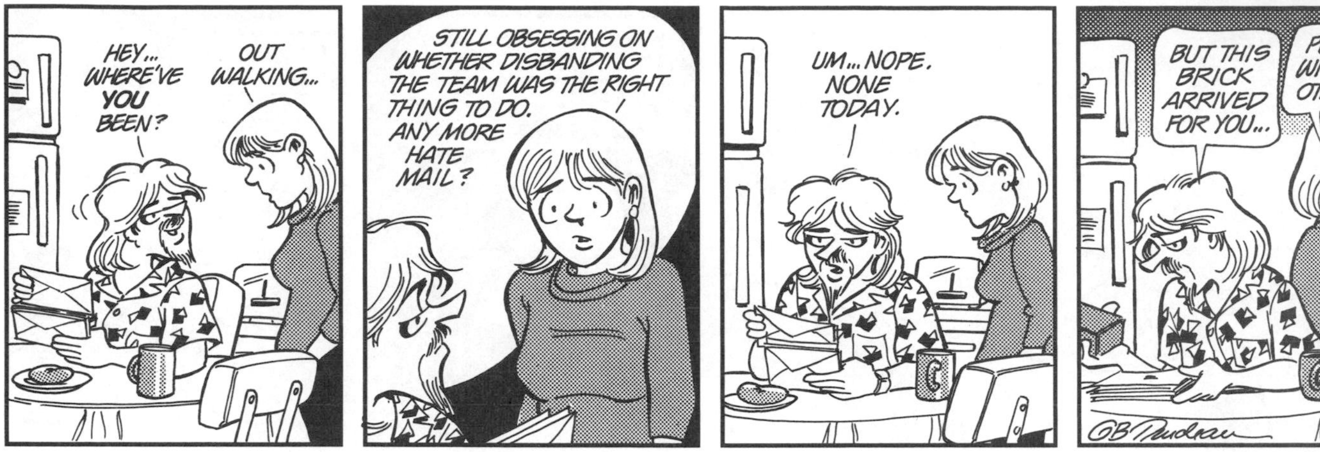
HEY... WHERE'VE **YOU** BEEN?
OUT WALKING...
STILL OBSESSING ON WHETHER DISBANDING THE TEAM WAS THE RIGHT THING TO DO. ANY MORE HATE MAIL?
UM... NOPE. NONE TODAY.
BUT THIS BRICK ARRIVED FOR YOU...
PUT IT WITH THE OTHERS.

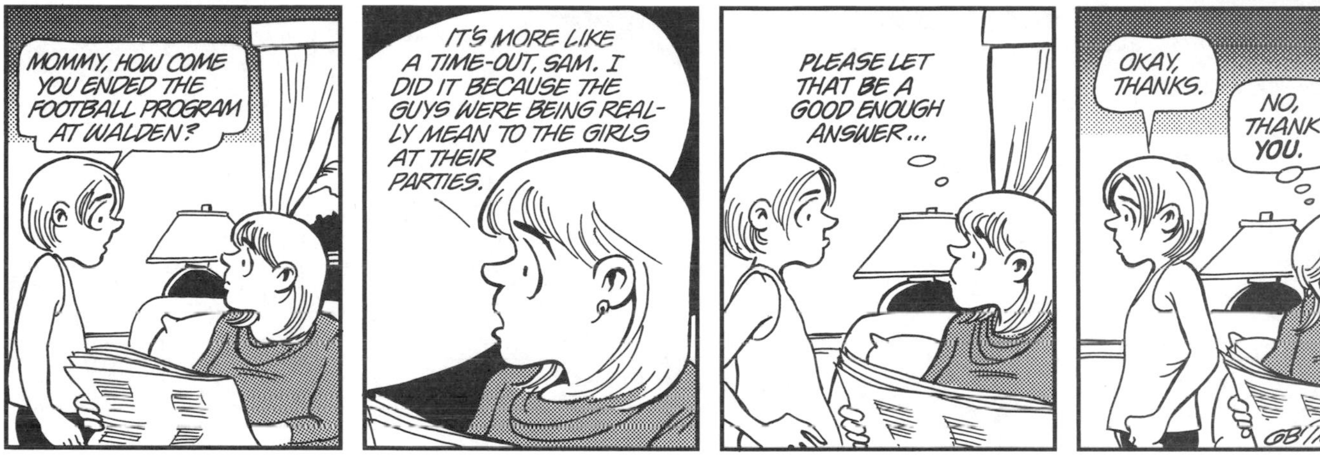
MOMMY, HOW COME YOU ENDED THE FOOTBALL PROGRAM AT WALDEN?
IT'S MORE LIKE A TIME-OUT, SAM. I DID IT BECAUSE THE GUYS WERE BEING REALLY MEAN TO THE GIRLS AT THEIR PARTIES.
PLEASE LET THAT BE A GOOD ENOUGH ANSWER...
OKAY, THANKS.
NO, THANK **YOU**.

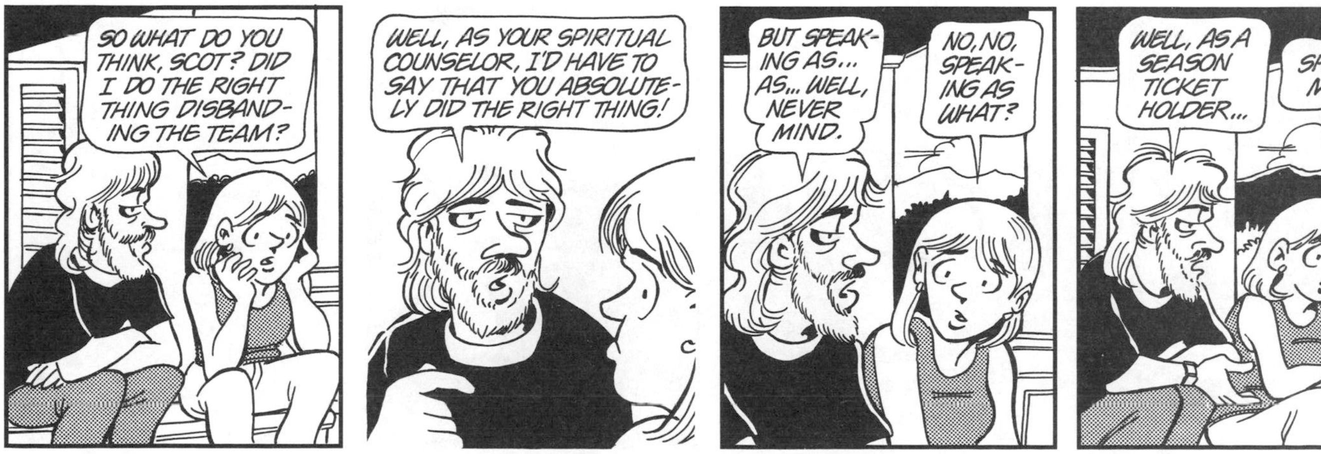
SO WHAT DO YOU THINK, SCOT? DID I DO THE RIGHT THING DISBANDING THE TEAM?
WELL, AS YOUR SPIRITUAL COUNSELOR, I'D HAVE TO SAY THAT YOU ABSOLUTELY DID THE RIGHT THING!
BUT SPEAKING AS... AS... WELL, NEVER MIND.
NO, NO, SPEAKING AS WHAT?
WELL, AS A SEASON TICKET HOLDER...
SPARE ME.

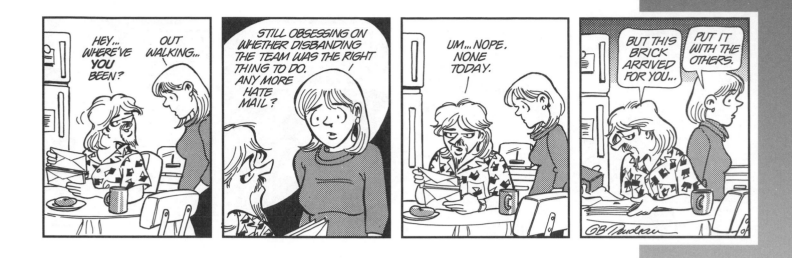

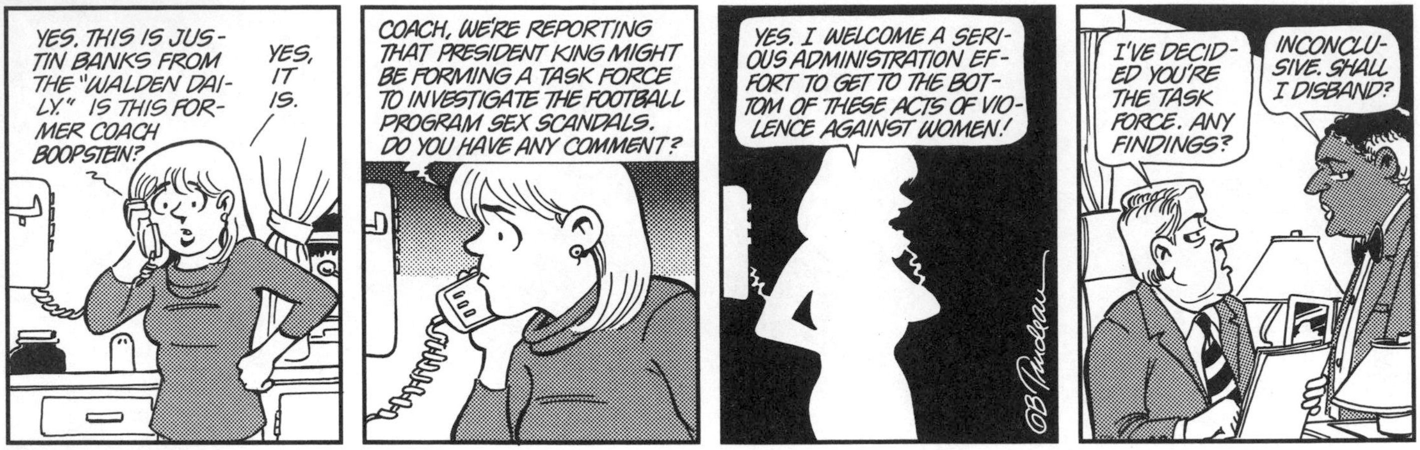
YES. THIS IS JUSTIN BANKS FROM THE "WALDEN DAILY." IS THIS FORMER COACH BOOPSTEIN?
YES, IT IS.
COACH, WE'RE REPORTING THAT PRESIDENT KING MIGHT BE FORMING A TASK FORCE TO INVESTIGATE THE FOOTBALL PROGRAM SEX SCANDALS. DO YOU HAVE ANY COMMENT?
YES. I WELCOME A SERIOUS ADMINISTRATION EFFORT TO GET TO THE BOTTOM OF THESE ACTS OF VIOLENCE AGAINST WOMEN!
I'VE DECIDED YOU'RE THE TASK FORCE. ANY FINDINGS?
INCONCLUSIVE. SHALL I DISBAND?

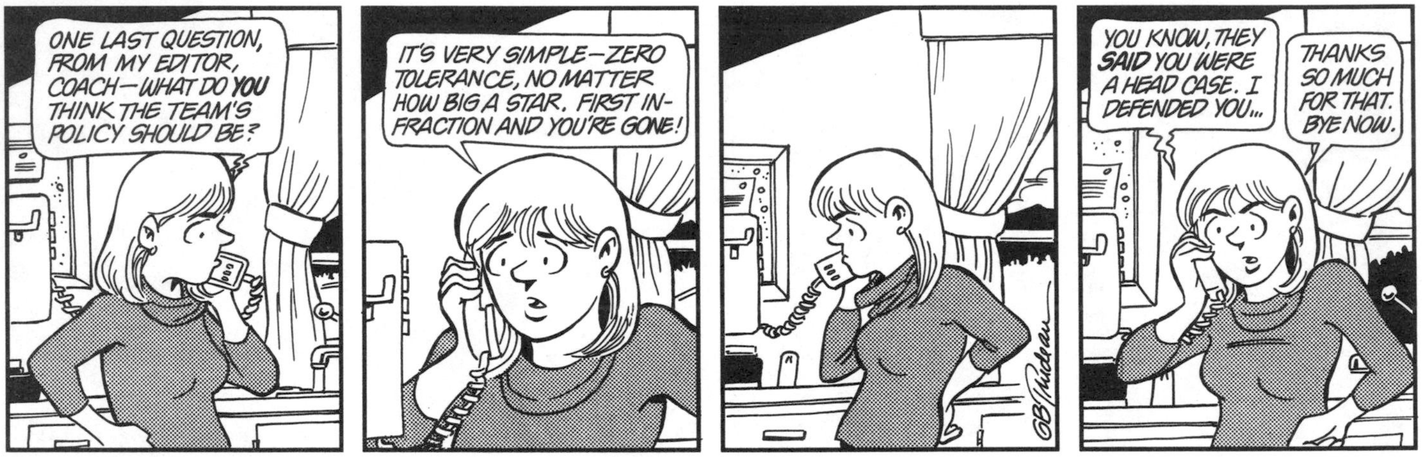
ONE LAST QUESTION, FROM MY EDITOR, COACH—WHAT DO YOU THINK THE TEAM'S POLICY SHOULD BE?
IT'S VERY SIMPLE—ZERO TOLERANCE, NO MATTER HOW BIG A STAR. FIRST INFRACTION AND YOU'RE GONE!
YOU KNOW, THEY SAID YOU WERE A HEAD CASE. I DEFENDED YOU...
THANKS SO MUCH FOR THAT. BYE NOW.

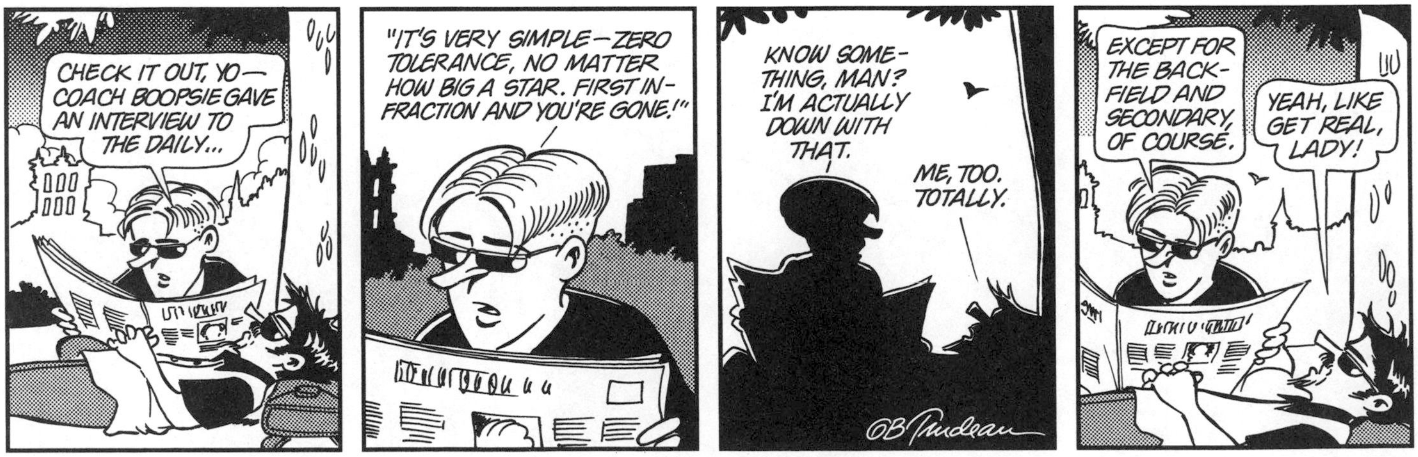
CHECK IT OUT, YO—COACH BOOPSIE GAVE AN INTERVIEW TO THE DAILY...
"IT'S VERY SIMPLE—ZERO TOLERANCE, NO MATTER HOW BIG A STAR. FIRST INFRACTION AND YOU'RE GONE!"
KNOW SOMETHING, MAN? I'M ACTUALLY DOWN WITH THAT.
ME, TOO. TOTALLY.
EXCEPT FOR THE BACKFIELD AND SECONDARY, OF COURSE.
YEAH, LIKE GET REAL, LADY!

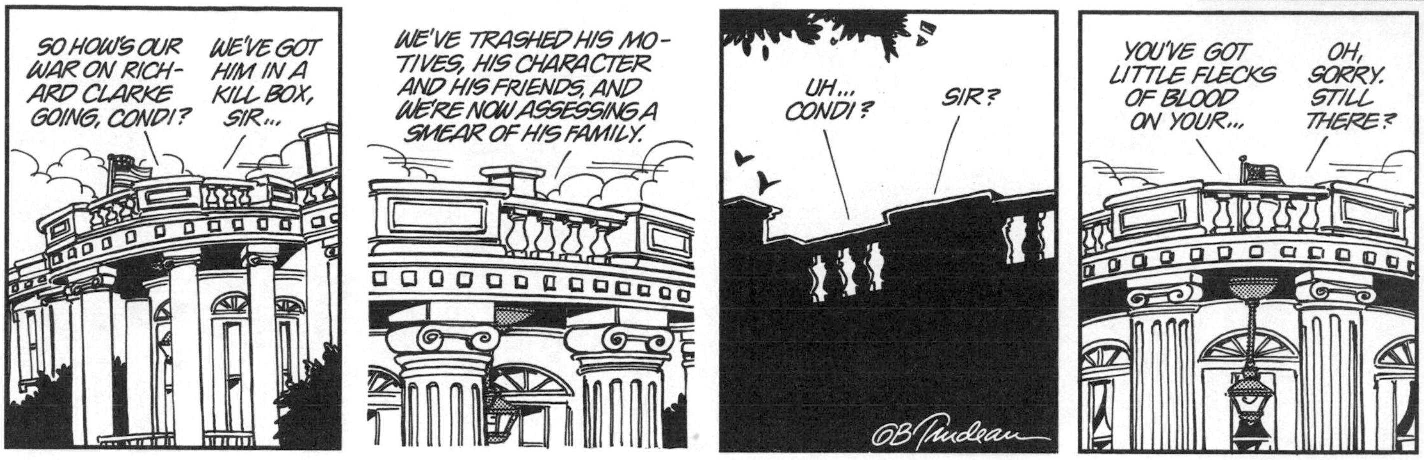
SO HOW'S OUR WAR ON RICHARD CLARKE GOING, CONDI?
WE'VE GOT HIM IN A KILL BOX, SIR...
WE'VE TRASHED HIS MOTIVES, HIS CHARACTER AND HIS FRIENDS, AND WE'RE NOW ASSESSING A SMEAR OF HIS FAMILY.
UH... CONDI?
SIR?
YOU'VE GOT LITTLE FLECKS OF BLOOD ON YOUR...
OH, SORRY. STILL THERE?

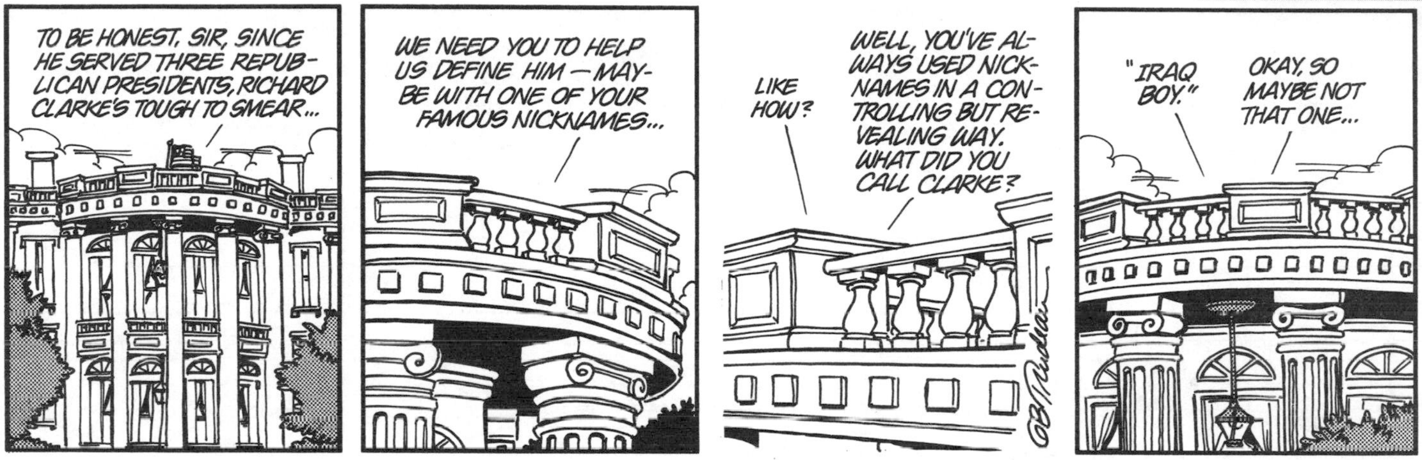
TO BE HONEST, SIR, SINCE HE SERVED THREE REPUBLICAN PRESIDENTS, RICHARD CLARKE'S TOUGH TO SMEAR...
WE NEED YOU TO HELP US DEFINE HIM — MAYBE WITH ONE OF YOUR FAMOUS NICKNAMES...
LIKE HOW?
WELL, YOU'VE ALWAYS USED NICKNAMES IN A CONTROLLING BUT REVEALING WAY. WHAT DID YOU CALL CLARKE?
"IRAQ BOY."
OKAY, SO MAYBE NOT THAT ONE...

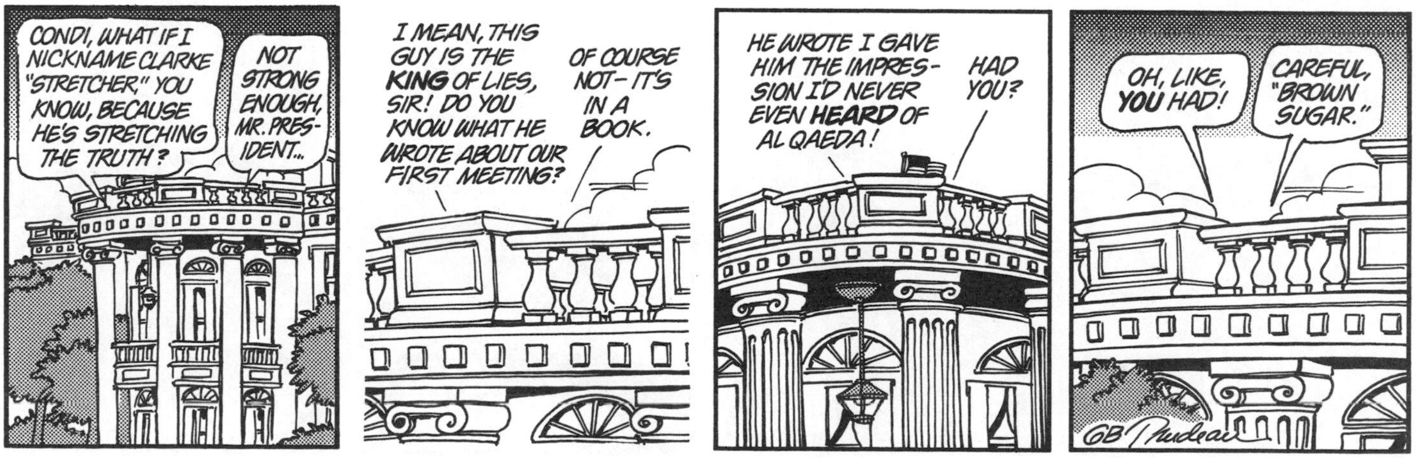
CONDI, WHAT IF I NICKNAME CLARKE "STRETCHER," YOU KNOW, BECAUSE HE'S STRETCHING THE TRUTH?
NOT STRONG ENOUGH, MR. PRESIDENT...
I MEAN, THIS GUY IS THE **KING** OF LIES, SIR! DO YOU KNOW WHAT HE WROTE ABOUT OUR FIRST MEETING?
OF COURSE NOT– IT'S IN A BOOK.
HE WROTE I GAVE HIM THE IMPRESSION I'D NEVER EVEN **HEARD** OF AL QAEDA!
HAD YOU?
OH, LIKE, **YOU** HAD!
CAREFUL, "BROWN SUGAR."

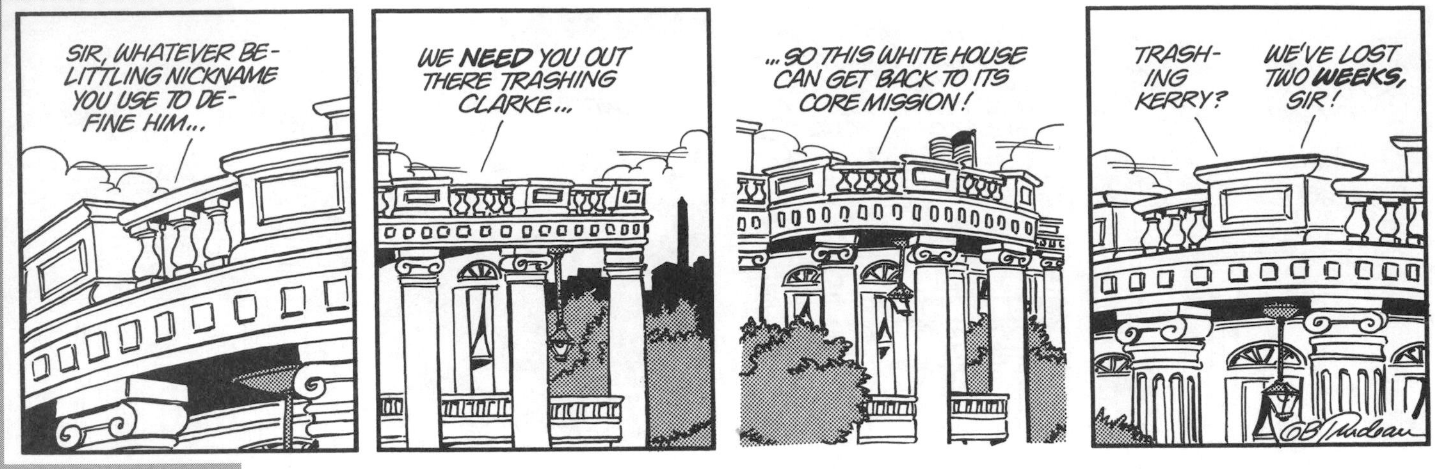
SIR, WHATEVER BE-LITTLING NICKNAME YOU USE TO DE-FINE HIM...
WE NEED YOU OUT THERE TRASHING CLARKE...
...SO THIS WHITE HOUSE CAN GET BACK TO ITS CORE MISSION!
TRASH-ING KERRY?
WE'VE LOST TWO WEEKS, SIR!
©B Trudeau

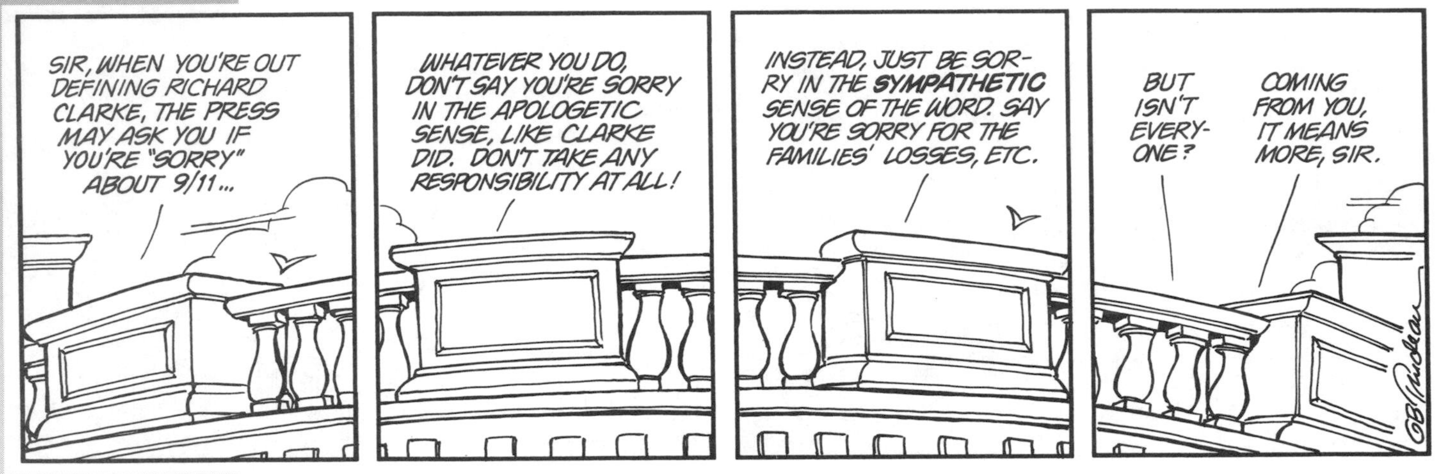
SIR, WHEN YOU'RE OUT DEFINING RICHARD CLARKE, THE PRESS MAY ASK YOU IF YOU'RE "SORRY" ABOUT 9/11...
WHATEVER YOU DO, DON'T SAY YOU'RE SORRY IN THE APOLOGETIC SENSE, LIKE CLARKE DID. DON'T TAKE ANY RESPONSIBILITY AT ALL!
INSTEAD, JUST BE SOR-RY IN THE SYMPATHETIC SENSE OF THE WORD. SAY YOU'RE SORRY FOR THE FAMILIES' LOSSES, ETC.
BUT ISN'T EVERY-ONE?
COMING FROM YOU, IT MEANS MORE, SIR.
©B Trudeau

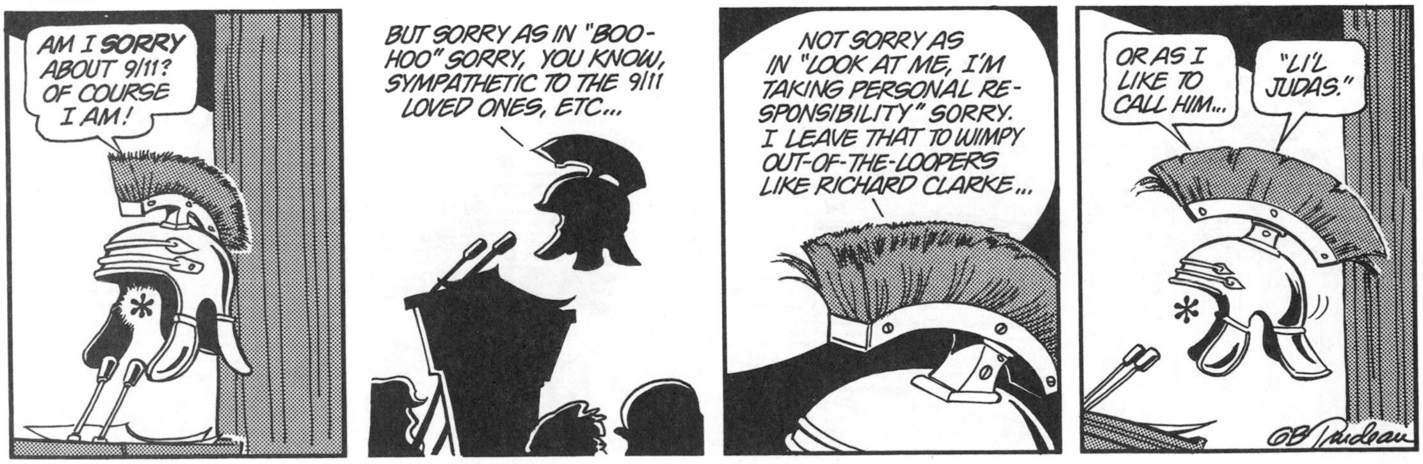
AM I SORRY ABOUT 9/11? OF COURSE I AM!
BUT SORRY AS IN "BOO-HOO" SORRY, YOU KNOW, SYMPATHETIC TO THE 9/11 LOVED ONES, ETC...
NOT SORRY AS IN "LOOK AT ME, I'M TAKING PERSONAL RE-SPONSIBILITY" SORRY. I LEAVE THAT TO WIMPY OUT-OF-THE-LOOPERS LIKE RICHARD CLARKE...
OR AS I LIKE TO CALL HIM...
"LI'L JUDAS."
©B Trudeau

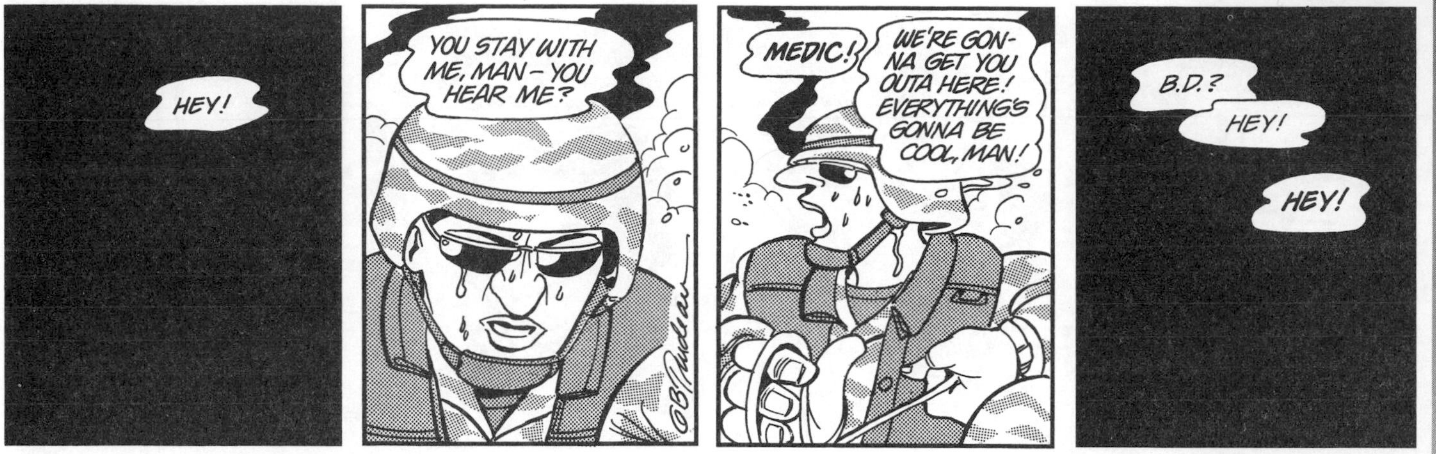
HEY!
YOU STAY WITH ME, MAN – YOU HEAR ME?
MEDIC!
WE'RE GON-NA GET YOU OUTA HERE! EVERYTHING'S GONNA BE COOL, MAN!
B.D.?
HEY!
HEY!

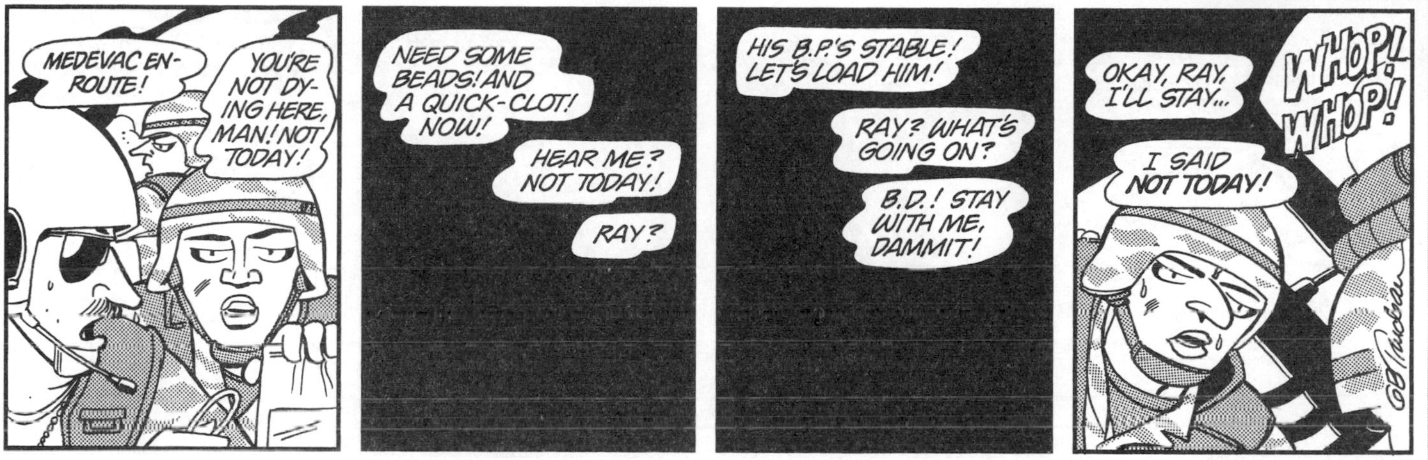
MEDEVAC EN-ROUTE!
YOU'RE NOT DY-ING HERE, MAN! NOT TODAY!
NEED SOME BEADS! AND A QUICK-CLOT! NOW!
HEAR ME? NOT TODAY!
RAY?
HIS B.P.'S STABLE! LET'S LOAD HIM!
RAY? WHAT'S GOING ON?
B.D.! STAY WITH ME, DAMMIT!
OKAY, RAY, I'LL STAY...
WHOP! WHOP!
I SAID NOT TODAY!

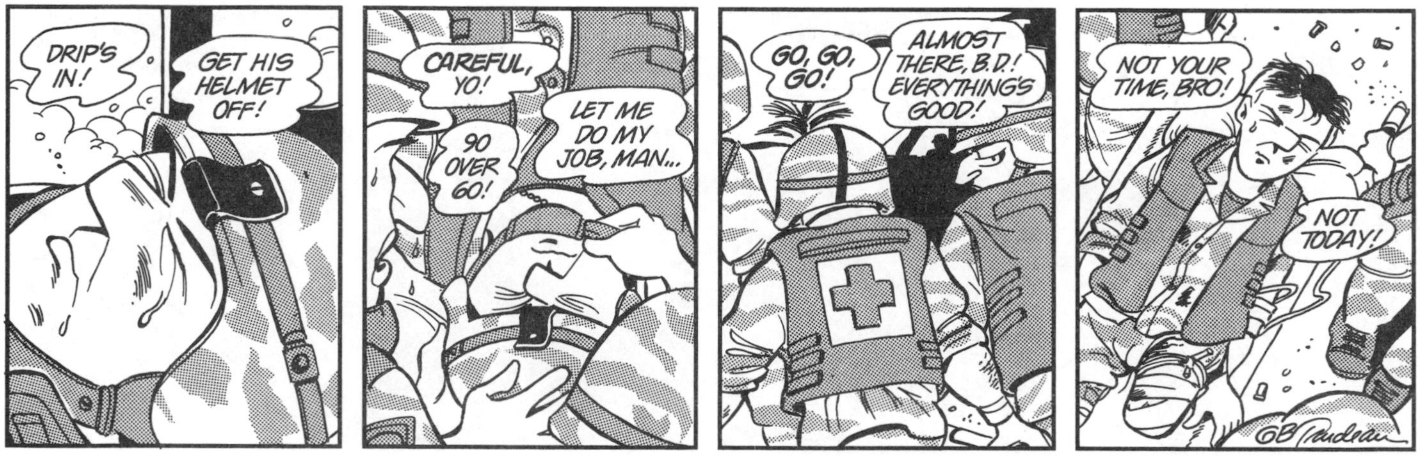
DRIP'S IN!
GET HIS HELMET OFF!
CAREFUL, YO!
90 OVER 60!
LET ME DO MY JOB, MAN...
GO, GO, GO!
ALMOST THERE, B.D.! EVERYTHING'S GOOD!
NOT YOUR TIME, BRO!
NOT TODAY!

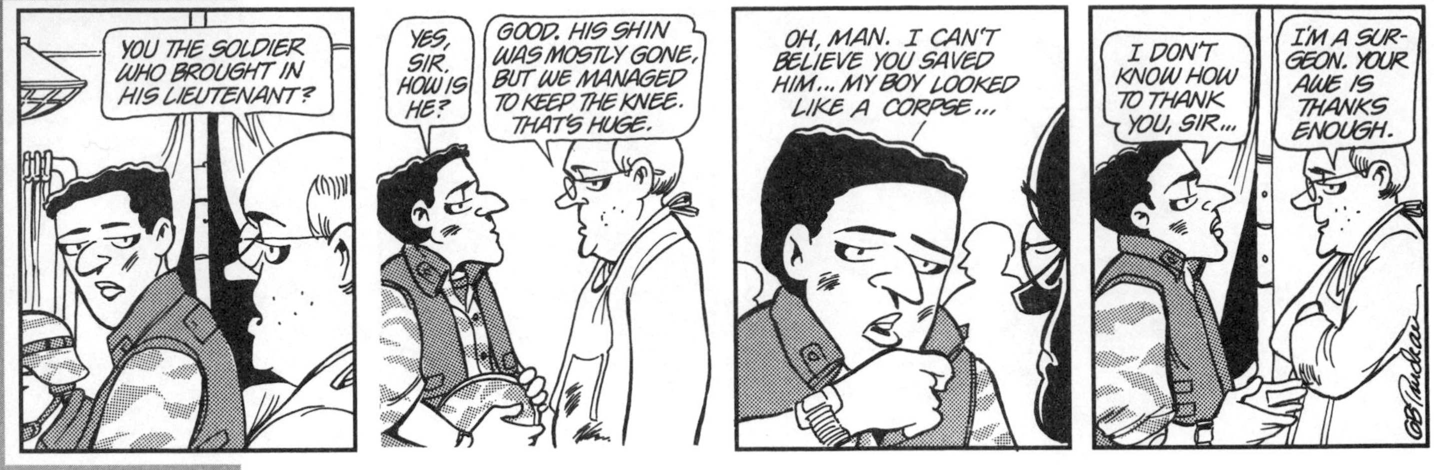
YOU THE SOLDIER WHO BROUGHT IN HIS LIEUTENANT?
YES, SIR. HOW IS HE?
GOOD. HIS SHIN WAS MOSTLY GONE, BUT WE MANAGED TO KEEP THE KNEE. THAT'S HUGE.
OH, MAN. I CAN'T BELIEVE YOU SAVED HIM... MY BOY LOOKED LIKE A CORPSE...
I DON'T KNOW HOW TO THANK YOU, SIR...
I'M A SURGEON. YOUR AWE IS THANKS ENOUGH.

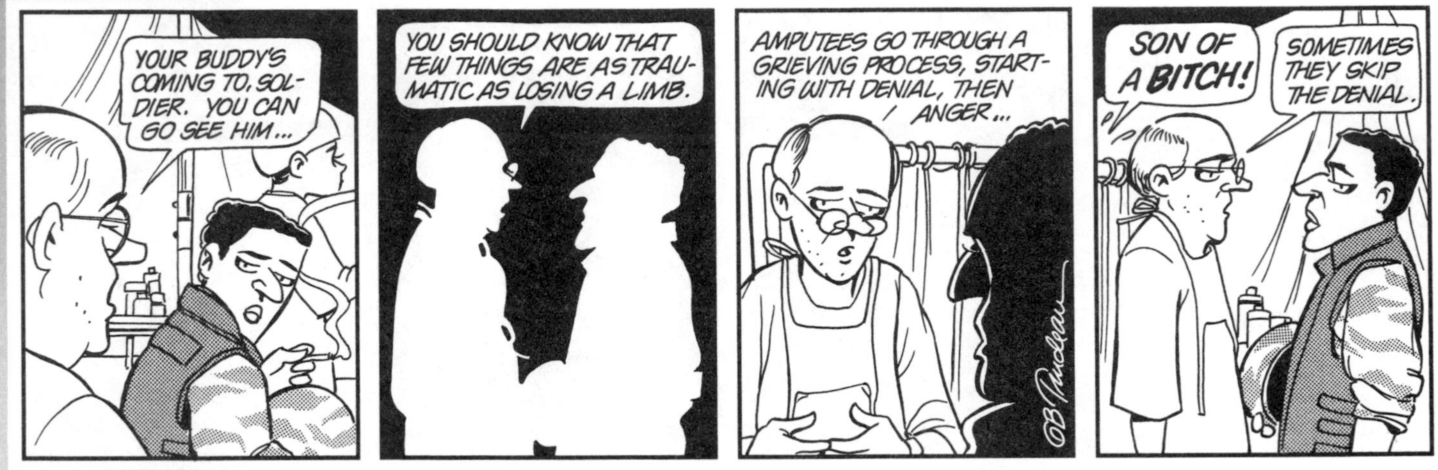
YOUR BUDDY'S COMING TO, SOLDIER. YOU CAN GO SEE HIM...
YOU SHOULD KNOW THAT FEW THINGS ARE AS TRAUMATIC AS LOSING A LIMB.
AMPUTEES GO THROUGH A GRIEVING PROCESS, STARTING WITH DENIAL, THEN ANGER...
SON OF A BITCH!
SOMETIMES THEY SKIP THE DENIAL.

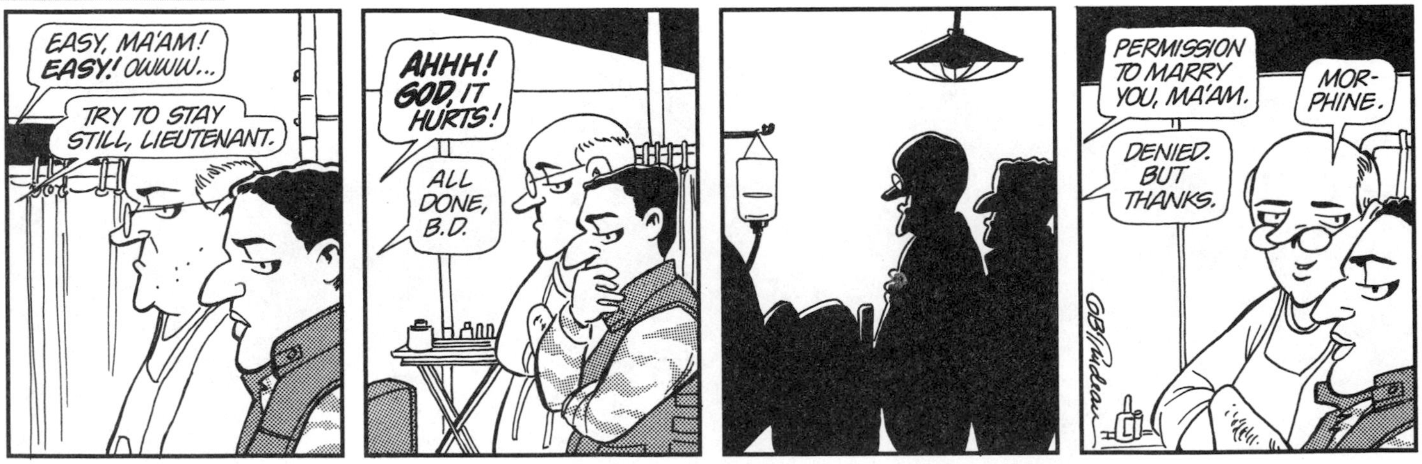
EASY, MA'AM! EASY! OWWW...
TRY TO STAY STILL, LIEUTENANT.
AHHH! GOD, IT HURTS!
ALL DONE, B.D.
PERMISSION TO MARRY YOU, MA'AM.
MORPHINE.
DENIED. BUT THANKS.

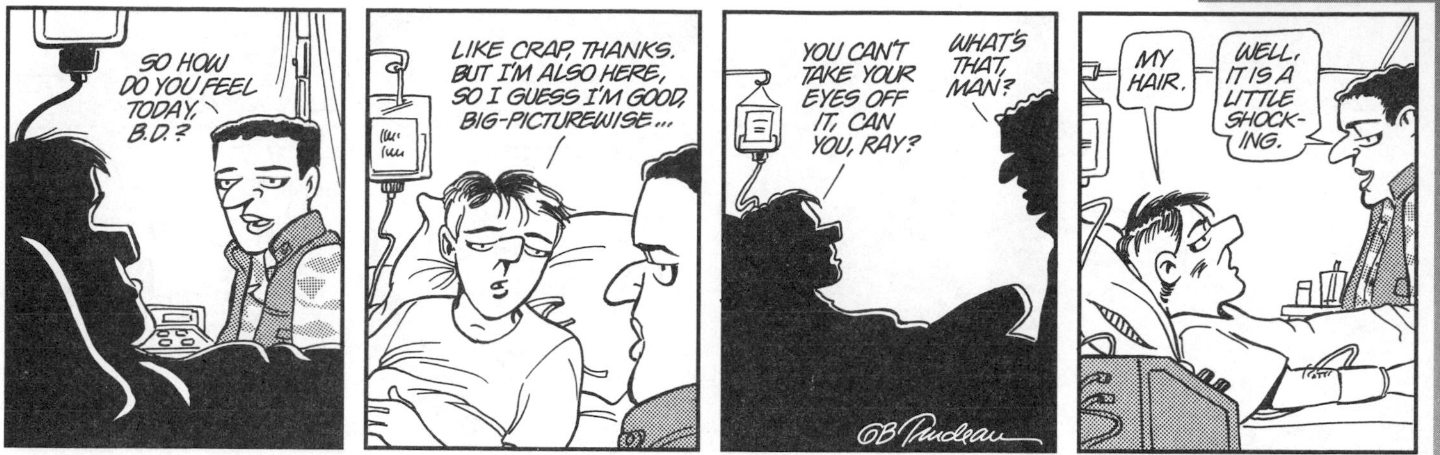
SO HOW DO YOU FEEL TODAY, B.D.?
LIKE CRAP, THANKS. BUT I'M ALSO HERE, SO I GUESS I'M GOOD, BIG-PICTUREWISE...
YOU CAN'T TAKE YOUR EYES OFF IT, CAN YOU, RAY?
WHAT'S THAT, MAN?
MY HAIR.
WELL, IT IS A LITTLE SHOCKING.
GB Trudeau

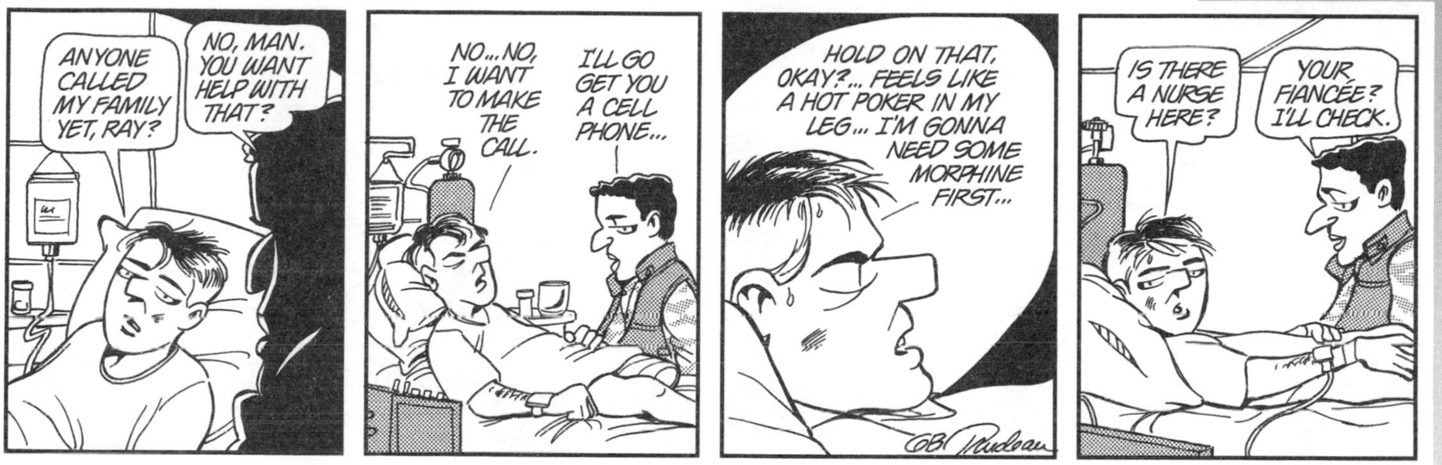
ANYONE CALLED MY FAMILY YET, RAY?
NO, MAN. YOU WANT HELP WITH THAT?
NO... NO, I WANT TO MAKE THE CALL.
I'LL GO GET YOU A CELL PHONE...
HOLD ON THAT. OKAY?... FEELS LIKE A HOT POKER IN MY LEG... I'M GONNA NEED SOME MORPHINE FIRST...
IS THERE A NURSE HERE?
YOUR FIANCÉE? I'LL CHECK.
GB Trudeau

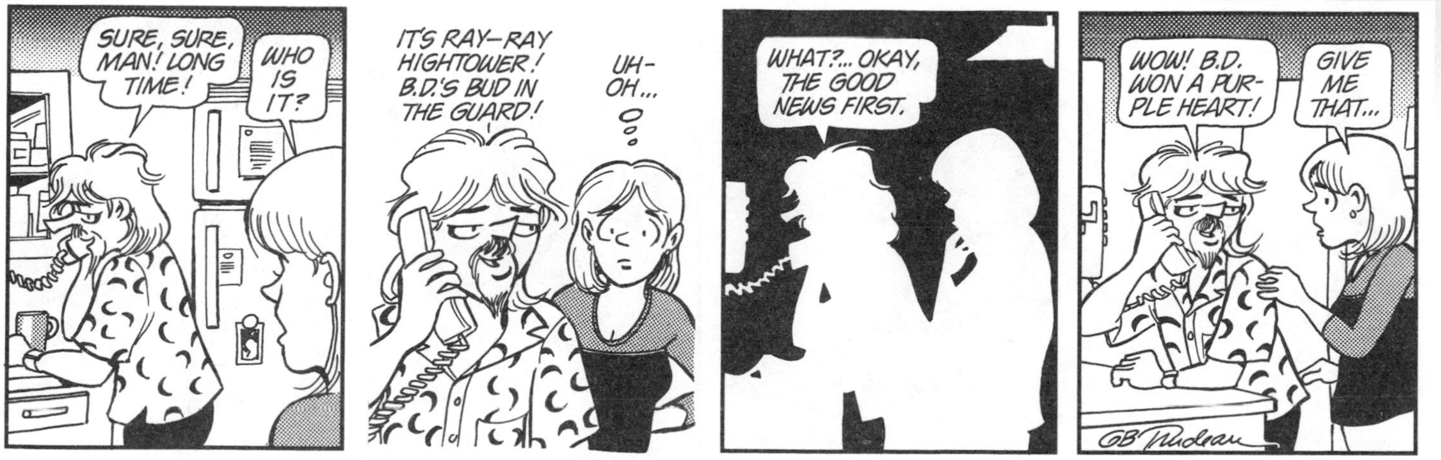
SURE, SURE, MAN! LONG TIME!
WHO IS IT?
IT'S RAY-RAY HIGHTOWER! B.D.'S BUD IN THE GUARD!
UH-OH...
WHAT?... OKAY, THE GOOD NEWS FIRST.
WOW! B.D. WON A PURPLE HEART!
GIVE ME THAT...
GB Trudeau

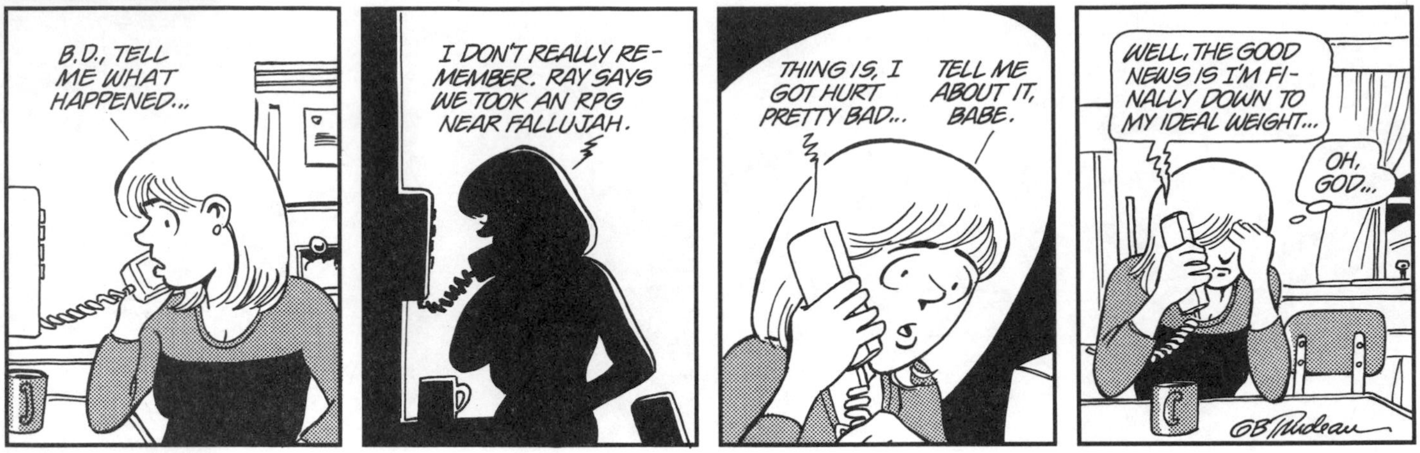
B.D., TELL ME WHAT HAPPENED...
I DON'T REALLY RE-MEMBER. RAY SAYS WE TOOK AN RPG NEAR FALLUJAH.
THING IS, I GOT HURT PRETTY BAD...
TELL ME ABOUT IT, BABE.
WELL, THE GOOD NEWS IS I'M FI-NALLY DOWN TO MY IDEAL WEIGHT...
OH, GOD...

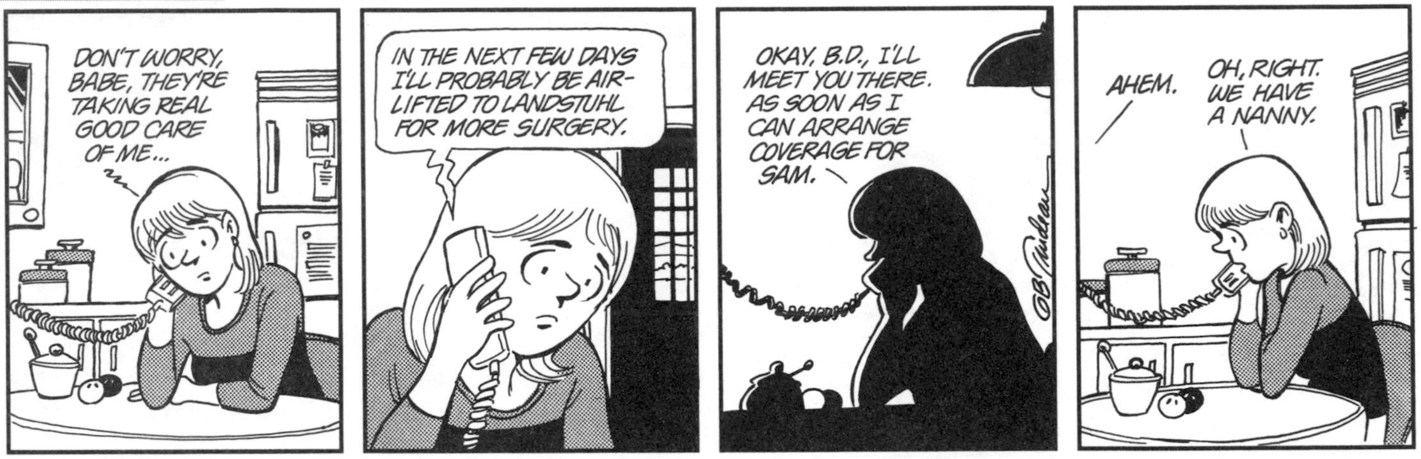
DON'T WORRY, BABE, THEY'RE TAKING REAL GOOD CARE OF ME...
IN THE NEXT FEW DAYS I'LL PROBABLY BE AIR-LIFTED TO LANDSTUHL FOR MORE SURGERY.
OKAY, B.D., I'LL MEET YOU THERE. AS SOON AS I CAN ARRANGE COVERAGE FOR SAM.
AHEM.
OH, RIGHT. WE HAVE A NANNY.

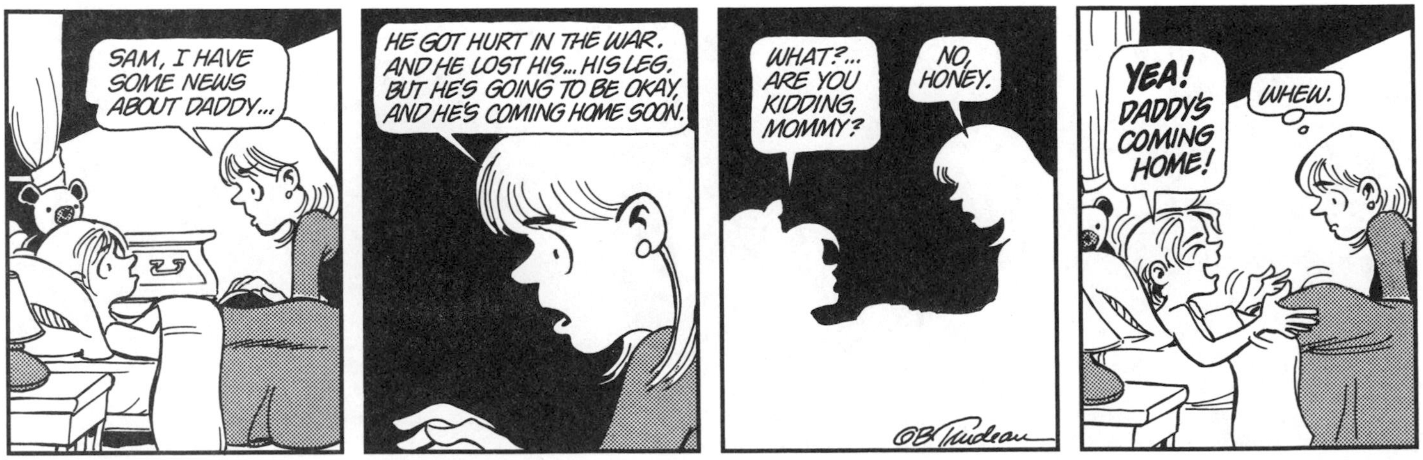
SAM, I HAVE SOME NEWS ABOUT DADDY...
HE GOT HURT IN THE WAR. AND HE LOST HIS... HIS LEG. BUT HE'S GOING TO BE OKAY, AND HE'S COMING HOME SOON.
WHAT?... ARE YOU KIDDING, MOMMY?
NO, HONEY.
YEA! DADDY'S COMING HOME!
WHEW.

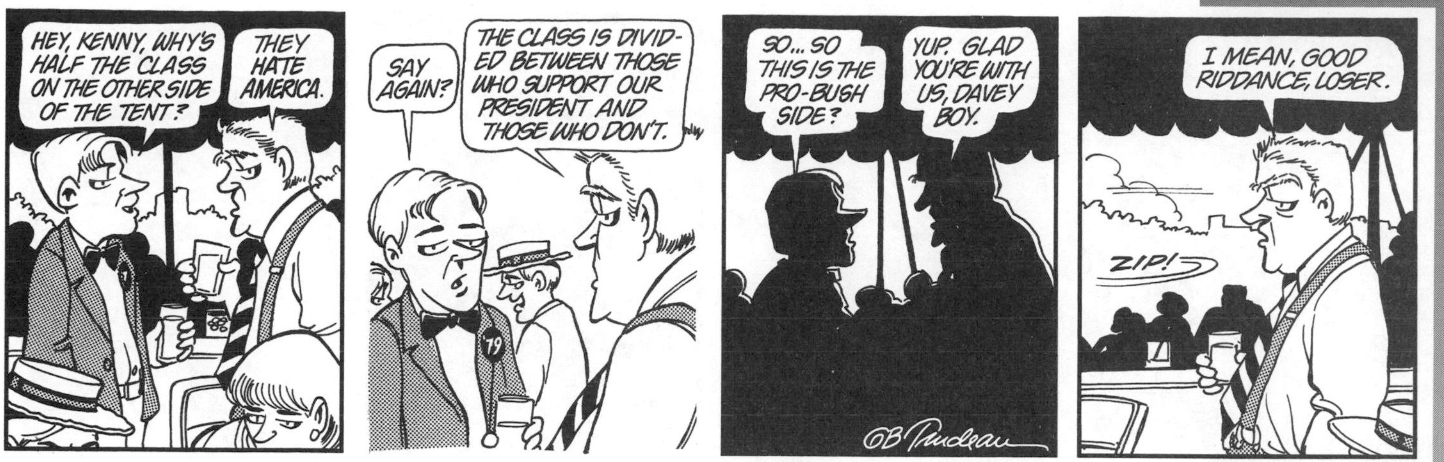
HEY, KENNY, WHY'S HALF THE CLASS ON THE OTHER SIDE OF THE TENT?
THEY HATE AMERICA.
SAY AGAIN?
THE CLASS IS DIVIDED BETWEEN THOSE WHO SUPPORT OUR PRESIDENT AND THOSE WHO DON'T.
SO... SO THIS IS THE PRO-BUSH SIDE?
YUP. GLAD YOU'RE WITH US, DAVEY BOY.
I MEAN, GOOD RIDDANCE, LOSER.
ZIP!

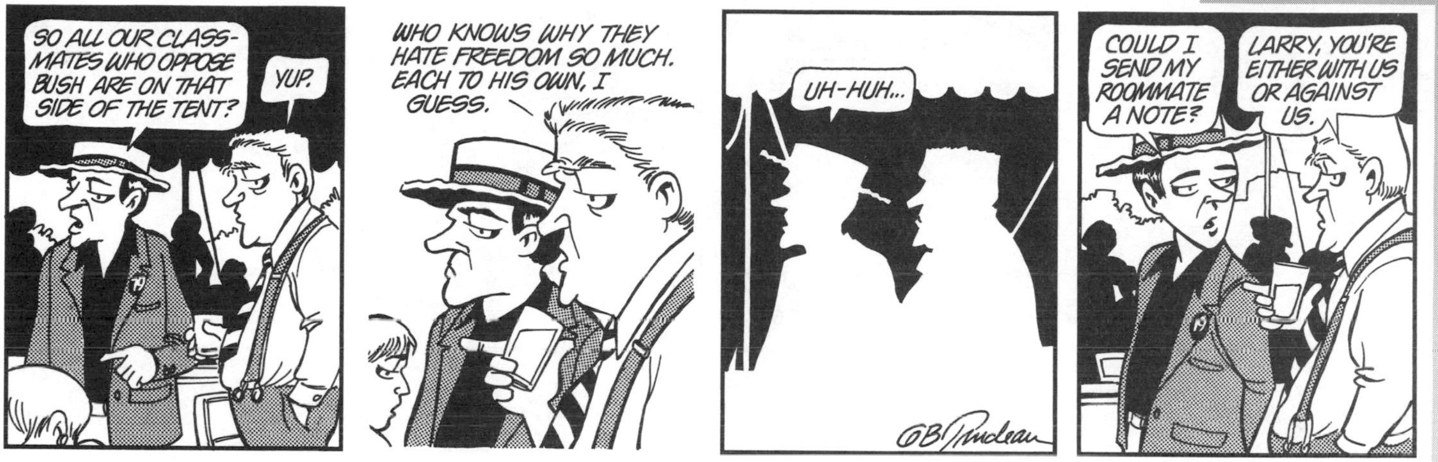
SO ALL OUR CLASSMATES WHO OPPOSE BUSH ARE ON THAT SIDE OF THE TENT?
YUP.
WHO KNOWS WHY THEY HATE FREEDOM SO MUCH. EACH TO HIS OWN, I GUESS.
UH-HUH...
COULD I SEND MY ROOMMATE A NOTE?
LARRY, YOU'RE EITHER WITH US OR AGAINST US.

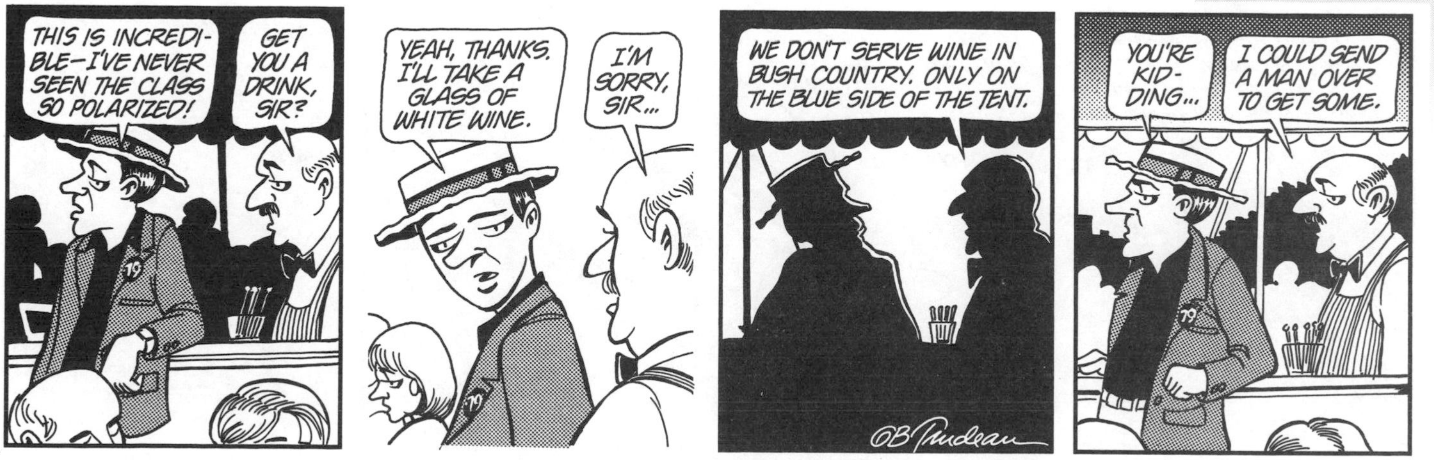
THIS IS INCREDIBLE—I'VE NEVER SEEN THE CLASS SO POLARIZED!
GET YOU A DRINK, SIR?
YEAH, THANKS. I'LL TAKE A GLASS OF WHITE WINE.
I'M SORRY, SIR...
WE DON'T SERVE WINE IN BUSH COUNTRY. ONLY ON THE BLUE SIDE OF THE TENT.
YOU'RE KIDDING...
I COULD SEND A MAN OVER TO GET SOME.

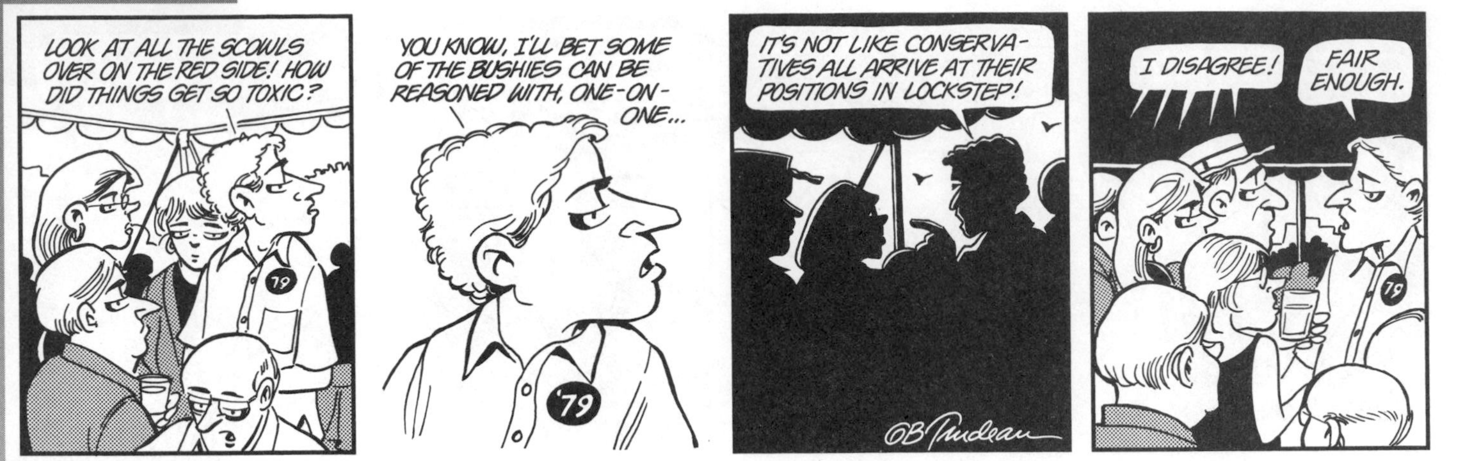
LOOK AT ALL THE SCOWLS OVER ON THE RED SIDE! HOW DID THINGS GET SO TOXIC?
YOU KNOW, I'LL BET SOME OF THE BUSHIES CAN BE REASONED WITH, ONE-ON-ONE...
IT'S NOT LIKE CONSERVA-TIVES ALL ARRIVE AT THEIR POSITIONS IN LOCKSTEP!
I DISAGREE!
FAIR ENOUGH.

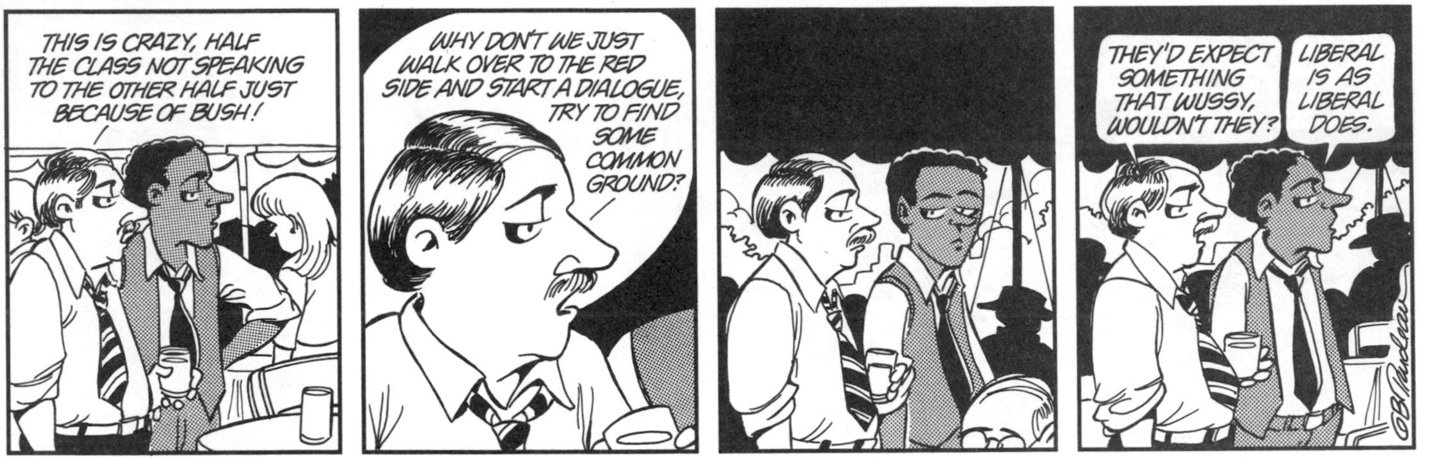
THIS IS CRAZY, HALF THE CLASS NOT SPEAKING TO THE OTHER HALF JUST BECAUSE OF BUSH!
WHY DON'T WE JUST WALK OVER TO THE RED SIDE AND START A DIALOGUE, TRY TO FIND SOME COMMON GROUND?
THEY'D EXPECT SOMETHING THAT WUSSY, WOULDN'T THEY?
LIBERAL IS AS LIBERAL DOES.

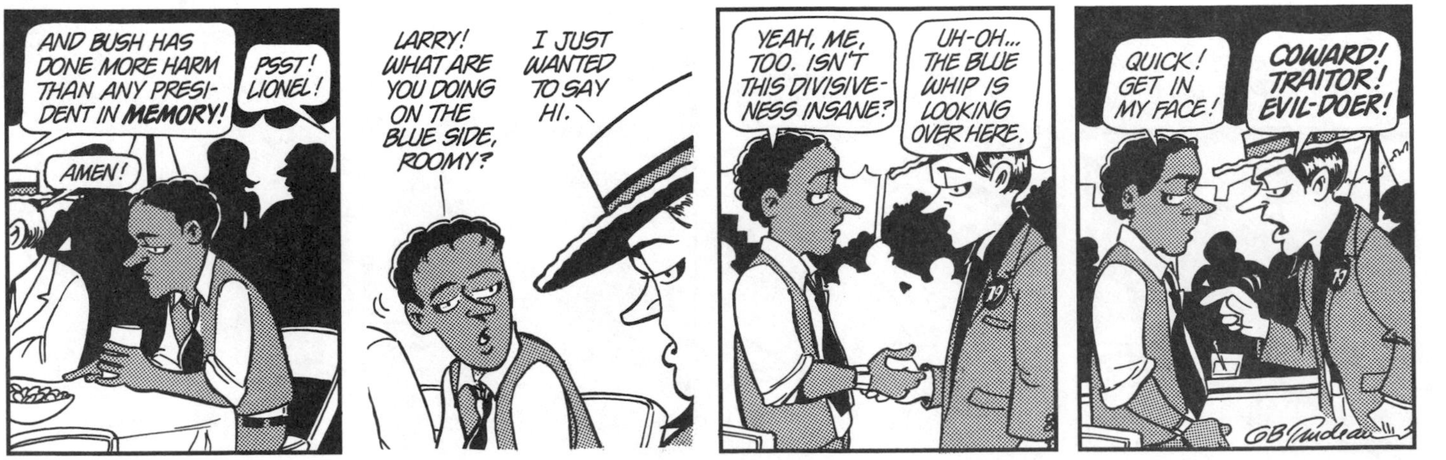
AND BUSH HAS DONE MORE HARM THAN ANY PRESI-DENT IN **MEMORY**!
PSST! LIONEL!
AMEN!
LARRY! WHAT ARE YOU DOING ON THE BLUE SIDE, ROOMY?
I JUST WANTED TO SAY HI.
YEAH, ME, TOO. ISN'T THIS DIVISIVE-NESS INSANE?
UH-OH... THE BLUE WHIP IS LOOKING OVER HERE.
QUICK! GET IN MY FACE!
COWARD! TRAITOR! EVIL-DOER!

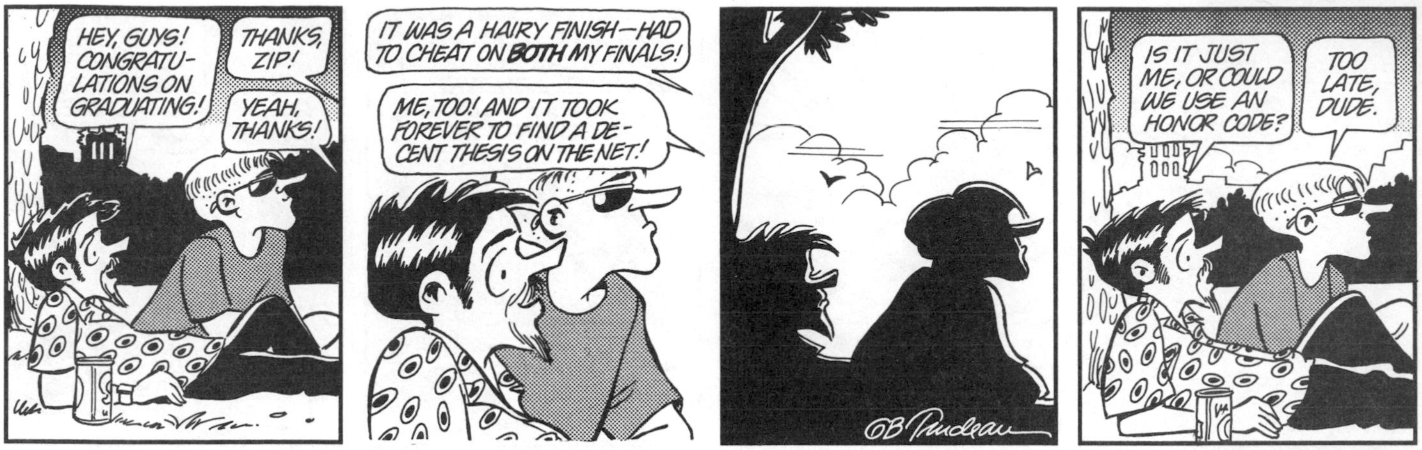
HEY, GUYS! CONGRATULATIONS ON GRADUATING!
THANKS, ZIP!
YEAH, THANKS!
IT WAS A HAIRY FINISH—HAD TO CHEAT ON **BOTH** MY FINALS!
ME, TOO! AND IT TOOK FOREVER TO FIND A DECENT THESIS ON THE NET!
GB Trudeau
IS IT JUST ME, OR COULD WE USE AN HONOR CODE?
TOO LATE, DUDE.

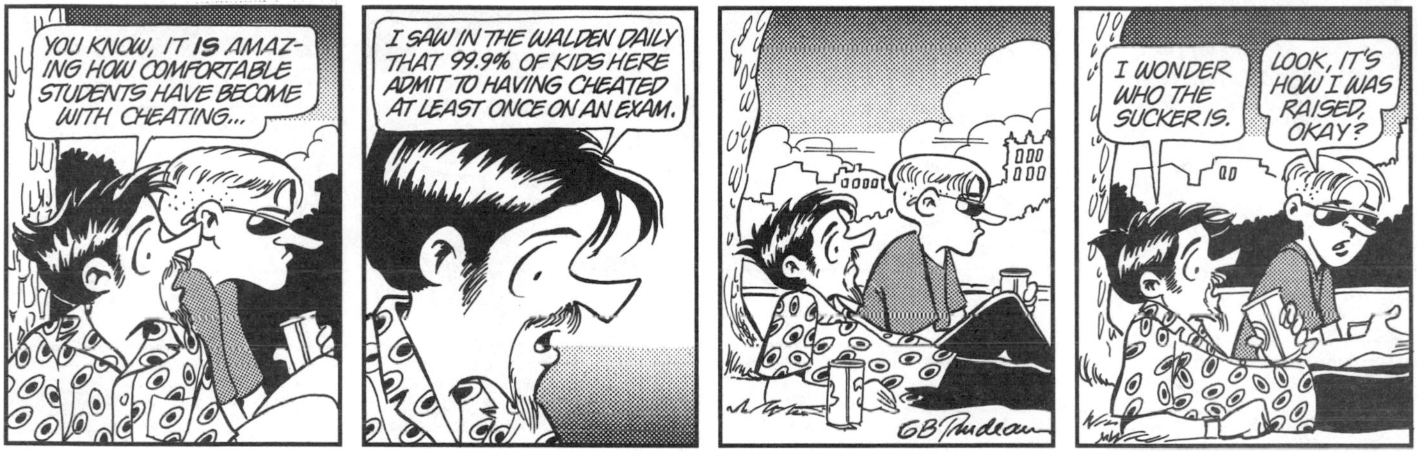
YOU KNOW, IT **IS** AMAZING HOW COMFORTABLE STUDENTS HAVE BECOME WITH CHEATING...
I SAW IN THE WALDEN DAILY THAT 99.9% OF KIDS HERE ADMIT TO HAVING CHEATED AT LEAST ONCE ON AN EXAM.
GB Trudeau
I WONDER WHO THE SUCKER IS.
LOOK, IT'S HOW I WAS RAISED, OKAY?

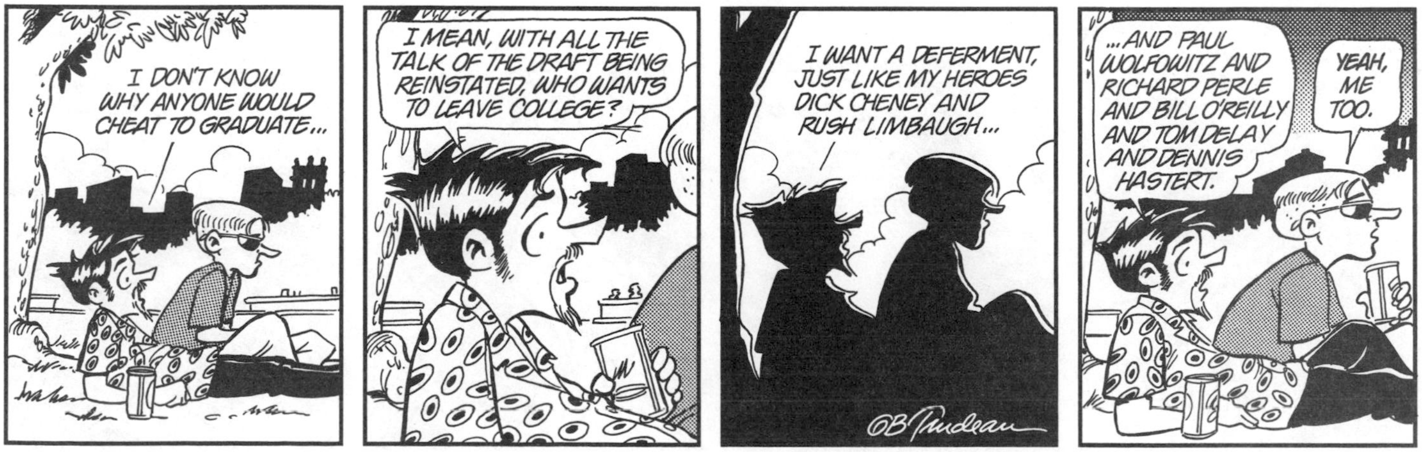
I DON'T KNOW WHY ANYONE WOULD CHEAT TO GRADUATE...
I MEAN, WITH ALL THE TALK OF THE DRAFT BEING REINSTATED, WHO WANTS TO LEAVE COLLEGE?
I WANT A DEFERMENT, JUST LIKE MY HEROES DICK CHENEY AND RUSH LIMBAUGH...
GB Trudeau
...AND PAUL WOLFOWITZ AND RICHARD PERLE AND BILL O'REILLY AND TOM DELAY AND DENNIS HASTERT.
YEAH, ME TOO.

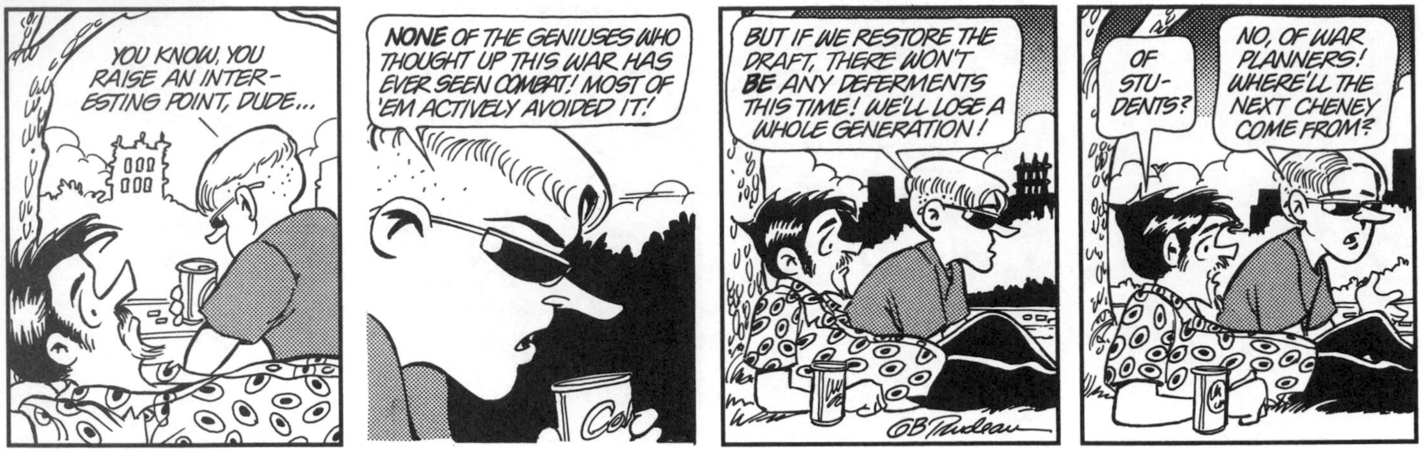
YOU KNOW, YOU RAISE AN INTER-ESTING POINT, DUDE...
NONE OF THE GENIUSES WHO THOUGHT UP THIS WAR HAS EVER SEEN COMBAT! MOST OF 'EM ACTIVELY AVOIDED IT!
BUT IF WE RESTORE THE DRAFT, THERE WON'T BE ANY DEFERMENTS THIS TIME! WE'LL LOSE A WHOLE GENERATION!
OF STU-DENTS?
NO, OF WAR PLANNERS! WHERE'LL THE NEXT CHENEY COME FROM?

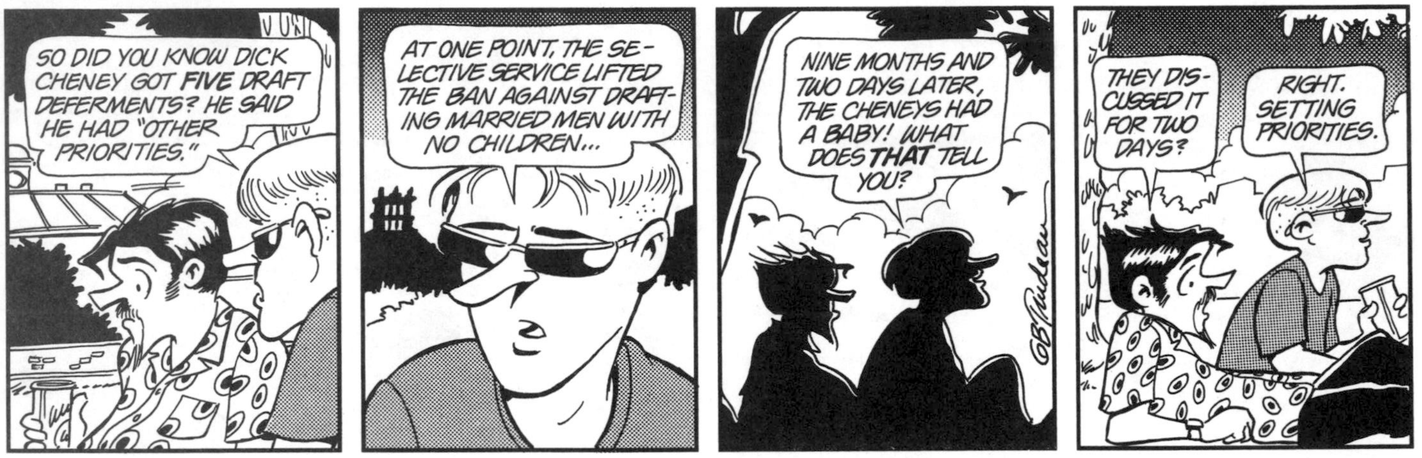
SO DID YOU KNOW DICK CHENEY GOT FIVE DRAFT DEFERMENTS? HE SAID HE HAD "OTHER PRIORITIES."
AT ONE POINT, THE SE-LECTIVE SERVICE LIFTED THE BAN AGAINST DRAFT-ING MARRIED MEN WITH NO CHILDREN...
NINE MONTHS AND TWO DAYS LATER, THE CHENEYS HAD A BABY! WHAT DOES THAT TELL YOU?
THEY DIS-CUSSED IT FOR TWO DAYS?
RIGHT. SETTING PRIORITIES.

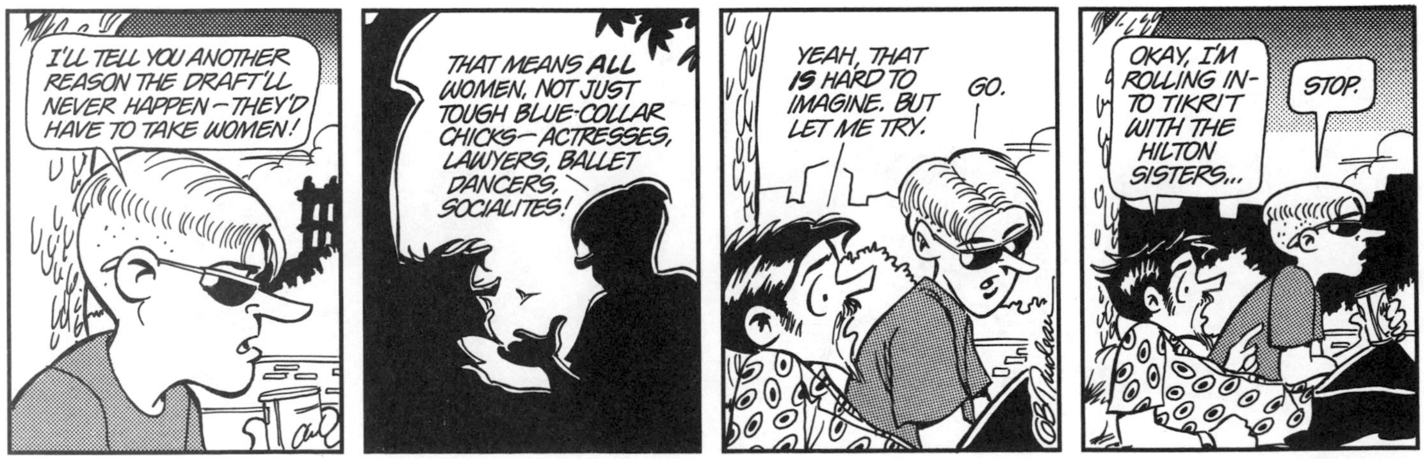
I'LL TELL YOU ANOTHER REASON THE DRAFT'LL NEVER HAPPEN—THEY'D HAVE TO TAKE WOMEN!
THAT MEANS ALL WOMEN, NOT JUST TOUGH BLUE-COLLAR CHICKS—ACTRESSES, LAWYERS, BALLET DANCERS, SOCIALITES!
YEAH, THAT IS HARD TO IMAGINE. BUT LET ME TRY.
GO.
OKAY, I'M ROLLING IN-TO TIKRIT WITH THE HILTON SISTERS...
STOP.

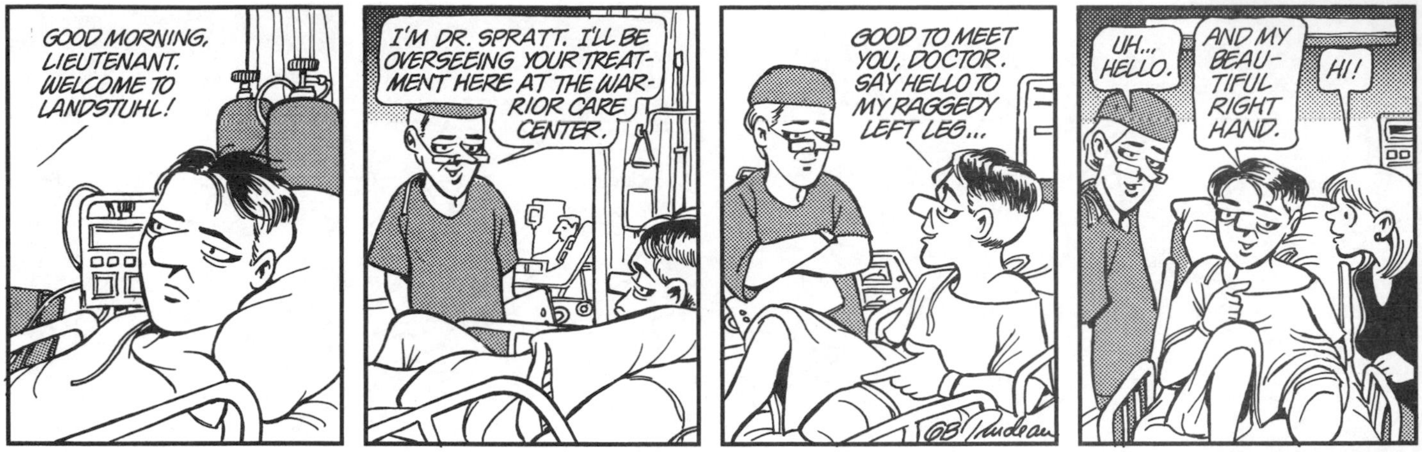
GOOD MORNING, LIEUTENANT. WELCOME TO LANDSTUHL!
I'M DR. SPRATT. I'LL BE OVERSEEING YOUR TREATMENT HERE AT THE WARRIOR CARE CENTER.
GOOD TO MEET YOU, DOCTOR. SAY HELLO TO MY RAGGEDY LEFT LEG...
UH... HELLO.
AND MY BEAUTIFUL RIGHT HAND.
HI!
©B Trudeau

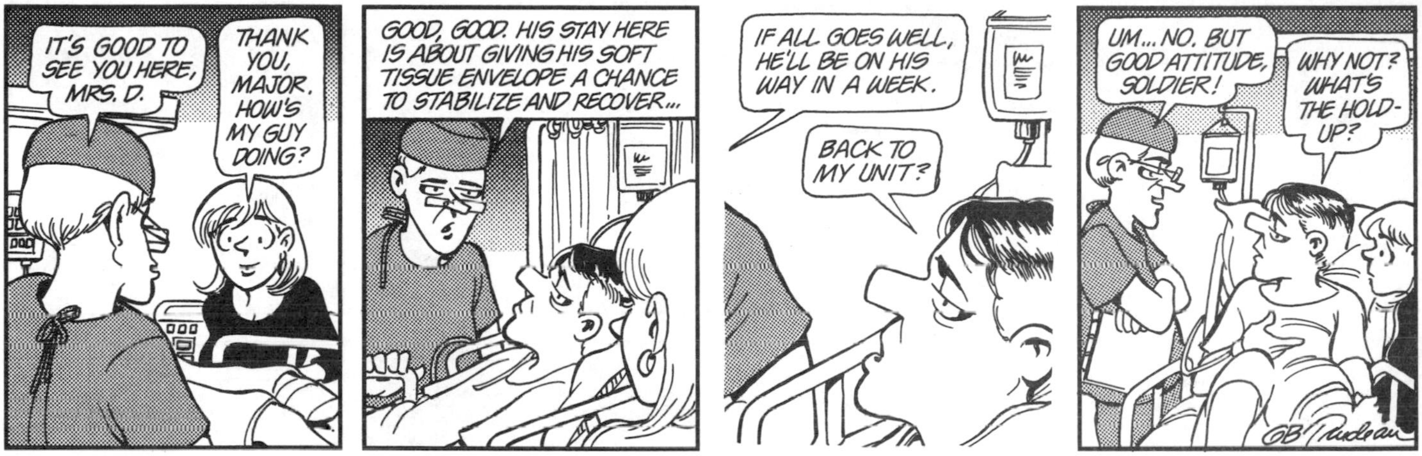
IT'S GOOD TO SEE YOU HERE, MRS. D.
THANK YOU, MAJOR. HOW'S MY GUY DOING?
GOOD, GOOD. HIS STAY HERE IS ABOUT GIVING HIS SOFT TISSUE ENVELOPE A CHANCE TO STABILIZE AND RECOVER...
IF ALL GOES WELL, HE'LL BE ON HIS WAY IN A WEEK.
BACK TO MY UNIT?
UM... NO. BUT GOOD ATTITUDE, SOLDIER!
WHY NOT? WHAT'S THE HOLD-UP?
©B Trudeau

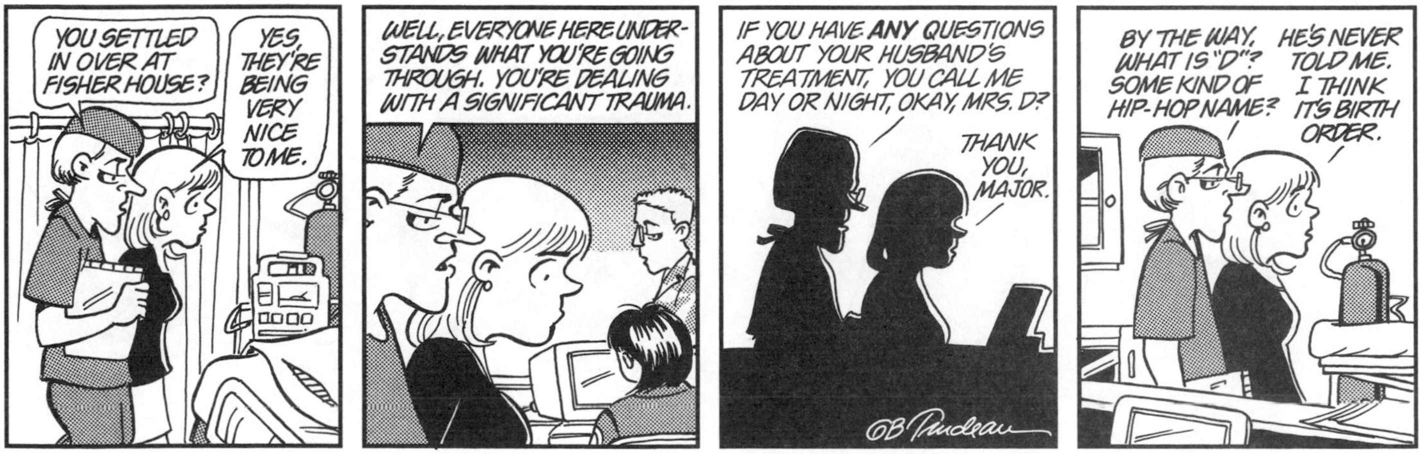
YOU SETTLED IN OVER AT FISHER HOUSE?
YES, THEY'RE BEING VERY NICE TO ME.
WELL, EVERYONE HERE UNDERSTANDS WHAT YOU'RE GOING THROUGH. YOU'RE DEALING WITH A SIGNIFICANT TRAUMA.
IF YOU HAVE ANY QUESTIONS ABOUT YOUR HUSBAND'S TREATMENT, YOU CALL ME DAY OR NIGHT, OKAY, MRS. D?
THANK YOU, MAJOR.
©B Trudeau
BY THE WAY, WHAT IS "D"? SOME KIND OF HIP-HOP NAME?
HE'S NEVER TOLD ME. I THINK IT'S BIRTH ORDER.

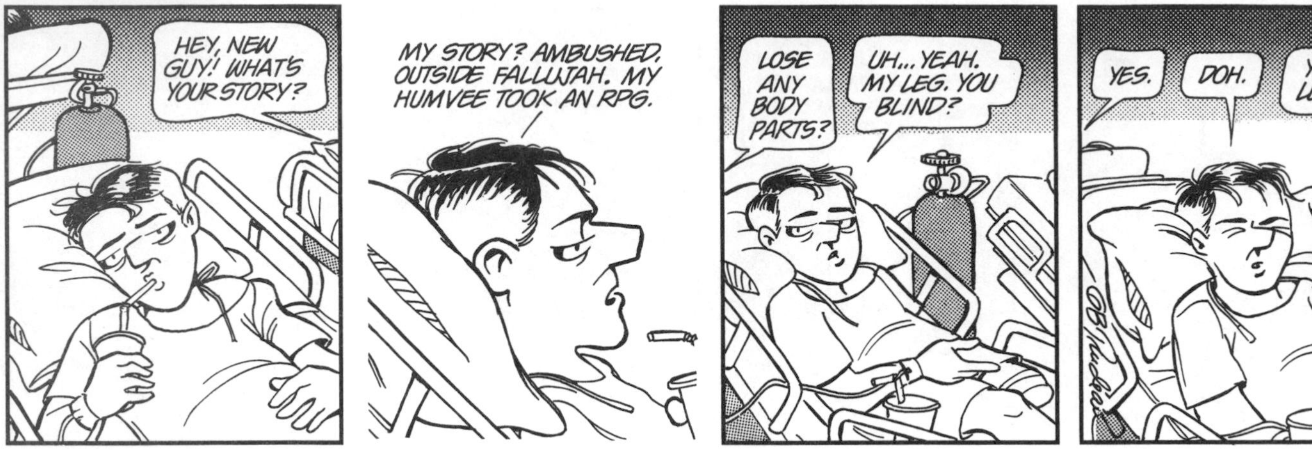
HEY, NEW GUY! WHAT'S YOUR STORY?
MY STORY? AMBUSHED, OUTSIDE FALLUJAH. MY HUMVEE TOOK AN RPG.
LOSE ANY BODY PARTS?
UH... YEAH. MY LEG. YOU BLIND?
YES.
DOH.
YOU'LL LEARN.

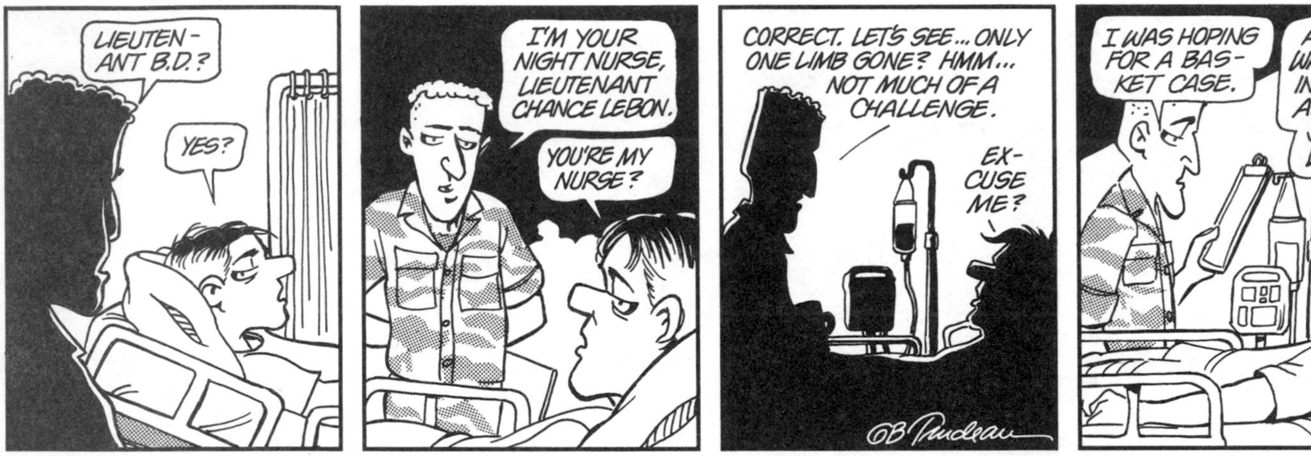
LIEUTEN-ANT B.D.?
YES?
I'M YOUR NIGHT NURSE, LIEUTENANT CHANCE LEBON.
YOU'RE MY NURSE?
CORRECT. LET'S SEE... ONLY ONE LIMB GONE? HMM... NOT MUCH OF A CHALLENGE.
EX-CUSE ME?
I WAS HOPING FOR A BAS-KET CASE.
AND I WAS HOP-ING FOR ASHLEY JUDD. DEAL.

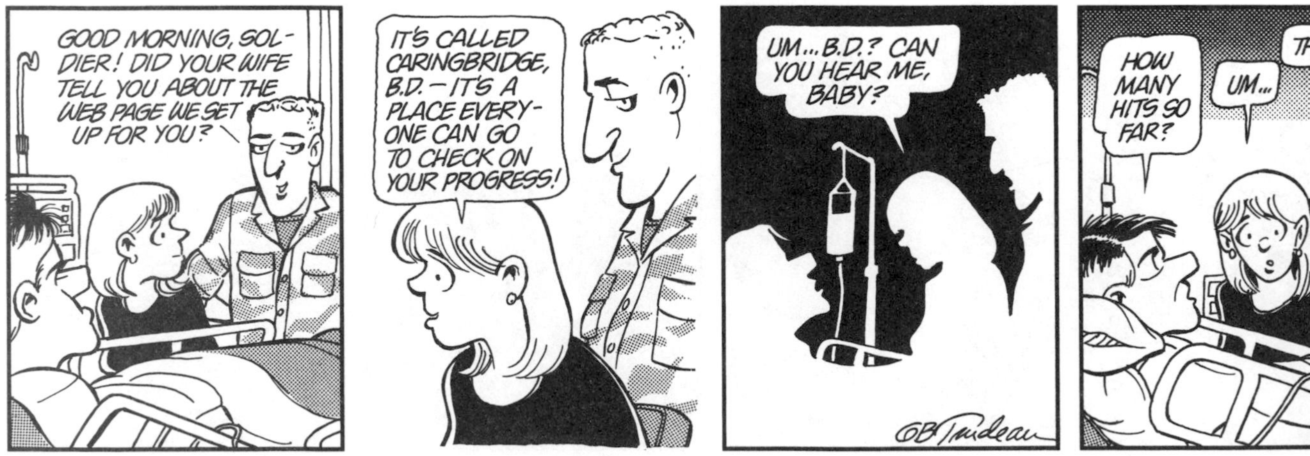
GOOD MORNING, SOL-DIER! DID YOUR WIFE TELL YOU ABOUT THE WEB PAGE WE SET UP FOR YOU?
IT'S CALLED CARINGBRIDGE, B.D.—IT'S A PLACE EVERY-ONE CAN GO TO CHECK ON YOUR PROGRESS!
UM... B.D.? CAN YOU HEAR ME, BABY?
HOW MANY HITS SO FAR?
UM...
THOUSANDS.

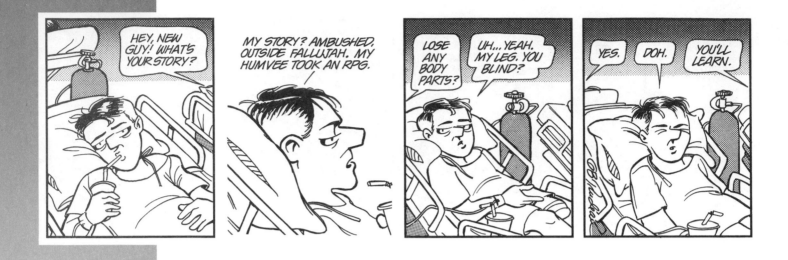

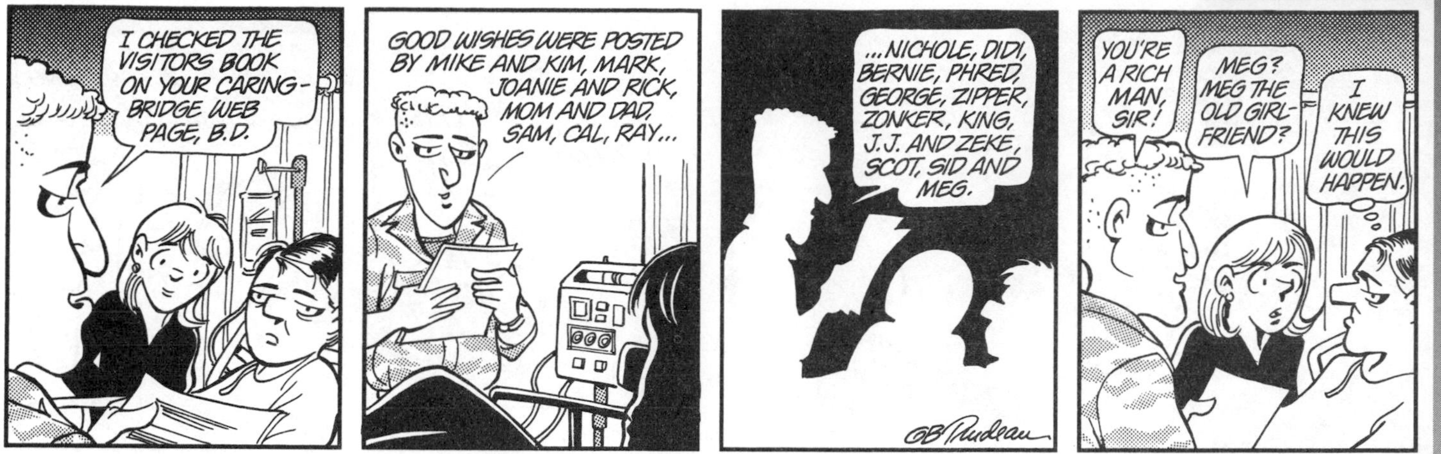
I CHECKED THE VISITORS BOOK ON YOUR CARING-BRIDGE WEB PAGE, B.D.
GOOD WISHES WERE POSTED BY MIKE AND KIM, MARK, JOANIE AND RICK, MOM AND DAD, SAM, CAL, RAY...
...NICHOLE, DIDI, BERNIE, PHRED, GEORGE, ZIPPER, ZONKER, KING, J.J. AND ZEKE, SCOT, SID AND MEG.
YOU'RE A RICH MAN, SIR!
MEG? MEG THE OLD GIRL-FRIEND?
I KNEW THIS WOULD HAPPEN.

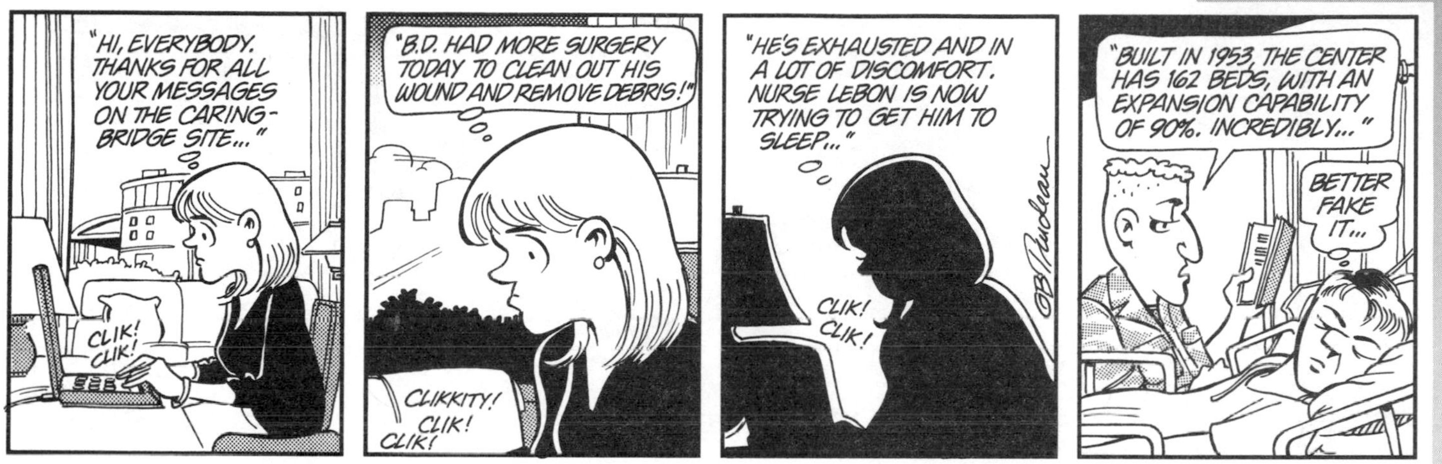
"HI, EVERYBODY. THANKS FOR ALL YOUR MESSAGES ON THE CARING-BRIDGE SITE..."
CLIK! CLIK!
"B.D. HAD MORE SURGERY TODAY TO CLEAN OUT HIS WOUND AND REMOVE DEBRIS!"
CLIKKITY! CLIK! CLIK!
"HE'S EXHAUSTED AND IN A LOT OF DISCOMFORT. NURSE LEBON IS NOW TRYING TO GET HIM TO SLEEP..."
CLIK! CLIK!
"BUILT IN 1953, THE CENTER HAS 162 BEDS, WITH AN EXPANSION CAPABILITY OF 90%. INCREDIBLY..."
BETTER FAKE IT...

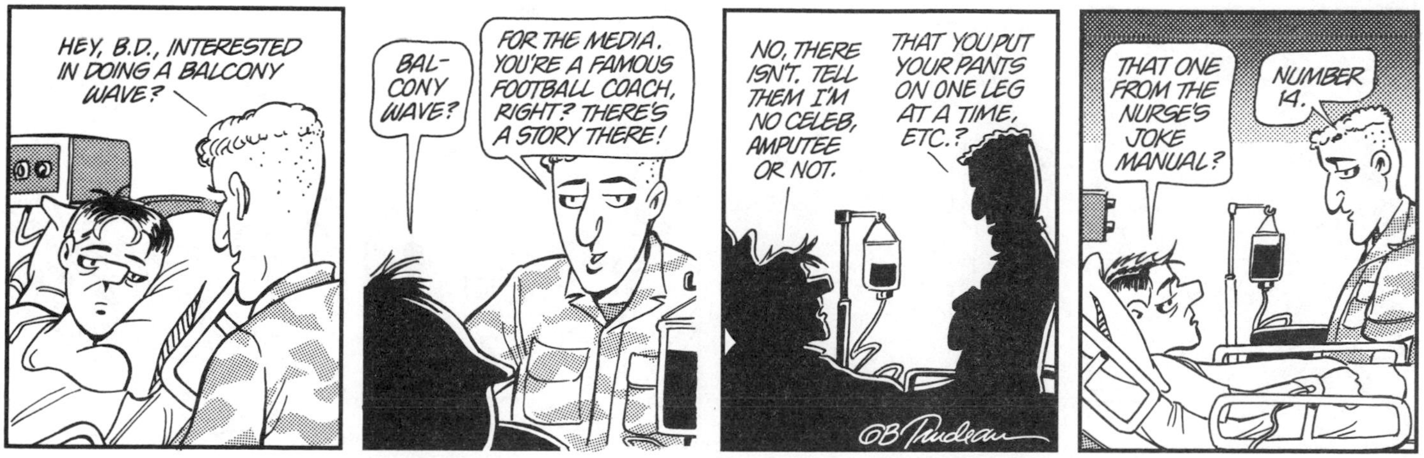
HEY, B.D., INTERESTED IN DOING A BALCONY WAVE?
BAL-CONY WAVE?
FOR THE MEDIA. YOU'RE A FAMOUS FOOTBALL COACH, RIGHT? THERE'S A STORY THERE!
NO, THERE ISN'T. TELL THEM I'M NO CELEB, AMPUTEE OR NOT.
THAT YOU PUT YOUR PANTS ON ONE LEG AT A TIME, ETC.?
THAT ONE FROM THE NURSE'S JOKE MANUAL?
NUMBER 14.

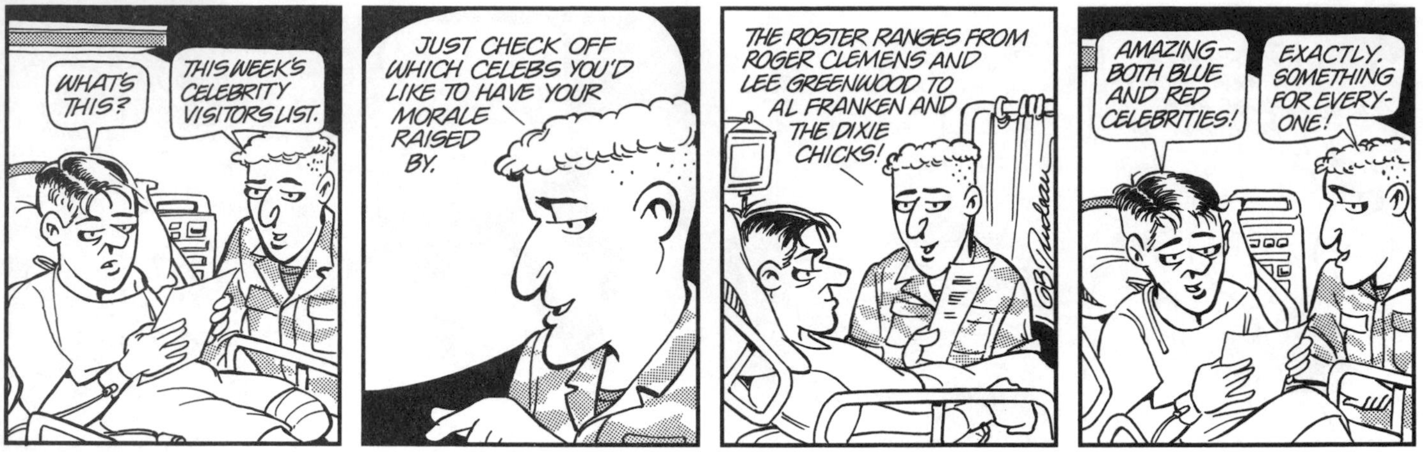
WHAT'S THIS?
THIS WEEK'S CELEBRITY VISITORS LIST.
JUST CHECK OFF WHICH CELEBS YOU'D LIKE TO HAVE YOUR MORALE RAISED BY.
THE ROSTER RANGES FROM ROGER CLEMENS AND LEE GREENWOOD TO AL FRANKEN AND THE DIXIE CHICKS!
AMAZING— BOTH BLUE AND RED CELEBRITIES!
EXACTLY. SOMETHING FOR EVERY-ONE!

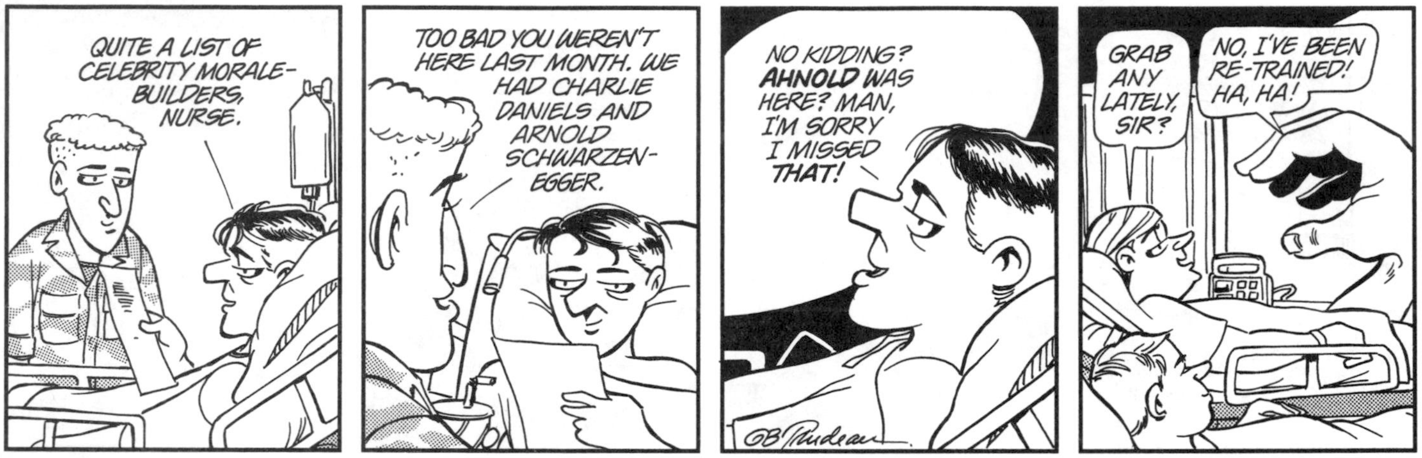
QUITE A LIST OF CELEBRITY MORALE-BUILDERS, NURSE.
TOO BAD YOU WEREN'T HERE LAST MONTH. WE HAD CHARLIE DANIELS AND ARNOLD SCHWARZEN-EGGER.
NO KIDDING? **AHNOLD** WAS HERE? MAN, I'M SORRY I MISSED **THAT!**
GRAB ANY LATELY, SIR?
NO, I'VE BEEN RE-TRAINED! HA, HA!

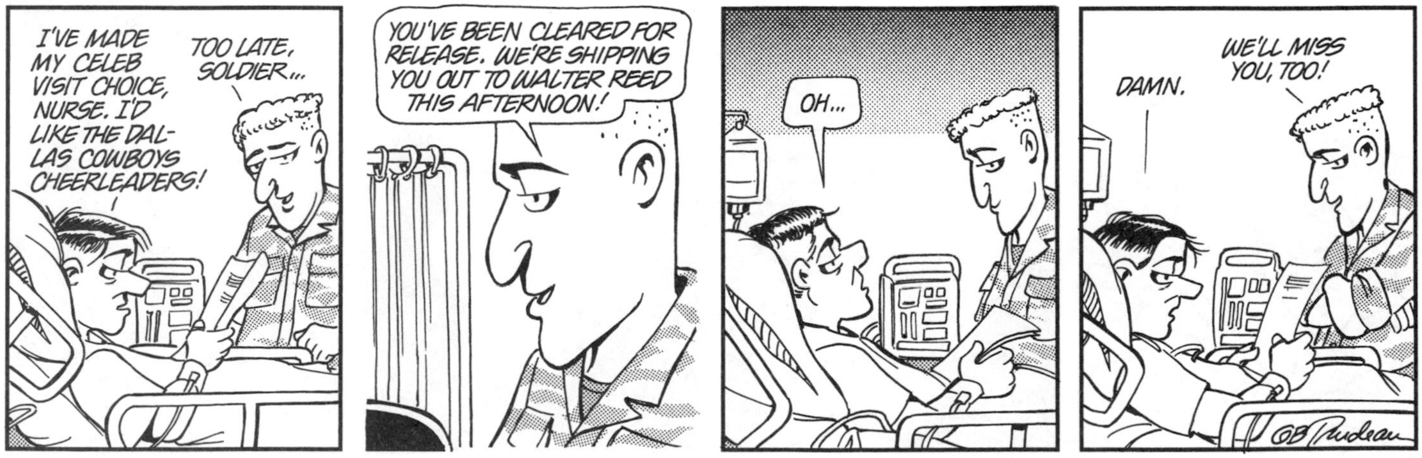
I'VE MADE MY CELEB VISIT CHOICE, NURSE. I'D LIKE THE DAL-LAS COWBOYS CHEERLEADERS!
TOO LATE, SOLDIER...
YOU'VE BEEN CLEARED FOR RELEASE. WE'RE SHIPPING YOU OUT TO WALTER REED THIS AFTERNOON!
OH...
DAMN.
WE'LL MISS YOU, TOO!

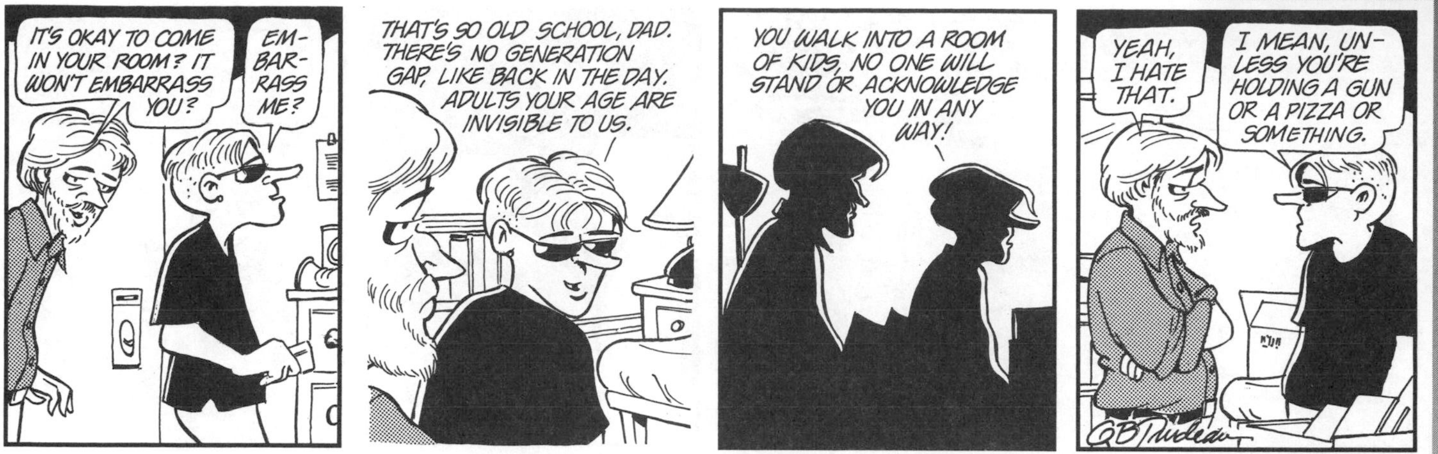
IT'S OKAY TO COME IN YOUR ROOM? IT WON'T EMBARRASS YOU?
EM-BAR-RASS ME?
THAT'S SO OLD SCHOOL, DAD. THERE'S NO GENERATION GAP, LIKE BACK IN THE DAY. ADULTS YOUR AGE ARE INVISIBLE TO US.
YOU WALK INTO A ROOM OF KIDS, NO ONE WILL STAND OR ACKNOWLEDGE YOU IN ANY WAY!
YEAH, I HATE THAT.
I MEAN, UN-LESS YOU'RE HOLDING A GUN OR A PIZZA OR SOMETHING.
©B Trudeau

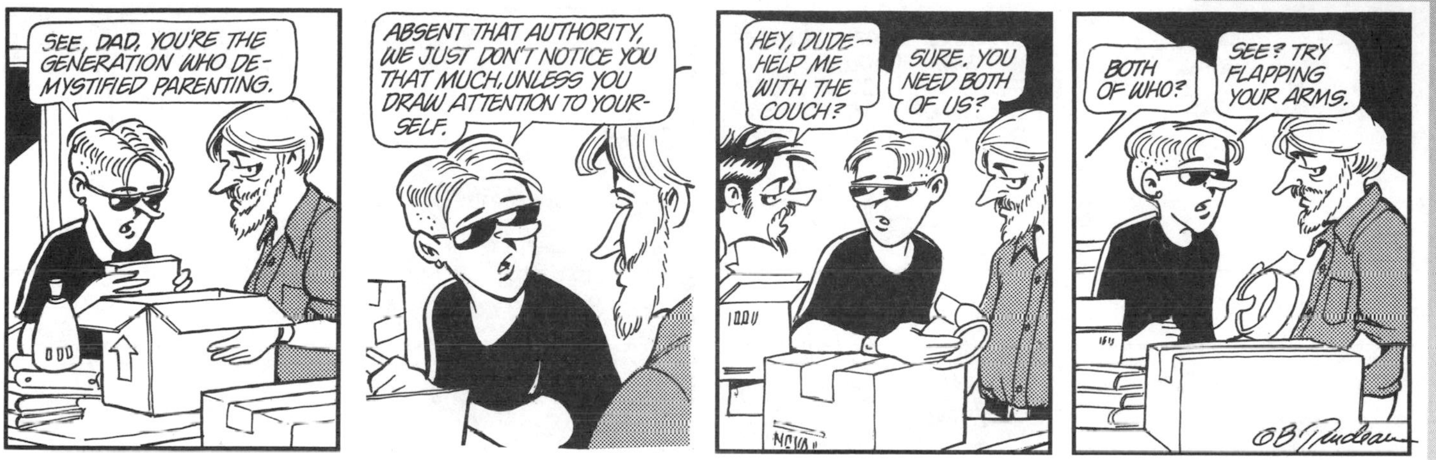
SEE, DAD, YOU'RE THE GENERATION WHO DE-MYSTIFIED PARENTING.
ABSENT THAT AUTHORITY, WE JUST DON'T NOTICE YOU THAT MUCH, UNLESS YOU DRAW ATTENTION TO YOUR-SELF.
HEY, DUDE-HELP ME WITH THE COUCH?
SURE. YOU NEED BOTH OF US?
BOTH OF WHO?
SEE? TRY FLAPPING YOUR ARMS.
©B Trudeau

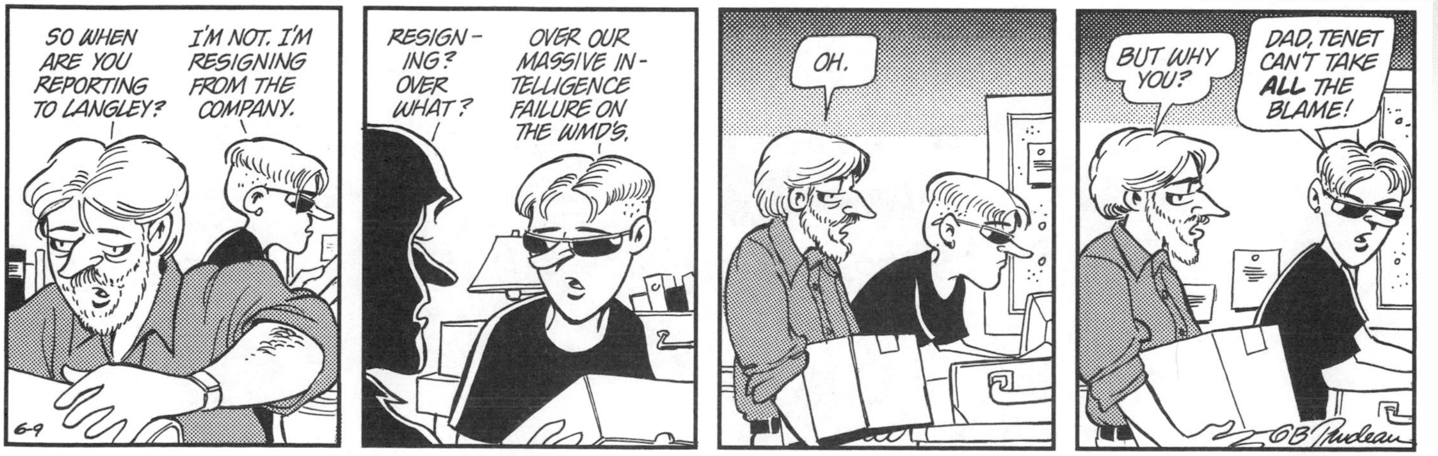
SO WHEN ARE YOU REPORTING TO LANGLEY?
I'M NOT. I'M RESIGNING FROM THE COMPANY.
6-9
RESIGN-ING? OVER WHAT?
OVER OUR MASSIVE IN-TELLIGENCE FAILURE ON THE WMD'S.
OH.
BUT WHY YOU?
DAD, TENET CAN'T TAKE ALL THE BLAME!
©B Trudeau

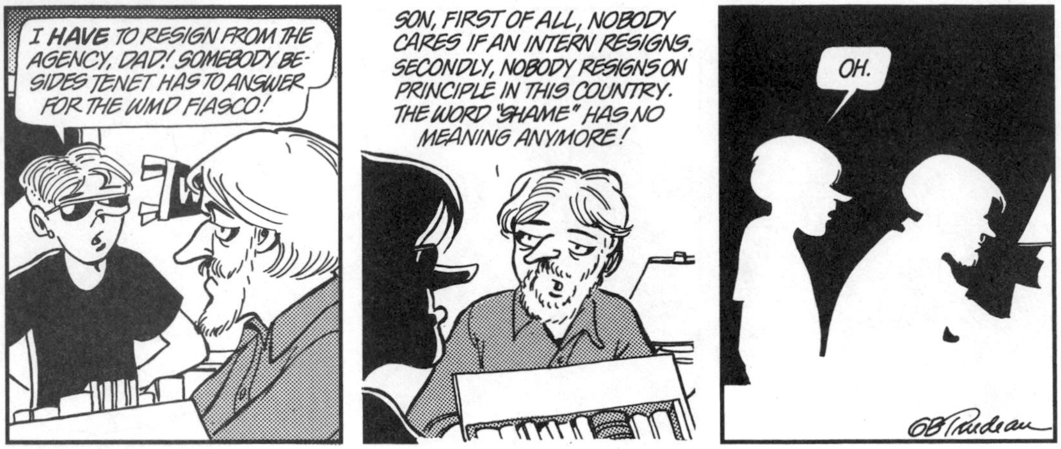
I HAVE TO RESIGN FROM THE AGENCY, DAD! SOMEBODY BESIDES TENET HAS TO ANSWER FOR THE WMD FIASCO!
SON, FIRST OF ALL, NOBODY CARES IF AN INTERN RESIGNS. SECONDLY, NOBODY RESIGNS ON PRINCIPLE IN THIS COUNTRY. THE WORD "SHAME" HAS NO MEANING ANYMORE!
OH.
SO WHY'S IT STILL IN THE LANGUAGE?
SO WE CAN DISCUSS THE JAPANESE.
GB Trudeau

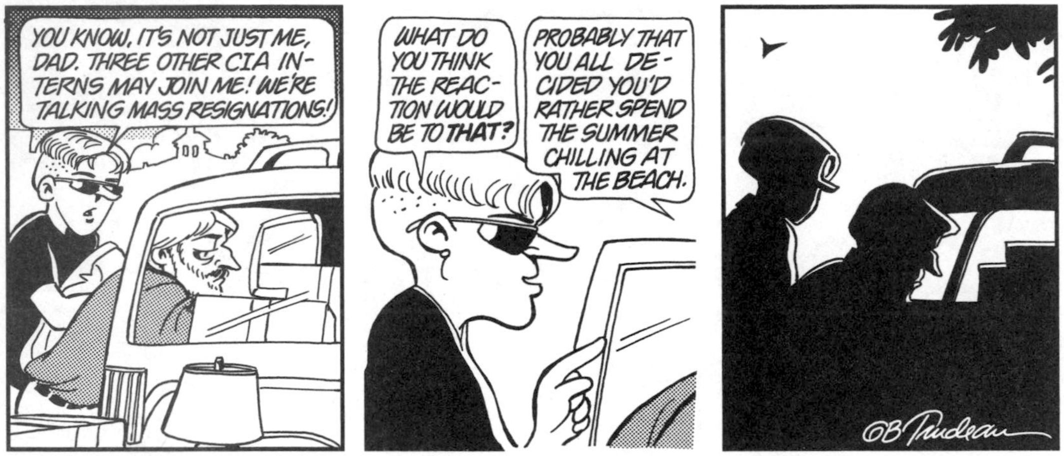
YOU KNOW, IT'S NOT JUST ME, DAD. THREE OTHER CIA INTERNS MAY JOIN ME! WE'RE TALKING MASS RESIGNATIONS!
WHAT DO YOU THINK THE REACTION WOULD BE TO THAT?
PROBABLY THAT YOU ALL DECIDED YOU'D RATHER SPEND THE SUMMER CHILLING AT THE BEACH.
GB Trudeau
OKAY, LUCKY GUESS. BUT MOST PEOPLE WOULDN'T PICK UP ON THAT.
YEAH, PROBABLY NOT.

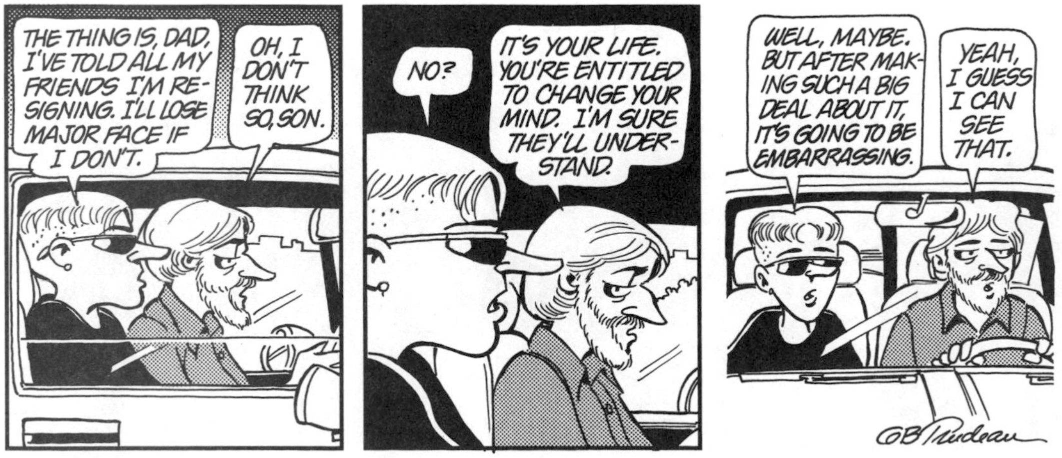
THE THING IS, DAD, I'VE TOLD ALL MY FRIENDS I'M RESIGNING. I'LL LOSE MAJOR FACE IF I DON'T.
OH, I DON'T THINK SO, SON.
NO?
IT'S YOUR LIFE. YOU'RE ENTITLED TO CHANGE YOUR MIND. I'M SURE THEY'LL UNDERSTAND.
WELL, MAYBE. BUT AFTER MAKING SUCH A BIG DEAL ABOUT IT, IT'S GOING TO BE EMBARRASSING.
YEAH, I GUESS I CAN SEE THAT.
GB Trudeau
GOOD. COULD YOU CANCEL MY PRESS CONFERENCE FOR ME?
ANYTHING TO HELP.

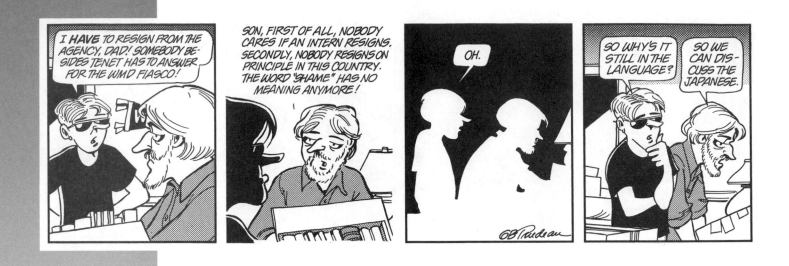

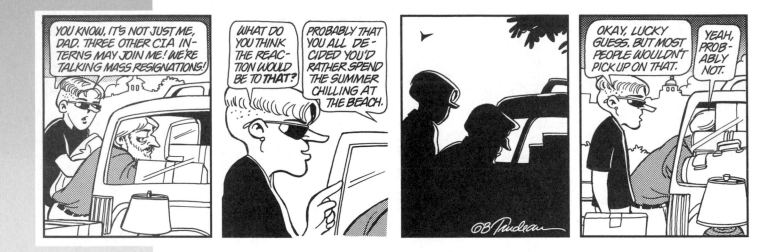

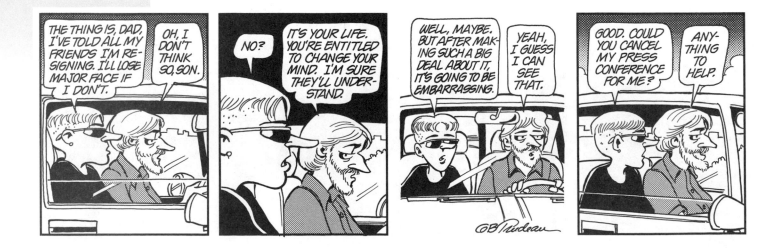

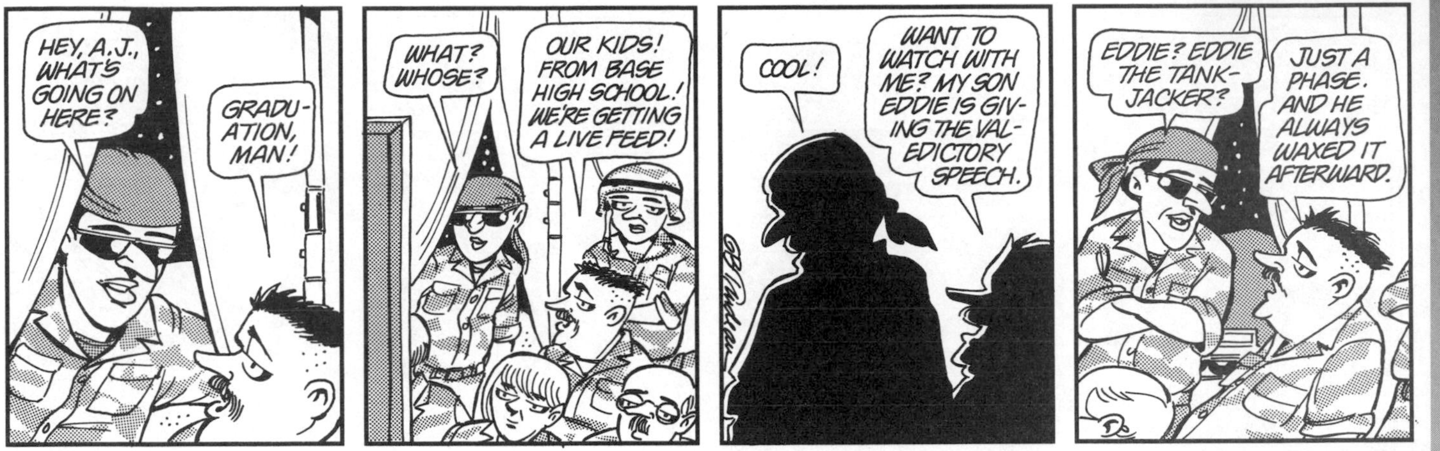
HEY, A.J., WHAT'S GOING ON HERE?
GRADUATION, MAN!
WHAT? WHOSE?
OUR KIDS! FROM BASE HIGH SCHOOL! WE'RE GETTING A LIVE FEED!
COOL!
WANT TO WATCH WITH ME? MY SON EDDIE IS GIVING THE VALEDICTORY SPEECH.
EDDIE? EDDIE THE TANK-JACKER?
JUST A PHASE. AND HE ALWAYS WAXED IT AFTERWARD.

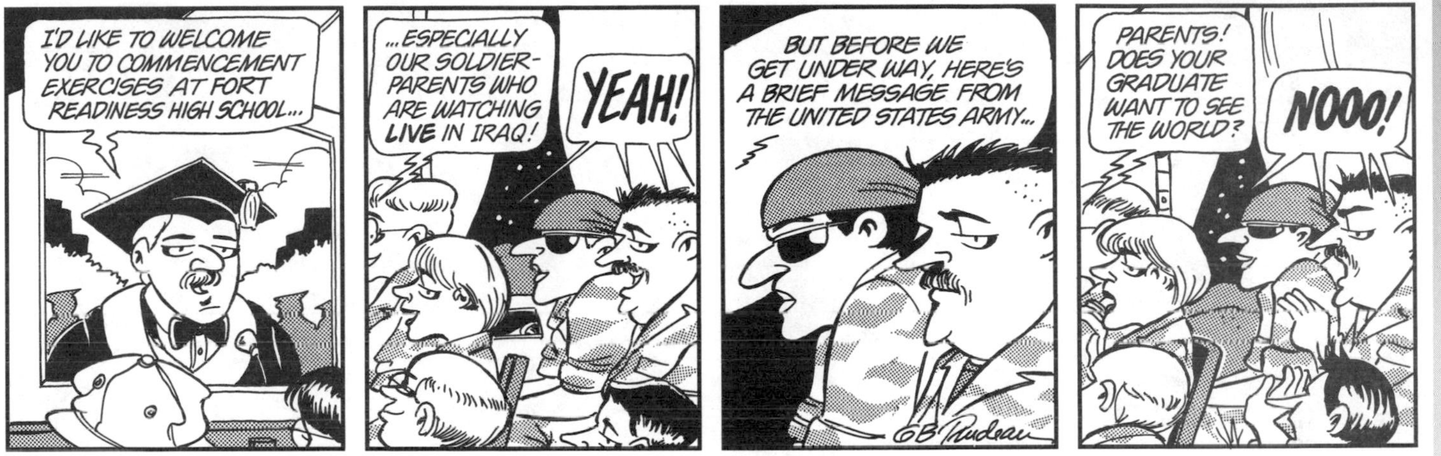
I'D LIKE TO WELCOME YOU TO COMMENCEMENT EXERCISES AT FORT READINESS HIGH SCHOOL...
...ESPECIALLY OUR SOLDIER-PARENTS WHO ARE WATCHING LIVE IN IRAQ!
YEAH!
BUT BEFORE WE GET UNDER WAY, HERE'S A BRIEF MESSAGE FROM THE UNITED STATES ARMY...
PARENTS! DOES YOUR GRADUATE WANT TO SEE THE WORLD?
NOOO!

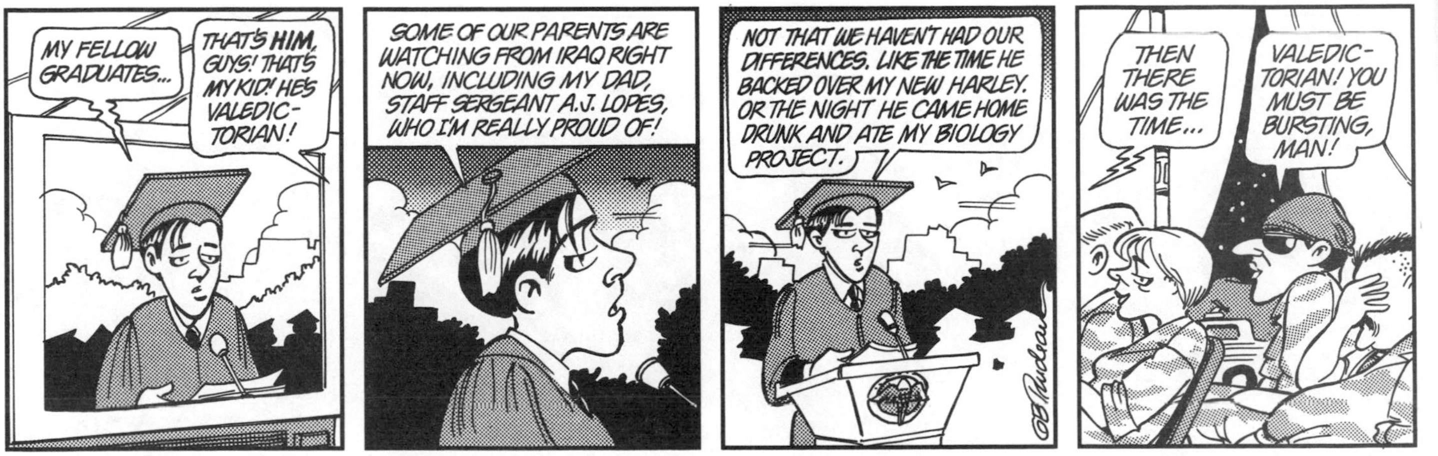
MY FELLOW GRADUATES...
THAT'S HIM, GUYS! THAT'S MY KID! HE'S VALEDICTORIAN!
SOME OF OUR PARENTS ARE WATCHING FROM IRAQ RIGHT NOW, INCLUDING MY DAD, STAFF SERGEANT A.J. LOPES, WHO I'M REALLY PROUD OF!
NOT THAT WE HAVEN'T HAD OUR DIFFERENCES. LIKE THE TIME HE BACKED OVER MY NEW HARLEY. OR THE NIGHT HE CAME HOME DRUNK AND ATE MY BIOLOGY PROJECT.
THEN THERE WAS THE TIME...
VALEDICTORIAN! YOU MUST BE BURSTING, MAN!

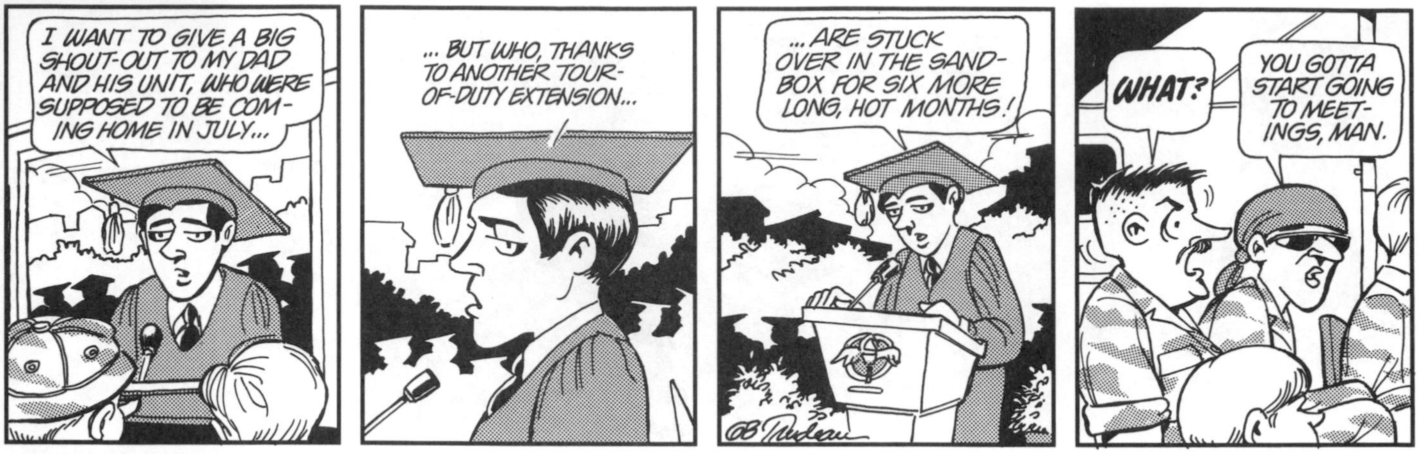
I WANT TO GIVE A BIG SHOUT-OUT TO MY DAD AND HIS UNIT, WHO WERE SUPPOSED TO BE COMING HOME IN JULY...
... BUT WHO, THANKS TO ANOTHER TOUR-OF-DUTY EXTENSION...
...ARE STUCK OVER IN THE SANDBOX FOR SIX MORE LONG, HOT MONTHS!
WHAT?
YOU GOTTA START GOING TO MEETINGS, MAN.

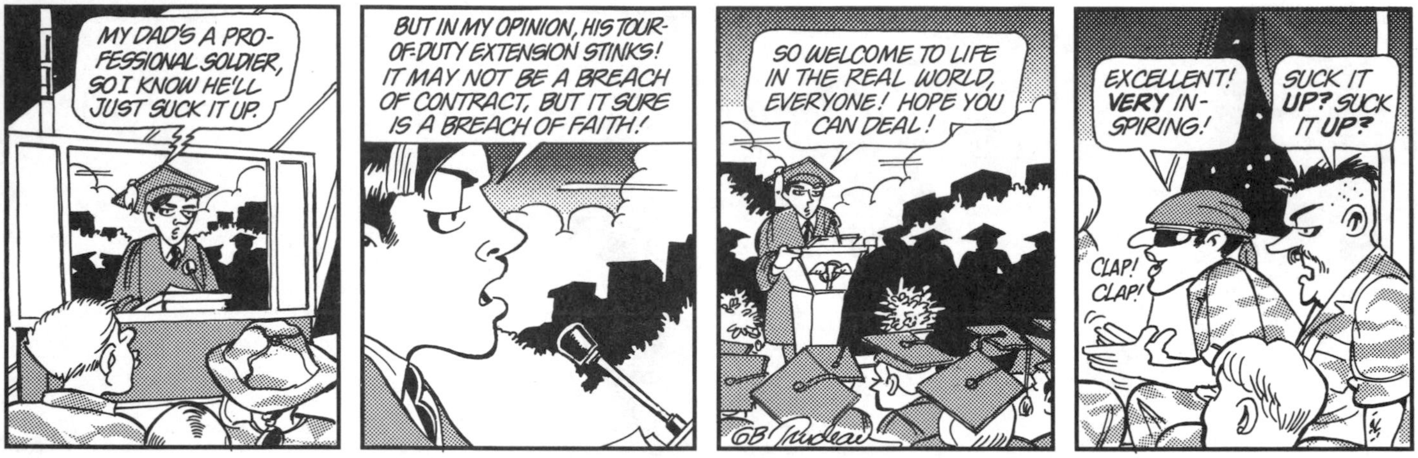
MY DAD'S A PROFESSIONAL SOLDIER, SO I KNOW HE'LL JUST SUCK IT UP.
BUT IN MY OPINION, HIS TOUR-OF-DUTY EXTENSION STINKS! IT MAY NOT BE A BREACH OF CONTRACT, BUT IT SURE IS A BREACH OF FAITH!
SO WELCOME TO LIFE IN THE REAL WORLD, EVERYONE! HOPE YOU CAN DEAL!
EXCELLENT! VERY INSPIRING!
CLAP! CLAP!
SUCK IT UP? SUCK IT UP?

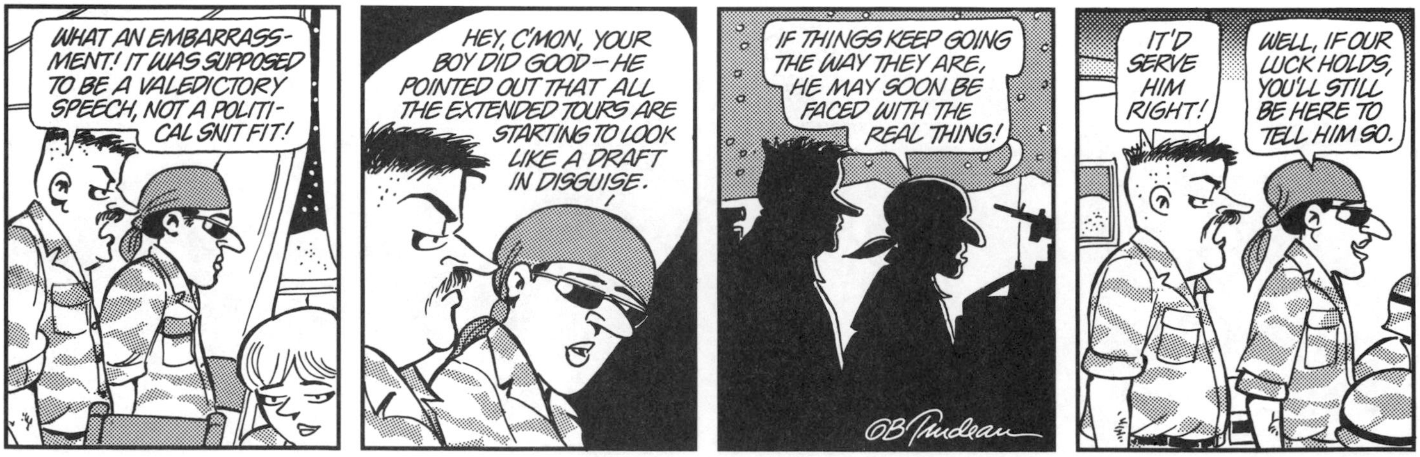
WHAT AN EMBARRASSMENT! IT WAS SUPPOSED TO BE A VALEDICTORY SPEECH, NOT A POLITICAL SNIT FIT!
HEY, C'MON, YOUR BOY DID GOOD—HE POINTED OUT THAT ALL THE EXTENDED TOURS ARE STARTING TO LOOK LIKE A DRAFT IN DISGUISE.
IF THINGS KEEP GOING THE WAY THEY ARE, HE MAY SOON BE FACED WITH THE REAL THING!
IT'D SERVE HIM RIGHT!
WELL, IF OUR LUCK HOLDS, YOU'LL STILL BE HERE TO TELL HIM SO.

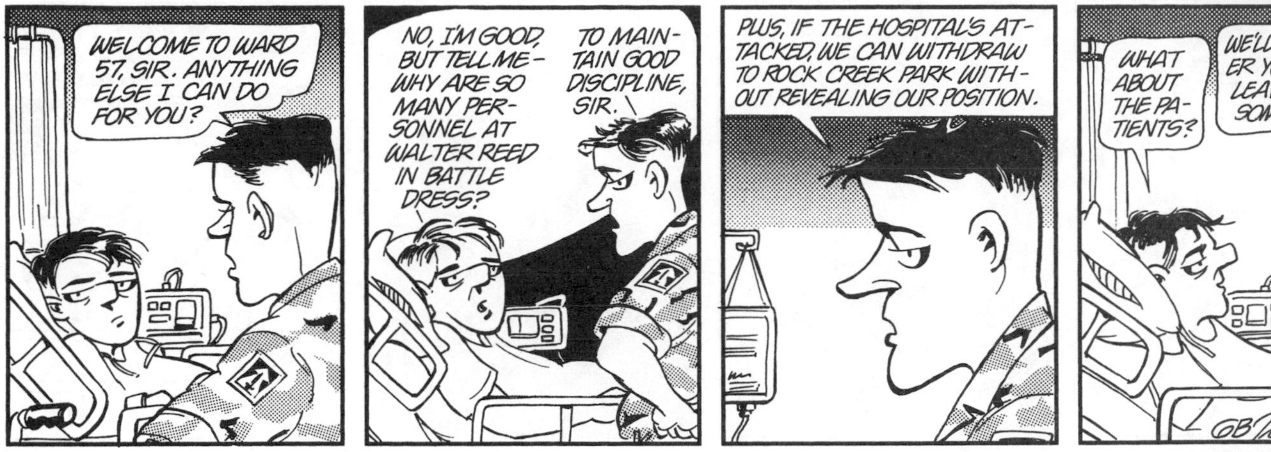
WELCOME TO WARD 57, SIR. ANYTHING ELSE I CAN DO FOR YOU?
NO, I'M GOOD, BUT TELL ME– WHY ARE SO MANY PERSONNEL AT WALTER REED IN BATTLE DRESS?
TO MAINTAIN GOOD DISCIPLINE, SIR.
PLUS, IF THE HOSPITAL'S ATTACKED, WE CAN WITHDRAW TO ROCK CREEK PARK WITHOUT REVEALING OUR POSITION.
WHAT ABOUT THE PATIENTS?
WE'LL JUST COVER YOU UP WITH LEAVES OR SOMETHING.

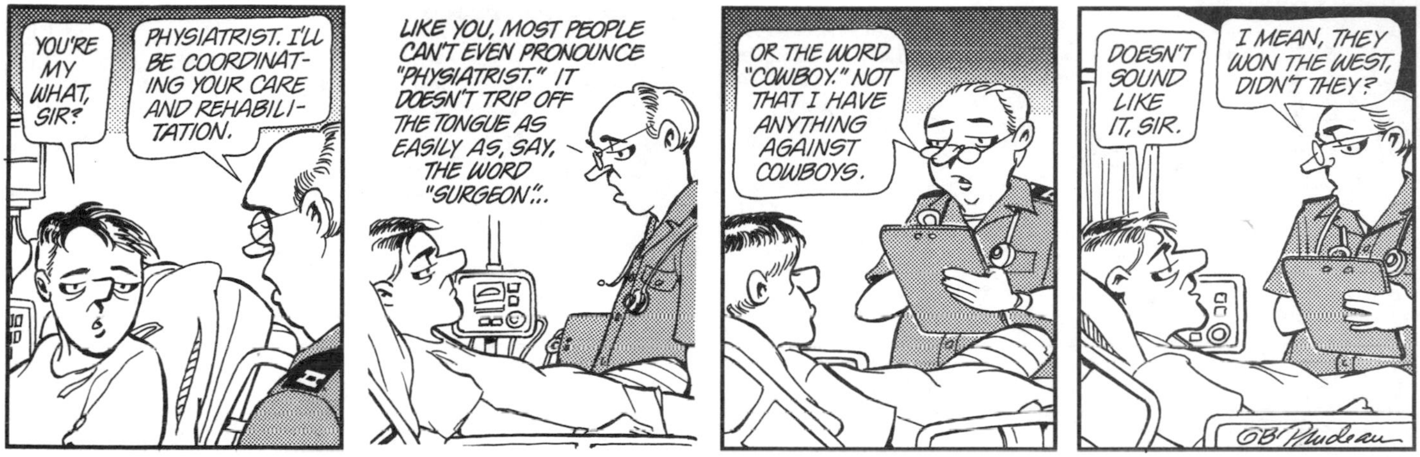
YOU'RE MY WHAT, SIR?
PHYSIATRIST. I'LL BE COORDINATING YOUR CARE AND REHABILITATION.
LIKE YOU, MOST PEOPLE CAN'T EVEN PRONOUNCE "PHYSIATRIST." IT DOESN'T TRIP OFF THE TONGUE AS EASILY AS, SAY, THE WORD "SURGEON"...
OR THE WORD "COWBOY." NOT THAT I HAVE ANYTHING AGAINST COWBOYS.
DOESN'T SOUND LIKE IT, SIR.
I MEAN, THEY WON THE WEST, DIDN'T THEY?

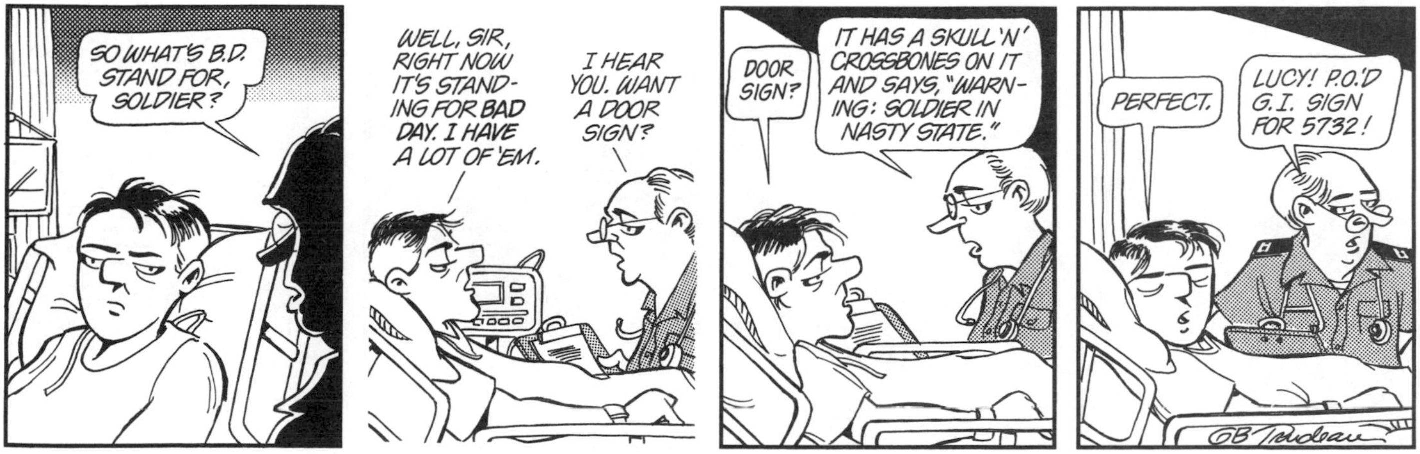
SO WHAT'S B.D. STAND FOR, SOLDIER?
WELL, SIR, RIGHT NOW IT'S STANDING FOR BAD DAY. I HAVE A LOT OF 'EM.
I HEAR YOU. WANT A DOOR SIGN?
DOOR SIGN?
IT HAS A SKULL 'N' CROSSBONES ON IT AND SAYS, "WARNING: SOLDIER IN NASTY STATE."
PERFECT.
LUCY! P.O.'D G.I. SIGN FOR 5732!

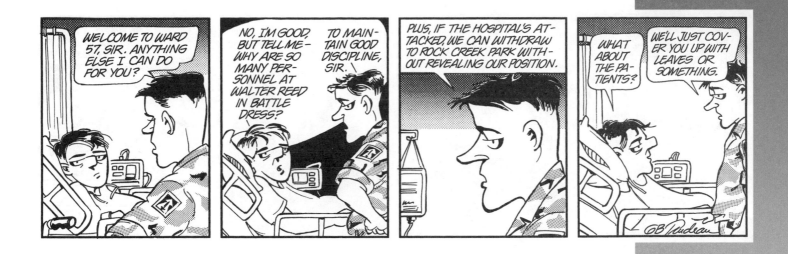

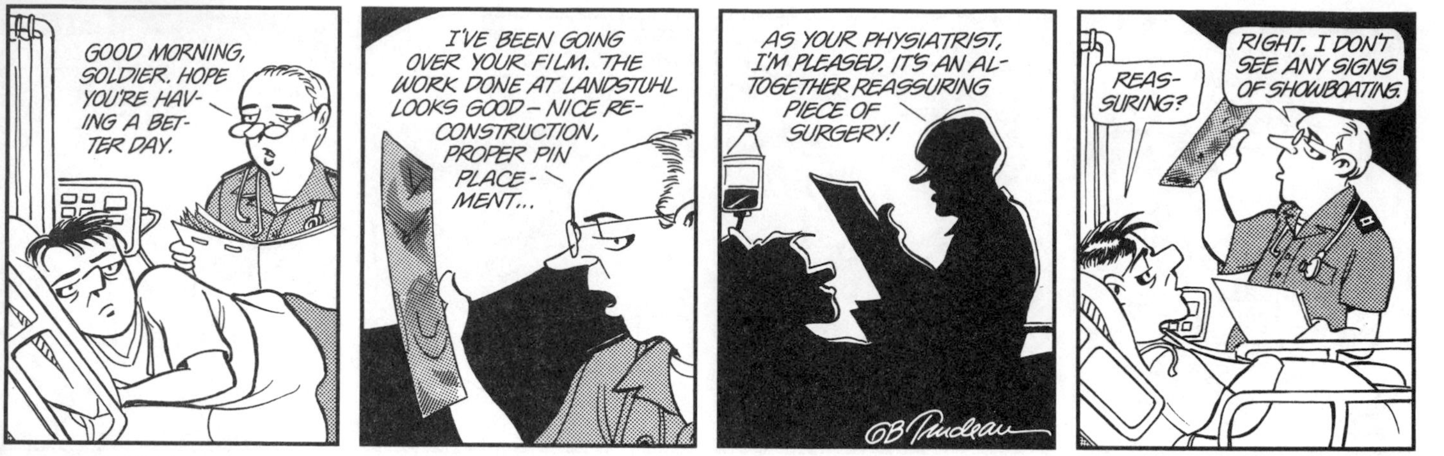
GOOD MORNING, SOLDIER. HOPE YOU'RE HAVING A BETTER DAY.
I'VE BEEN GOING OVER YOUR FILM. THE WORK DONE AT LANDSTUHL LOOKS GOOD – NICE RECONSTRUCTION, PROPER PIN PLACEMENT...
AS YOUR PHYSIATRIST, I'M PLEASED. IT'S AN ALTOGETHER REASSURING PIECE OF SURGERY!
REASSURING?
RIGHT. I DON'T SEE ANY SIGNS OF SHOWBOATING.
GB Trudeau

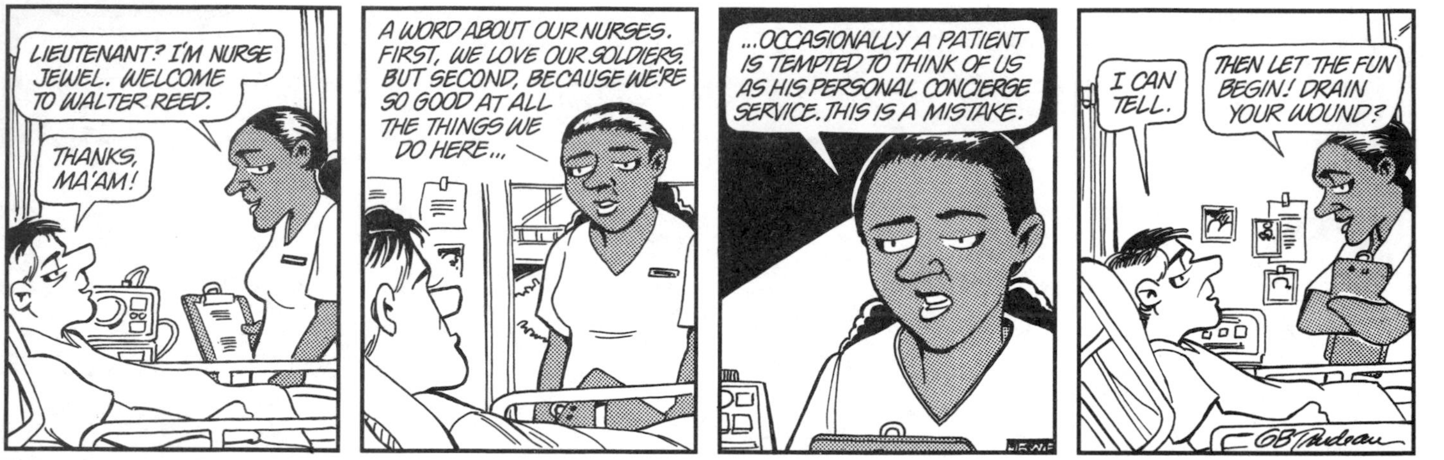
LIEUTENANT? I'M NURSE JEWEL. WELCOME TO WALTER REED.
THANKS, MA'AM!
A WORD ABOUT OUR NURSES. FIRST, WE LOVE OUR SOLDIERS. BUT SECOND, BECAUSE WE'RE SO GOOD AT ALL THE THINGS WE DO HERE...
...OCCASIONALLY A PATIENT IS TEMPTED TO THINK OF US AS HIS PERSONAL CONCIERGE SERVICE. THIS IS A MISTAKE.
I CAN TELL.
THEN LET THE FUN BEGIN! DRAIN YOUR WOUND?
GB Trudeau

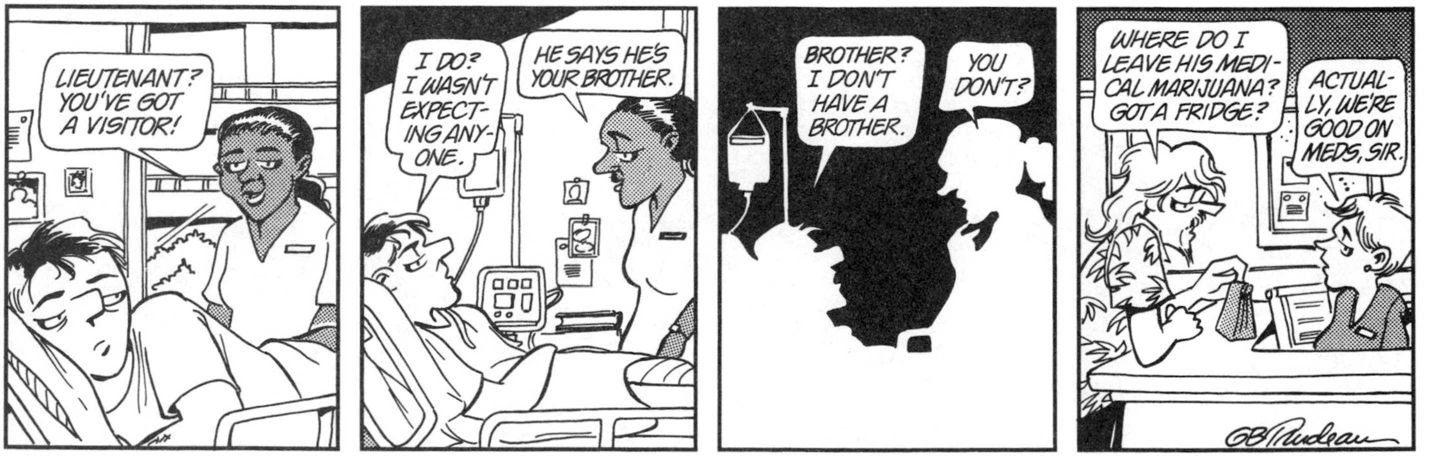
LIEUTENANT? YOU'VE GOT A VISITOR!
I DO? I WASN'T EXPECTING ANYONE.
HE SAYS HE'S YOUR BROTHER.
BROTHER? I DON'T HAVE A BROTHER.
YOU DON'T?
WHERE DO I LEAVE HIS MEDICAL MARIJUANA? GOT A FRIDGE?
ACTUALLY, WE'RE GOOD ON MEDS, SIR.
GB Trudeau

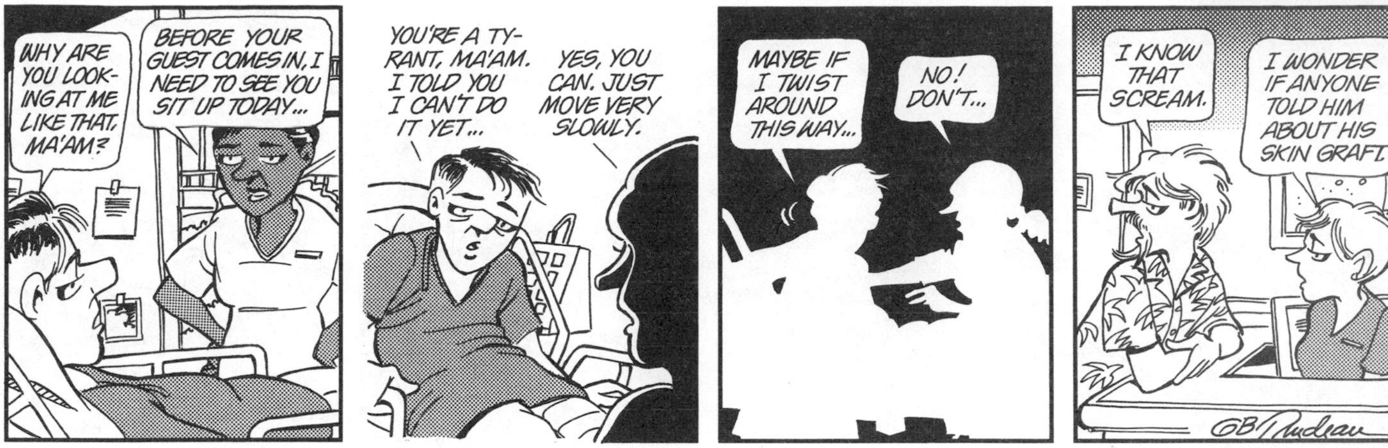
WHY ARE YOU LOOKING AT ME LIKE THAT, MA'AM?
BEFORE YOUR GUEST COMES IN, I NEED TO SEE YOU SIT UP TODAY...
YOU'RE A TYRANT, MA'AM. I TOLD YOU I CAN'T DO IT YET...
YES, YOU CAN. JUST MOVE VERY SLOWLY.
MAYBE IF I TWIST AROUND THIS WAY...
NO! DON'T...
I KNOW THAT SCREAM.
I WONDER IF ANYONE TOLD HIM ABOUT HIS SKIN GRAFT.

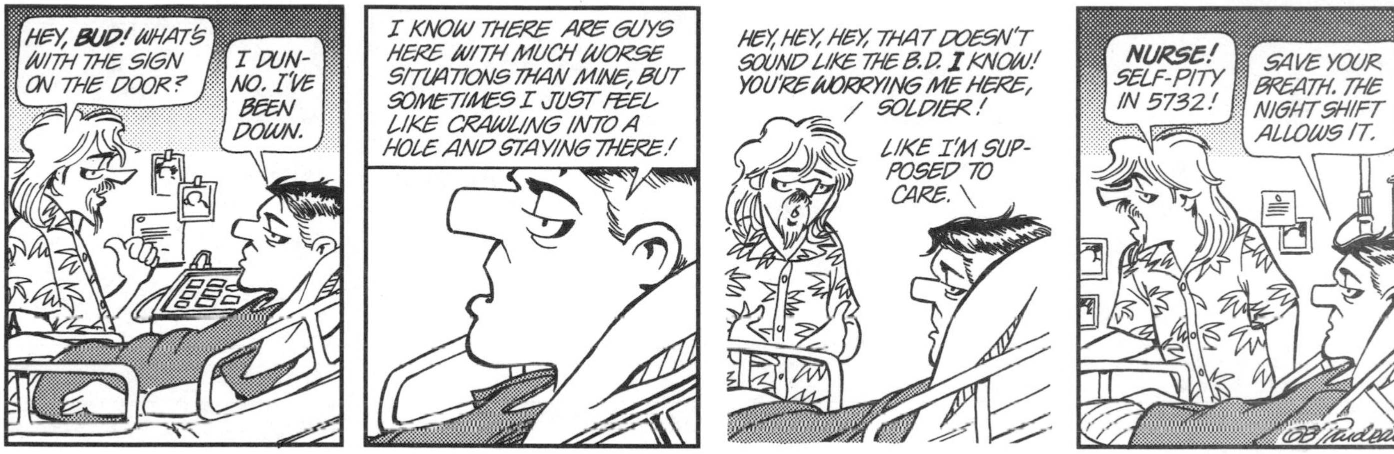
HEY, BUD! WHAT'S WITH THE SIGN ON THE DOOR?
I DUNNO. I'VE BEEN DOWN.
I KNOW THERE ARE GUYS HERE WITH MUCH WORSE SITUATIONS THAN MINE, BUT SOMETIMES I JUST FEEL LIKE CRAWLING INTO A HOLE AND STAYING THERE!
HEY, HEY, HEY, THAT DOESN'T SOUND LIKE THE B.D. I KNOW! YOU'RE WORRYING ME HERE, SOLDIER!
LIKE I'M SUPPOSED TO CARE.
NURSE! SELF-PITY IN 5732!
SAVE YOUR BREATH. THE NIGHT SHIFT ALLOWS IT.

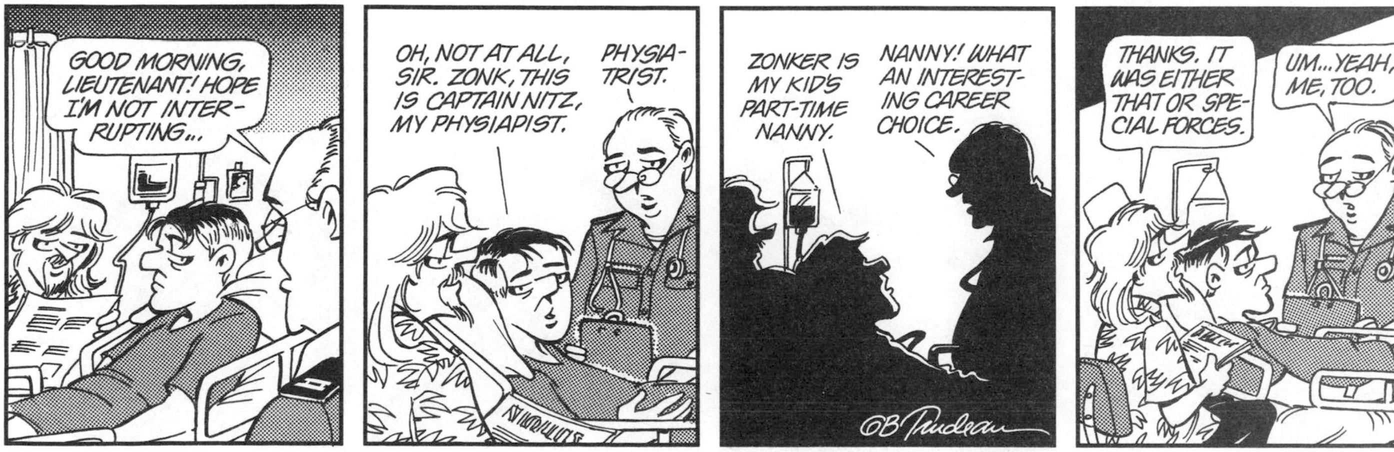
GOOD MORNING, LIEUTENANT! HOPE I'M NOT INTERRUPTING...
OH, NOT AT ALL, SIR. ZONK, THIS IS CAPTAIN NITZ, MY PHYSIAPIST.
PHYSIATRIST.
ZONKER IS MY KID'S PART-TIME NANNY.
NANNY! WHAT AN INTERESTING CAREER CHOICE.
THANKS. IT WAS EITHER THAT OR SPECIAL FORCES.
UM...YEAH, ME, TOO.

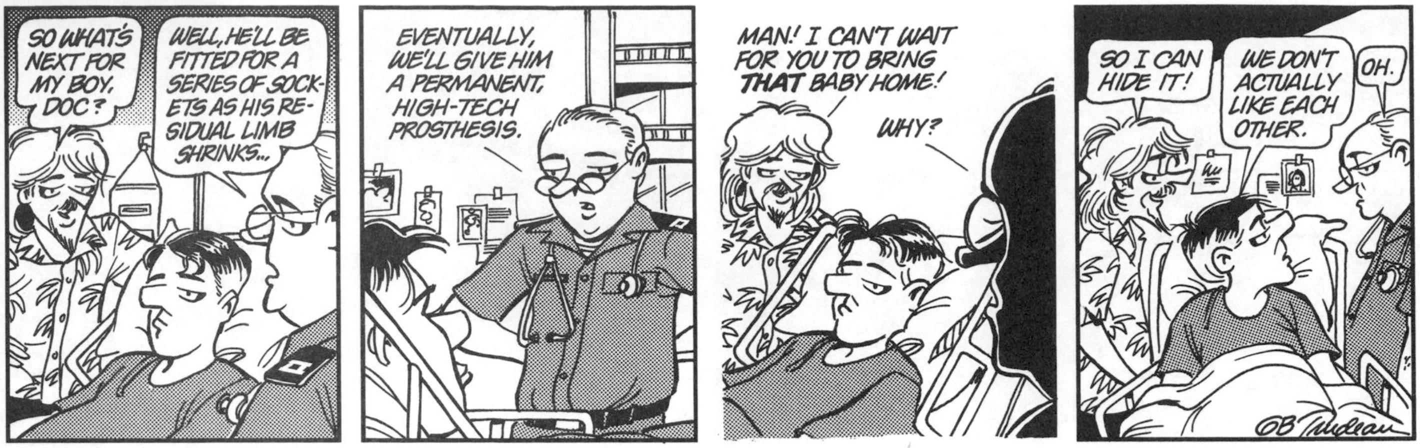
SO WHAT'S NEXT FOR MY BOY, DOC?
WELL, HE'LL BE FITTED FOR A SERIES OF SOCKETS AS HIS RESIDUAL LIMB SHRINKS...
EVENTUALLY, WE'LL GIVE HIM A PERMANENT, HIGH-TECH PROSTHESIS.
MAN! I CAN'T WAIT FOR YOU TO BRING **THAT** BABY HOME!
WHY?
SO I CAN HIDE IT!
WE DON'T ACTUALLY LIKE EACH OTHER.
OH.

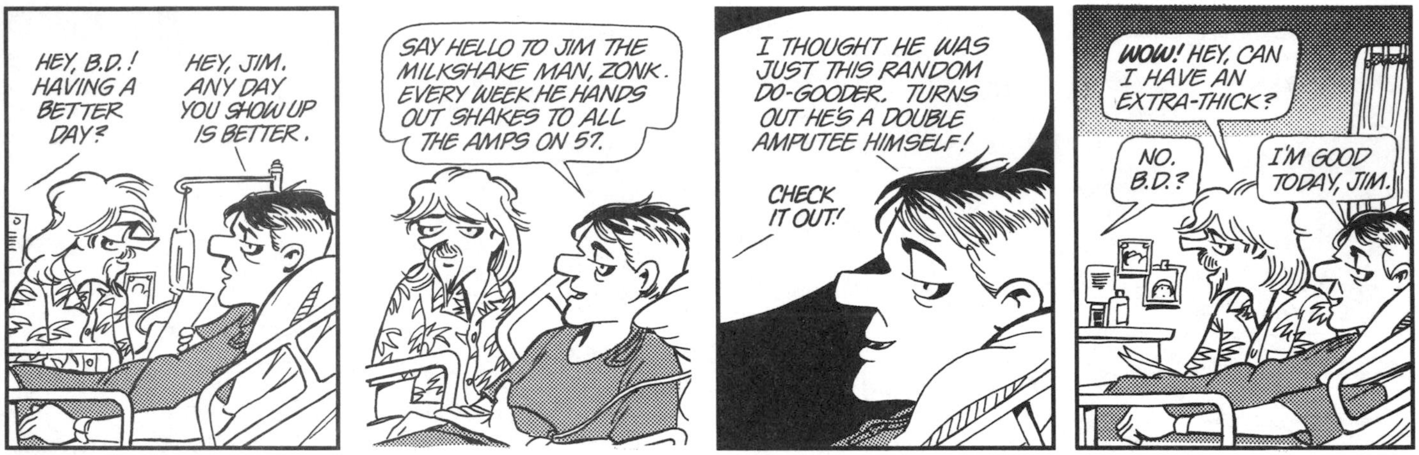
HEY, B.D.! HAVING A BETTER DAY?
HEY, JIM. ANY DAY YOU SHOW UP IS BETTER.
SAY HELLO TO JIM THE MILKSHAKE MAN, ZONK. EVERY WEEK HE HANDS OUT SHAKES TO ALL THE AMPS ON 57.
I THOUGHT HE WAS JUST THIS RANDOM DO-GOODER. TURNS OUT HE'S A DOUBLE AMPUTEE HIMSELF!
CHECK IT OUT!
WOW! HEY, CAN I HAVE AN EXTRA-THICK?
NO. B.D.?
I'M GOOD TODAY, JIM.

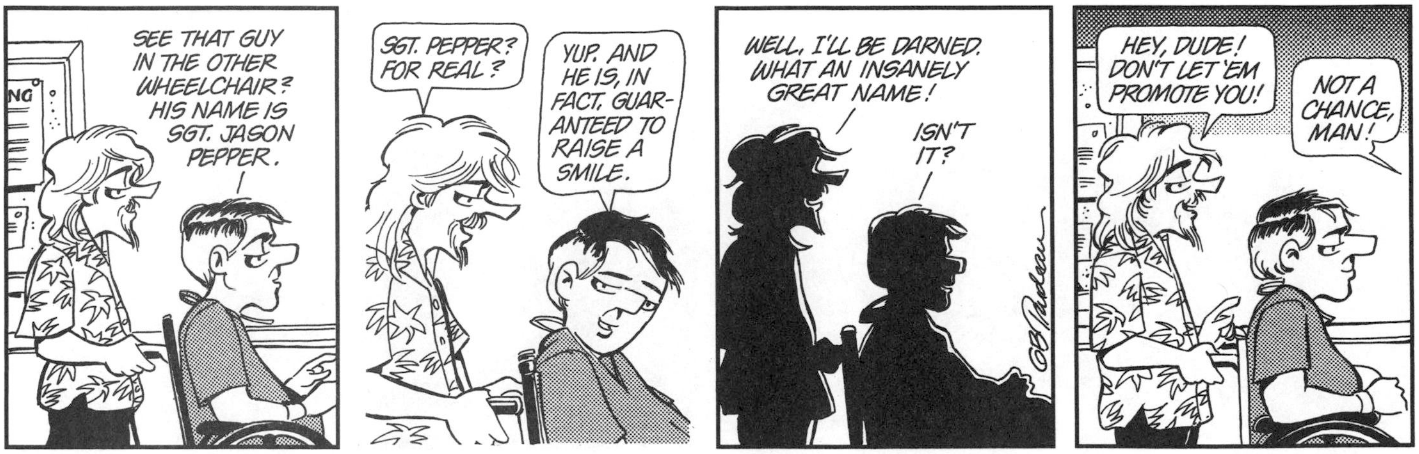
SEE THAT GUY IN THE OTHER WHEELCHAIR? HIS NAME IS SGT. JASON PEPPER.
SGT. PEPPER? FOR REAL?
YUP. AND HE IS, IN FACT, GUARANTEED TO RAISE A SMILE.
WELL, I'LL BE DARNED. WHAT AN INSANELY GREAT NAME!
ISN'T IT?
HEY, DUDE! DON'T LET 'EM PROMOTE YOU!
NOT A CHANCE, MAN!

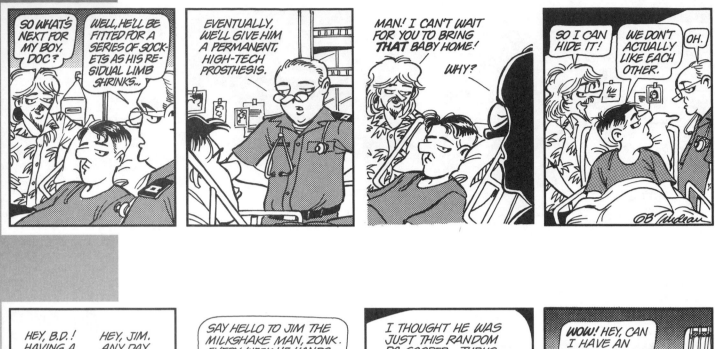

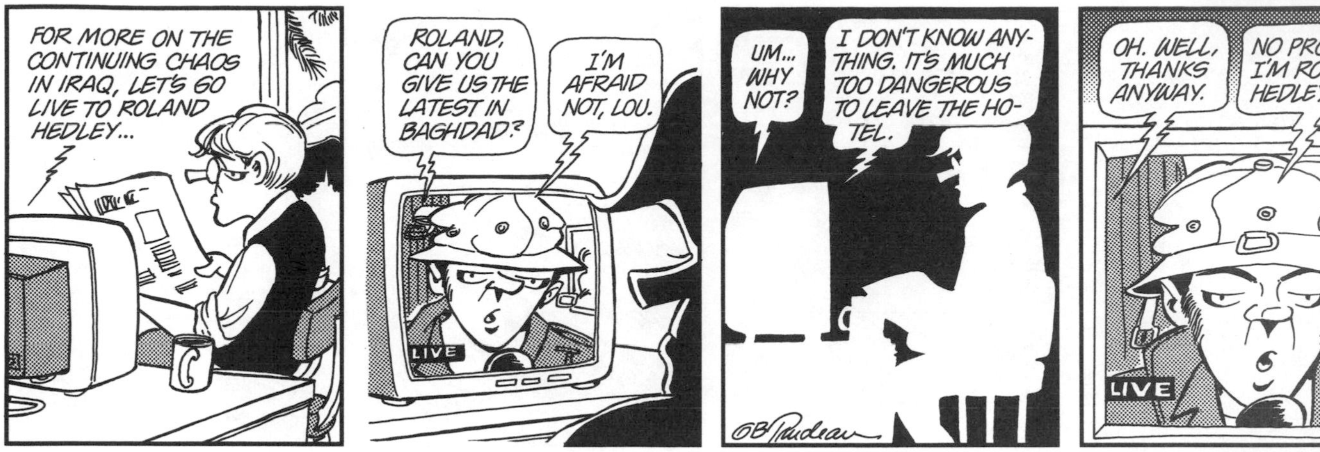
FOR MORE ON THE CONTINUING CHAOS IN IRAQ, LET'S GO LIVE TO ROLAND HEDLEY...
ROLAND, CAN YOU GIVE US THE LATEST IN BAGHDAD?
I'M AFRAID NOT, LOU.
LIVE
UM... WHY NOT?
I DON'T KNOW ANYTHING. IT'S MUCH TOO DANGEROUS TO LEAVE THE HOTEL.
OH. WELL, THANKS ANYWAY.
NO PROBLEM! I'M ROLAND HEDLEY, LIVE!
LIVE

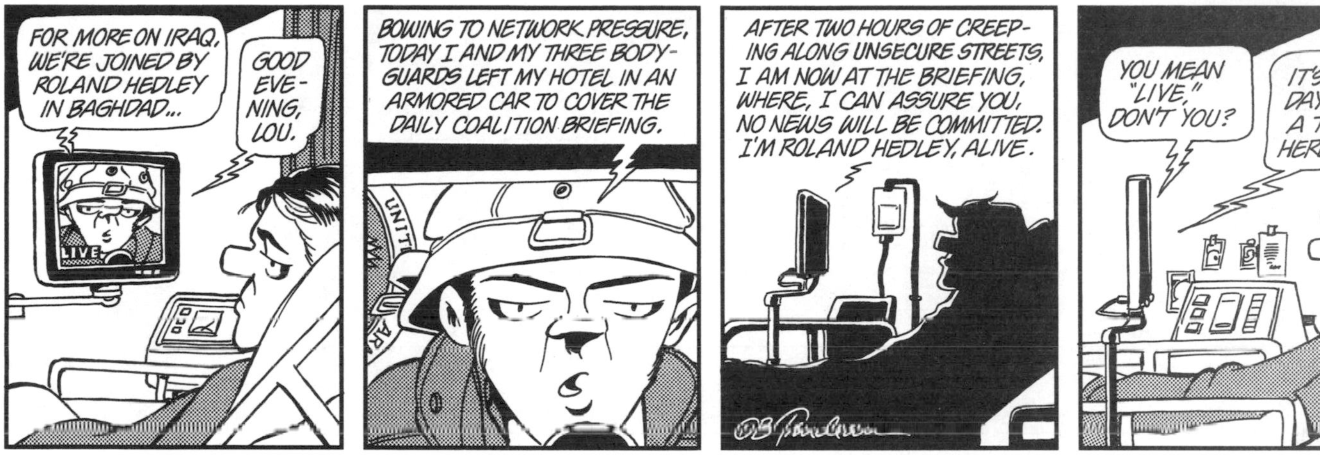
FOR MORE ON IRAQ, WE'RE JOINED BY ROLAND HEDLEY IN BAGHDAD...
GOOD EVENING, LOU.
LIVE
BOWING TO NETWORK PRESSURE, TODAY I AND MY THREE BODYGUARDS LEFT MY HOTEL IN AN ARMORED CAR TO COVER THE DAILY COALITION BRIEFING.
AFTER TWO HOURS OF CREEPING ALONG UNSECURE STREETS, I AM NOW AT THE BRIEFING, WHERE, I CAN ASSURE YOU, NO NEWS WILL BE COMMITTED. I'M ROLAND HEDLEY, ALIVE.
YOU MEAN "LIVE," DON'T YOU?
IT'S ONE DAY AT A TIME HERE, LOU.

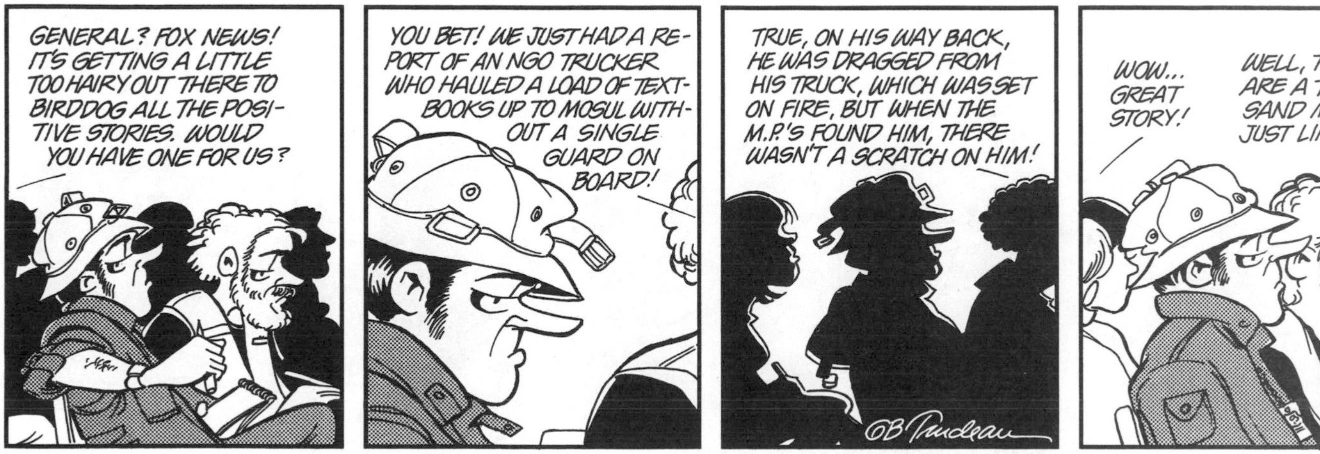
GENERAL? FOX NEWS! IT'S GETTING A LITTLE TOO HAIRY OUT THERE TO BIRDDOG ALL THE POSITIVE STORIES. WOULD YOU HAVE ONE FOR US?
YOU BET! WE JUST HAD A REPORT OF AN NGO TRUCKER WHO HAULED A LOAD OF TEXTBOOKS UP TO MOSUL WITHOUT A SINGLE GUARD ON BOARD!
TRUE, ON HIS WAY BACK, HE WAS DRAGGED FROM HIS TRUCK, WHICH WAS SET ON FIRE, BUT WHEN THE M.P.'S FOUND HIM, THERE WASN'T A SCRATCH ON HIM!
WOW... GREAT STORY!
WELL, THERE ARE A THOUSAND MORE JUST LIKE IT!

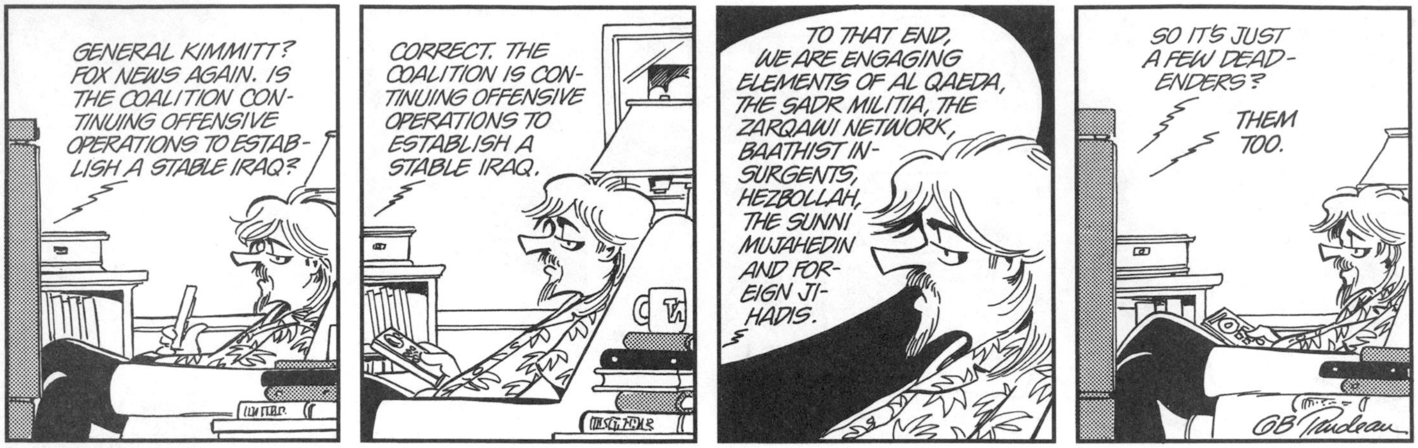
GENERAL KIMMITT? FOX NEWS AGAIN. IS THE COALITION CONTINUING OFFENSIVE OPERATIONS TO ESTABLISH A STABLE IRAQ?
CORRECT. THE COALITION IS CONTINUING OFFENSIVE OPERATIONS TO ESTABLISH A STABLE IRAQ.
TO THAT END, WE ARE ENGAGING ELEMENTS OF AL QAEDA, THE SADR MILITIA, THE ZARQAWI NETWORK, BAATHIST INSURGENTS, HEZBOLLAH, THE SUNNI MUJAHEDIN AND FOREIGN JIHADIS.
SO IT'S JUST A FEW DEAD-ENDERS?
THEM TOO.
GB Trudeau

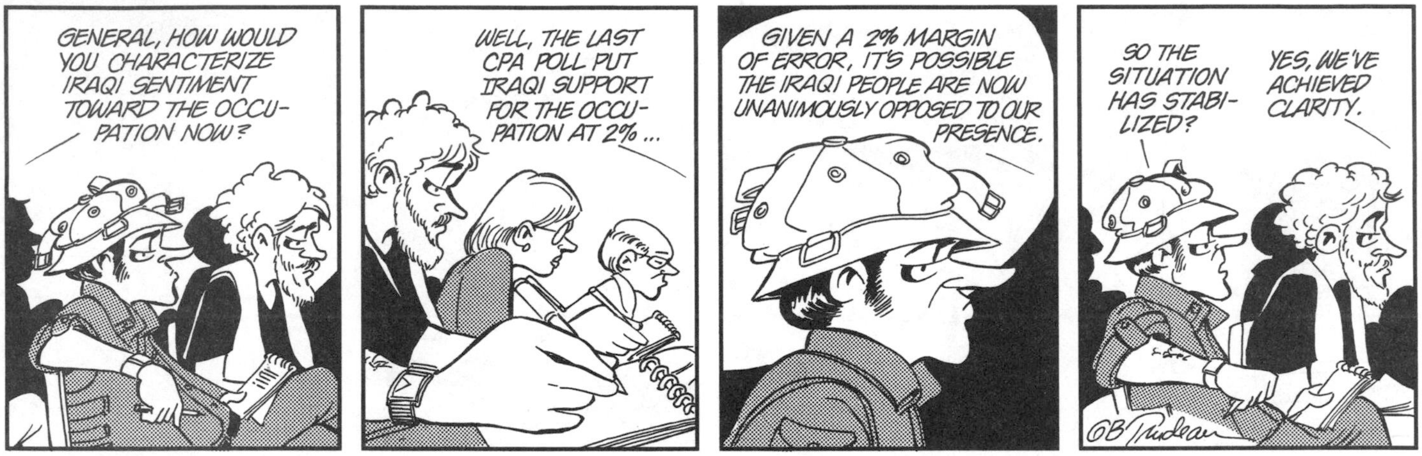
GENERAL, HOW WOULD YOU CHARACTERIZE IRAQI SENTIMENT TOWARD THE OCCUPATION NOW?
WELL, THE LAST CPA POLL PUT IRAQI SUPPORT FOR THE OCCUPATION AT 2% ...
GIVEN A 2% MARGIN OF ERROR, IT'S POSSIBLE THE IRAQI PEOPLE ARE NOW UNANIMOUSLY OPPOSED TO OUR PRESENCE.
SO THE SITUATION HAS STABILIZED?
YES, WE'VE ACHIEVED CLARITY.
GB Trudeau

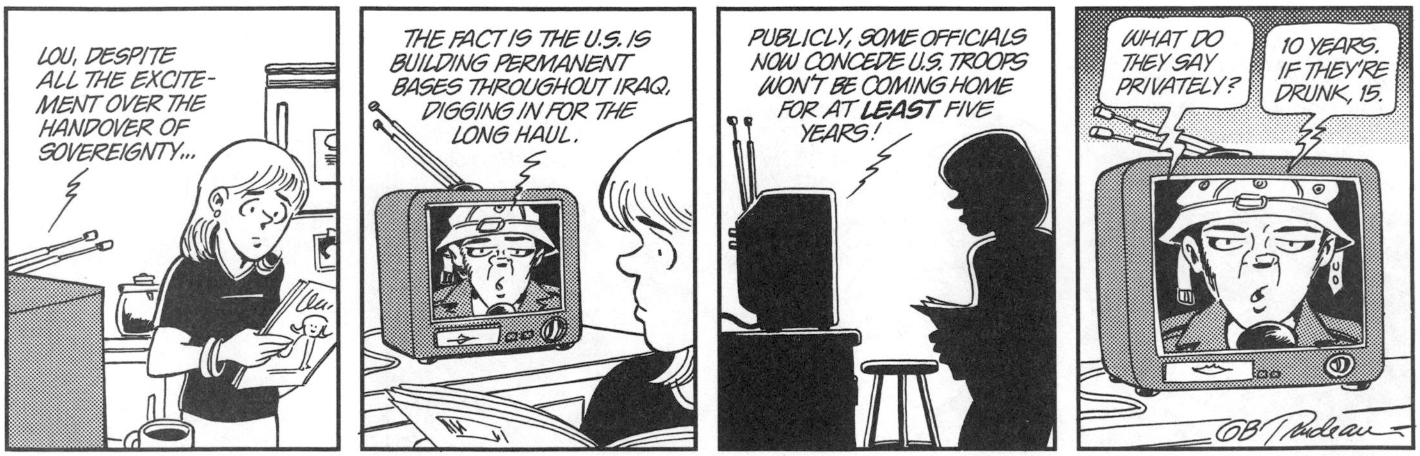
LOU, DESPITE ALL THE EXCITEMENT OVER THE HANDOVER OF SOVEREIGNTY...
THE FACT IS THE U.S. IS BUILDING PERMANENT BASES THROUGHOUT IRAQ, DIGGING IN FOR THE LONG HAUL.
PUBLICLY, SOME OFFICIALS NOW CONCEDE U.S. TROOPS WON'T BE COMING HOME FOR AT LEAST FIVE YEARS!
WHAT DO THEY SAY PRIVATELY?
10 YEARS. IF THEY'RE DRUNK, 15.
GB Trudeau

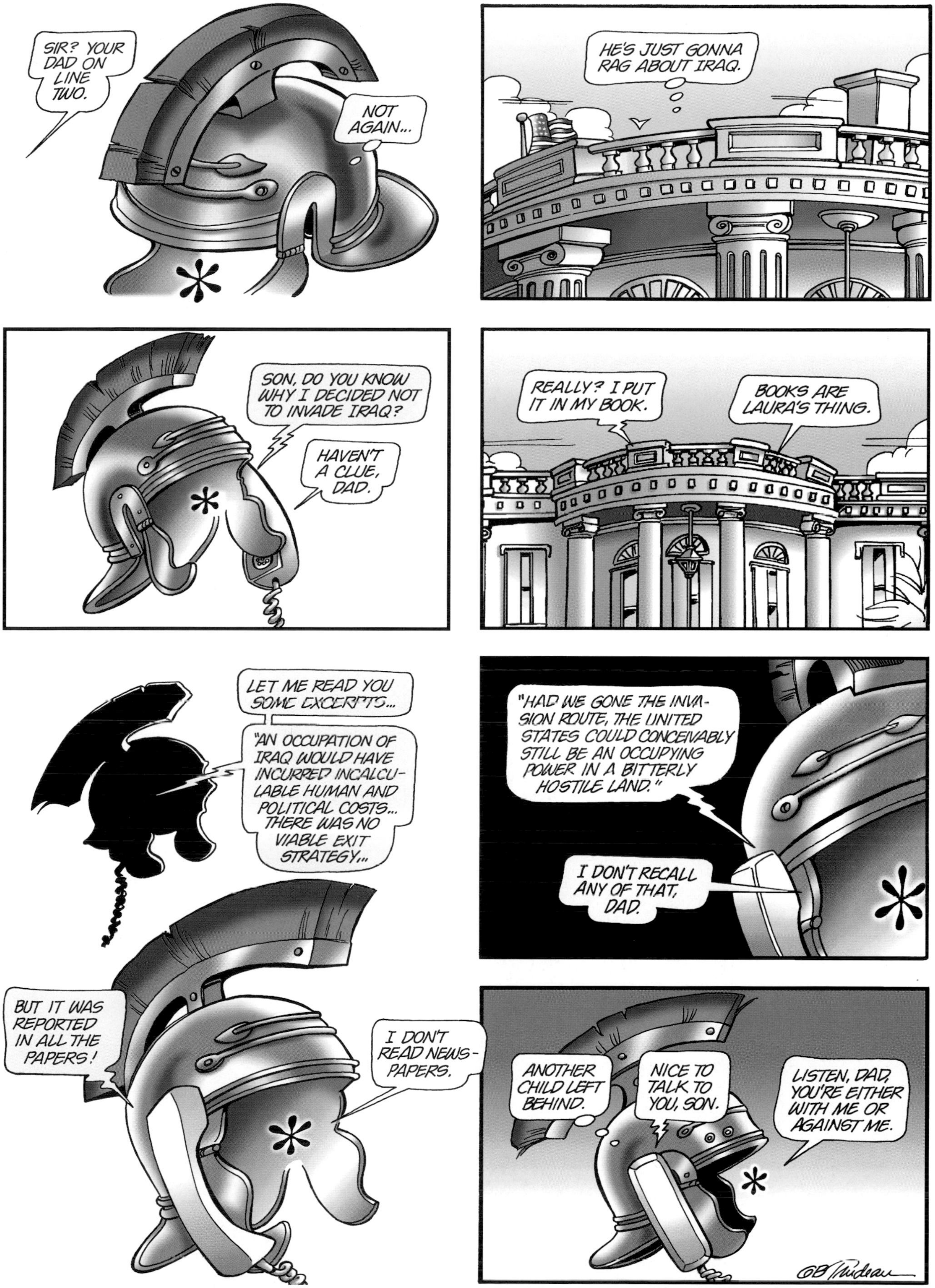

SIR? YOUR DAD ON LINE TWO.
NOT AGAIN...
HE'S JUST GONNA RAG ABOUT IRAQ.
SON, DO YOU KNOW WHY I DECIDED NOT TO INVADE IRAQ?
HAVEN'T A CLUE, DAD.
REALLY? I PUT IT IN MY BOOK.
BOOKS ARE LAURA'S THING.
LET ME READ YOU SOME EXCERPTS...
"AN OCCUPATION OF IRAQ WOULD HAVE INCURRED INCALCU-LABLE HUMAN AND POLITICAL COSTS... THERE WAS NO VIABLE EXIT STRATEGY...
"HAD WE GONE THE INVA-SION ROUTE, THE UNITED STATES COULD CONCEIVABLY STILL BE AN OCCUPYING POWER IN A BITTERLY HOSTILE LAND."
I DON'T RECALL ANY OF THAT, DAD.
BUT IT WAS REPORTED IN ALL THE PAPERS!
I DON'T READ NEWS-PAPERS.
ANOTHER CHILD LEFT BEHIND.
NICE TO TALK TO YOU, SON.
LISTEN, DAD, YOU'RE EITHER WITH ME OR AGAINST ME.

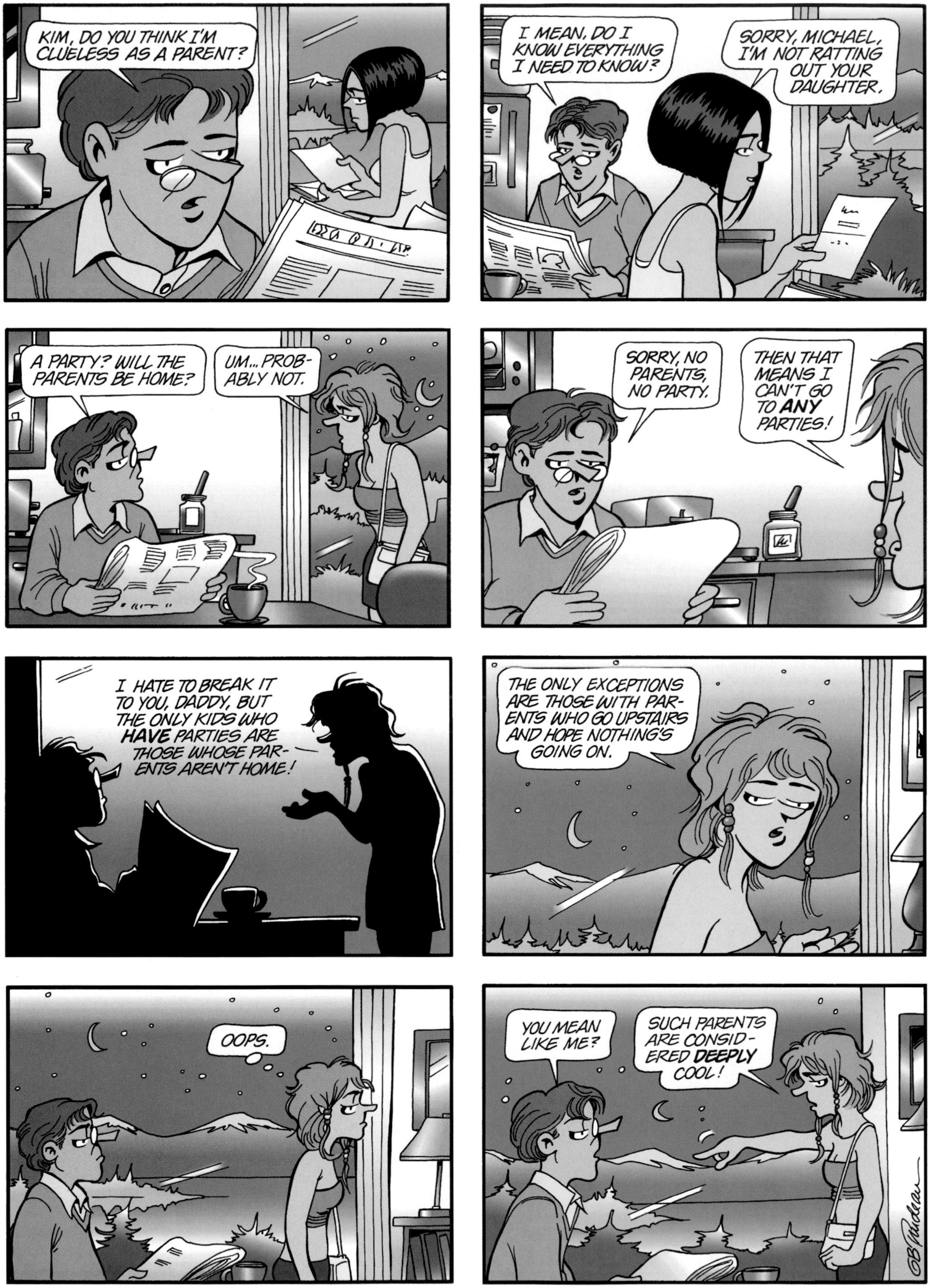
KIM, DO YOU THINK I'M CLUELESS AS A PARENT?
I MEAN, DO I KNOW EVERYTHING I NEED TO KNOW?
SORRY, MICHAEL, I'M NOT RATTING OUT YOUR DAUGHTER.
A PARTY? WILL THE PARENTS BE HOME?
UM... PROBABLY NOT.
SORRY, NO PARENTS, NO PARTY.
THEN THAT MEANS I CAN'T GO TO **ANY** PARTIES!
I HATE TO BREAK IT TO YOU, DADDY, BUT THE ONLY KIDS WHO **HAVE** PARTIES ARE THOSE WHOSE PARENTS AREN'T HOME!
THE ONLY EXCEPTIONS ARE THOSE WITH PARENTS WHO GO UPSTAIRS AND HOPE NOTHING'S GOING ON.
OOPS.
YOU MEAN LIKE ME?
SUCH PARENTS ARE CONSIDERED **DEEPLY** COOL!

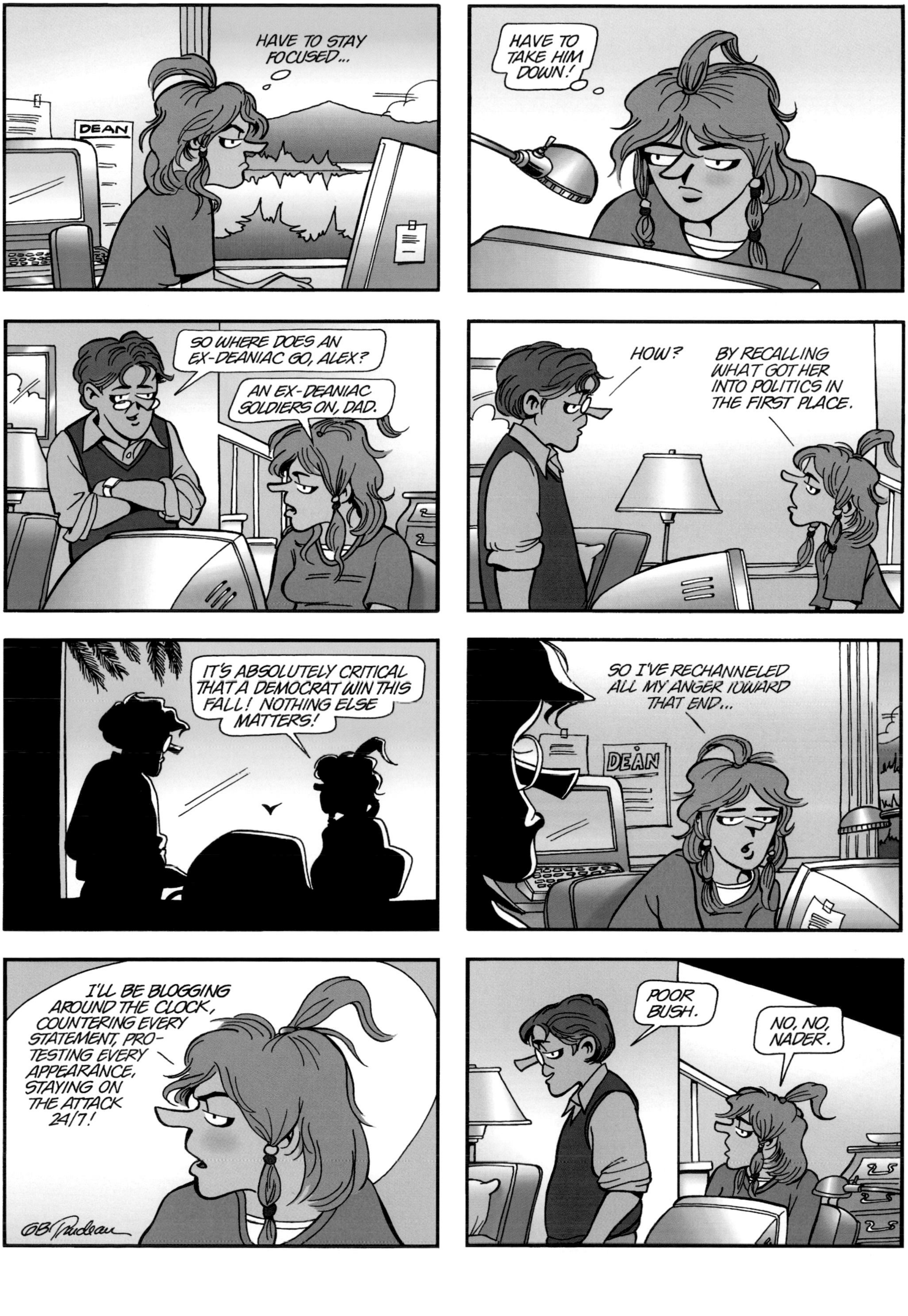
HAVE TO STAY FOCUSED...
HAVE TO TAKE HIM DOWN!
SO WHERE DOES AN EX-DEANIAC GO, ALEX?
AN EX-DEANIAC SOLDIERS ON, DAD.
HOW?
BY RECALLING WHAT GOT HER INTO POLITICS IN THE FIRST PLACE.
IT'S ABSOLUTELY CRITICAL THAT A DEMOCRAT WIN THIS FALL! NOTHING ELSE MATTERS!
SO I'VE RECHANNELED ALL MY ANGER TOWARD THAT END...
I'LL BE BLOGGING AROUND THE CLOCK, COUNTERING EVERY STATEMENT, PROTESTING EVERY APPEARANCE, STAYING ON THE ATTACK 24/7!
POOR BUSH.
NO, NO, NADER.

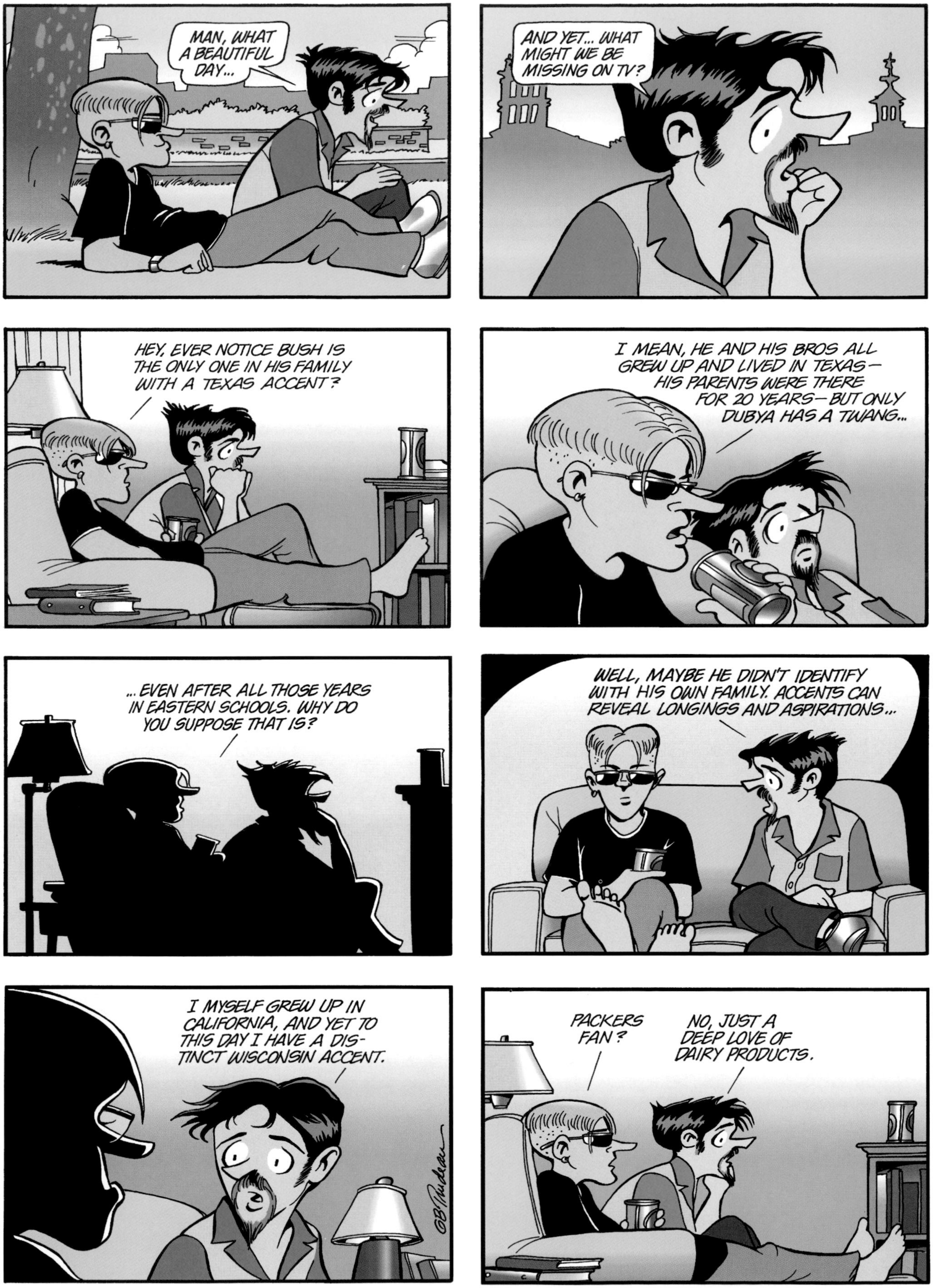
MAN, WHAT A BEAUTIFUL DAY...
AND YET... WHAT MIGHT WE BE MISSING ON TV?
HEY, EVER NOTICE BUSH IS THE ONLY ONE IN HIS FAMILY WITH A TEXAS ACCENT?
I MEAN, HE AND HIS BROS ALL GREW UP AND LIVED IN TEXAS— HIS PARENTS WERE THERE FOR 20 YEARS—BUT ONLY DUBYA HAS A TWANG...
...EVEN AFTER ALL THOSE YEARS IN EASTERN SCHOOLS. WHY DO YOU SUPPOSE THAT IS?
WELL, MAYBE HE DIDN'T IDENTIFY WITH HIS OWN FAMILY. ACCENTS CAN REVEAL LONGINGS AND ASPIRATIONS...
I MYSELF GREW UP IN CALIFORNIA, AND YET TO THIS DAY I HAVE A DISTINCT WISCONSIN ACCENT.
PACKERS FAN?
NO, JUST A DEEP LOVE OF DAIRY PRODUCTS.

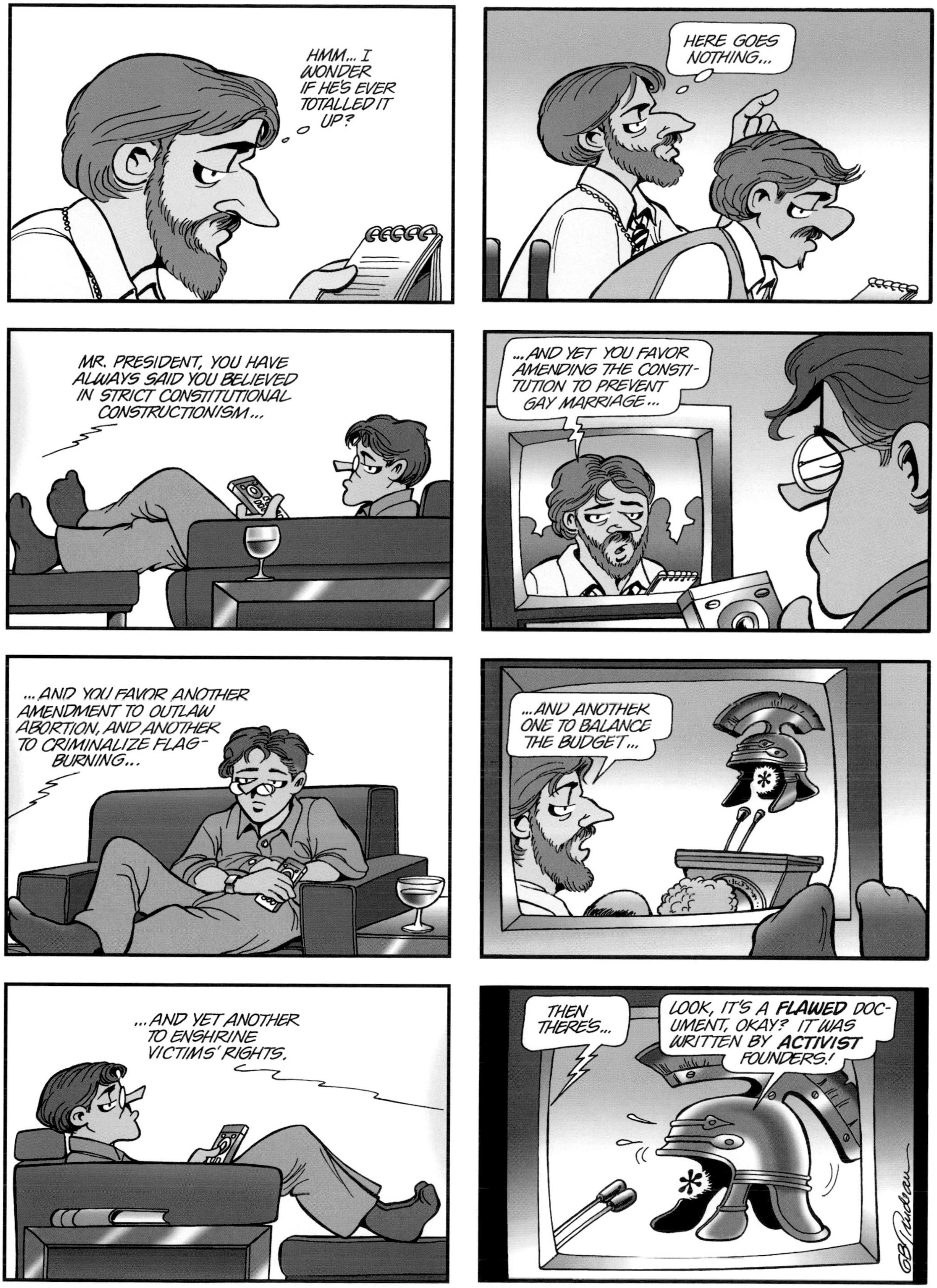
HMM... I WONDER IF HE'S EVER TOTALLED IT UP?
HERE GOES NOTHING...
MR. PRESIDENT, YOU HAVE ALWAYS SAID YOU BELIEVED IN STRICT CONSTITUTIONAL CONSTRUCTIONISM...
...AND YET YOU FAVOR AMENDING THE CONSTITUTION TO PREVENT GAY MARRIAGE...
...AND YOU FAVOR ANOTHER AMENDMENT TO OUTLAW ABORTION, AND ANOTHER TO CRIMINALIZE FLAG-BURNING...
...AND ANOTHER ONE TO BALANCE THE BUDGET...
...AND YET ANOTHER TO ENSHRINE VICTIMS' RIGHTS.
THEN THERE'S...
LOOK, IT'S A **FLAWED** DOCUMENT, OKAY? IT WAS WRITTEN BY **ACTIVIST** FOUNDERS!

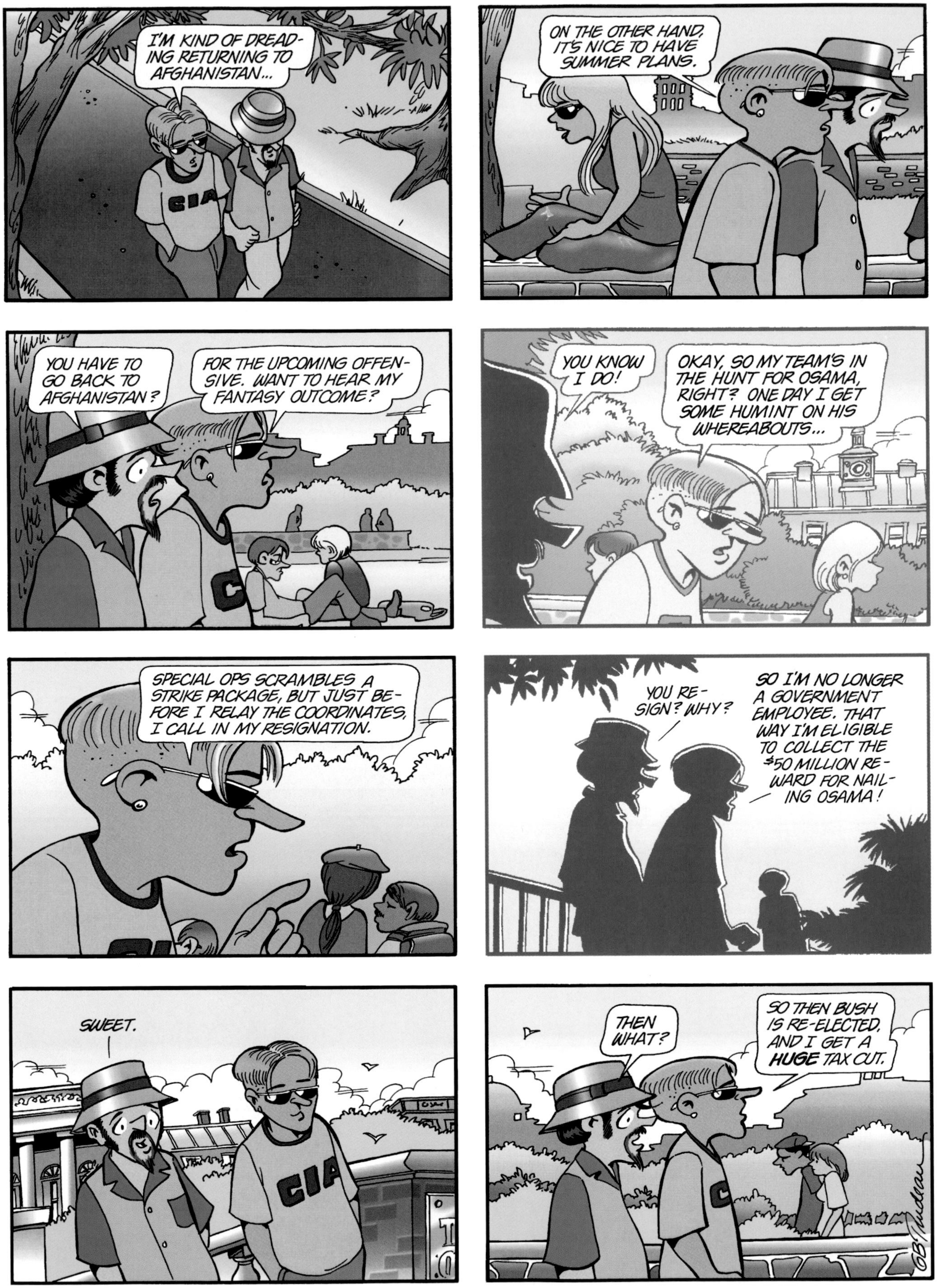
I'M KIND OF DREADING RETURNING TO AFGHANISTAN...
ON THE OTHER HAND, IT'S NICE TO HAVE SUMMER PLANS.
YOU HAVE TO GO BACK TO AFGHANISTAN?
FOR THE UPCOMING OFFENSIVE. WANT TO HEAR MY FANTASY OUTCOME?
YOU KNOW I DO!
OKAY, SO MY TEAM'S IN THE HUNT FOR OSAMA, RIGHT? ONE DAY I GET SOME HUMINT ON HIS WHEREABOUTS...
SPECIAL OPS SCRAMBLES A STRIKE PACKAGE, BUT JUST BEFORE I RELAY THE COORDINATES, I CALL IN MY RESIGNATION.
YOU RESIGN? WHY?
SO I'M NO LONGER A GOVERNMENT EMPLOYEE. THAT WAY I'M ELIGIBLE TO COLLECT THE $50 MILLION REWARD FOR NAILING OSAMA!
SWEET.
THEN WHAT?
SO THEN BUSH IS RE-ELECTED, AND I GET A **HUGE** TAX CUT.

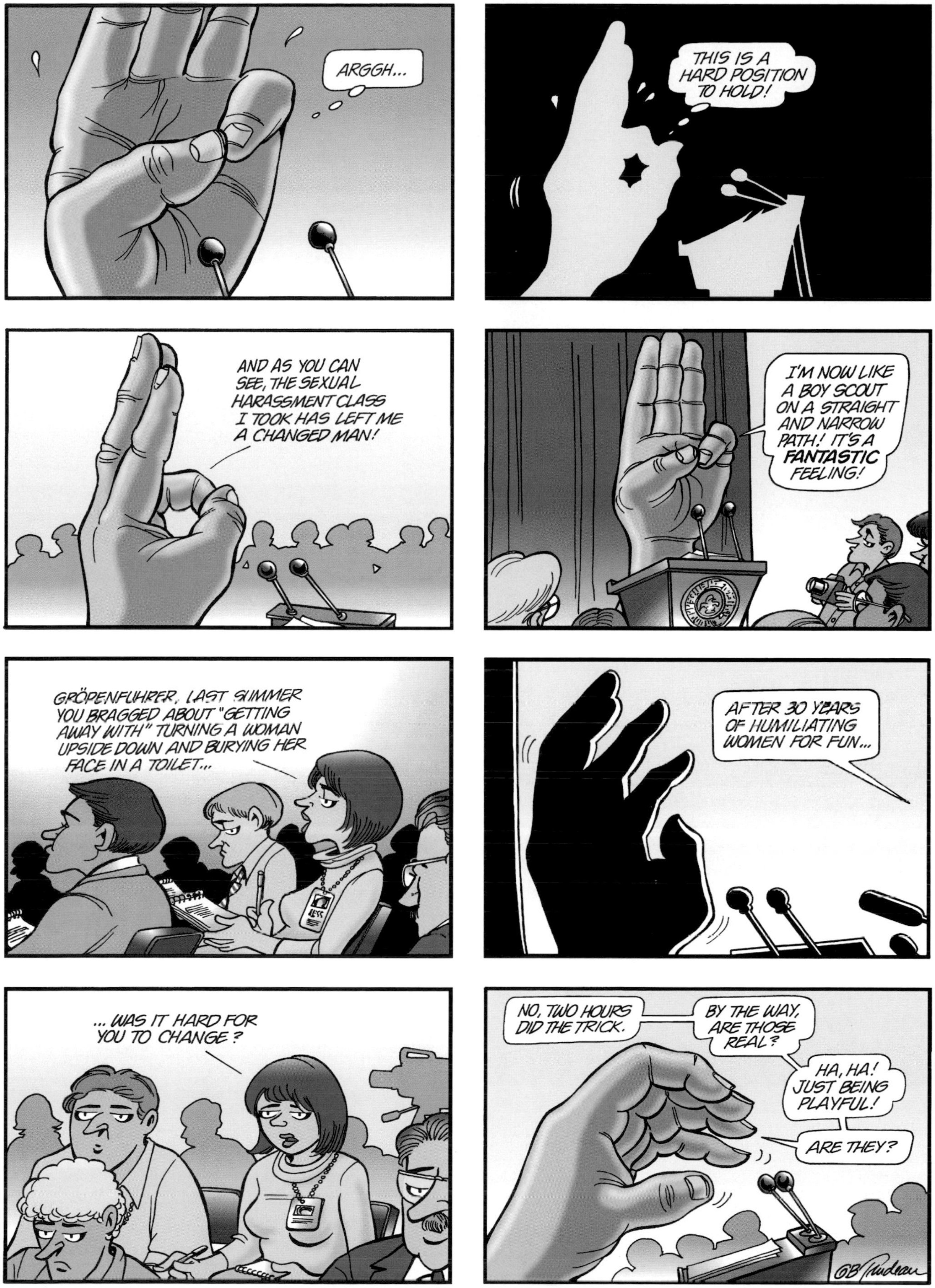
ARGGH...
THIS IS A HARD POSITION TO HOLD!
AND AS YOU CAN SEE, THE SEXUAL HARASSMENT CLASS I TOOK HAS LEFT ME A CHANGED MAN!
I'M NOW LIKE A BOY SCOUT ON A STRAIGHT AND NARROW PATH! IT'S A FANTASTIC FEELING!
GRÖPENFUHRER, LAST SUMMER YOU BRAGGED ABOUT "GETTING AWAY WITH" TURNING A WOMAN UPSIDE DOWN AND BURYING HER FACE IN A TOILET...
AFTER 30 YEARS OF HUMILIATING WOMEN FOR FUN...
...WAS IT HARD FOR YOU TO CHANGE?
NO, TWO HOURS DID THE TRICK.
BY THE WAY, ARE THOSE REAL?
HA, HA! JUST BEING PLAYFUL!
ARE THEY?
©B. Trudeau

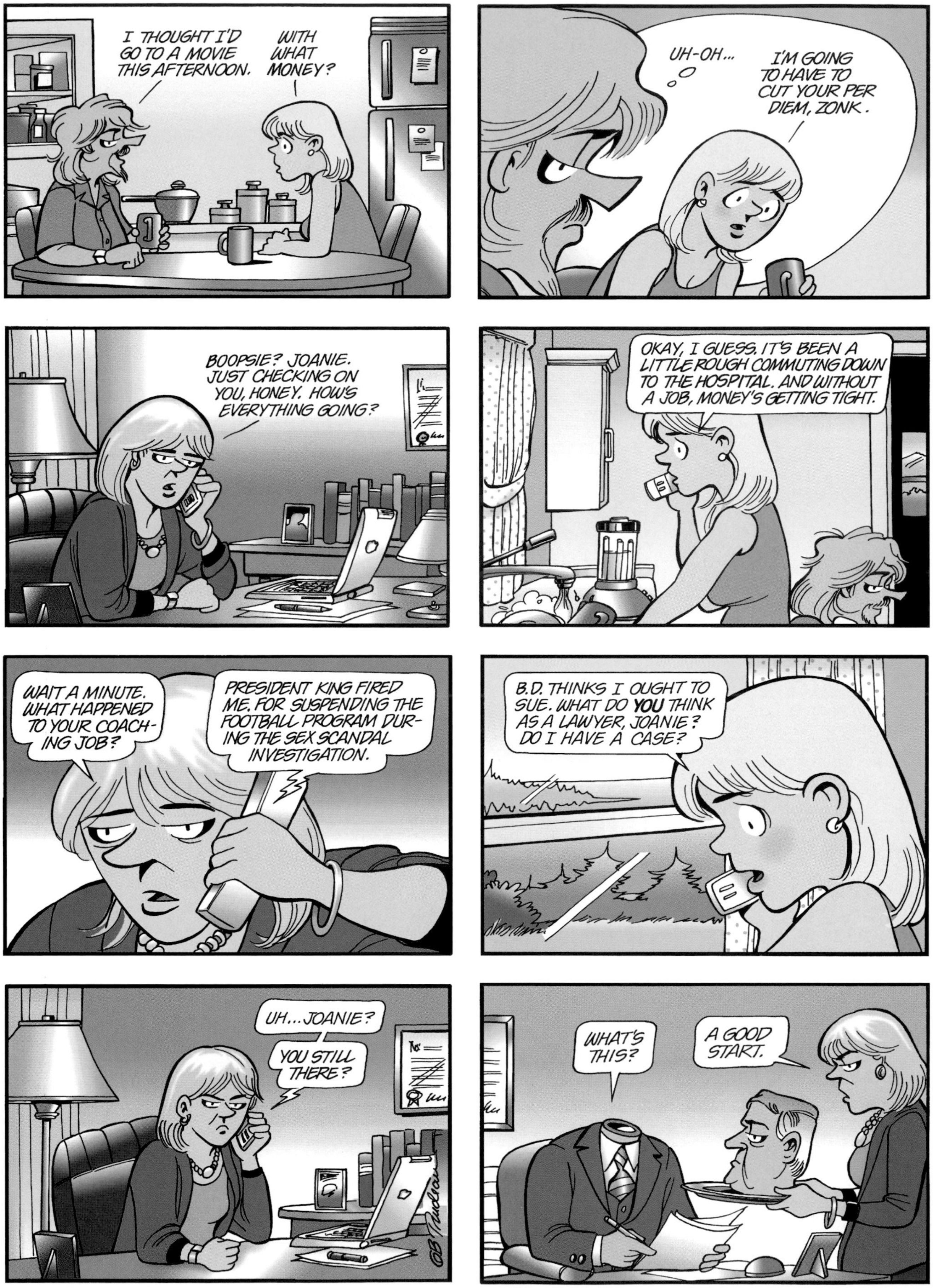
I THOUGHT I'D GO TO A MOVIE THIS AFTERNOON.
WITH WHAT MONEY?
UH-OH...
I'M GOING TO HAVE TO CUT YOUR PER DIEM, ZONK.
BOOPSIE? JOANIE. JUST CHECKING ON YOU, HONEY. HOW'S EVERYTHING GOING?
OKAY, I GUESS. IT'S BEEN A LITTLE ROUGH COMMUTING DOWN TO THE HOSPITAL. AND WITHOUT A JOB, MONEY'S GETTING TIGHT.
WAIT A MINUTE. WHAT HAPPENED TO YOUR COACHING JOB?
PRESIDENT KING FIRED ME. FOR SUSPENDING THE FOOTBALL PROGRAM DURING THE SEX SCANDAL INVESTIGATION.
B.D. THINKS I OUGHT TO SUE. WHAT DO **YOU** THINK AS A LAWYER, JOANIE? DO I HAVE A CASE?
UH...JOANIE?
YOU STILL THERE?
WHAT'S THIS?
A GOOD START.

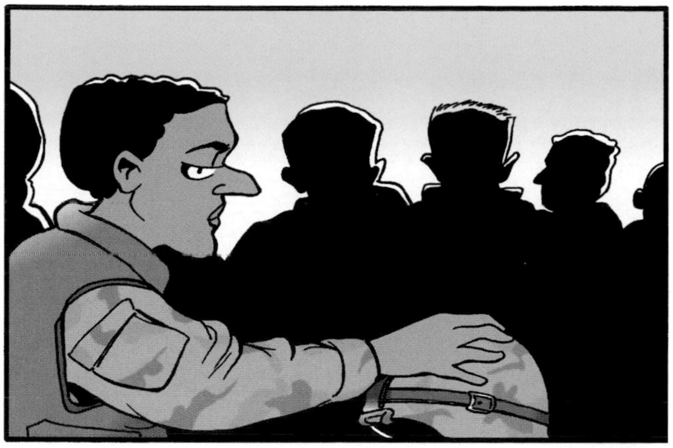

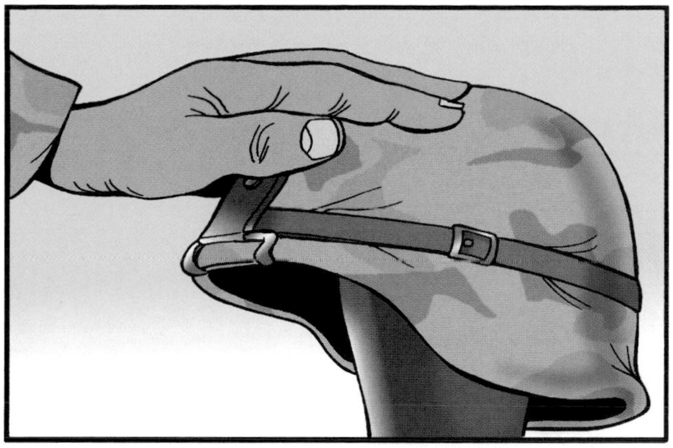

IN MEMORIAM
THE WAR IN IRAQ

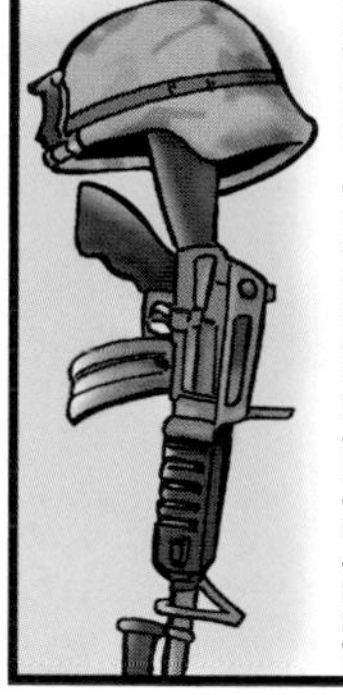

Therrel Childers • Jay Aubin • Ryan Beaupre • Brian Kennedy Kendall Waters-Bey • Jose Gutierrez • Eric Orlowski • Brandon Tobler • Thomas Adams • Nicolas Hodson • Christopher Scott Seifert • Jamaal Addison • Frederick Pokorney Jr. • George Buggs Robert Dowdy • Ruben Estrella-Soto • Howard Johnson II • James Kiehl • Johnny Mata • Lori Ann Piestewa • Brandon Sloan • Donald Walters • Edward Anguiano • Michael Bitz • David Fribley • Jose Garibay • Jose Gonzalez • Phillip Jordan • Thomas Slocum • Brian Buesing • Randal Rosacker • Michael Williams • Patrick Nixon Brendon Reiss • Tamario Burkett • Donald Cline • Nolen Hutchings Jonathan Gifford • Kemaphoom Chanwongse • Evan James Bradley Korthaus • Gregory Sanders • Thomas Blair • Gregory Stone • Michael Johnson Jr. • Kevin Nave • Donald May Jr. • Patrick O'Day • Francisco Martinez-Flores • Robert Rodriguez • Joseph Menusa • Jesus Suarez del Solar • Fernando Padilla-Ramirez Roderic Solomon • James Cawley • Russell Creighton-Weldon Michael Curtin • Diego Rincon • Eugene Williams • William White Michael Lalush • Brian McGinnis • Aaron Contreras • William Jeffries • Brandon Rowe • Jacob Butler • Joseph Maglione III Brian Anderson • Patrick O'Day • George Fernandez • Nathan White James Adamouski • Erik Halvorsen • Scott Jamar • Michael Pedersen • Eric Smith • Matthew Boule • Chad Bales • Donald Oaks Jr. • Randall Rehn • Todd Robbins • Nino Livaudais • Ryan Long Russell Rippetoe • Mark Evnin • Erik Silva • Wilbert Davis • Edward Korn • Travis Ford • Benjamin Sammis • Tristan Aitken Wilfred Bellard • Daniel Cunningham • Devon Jones • Paul Smith

Bernard Gooden • Brian McPhillips • Duane Rios • Stevon Booker • Larry Brown • Edward Smith • Gregory Huxley Jr. • Kelley Prewitt • Andrew Aviles • Jesus Medellin • Lincoln Hollinsaid • Jeffrey Kaylor • Anthony Miller • George Mitchell • William Watkins III • Eric Das • Henry Brown • Juan Garza Jr. • John Marshall • Jason Meyer • Robert Stever • Scott Sather • Jeffrey Bohr Jr. • Terry Hemingway • Riayan Tejeda • Jesus Gonzalez • David Owens Jr. • Gil Mercado • Thomas Foley III • Joseph Mayek • Armando Gonzalez Richard Goward • Jason Mileo • John Brown • John Rivero • Andrew Arnold • Robert Channell Jr. • Alan Lam Roy Buckley • Troy Jenkins • Osbaldo Orozco • Narson Sullivan Joe Garza • Jesse Givens • Sean Reynolds • Jason Deibler • Marlin Rockhold • Cedric Bruns • Richard Carl Hans Gukeisen • Brian Van Dusen • Matthew Smith • Jakub Kowalik Jose Rodriguez Patrick Griffin Jr. • Nicholas Kleiboeker • David Nutt • William Payne Douglas Marencoreyes • Rasheed Sahib • Dominic Baragona • Andrew LaMont • Timothy Ryan Aaron White • Kirk Straseskie • Jason Moore • Nathaniel Caldwell • David Evans Jr. Keman Mitchell • Kenneth Nalley • Brett Petriken • Jeremiah Smith • Matthew Schram Thomas Broomhead • Michael Quinn • Kenneth Bradley • Jose Perez III • Michael Gleason Kyle Griffin • Zachariah Long • Jonathan Lambert • Atanasio Haro Marin Jr. • Branden Oberleitner • Doyle Bollinger Jr. • Travis Burkhardt • David Sisung • Jesse Halling Michael Dooley • Gavin Neighbor • John Klinesmith Jr. • Andrew Pokorny • Ryan Cox Joseph Suell • Shawn Pahnke • Robert Frantz • Michael Tosto • Michael Deuel • William Latham • Paul Nakamura • Orenthial Smith • Cedric Lennon • Gregory MacDonald Andrew Chris • Gladimir Philippe • Kevin Ott • Richard Orengo • Corey Hubbell • Joshua McIntosh • Tomas Sotelo Jr. • Timothy Conneway • Christopher Coffin • Travis Bradachnall • Corey Small • Edward Herrgott • Jeffrey Wershow • David Parson • Chad Keith • Barry Sanford Sr. • Craig Boling • Robert McKinley • Roger Rowe • Jason Tetrault Melissa Valles • Dan Gabrielson • Christian Schultz • Joshua Neusche • Paul Cassidy Jaror Puello-Coronado • Michael Crockett • Cory Geurin • Ramon Torres • David Moreno

Mason Whetstone • Joel Bertoldie • Jonathan Rozier • Jason Jordan • Justin Garvey Christopher Willoughby • David Scott • Mark Bibby • Jon Fettig • Brett Christian • Joshua Byers • Evan Ashcraft • Hector Perez • Juan Serrano • Raheen Heighter • Jonathan Barnes • Daniel Methvin • Wilfredo Perez Jr. • Jonathan Cheatham • Heath McMillin William Maher III • Nathaniel Hart Jr. • Leif Nott • Michael Deutsch • James Lambert III Justin Hebert • David Loyd • Faraa Letufuga • Kyle Gilbert • Zeferino Colunga • Leonard Simmons • Brian Hellerman • Duane Longstreth • Matthew Bush • Brandon Ramsey Floyd Knighten Jr. • Levi Kinchen • David Perry • Taft Williams • Richard Eaton Jr. • Timmy Brown Jr. • Daniel Parker • Steven White • David Kirchhoff • Craig Ivory • Eric Hull Kenneth Harris Jr. • Bobby Franklin • Michael Adams • Kylan Jones-Huffman • Vorn Mack Stephen Scott • Ronald Allen Jr. • Pablo Manzano • Darryl Dent • Rafael Navea • Gregory Belanger • Anthony Sherman • Mark Lawton • Sean Cataudella • Cameron Sarno • Joseph Camara • Charles Caldwell • Christopher Sisson • Bruce Brown • Jarrett Thompson Ryan Carlock • Joseph Robsky Jr. • Henry Ybarra III • William Bennett • Kevin Morehead Trevor Blumberg • Kevin Kimmerly • Alyssa Peterson • James Wright • Brian Faunce Anthony Thompson • Richard Arriaga • David Friedrich • Lunsford Brown II • Frederick Miller Jr. • Paul Sturino • Michael Andrade • Robert Lucero • Kyle Thomas • Robert Rooney • Christopher Cutchall • Andrew Baddick • Darrin Potter • Dustin McGaugh Simeon Hunte • Analaura Gutierrez • James Blankenbecler • Tamarra Ramos • Charles Sims • James Pirtle • Kerry Scott • Spencer Karol • Richard Torres • Joseph Norquist Christopher Swisher • Sean Silva • James Powell • Jose Casanova • Stephen Wyatt Donald Wheeler • Douglas Weismantle • Benjamin Freeman • Kim Orlando • Joseph Bellavia • Sean Grilley • Michael Williams • John D. Hart • David Bernstein • Paul Johnson Paul Bueche • Jason Ward • John Johnson • John Teal • Artimus Brassfield • Jose Mora Michael Hancock • Joseph Guerrera • Rachel Bosveld • Charles Buehring Jamie Huggins • Steven Acosta • Aubrey Bell • Jonathan Falaniko • Algernon Adams

Michael Barrera • Isaac Campoy • Todd Bryant • Joshua Hurley • Maurice Johnson Benjamin Colgan • Paul Velasquez • Ernest Bucklew • Anthony Dagostino • Karina Lau Keelan Moss • Ross Pennanen • Brian Slavenas • Frances Vega • Joe Wilson • Darius Jennings • Daniel Bader • Steven Conover • Brian Penisten • Joel Perez • Bruce Smith Rayshawn Johnson • Francisco Martinez • Robert Benson • Jose Rivera • James Chance III Paul Fisher • James Wolf • Sharon Swartworth • Kyran Kennedy • Paul Neff II • Scott Rose Benedict Smith • Cornell Gilmore I • Morgan Kennon • Mark Vasquez • Gary Collins • Kurt Frosheiser • Linda Jimenez • Nicholas Tomko • Genaro Acosta • Marlon Jackson • Robert Wise • Nathan Bailey • Joseph Minucci II • Jacob Fletcher • Irving Medina • Timothy Hayslett • Michael Acklin II • Ryan Baker • William Dusenbery • Warren Hansen • Eugene Uhl III • Sheldon Hawk Eagle • Erik Kooteroon • John Sullivan • Jeremy Wolfe • Kelly Bolor John Russell • Scott Saboe • Damian Heidelberg • Jeremiah DiGiovanni • Richard Hafer Pierre Piche • Joey Whitener • Dale Panchot • Alexander Coulter • James Shull • Nathan Dalley • Joseph Lister • George Wood • Scott Tyrrell • Gary Coleman • Damian Bushart Robert Roberts • Jerry Wilson • Rel Ravago IV • Eddie Menyweather • Darrell Smith Christopher Nason • David Goldberg • Thomas Sweet II • Ariel Rico • Aaron Sissel Stephen Bertolino • Uday Singh • Raphael Davis • Ryan Young • Clarence Boone • Arron Clark • Ray Hutchinson • Jason Wright • Steven Bridges • Joseph Blickenstaff Christopher Wesley • Jerrick Petty • Richard Burdick • Aaron Reese • Todd Bates Marshall Edgerton • Jeffrey Braun • Jarrod Black • Rian Ferguson • Kimberly Voelz Kenneth Souslin • Nathan Nakis • Christopher Holland • Glenn Allison • Charles Bush Jr. Edward Saltz • Stuart Moore • Christopher Splinter • Christopher Soelzer • Benjamin Biskie • Eric Cooke • Michael Yashinski • Thomas Christensen • Stephen Hattamer Charles Haight • Michael Sutter • Michael Mihalakis • Rey Cuervo • Ernesto Blanco • Curt Jordan Jr. • Justin Pollard • Dennis Corral • Kimberly Hampton • Eric Paliwoda Solomon Bangayan • Marc Seiden • Luke Frist • Jesse Mizener • Aaron Weaver

Jeffrey Walker • Michael Diraimondo • Gregory Hicks • Nathaniel Johnson • Christopher Golby • Craig Davis • Philip Johnson Jr. • Ian Manuel • Ricky Crockett • Keicia Hines Roland Castro • Edmond Randle Jr. • Larry Polley Jr. • Cody Orr • Kelly Hornbeck • Gabriel Palacios • James Parker • Michael Blaise • Brian Hazelgrove • Kenneth Hendrickson Keith Smette • Jason Chappell • William Sturges Jr. • Randy Rosenberg • Ervin Dervishi Patrick Dorff • Christopher Bunda • Adam Mooney • Matthew August • Cory Mracek • Luke James • James Hoffman • Lester Kinney II • Travis Moothart • Sean Landrus • Luis Moreno • Eliu Miersandoval • Juan Cabralbanuelos • Holly McGeogh • Roger C. Turner Jr. Armando Soriano • Seth Dvorin • Joshua Knowles • Richard Ramey • Thomas Robbins Elijah Wong • Jude Mariano • Patrick Tainsh • William Ramirez • Eric Ramirez • Bryan Spry Nichole Frye • Christopher Taylor • Michael Merila • Jeffrey Graham • Roger Ling • Henry Bacon • Stephen Wells • Matthew Laskowski • Michael Woodliff • Michael Gray • Gussie Jones • Matthew Milczark • Richard Gottfried • Edward Brabazon • Fern Holland • Robert Zangas • Bert Hoyer • Joe Dunigan Jr. • Christopher Hill • John Kurth • Jason Ford • Clint Ferrin • Daniel Londono • Joel Brattain • Jocelyn Carrasquillo • William Normandy Michael Adams • Thomas Thigpen Sr. • Tracy Laramore • Ivory Phipps • Brandon Smith Ricky Morris Jr. • Ernest Sutphin • Andrew Brownfield • Doron Chan • Clint Matthews Jason Ludlam • David Vicente • Matthew Sandri • Mark Taylor • Michael Vega • Dustin Kreider • Christopher Hudson • Andrew Dang • Bruce Miller Jr. • Wentz Shanaberger III Adam Froehlich • Jeffrey Burgess • James Casper • Leroy Sandoval Jr. • Timothy Toney Sean Schneider • Jeremiah Holmes • William Wiscowiche • Richard Ferguson • Doyle Hufstedler • Sean Mitchell • Michael Karr Jr. • Cleston Raney • Brandon Davis • Dustin Sekula • William Strange • Geoffrey Morris • Aric Barr • Tyler Fey • Robert Arsiaga • Israel Garza • Forest Jostes • Casey Sheehan • Ahmed Cason • Stephen Hiller • Yihiyh Chen Michael Mitchell • John Amos II • Phillip Rogers • Deryk Hallal • Moises Langhorst Matthew Serio • Christopher Ramos • Jesse Thiry • Shane Goldman • David McKeever

Scott Larson Jr. • Gerardo Moreno • Christopher Cobb • Ryan Jerabek • Travis Layfield Allan Walker • Kyle Crowley • Anthony Roberts • Marcus Cherry • Benjamin Carman Fernando Mendezaceves • Christopher Mabry • Lee Todacheene • John Wroblewski George Rentschler • Tyanna Felder • William Labadie Jr. • Marvin Miller Brent Morel • Isaac Nieves • Levi Angell • William Harrell • Joshua Palmer Michael Wafford • Nicholas Dieruf • Christopher Wasser • Phillip Frank Felix Delgreco • Gregory Goodrich • Jonathan Kephart • Matthew Matula • Elias Torrez III • Michael Speer • Don McMahan • Peter Enos • Toby Mallet • Raymond Jones Jr. • Michelle Witmer Allen Vandayburg • Eric Ayon • Chance Phelps • Antoine Holt • John Sims Jr. • William Eckhart • Adolf Carballo Wesley Fortenberry • Lawrence Colton • Oscar Jimenez • Daniel Amaya • Torrey Gray • George Torres • Justin Johnson • Nathan Brown • Michael Stack • Robert Zurheide Jr. • Brad Shuder • Victor Rosaleslomeli • Noah Boye • Kevin Kolm • Frank Rivers Jr. • Richard Trevithick • Christopher Ramirez • Jimmy Arroyave • Brian Wood • Michael McGlothin • Robert Henderson II • Clayton Henson Jonathan Hartman • Richard Gannon II • Michael Smith Jr. • Ruben Valdez Jr. • Gary Van Leuven Chris Gibson • Edward Carman • Marvin Camposiles Dennis Morgan • Christopher Gelineau

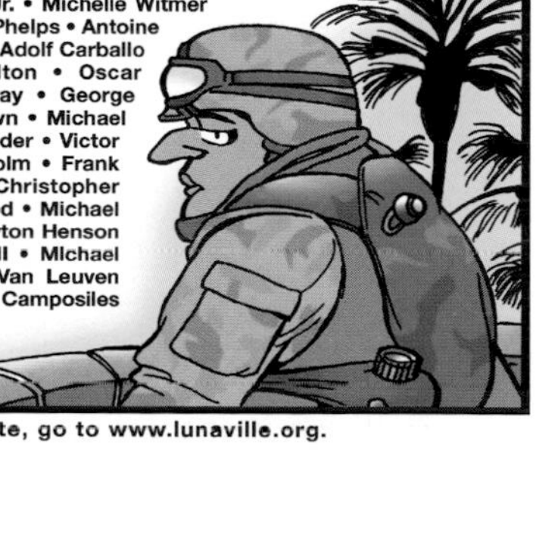

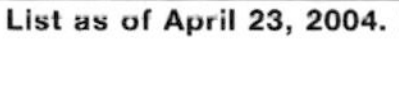

List as of April 23, 2004. For update, go to www.lunaville.org.

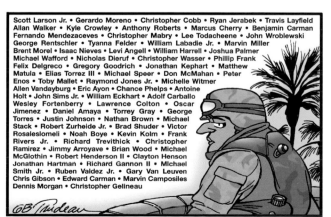

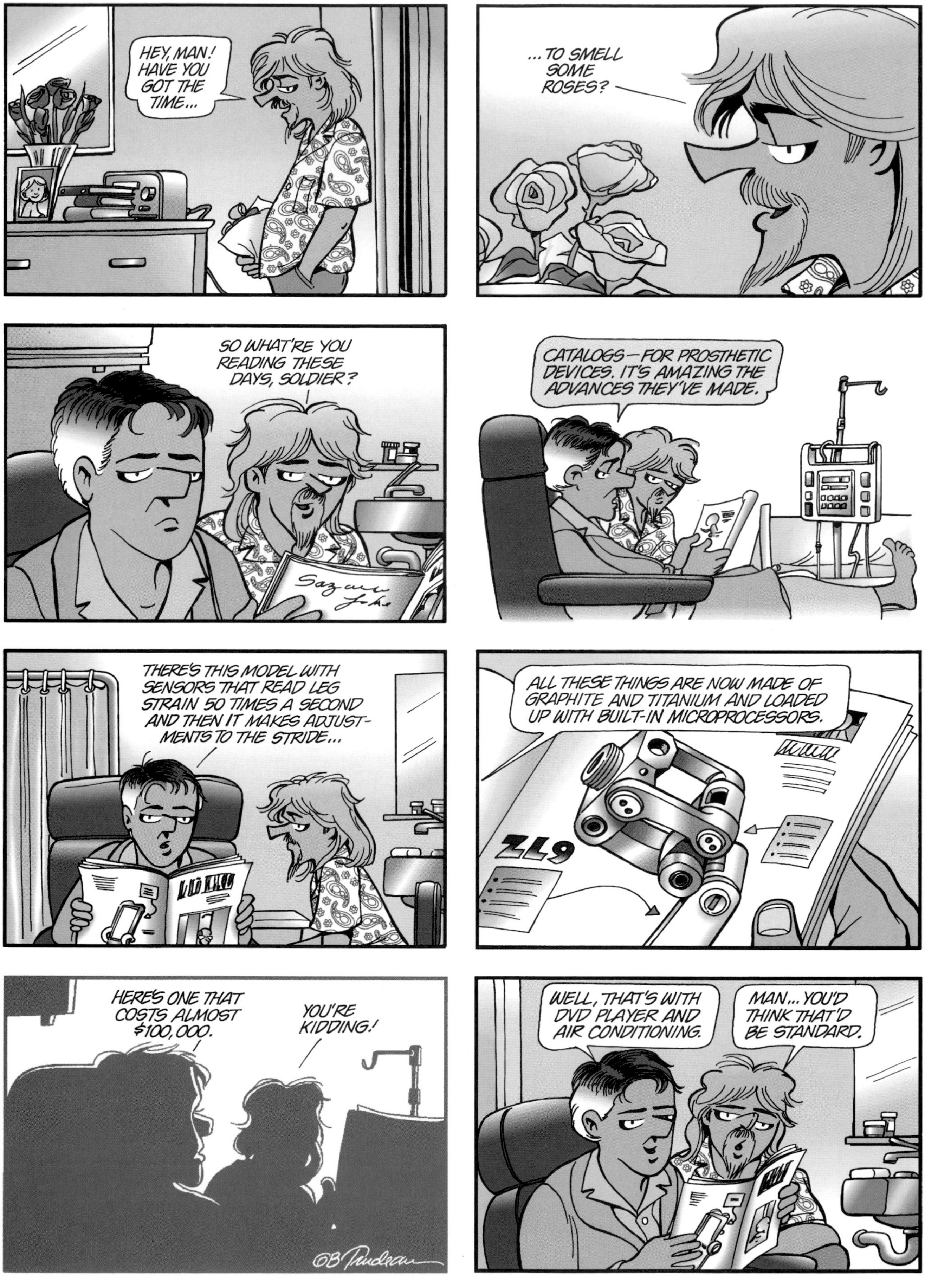
HEY, MAN! HAVE YOU GOT THE TIME...
...TO SMELL SOME ROSES?
SO WHAT'RE YOU READING THESE DAYS, SOLDIER?
CATALOGS—FOR PROSTHETIC DEVICES. IT'S AMAZING THE ADVANCES THEY'VE MADE.
THERE'S THIS MODEL WITH SENSORS THAT READ LEG STRAIN 50 TIMES A SECOND AND THEN IT MAKES ADJUSTMENTS TO THE STRIDE...
ALL THESE THINGS ARE NOW MADE OF GRAPHITE AND TITANIUM AND LOADED UP WITH BUILT-IN MICROPROCESSORS.
HERE'S ONE THAT COSTS ALMOST $100,000.
YOU'RE KIDDING!
WELL, THAT'S WITH DVD PLAYER AND AIR CONDITIONING.
MAN... YOU'D THINK THAT'D BE STANDARD.
©B Trudeau

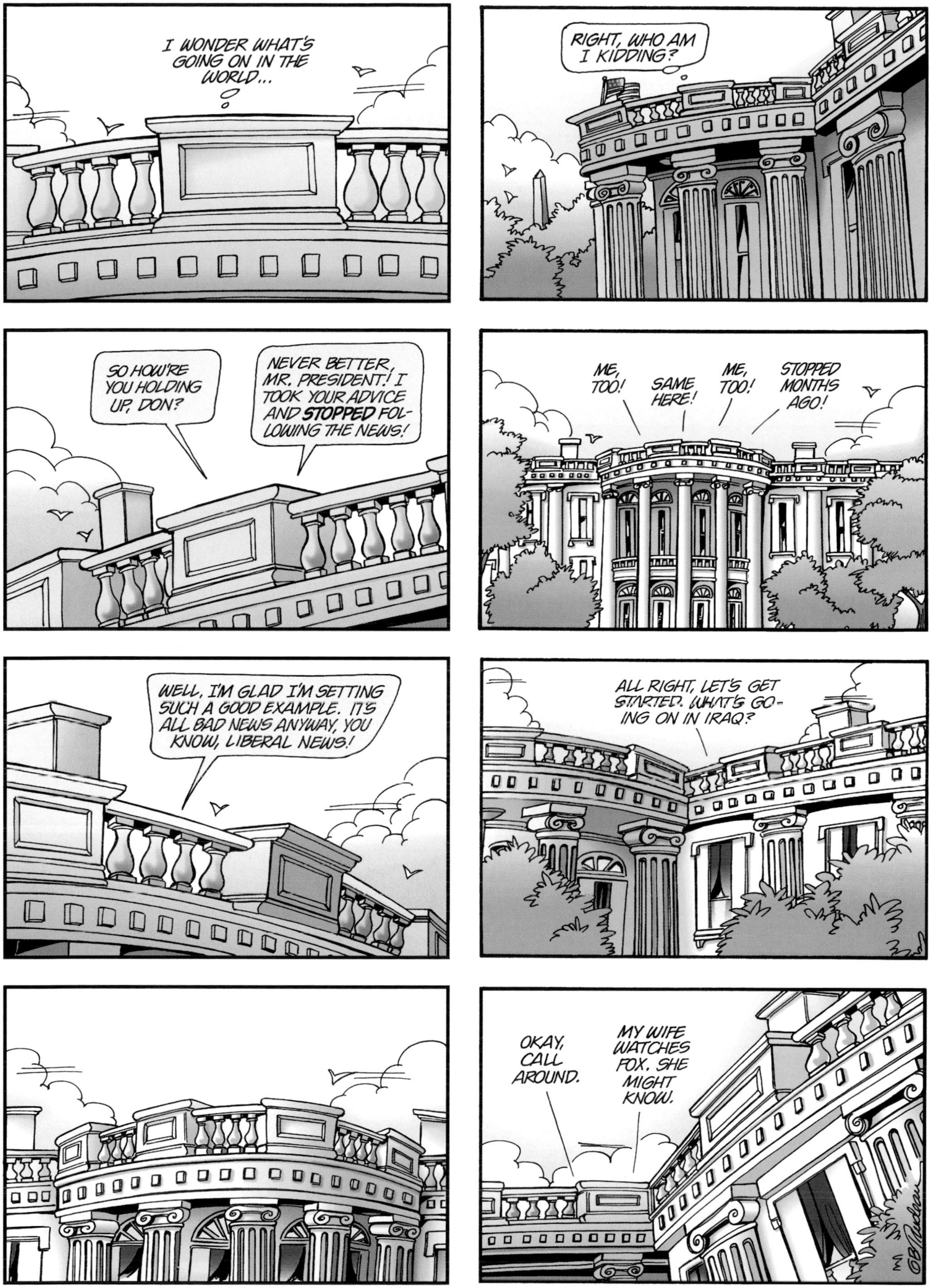
I WONDER WHAT'S GOING ON IN THE WORLD...
RIGHT, WHO AM I KIDDING?
SO HOW'RE YOU HOLDING UP, DON?
NEVER BETTER, MR. PRESIDENT! I TOOK YOUR ADVICE AND STOPPED FOLLOWING THE NEWS!
ME, TOO!
SAME HERE!
ME, TOO!
STOPPED MONTHS AGO!
WELL, I'M GLAD I'M SETTING SUCH A GOOD EXAMPLE. IT'S ALL BAD NEWS ANYWAY, YOU KNOW, LIBERAL NEWS!
ALL RIGHT, LET'S GET STARTED. WHAT'S GOING ON IN IRAQ?
OKAY, CALL AROUND.
MY WIFE WATCHES FOX. SHE MIGHT KNOW.

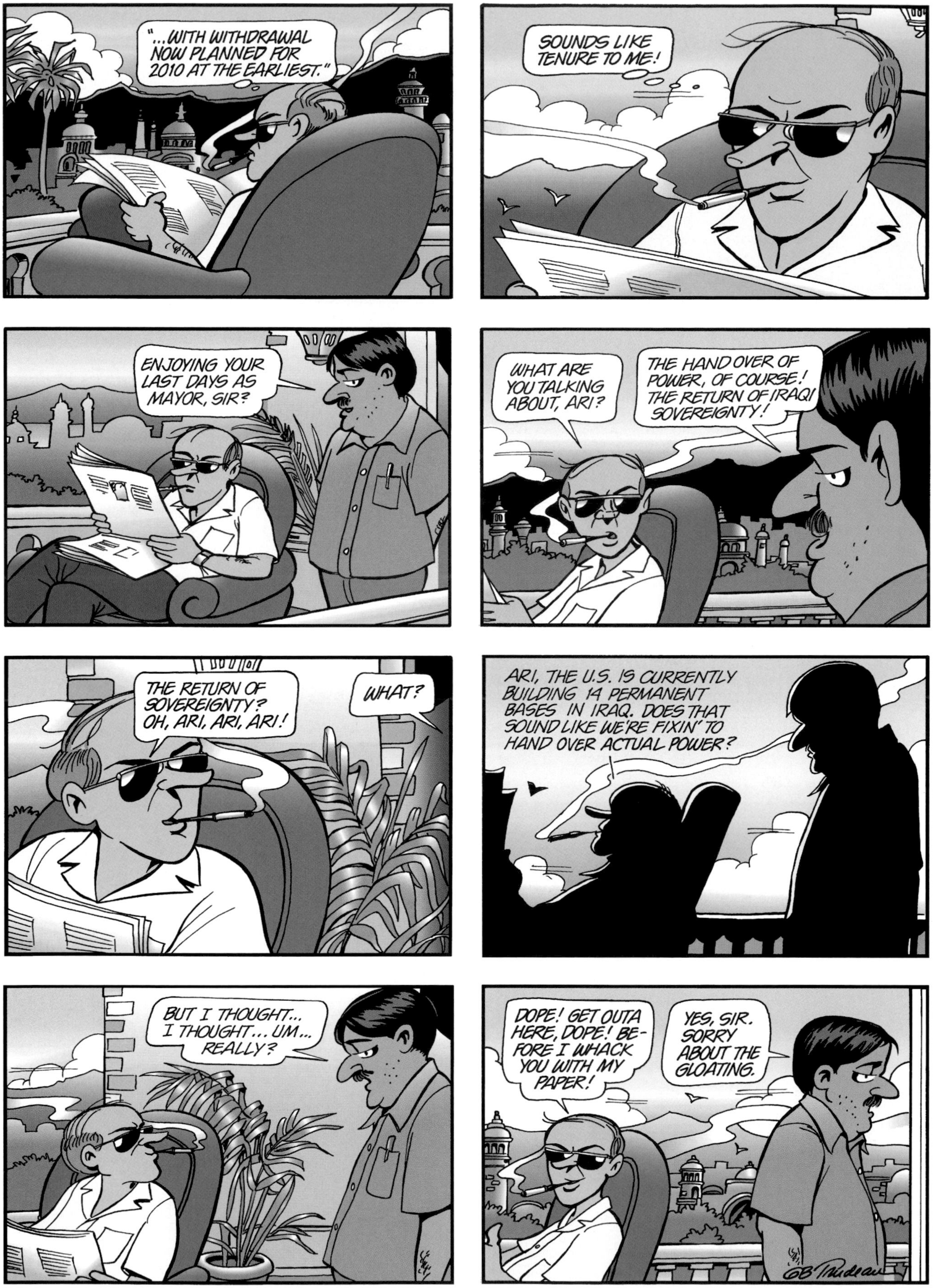
"...WITH WITHDRAWAL NOW PLANNED FOR 2010 AT THE EARLIEST."
SOUNDS LIKE TENURE TO ME!
ENJOYING YOUR LAST DAYS AS MAYOR, SIR?
WHAT ARE YOU TALKING ABOUT, ARI?
THE HAND OVER OF POWER, OF COURSE! THE RETURN OF IRAQI SOVEREIGNTY!
THE RETURN OF SOVEREIGNTY? OH, ARI, ARI, ARI!
WHAT?
ARI, THE U.S. IS CURRENTLY BUILDING 14 PERMANENT BASES IN IRAQ. DOES THAT SOUND LIKE WE'RE FIXIN' TO HAND OVER ACTUAL POWER?
BUT I THOUGHT... I THOUGHT... UM... REALLY?
DOPE! GET OUTA HERE, DOPE! BEFORE I WHACK YOU WITH MY PAPER!
YES, SIR. SORRY ABOUT THE GLOATING.
GB Trudeau

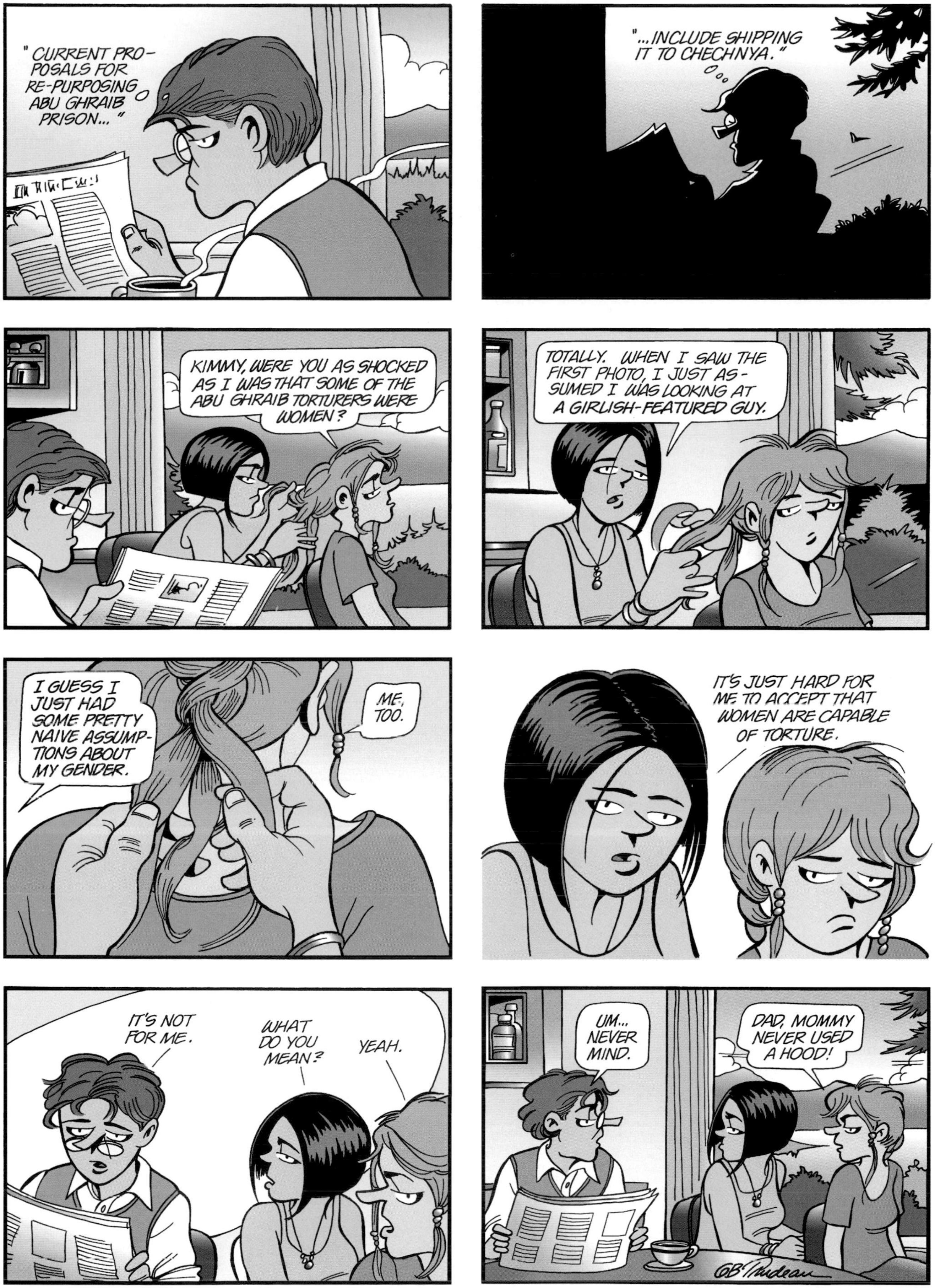
"CURRENT PROPOSALS FOR RE-PURPOSING ABU GHRAIB PRISON..."
"...INCLUDE SHIPPING IT TO CHECHNYA."
KIMMY, WERE YOU AS SHOCKED AS I WAS THAT SOME OF THE ABU GHRAIB TORTURERS WERE WOMEN?
TOTALLY. WHEN I SAW THE FIRST PHOTO, I JUST ASSUMED I WAS LOOKING AT A GIRLISH-FEATURED GUY.
I GUESS I JUST HAD SOME PRETTY NAIVE ASSUMPTIONS ABOUT MY GENDER.
ME, TOO.
IT'S JUST HARD FOR ME TO ACCEPT THAT WOMEN ARE CAPABLE OF TORTURE.
IT'S NOT FOR ME.
WHAT DO YOU MEAN?
YEAH.
UM... NEVER MIND.
DAD, MOMMY NEVER USED A HOOD!
GB Trudeau

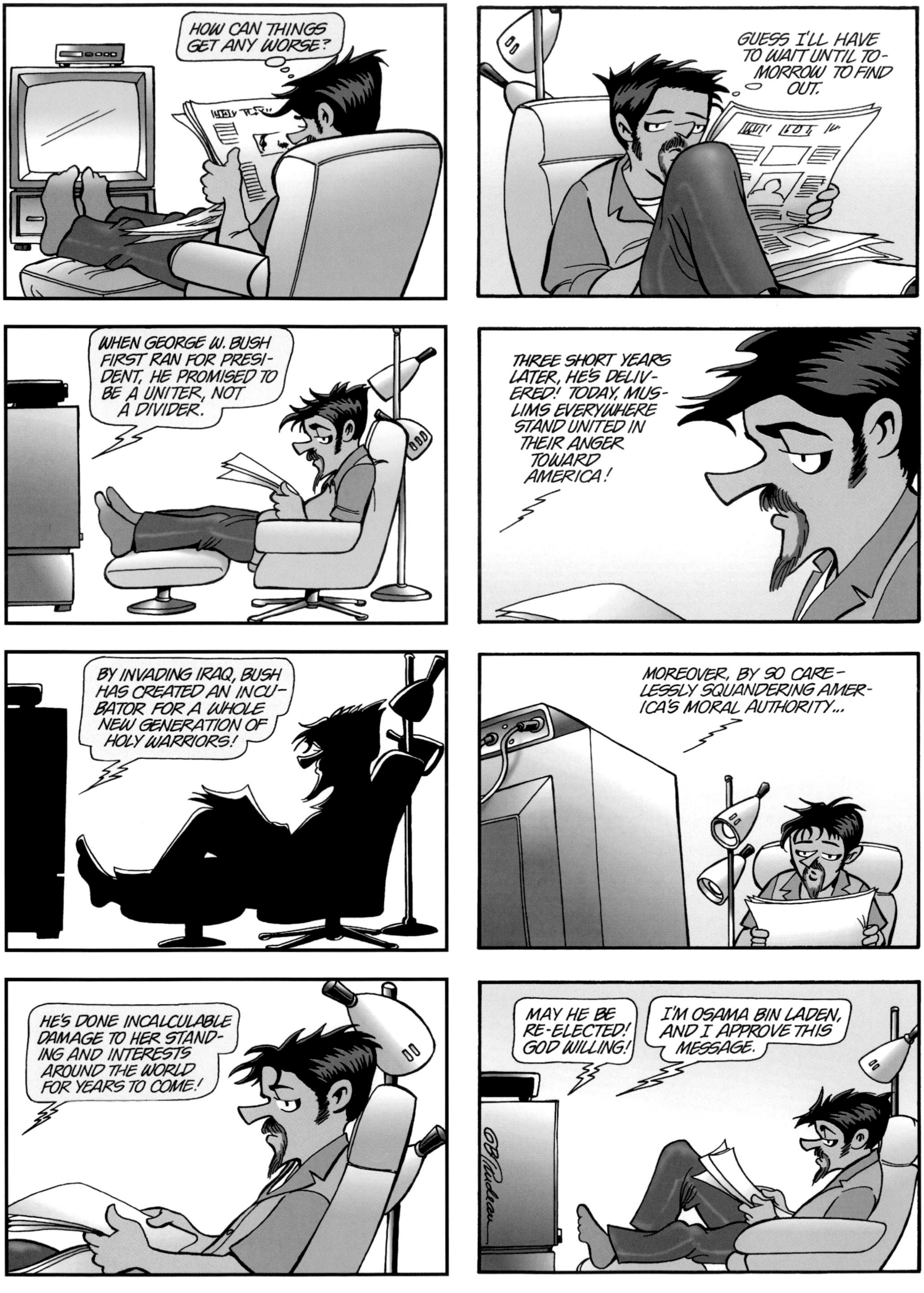
HOW CAN THINGS GET ANY WORSE?
GUESS I'LL HAVE TO WAIT UNTIL TO-MORROW TO FIND OUT.
WHEN GEORGE W. BUSH FIRST RAN FOR PRESI-DENT, HE PROMISED TO BE A UNITER, NOT A DIVIDER.
THREE SHORT YEARS LATER, HE'S DELIV-ERED! TODAY, MUS-LIMS EVERYWHERE STAND UNITED IN THEIR ANGER TOWARD AMERICA!
BY INVADING IRAQ, BUSH HAS CREATED AN INCU-BATOR FOR A WHOLE NEW GENERATION OF HOLY WARRIORS!
MOREOVER, BY SO CARE-LESSLY SQUANDERING AMER-ICA'S MORAL AUTHORITY...
HE'S DONE INCALCULABLE DAMAGE TO HER STAND-ING AND INTERESTS AROUND THE WORLD FOR YEARS TO COME!
MAY HE BE RE-ELECTED! GOD WILLING!
I'M OSAMA BIN LADEN, AND I APPROVE THIS MESSAGE.

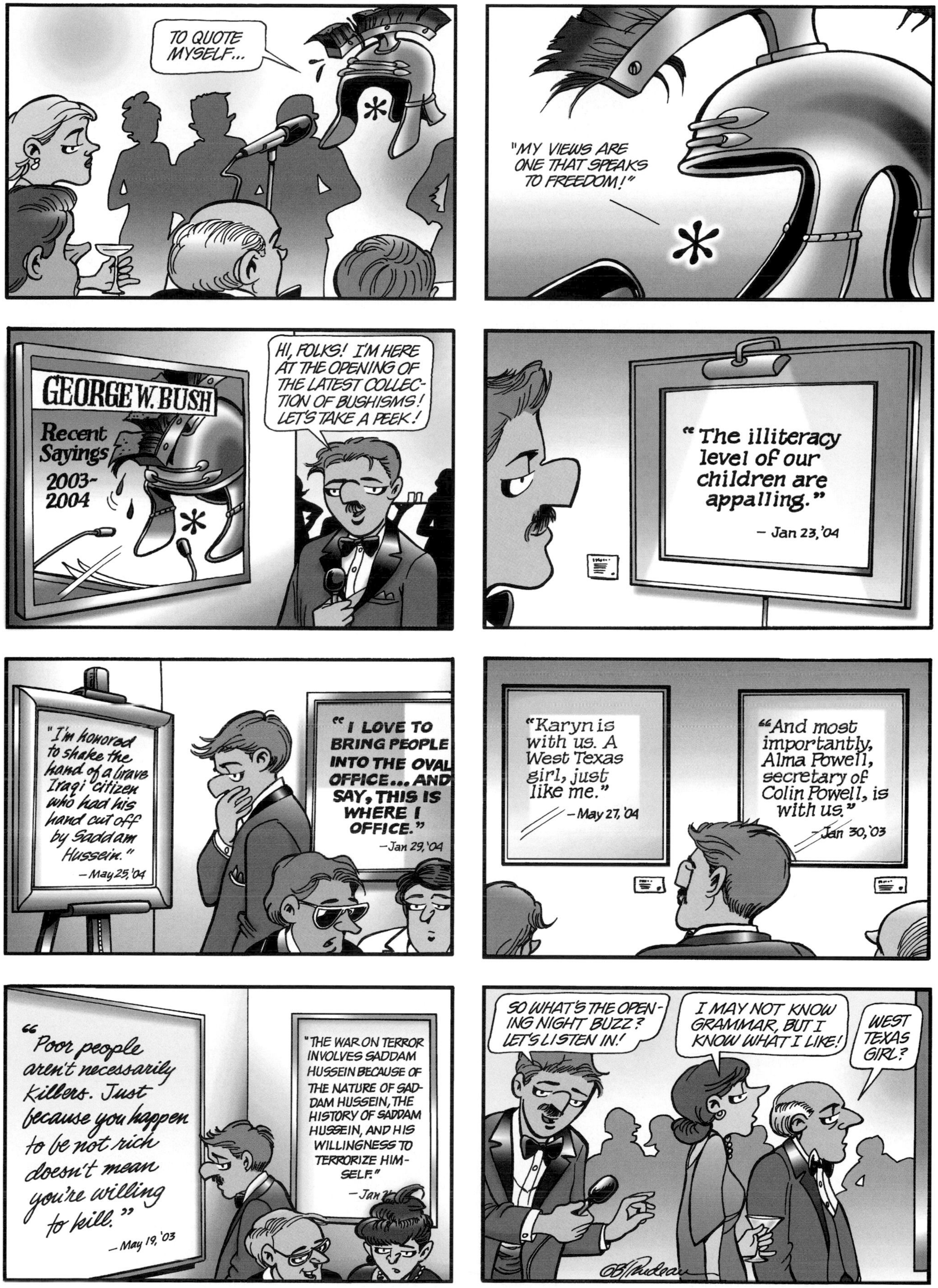

TO QUOTE MYSELF...
"MY VIEWS ARE ONE THAT SPEAKS TO FREEDOM!"
GEORGE W. BUSH
Recent Sayings
2003-2004
HI, FOLKS! I'M HERE AT THE OPENING OF THE LATEST COLLECTION OF BUSHISMS! LET'S TAKE A PEEK!
"The illiteracy level of our children are appalling."
– Jan 23, '04
"I'm honored to shake the hand of a brave Iraqi citizen who had his hand cut off by Saddam Hussein."
– May 25, '04
"I LOVE TO BRING PEOPLE INTO THE OVAL OFFICE... AND SAY, THIS IS WHERE I OFFICE."
– Jan 29, '04
"Karyn is with us. A West Texas girl, just like me."
– May 27, '04
"And most importantly, Alma Powell, secretary of Colin Powell, is with us."
– Jan 30, '03
"Poor people aren't necessarily killers. Just because you happen to be not rich doesn't mean you're willing to kill."
– May 19, '03
"THE WAR ON TERROR INVOLVES SADDAM HUSSEIN BECAUSE OF THE NATURE OF SADDAM HUSSEIN, THE HISTORY OF SADDAM HUSSEIN, AND HIS WILLINGNESS TO TERRORIZE HIMSELF."
SO WHAT'S THE OPENING NIGHT BUZZ? LET'S LISTEN IN!
I MAY NOT KNOW GRAMMAR, BUT I KNOW WHAT I LIKE!
WEST TEXAS GIRL?

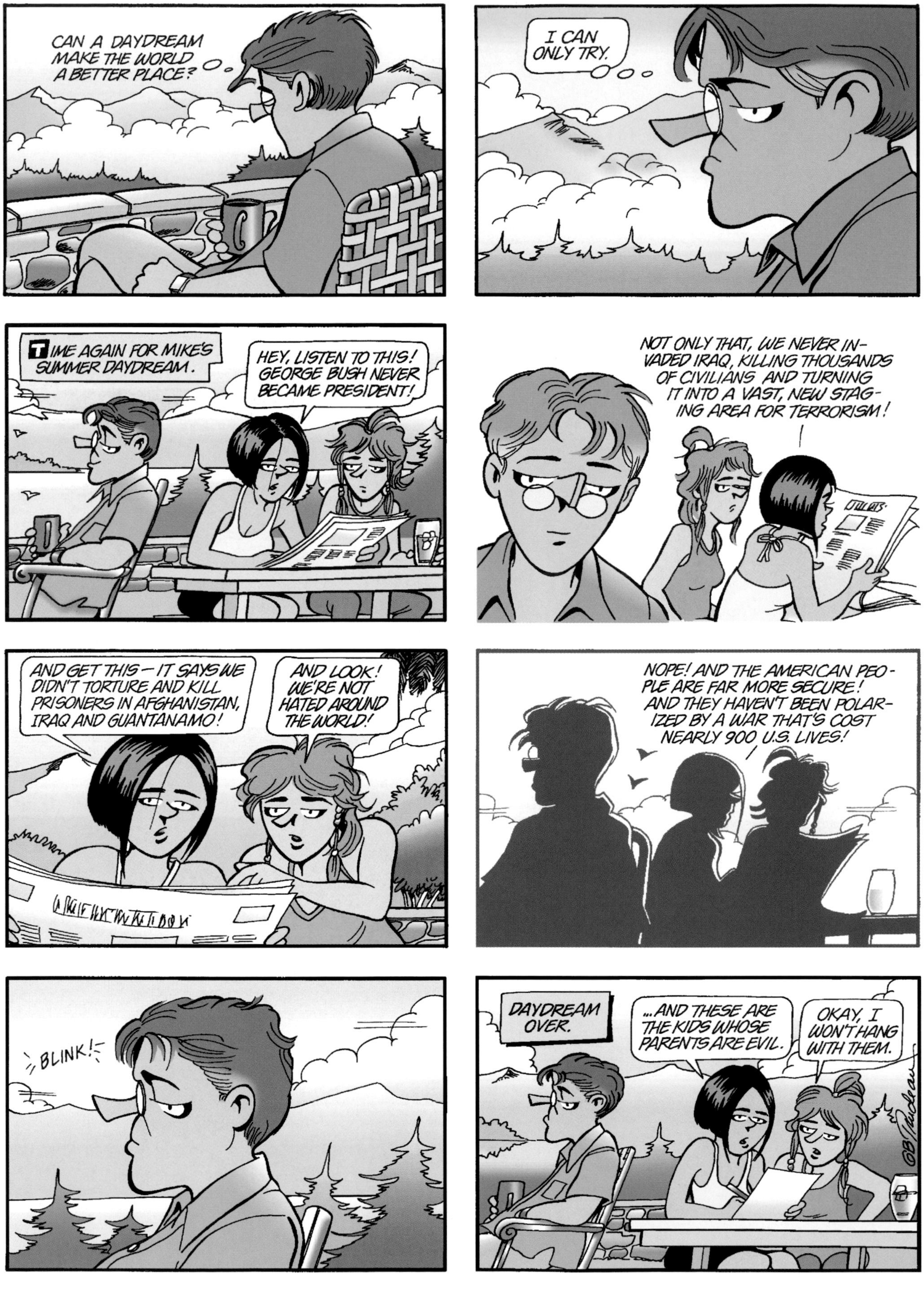
CAN A DAYDREAM MAKE THE WORLD A BETTER PLACE?
I CAN ONLY TRY.
TIME AGAIN FOR MIKE'S SUMMER DAYDREAM.
HEY, LISTEN TO THIS! GEORGE BUSH NEVER BECAME PRESIDENT!
NOT ONLY THAT, WE NEVER INVADED IRAQ, KILLING THOUSANDS OF CIVILIANS AND TURNING IT INTO A VAST, NEW STAGING AREA FOR TERRORISM!
AND GET THIS — IT SAYS WE DIDN'T TORTURE AND KILL PRISONERS IN AFGHANISTAN, IRAQ AND GUANTANAMO!
AND LOOK! WE'RE NOT HATED AROUND THE WORLD!
NOPE! AND THE AMERICAN PEOPLE ARE FAR MORE SECURE! AND THEY HAVEN'T BEEN POLARIZED BY A WAR THAT'S COST NEARLY 900 U.S. LIVES!
BLINK!
DAYDREAM OVER.
...AND THESE ARE THE KIDS WHOSE PARENTS ARE EVIL.
OKAY, I WON'T HANG WITH THEM.

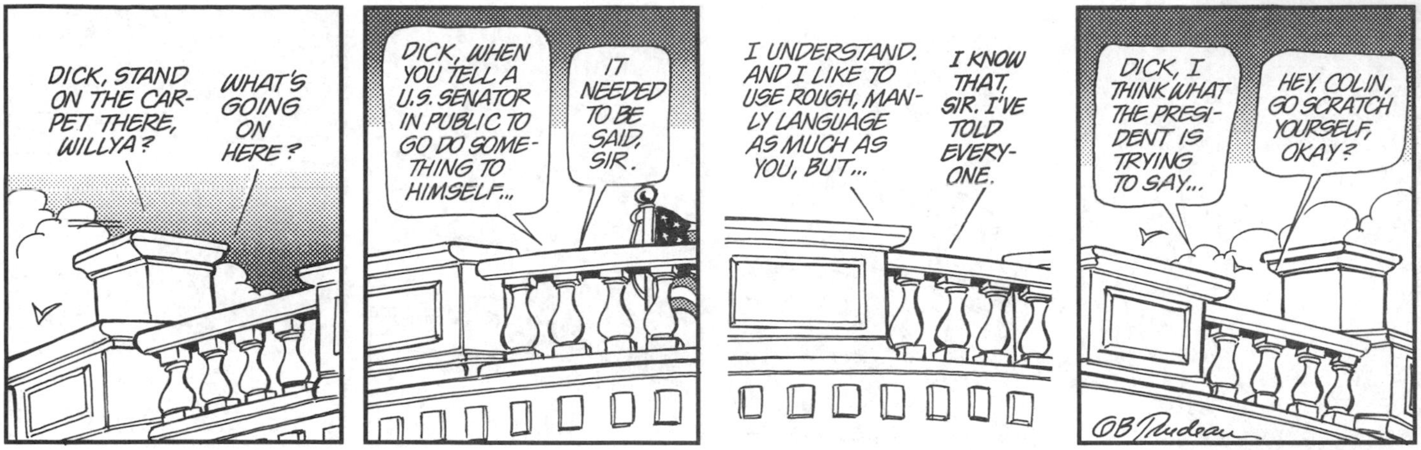
DICK, STAND ON THE CARPET THERE, WILLYA?
WHAT'S GOING ON HERE?
DICK, WHEN YOU TELL A U.S. SENATOR IN PUBLIC TO GO DO SOMETHING TO HIMSELF...
IT NEEDED TO BE SAID, SIR.
I UNDERSTAND. AND I LIKE TO USE ROUGH, MANLY LANGUAGE AS MUCH AS YOU, BUT...
I KNOW THAT, SIR. I'VE TOLD EVERYONE.
DICK, I THINK WHAT THE PRESIDENT IS TRYING TO SAY...
HEY, COLIN, GO SCRATCH YOURSELF, OKAY?

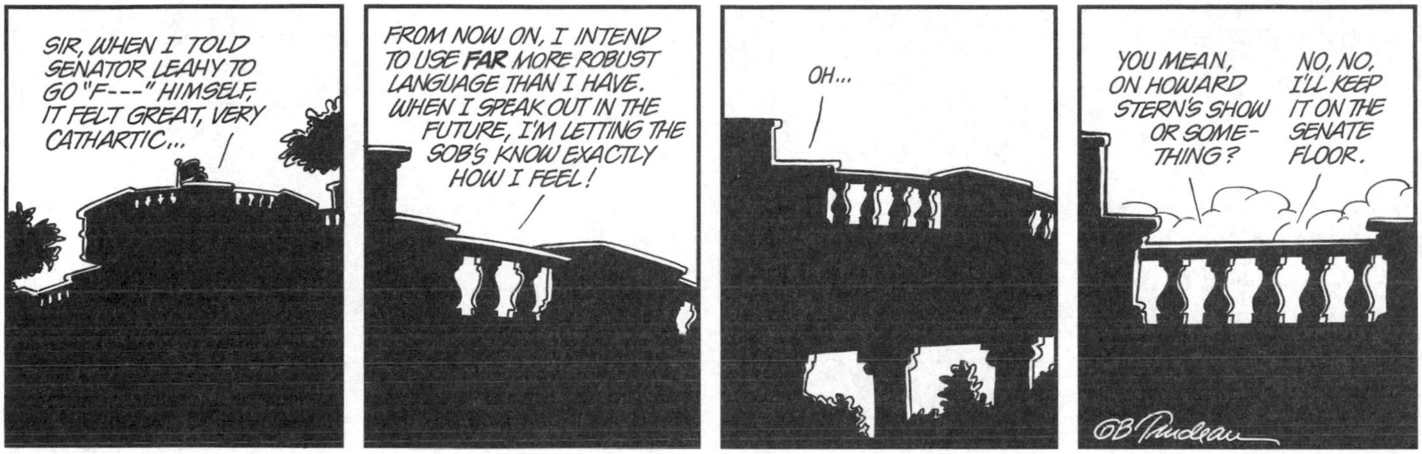
SIR, WHEN I TOLD SENATOR LEAHY TO GO "F---" HIMSELF, IT FELT GREAT, VERY CATHARTIC...
FROM NOW ON, I INTEND TO USE FAR MORE ROBUST LANGUAGE THAN I HAVE. WHEN I SPEAK OUT IN THE FUTURE, I'M LETTING THE SOB'S KNOW EXACTLY HOW I FEEL!
OH...
YOU MEAN, ON HOWARD STERN'S SHOW OR SOMETHING?
NO, NO, I'LL KEEP IT ON THE SENATE FLOOR.

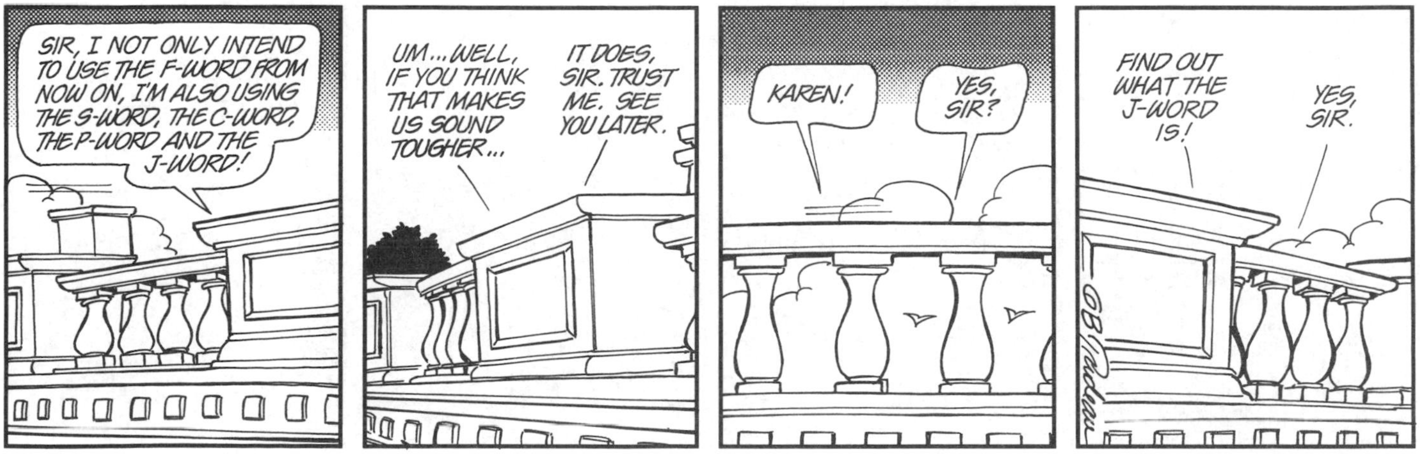
SIR, I NOT ONLY INTEND TO USE THE F-WORD FROM NOW ON, I'M ALSO USING THE S-WORD, THE C-WORD, THE P-WORD AND THE J-WORD!
UM... WELL, IF YOU THINK THAT MAKES US SOUND TOUGHER...
IT DOES, SIR. TRUST ME. SEE YOU LATER.
KAREN!
YES, SIR?
FIND OUT WHAT THE J-WORD IS!
YES, SIR.

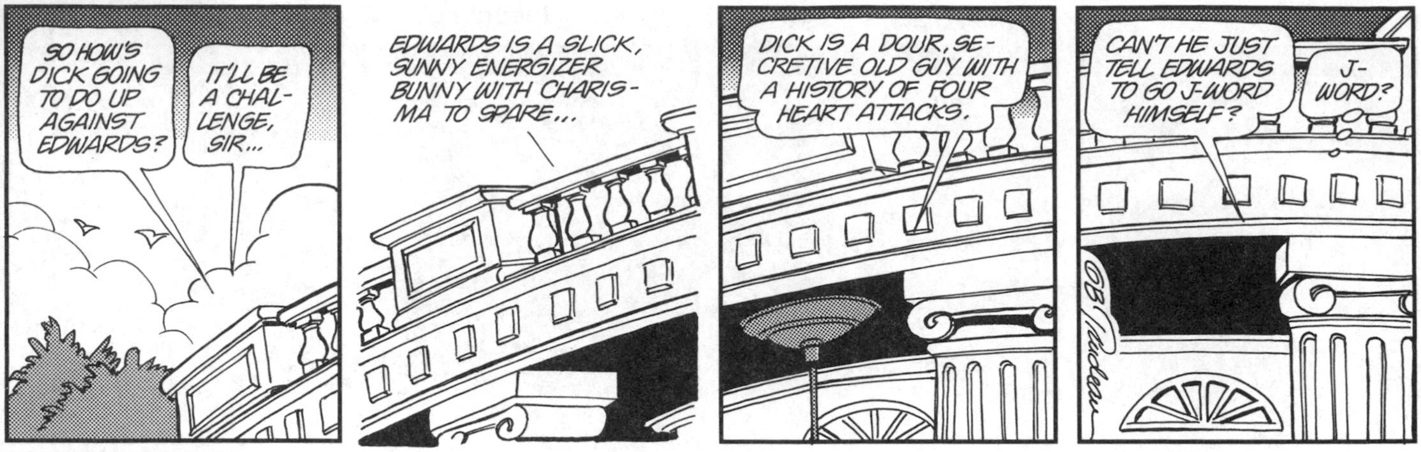
SO HOW'S DICK GOING TO DO UP AGAINST EDWARDS?
IT'LL BE A CHAL-LENGE, SIR...
EDWARDS IS A SLICK, SUNNY ENERGIZER BUNNY WITH CHARIS-MA TO SPARE...
DICK IS A DOUR, SE-CRETIVE OLD GUY WITH A HISTORY OF FOUR HEART ATTACKS.
CAN'T HE JUST TELL EDWARDS TO GO J-WORD HIMSELF?
J-WORD?

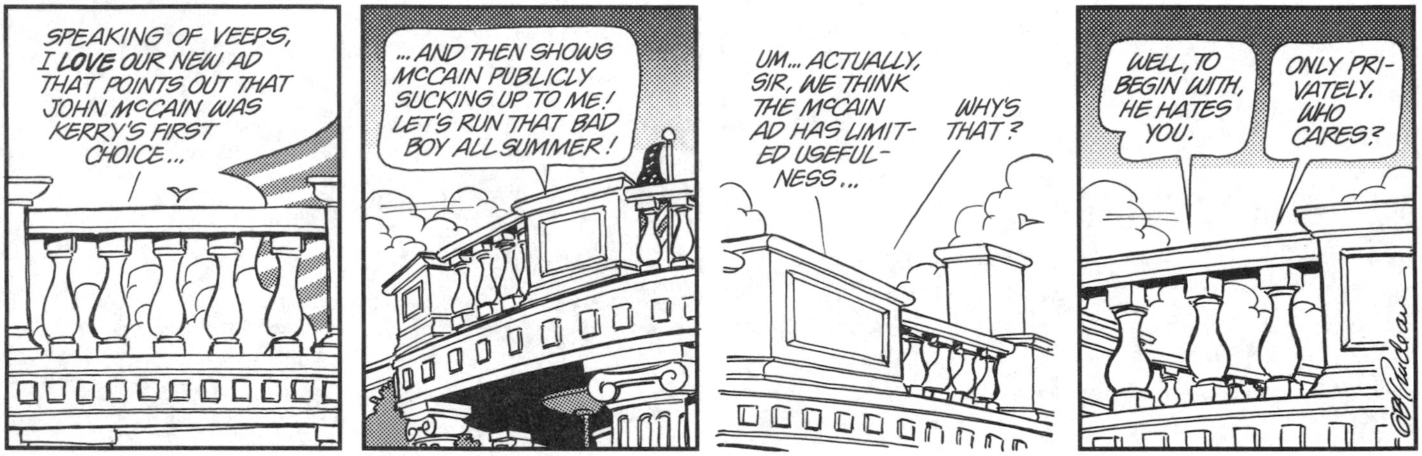
SPEAKING OF VEEPS, I **LOVE** OUR NEW AD THAT POINTS OUT THAT JOHN McCAIN WAS KERRY'S FIRST CHOICE...
...AND THEN SHOWS McCAIN PUBLICLY SUCKING UP TO ME! LET'S RUN THAT BAD BOY ALL SUMMER!
UM... ACTUALLY, SIR, WE THINK THE McCAIN AD HAS LIMIT-ED USEFUL-NESS...
WHY'S THAT?
WELL, TO BEGIN WITH, HE HATES YOU.
ONLY PRI-VATELY. WHO CARES?

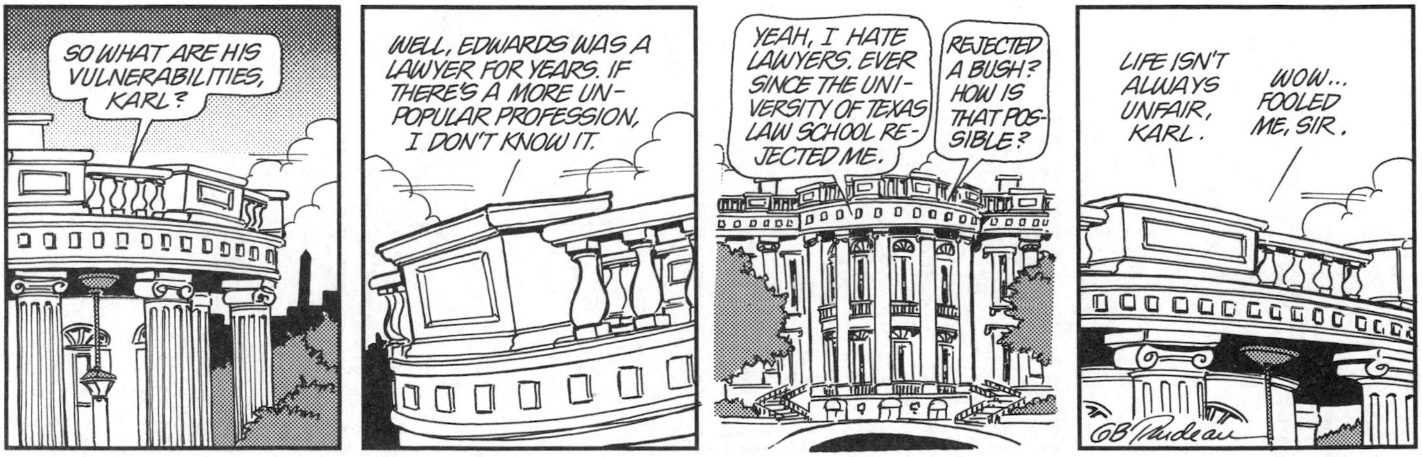
SO WHAT ARE HIS VULNERABILITIES, KARL?
WELL, EDWARDS WAS A LAWYER FOR YEARS. IF THERE'S A MORE UN-POPULAR PROFESSION, I DON'T KNOW IT.
YEAH, I HATE LAWYERS. EVER SINCE THE UNI-VERSITY OF TEXAS LAW SCHOOL RE-JECTED ME.
REJECTED A BUSH? HOW IS THAT POS-SIBLE?
LIFE ISN'T ALWAYS UNFAIR, KARL.
WOW... FOOLED ME, SIR.

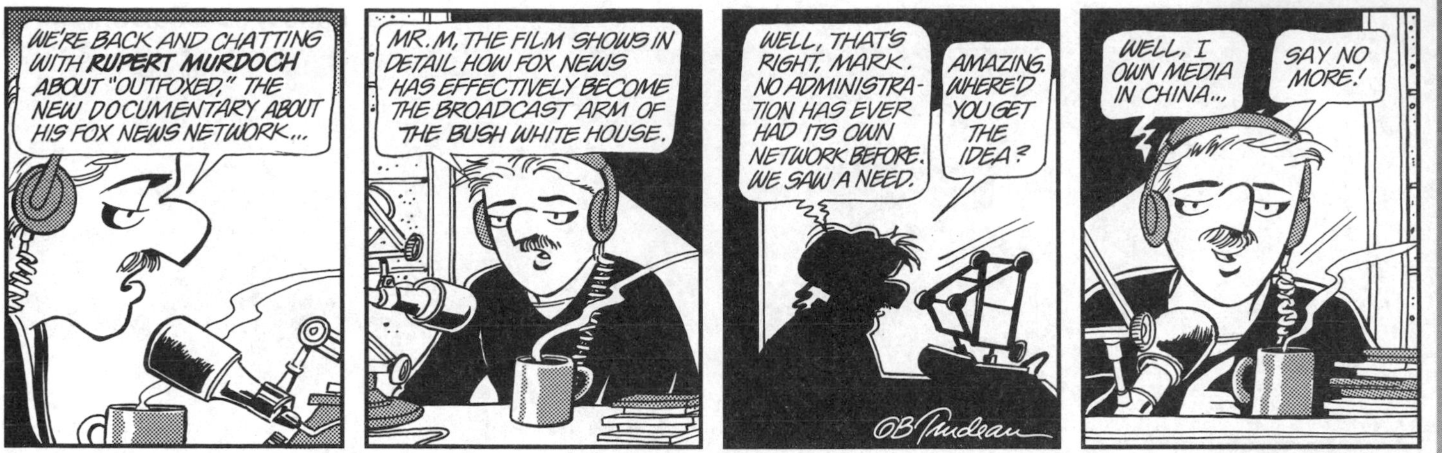
WE'RE BACK AND CHATTING WITH RUPERT MURDOCH ABOUT "OUTFOXED," THE NEW DOCUMENTARY ABOUT HIS FOX NEWS NETWORK...
MR. M, THE FILM SHOWS IN DETAIL HOW FOX NEWS HAS EFFECTIVELY BECOME THE BROADCAST ARM OF THE BUSH WHITE HOUSE.
WELL, THAT'S RIGHT, MARK. NO ADMINISTRATION HAS EVER HAD ITS OWN NETWORK BEFORE. WE SAW A NEED.
AMAZING. WHERE'D YOU GET THE IDEA?
WELL, I OWN MEDIA IN CHINA...
SAY NO MORE!

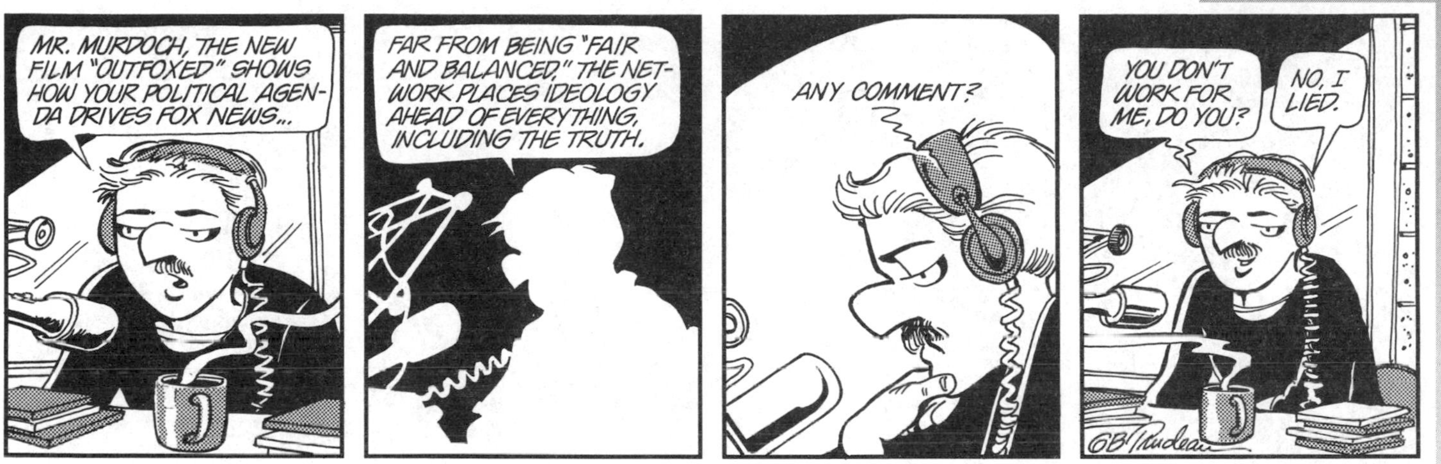
MR. MURDOCH, THE NEW FILM "OUTFOXED" SHOWS HOW YOUR POLITICAL AGENDA DRIVES FOX NEWS...
FAR FROM BEING "FAIR AND BALANCED," THE NETWORK PLACES IDEOLOGY AHEAD OF EVERYTHING, INCLUDING THE TRUTH.
ANY COMMENT?
YOU DON'T WORK FOR ME, DO YOU?
NO, I LIED.

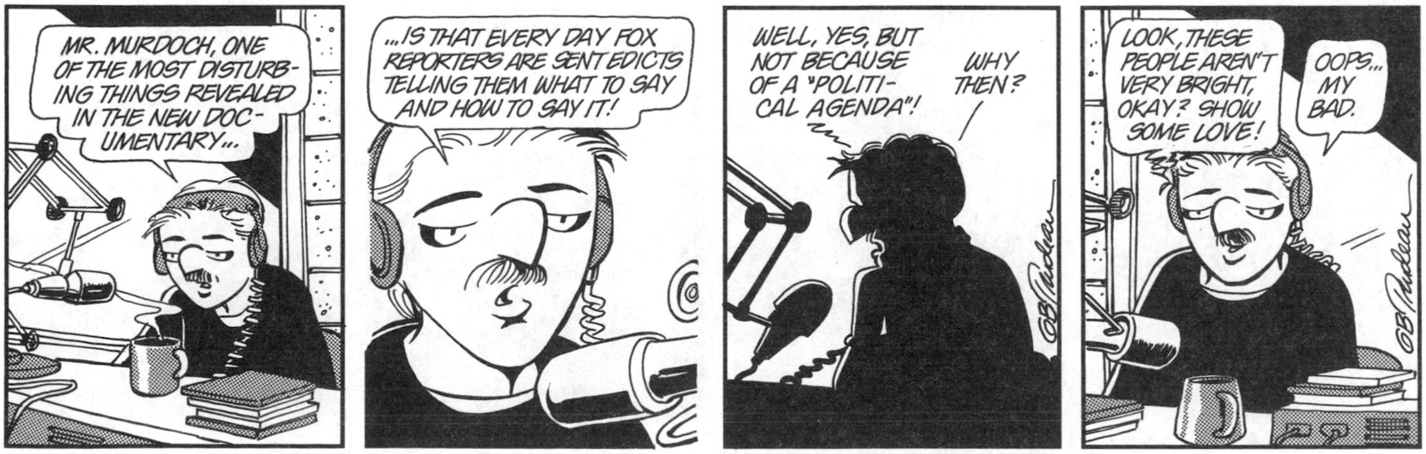
MR. MURDOCH, ONE OF THE MOST DISTURBING THINGS REVEALED IN THE NEW DOCUMENTARY...
...IS THAT EVERY DAY FOX REPORTERS ARE SENT EDICTS TELLING THEM WHAT TO SAY AND HOW TO SAY IT!
WELL, YES, BUT NOT BECAUSE OF A "POLITICAL AGENDA"!
WHY THEN?
LOOK, THESE PEOPLE AREN'T VERY BRIGHT, OKAY? SHOW SOME LOVE!
OOPS... MY BAD.

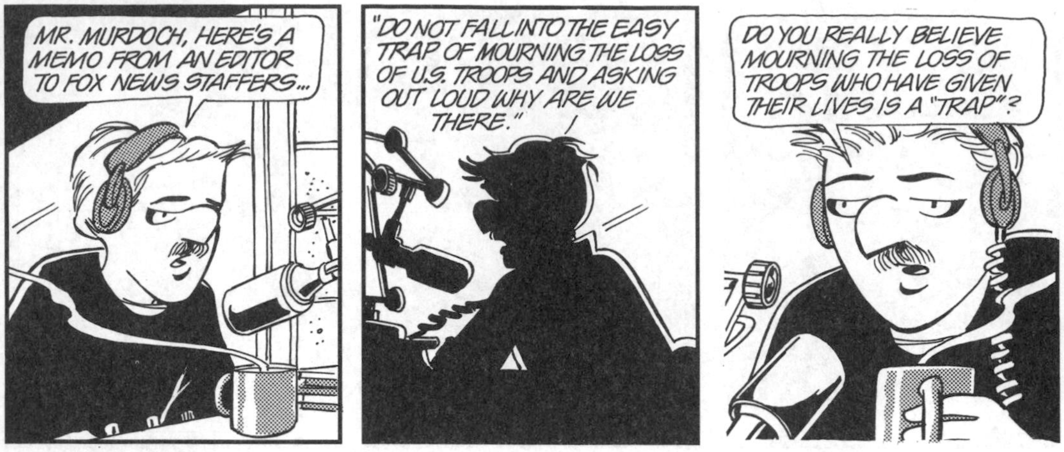
MR. MURDOCH, HERE'S A MEMO FROM AN EDITOR TO FOX NEWS STAFFERS...
"DO NOT FALL INTO THE EASY TRAP OF MOURNING THE LOSS OF U.S. TROOPS AND ASKING OUT LOUD WHY ARE WE THERE."
DO YOU REALLY BELIEVE MOURNING THE LOSS OF TROOPS WHO HAVE GIVEN THEIR LIVES IS A "TRAP"?
YES. EVERYBODY ALREADY KNOWS ABOUT THE 200-PLUS DEAD GUYS!
PLUS?

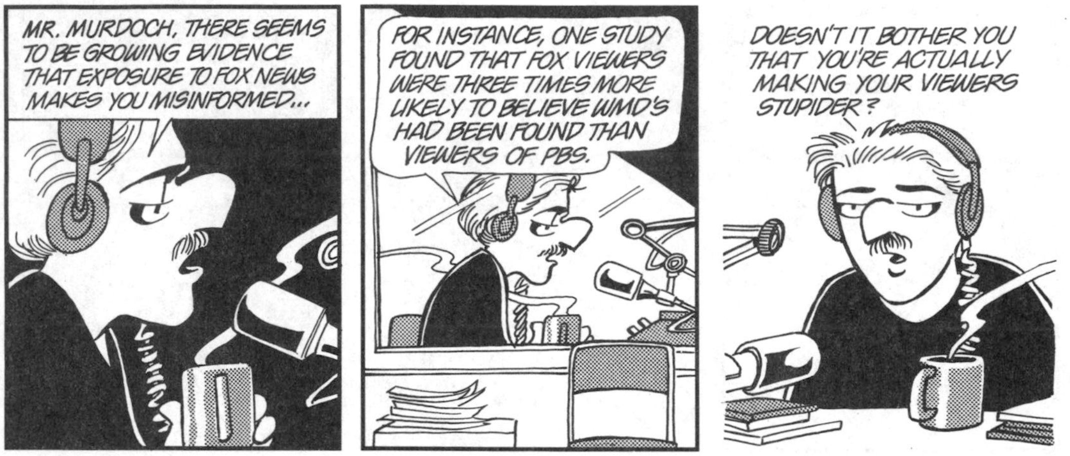
MR. MURDOCH, THERE SEEMS TO BE GROWING EVIDENCE THAT EXPOSURE TO FOX NEWS MAKES YOU MISINFORMED...
FOR INSTANCE, ONE STUDY FOUND THAT FOX VIEWERS WERE THREE TIMES MORE LIKELY TO BELIEVE WMD'S HAD BEEN FOUND THAN VIEWERS OF PBS.
DOESN'T IT BOTHER YOU THAT YOU'RE ACTUALLY MAKING YOUR VIEWERS STUPIDER?
NO. WE REPORT, THEY DECIDE.
BUT SHOULDN'T YOUR GUYS WINK OR SOMETHING?

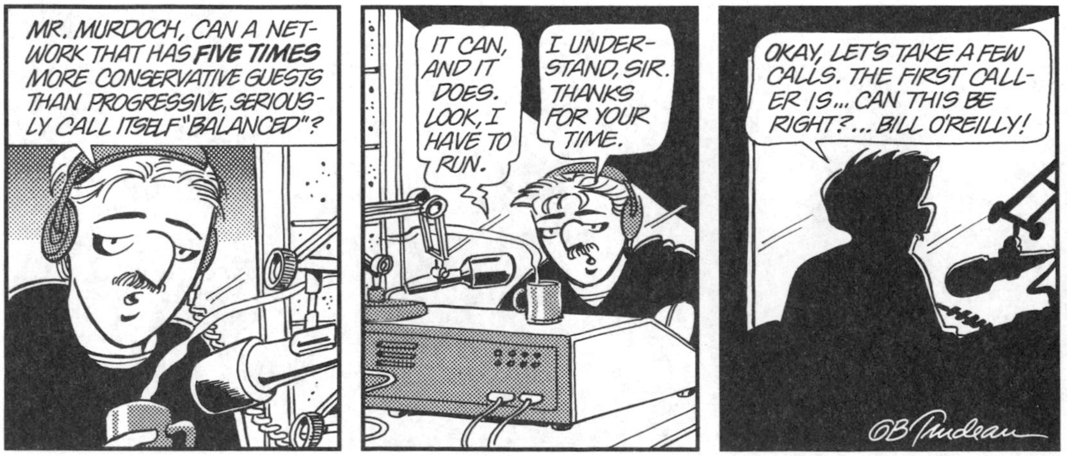
MR. MURDOCH, CAN A NETWORK THAT HAS FIVE TIMES MORE CONSERVATIVE GUESTS THAN PROGRESSIVE, SERIOUSLY CALL ITSELF "BALANCED"?
IT CAN, AND IT DOES. LOOK, I HAVE TO RUN.
I UNDERSTAND, SIR. THANKS FOR YOUR TIME.
OKAY, LET'S TAKE A FEW CALLS. THE FIRST CALLER IS... CAN THIS BE RIGHT?... BILL O'REILLY!
MR. O'REILLY! WHAT AN HONOR TO...
SHUT UP! OKAY? JUST SHUT UP!

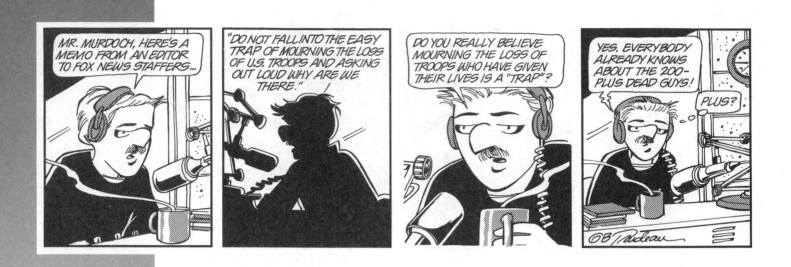

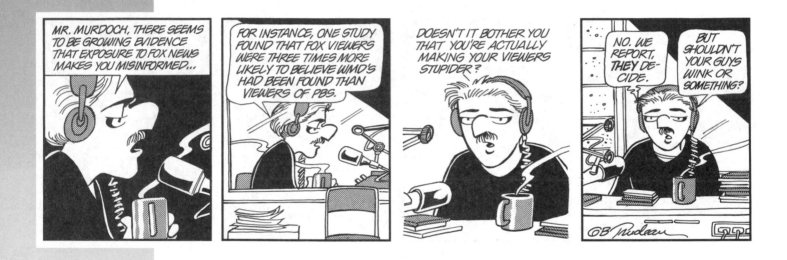

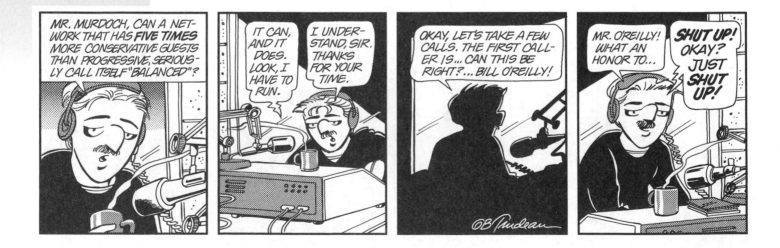

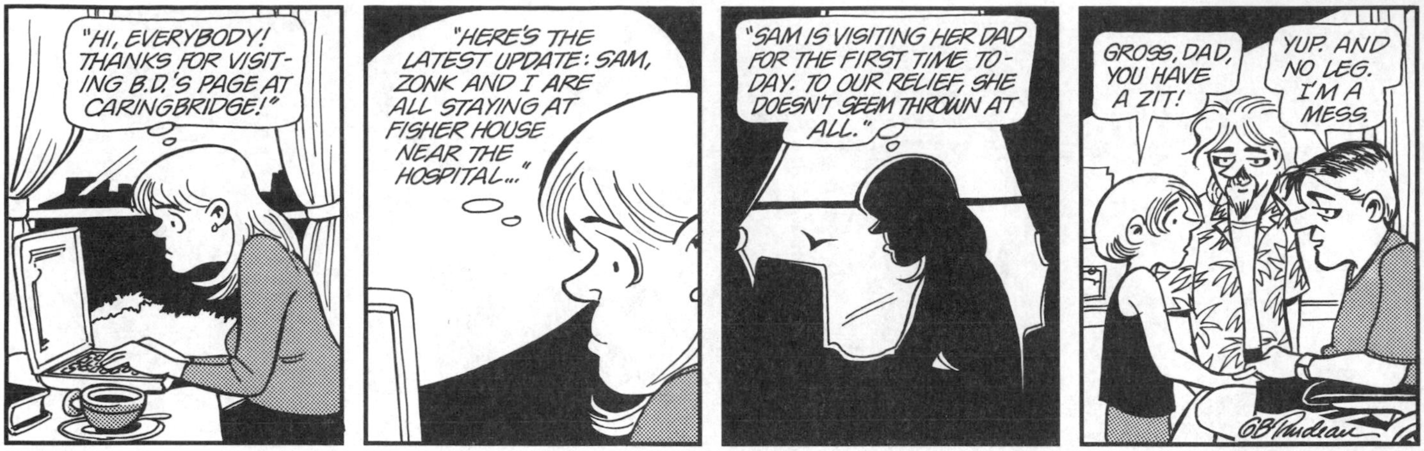
"HI, EVERYBODY! THANKS FOR VISITING B.D.'S PAGE AT CARINGBRIDGE!"
"HERE'S THE LATEST UPDATE: SAM, ZONK AND I ARE ALL STAYING AT FISHER HOUSE NEAR THE HOSPITAL..."
"SAM IS VISITING HER DAD FOR THE FIRST TIME TODAY. TO OUR RELIEF, SHE DOESN'T SEEM THROWN AT ALL."
GROSS, DAD, YOU HAVE A ZIT!
YUP. AND NO LEG. I'M A MESS.

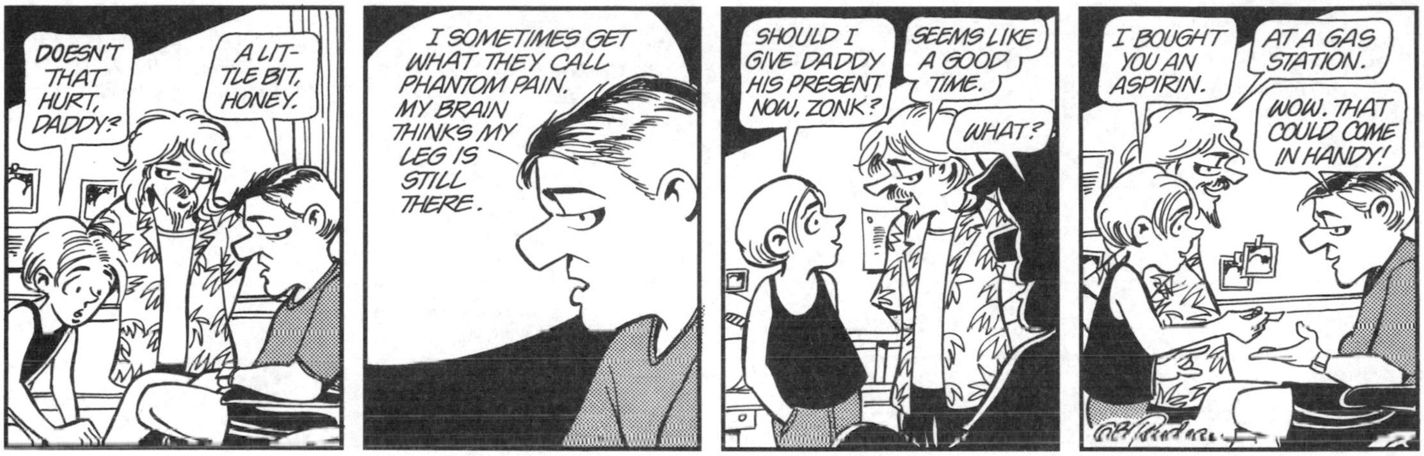
DOESN'T THAT HURT, DADDY?
A LITTLE BIT, HONEY.
I SOMETIMES GET WHAT THEY CALL PHANTOM PAIN. MY BRAIN THINKS MY LEG IS STILL THERE.
SHOULD I GIVE DADDY HIS PRESENT NOW, ZONK?
SEEMS LIKE A GOOD TIME.
WHAT?
I BOUGHT YOU AN ASPIRIN.
AT A GAS STATION.
WOW. THAT COULD COME IN HANDY!

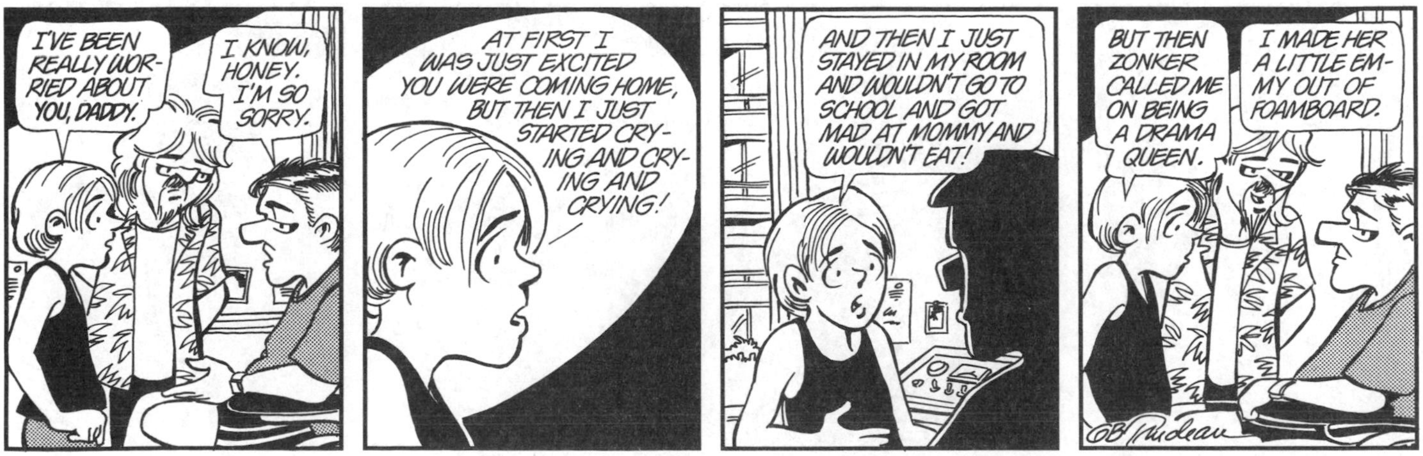
I'VE BEEN REALLY WORRIED ABOUT YOU, DADDY.
I KNOW, HONEY. I'M SO SORRY.
AT FIRST I WAS JUST EXCITED YOU WERE COMING HOME, BUT THEN I JUST STARTED CRYING AND CRYING AND CRYING!
AND THEN I JUST STAYED IN MY ROOM AND WOULDN'T GO TO SCHOOL AND GOT MAD AT MOMMY AND WOULDN'T EAT!
BUT THEN ZONKER CALLED ME ON BEING A DRAMA QUEEN.
I MADE HER A LITTLE EMMY OUT OF FOAMBOARD.

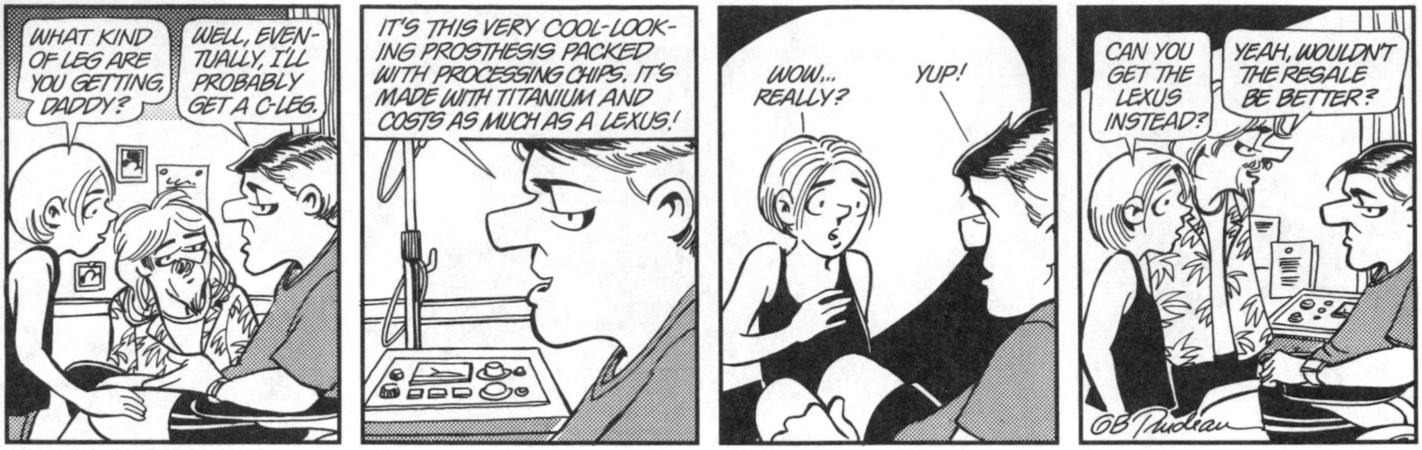
WHAT KIND OF LEG ARE YOU GETTING, DADDY?
WELL, EVENTUALLY, I'LL PROBABLY GET A C-LEG.
IT'S THIS VERY COOL-LOOKING PROSTHESIS PACKED WITH PROCESSING CHIPS. IT'S MADE WITH TITANIUM AND COSTS AS MUCH AS A LEXUS!
WOW... REALLY?
YUP!
CAN YOU GET THE LEXUS INSTEAD?
YEAH, WOULDN'T THE RESALE BE BETTER?
©B Trudeau

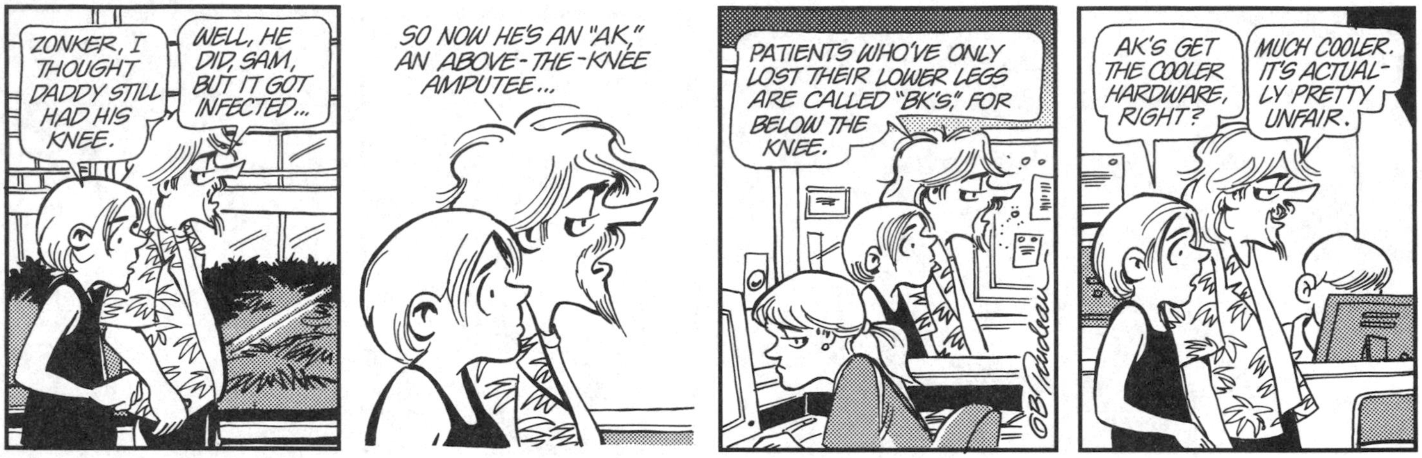
ZONKER, I THOUGHT DADDY STILL HAD HIS KNEE.
WELL, HE DID, SAM, BUT IT GOT INFECTED...
SO NOW HE'S AN "AK," AN ABOVE-THE-KNEE AMPUTEE...
PATIENTS WHO'VE ONLY LOST THEIR LOWER LEGS ARE CALLED "BK'S," FOR BELOW THE KNEE.
©B Trudeau
AK'S GET THE COOLER HARDWARE, RIGHT?
MUCH COOLER. IT'S ACTUALLY PRETTY UNFAIR.

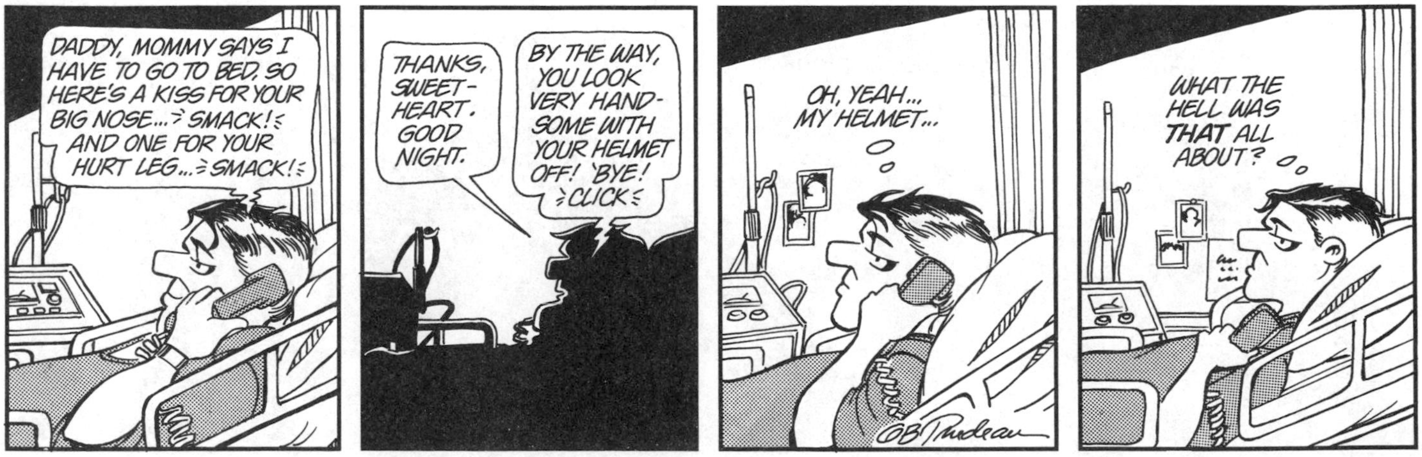
DADDY, MOMMY SAYS I HAVE TO GO TO BED, SO HERE'S A KISS FOR YOUR BIG NOSE... SMACK! AND ONE FOR YOUR HURT LEG... SMACK!
THANKS, SWEETHEART. GOOD NIGHT.
BY THE WAY, YOU LOOK VERY HANDSOME WITH YOUR HELMET OFF! 'BYE! CLICK
OH, YEAH... MY HELMET...
©B Trudeau
WHAT THE HELL WAS THAT ALL ABOUT?

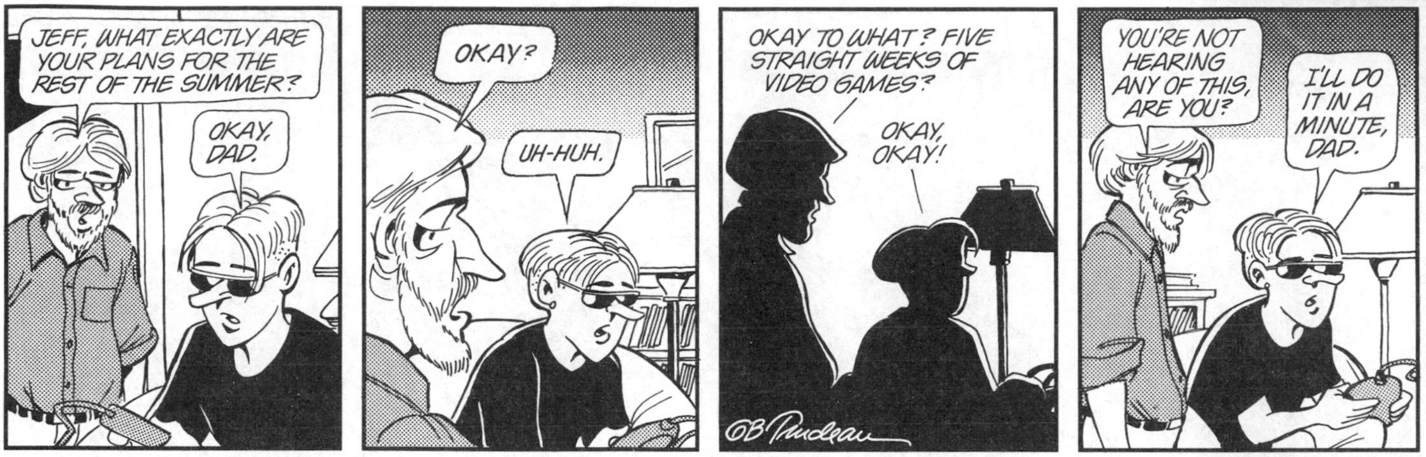

JEFF, WHAT EXACTLY ARE YOUR PLANS FOR THE REST OF THE SUMMER?
OKAY, DAD.
OKAY?
UH-HUH.
OKAY TO WHAT? FIVE STRAIGHT WEEKS OF VIDEO GAMES?
OKAY, OKAY!
©B Trudeau
YOU'RE NOT HEARING ANY OF THIS, ARE YOU?
I'LL DO IT IN A MINUTE, DAD.

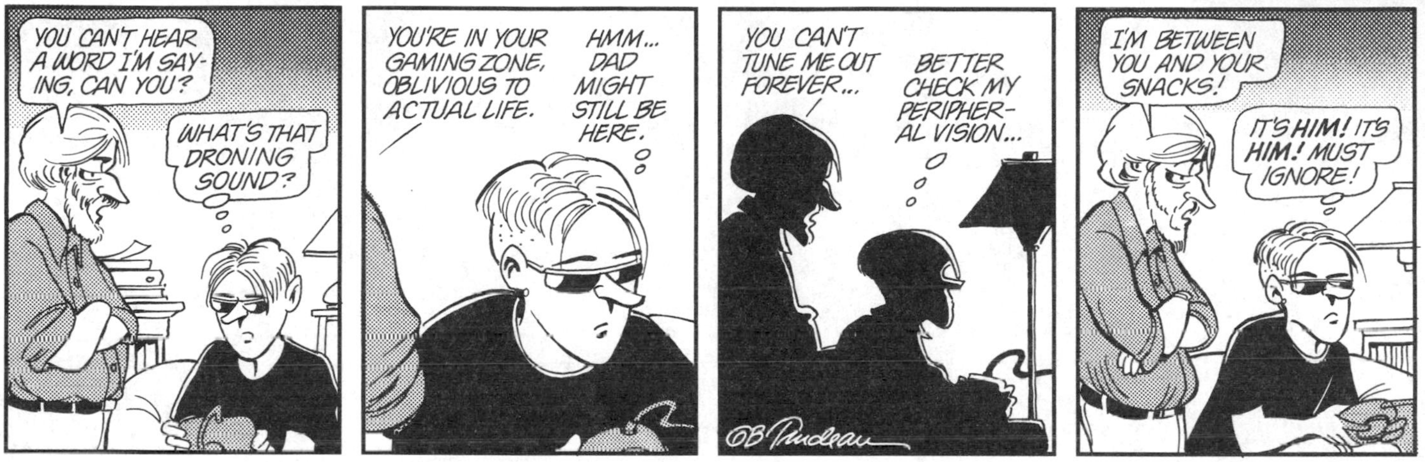

YOU CAN'T HEAR A WORD I'M SAYING, CAN YOU?
WHAT'S THAT DRONING SOUND?
YOU'RE IN YOUR GAMING ZONE, OBLIVIOUS TO ACTUAL LIFE.
HMM... DAD MIGHT STILL BE HERE.
YOU CAN'T TUNE ME OUT FOREVER...
BETTER CHECK MY PERIPHERAL VISION...
©B Trudeau
I'M BETWEEN YOU AND YOUR SNACKS!
IT'S **HIM!** IT'S **HIM!** MUST IGNORE!

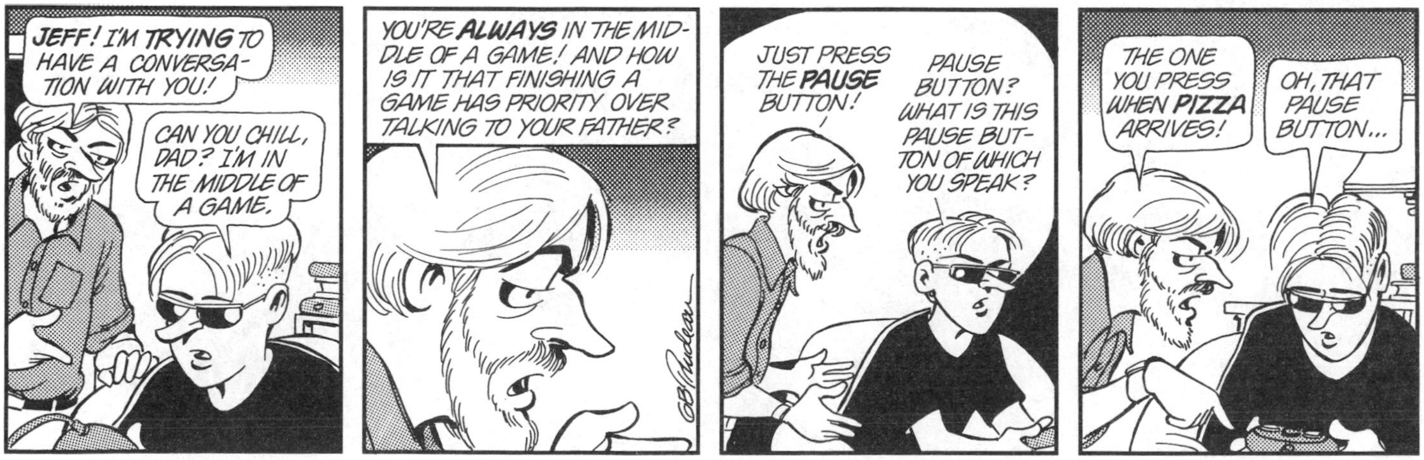

JEFF! I'M **TRYING** TO HAVE A CONVERSATION WITH YOU!
CAN YOU CHILL, DAD? I'M IN THE MIDDLE OF A GAME.
YOU'RE **ALWAYS** IN THE MIDDLE OF A GAME! AND HOW IS IT THAT FINISHING A GAME HAS PRIORITY OVER TALKING TO YOUR FATHER?
©B Trudeau
JUST PRESS THE **PAUSE** BUTTON!
PAUSE BUTTON? WHAT IS THIS PAUSE BUTTON OF WHICH YOU SPEAK?
THE ONE YOU PRESS WHEN **PIZZA** ARRIVES!
OH, THAT PAUSE BUTTON...

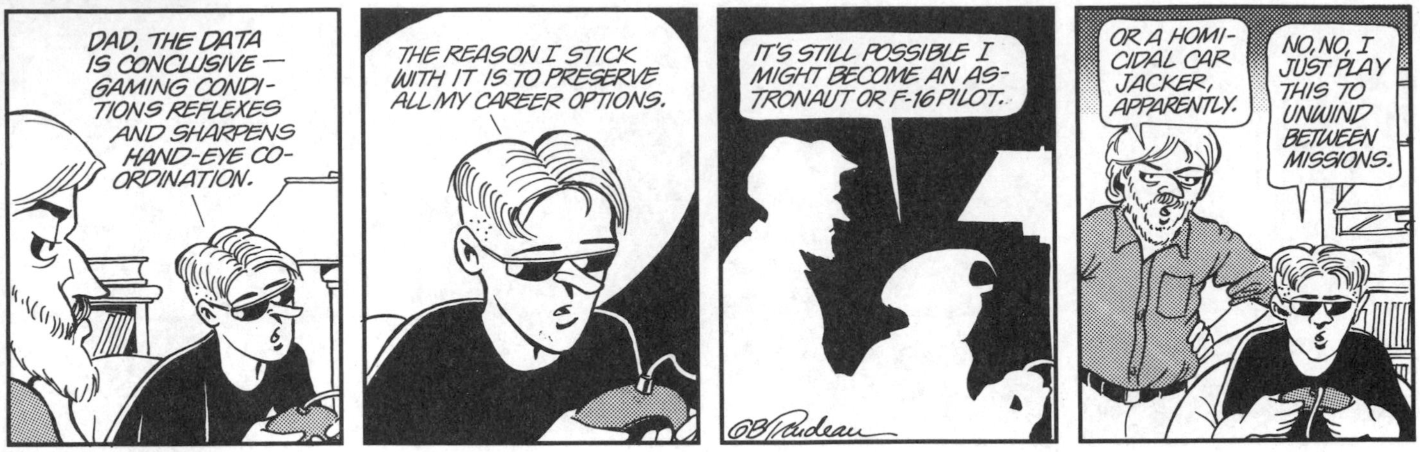
DAD, THE DATA IS CONCLUSIVE — GAMING CONDITIONS REFLEXES AND SHARPENS HAND-EYE CO-ORDINATION.
THE REASON I STICK WITH IT IS TO PRESERVE ALL MY CAREER OPTIONS.
IT'S STILL POSSIBLE I MIGHT BECOME AN ASTRONAUT OR F-16 PILOT.
©B Trudeau
OR A HOMICIDAL CAR JACKER, APPARENTLY.
NO, NO, I JUST PLAY THIS TO UNWIND BETWEEN MISSIONS.

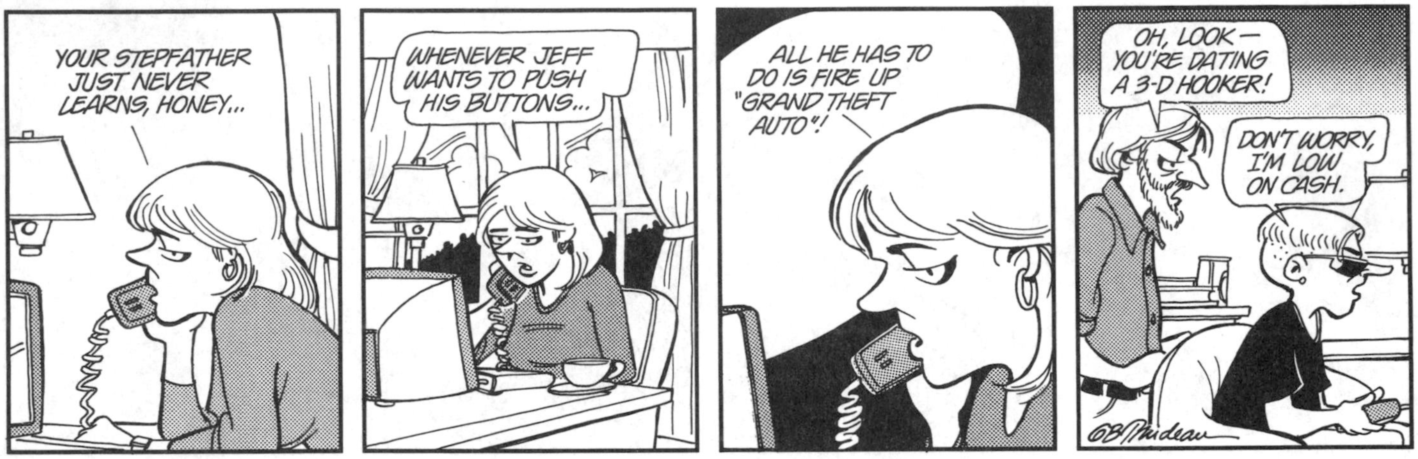
YOUR STEPFATHER JUST NEVER LEARNS, HONEY...
WHENEVER JEFF WANTS TO PUSH HIS BUTTONS...
ALL HE HAS TO DO IS FIRE UP "GRAND THEFT AUTO"!
OH, LOOK — YOU'RE DATING A 3-D HOOKER!
DON'T WORRY, I'M LOW ON CASH.
©B Trudeau

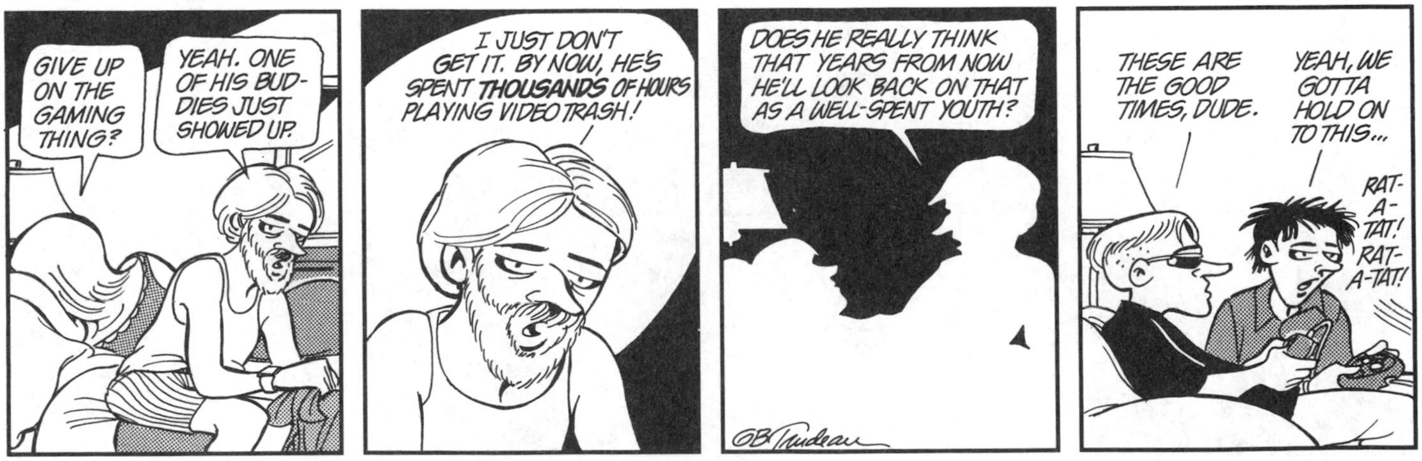
GIVE UP ON THE GAMING THING?
YEAH. ONE OF HIS BUDDIES JUST SHOWED UP.
I JUST DON'T GET IT. BY NOW, HE'S SPENT THOUSANDS OF HOURS PLAYING VIDEO TRASH!
DOES HE REALLY THINK THAT YEARS FROM NOW HE'LL LOOK BACK ON THAT AS A WELL-SPENT YOUTH?
©B Trudeau
THESE ARE THE GOOD TIMES, DUDE.
YEAH, WE GOTTA HOLD ON TO THIS...
RAT-A-TAT! RAT-A-TAT!